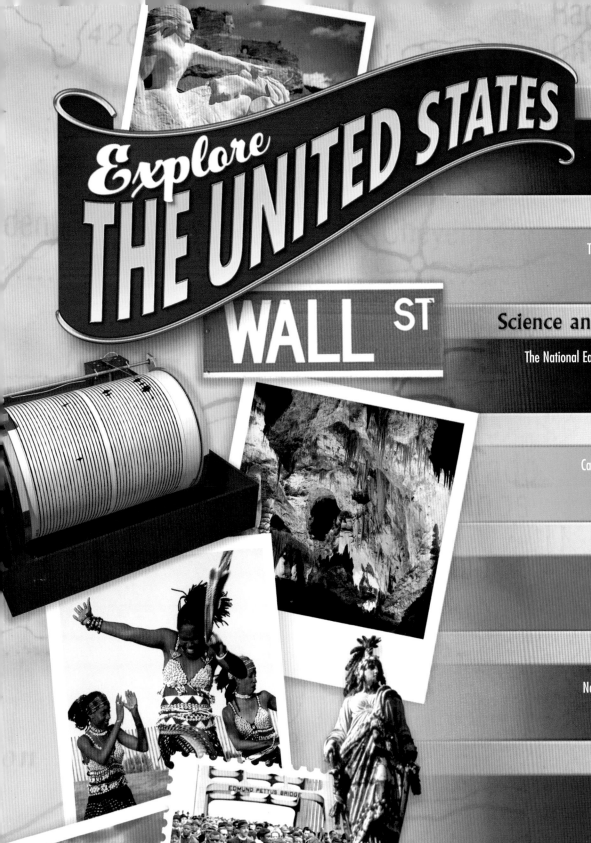

Explore THE UNITED STATES

WALL ST

History

Crazy Horse Memorial
Black Hills, South Dakota
p. E2

Economics

The New York Stock Exchange
New York City, New York
p. E4

Science and Technology

The National Earthquake Information Center
Golden, Colorado
p. E6

Geography

Carlsbad Caverns National Park
New Mexico
p. E8

Culture

The Kunta Kinte Festival
Annapolis, Maryland
p. E10

Citizenship

National Voting Rights Museum
Selma, Alabama
p. E12

Government

The United States Capitol
Washington, D.C.
p. E14

National Symbols

U.S. Supreme Court, Washington, D.C.
The Great Seal and Motto
Ellis Island, New York Harbor, NY
p. E16

History

History is the study of people and events from the past.

Crazy Horse Memorial
Black Hills, South Dakota

You Are There
You're tired. Your muscles ache. You've been climbing for three hours to reach the top of Crazy Horse Monument. You feel honored to be here. People are allowed to walk up to the monument only one weekend a year. Looking out over the Black Hills and beyond, you picture Crazy Horse riding across the Great Plains more than 100 years ago. You turn toward the giant, stone-faced monument. Once it's complete, it will be the largest monument on Earth.

VISIT HISTORY AT

CRAZY HORSE MEMORIAL

The main feature of Crazy Horse Memorial is a monument carved into the rock of the Black Hills of South Dakota. The monument **honors**, or shows respect for, Crazy Horse. It also honors the culture and heritage of all Native Americans of North America. Crazy Horse was an Oglala Sioux chief who fought to preserve Sioux lands and traditions. He died in 1877—more than a **century**, or 100 years, ago. In 1939, Chief Standing Bear and other Native American elders began to plan the Crazy Horse monument. Work on the monument continues to this day.

◄ Native Americans invited sculptor, Koczak Ziolkowski (KOR-chok jewel-CUFF-ski), to carve the giant statue of Crazy Horse. The monument became his life's work, until he died in 1982. Today, his wife and seven of their sons and daughters work to finish his dream.

1987 April 1990 February 1991

Black Hills

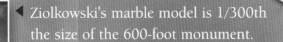
◀ Ziolkowski's marble model is 1/300th the size of the 600-foot monument.

Fast Facts

- The finished monument will be 641 feet long by 563 feet high.

- The Crazy Horse Memorial Foundation does not know when the monument will be finished. It might take decades to complete.

Link to You

Tell about a memorial you have visited or know about that honors a person's role in history. Why do we honor this person?

June 1991
August 1993

July 1994

August 1996

Economics

Economics is the study of the production, distribution, and consumption, or use, of goods and services.

The New York Stock Exchange
New York City, New York

You Are There You can't believe you're standing on the Trading Floor of the New York Stock Exchange (NYSE), the heart of buying and selling shares of ownership in companies. You're a broker who buys and sells shares for others. It's your first day on the job, and you're feeling the pressure. "Calm down," you tell yourself. "Remember, it's simple. Match buyers with sellers and do it fast. How hard can that be?" You take a deep breath and wait for the opening bell to ring.

Economics in Action at the

NYSE NEW YORK

The New York Stock Exchange (NYSE) is where people can buy and sell pieces or shares of companies called **stocks**. The Trading Floor is where all this buying and selling, or **trading**, takes place. Customers don't make their own trades on the Trading Floor. The people who buy and sell stocks for customers are called **brokers**. Brokers at the NYSE make more than one million trades on an average day. The Trading Floor is one of the fastest-paced, busiest places in the world. Stock prices can change quickly. If many people compete over shares in the same company, the price of the share rises. If no one wants the shares of a company, the share price drops. A good broker works quickly and tries to get the best price.

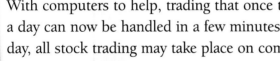

New York City

STOCK EXCHANGE

Fast Facts

- Every weekday, nearly two billion shares of stock are traded on the NYSE.

- The stock exchange works like an auction. Customers are actually buying and selling stocks to and from one another, with brokers negotiating the price.

With computers to help, trading that once took a day can now be handled in a few minutes. Some day, all stock trading may take place on computers.

The NYSE is on Wall Street in New York City. It is one of the most important financial centers in the world.

Link to You

What businesses would you like to own shares of stock in? Why?

Science and Technology

Science and technology change people's lives. These changes bring opportunities and challenges.

National Earthquake Information Center

The National Earthquake Information Center
Golden, Colorado

You Are There

Your class is touring the National Earthquake Information Center (NEIC). Seismographs that measure and record the strength of earthquakes are humming and scribbling calmly. Suddenly, one of the seismographs starts to scratch out a different pattern, a series of scribbles going back and forth in a wider arc. The scientists spring into action. They call government officials, railroad personnel, and safety organizations in the affected area. "This must be pretty unusual," you say to one of the scientists. "Not really," she says. "We get about 50 of these per day."

Scientists who study earthquakes are called **seismologists**. The seismologists at the NEIC use various instruments to study and record earthquakes around the world as they happen. They can help people understand why earthquakes happen, and how to build homes and cities that will be better able to withstand them. No one, not even seismologists, can prevent or predict earthquakes. They can study **data**, or factual information, to determine places that are more likely to have earthquakes. Based on the information they gather, they are able to understand the Earth's structure in an area that might lead to an earthquake.

Golden

U.S. Geological Survey Chief of Seismology Bill Ellsworth uses a seismometer to study earthquakes.

The National Earthquake Information Center holds the world's largest collection of earthquake data in the world.

This building in San Francisco, California, collapsed in a large earthquake in 1989.

Fast Facts

- Earthquake monitoring shows that Alaska has more earthquakes than any other state, while Florida and North Dakota have the fewest.

- Scientists shoot laser beams across the San Andreas Fault at Parkfield, California, to monitor the movement of that dangerous fault.

FIRST AID

Link to You

What natural disasters occur in your region? How can technology help us prepare for them?

Geography

Geography is the study of Earth's surface, features, and climates, and the way they impact people in different regions.

Carlsbad Caverns National Park
New Mexico

You Are There It's taken you about an hour to walk the winding path from the natural entrance down to the Big Room of Carlsbad Caverns. Now you stand about 750 feet beneath the desert. Instead of the dry, sunny heat of the surface, the Big Room is dim, cool, and damp. It is also huge—the area of more than six football fields! You set off along the trail to explore the fascinating cave formations that lie within: towering stalagmites; long, slender stalactites; sturdy columns, and walls of flowstone that look as delicate as folded fabric. How different this is from Juniper Ridge, where you hiked yesterday!

Welcome to Carlsbad

Carlsbad Caverns National Park is best known for its series of huge caverns. Nearly half a million people come each year to tour the park's underground wonders and see the famous evening bat flight. However, the park is also known as prime habitat for many desert species. A **habitat** is a place where an animal or plant naturally lives. Carlsbad Caverns National Park lies in the Chihuahuan (chi WAH wahn) Desert. This desert extends from southern New Mexico and western Texas south into Mexico. Desert shrubs and different types of cactus grow in the park's rugged canyons and atop its mesas. A **mesa** is a small, high plateau with a flat top and steep sides. Mule deer, coyote, mountain lions, hawks, and roadrunners are among the wildlife that lives in the park.

▶ This view of Rattlesnake Canyon shows the rugged desert of Carlsbad Caverns National Park.

Carlsbad Caverns National Park

Caverns
National Park!

Each summer evening, hundreds of thousands of Mexican free-tailed bats fly out of Carlsbad Caverns to hunt for insects in the desert night.

Visitors to Carsbad Caverns can tour some of the cave's largest and most spectacular chambers.

Visitors to the park may see a roadrunner. This desert bird is also the state bird of New Mexico.

Fast Facts

- Ancient pictographs, or rock paintings, have been found at the entrances to caves in Carlsbad Caverns National Park. Humans found shelter in these caves hundreds or perhaps even thousands of years ago.

- Today, elevators take visitors from the visitor center on the surface to the Big Room 750 feet below in less than a minute.

Link to You

How would you describe the geography of the region where you live? What plant and animal habitats are in your region?

E9

Culture

Culture is the customs, traditions, habits and values of a group of people.

Roots is a bestselling book. It has been published in thirty languages, and more than six million copies have been sold.

The Kunta Kinte Festival
Annapolis, Maryland

You Are There It's a hot day in August and drums are pounding. The aroma of African foods, such as chicken imoyo and plantain fritters, drifts in from every direction. Vendors are selling food, art, clothing, and crafts. It seems as if you are in the middle of an African market. A woman's voice catches your attention. It's the griot (GREE oh). She is telling traditional African stories. Her voice rises and falls as she tells her tales, and you cannot help but listen. She brings people from the past alive.

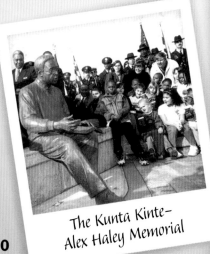

The Kunta Kinte–Alex Haley Memorial

Annapolis★

Preserving Culture at the

Kunta Kinte Festival

In 1976 Alex Haley wrote a book called *Roots*. The book told the story of a man named Kunta Kinte, an ancestor of Haley. An **ancestor** is a person who is related to you from the past. Kunta Kinte was kidnapped from his home in Africa when he was 17 years old. He was put on a boat headed for Maryland, where he was sold into slavery. He spent much of his life enslaved but managed to keep the customs of his homeland and family alive. **Customs** are long established ways people have of doing things. The Kunta Kinte Festival honors Kinte's struggle to **preserve**, or keep, his cultural roots.

The Kunta Kinte Heritage Festival is a celebration of the preservation of culture. More than 125,000 people have visited the Kunta Kinte Festival since 1989.

Fast Facts

- Alex Haley began researching Kunta Kinte's life after hearing stories about his ancestors from his grandmother, a griot.

- Before they are allowed to sell at the festival, craftspeople and artists are reviewed for cultural authenticity and historical value.

Link to You

Describe customs from countries outside the United States that you have seen practiced in your community.

Citizenship

Citizenship is all the rights and privileges of being a member of a community, state, or nation.

National Voting Rights Museum,
Selma, Alabama

You Are There You are standing on the Edmund Pettus Bridge. Beneath the bridge, the Alabama River flows peacefully by. Your grandparents have told you about this bridge—it is a place where people made a stand to protect their right to vote. Even violence could not stop them. You turn and walk the few steps back to the National Voting Rights Museum, where you will learn about brave American citizens who risked their lives to protect their rights.

Learn about citizenship rights at the
National Voting

The National Voting Rights Museum honors the citizens of Alabama and the nation who risked their own safety to gain civil rights for all. A **civil right** is a right guaranteed equally to every eligible citizen. Voting is a civil right. Throughout the history of our nation people have fought for this right, because it is the basis of our power as citizens of a republic. In a **republic**, citizens vote to choose leaders to represent them in the government. Exhibits at the National Voting Rights Museum honor the struggle African Americans, women, and others have made to win and keep the right to vote. The museum encourages all of us to use our right to vote.

Suffrugists, or those who were for women's suffrage, handed out information on their cause. This booth was set up in New York City in 1914.

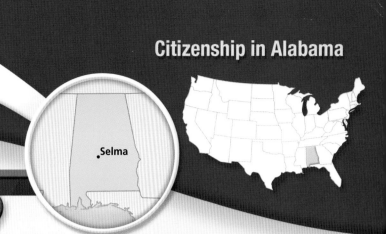

Rights Museum

Suffragists protested at the White House.

People from around the country travel to Selma each year to celebrate the anniversary of the march to Montgomery.

WE MARCH FOR FIRST CLASS CITIZENSHIP NOW!

EDMUND PETTUS BRIDGE

sclc If You Don't Vote You Don't Count

I HAVE A DREAM LET FREEDOM RING
JAN. 15, 1929
APRIL 4, 1968
REV. MARTIN LUTHER KING
A GREAT AMERICAN

In 1963, thousands of people in Washington, D.C., marched in support of civil rights, including voting rights.

Fast Facts

- Women gained the right to vote in national elections in 1920.

- The Voting Rights Act of 1965 made it illegal to deny voting rights because of race.

- The museum's annual "Bridge Crossing Jubilee," an outdoor festival held on the first weekend in March, attracts as many as 25,000 people.

★ Link to You ★

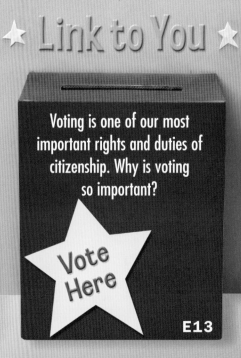

Voting is one of our most important rights and duties of citizenship. Why is voting so important?

Vote Here

Government

Government is a system for running a community, state, or country.

The United States Capitol
Washington, D.C.

You Are There From your seat in the public gallery, you can watch all the activity below. The Chamber of the House of Representatives is large. It smells of polished wood and leather. You hear the sharp crack of a gavel. The representatives take their seats and begin to discuss a bill to fund solar energy research. You watch as members rise to speak and debate. Even though the speakers hold different points of view, you think they all make sense. You wonder whether this bill will pass.

Watch Government in Action at the

United States Capitol

The U.S. Capitol is one of the most recognizable buildings in the world. Its gleaming white dome has become a symbol of our nation. The Capitol is the central building of the Capitol Complex, which houses the legislative branch of the United States government. The **legislative branch** makes our laws. Both the House of Representatives and the Senate are part of the legislative branch. Visitors to the Capitol can arrange in advance to watch either the House or the Senate in session.

Washington, ⊛ D.C.

Visitors can also tour the Capitol to see historical paintings, statues, exhibits, and the **rotunda**, a round ceremonial area that lies beneath the dome.

On top of the U.S. Capitol dome is the *Statue of Freedom*.

Fast Facts

- During the Civil War, a part of the Capitol was used as a Union hospital.

- The first electric lights in the Capitol were installed in the Senate cloakroom, lobby, and stairways in 1885.

Link to You

How does the United States government work for your state or community?

National Symbols

U.S. Supreme Court
Washington, D.C.

◀ The Supreme Court is the highest court of the United States, and a symbol of the American justice system. The words "Equal Justice Under Law" are engraved over the doors of the Supreme Court Building. The nine justices of the Supreme Court make their rulings based on whether the law upholds the principles outlined in the U.S. Constitution.

The Great Seal and Motto

Ellis Island
New York Harbor, NY

▲ Opened in 1892, Ellis Island became known as the "gateway to America." For more than 50 years, the island was used as a Federal Immigration Station. Millions of immigrants arriving in the United States from Europe were questioned, inspected, and recorded here.

▲ On July 4, 1776, the Continental Congress appointed Benjamin Franklin, John Adams, and Thomas Jefferson to create an official seal for the United States of America. The seal is a symbol of the hopes and values of the nation. The Great Seal has two sides. On one side, a bald eagle holds a scroll in its beak, bearing the Latin inscription E pluribus unum, our nation's motto. The motto means "out of many, one." The image of the seal is printed on the one dollar bill and on many important government documents.

SCOTT FORESMAN

SOCIAL STUDIES

GROWTH OF A NATION

SCOTT FORESMAN

SOCIAL STUDIES

GROWTH OF A NATION

ISBN: 0-328-23977-1

5 6 7 8 9 10 V057 15 14 13 12 11 10 09 08

www.sfsocialstudies.com

CLASSROOM REVIEWERS

Nancy Neff Burgess
Upshur County Schools
Buckhannon-Upshur Middle School
Upshur County, West Virginia

Stephen Corsini
Content Specialist in Elementary
Social Studies
School District 5 of Lexington and
Richland Counties
Ballentine, South Carolina

Deanna Crews
Millbrook Middle School
Elmore County
Millbrook, Alabama

Kevin L. Curry
Social Studies Curriculum Chair
Hickory Flat Elementary School
Henry County, McDonough, Georgia

Sheila A. Czech
Sky Oaks Elementary School
Burnsville, Minnesota

Rebecca Eustace Mills
Supervisor of Social Studies
Spotsylvania County Schools
Spotsylvania, Virginia

Cynthia K. Reneau
Muscogee County School District
Columbus, Georgia

Brandon Dale Rice
Secondary Education Social Science
Mobile County Public School System
Mobile, Alabama

Teresa L. Wilson
NBCT (MCGEN)
Neale Elementary School
Vienna, West Virginia

CONTENT REVIEWERS

The Colonial Williamsburg
Foundation
History Education Initiative
Williamsburg, Virginia

Dr. William E. White
Director, Educational Program
Development
The Colonial Williamsburg Foundation
Williamsburg, Virginia

Steve Sheinkin
Curriculum Writer
New York, New York

Editorial Offices:
• Glenview, Illinois • Parsippany, New
Jersey • New York, New York

Sales Offices:
• Boston, Massachusetts • Duluth, Georgia
• Glenview, Illinois • Coppell, Texas
• Sacramento, California • Mesa, Arizona

Contents

Social Studies Handbook

H2   Citizenship Skills

H4   Colonial Williamsburg

H6   Research Skills

H10 Geography Skills

Overview   1   **Establishing a Nation**

2   **Begin with a Primary Source**

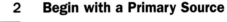
4   Reading Social Studies: Summarize

6   **Lesson 1 Connections Across Continents**

9   **Here and There** Connections Among Continents

12   **Lesson 2 Life in the Colonies**

14   **Then and Now** The Jamestown Colony

19   Biography *John Rolfe*

20   **Map and Globe Skills:** Compare Maps at Different Scales

22   **Lesson 3 Revolution and Constitution**

24   **Literature and Social Studies** The Declaration of Independence

29   Biography *Abigail Adams*

30   **Lesson 4 A Growing Nation**

32   **Map Adventure** Lewis and Clark

37   Biography *Sequoyah*

38   **Chart and Graph Skills:** Use Parallel Time Lines

40   ⭐ **Citizen Heroes:** Respecting the Flag

42   **Overview Review**

44   **Discovery Channel School:** Overview Project

UNIT 1

War Divides the Nation

46 **Begin with a Primary Source**

48 **Meet the People**

50 **Reading Social Studies:** Main Idea and Details

Chapter 1　52　**A Divided Nation**

54 **Lesson 1 North and South Grow Apart**

58 **Thinking Skills:** Recognize Point of View

60 **Lesson 2 Resisting Slavery**

62 **Then and Now** The *Amistad*

65 **Biography** *Harriet Tubman*

66 **Lesson 3 The Struggle over Slavery**

70 **Literature and Social Studies** *Uncle Tom's Cabin*

73 **Biography** *Abraham Lincoln*

74 **Lesson 4 The First Shots Are Fired**

78 **Chapter 1 Review**

Chapter 2　80　**War and Reconstruction**

82 **Lesson 1 The Early Stages of the War**

87 **Biography** *Robert E. Lee*

88 **Lesson 2 Life During the War**

90 **Here and There** Slaves and Serfs

94 ★ **Citizen Heroes:** Working for Lasting Peace

96 **Lesson 3 How the North Won**

97 **Map Adventure** Battle of Gettysburg, 1863

102 **Map and Globe Skills:** Read a Road Map

104 **DK Communications During the Civil War**

106 **Lesson 4 The End of Slavery**

112 **Chapter 2 Review**

114 **End with a Song:** "When Johnny Comes Marching Home"

116 **Unit 1 Review**

118 **Discovery Channel School:** Unit 1 Project

UNIT 2

An Expanding Nation

120 **Begin with a Primary Source**

122 **Meet the People**

124 **Reading Social Studies:** Sequence

Chapter 3

126 **Crossing the Continent**

128 **Lesson 1 Rails Across the Nation**

134 **Map and Globe Skills:** Read a Time Zone Map

136 *Colonial Williamsburg* Westward Growth of America, 1607–1862

138 **Lesson 2 Pioneers on the Plains**

141 **Then and Now** Nicodemus, Kansas

145 **Biography** *George Shima*

146 **Chart and Graph Skills:** Read Climographs

148 **Lesson 3 Cowboys and Miners**

150 **Map Adventure** The Long Cattle Drives

152 **Literature and Social Studies** *Roughing It*

154 **Lesson 4 War in the West**

160 ★ **Citizen Heroes:** Fighting for a Homeland

162 **Chapter 3 Review**

Chapter 4

164 **Industry and Immigration**

166 **Lesson 1 Inventors Change the World**

174 **Research and Writing Skills:** Write an Outline

176 **Lesson 2 The Rise of Big Business**

183 **Biography** *Andrew Carnegie*

184 **Lesson 3 New Americans**

185 **Here and There** The Irish Potato Famine

191 **Biography** *Mary Antin*

192 **Lesson 4 The Labor Movement**

198 **Issues and Viewpoints:** Working Against Child Labor

200 **Chapter 4 Review**

202 **End with a Song:** "Red River Valley"

204 **Unit 2 Review**

206 **Discovery Channel School:** Unit 2 Project

UNIT 3

Expansion and Change

208 **Begin with a Primary Source**

210 **Meet the People**

212 **Reading Social Studies:** Compare and Contrast

Chapter 5   214 **Changing Ways of Life**

216 **Lesson 1 Rural Life Changes**

218 **Then and Now** Mail-Order Catalogs

222 **Lesson 2 Life in the Growing Cities**

230 **Chart and Graph Skills:** Read Line and Circle Graphs

232 **Lesson 3 Unequal Opportunities**

239 **Biography** *Booker T. Washington*

240 **Lesson 4 Women's Rights**

245 **Biography** *Susan B. Anthony*

246 **Chapter 5 Review**

Chapter 6   248 **Becoming a World Power**

250 **Lesson 1 Expanding Overseas**

251 **Literature and Social Studies** "To Build a Fire"

256 **Map Adventure** Swimming the Panama Canal

259 **Biography** *Theodore Roosevelt*

260 **Thinking Skills:** Credibility of a Source

262 **Lesson 2 The Progressive Movement**

268 **Research and Writing Skills:** Interpret Political Cartoons

270 ⭐ **Citizen Heroes:** Investigating and Sharing the Truth

272 **Lesson 3 World War I**

277 **Here and There** ANZACs at Gallipoli

279 **Literature and Social Studies:** "In Flanders Fields"

281 DK **War in the Air**

282 **Chapter 6 Review**

284 **End with a Song:** "Over There"

286 **Unit 3 Review**

288 Discovery SCHOOL **Discovery Channel School:** Unit 3 Project

UNIT 4

Prosperity, Depression, and War

290 **Begin with a Primary Source**

292 **Meet the People**

294 **Reading Social Studies:** Draw Conclusions

Chapter 7

296 **Times of Plenty, Times of Hardship**

298 **Lesson 1 An Industrial Nation**

301 **Map Adventure** Natural Resources for Detroit's Automobile Industry, 1920

306 **Thinking Skills:** Fact and Opinion

308 **Inventions of the Early 1900s**

310 **Lesson 2 The Roaring Twenties**

314 **Literature and Social Studies** "I, Too"

317 **Biography** *Georgia O'Keeffe*

318 **Citizen Heroes** A Different Kind of Story

320 **Lesson 3 The Good Times End**

327 **Biography** *Franklin Delano Roosevelt*

328 **Lesson 4 The New Deal**

336 **Chapter 7 Review**

Chapter 8

338 **World War II**

340 **Lesson 1 World War II Begins**

344 **Then and Now** Pearl Harbor, Hawaii

348 **Lesson 2 The Home Front**

351 **Here and There** The Home Front in Great Britain

356 **Lesson 3 The World at War**

365 **Biography** *Dwight David Eisenhower*

366 **Map and Globe Skills:** Understand Key Lines of Latitude and Longitude

368 **Chapter 8 Review**

370 **End with Literature:** *The Grapes of Wrath*

372 **Unit 4 Review**

374 **Discovery Channel School:** Unit 4 Project

UNIT 5

Challenges at Home and Abroad

376 **Begin with a Primary Source**

378 **Meet the People**

380 **Reading Social Studies:** Cause and Effect

Chapter 9   382   **The Postwar World**

384 **Lesson 1 The World Is Divided**

392 **Research and Writing Skills:** Compare Primary and Secondary Sources

394 **Lesson 2 Boom Years at Home**

401 **Map Adventure** Family Vacation Along Route 66, 1955

404 **The Roots of Rock and Roll**

406 **Lesson 3 Cold War Conflicts**

408 **Then and Now** South Korea

413 **Biography** *John F. Kennedy*

414 **Chapter 9 Review**

Chapter 10   416   **A Changing Nation**

418 **Lesson 1 African Americans and Civil Rights**

427 **Biography** *Martin Luther King, Jr.*

428 **Lesson 2 The Cold War Continues**

436 **Citizen Heroes:** Honoring the Veteran

438 **Lesson 3 Years of Change**

443 **Literature and Social Studies** *Silent Spring*

445 **Biography** *Dolores Huerta*

446 **Lesson 4 Changing World, Changing Roles**

451 **Here and There** South Africa

454 **Map and Globe Skills:** Understand Map Projections

456 **Chapter 10 Review**

458 **End with a Transcript:** Apollo 11

460 **Unit 5 Review**

462 **Discovery Channel School:** Unit 5 Project

UNIT 6

Moving into the Twenty-first Century

464 **Begin with a Primary Source**

466 **Meet the People**

468 **Reading Social Studies:** Summarize

Chapter 11 470 **The United States Today**

472 **Lesson 1 The Fifty States**

475 **Here and There** Immigration to Brazil

476 **Literature and Social Studies** *When I Was Puerto Rican*

478 **Map and Globe Skills:** Compare Population Density Maps

480 **Lesson 2 Government of the People**

483 **Map Adventure** Counting the Votes

485 **Biography** *Sandra Day O'Connor*

486 **Issues and Viewpoints:** Becoming a United States Citizen

488 **Lesson 3 Economy and Trade**

495 **Biography** *An Wang*

496 **Research and Writing Skills:** Internet Research

498 **Chapter 11 Review**

Chapter 12 500 **Global Challenges**

502 **Lesson 1 New Dangers**

509 **Biography** *Daniel Libeskind*

510 ⭐ **Citizen Heroes:** Racing to the Rescue

512 **Lesson 2 Looking Ahead**

516 **Then and Now** Visions of the Future

518 **Thinking Skills:** Make Generalizations

520 **The Future and Technology**

522 **Chapter 12 Review**

524 **End with a Song:** "You're a Grand Old Flag"

526 **Unit 6 Review**

528 **Discovery Channel School:** Unit 6 Project

A Visual Introduction • Western Hemisphere　529

Canada	530
Mexico	534
The Countries of Central America	538
The Countries of the Caribbean Region	540
The Countries of South America	542

Reference Guide

Atlas	R2
Geography Terms	R16
Facts About Our 50 States	R18
Facts About Our Presidents	R22
United States Documents	R26
Gazetteer	R53
Biographical Dictionary	R59
Glossary	R68
Index	R80

★ BIOGRAPHY ★

John Rolfe	19	Theodore Roosevelt	259
Abigail Adams	29	Georgia O'Keeffe	317
Sequoyah	37	Franklin Delano Roosevelt	327
Harriet Tubman	65	Dwight David Eisenhower	365
Abraham Lincoln	73	John F. Kennedy	413
Robert E. Lee	87	Martin Luther King, Jr.	427
George Shima	145	Dolores Huerta	445
Andrew Carnegie	183	Sandra Day O'Connor	485
Mary Antin	191	An Wang	495
Booker T. Washington	239	Daniel Libeskind	509
Susan B. Anthony	245		

Maps

Connections Across Continents 6
Routes of Early Americans 7
Native American Cultural Regions 8
Connections Among Continents 9
Life in the Colonies 12
Major European Colonies in North America, 1638 13
13 English Colonies 16
Triangular Trade Routes 17
Small-Scale Map: Virginia 20
Large-Scale Map: Colonial National Historical Park 21
Revolution and Constitution 22
A Growing Nation 30
Lewis and Clark 32
Expansion of the United States, 1783–1898 35
A Divided Nation 53
North and South Grow Apart 54
Resisting Slavery 60
Routes of the Underground Railroad 63
The Struggle over Slavery 66
The Missouri Compromise, 1820 67
The Kansas-Nebraska Act, 1854 69
The First Shots Are Fired 74
The Union and the Confederacy, 1861–1865 76
War and Reconstruction 81
The Early Stages of the War 82
Life During the War 88
Slaves and Serfs 90
How the North Won 96
Battle of Gettysburg, 1863 97
Major Battles of the Civil War, 1861–1865 99
Road Map 103
The End of Slavery 106
Road Map 113
Crossing the Continent 127
Rails Across the Nation 128
Transcontinental Railroads, 1869–1893 130
United States Time Zones 134
Westward Growth of America, 1607–1862 136
Pioneers on the Plains 138
Cowboys and Miners 148
The Long Cattle Drives 150
War in the West 154
Major Native American Reservations, 1890 158
Industry and Immigration 165

Inventors Change the World 166
The Rise of Big Business 176
Major Railroad Lines, 1880 178
New Americans 184
The Irish Potato Famine 185
The Labor Movement 192
Changing Ways of Life 215
Rural Life Changes 216
Life in the Growing Cities 222
The Country's Fastest-Growing Cities, 1890–1910 223
New York Neighborhoods in 1910 227
Unequal Opportunities 232
The Great Migration 235
Women's Rights 240
Becoming a World Power 249
Expanding Overseas 250
New United States Territories, 1898 255
Swimming the Panama Canal 256
The Progressive Movement 262
World War I 272
The Allied Powers and Central Powers in 1915 273
ANZACs at Gallipoli 277
Times of Plenty, Times of Hardship 297
An Industrial Nation 298
Natural Resources for Detroit's Automobile Industry, 1920 301
The Roaring Twenties 310
The Good Times End 320
The New Deal 328
The Dust Bowl, 1930s 332
World War II 339
World War II Begins 340
Pearl Harbor, Hawaii 344
World War II, 1939–1945 346
The Home Front 348
The Home Front in Great Britain 351
The World at War 356
Major Battles of World War II 358
Normandy Invasion 360
Latitude 366
Longitude 366
Major Pacific Battles, World War II 367
The Postwar World 383
The World Is Divided 384
The Iron Curtain in Europe, 1945–1989 389
Boom Years at Home 394
Family Vacation Along Route 66, 1955 401
Cold War Conflicts 406
North and South Korea 407

Range of Soviet Nuclear Missiles 411
A Changing Nation 417
African Americans and Civil Rights 418
Segregation in 1952 419
The Cold War Continues 428
North and South Vietnam 431
Years of Change 438
How States Voted on the ERA 440
Changing World, Changing Roles 446
The End of Soviet Control 449
South Africa 451
Mercator Projection 454
Equal-Area Projection 455
Equal-Area Projection 457
The United States Today 471
The Fifty States 472
Regions of the United States 473
Immigration to Brazil 475
Population Density in the Midwest, 2000 478
Population Density in the Southeast, 2000 479
Government of the People 480
Counting the Votes 483
Economy and Trade 488
Global Challenges 501
New Dangers 502
Iraq and Afghanistan 506
Western Hemisphere 529
Canada 530
Mexico 534
Central America 538
Caribbean Region 541
South America 543
World: Political R4
Western Hemisphere: Political R6
Western Hemisphere: Physical R7
North America: Political R8
North America: Physical R9
United States of America R10
Our Fifty States: Political R12
Our Fifty States: Physical R14

Skills

Reading Social Studies

Summarize 4
Main Idea and Details 50
Sequence 124
Compare and Contrast 212
Draw Conclusions 294
Cause and Effect 380
Summarize 468

Map and Globe Skills

Compare Maps at Different Scales   20
Read a Road Map   102
Read a Time Zone Map   134
Understand Key Lines of Latitude and Longitude   366
Understand Map Projections   454
Compare Population Density Maps   478

Thinking Skills

Recognize Point of View   58
Credibility of a Source   260
Fact and Opinion   306
Make Generalizations   518

Research and Writing Skills

Write an Outline   174
Interpret Political Cartoons   268
Compare Primary and Secondary Sources   392
Internet Research   496

Chart and Graph Skills

Use Parallel Time Lines   38
Read Climographs   146
Read Line and Circle Graphs   230

Fact File

The Road to Revolution   23
The Three Branches of Government   27
Years of Growth and Conflict   33
Union and Confederacy, 1861   83
Technology on the Plains   143
Invention Time Line   171
Electric Appliances Change Work   220
Growing Concern for Worker Safety   265
New Deal Programs   330
Major Powers of the Axis and Allies   345
Baby Boomers   400
African American Voters Before and After the Voting Rights Act of 1965   425
Heroes Help Others   505
Challenges of the Twenty-first Century   515

Citizen Heroes

Respecting the Flag   40
Working for Lasting Peace   94
Fighting for a Homeland   160
Investigating and Sharing the Truth   270
A Different Kind of Story   318
Honoring the Veteran   436
Racing to the Rescue   510

Issues and Viewpoints

Working Against Child Labor   198
Becoming a United States Citizen   486

Then and Now

The Jamestown Colony   14
The *Amistad*   62
Nicodemus, Kansas   141
Mail-Order Catalogs   218
Pearl Harbor, Hawaii   344
South Korea   408
Visions of the Future   516

Here and There

Connections Among Continents   9
Slaves and Serfs   90
The Irish Potato Famine   185
ANZACs at Gallipoli   277
The Home Front in Great Britain   351
South Africa   451
Immigration to Brazil   475

Literature and Social Studies

The Declaration of Independence   24
Uncle Tom's Cabin   70
Roughing It   152
"To Build a Fire"   251
"In Flanders Fields"   279
"I, Too"   314
Silent Spring   443
When I Was Puerto Rican   476

Map Adventure

Lewis and Clark   32
Battle of Gettysburg, 1863   97
The Long Cattle Drives   150
Swimming the Panama Canal   256
Natural Resources for Detroit's Automobile Industry, 1920   301
Family Vacation Along Route 66, 1955   401
Counting the Votes   483

Graphic Organizers

Summarize   4
Summarize   11
Summarize   18
Summarize   28
Summarize   36
Main Idea and Details   50
Main Idea and Details   57
Main Idea and Details   64
Main Idea and Details   72
Sequence   77
Main Idea and Details   78
Main Idea and Details   86
Main Idea and Details   93
Main Idea and Details   101
Main Idea and Details   111
Main Idea and Details   112
Sequence   124
Sequence   133
Sequence   144
Sequence   153
Sequence   159
Sequence   162
Sequence   173
Main Idea and Details   182
Summarize   190
Draw Conclusions   197
Sequence   200
Compare and Contrast   212
Compare and Contrast   221
Cause and Effect   229
Main Idea and Details   238
Sequence   244
Compare and Contrast   246
Cause and Effect   258
Compare and Contrast   267
Compare and Contrast   280
Compare and Contrast   282
Draw Conclusions   294
Draw Conclusions   305
Draw Conclusions   316
Cause and Effect   326
Main Idea and Details   335
Draw Conclusions   336
Draw Conclusions   347
Main Idea and Details   355
Sequence   364
Draw Conclusions   368
Cause and Effect   380
Cause and Effect   391
Cause and Effect   403

Summarize	412
Cause and Effect	414
Cause and Effect	426
Summarize	435
Cause and Effect	444
Cause and Effect	453
Cause and Effect	456
Summarize	468
Summarize	477
Summarize	484
Cause and Effect	494
Summarize	498
Summarize	508
Main Idea and Details	517
Summarize	522

Charts, Graphs, Tables & Diagrams

Diagram: An Iroquois Longhouse	9
Chart: The Columbian Exchange	10
Chart: The Three Branches of Government	27
Pictograph: Cotton Production in the United States, 1800–1850	34
Circle and Bar Graphs: North and South Population, 1850	55
Line Graph: Free and Enslaved African Americans, 1820–1860	56
Bar Graphs: Union and Confederacy, 1861	83
Chart: Reconstruction Amendments	109
Climograph: Omaha, Nebraska	146
Climograph: Winchester, Virginia	147
Climograph: Houston, Texas	163
Line Graph: Percentage of Homes with Electrical Service	169
Bar Graph: Immigration in the Twentieth Century	188
Bar Graph: Growth of 3 Largest Cities, 1890–1910	223
Line Graph: United States Population 1790–2000	230
Circle Graph: United State Labor Force 1900	231
Circle Graph: United State Labor Force 2000	231
Line Graph: Weekly Movie Attendance	304
Line Graph: Average Value of Selected Stocks, 1920–1932	322
Line Graph: Looking for Work	349
Line Graph: Birth Rate by Year, 1945–1965	400
Circle Graph: African American Voters in the United States, 1964	425
Circle Graph: African American Voters in the United States, 1969	425
Circle Graph: African American Voters in Mississippi, 1964	425
Circle Graph: African American Voters in Mississippi, 1969	425
Bar Graph: Labor Force Participation of Women by Age, 1950 and 1998	439
Bar Graph: Changing Population of United States Cities, 1950–2000	474
Table: Changing Population of United States Cities, 1950 and 2000	474
Table: Five Fastest-Growing Job Types	490
Diagram: Satellite Communication	491
Bar Graph: Major United States Imports, 2001	492
Diagram: International Trade	492
Bar Graph: Major United States Exports, 2001	493
Circle Graph: Sources of Energy in the United States, 2000	513

Time Lines

Establishing a Nation	2
Connections Across Continents	6
Life in the Colonies	12
Revolution and Constitution	22
The Road to Revolution	23
A Growing Nation	30
Years of Growth and Conflict	33
New England Colonies	38
Middle Colonies	38
Southern Colonies	38
War Divides the Nation	46
Unit 1 Meet the People	48
North and South Grow Apart	54
Resisting Slavery	60
The Struggle over Slavery	66
The First Shots Are Fired	74
Chapter 1 Review	78
The Early Stages of the War	82
Life During the War	88
How the North Won	96
The End of Slavery	106
Chapter 2 Review	112
An Expanding Nation	120
Unit 2 Meet the People	122
Rails Across the Nations	128
Westward Growth of America, 1607–1862	137
Pioneers on the Plains	138
Cowboys and Miners	148
War in the West	154
Chapter 3 Review	162
Inventors Change the World	166
Invention Time Line	171
The Rise of Big Business	176
New Americans	184
The Labor Movement	192
Chapter 4 Review	200
Expansion and Change	208
Unit 3 Meet the People	210
Rural Life Changes	216
Life in the Growing Cities	222
Unequal Opportunities	232
Women's Rights	240
Chapter 5 Review	246
Expanding Overseas	250
The Progressive Movement	262
World War I	272
Chapter 6 Review	282
Prosperity, Depression, and War	290
Unit 4 Meet the People	292
An Industrial Nation	298
The Roaring Twenties	310
The Good Times End	320
The New Deal	328
Chapter 7 Review	336
World War II Begins	340
The Home Front	348
The World at War	356
Chapter 8 Review	368
Challenges at Home and Abroad	376
Unit 5 Meet the People	378
The World Is Divided	384
Boom Years at Home	394
Cold War Conflicts	406
Chapter 9 Review	414
African Americans and Civil Rights	418
The Cold War Continues	428
Years of Change	438
Changing World, Changing Roles	446
Chapter 10 Review	456
Moving into the Twenty-first Century	464
Unit 6 Meet the People	466
New Dangers	502
Looking Ahead	512
Chapter 12 Review	522

Citizenship Skills

There are six ways to show good citizenship: caring, respect, responsibility, fairness, honesty, and courage. In your textbook, you will learn about people who used these ways to help their community, state, and country.

Caring
Think about what someone else needs.

Respect
Treat others as you would want to be treated, and welcome differences among people.

Responsibility
Do what you are supposed to do and think before you act.

Fairness
Take turns and follow the rules. Listen to other people and treat them fairly.

Honesty
Tell the truth and do what you say you will do.

Courage
Do what is right even when the task might be hard.

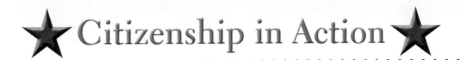

★ Citizenship in Action ★

Good citizens make careful decisions. They solve problems in a logical way. How will the fifth-graders handle each situation as good citizens?

Decision Making

These students are voting in the school election. Before making a decision, each student follows these steps:

1. **Tell what decision you need to make.**
2. **Gather information.**
3. **List your choices.**
4. **Tell what might happen with each choice.**
5. **Make your decision.**
6. **Act according to your decision.**

Problem Solving

These students broke a window near the playground. They follow these steps to solve the problem.

1. **Name the problem.**
2. **Find out more about the problem.**
3. **List ways to solve the problem.**
4. **Talk about the best way to solve the problem.**
5. **Solve the problem.**
6. **Figure out how well the problem was solved.**

Living History from
Colonial Williamsburg
www.history.org

Think Like a Historian

At Colonial Williamsburg, we work to learn what life was like in the 1700s. To do this, we study artifacts from that time period. Artifacts and documents created by the people who lived in a time period and witnessed its events are called primary sources. Primary sources help us learn about people and places from the past. They help us understand events that happened before our time.

► Many artifacts survive and allow us to explore the past. We collect artifacts, such as this gown, that tell us how people lived.

Letters and diaries give us information about how people thought and acted. This description of Frances Carter was written by her children's teacher, Philip Vickers Fithian. ▼

Tuesday, January 4, 1774

"Mrs. Carter is prudent, always cheerful, never without something pleasant, a remarkable Economist, perfectly acquainted with the good management of children...."

H4

▶ Many family stories are passed down from generation to generation over time. We call these oral histories.

Documents such as court records and newspapers tell us the types of things people owned and used. Look at this store advertisement from the *Virginia Gazette*, the local newspaper.

Archaeologists find many artifacts by excavating the ground where people lived. Pieces of plates, cups, and teapots help us learn what people once used in their homes. ◀

"Just IMPORTED, and to be sold by the subscriber, in Williamsburg, THE FOLLOWING ARTICLES, VIZ. Irish linens, . . . children's shoes and stays, flannel waistcoats, new rosebags, paste necklaces and earrings . . . dolls and toys, and many other things too numerous to insert. The above GOODS to be sold on reasonable terms for ready money.

C. RATHELL."

By carefully studying many primary sources, we are able to form an idea of what life was like in colonial times. ◀

Find primary sources that describe your family or your school in the past. You might look for yearbooks, newspapers, articles that have been saved, or pictures that were taken. Use those primary sources to write a description of what your family or school was like in the past.

When gathering information for written reports and research projects, you will need to use resources in addition to your textbook. You can use print technology resources, and community resources. These sources can be of two different kinds.

Primary sources are firsthand documents produced by people who were involved in the event. Primary sources include journals, diaries, letters, speeches, autobiographies, photographs, interviews, and eyewitness accounts.

Secondary sources are descriptions of an event written by people who did not participate in the event. Secondary sources include history books, encyclopedias, and biographies.

Print Resources

Libraries often have books, periodicals, and reference books such as atlases, almanacs, and encyclopedias.

An *encyclopedia* is a collection of articles, listed alphabetically, on various topics. Electronic encyclopedias often have sound and video clips in addition to words.

A *dictionary* is an alphabetical collection of words that includes the meanings of each word. A dictionary is the best source for checking the correct spelling of a word.

An *atlas* is a collection of maps. Some atlases have a variety of maps showing elevation, natural resources, historical events, and so on.

An *almanac* is a book or computer resource that contains facts about a variety of subjects. Almanacs are updated every year, so they usually have the latest statistics on populations, weather, and other number-based facts.

A *nonfiction book* is a factual book about a specific topic. In a library you can search for books by subject, by title, or by author. Once you find a book that you want, the book's catalog number will guide you to the area of the library where you will find the book.

A *periodical,* such as a newspaper or magazine, has information that is usually more up-to-date than that found in an older book. Most libraries have a special periodical section.

Technology Resources

The Internet, CD-ROMs, and TV programs are some technology sources that you can use for research.

The Internet is a system of linked computers that store information to be accessed by others. There are online encyclopedias, dictionaries, almanacs, and Web sites for many different companies, individuals, projects, and museums.

Anyone can create a Web site and post information on the Internet. As a researcher, you must determine which information is accurate. It is important to know who put together the information. It is wise to check information by finding several different reliable sources that give the same facts.

Before you turn on your computer, you should plan your research. What do you need to find out? For example, to begin the research project that appears on page H5, list names of communities or schools you want to research. Then use a *search engine* to find more information about these places. If you have not used the Internet before, ask a librarian, teacher, or parent for help.

Searching by Subject To find a search engine, click on SEARCH at the top of your screen. Choose a search engine from the list. Type one of your subject words into the search engine field. Then click SEARCH or GO. Click on the site you are most interested in.

Searching by Address URLs, or Web addresses, are found in many places. Magazines, newspapers, TV programs, and books often give Web addresses. You will see URLs written in this form: *www.sfsocialstudies.com*. Type the URL in the long address field at the top of the screen. Then press ENTER or RETURN.

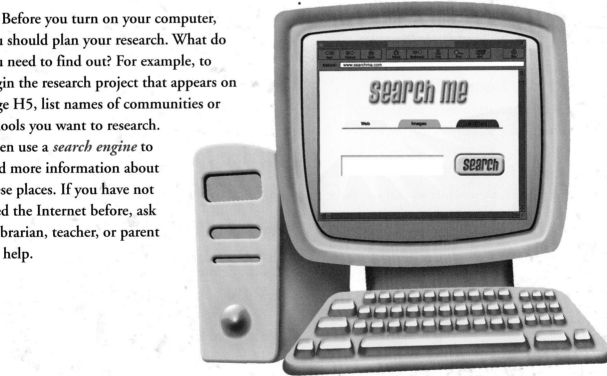

Community Resources

The people of your community are good sources of information.

Interviews

One way to find out what the people in your community know is to interview them. This means to ask them questions about the topic you are studying. If you want to conduct an interview, follow these steps.

Plan Ahead

- List the people you want to interview.
- Call or write to ask permission. Let the person know who you are and why you need information.
- Agree on a time and place for the interview.
- Find out background information about your topic.
- Write down questions you want to ask.

Ask/Listen/Record

- Ask questions clearly.
- Listen carefully.
- Be polite.
- Take notes to remember important ideas. If possible, use a tape recorder so that you have a recording of what was said.

Wrap-up

- Thank the person for his or her time.
- Send a follow-up thank-you note.

Surveys

Another way to find information in your community is to conduct a survey. A survey is a list of questions that you ask people and a record of their answers. You can use either yes/no questions or short-answer questions. To record the information you find out, make a chart with a column for each question.

The following steps will help you plan a survey:

- Make a list of questions.
- Decide where you want to conduct the survey and how many people you want to ask.
- Use a tally sheet to record people's answers.
- After the survey, look through the responses and write down what you found out.

When did you go to school?	How many kids were in your class?	What is your best memory?	Describe your favorite teacher.
1965-1968	around 15	recess	Mrs. Summers She was smart and fair.
1952-1956	around 20	winning the spelling bee	Mr. Shifflet He was a great storyteller.

Write for Information

Another way to use the people in your community as resources is to e-mail or write a letter asking for information. Use the following steps:

- Plan before you write.
- Tell who you are and why you are writing.
- Be neat and careful about spelling and punctuation.
- Thank the person.

Writing a Research Report

Prewrite

- Decide on a topic for your report. Your teacher may tell you what kind of report to write and how long it should be.
- Generate questions about your topic to help focus your report.
- Use a variety of sources to find information and answer your questions.
- Evaluate your sources to determine which will be the most helpful.
- Take notes from your sources.
- Review your notes and write down the main ideas related to the topic that you want to present in your report. Two or three main ideas are enough for most reports.
- Organize your notes into an outline, listing each main idea and the details that support it.

Write a First Draft

- Using your outline and your notes, write a draft report of what you have learned. You can correct mistakes at the revising step.
- Write in paragraph form. Each paragraph should be about a new idea.
- When you quote something directly from your sources, write down which source the quote came from.
- Your report should be organized with a strong introduction, a solid summary of information, a conclusion, and the list of sources you used.

Revise

- Read over your first draft. Does it make sense? Does it answer the questions you asked? Does it clearly explain facts and ideas? Do your ideas flow from one to the other in an organized way? Do you need more information about any main idea? Will the report hold a reader's interest?
- Change any sentences or paragraphs that do not make sense. Add anything that will make your ideas clear.
- Check your quotations to make sure you have used people's exact words and that you have noted the source.

Edit

- Proofread your report. Correct any errors in spelling, capitalization, or punctuation.

Publish

- Include illustrations, maps, time lines, or other graphics that will add to the report.
  - Write a table of contents.
  - Write or type a final copy of your report as neatly as possible.

My School

Geography Skills

Five Themes of Geography

Geography is the study of Earth and the relationship of Earth's physical features, climate, and people. This study can be divided into five themes that help you understand why Earth has such a wide variety of places. Each theme reveals something different about a spot, as this example of Yellowstone National Park, the nation's first national park, shows.

Location

Where can this park be found?
Yellowstone National Park is located at about 45°N, between 110°W and 111°W.

Place

How is this place different from others?
Yellowstone National Park is an area of volcanic activity, with hot springs, mudpots, and geysers such as Old Faithful.

Human/Environment Interaction

How have people changed this place?
People have built visitor centers and lodgings in Yellowstone National Park, as well as special walkways so tourists can hike safely among hot springs and geysers.

Movement

Millions of people travel to and through Yellowstone National Park each year to see its beauty and natural wonders.

Region

What is special about the region in which Yellowstone National Park is located? Yellowstone National Park is located in the Rocky Mountains, a system of mountain ranges that stretches from New Mexico north into Canada and Alaska.

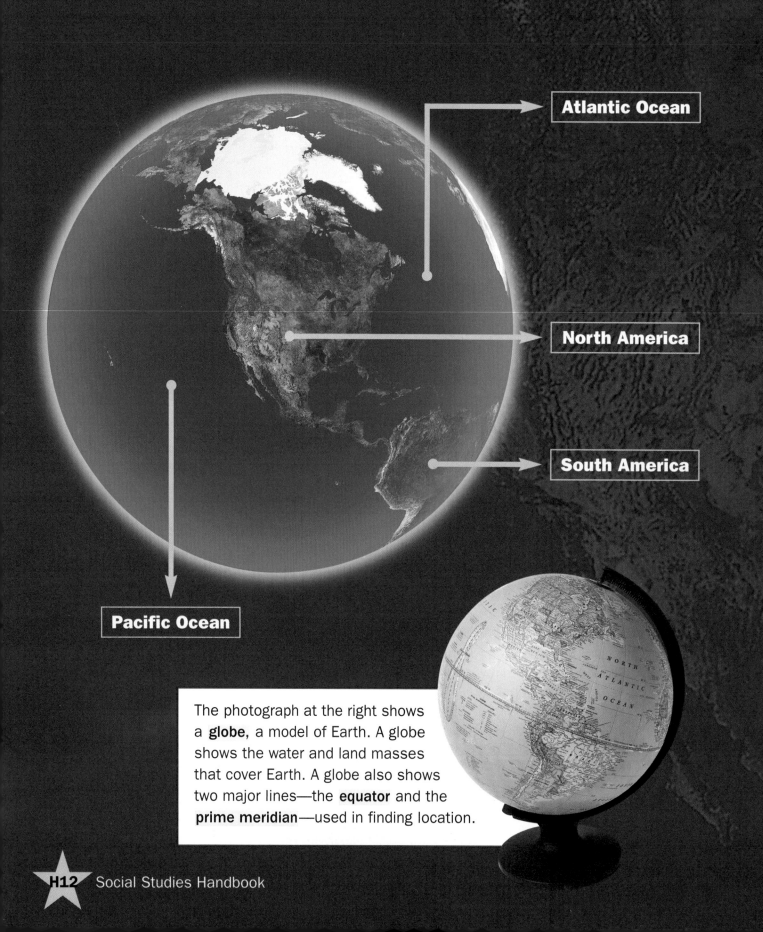

Atlantic Ocean

North America

South America

Pacific Ocean

The photograph at the right shows a **globe,** a model of Earth. A globe shows the water and land masses that cover Earth. A globe also shows two major lines—the **equator** and the **prime meridian**—used in finding location.

Hemispheres: Northern and Southern

A globe, like Earth, is shaped like a sphere, or ball, so it can only show one half of Earth at a time. People commonly speak of Earth as being divided into half-spheres called hemispheres. The **Northern Hemisphere** is the half north of the equator, an imaginary line that circles Earth at its widest point between the North and South poles. The **Southern Hemisphere** is the half south of the equator.

Complete views of these hemispheres are not possible when you are looking at a globe only from the side. For a complete view, you have to turn a globe until you are looking down directly at either the North or South Pole. The illustration below shows you these views.

Northern Hemisphere

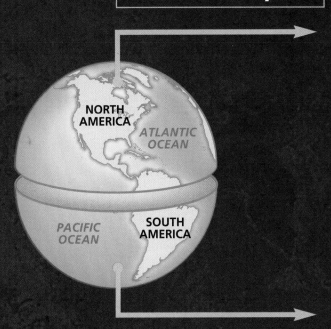

Southern Hemisphere

Vocabulary

globe

equator

prime meridian

hemisphere

Geography Skills

Hemispheres: Western and Eastern

Earth has two other hemispheres—the **Eastern Hemisphere** and the **Western Hemisphere.** These are formed by dividing the globe into halves along the prime meridian. The prime meridian is an imaginary line that extends from pole to pole and passes through Greenwich, England. To the east of the prime meridian, halfway around Earth, is the Eastern Hemisphere. To the west of the prime meridian is the Western Hemisphere. The illustration below shows you these views.

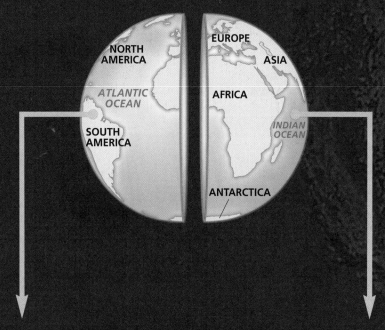

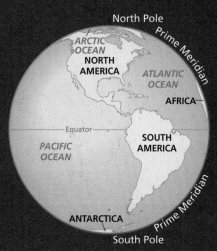

Western Hemisphere

Eastern Hemisphere

Latitude and Longitude on a Globe

Latitude and longitude are imaginary lines that help us find locations on Earth. The lines are found only on globes and maps.

Lines of latitude circle Earth in an east-west direction. They are also called parallels because they are parallel to the equator and to one another. These lines are measured in units called degrees. The equator is the latitude line of 0 degrees (0°) where measurements begin. Latitude lines tell how many degrees north or south of the equator a location is. A change of one degree of latitude in any direction on Earth is equal to about 69 miles.

Lines of longitude circle Earth in a north-south direction. They are also called meridians. The prime meridian is 0 degrees (0°) longitude. Longitude lines tell how many degrees east or west of the prime meridian a location is. Unlike latitude, longitude lines are not parallel. They are farthest apart at the middle of Earth but become closer together as they move toward the poles.

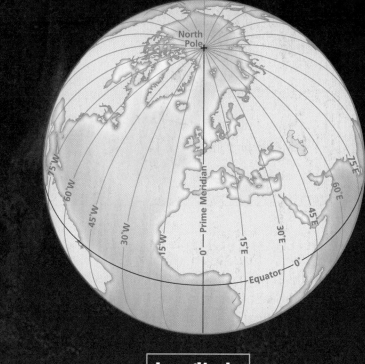

Longitude

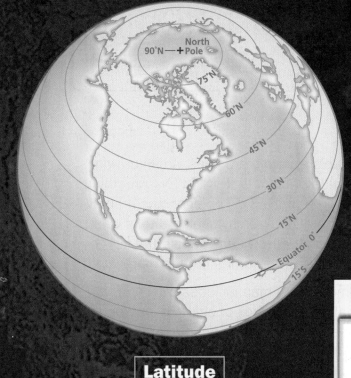

Latitude

Vocabulary

latitude
longitude
parallel
degree
meridian

Geography Skills

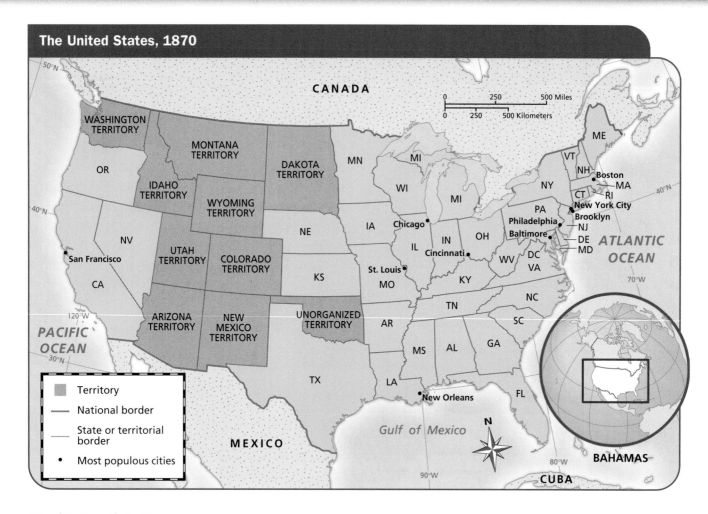

The United States, 1870

Territory
National border
State or territorial border
• Most populous cities

Political Map

A **political map** shows what humans have created on Earth's surface. This means that a political map can show borders that divide an area into countries, states, and counties. It can also show where cities, roads, buildings, and other human-made elements once were or still are today. Like other kinds of maps, political maps have many of the features below that help us read and use them.

A map's **title** tells what a map is about. What is the title of the historical map on this page?

A map's **symbols** are lines, small drawings, or fields of color that stand for something else. The map's **key**, or legend, is a small box that lists each symbol and tells what it stands for. How can you use the key to identify U.S. territories on this map?

Sometimes a map includes a **locator**, a small map in a box or circle. It locates the subject of the main map in a larger area such as a state, country, continent, or hemisphere. In what larger area is the United States of 1870 shown?

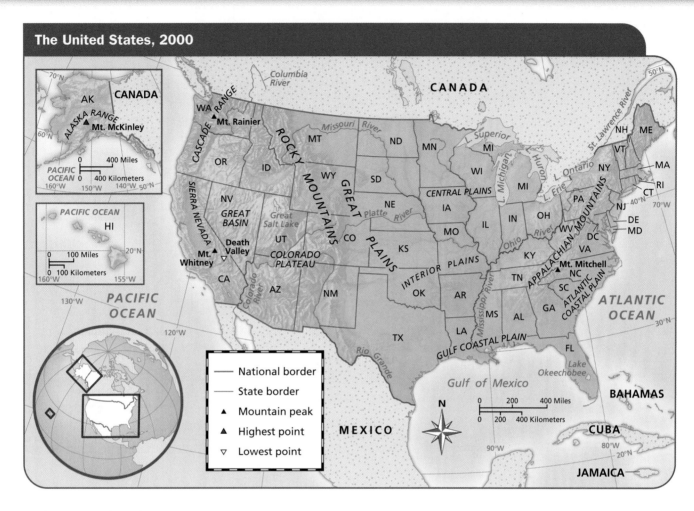

The United States, 2000

Key:
— National border
— State border
▲ Mountain peak
▲ Highest point
▽ Lowest point

Physical Map

A **physical map** shows the major landforms and water features on an area of Earth's surface. What are some examples of mountains, plains, rivers, gulfs, and oceans on the physical map of the United States on this page? Notice that a physical map can have a few elements of a political map.

A **compass rose** is a fancy design with four large pointers that show the cardinal directions. The north pointer, which points toward the North Pole, is marked with an "N." East is to the right, south is opposite north, and west is to the left. The compass rose also shows **intermediate directions,** which are smaller pointers halfway between the cardinal directions. Intermediate directions are northeast, southeast, southwest, and northwest. What direction is the Gulf of Mexico from the Cascade Range?

Four other common features on maps are a scale, inset maps, latitude and longitude, and elevation. These and other features are covered in detail on the next five pages of this handbook.

Vocabulary

political map

title

symbol

key

locator

physical map

compass rose

intermediate direction

Social Studies Handbook **H17**

Geography Skills

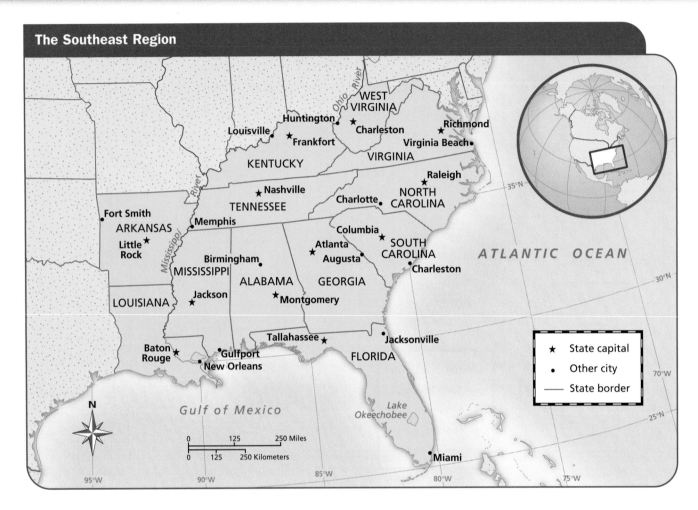

The Southeast Region

Scale

Usually a map has a **scale**, a set of lines marked off in miles and kilometers. A scale allows you to estimate the actual distances between points on a map. It tells you what a small distance on a map equals in actual miles on Earth. For example, one inch on a map may equal one mile, hundreds of miles, or even thousands of miles. On the scale above, one inch equals 250 miles. If two points on the map are two inches apart, about how many miles apart are they? How many miles apart are Little Rock, Arkansas, and Richmond, Virginia?

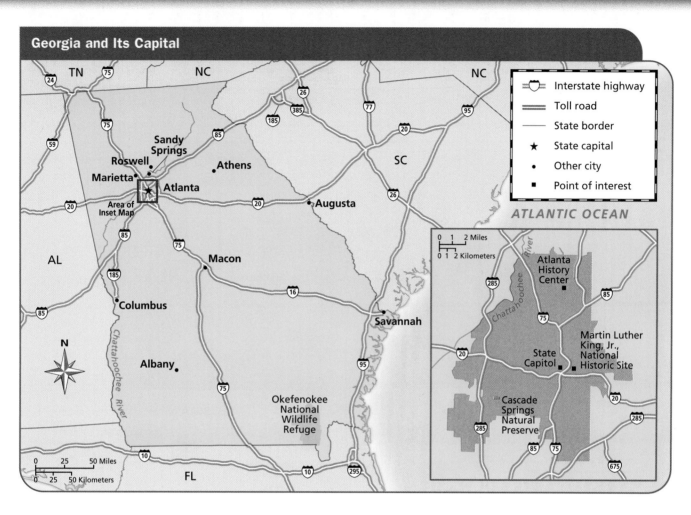

Georgia and Its Capital

Interstate highway
Toll road
State border
★ State capital
• Other city
■ Point of interest

ATLANTIC OCEAN

Sandy Springs
Roswell
Marietta
Athens
Atlanta
Area of Inset Map
Augusta
Macon
Columbus
Savannah
Albany
Okefenokee National Wildlife Refuge

TN NC NC SC AL FL

N

Chattahoochee River

0   25   50 Miles
0   25   50 Kilometers

0   1   2 Miles
0 1 2 Kilometers

Atlanta History Center
Martin Luther King, Jr., National Historic Site
State Capitol
Cascade Springs Natural Preserve
Chattahoochee River

Inset Map

An **inset map** is a small map in a box that is set inside a main map. An inset map is not the same as a locator map. It is not the purpose of an inset map to locate the main map in a larger area. Instead, an inset map shows either more of the main map or details about the main map. The map of the United States on page H17 has two inset maps. They show Alaska and Hawaii, which otherwise would be outside the area shown on the main map. The inset map has its own scale, and this often lets you see something in greater detail. What do you see on the inset map of Atlanta that you cannot see on the main map?

Vocabulary

scale
inset map

Geography Skills

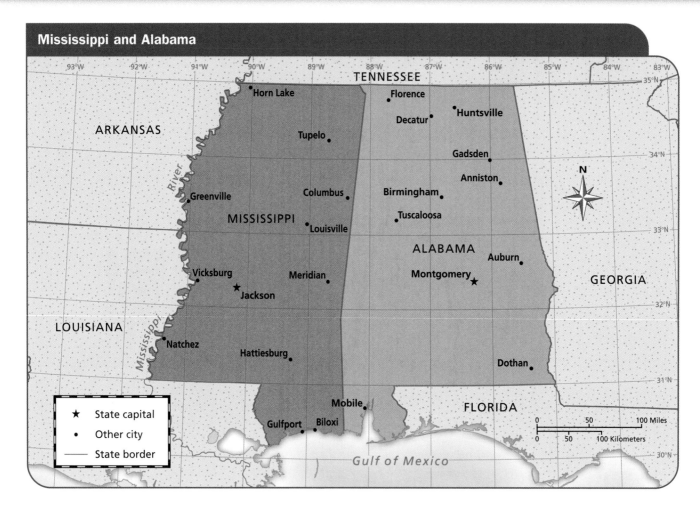

Mississippi and Alabama

Latitude and Longitude on a Map

Lines of latitude and longitude can appear on maps as well as on globes. They are usually drawn as thin, light blue lines, with numbers at the edge of the map. The point where these horizontal and vertical lines cross shows the exact location of a place. We can find the location of a place by knowing its latitude and longitude.

We refer to degrees (°) east and west (for longitude) and degrees north and south (for latitude). Although this map shows every degree, maps of larger areas do not. That would make them too cluttered and hard to read. So mapmakers usually place the lines at intervals of every 5°, 10°, 15°, 20°, or 30°. On this map, Gadsden, Alabama, is nearly exactly at the point where which lines cross? Which city lies nearest the point at which 35°N and 90°W cross?

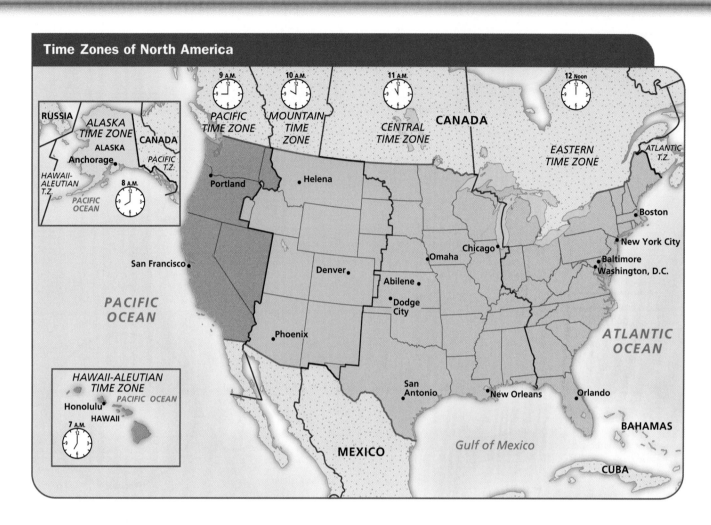

Time Zones of North America

Time Zone Map

The world is divided into 24 time zones, one for each hour of the day. A **time zone map** shows a given region's time zones. A time zone map of the world can show all 24 of the world's time zones. The United States has six times zones. Within a time zone, almost every place has the same time. Look at the map above. What is the name of the time zone in which Anchorage is located? If it is 11 A.M. in Orlando, what time is it in Phoenix?

Vocabulary

time zone map

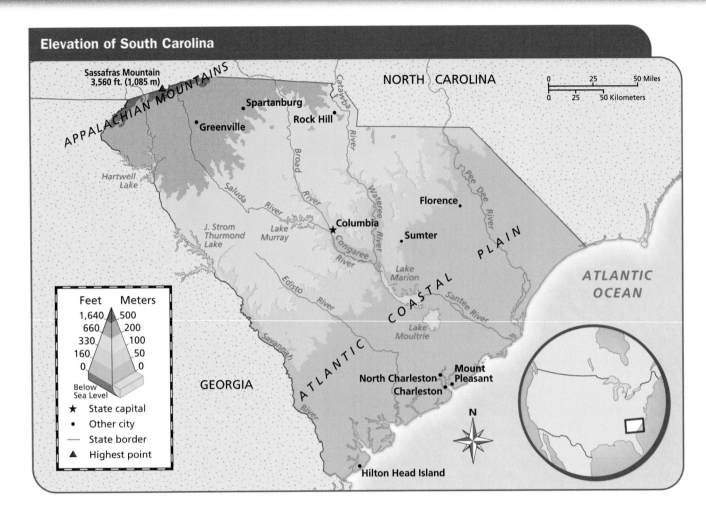

Elevation of South Carolina

Elevation Map

Elevation is the height of land above sea level. The measurement is usually given in both feet and meters.

An **elevation map** like the one on this page uses colors to show different elevations across a landscape. You can see the general heights of mountains, plateaus, and other landforms.

The key on an elevation map often contains a pyramid-shaped graphic to emphasize height. Different colors are used to stand for certain ranges of

elevation in feet and meters. For example, the darker green color stands for land that ranges between sea level and 160 feet above sea level.

On the key, which color shows the highest elevation range? What is the highest elevation range shown on the map? In which elevation range is South Carolina's capital city of Columbia? On average, is the land in South Carolina higher in the east or in the west of the state?

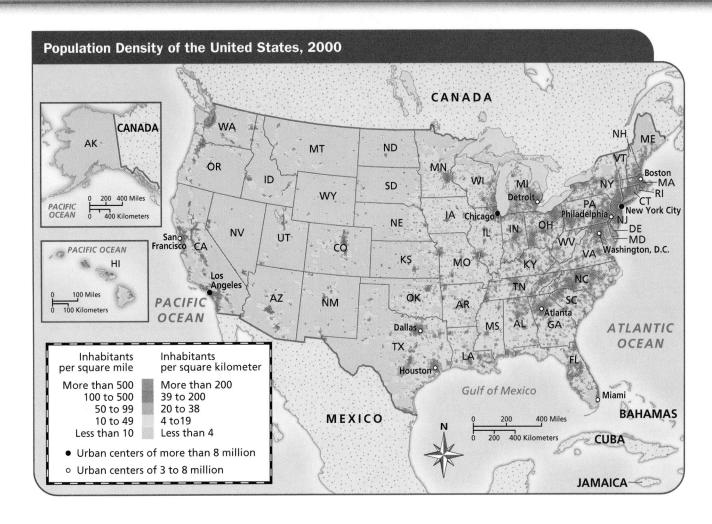

Population Density of the United States, 2000

Inhabitants per square mile	Inhabitants per square kilometer
More than 500	More than 200
100 to 500	39 to 200
50 to 99	20 to 38
10 to 49	4 to 19
Less than 10	Less than 4

● Urban centers of more than 8 million
○ Urban centers of 3 to 8 million

Population Density Map

A **distribution map** shows the pattern of data, or specific information, spread out over an area. Such a map can show this pattern for a city, a region, a country, a continent, and even the whole world at a time. This distribution map shows **population density,** or the average number of people who live in a given area.

Similar to an elevation key, the key in this population density map has boxes of color and a few other symbols. Do more people live in North Carolina or in Kansas? Which region has the higher population density, the Northwest or the Northeast? Which United States cities have more than 3 million inhabitants? Where would you guess that the mountain and desert regions of the United States are located? What hints at this fact?

Vocabulary

elevation
elevation map
distribution map
population density

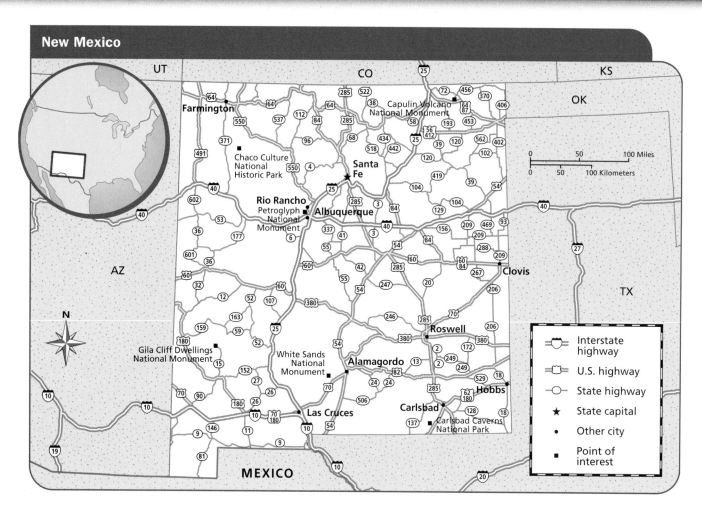

New Mexico

Road Map

A **road map** shows automobile routes between towns and cities for a region, county, state, or country. Major and minor roads or paved and unpaved roads are usually shown with thick or thin lines or with different colors. Most roads are numbered or lettered to make following them easier. Road maps may also show points of interest within a region.

The United States has several types of roads. The largest are Interstate highways that connect states and have the most lanes for traveling. The map key shows you the different types of roads.

The map on this page is a road map of New Mexico. If you lived in Alamagordo and wanted to drive southwest to Las Cruces, which numbered highway would you take? What is the number of the road that is the most direct route from Roswell north to Santa Fe? Which highways would you take from Farmington to Albuquerque?

Vocabulary

road map

Why do Americans celebrate the Fourth of July?

Begin With a Primary Source

40,000 years ago — 1500 — 1600 — 1700

40,000–10,000 years ago
People migrate from Asia to North America, scientists now believe.

1492
Christopher Columbus reaches the Americas.

1607
English settlers establish Jamestown.

1620
Pilgrims sail from Europe to North America.

This painting shows leaders from the original 13 Colonies signing the Declaration of Independence. The document declared that the United States was an independent country and was adopted by the leaders on July 4, 1776.

1800

1900

1776
The 13 Colonies declare independence from Britain.

1787
The United States Constitution is signed.

1803
The Louisiana Purchase doubles the size of the United States.

1848
The United States stretches from the Atlantic to the Pacific Ocean.

3

Establishing a Nation

Summarize

Summarizing means telling the main idea of a paragraph, section, or story. Writers use summarizing sentences to describe a main idea.

- A good summary is short. It tells the most important ideas. It should not include many words or details.

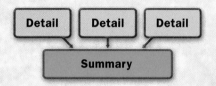

Sometimes a paragraph's **topic sentence** provides a summary. **Details** can be found in other parts of the paragraph.

During the American Revolution, the American colonists and the British fought major battles throughout the colonies. The British won battles at White Plains, New York, and Charleston, South Carolina. The Americans won battles at Saratoga, New York, and Trenton, New Jersey. The American victory at Yorktown, Virginia, was the last major battle of the war.

Word Exercise

Meaning from Context Some words have more than one meaning. You can figure out which meaning is correct by looking at how a word relates to other words in the sentence.

- She **upset** (tipped over) the glass and spilled the water.
- The loss of his wallet **upset** (troubled) him.
- The Colts **upset** (unexpectedly defeated) the Bears and easily won the game.

The Battle of Yorktown

The American victory at Yorktown, Virginia, was the last major battle of the American Revolution. In September 1781, British General Charles Cornwallis and his army were trapped in Yorktown near the Chesapeake Bay. American and French soldiers, led by General George Washington, surrounded the town by land. The French navy blocked the British from escaping by sea. Washington wrote, "The present moment will decide American independence. . . . The liberties of America . . . are in our hands."

The American and French soldiers fired on the British constantly. The British hoped help would arrive, but it never did. Cornwallis realized that the situation was hopeless. Outnumbered and running out of food, he surrendered on October 19. About 100 American and French soldiers, and 156 British soldiers, were killed in the Battle of Yorktown.

For the official surrender, soldiers on each side put on their best uniforms. American and French soldiers lined up along the road that the British soldiers would walk down. When the British came out of their camp, General Cornwallis was not leading them. He was too upset to attend the surrender ceremony.

One by one, the British soldiers laid down their guns in a large circle. The British band played the song "The World Turned Upside Down." For the British, it seemed as if the world really had been turned upside down.

Use the reading strategy of summarizing to answer the first two questions. Then answer the vocabulary question.

1 Which sentence gives a summary of the ideas in the passage?

2 How did the Americans and French defeat the British at Yorktown?

3 Find this sentence in the selection: *He was too upset to attend the surrender ceremony*. Was he tipped over, troubled, or unexpectedly defeated?

50,000 years ago   10,000 years ago   1400

40,000–10,000 years ago
People migrate from Asia to North America, scientists believe.

1400s
Native Americans develop a wide variety of cultures in North America.

1492
Columbus reaches the Americas.

PREVIEW

Focus on the Main Idea
A wide variety of Native American groups lived in North America when European explorers began arriving in the late 1400s.

PLACES
Bering Strait
Asia
North America

PEOPLE
Christopher Columbus

VOCABULARY
Ice Age
glacier
migrate
agriculture
culture
colony
Columbian
  Exchange

▶ Woolly mammoth hunters used tools like this spear thrower to make spears go farther.

Connections Across Continents

You Are There
You crouch behind a large rock, shivering in the morning wind. You look at the spear in your hand. It's made of solid wood, with a sharpened stone fastened to the end. You look around at the older members of your small band. They're all watching the snowy field in front of you.

You look out at the field, and there it is—a woolly mammoth. It's a massive elephant-like creature with long, sharp tusks and legs bigger than your whole body. You watch the mammoth walk closer and closer to your hiding place. If you can kill the animal, it will mean weeks of meat for your group.

The leader of your band gives a silent signal. All together, you lift your spears, stand, and throw.

Summarize As you read, look for details that will help you summarize the changing ways of life in North America.

6

From Asia to the Americas

The scene you just read about could have occurred about 20,000 years ago, during the **Ice Age.** This was a long period of time during which Earth's climate was colder than it is today. Low temperatures caused much of Earth's water to freeze into **glaciers,** or thick sheets of ice. In fact, so much of Earth's water was frozen in glaciers that the level of the oceans became lower.

Some areas that had been underwater now became dry land. As the map on this page shows, a strip of land called the **Bering Strait** land bridge connected **Asia** and **North America.** This land bridge allowed people to **migrate,** or move, from Asia to the Americas. Many scholars believe that people began to migrate to the Americas between 40,000 and 10,000 years ago.

Over thousands of years, people migrated throughout North America and South America. Getting enough food to eat was often a challenge for these early Americans. People traveled together in small bands, or groups, using stone tools to hunt wandering herds of animals.

About 10,000 years ago, the Ice Age gradually came to an end. The woolly mammoth and some of the other large Ice Age animals became extinct, or died out.

People continued to hunt for smaller animals and to fish. They also gathered wild plants, such as grains, berries, and nuts.

About 7,000 years ago, in present-day Mexico, people began to learn how to grow food themselves. **Agriculture,** or the growing of crops and the raising of farm animals, made it possible for people to settle in one place. Now wandering bands of hunter-gatherers could become members of settled communities.

REVIEW How did the end of the Ice Age change life for early Americans?
↻ **Summarize**

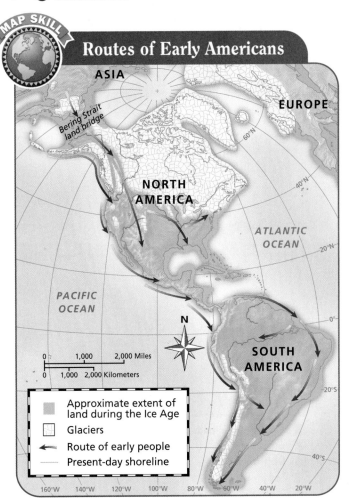

MAP SKILL

Routes of Early Americans

ASIA

EUROPE

Bering Strait land bridge

NORTH AMERICA

ATLANTIC OCEAN

PACIFIC OCEAN

N

SOUTH AMERICA

0   1,000   2,000 Miles
0 1,000 2,000 Kilometers

■ Approximate extent of land during the Ice Age
□ Glaciers
← Route of early people
— Present-day shoreline

160°W 140°W 120°W 100°W 80°W 60°W 40°W 20°W

▶ Early people adapted to different environments throughout the Americas.

MAP SKILL Movement *In which main direction were people moving as they traveled through the Americas?*

7

Native American Cultures

Early Americans developed a variety of cultures over the course of many centuries. A **culture** is the way of life of a group of people. Culture can include religion, customs, and language.

By the 1400s, Native Americans, also known as American Indians, had developed into a huge variety of groups that lived all over what is now the United States. While each group had its own culture and traditions, groups that lived in the same region often developed similar cultures. The map on this page shows some of these cultural regions.

In the Eastern Woodlands, Native American groups such as the Iroquois hunted deer, bear, and beaver in the thick forests. They

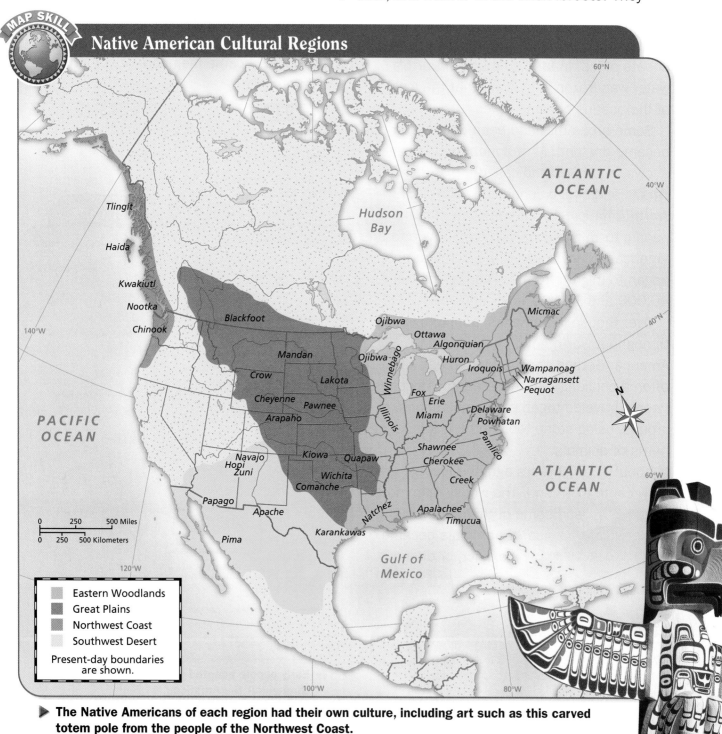

Native American Cultural Regions

Tlingit
Haida
Kwakiutl
Nootka
Chinook
PACIFIC OCEAN
Blackfoot
Mandan
Crow
Lakota
Cheyenne
Pawnee
Arapaho
Navajo
Hopi
Zuni
Papago
Apache
Pima
Kiowa
Comanche
Wichita
Karankawas
Quapaw
Natchez
Ojibwa
Winnebago
Illinois
Fox
Erie
Miami
Shawnee
Cherokee
Creek
Apalachee
Timucua
Ottawa
Algonquian
Huron
Iroquois
Delaware
Powhatan
Pamlico
Micmac
Wampanoag
Narragansett
Pequot
Hudson Bay
ATLANTIC OCEAN
Gulf of Mexico

0   250   500 Miles
0   250   500 Kilometers

Legend:
- Eastern Woodlands
- Great Plains
- Northwest Coast
- Southwest Desert

Present-day boundaries are shown.

▶ The Native Americans of each region had their own culture, including art such as this carved totem pole from the people of the Northwest Coast.

MAP SKILL Location *Which region extended the farthest north?*

used plentiful supplies of wood to build longhouses—long buildings that were shared by as many as 12 families.

On the flat, grass-covered Great Plains, huge herds of buffalo helped shape life for groups such as the Lakota and Pawnee. In summer and fall, Plains Indians traveled to hunt the buffalo. While on the hunt, they lived in tepees made from buffalo hides.

In the hot and dry Southwest, groups including the Hopi and Zuni developed a village way of life based on farming. By digging ditches to carry water from streams, people were able to grow corn, squash, and beans in this dry region.

The forests of the Northwest Coast were rich in animals that could be hunted. Coastal waters and rivers were filled with fish and seals. Groups including the Kwakiutl (kwah kee OO tuhl) and Tlingit (TLIN git) got all they needed from hunting and gathering. They did not have to grow crops for food.

REVIEW What are two ways Native Americans used natural resources? 🔄 Summarize

An Iroquois Longhouse

Elm-bark covering

Cobs of corn drying on storage racks in roof rafters

All families in a longhouse were related through the women

Poles for the frame

▶ This model shows an eight-family Iroquois longhouse. There were four shared cooking fires along the central aisle.

DIAGRAM SKILL *Where were the drying cobs of corn kept?*

HERE AND THERE Connections Among Continents

At the same time that Native American cultures were thriving in North America, connections were growing among Asia, Africa, and Europe. The Chinese developed valuable trade goods, such as silk cloth, tea, and spices. A network of trade routes called the Silk Road connected China to other lands, where demand for Chinese goods was high. Along with trade goods, ideas, skills, and customs moved back and forth along the Silk Road.

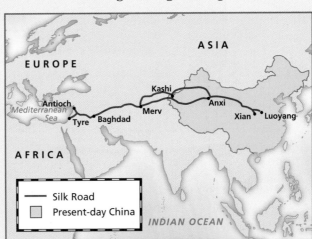

▶ This Chinese vase was carried along the Silk Road to Africa.

EUROPE
ASIA
AFRICA
Mediterranean Sea
Antioch
Tyre
Baghdad
Merv
Kashi
Anxi
Xian
Luoyang
INDIAN OCEAN

— Silk Road
☐ Present-day China

East Meets West

In the 1200s and 1300s, trade was increasing among the peoples of Asia, Africa, and Europe. New inventions were making it easier for people to travel by ship. For example, the magnetic compass, invented in China, made it possible for sailors to determine their direction far out at sea.

In Europe, these new tools were combined with advances in ship design. Explorers could now sail farther from home. This fact, along with the desire to find new trade routes, led to an age of exploration.

▶ **An early Chinese compass.**

Sailing for Spain, **Christopher Columbus** led an expedition of three ships west across the Atlantic Ocean. Columbus was hoping to find a sea route to Asia. When he sighted land in October 1492, he thought he had reached India. But historians believe that Columbus had really reached the Bahama Islands, off the coast of North America.

Spain, followed by other European countries, began establishing colonies in North and South America. A **colony** is a settlement far from the country that rules it. This was the beginning of the **Columbian Exchange**—a movement of people, animals, plants, and

▶ **The Columbian Exchange brought changes to both the Eastern and Western Hemispheres.**

CHART SKILL *In which direction did horses move?*

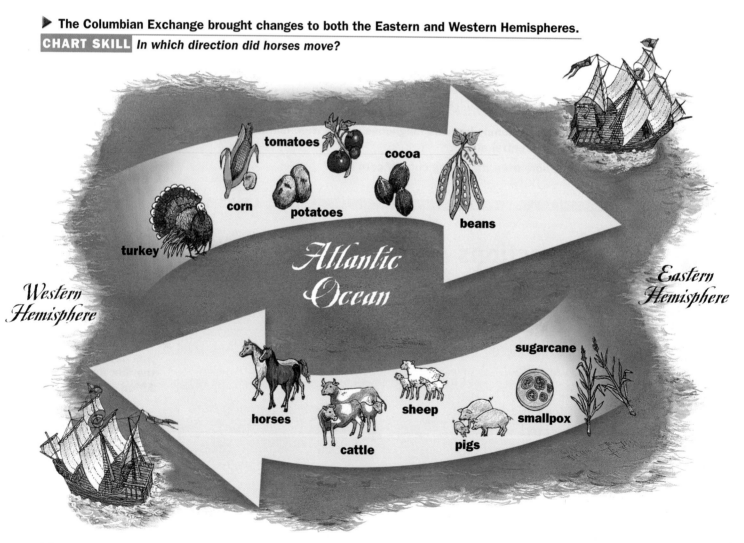

tomatoes
cocoa
corn
potatoes
beans
turkey

Atlantic Ocean

Western Hemisphere

Eastern Hemisphere

horses
cattle
sheep
pigs
smallpox
sugarcane

10

ways of life between the Eastern Hemisphere and Western Hemisphere. As the chart shows, European farm animals, such as horses and cattle, were brought to the Americas. Native American foods, such as corn and potatoes, were brought to Europe.

Not all the effects of the Columbian Exchange were positive. Without knowing it, Europeans brought disease germs to the Americas. Many Native Americans died because they had no defense against diseases such as smallpox and measles. As European colonies grew, many Native Americans were enslaved or forced off their land. The Indian way of life was changed forever.

REVIEW What changes did the Columbian Exchange bring to the Eastern and Western Hemispheres?  Summarize

▶ Columbus made contact with the people of several islands off the coast of North America.

Summarize the Lesson

- **40,000–10,000 years ago** During the Ice Age, people migrated across a land bridge from Asia to North America.

- **1400s** Native Americans had developed a wide variety of cultures in North America.

- **1492** Columbus reached the Americas, beginning a time of exchange between the Eastern and Western Hemispheres.

LESSON 1   REVIEW

Check Facts and Main Ideas

1. **Summarize** On a separate sheet of paper, fill in two details that support the summary below.

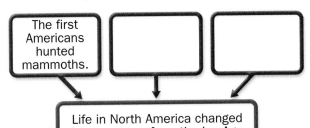

The first Americans hunted mammoths.

Life in North America changed in many ways from the Ice Age to the arrival of Europeans.

2. How did **Ice Age glaciers** allow people to **migrate** from Asia to the Americas?

3. How did Native Americans of the different geographical regions get their food?

4. How did life for Native Americans change after Columbus's voyage to the Americas?

5. **Critical Thinking: *Interpret Charts*** Based on the chart on page 10, do you think Europe benefited from the **Columbian Exchange**? Explain your answer.

Link to ⟷ Science

Identify Ice Age Animals Using a library or the Internet, find out more about Ice Age animals of North America. Identify three animals that lived here during the Ice Age and later became extinct. According to scientists, what caused these animals to disappear?

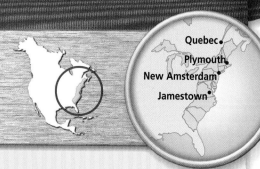

1600   **1700**   **1800**

1607
English settlers establish Jamestown.

1626
Dutch settlers establish New Amsterdam.

1733
England has 13 colonies along the Atlantic coast.

PREVIEW

Focus on the Main Idea
By the early 1600s, many European countries had established colonies in North America.

PLACES
Quebec
New Amsterdam
Jamestown
Plymouth

PEOPLE
John Smith
John Rolfe
Pocahontas
Squanto

VOCABULARY
cash crop
House of Burgesses
natural resource
economy
plantation
triangular trade route
French and Indian War

Life in the Colonies

You Are There
Do you think you would like to settle in New Amsterdam? The year is 1655, and you're here to check out this Dutch colonial town on the island of Manhattan.

As you walk from the busy port, you see a few dirt streets lined with wooden houses and workshops. Some of the buildings have wooden chimneys, which are a serious fire hazard. That's why leather water buckets are kept on the street corners.

You pass by people from many different countries. They're all working, trading goods, and shouting to one another in more languages than you can identify. You also pass lots of pigs, goats, and cows. People let their animals run free. It's cheaper to let the animals feed on garbage in the street than to buy food for them!

Summarize As you read, keep track of the factors that caused European colonies in North America to grow quickly.

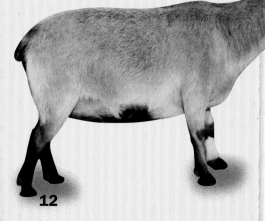

▶ Settlers relied on farm animals such as goats for meat and milk.

Founding Colonies

By the early 1600s, Spain, England, France, Sweden, and the Netherlands had all established colonies in North America. Many colonial towns became busy trading centers. The French town of **Quebec,** for example, thrived on the beaver fur trade. Quebec was founded in 1608 on the St. Lawrence River in present-day Canada. This proved to be a good location for a colony, because millions of beavers lived in the forests of this region.

Huron Native Americans trapped the beavers and brought the furs to Quebec for trading. These furs could then be sold for huge profits in Europe. A profit is the money a business has left over after it has paid all its costs.

By 1626 Dutch settlers, from the Netherlands, had established the town of **New Amsterdam** on Manhattan Island. Settlers here also traded with local Native Americans for beaver furs. With an ideal location for trade, New Amsterdam attracted settlers from many countries. By the 1640s, about 18 different languages could be heard on the streets of New Amsterdam. In addition to Dutch, people spoke languages such as French, English, German, Spanish, Portuguese, and Polish.

With thriving industries such as the fur trade, there was money to be made in North America. This attracted new settlers from Europe, causing many colonies to grow quickly. Settlers also had other reasons for moving from Europe to North America. Some came to explore and to spread their religion. Others came in search of land of their own and religious freedom.

Some people came to North America against their will. In the 1500s, European ships began bringing captive Africans to work as slaves in the colonies. However, not all Africans in North America were slaves. In places such as New Amsterdam, some Africans came to the colony as free people and some enslaved people were able to earn their freedom. The son of a former slave, Lucas Santomee, became New Amsterdam's first black doctor.

REVIEW What effect did the beaver fur trade have on the town of Quebec?
Cause and Effect

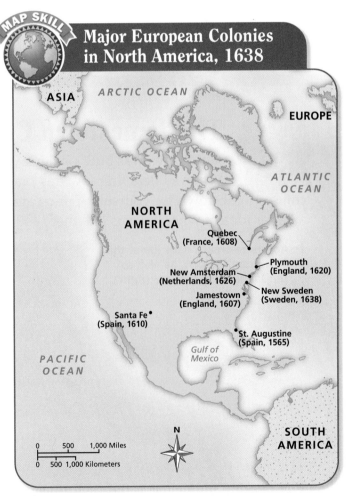

MAP SKILL

Major European Colonies in North America, 1638

ASIA
ARCTIC OCEAN
EUROPE
ATLANTIC OCEAN
NORTH AMERICA
Quebec (France, 1608)
Plymouth (England, 1620)
New Amsterdam (Netherlands, 1626)
New Sweden (Sweden, 1638)
Jamestown (England, 1607)
Santa Fe (Spain, 1610)
St. Augustine (Spain, 1565)
Gulf of Mexico
PACIFIC OCEAN
N
SOUTH AMERICA
0   500   1,000 Miles
0   500 1,000 Kilometers

► **Look at each colony to see what year it was founded and by which country.**

MAP SKILL Use a Historical Map *According to the map, what was the first colony to be founded in North America? Which country established it?*

The First Permanent English Colony

In 1607 English settlers established the colony of **Jamestown** on the east coast of present-day Virginia. This was the first permanent English settlement in what is now the United States. Lacking food and fresh water, many of the settlers died of starvation and disease during the first year. Then, under the leadership of **John Smith,** the colonists built houses, planted crops, and dug wells. Corn from the Powhatan Indians helped keep the settlers alive during this difficult time.

In about 1612, an English settler named **John Rolfe** began raising tobacco in the rich Virginia soil. You will read more about John Rolfe in the biography on page 19. Tobacco soon became Virginia's first **cash crop,** or crop grown for profit. Profits from tobacco exports to England helped the Jamestown colony grow. John Rolfe's marriage to a Powhatan woman named **Pocahontas** helped ensure a time of peace between the English and Powhatan people.

Hoping to attract more settlers from England, leaders of the colony decided to give colonists the right to govern themselves. In 1619 the Virginia **House of Burgesses** met for the first time. This was the first lawmaking assembly in an English colony. It was organized much like small-town governments in England. The House of Burgesses began to establish self-government in the English colonies.

REVIEW Why do you think self-government might have attracted new settlers to Virginia?
Draw Conclusions

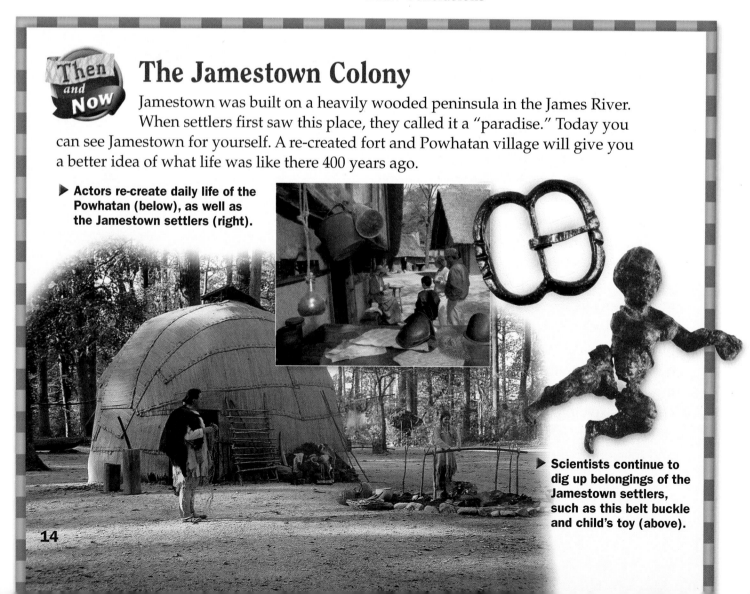

Then and Now

The Jamestown Colony

Jamestown was built on a heavily wooded peninsula in the James River. When settlers first saw this place, they called it a "paradise." Today you can see Jamestown for yourself. A re-created fort and Powhatan village will give you a better idea of what life was like there 400 years ago.

▶ Actors re-create daily life of the Powhatan (below), as well as the Jamestown settlers (right).

▶ Scientists continue to dig up belongings of the Jamestown settlers, such as this belt buckle and child's toy (above).

> After the long journey across the Atlantic Ocean in the *Mayflower* (left), Pilgrim leaders met to establish a government for their new colony (above).

Religious Freedom

In the early 1600s, the search for religious freedom led to the founding of new colonies in what is now Massachusetts. Members of a group called the Pilgrims sailed from Europe to North America in 1620. They had faced persecution, or unjust treatment because of their beliefs, in England. Now they hoped to find a place where they could practice their religion as they pleased.

About 100 Pilgrims crossed the Atlantic Ocean in a small ship called the *Mayflower.* The *Mayflower* landed in a rocky harbor the English called **Plymouth.**

The Pilgrims enjoyed a period of friendly relations with the Wampanoag Indians. A Native American named **Squanto** showed the Pilgrims the best hunting and fishing areas, and he taught them how to grow corn in the rocky New England soil. In the fall of 1621, Pilgrims gathered their first harvest in Plymouth. They invited the Wampanoag to a thanksgiving feast.

In 1630 a group called the Puritans sailed from England to Massachusetts. Like the Pilgrims, they came in search of religious freedom. Puritans founded the Massachusetts Bay Colony. The main settlement was named Boston, which thrived on fishing and trade. It remained the largest city in the English colonies for more than 100 years.

REVIEW Why did the Pilgrims and Puritans come to North America? Summarize

> The Wampanoag taught the Pilgrims how to grow corn.

The 13 English Colonies

By 1733 the English had established 13 colonies along the east coast of North America. The colonies can be divided into three regions—the New England Colonies, the Middle Colonies, and the Southern Colonies.

Each region was rich in different natural resources. **Natural resources** are materials found in nature that people can use, such as trees or water. The New England, Middle, and Southern Colonies each developed a different type of economy. An **economy** is a system for producing and distributing goods and services. In New England, for example, trees from the thick forests were used to build houses, ships, and barrels. With ships, colonists could fish in the waters off the New England coast.

Farmers in the Middle Colonies grew so much wheat that the region became known as "the breadbasket of the colonies." Flour from the Middle Colonies was shipped to the New England and Southern Colonies, and sent to other countries. Iron from mines in the Middle Colonies was made into tools.

With rich soil, a warm climate, and plentiful rain, the Southern Colonies developed an economy based on cash crops, such as tobacco and rice. Farms ranged in size from small family farms to large **plantations**, or large farms with many workers who lived on the land they worked. Many of the workers on plantations were enslaved Africans.

REVIEW Compare the important products of the New England, Middle, and Southern Colonies. Compare and Contrast

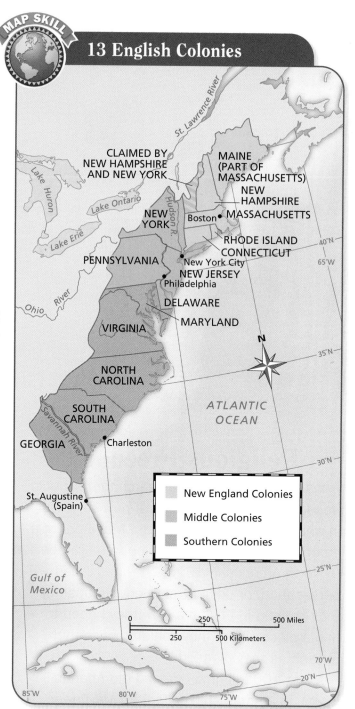

13 English Colonies

▶ The 13 English Colonies were all on the Atlantic coast.

MAP SKILL Location *Name the Southern Colonies.*

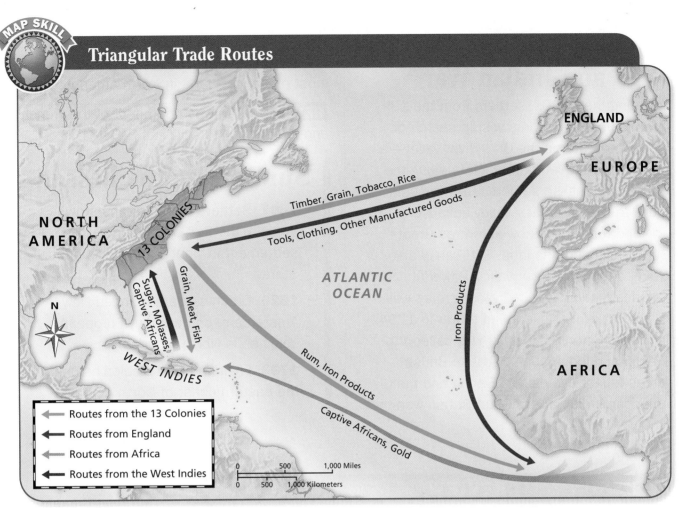

▶ The shipping routes among the colonies, England, and Africa were known as triangular trade routes.

MAP SKILL Use Routes *From where were tools and clothing shipped? To where were these products shipped?*

Slavery and the Slave Trade

As the colonial economies grew, cities such as Boston, New York, Philadelphia, and Charleston became thriving trading centers. An important part of colonial trade was the slave trade. Ships brought captive Africans to the colonies. These enslaved people were sold and then forced to work without wages.

Some trade routes became known as **triangular trade routes,** because they were shaped like giant triangles. Look at the map on this page and you will see examples of the slave trade and triangular trade routes.

Slavery expanded rapidly in the 13 Colonies during the 1700s. By 1760 about 40,000 enslaved people lived in the New England and Middle Colonies, mostly in towns and cities. They worked in people's homes, as well as in stores and, inns, and as skilled artisans.

The largest number of enslaved people—about 250,000 by 1760—lived in the Southern Colonies. Most slaves in the South worked on plantations. Sometimes hundreds of enslaved people worked on a single large plantation.

REVIEW In which region of the colonies did the largest number of enslaved people live? **Compare and Contrast**

17

The French and Indian War

During the 1700s, settlers from the 13 Colonies began moving west in search of land. They entered the Ohio River valley—a region of fertile land and forests along the Ohio River. English settlers felt they could move to the Ohio River valley because England, which was now known as Great Britain, claimed this land. But France also claimed the Ohio River valley. Powerful American Indian groups lived there as well.

Conflict over this land led to war in 1754. In the 13 Colonies, the war was called the **French and Indian War,** because British forces fought against the French and their American Indian allies. Great Britain won the war. In 1763 Britain and France signed a peace treaty that gave Britain control over most of France's land in North America.

REVIEW What was one effect of the French and Indian War? *Cause and Effect*

Summarize the Lesson

1607 Settlers founded Jamestown, Virginia, the first permanent English settlement in what is now the United States.

1626 Dutch settlers founded New Amsterdam, one of many European colonies in North America.

1733 England had 13 colonies on the eastern coast of North America.

LESSON 2 ⟩ REVIEW

Check Facts and Main Ideas

1. **Summarize** On a separate sheet of paper, fill in three details that support the summary below.

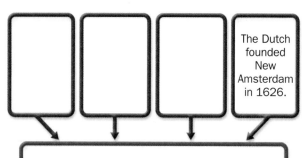

The Dutch founded New Amsterdam in 1626.

By the 1600s, Europeans had established many colonies in North America.

2. Identify reasons that European settlers moved to North America.

3. What **cash crop** was important to Jamestown, and how did it help the colony grow?

4. How was slavery in the New England and Middle Colonies different from slavery in the Southern Colonies?

5. **Critical Thinking:** *Apply Information* Explain how **natural resources** helped shape the different **economies** of the New England, Middle, and Southern Colonies.

Link to ⟨∞⟩ Mathematics

Draw a Bar Graph Use the information below to draw a bar graph. Your graph should show the rapid growth of the population of the 13 Colonies.

Year	Population of the 13 Colonies
1730	629,445
1750	1,170,760
1770	2,148,076

John Rolfe
1585–1622

When John Rolfe arrived in Jamestown from England in 1610, the colony was in trouble. Many people had left the colony. There was also tension between the colonists and the Powhatan. But by the time Rolfe left Jamestown in 1616, the colony was making money and had maintained peace with the Powhatan. How did this happen?

Rolfe wanted to find a product to sell to England that would make a profit. He knew tobacco sold by Spain was popular in England. But the English found the tobacco grown by the Powhatan to be too bitter. In 1612 Rolfe planted tobacco seeds that came from islands in the Caribbean Sea. He also experimented with different ways to dry and prepare tobacco leaves. People in England liked the new tobacco's sweeter taste.

BIOFACT

Rolfe was a member of the Virginia House of Burgesses, which first met in the Jamestown Church. Rolfe and Pocahontas were also married there.

Around the same time, Rolfe fell in love with the Powhatan princess Pocahontas. He asked both the Virginia governor and the Powhatan chief for permission to marry her. Rolfe described Pocahontas as one,

"To whom my heart and best thoughts are, and have a long time been so entangled [involved with]."

Rolfe and Pocahontas were married in 1614. Two years later they toured England to attract more settlers to Jamestown.

Rolfe's actions had a lasting effect on the colony. He developed the first product sold to England to make a profit. In 1617 colonists sent 20,000 pounds of tobacco to England. In 1630 they shipped 500,000 pounds. Rolfe's marriage to Pocahontas also created a peace between colonists and the Powhatan that lasted eight years. This gave the settlement enough time to become permanent and for its tobacco industry to grow.

Learn from Biographies

How did John Rolfe help the Jamestown colonists?

For more information, go to *Meet the People* at **www.sfsocialstudies.com.**

Map and Globe Skills

Compare Maps at Different Scales

What? A map scale uses a unit of measurement, such as one inch, to represent an actual larger distance on Earth, such as one mile. On a **small-scale map,** an inch on the map represents a very large distance on Earth. Therefore, a small-scale map shows a big area of Earth, such as a state or a country. Map A is a small-scale map.

On a **large-scale map,** an inch represents a shorter distance on Earth. Therefore, this kind of map can show more details than a small-scale map. Map B is a large-scale map.

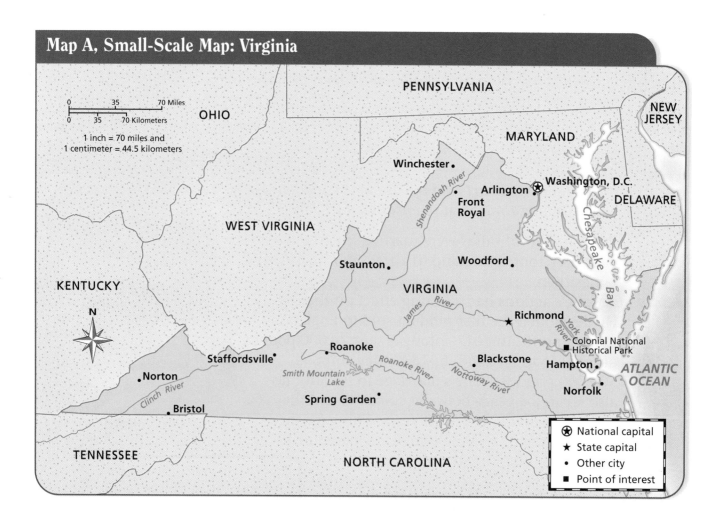

Map A, Small-Scale Map: Virginia

1 inch = 70 miles and
1 centimeter = 44.5 kilometers

Legend:
- ⊛ National capital
- ★ State capital
- • Other city
- ■ Point of interest

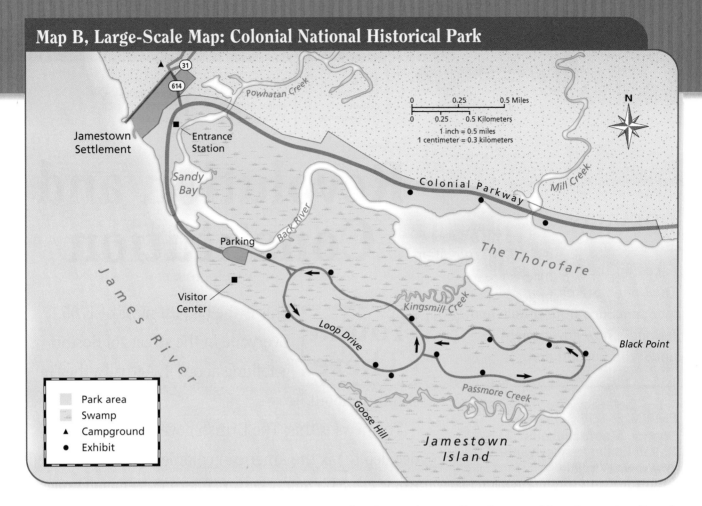

Powhatan Creek

0   0.25   0.5 Miles

.0   0.25   .0.5 Kilometers
1 inch = 0.5 miles
1 centimeter = 0.3 kilometers

N

Jamestown Settlement

Entrance Station

Sandy Bay

Colonial Parkway

Mill Creek

Back River

Parking

The Thorofare

Visitor Center

Loop Drive

Kingsmill Creek

Black Point

Passmore Creek

Goose Hill

Jamestown Island

Park area
Swamp
▲ Campground
● Exhibit

Why? In Lesson 2, you read about the founding of Jamestown. Map B shows Jamestown, which is part of the Colonial National Historical Park. To locate the park in relation to other places in present-day Virginia, you need a small-scale map. To see places in Jamestown and other details of the historical park, you need a large-scale map.

How? You can compare Map A and Map B to see the difference between a large-scale map and a small-scale map. Look at the scale on Map A. How many miles does one inch represent? Measure the distance between the Colonial National Historical Park and Woodford. The park is about 70 miles southeast of Woodford. Now measure the distance between the park and Staunton. How far apart are these places?

Look at the scale on Map B. On this map, one inch represents 1/2 mile. The area

shown is smaller than on Map A, so details of the Colonial National Historical Park can be shown. Find the Visitor Center on this map.

Think and Apply

1. Which map would you use to locate Roanoke?

2. Which map would you use to locate the Colonial Parkway?

3. Turn to the map of the 13 English Colonies on page 16. Is this a large-scale map or a small-scale map?

Internet Activity

For more information, go online to the Atlas at www.sfsocialstudies.com.

MA
Boston
PA Philadelphia
VA Yorktown

1775   1785   1795

1776
13 Colonies declare independence from Britain

1781
Americans defeat British at Yorktown

1787
United States Constitution is signed

Revolution and Constitution

PREVIEW

Focus on the Main Idea
The United States won independence from Britain and formed a new government under the Constitution.

PLACES
Boston, Massachusetts
Philadelphia, Pennsylvania
Yorktown, Virginia

PEOPLE
Samuel Adams
George Washington
John Adams
Benjamin Franklin
Thomas Jefferson
Abigail Adams
Peter Salem

VOCABULARY
Stamp Act
Declaration of Independence
republic
constitution
checks and balances
Bill of Rights

You Are There

This is the biggest news of 1765. Everyone in the streets of Boston is talking about it. Actually, they're shouting about it.

The news is this: The British government has decided to tax the American colonies. A new law called the Stamp Act will place a tax on newspapers, legal documents, even playing cards! You know the British government needs money—it has huge debts from the French and Indian War. But you never thought the British would try to tax the American colonists directly.

How will colonists react to the Stamp Act? Just listen to those angry voices all around you. It is beginning to sound like there might be trouble. What will people do? How will the British react?

▶ The Stamp Act required that stamps like this be placed on all printed materials.

Summarize As you read, think of ways to summarize the events that led to the founding of the United States of America.

Taxes and Protests

When news of the **Stamp Act** reached the 13 Colonies, many colonists reacted with anger. By 1765 the colonies had a long tradition of self-government. Since colonists could not vote for members of the British government, they believed that the British government had no right to tax them. This led to the popular protest cry: "No taxation without representation!"

Samuel Adams became an outspoken opponent of British taxes. In **Boston, Massachusetts,** Adams organized the Sons of Liberty, a group that led protests against the Stamp Act. Soon Sons of Liberty groups were started in towns throughout the colonies.

In response to these protests, the British government repealed, or ended, the Stamp Act. But British leaders insisted that they still had the right to tax the colonies. When the British government passed a new act demanding taxes, the 13 Colonies began to unite against the British. Colonists who opposed British rule became known as Patriots.

In 1774 Patriot leaders from every colony except Georgia met at the Continental Congress in **Philadelphia, Pennsylvania.** Leaders agreed that each colony should begin training militias, or volunteer armies. However, most colonists still hoped their dispute with Britain could be settled peacefully.

REVIEW Explain the meaning of the protest cry: "No taxation without representation."
⟳ **Summarize**

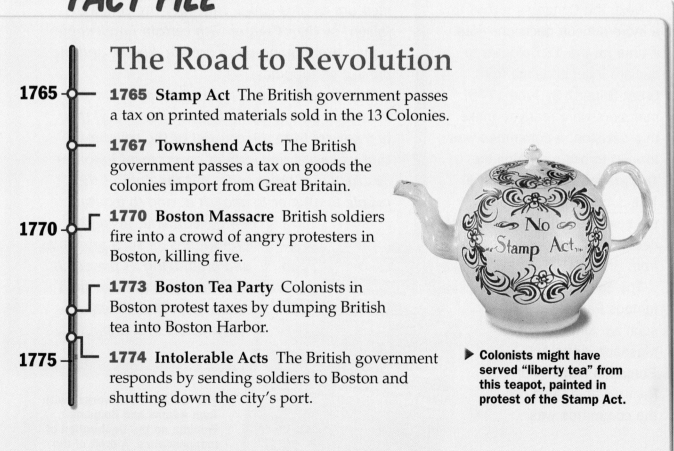

FACT FILE

The Road to Revolution

1765

1765 Stamp Act The British government passes a tax on printed materials sold in the 13 Colonies.

1767 Townshend Acts The British government passes a tax on goods the colonies import from Great Britain.

1770

1770 Boston Massacre British soldiers fire into a crowd of angry protesters in Boston, killing five.

1773 Boston Tea Party Colonists in Boston protest taxes by dumping British tea into Boston Harbor.

1775

1774 Intolerable Acts The British government responds by sending soldiers to Boston and shutting down the city's port.

▶ **Colonists might have served "liberty tea" from this teapot, painted in protest of the Stamp Act.**

Declaring Independence

On April 19, 1775, tensions around Boston exploded into war. British soldiers marched from Boston to the nearby towns of Lexington and Concord. Their goal was to destroy militia weapons that colonists had been collecting. But militia members in both Lexington and Concord stood up to the British, and the result was a long, bloody day of fighting. This was the beginning of the American Revolution.

Members of the Continental Congress decided it was time to form the Continental Army, an army with soldiers from all 13 Colonies. They selected **George Washington** to lead the new army. General Washington had gained military experience as a Virginia militia officer during the French and Indian War.

Next, the Congress turned to a more difficult decision—was it time for the 13 Colonies to declare independence from Great Britain? By June 1776, members were ready to make this decision. A committee was formed to begin drafting the **Declaration of Independence.** This document explained why the colonies believed they must declare independence from Britain.

The committee included famous Patriot leaders such as **John Adams** of Massachusetts and **Benjamin Franklin** of Pennsylvania. Also on the committee was

Thomas Jefferson, a 33-year-old lawyer from Virginia who had a reputation as an excellent writer. Jefferson was given the job of writing the first draft of the Declaration. After making a few changes to Jefferson's draft, the Continental Congress voted to approve the Declaration of Independence on July 4, 1776.

REVIEW What was the purpose of the Declaration of Independence?
Main Idea and Details

Literature and Social Studies

The Declaration of Independence

For more than 200 years, Jefferson's bold words have inspired people all over the world. Below is one of the most famous sections of the Declaration of Independence.

We hold these truths to be self-evident; that all men are created equal, that they are endowed [given] by their Creator with certain unalienable rights, that among these are life, liberty, and the pursuit of happiness.

That to secure these rights, governments are instituted among men, deriving [receiving] their just powers from the consent of the governed; that whenever any form of government becomes destructive of these ends, it is the right of the people to alter or to abolish it, and to institute new government, laying its foundations on such principles, and organizing its powers in such form, as to them shall seem most likely to effect their safety and happiness.

▶ **Thomas Jefferson worked with John Adams and Benjamin Franklin on the Declaration of Independence. A draft of the Declaration is shown here.**

▶ The British surrendered to American and French forces at Yorktown.

Winning the War

The Americans had declared their independence, but they still faced a British government that was determined to hold onto its colonies. In early battles, Washington's army suffered several defeats. The army also faced constant shortages of soldiers and supplies.

An important turning point came in 1777, when Americans defeated a large British army at the Battle of Saratoga in northern New York State. This convinced French leaders that the Continental Army could win the war. France agreed to help the Americans defeat Britain.

Even with this help, victory over Britain still seemed far away. Patriot women helped keep the Revolution alive by collecting food, raising money, and making clothing for the soldiers. **Abigail Adams,** the wife of John Adams, helped the struggle for independence with her pen. She wrote bold letters supporting American independence. You'll read more about Abigail Adams in the Biography after this lesson.

Peter Salem was one of about 5,000 African Americans who served in the Continental Army. Salem gained fame for his heroism at the Battles of Bunker Hill and Saratoga. Many African American Patriots hoped that victory in the Revolution would mean freedom for all Americans—including those who were enslaved.

In September 1781, American and French forces trapped a large British army at **Yorktown, Virginia.** The British were forced to surrender to Washington in October. This was the last major battle of the American Revolution. The Americans had finally defeated mighty Great Britain.

REVIEW Which two major victories helped the Americans win the Revolution?
↩ Summarize

James Madison

George Washington

Ben Franklin

The Granger Collection

▶ The 55 delegates to the Constitutional Convention included many of the country's most important men. They elected George Washington as leader of the convention.

A New Constitution

After winning independence, Americans had to create new plans for a government of their own. Leaders knew that they wanted their new nation to be a republic. In a **republic,** the people elect representatives to make laws and run the government. Leaders did not want their new government to have too much power, however. They remembered what it was like to live under the very powerful British government.

In 1781 the Continental Congress approved a new plan of government called the Articles of Confederation. The Articles set up a weak national government. As the main governing body, Congress had the power to make laws but not to collect taxes to run the government. This weak government soon faced problems. Paper money printed by Congress became almost worthless. Many leaders decided that it was time to form a stronger national government.

In May 1787, 55 delegates, or representatives, met in Philadelphia. After months of argument, discussion, and compromise, the delegates agreed on a constitution for the United States. A **constitution** is a written plan of government. This meeting became known as the Constitutional Convention.

The Preamble, or introduction, to the United States Constitution sets out the major goals of the new government: to establish justice, to ensure peace, to defend the nation, and to protect the people's well-being and liberty.

The Constitution divides the government into three branches, or parts—the Legislative Branch, Executive Branch, and Judicial Branch. To guard against any one branch becoming too powerful, the Constitution provides a system of **checks and balances.** The chart on the next page shows which powers belong to each branch of government. You will also see how the system of checks and balances works.

REVIEW Why do you think Americans were worried about forming a government that had too much power? **Draw Conclusions**

▶ Congress and the states printed paper money during and after the Revolution.

The Three Branches of Government

The Constitution of the United States divides our federal, or national, government into three branches. A system of checks and balances limits the power of each branch. The people provide the final check over all three branches.

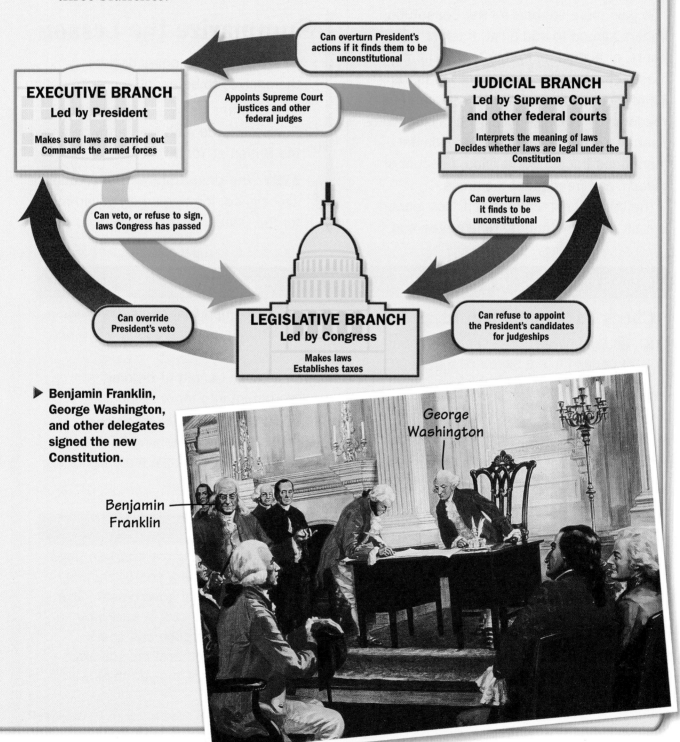

Can overturn President's actions if it finds them to be unconstitutional

EXECUTIVE BRANCH
Led by President

Makes sure laws are carried out
Commands the armed forces

Appoints Supreme Court justices and other federal judges

JUDICIAL BRANCH
Led by Supreme Court and other federal courts

Interprets the meaning of laws
Decides whether laws are legal under the Constitution

Can veto, or refuse to sign, laws Congress has passed

Can overturn laws it finds to be unconstitutional

Can override President's veto

LEGISLATIVE BRANCH
Led by Congress

Makes laws
Establishes taxes

Can refuse to appoint the President's candidates for judgeships

▶ Benjamin Franklin, George Washington, and other delegates signed the new Constitution.

George Washington

Benjamin Franklin

27

The Bill of Rights

Delegates at the Constitutional Convention signed the Constitution on September 17, 1787. Next, it had to be ratified, or officially approved, by at least 9 of the 13 states. Around the country, however, some people worried that the Constitution gave the national government too much power.

To gain more support for the Constitution, leaders agreed to add a list of ten amendments, or additions, to the Constitution. These ten amendments are known as the **Bill of Rights.** The Bill of Rights guarantees freedoms by placing specific limits on government. For example, the First Amendment guarantees freedom of religion, freedom of speech, and freedom of the press.

The Bill of Rights helped convince leaders to ratify the Constitution. Nine states had ratified the Constitution by 1788. The new government of the United States of America took effect on March 4, 1789. The following year, all 13 states had ratified the Constitution.

REVIEW How did the Bill of Rights help convince many people to support the Constitution? ◔ Summarize

Summarize the Lesson

1776 The 13 Colonies declared themselves to be an independent nation.

1781 In the last major battle of the Revolution, the American army defeated the British at Yorktown.

1787 The United States Constitution was signed, forming a new government for the United States of America.

LESSON 3 ⏵ REVIEW

Check Facts and Main Ideas

1. ◔ Summarize On a separate sheet of paper, fill in a sentence that summarizes the details given below.

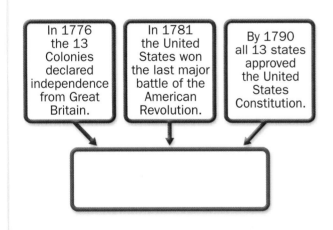

In 1776 the 13 Colonies declared independence from Great Britain.

In 1781 the United States won the last major battle of the American Revolution.

By 1790 all 13 states approved the United States Constitution.

2. Why did the **Stamp Act** and other British taxes cause conflict in the 13 Colonies?

3. Name two important decisions made by the Continental Congress in 1775 and 1776.

4. What is one benefit of dividing government into three branches?

5. Critical Thinking: *Make Decisions* Suppose you were helping to write the **Bill of Rights.** What are three rights you would want to include?

Link to ⛓ Art

Create a Poster Using the chart on page 27 as a guide, create a poster showing the three branches of government. Give the name and main jobs of each branch. Explain how each branch can check the powers of the others. Include any drawings or photographs you think will improve the poster.

Abigail Adams
1744–1818

"**I** never went to school. I was always sick," wrote Abigail Adams about her childhood. With the help of her father's book collection and her grandmother's instruction, young Abigail Smith was educated entirely at home. Since distance separated Abigail from her friends, she also became a frequent letter writer.

In 1764 Abigail Smith married John Adams, a Massachusetts lawyer. He helped to create the new government of the United States during and after the American Revolution. John Adams was often far from home. In his absence, Abigail ran the family farm and raised their five children.

Through it all, Abigail constantly wrote letters to her husband and other important people of her day, including Thomas Jefferson. John valued her opinion and often asked her advice. In many of her letters, Abigail explained how important it was that women and men have an equal education. When the Declaration of Independence was being written, she asked John to "remember the ladies." Abigail wrote to him,

BIOFACT

John and Abigail Adams were the first President and First Lady to live in the Presidential Mansion, now called the White House, in Washington, D.C.

The Granger Collection

> "*. . . and be more generous and favorable to them than your ancestors. Do not put such unlimited power into the hands of the husbands.*"

In 1797 John Adams became the second President of the United States. As First Lady, Abigail continued to help her husband. John wrote to her, "I never wanted your advice and assistance more in my life."

Learn from Biographies

Why do you think it was so important to Abigail Adams that women have a better chance for education?

For more information, go to *Meet the People* at **www.sfsocialstudies.com**.

1789
George Washington becomes the first President of the United States.

1790
The first factory in the United States is built.

1848
The United States stretches from the Atlantic Ocean to the Pacific Ocean.

Washington, D.C.

PREVIEW

Focus on the Main Idea
During the first half of the 1800s, the United States expanded west to the Pacific Ocean, and the Industrial Revolution changed the way Americans lived and worked.

PLACES
Washington, D.C.

PEOPLE
Alexander Hamilton
Meriwether Lewis
William Clark
Sacagawea
Sequoyah
James Monroe
Andrew Jackson
Samuel Slater
Frederick Douglass

VOCABULARY
Cabinet
political party
Industrial Revolution
manifest destiny
abolitionist

A Growing Nation

You Are There

What's going on in New York City? The date is April 30, 1789. There are pictures of George Washington everywhere. People are wearing buttons with the initials G. W. on them. The city is so crowded with visitors, many people have been forced to stay in campgrounds.

At about noon, you follow the crowds to Federal Hall. There, up on the balcony, is George Washington. That explains what everyone is doing in New York. They are here to see George Washington sworn in as the first President of the United States.

Washington places one hand on a Bible, raises his other hand, and vows to "preserve, protect and defend the Constitution of the United States." The crowd cheers their new President, shouting "Long live George Washington!"

Summarize As you read, look for ways to summarize important changes that took place in the United States in the early 1800s.

▶ This button was made in honor of George Washington becoming the first President of the United States. His inauguration was originally scheduled for "March the fourth," as shown on the button.

George Washington
Henry Knox
Alexander Hamilton
Thomas Jefferson
Edmund Randolph

Lithograph by Currier and Ives

▶ **President Washington chose well-known leaders to serve in his Cabinet.**

President Washington

In 1789 George Washington became the first President of the United States. As President, Washington began dividing the work of the Executive Branch into different departments. Conducting foreign affairs, or relations with other countries, became the job of the Department of State. Washington picked Thomas Jefferson to be secretary of state, the head of the Department of State. The job of handling money matters went to the Department of the Treasury. Washington picked **Alexander Hamilton** to be secretary of the treasury.

The heads of these and other departments became part of the President's **Cabinet.** Their job was to advise the President and help him govern.

Members of Washington's Cabinet had very different ideas on how to run the new government. Alexander Hamilton believed in a strong national government. He argued that government should be active in encouraging the growth of cities and trade. Thomas Jefferson, on the other hand, wanted the

nation to remain a land of small farmers and skilled workers. He believed that such a country would not need the strong government that Hamilton supported.

Hamilton and Jefferson each had a large following among Americans. Eventually, the two sides organized themselves into two political parties. A **political party** is an organized group of people who share a view of what government should do. Political parties work to elect their members to government offices.

The new government met in New York City. This was just a temporary capital for the United States. In 1790, Congress chose a site on the Potomac River for the nation's permanent capital. After Washington's death in 1799, this new city was named **Washington, D.C.** The letters D.C. stand for District of Columbia. The federal government moved to Washington, D.C., in 1800.

REVIEW How were Hamilton's ideas about government different from Jefferson's?
Compare and Contrast

The Louisiana Purchase

In 1801 Thomas Jefferson became the third President of the United States. One of Jefferson's most important acts was the Louisiana Purchase in 1803. For a cost of $15 million, the United States bought the vast Louisiana Territory from France. This territory stretched from the Mississippi River west to the Rocky Mountains. The Louisiana Purchase doubled the size of the United States.

Jefferson wanted to find out more about the geography, resources, and Native Americans of this newly acquired land. He chose **Meriwether Lewis**, an army captain, for the job of exploring the West. Lewis chose a fellow army captain, his friend **William Clark**, to share command of the expedition.

Lewis and Clark began their expedition in May 1804. They hired a French Canadian fur trapper and his Shoshone wife, **Sacagawea** (sah KAH gah way ah), to act as interpreters and guides. Sacagawea helped Lewis and Clark establish good relations with Native Americans along the way.

By the time the expedition ended in 1806, Lewis and Clark had explored and mapped a vast area. This helped open the West to new settlers from the United States.

REVIEW What did Jefferson want Lewis and Clark to accomplish? ↻ Summarize

---

Map Adventure

Lewis and Clark

1. **What river did Lewis and Clark follow at the beginning of their trip?**

2. **Were Lewis and Clark the first people to travel through this area? How can you tell?**

3. **What natural feature might have made it difficult for Lewis and Clark to reach the West Coast?**

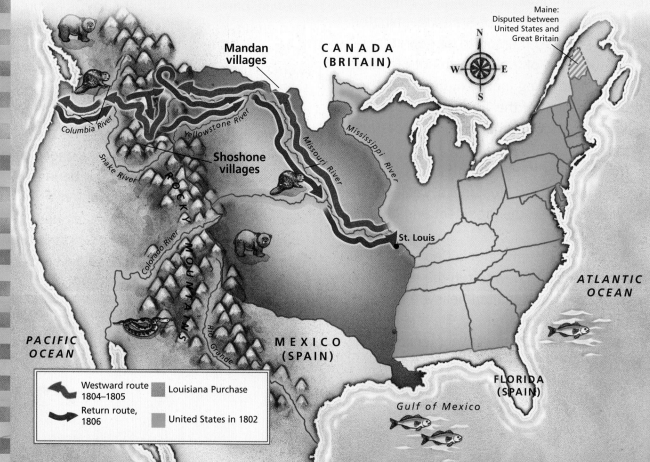

Maine: Disputed between United States and Great Britain

Mandan villages

CANADA (BRITAIN)

Columbia River

Yellowstone River

Snake River

Shoshone villages

Missouri River

Mississippi River

ROCKY MOUNTAINS

Colorado River

Rio Grande

St. Louis

MEXICO (SPAIN)

PACIFIC OCEAN

ATLANTIC OCEAN

FLORIDA (SPAIN)

Gulf of Mexico

Westward route 1804–1805
Return route, 1806
Louisiana Purchase
United States in 1802

Years of Growth and Conflict

1790

1791 **New States** Vermont became the fourteenth state in 1791. By 1821, the United States had grown to 24 states.

1812 **War of 1812** The United States and Great Britain fought in the War of 1812. Neither side won, but the United States showed the world that it could defend itself at sea and on land.

1800

1821 **Sequoyah** A Cherokee named Sequoyah developed an alphabet for the Cherokee language in 1821.

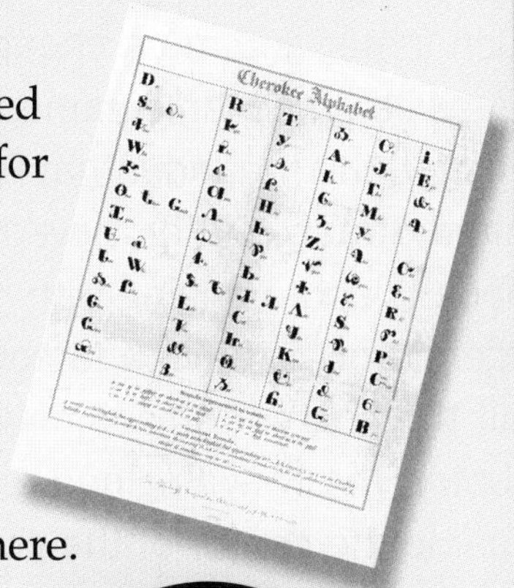

1823 **Monroe Doctrine** President James Monroe issued the Monroe Doctrine in 1823. This statement warned European nations against interfering in the Western Hemisphere.

1810

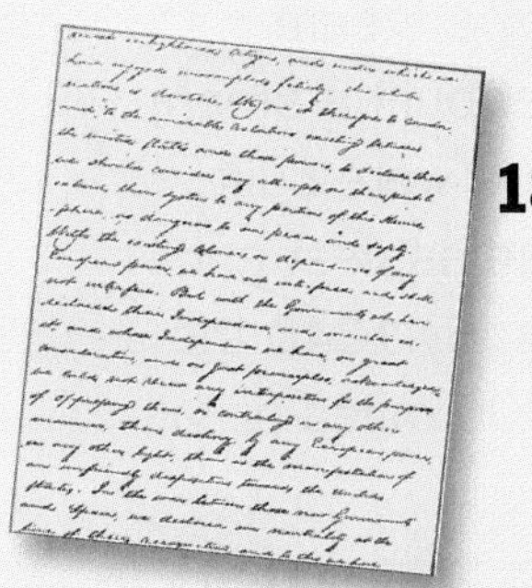

Peter Newark's American Pictures

1828 **Andrew Jackson** After gaining fame as a hero in the War of 1812, Andrew Jackson was elected President in 1828. The son of poor Tennessee settlers, Jackson was the first President who was not from a wealthy Virginia or Massachusetts family.

1820

1830s **American Indian Removal** In the 1830s, the United States government forced five major American Indian groups in the Southeast to leave their land and move to Indian Territory, in present-day Oklahoma.

1830

The Industrial Revolution

In Great Britain in the middle 1700s, the Industrial Revolution began to change the world. The **Industrial Revolution** was a change in the way goods were produced. Before the Industrial Revolution, goods were made by hand in small workshops or at home. During the Industrial Revolution, people began making goods by machine in factories. Machines helped businesses manufacture clothing and other goods much faster and more cheaply than before.

A skilled mechanic named **Samuel Slater** helped bring the Industrial Revolution to the United States. Slater moved from Britain to Rhode Island, bringing with him his knowledge of how to build a factory. In 1790 he built the first cotton-spinning factory in the country. The New England region soon became the center of the country's new clothing industry.

The Industrial Revolution dramatically changed the way Americans lived and worked. Inventors developed new machines that could help produce goods more quickly than ever before. In 1793 Eli Whitney invented the cotton gin, which could clean 50 times as much cotton a day as could be done by hand. With more cotton available, factories could manufacture more goods, often more cheaply than before.

▶ **In the 1800s, many children such as this girl worked long hours in factories.**

With all of these goods being produced, people needed better ways to get their products to market. This need led to major advances in transportation. In 1807 an engineer named Robert Fulton successfully tested a riverboat powered by a steam engine. In 1830 Peter Cooper built a steam-powered locomotive. Railroads were built, and trains quickly became the easiest and cheapest way to move goods. By 1840 the United States had about 3,000 miles of railroad track.

REVIEW How did the Industrial Revolution change the way goods were produced?
Main Idea and Details

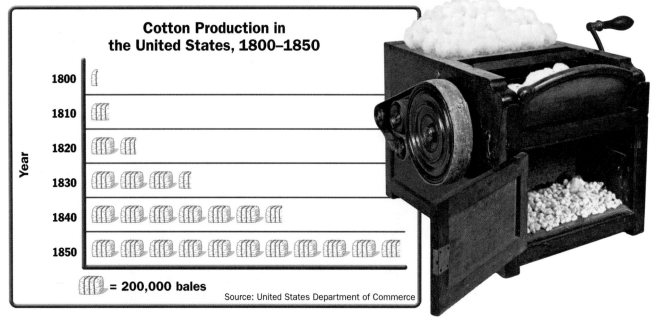

Cotton Production in the United States, 1800–1850

Year	
1800	
1810	
1820	
1830	
1840	
1850	

= 200,000 bales

Source: United States Department of Commerce

▶ **Eli Whitney's cotton gin led to a rapid increase in cotton production.**

GRAPH SKILL *By about how many bales did cotton production increase from 1830 to 1840?*

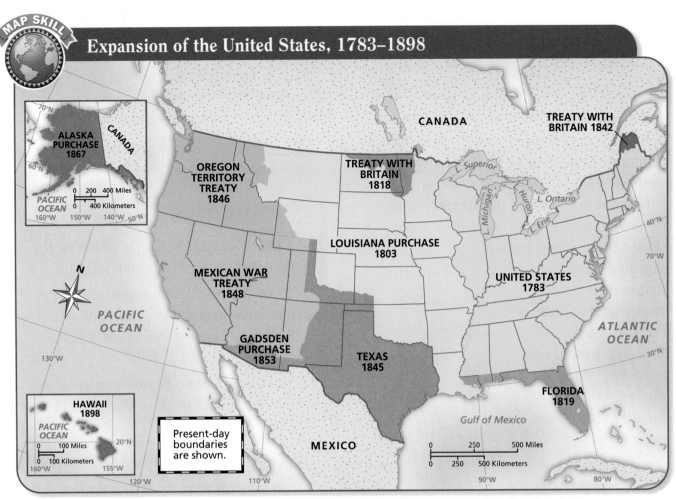

MAP SKILL
Expansion of the United States, 1783–1898

ALASKA PURCHASE 1867

OREGON TERRITORY TREATY 1846

MEXICAN WAR TREATY 1848

GADSDEN PURCHASE 1853

HAWAII 1898

PACIFIC OCEAN

Present-day boundaries are shown.

MEXICO

CANADA

TREATY WITH BRITAIN 1818

TREATY WITH BRITAIN 1842

LOUISIANA PURCHASE 1803

UNITED STATES 1783

TEXAS 1845

FLORIDA 1819

Gulf of Mexico

ATLANTIC OCEAN

▶ As a result of the Mexican War, the territory of the United States extended to the Pacific Ocean.

MAP SKILL Place *What was the last territory or area to become part of the United States?*

An Expanding Nation

In the 1820s settlers from the United States began moving to Texas, which was part of the country of Mexico. At the time, Mexico welcomed settlers to build towns, farms, and cattle ranches in Texas. But settlers soon clashed with the Mexican government over how Texas should be governed. The Texas Revolution began in 1835. By winning this war, Texans won independence from Mexico.

Many Texans wanted the United States to annex, or add, Texas as a new state. In the United States, supporters of annexing Texas talked about the idea of **manifest destiny.** This was the belief that the United States should expand west to the Pacific Ocean.

The United States Congress voted to make Texas a state in 1845. This quickly led to war with Mexico, which still thought of Texas as part of Mexico's territory. The Mexican War lasted from 1846 to 1848. The United States defeated Mexico. Mexico had to give up most of its northern territory to the United States. In return, the United States paid Mexico $15 million. The map on this page shows the land that became part of the United States after the Mexican War.

The map also shows the Oregon Territory, which became part of the United States as a result of a treaty with Great Britain in 1846. Before this treaty, both the United States and Great Britain had claimed this land. The territory of the United States now stretched across the continent, from the Atlantic to the Pacific.

REVIEW What effect did the Mexican War have on the size of the United States?
Cause and Effect

35

The Abolitionist Movement

As the United States gained new territory, questions about slavery began causing fierce debate. Should slavery be allowed in the new territories? Should it be abolished, or ended, everywhere in the United States?

Reformers known as **abolitionists** called for an end to slavery everywhere in the United States. Abolitionists attacked slavery as an evil that must be ended. **Frederick Douglass,** who escaped from slavery as a young man, was a powerful voice for the abolitionists. Douglass's stories of his own experience as a slave won many supporters for the abolitionist movement.

Questions about slavery would not be easily settled, however. As you will read in Unit 1, this issue would soon tear the country apart.

REVIEW What was the goal of the abolitionist movement? ⟳ Summarize

Summarize the Lesson

- **1789** George Washington became the first President of the United States.

- **1790** Samuel Slater helped bring the Industrial Revolution to the United States by building the nation's first factory.

- **1848** The United States stretched to the Pacific Ocean after its victory in the Mexican War.

▶ **Frederick Douglass gave speeches and wrote articles and books that convinced many people to support the abolitionist movement.**

LESSON 4 · REVIEW

Check Facts and Main Ideas

1. ⟳ Summarize On a separate sheet of paper, fill in three details that support the summary below.

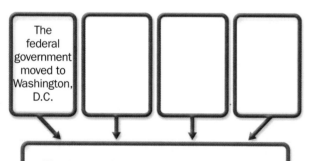

| The federal government moved to Washington, D.C. | | | |

↓

The United States changed in important ways during the first half of the 1800s.

2. What is the President's **Cabinet**? Describe the role of the Cabinet.

3. What did Lewis and Clark accomplish?

4. How did the **Industrial Revolution** create the need for better transportation?

5. Critical Thinking: *Compare and Contrast* Describe the different ways the United States gained territory from 1803 to 1848.

Link to · Writing

Write a Biography Using a library or the Internet, find out more about one person from this lesson. Write a one-page biography about this person. Explain why he or she is still remembered today.

Sequoyah
1770?–1843

Sequoyah was born into the Cherokee, a Native American group in which many young men grew up to be fighters. But Sequoyah's leg was injured in a hunting accident, so he became a trader and silversmith. He noticed that white traders had a way to communicate with each other on paper, which many Native Americans called "talking leaves." Sequoyah wanted to create a system of writing for the Cherokee. He believed it would help the Cherokee keep their history and culture.

Sequoyah worked for more than ten years on his writing system. Some people criticized him, believing his work was not worthwhile. But Sequoyah defended himself, saying,

BIOFACT

The first Native American newspaper, the Cherokee Phoenix, was published in 1828 using Sequoyah's writing system.

"It is not our people that have advised me to [do] this and it is not therefore our people who can be blamed if I am wrong. What I have done I have done from myself."

To create a writing system, Sequoyah created 86 symbols to represent the sounds of the Cherokee language.

After finishing his writing system in 1821, Sequoyah had to convince the major Cherokee chiefs that his writing system was useful. The chiefs asked Sequoyah to teach a group of Cherokees the system. The students were moved far from each other and given messages to write down. When each student could read the other students' notes easily, the chiefs were convinced.

Soon thousands of Cherokee learned how to write their language using Sequoyah's system. Books and newspapers were printed in the Cherokee language. Today Sequoyah is remembered for being the first person known to have created an entire written language alone.

Learn from Biographies
How did not giving up help Sequoyah achieve his goal?

For more information, go to *Meet the People* at **www.sfsocialstudies.com.**

Chart and Graph Skills

Use Parallel Time Lines

New England Colonies

1600 — 1620 — 1640 — 1660 — 1680 — 1700

1620
Pilgrims arrive in Plymouth.

1630
Puritans establish Boston.

1647
Massachusetts law requires towns to build public schools.

Middle Colonies

1600 — 1620 — 1640 — 1660 — 1680 — 1700

1626
Dutch establish New Amsterdam.

1664
New Amsterdam becomes New York City.

1681
William Penn founds the colony of Pennsylvania.

Southern Colonies

1600 — 1620 — 1640 — 1660 — 1680 — 1700

1607
English establish settlement in Jamestown.

1619
Virginia House of Burgesses meets for the first time.

1693
The College of William and Mary opens in Virginia.

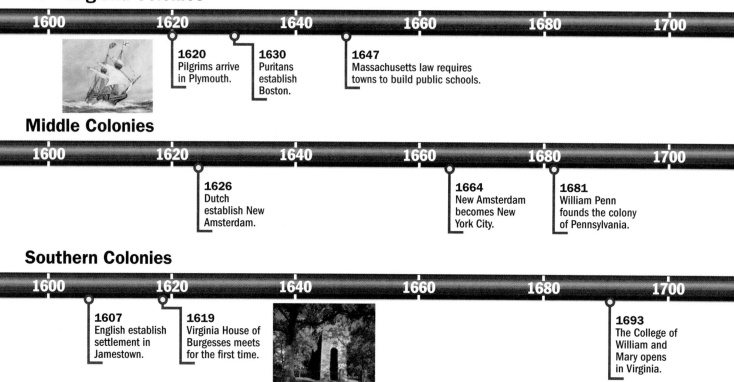

What? A time line is a diagram that shows the sequence of historical events. **Parallel time lines** are two or more time lines grouped together. They show major events in different places during the same period of time. Time lines are divided into equal spans of time such as a **decade**, 10 years, or a **century**, 100 years. The time lines above are divided into 20-year intervals.

Why? As you know from the map on page 16, the 13 English colonies were divided into three regions—the New England Colonies, the Middle Colonies, and the Southern Colonies. The parallel time lines on these pages show events that took place in each region between 1600 and 1800. By comparing parallel time lines, you can recognize patterns in the development of the different regions.

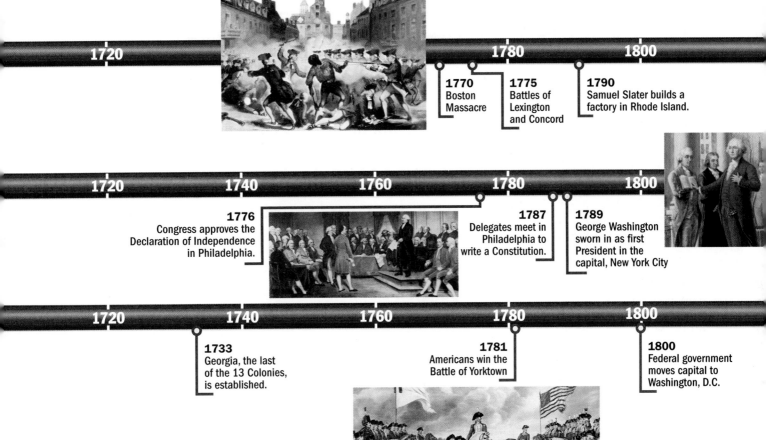

1720

1770
Boston
Massacre

1780

1775
Battles of
Lexington
and Concord

1800

1790
Samuel Slater builds a
factory in Rhode Island.

1720   **1740**   **1760**   **1780**   **1800**

1776
Congress approves the
Declaration of Independence
in Philadelphia.

1787
Delegates meet in
Philadelphia to
write a Constitution.

1789
George Washington
sworn in as first
President in the
capital, New York City

1720   **1740**   **1760**   **1780**   **1800**

1733
Georgia, the last
of the 13 Colonies,
is established.

1781
Americans win the
Battle of Yorktown

1800
Federal government
moves capital to
Washington, D.C.

How? Look at the three parallel time lines and compare them. Although the time lines show the same period of time, different events were taking place in each region. Sometimes events that began in one region reached another region.

To use the time lines, first look at each one separately. Then compare what was taking place in two or three different regions during a particular time period. Think about how these events may have been related or may have affected other areas.

Think and Apply

1 What event was taking place in all three regions in the 1600s?

2 What occurred in Philadelphia in the same decade that Americans defeated the British at Yorktown?

3 According to the time lines, which city was one of the capitals of the United States before Washington, D.C.?

Respecting the Flag

▶ **Francis Scott Key witnessed the British attack on Fort McHenry.**

You know that it is important to show respect for our country's flag. For example, when the flag passes in a parade, you stand and place your right hand over your heart. When people show respect for a flag, it is because they want to show respect for the ideals it represents. For Francis Scott Key, the United States flag represented hope and freedom in a moment of crisis. The flag even inspired him to write what became our country's national anthem—"The Star-Spangled Banner."

In 1812 Great Britain was fighting a war against France. The crews of British ships often stopped American ships, forcing the men on board to fight for Britain against their will. Soon the United States was fighting the British in what was sometimes called a "second war for independence"—the War of 1812. In August 1814, the British invaded Washington, D.C., and set fire to the White House and the Capitol.

At this time, Francis Scott Key was a lawyer working near Washington, D.C. His friend William Beanes was taken prisoner by the British after they left Washington. In September United States military leaders sent Key to try to persuade the British to release Beanes, who was held on a ship in Chesapeake Bay near Baltimore, Maryland. The British agreed to release Key's friend. However, they were about to attack Fort McHenry in Baltimore and did not want Key or Beanes to warn the Americans. Key and Beanes were forced to wait aboard a ship. On September 13, the British began firing on Fort McHenry. When the fighting finally stopped, it was too dark for Key to see what had happened to the fort. He waited anxiously for the sun to rise. In the morning, he saw the American flag flying over Fort McHenry. It was torn but still waving. The fort had not been captured.

▶ **Francis Scott Key**

BUILDING
CITIZENSHIP
Caring
⭐ Respect
Responsibility
Fairness
Honesty
Courage

Key was overjoyed to see the flag. He was immediately inspired to write a poem about the event. The first part of his poem says,

Oh, say can you see, by the dawn's early light,
What so proudly we hailed at the twilight's
*   last gleaming?*
Whose broad stripes and bright stars,
*   through the perilous fight,*
O'er the ramparts we watched, were so
*   gallantly streaming?*
And the rockets' red glare, the bombs
*   bursting in air,*
Gave proof through the night that our
*   flag was still there.*
Oh say, does that star-spangled banner
*   yet wave*
O'er the land of the free and the home of
*   the brave?*

▶ The original flag that flew over Fort McHenry is located at the National Museum of American History of the Smithsonian Institution in Washington, D.C.

Within a week, the poem, first called "The Defense of Fort McHenry," was published in a Baltimore newspaper. Soon other newspapers all over the country also published the poem. Set to a popular tune of the time, Key's song became known as "The Star-Spangled Banner." Congress officially adopted the song as the national anthem in 1931. Today the very flag that inspired Key to write the anthem is on display at the Smithsonian Institution in Washington, D.C.

Respect in Action

When "The Star-Spangled Banner" is sung at a sports game or other event, people stand and men remove their hats. Why do you think this is the custom? In what other ways can you show respect for our country?

Main Ideas and Vocabulary

Read the passage below and use it to answer the questions that follow.

During the Ice Age, about 40,000 to 10,000 years ago, people from Asia began moving to North America over a land bridge. After the Ice Age, different cultures developed among Native American groups.

In 1492 Christopher Columbus sailed to an island off the coast of North America. Soon, Spain, England, France, Sweden, and the Netherlands began establishing colonies in North and South America. By 1733 Great Britain had 13 colonies in North America. When the French and Indian War ended in 1763, Britain gained more land from France.

During the American Revolution, from 1775 to 1781, Americans living in the 13 Colonies fought against Great Britain to gain independence. After the Americans won the war, delegates met in Philadelphia to write a constitution for the new United States of America. They formed a government based on three branches of government.

In the early years of the nation, the Industrial Revolution dramatically changed the way Americans lived. New forms of transportation made travel easier and provided cheaper and faster ways to move goods to markets.

The issue of slavery soon divided the country. Abolitionists wanted it ended everywhere in the United States. Slavery became the central issue in the nation.

1 According to this passage, what was the effect of the French and Indian War?
  A Christopher Columbus was allowed to travel to North America.
  B The American colonists gained independence.
  C Britain gained land from France.
  D Spain acquired more colonies.

2 In the passage, the term Ice Age means—
  A a period of colder climate than today
  B a settlement
  C a period of warmer climate than today
  D a period of storms

3 In the passage, the word constitution means—
  A a book
  B a to-do list
  C a declaration of war
  D a written plan of government

4 Which sentence is true?
  A The French and Indian War came after the American Revolution.
  B Columbus landed in North America after the American Revolution.
  C Columbus arrived in North America before the Ice Age.
  D The French and Indian War came before the American Revolution.

People and Vocabulary

Match each person and term to its definition.

1. **migrate** (p. 7)
2. **Pocahontas** (p. 14)
3. **Thomas Jefferson** (p. 24)
4. **republic** (p. 26)
5. **manifest destiny** (p. 35)
6. **Frederick Douglass** (p. 36)

   a. government in which people elect representatives

   b. leader in the abolitionist movement

   c. belief that the United States should expand west to the Pacific Ocean

   d. brought peace between the English and the Powhatan with marriage

   e. to move

   f. wrote the Declaration of Independence

Write and Share

Present an Interview With the help of a classmate, choose one key person from this unit. Write a list of questions you would ask if that person were alive today. Conduct research in the library to answer as many of your questions as you can. Finally, share your findings with the class in the form of an interview. One of you will be the key person and the other will be the interviewer.

Read on Your Own

Look for books like these in the library.

Apply Skills

Create Parallel Time Lines Make a time line listing major events from your life in the order they occurred. Then ask a friend or family member about major events in his or her life and when they occurred. Make another time line for this person's events. Draw pictures illustrating events in both time lines. Do any events on the time lines match? What are some differences?

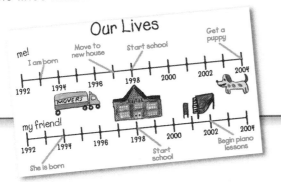

Project

This Just In

Report breaking news in American history.

1 Choose an important event that you have learned about American history.

2 Choose roles to play for a press conference about the event: government officials or experts, news reporters, eyewitnesses, and other participants.

3 Research the event, focusing on one or two important details of the event. Work together to write questions and answers about the event.

4 Create a poster that a TV news station might use to announce breaking news about an event.

5 Hold your press conference as a class activity.

Internet Activity

Find out more about history in North America. Go to **www.sfsocialstudies.com/activities** and select your grade and unit.

War Divides the Nation

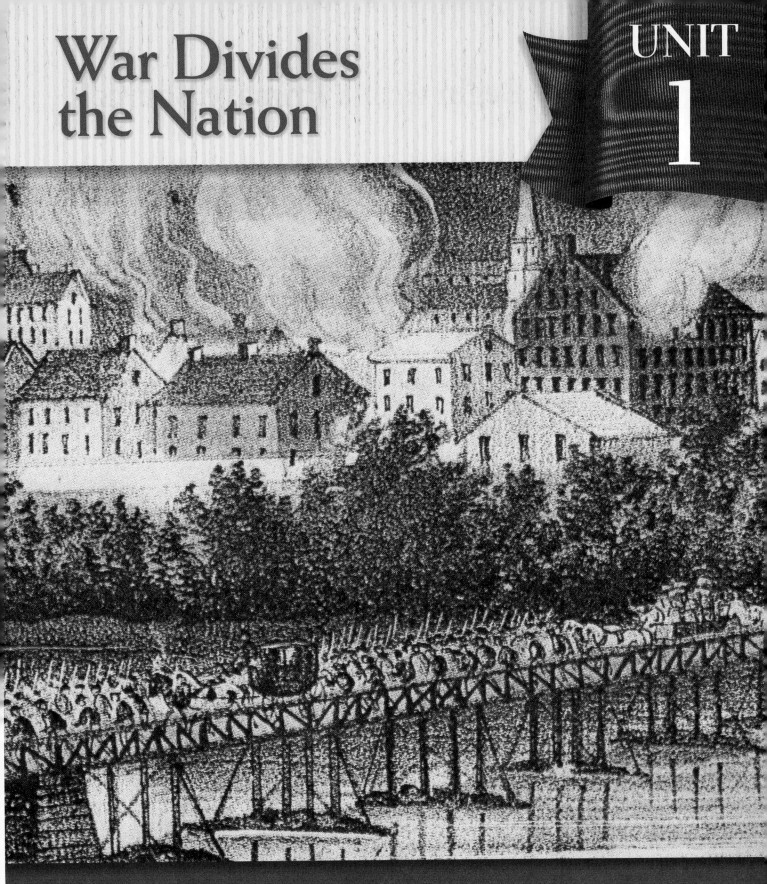

What might cause a nation to break apart?

1820

1850

1860

1820
Congress passes
Missouri Compromise.

1849
Harriet Tubman
escapes slavery
on the Underground
Railroad.

1860
Abraham Lincoln
is elected
President.

April 1861
Southern forces
fire on Fort
Sumter, beginning
the Civil War.

January 1863
Emancipation
Proclamation
takes effect.

> "...that these dead shall not have died in vain—that this nation, under God, shall have a new birth of freedom..."
>
> —Said by President Abraham Lincoln in the Gettysburg Address, November 19, 1863

This print by Currier and Ives shows the Fall of Richmond, Virginia, to Union forces in 1865.

1870

July 1863
Battle of Gettysburg is fought.

April 1865
Confederacy surrenders, ending the Civil War.

December 1865
The 13th Amendment ends slavery.

March 1867
Congress passes the first Reconstruction Act.

Meet the People

Henry Clay
1777–1852

Birthplace: Hanover County, Virginia

Lawyer, planter

- Nicknamed "The Great Compromiser"
- Helped create the Missouri Compromise in 1820
- Created the Compromise of 1850

Robert E. Lee
1807–1870

Birthplace: Stratford, Virginia

Army officer

- Fought in the Mexican War
- Turned down Lincoln's offer to command the Union army
- Became commander of the Army of Northern Virginia

Jefferson Davis
1808–1889

Birthplace: present-day Todd County, Kentucky

Plantation owner

- Served as United States Senator from Mississippi
- President of the Confederacy during the Civil War
- Wrote a book about the Confederate government

Abraham Lincoln
1809–1865

Birthplace: near Hodgenville, Kentucky

Lawyer, President

- Opposed the spread of slavery
- President of the United States from 1861 to 1865, during the Civil War
- Issued the Emancipation Proclamation

1770	1790	1810	1830

1777 • Henry Clay

1807 • Robert E. Lee

1808 • Jefferson Davis

1809 • Abraham Lincoln

about 1813 • Joseph Cinque

about 1820 • Harriet Tubman

1821 • Clara Barton

1822 • Ulysses S. Grant

Joseph Cinque

about 1813–about 1879

Birthplace: present-day Sierra Leone, West Africa

Rice farmer, leader of slave ship rebellion

- African name was Sengbe Pieh, which was pronounced by the Spanish as "Cinque"
- Led African captives in a revolt aboard the slave ship *Amistad*
- Served as key witness during the *Amistad* trial

Harriet Tubman

about 1820–1913

Birthplace: Dorchester County, Maryland

Conductor on the Underground Railroad, abolitionist

- Escaped from slavery in 1849 and settled in Philadelphia
- Made 19 trips to the South on the Underground Railroad and helped free more than 300 slaves
- Spoke out against slavery and for women's rights

Clara Barton

1821–1912

Birthplace: Oxford, Massachusetts

Teacher, nurse

- Volunteered as a nurse during the Civil War
- Nicknamed the "Angel of the Battlefield"
- Founded the American Red Cross

Ulysses S. Grant

1822–1885

Birthplace: Point Pleasant, Ohio

Army officer, President

- Won the first major Union victory of the Civil War at Fort Donelson
- Appointed to command the Union armies by President Lincoln
- Elected President of the United States in 1868

1850	1870	1890	1910

1852

1870

1889

1865

about 1879

1913

1912

1885

Reading Social Studies

War Divides the Nation

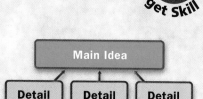

Target Skill

Main Idea and Details

Look at the diagram to see how details support a main idea. A main idea is the most important idea of a paragraph. Details are information related to the main idea. Each detail helps support the main idea.

Main Idea		
Detail	Detail	Detail

Read the following paragraph. The **main idea** and **details** have been highlighted.

In the 1800s the United States was growing and changing. The development of roads, waterways, and railroads allowed people to move west. The nation's land was expanding. The way people lived was also changing. In some places, cities were growing and attracting factory workers. In other parts of the country, people were still living on farms but changing the way they harvested their crops.

Word Exercise

Word Relationships One way to understand a word's meaning better and remember what you read is to look for word relationships. Seeing how key words and ideas from the reading are related can help you figure out a word's meaning and organize information.

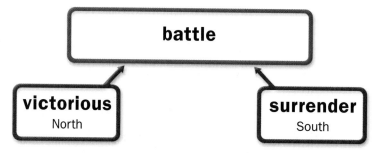

battle

victorious
North

surrender
South

Main Ideas and Details of War Divides a Nation

Differences between the Northern and Southern states led to many problems for the United States. The rural South depended on farming and slavery. The North had more factories and larger cities than the South.

Trouble grew when Abraham Lincoln became President in 1861. South Carolina broke away from the Union. Before long, eleven states in the South had done the same and formed the Confederate States of America. The country was divided and went to war. This war was called the Civil War.

Each side won some battles. In late 1863 Northern victories increased. In 1865 the North was victorious and the South surrendered.

Lincoln hoped to reunite the nation, but he was killed shortly after the Civil War. President Andrew Johnson and Congress fought over Reconstruction, or the plans for rebuilding the South. Amendments to the Constitution ended slavery and gave the vote to all male citizens, black and white.

Federal troops and Reconstruction laws governed Southern states. The Freedmen's Bureau, a federal agency, provided aid and set up schools for African Americans.

When Reconstruction ended in 1877, some Southerners tried to keep freed slaves from voting. A few people used violence to stop black men who tried to vote. Southern states also passed Jim Crow laws, which said African Americans could not use the same areas as whites in restaurants, trains, buses, hotels, and other public places.

Apply it!

Use the reading strategy of main idea and details to answer these questions.

1. What is the main idea of the first paragraph?

2. What details support that main idea?

3. How are these words from the selection related: *farming, cities, rural, factories?*

CHAPTER 1

A Divided Nation

1820

United States
About 1.5 million enslaved people live in the United States, most in the Southern states.

Lesson 1

1

1849

Philadelphia, Pennsylvania
Harriet Tubman escapes to freedom in Philadelphia on the Underground Railroad.

Lesson 2

2

March 1861

Washington, D.C.
Abraham Lincoln is inaugurated as President.

Lesson 3

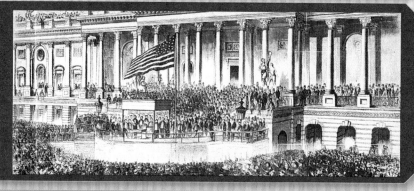

3

April 1861

Charleston, South Carolina
Southern troops fire on Fort Sumter.

Lesson 4

4

Why We Remember

"... one nation under God, indivisible, with liberty and justice for all."
These words are part of the Pledge of Allegiance, which Americans have said for many years. But there was a time when the words were not true for all Americans. In the middle 1800s, the United States was one nation divided into two parts, the North and the South. In the South, enslaved people grew crops such as cotton on plantations. In the North, where slavery was illegal in most states, many people worked in factories and lived in cities. Differences between the North and the South sparked serious conflicts, which in 1861 set off a terrible war. By the end of the war, Americans began the long task of rebuilding the country—"with liberty and justice for all."

1840   1860

1846
Congress votes
to lower tariffs
on imports.

1860
The number of enslaved African
Americans in the United States
reaches four million.

PREVIEW

Focus on the Main Idea
Differences between the
North and South led to
growing tensions between
the two regions.

PEOPLE
David Walker

VOCABULARY
sectionalism

North and South Grow Apart

You Are There

The year is 1850, and you are a sailor on a ship that carries goods to and from ports on the East Coast of the United States. Your ship glides into the port of Charleston, South Carolina, and ties up at a dock. You see hundreds of bundles of cotton waiting to be loaded onto your ship. The cotton has been grown on plantations across the South. You know that most of the work on those plantations is done by people who are enslaved.

You join the other sailors to unload your ship of its cargo of manufactured goods from Boston, Massachusetts. The cargo includes tools, machines, and cloth made by free workers in factories. You know that Charleston and Boston are part of the same country, the United States. Yet they are so different they might well be parts of different countries. Before long their differences will lead to war.

Main Idea and Details As you read, focus on how the North and South differed and how each of the differences pushed the two regions apart.

Two Regions

Many changes had taken place in the United States since the country was formed. The North and South were very different geographically, but after the start of the Industrial Revolution, other differences between the two regions increased dramatically. Southerners lived a mostly rural way of life. Most lived and worked on farms and in small towns. By the middle 1800s, few Southern cities had a population of more than 15,000.

In contrast, many Northerners at that time lived an urban way of life. Although most Northerners still lived on farms, more and more people worked in factories and lived in large towns and cities. In 1860 nine of the ten largest cities in the United States were located in the North. The bar graph and circle graphs below show how the populations of the North and South differed in 1850.

The goals of factory owners and factory workers in the North were different from those of plantation owners and farmers in the South. These differences led to a strong disagreement in 1846. A law passed by Congress in that year lowered the tariffs the United States charged for goods imported from other countries. This made Northern factory owners angry.

The Northern states had wanted higher tariffs, or taxes on imported goods. Higher prices on imported goods would encourage Americans to buy manufactured goods from the North.

The Southern states, however, wanted lower tariffs. They preferred to buy the cheaper goods made in Great Britain.

The way of life of one section of the United States was threatening the way of life in the other section of the United States. These differences caused sectionalism in our country. **Sectionalism** is a loyalty to a section or part of the country rather than to the whole country.

REVIEW Explain how differences between the North and South led to conflict between them. ⟳ **Main Idea and Details**

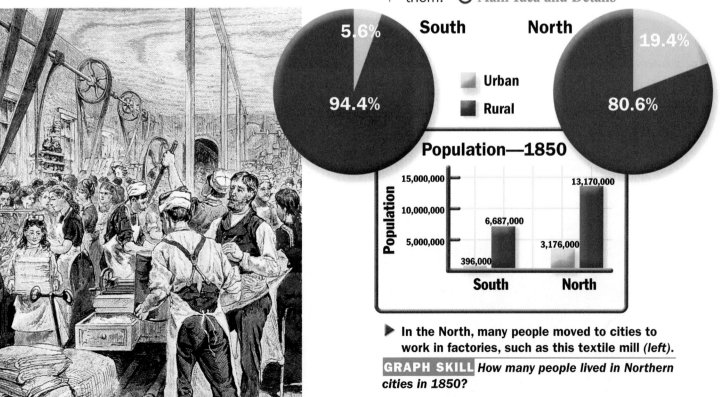

South

North

5.6%

94.4%

19.4%

80.6%

Urban

Rural

Population—1850

Population

15,000,000

10,000,000

5,000,000

396,000

6,687,000

South

3,176,000

13,170,000

North

▶ In the North, many people moved to cities to work in factories, such as this textile mill *(left)*.

GRAPH SKILL *How many people lived in Northern cities in 1850?*

Slavery in the South

One very important difference between the North and the South was slavery. Slavery was allowed in the Southern states, where enslaved people grew such crops as cotton, tobacco, and rice. By 1850 most Northern states had outlawed slavery. Northern workers were free and were paid for their work. In many Northern factories, however, workers put in long hours, under difficult conditions, for low pay.

Slavery was profitable to the economy of the South. The goods an enslaved person produced brought in at least twice as much money as the cost of owning the slave. In 1850 about six out of every ten slaves in the South worked in the cotton fields. Cotton was usually grown on large plantations. However, many slaves lived on small farms. On these smaller farms, the owner often worked in the fields alongside a small group of slaves. Still, only about one-third of Southern farmers owned slaves.

By 1860 enslaved African Americans in the United States totaled almost four million people. In some states, they outnumbered the free whites. The line graph on this page shows how the number of enslaved people changed between 1820 and 1860. It also shows changes in the population of free African Americans during the same time. Most of the enslaved African Americans lived in the South, while most of the free African Americans lived in the North.

Even free African Americans did not always have the same voting rights as whites. In some states, only people who owned property could vote, but in some states where this requirement had been dropped for whites, such as in New York, blacks still had to own land before they could vote. Throughout the country African Americans suffered from discrimination. They did not have the rights of full citizenship.

REVIEW Identify the main reason why the South wanted to keep slavery.

↻ **Main Idea and Details**

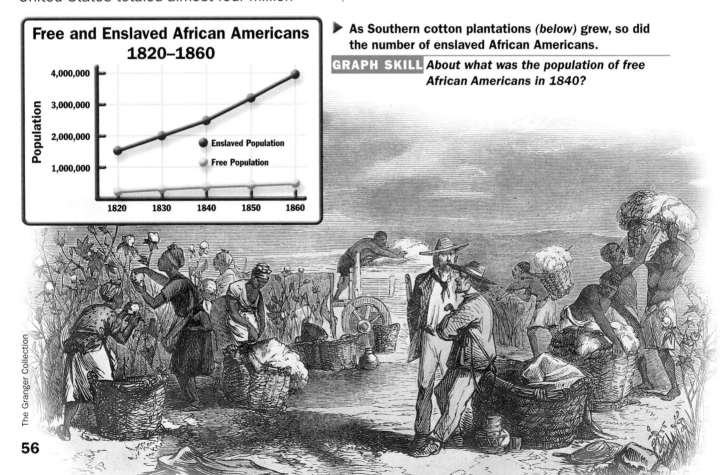

Free and Enslaved African Americans 1820–1860

- ● Enslaved Population
- ● Free Population

▶ As Southern cotton plantations (below) grew, so did the number of enslaved African Americans.

GRAPH SKILL *About what was the population of free African Americans in 1840?*

The Granger Collection

Different Views on Slavery

As you have read, abolitionists opposed the practice of slavery and fought to end slavery everywhere in the country. They insisted that slavery should be abolished because it was wrong for one human being to own another. One abolitionist, a free African American named **David Walker,** asked this about the Southern slave owners:

> *"How would they like us to make slaves of . . . them?"*

Southern slave owners continued to defend slavery. They pointed to the evils of factories in the North, where people worked long hours, in bad surroundings, for little pay. Slave owners argued that slaves were better off than Northern factory workers.

Debate continued throughout the middle 1800s. But, as you will read, words were not the only weapons to be used against slavery.

REVIEW Identify one argument that supported the idea that slavery should be abolished. Main Idea and Details

Summarize the Lesson

- **1846** Congress voted to lower the tariff on imports, which angered many Northerners.

- **1860** The number of enslaved African Americans in the United States reached almost four million.

LESSON 1   REVIEW

Check Facts and Main Ideas

1. Main Idea and Details On a sheet of paper, complete the graphic organizer to show details supporting the main idea.

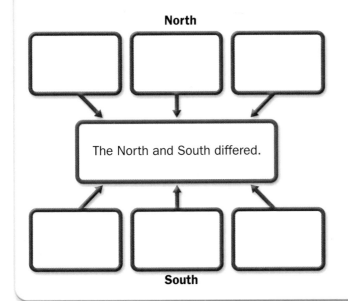

North

The North and South differed.

South

2. Describe how tariffs affected relations between the North and South. Use the word **sectionalism** in your answer.

3. In 1860 were more African Americans enslaved or free? How do you know?

4. **Critical Thinking:** *Make Inferences* What conditions existed in the North that might lead to problems at a later date?

5. Describe the main argument of people opposed to slavery.

Link to Art

Create a Graph or Illustration Choose one topic from the lesson. Then show with a graph or a picture how the North and the South were growing apart.

Thinking Skills

Recognize Point of View

What? **Point of view** is the way a person looks at or thinks about a topic or situation. A person's point of view may be affected by his or her experiences and way of life. As you have read in Lesson 1, people had very different points of view about slavery.

In the selections on these pages, two writers expressed their points of view about slavery. The writers tried to support their points of view with descriptions and details.

Selection A was written by George Fitzhugh, a lawyer who was a supporter of slavery. His family had lived in the South for many years and had owned a 500-acre plantation.

Selection B was written by Frances Anne (Fanny) Kemble, a famous British actress married to Pierce Butler, an American. In 1836 Butler inherited two Southern plantations and became one of the largest slaveholders in the country. His wife became an opponent of slavery and moved back to Britain. Years later she wrote of her experiences in *Journal of a Residence on a Georgian Plantation*.

George Fitzhugh

Fanny Kemble

Why? As a reader, you need to be able to identify a writer's point of view so that you can understand the writer's choice of details. Writers may use their own feelings and beliefs when they decide what to include and how to tell their story.

How? To recognize a writer's point of view, you may follow these steps:

1 Identify the topic.

2 Determine which statements are fact and which are opinions.

3 Look for words or phrases that tell how a writer feels about the topic.

4 Consider the writer's experiences and way of life. How might these affect the writer's point of view?

5 Describe the writer's point of view.

Selection B

"I have sometimes been haunted [worried] with the idea that it was . . . [a] duty, knowing what I know, and having seen what I have seen, to do all that lies in my power to show the dangers and the evils of this frightful institution [slavery]. . . . The handcuff, the lash—the tearing away of children from parents, of husbands from wives— the weary trudging [walking] . . . along the common highways, the labor of body, the despair of mind [hopelessness], the sickness of heart—these are the realities which belong to the system, and form the rule, rather than the exception, in the slave's experience."

—Fanny Kemble

Selection A

"The negro slaves of the South are the happiest, and in some sense, the freest people in the world. The children and the aged and infirm [sick or weak] work not at all, and yet have all the comforts and necessaries [needs] of life provided for them. They enjoy liberty, because they are oppressed [weighed down] neither by care nor labor. The women do little hard work, and are protected from . . . their husbands by their masters [slave owners]. The negro men and . . . boys work, on the average, in good weather, not more than nine hours a day. The balance of their time is spent in [relaxation]. Besides, they have their Sabbaths and holidays. . . . They can sleep at any hour. . . . We do not know whether free laborers [in the North] ever sleep."

—George Fitzhugh

Think and Apply

1. What is the subject of both of these writers?

2. What details does each writer use to support his or her point of view?

3. What are the points of view each writer reveals?

4. How might the experiences and way of life of each writer affect his or her point of view?

1830 | 1850

1831
Nat Turner leads a slave rebellion in Virginia.

1841
The Supreme Court frees the prisoners from the slave ship *Amistad*.

1849
Harriet Tubman escapes from slavery on the Underground Railroad.

New Haven

Southampton County

Resisting Slavery

PREVIEW

Focus on the Main Idea
Enslaved African Americans resisted slavery in many different ways.

PLACES
Southampton County, Virginia
New Haven, Connecticut

PEOPLE
Nat Turner
Joseph Cinque
Harriet Tubman
Levi Coffin
Catherine Coffin

VOCABULARY
slave codes
Underground Railroad

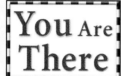

You Are There September 11, 1853, in Richmond, Virginia. In a house in the city, J.H. Hill, an escaped slave, waits for a message.

Later Hill wrote, "Nine months I was trying to get away. I was secreted [hidden] a long time in a kitchen of a merchant." And then the long awaited message arrives. He is to meet a guide who will try to lead him to freedom in the North. Early next morning, Hill leaves his hiding place and carefully makes his way to the guide. "I felt composed [calm]," Hill reports, "for I had started . . . that morning for liberty or for death." Hill reached the North where, at last, he found liberty.

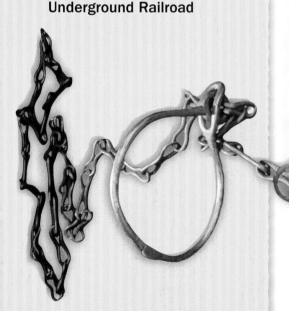

Main Idea and Details As you read, note the details that support the main idea that African Americans resisted slavery.

Target Skill

African Americans Resist Slavery

Some enslaved people, like J.H. Hill, resisted slavery by risking their lives in daring escapes. Other slaves found different ways to resist.

When enslaved people resisted slavery, they were fighting for freedom. They were also fighting against a cruel system. They had no choices. They would be moved when they were sold, and they could not control who bought them. Many owners treated slaves well, but some beat or abused their slaves.

Another form of cruelty was the breaking up of families. Abream Scriven, a slave sold by his owner in 1858, was forced to leave his wife, father, and mother. He wrote these words to his wife:

> *"Give my love to my father and mother and tell them good bye for me, and if we shall not meet in this world I hope to meet in heaven."*

Slave owners had almost complete control over slaves' lives. The owners told them when to start work and when to end work. Slaves could not leave the plantation without permission. Slave owners also decided whether slaves could marry and the age at which their children had to begin working.

Slave codes, or laws to control the behavior of slaves, also made life difficult for them. For example, most slave codes did not allow a slave to hit a white person, even in self-defense. Slaves were not allowed to own property, and few were allowed to buy and sell goods.

Resistance took many forms. Some slaves simply refused to obey the owner. Other slaves resisted by holding back the main thing they could control, their work. They worked more slowly or pretended to be sick. Others broke the tools that were needed to do work.

Many enslaved people resisted by breaking rules that were meant to keep them ignorant. For example, slaves often were not allowed to learn to read or write. Some slaves learned in secret, risking punishment if they were found out.

REVIEW Describe some ways enslaved African Americans resisted slavery.

🔁 **Main Idea and Details**

▶ **Family members were often separated when slaves were sold.**

61

Slave Rebellions

To prevent enslaved people from planning rebellions, slave owners tried to keep slaves from gathering and meeting with one another. Still, rebellions did occur. One was planned and led by **Nat Turner** in Virginia.

In August 1831, Turner and his followers killed about 60 whites in **Southampton County, Virginia.** United States and Virginia troops were called in to stop them. The soldiers killed more than 100 African Americans before the rebellion was ended. Turner escaped but was later captured. He was hanged on November 11, 1831.

A later rebellion had a different ending. In 1839, a group of 53 captive Africans seized control of the *Amistad,* a Spanish slave ship carrying them from one port to another in Cuba. The Africans were led by a farmer from West Africa who became known as **Joseph Cinque** (SEEN kay). He told the Africans: "We may as well die in trying to be free."

After taking control of the ship, the Africans told a Spanish sailor to sail them back to Africa. But the Spaniard tricked them and instead sailed the *Amistad* north along the coast of the United States. The United States Navy captured the *Amistad* near Long Island, New York. The Africans were taken as prisoners to **New Haven, Connecticut.**

At first, the United States planned to return the ship and the Africans to the Spanish. Abolitionists and Northern newspapers printed articles against this plan and in support of the Africans. With their help, the Africans' fight for freedom eventually came before the Supreme Court. There, former President John Quincy Adams presented the Africans' case. He argued that the Africans were not property but human beings and should not be returned to Spain.

On March 9, 1841, the Supreme Court reached its decision. It agreed with Adams and freed the Africans. All 35 of the Africans who survived the rebellion sailed back to Africa later that year.

REVIEW Contrast the Nat Turner and *Amistad* rebellions. **Compare and Contrast**

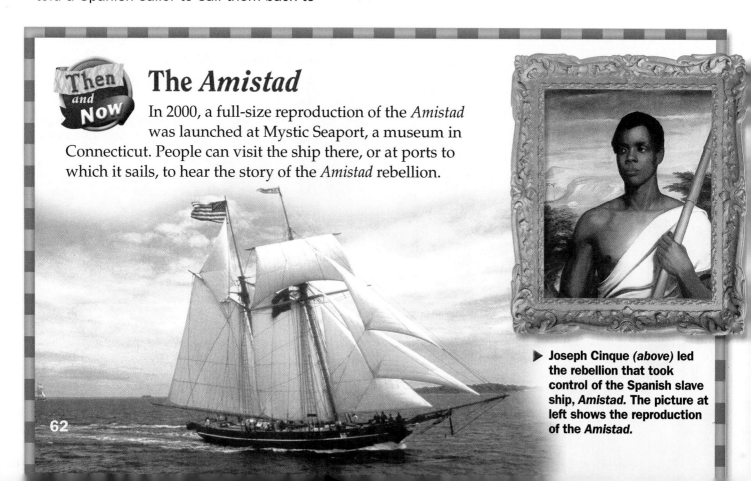

Then and Now

The *Amistad*

In 2000, a full-size reproduction of the *Amistad* was launched at Mystic Seaport, a museum in Connecticut. People can visit the ship there, or at ports to which it sails, to hear the story of the *Amistad* rebellion.

▶ **Joseph Cinque (above) led the rebellion that took control of the Spanish slave ship, *Amistad*. The picture at left shows the reproduction of the *Amistad*.**

Routes of the Underground Railroad

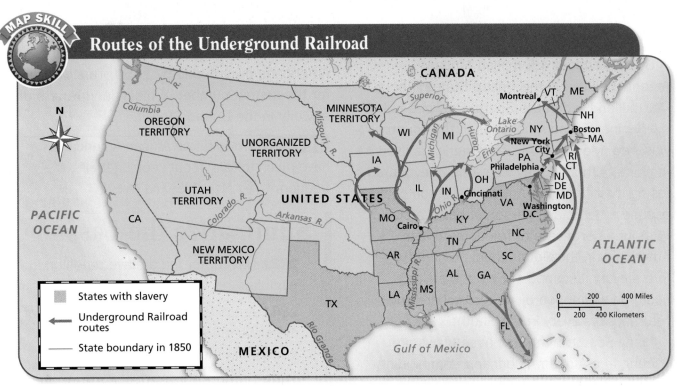

▶ This map shows some of the routes traveled by people escaping from slavery on the Underground Railroad.

MAP SKILL Use Routes *To what other country did many slaves escape?*

Underground Railroad

Thousands of enslaved African Americans resisted slavery by trying to escape. The **Underground Railroad** was an organized, secret system set up to help enslaved people escape from the South to freedom in the North or Canada. The map on this page shows its routes.

The Underground Railroad probably got its name when railroads became popular. The guides, or people who helped those escaping, were called "conductors." The houses, barns, and other places where runaways hid along their journey were known as "stations."

To find their way north, escaping slaves were guided by the North Star. On cloudy nights they felt for moss on tree trunks, because moss tends to grow on the north side of a tree. All along the journey, they faced the risk of capture, a severe beating, or death.

Between 40,000 and 100,000 slaves escaped using the Underground Railroad. **Harriet Tubman** was the most famous "conductor." In about 1849, Tubman escaped from slavery herself and settled in Philadelphia. Before the Civil War she returned south 19 times to lead more than 300 people, including her mother and father, to freedom. Tubman later said, "On my underground railroad, I never ran my train off the track and I never lost a passenger." You can read more about Tubman in the Biography on page 65.

Not all "conductors" on the Underground Railroad were African Americans. **Levi Coffin** was a white teacher who had opened a school for slaves in North Carolina. After slave owners closed his school, Coffin moved to Indiana. There he became one of the leading "conductors" of the Underground Railroad. He and his wife, **Catherine Coffin,** helped more than 2,000 slaves escape to freedom.

REVIEW Write a brief summary of the way the Underground Railroad helped people escape slavery. **Summarize**

Free African Americans

By 1860 about 4.5 million African Americans lived in the United States. About 4.1 million lived in the South. Only one out of every nine African Americans in the country was free. Most free African Americans lived in cities. Although they were free, they feared losing their freedom. Any white person could accuse a free black person of being a slave. Without a certificate of freedom, African Americans in the South could be sent back into slavery. Escaped slaves in the North could be kidnapped by slave catchers and returned to slavery in the South.

Many Southern states passed laws preventing free African Americans from holding certain jobs. In the North and the South, finding work was made more difficult by threats and violence from white workers. Still, thousands of free blacks found jobs and bought property. In New Orleans, 650 African Americans owned land by 1850. This was by far the largest number of black landowners of any city in the United States.

REVIEW Why did free African Americans have much to fear about keeping their freedom? **Main Idea and Details**

Summarize the Lesson

- **1831** Nat Turner led a slave rebellion in Virginia.

- **1841** Africans who had seized control of the slave ship *Amistad* gained their freedom in the Supreme Court.

- **1849** Harriet Tubman escaped slavery and began leading people to freedom on the Underground Railroad.

LESSON 2 REVIEW

Check Facts and Main Ideas

1. **Main Idea and Details** On a separate sheet of paper, complete the graphic organizer to show the details that support the main idea that enslaved African Americans resisted slavery.

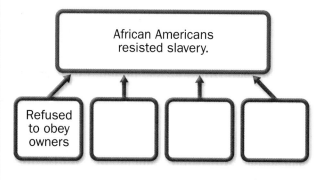

2. What was the purpose of the **slave codes**?

3. **Critical Thinking:** *Cause and Effect* Why would slave owners want to keep slaves from gathering or meeting one another?

4. Describe how enslaved African Americans escaped to freedom on the **Underground Railroad.**

5. What challenges were faced by free African Americans in the North and South?

Link to Science

Locate the North Star Escaping African Americans used the North Star to help them find the direction north. Do research to locate the North Star. Then one evening, when it is dark enough, look for the star and determine north.

Harriet Tubman
1820(?)–1913

As a teenager in Maryland, Harriet Tubman had only known a life of slavery, yet she grew tougher by resisting, or fighting back. She even survived a serious head injury that she suffered while helping another slave escape. As a result of the injury, for the rest of her life Harriet could not control falling asleep at odd times, suffered from bad headaches, and had a deep scar. Yet nothing could prevent her from seeking freedom.

When she was about 28 years old, Harriet Tubman escaped and made her way 90 miles on the Underground Railroad to Philadelphia. Although she was afraid, she later explained,

"I had reasoned this out in my mind. . . . I had a right to liberty or death; if I could not have one, I would have the other, for no man should take me alive."

Despite the dangers, before the Civil War Tubman returned again and again to the South to help lead other African Americans from slavery to freedom. No one in her care was ever caught.

BIOFACT

During the Civil War, Tubman served the United States Army as a nurse and a scout, helping to free almost 800 slaves in one attempt.

Learn from Biographies

How do you think Harriet Tubman's scar and trouble with sleeping could have made her escape more dangerous? Why do you think that she returned to the South so many times despite all of the dangers?

For more information, go online to *Meet the People* at **www.sfsocialstudies.com.**

1820   1860

1820
Missouri
Compromise

1850
Fugitive
Slave Law

1857
Dred Scott
case

1860
Abraham Lincoln is
elected President.

NEBRASKA TERR.
KANSAS TERR.
Harpers Ferry

PREVIEW

Focus on the Main Idea
Despite attempts to compromise, the struggle over slavery threatened to tear the United States apart.

PLACES
Nebraska Territory
Kansas Territory
Harpers Ferry, Virginia

PEOPLE
John C. Calhoun
Henry Clay
Daniel Webster
Stephen Douglas
Harriet Beecher Stowe
Dred Scott
John Brown
Abraham Lincoln

VOCABULARY
free state
slave state
states' rights
Missouri Compromise
Fugitive Slave Law
Compromise of 1850
Kansas-Nebraska Act

The Struggle over Slavery

You Are There
Your old home in Ohio lies hundreds of miles behind you as you ride into the Kansas Territory. On this spring day in 1854, you meet a group of 650 settlers from New England. They tell you they have all pledged to keep Kansas free of slavery.

You have also met other people coming to Kansas who have different views. One group is from neighboring Missouri, a slave state. Their aim is to make the Kansas Territory a place where people can own slaves.

Wherever you go, you hear arguments about whether or not Kansas should allow slavery. You also hear stories of violence between people on both sides of this argument. The issue of slavery is splitting Kansas apart. Soon it will threaten to split apart the entire country.

Main Idea and Details As you read, look for details that support the main idea that slavery was threatening to split apart the country in the middle 1800s.

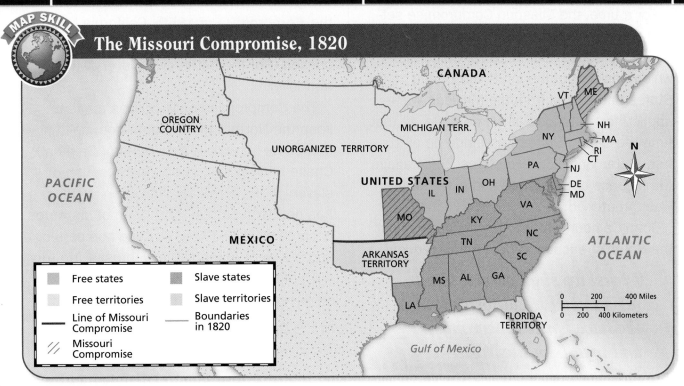

MAP SKILL

The Missouri Compromise, 1820

Free states

Free territories

Line of Missouri Compromise

Missouri Compromise

Slave states

Slave territories

Boundaries in 1820

▶ **The Missouri Compromise kept the balance between free states and slave states.**

MAP SKILL   Use a Map Key *Which two states were admitted as part of the Missouri Compromise?*

Missouri Compromise

In 1819 the United States was made up of 11 free states and 11 slave states. A **free state** was one in which slavery was not allowed. A **slave state** was one in which slavery was allowed. Since each state had two United States senators, the Senate was balanced evenly between senators that favored slavery and senators that opposed slavery.

In 1819 the people of Missouri asked for statehood as a slave state. Northern states did not want Missouri to be admitted as a slave state. Southern states took the opposite position.

John C. Calhoun from South Carolina was a leader of the Southerners in the Senate. Calhoun was a believer in **states' rights** — the idea that states have the right to make decisions about issues that concern them. According to Calhoun, slavery should be legal if a state's citizens wanted it to be.

Senator **Henry Clay** of Kentucky, who would become known as "The Great Compromiser," urged a solution called the **Missouri Compromise.** In 1820 Missouri was admitted as a slave state, and Maine was admitted as a free state. There were now 24 states, evenly balanced between free states and slave states.

What would happen when more new states were formed from land gained in the Louisiana Purchase? The Missouri Compromise tried to settle this question. Look at the map above and find the Missouri Compromise line. According to the Missouri Compromise, new states north of this line would be free states. New states south of this line could allow slavery.

REVIEW How did the Missouri Compromise affect the way in which future states would be admitted to the United States?

⟳ **Main Idea and Details**

The Compromise of 1850

For a time, the Missouri Compromise settled the question about the balance of free and slave states. But in 1849, California—which was part of the lands the United States had gained from the Mexican War—applied for statehood as a free state. At that time the United States was made up of 15 free states and 15 slave states. Once again, the balance between free and slave states was threatened.

John Calhoun wrote to his daughter about the South's reaction to California's request:

> *"I trust we shall persist in our resistance [to California]. . . . We have borne the wrongs and insults of the North long enough."*

Calhoun hoped that the Southern members of Congress would force the North to turn down California's request to enter as a free state.

Henry Clay again suggested a compromise. Clay proposed that the South accept California as a free state. In return, the North should agree to pass the **Fugitive Slave Law.** This law said that escaped slaves had to be returned to their owners, even if they had reached Northern states where slavery was not allowed. Clay's compromise also suggested a way to accept other new states from the territories gained from Mexico. He proposed that slavery be allowed in these territories if the people living there voted for it.

Daniel Webster, a senator from Massachusetts, spoke in favor of the compromise. Webster was an opponent of slavery. Yet like Clay, he wanted to keep the country together. Webster said, "We must view things as they are. Slavery does exist in the United States."

With the support of Calhoun and Webster, Congress passed Clay's plan. It was called the **Compromise of 1850.** California became a free state, and the Fugitive Slave Law was passed. But the battle over slavery was far from over.

The Compromise of 1850 was made to keep the North and the South from splitting apart over slavery. But as Senator Salmon P. Chase of Ohio said later, "The question of slavery in the territories has been avoided. It has not been settled." The truth of his words became clear in 1854, as huge numbers of settlers were entering the Nebraska Territory west of the Missouri River.

REVIEW What were the main proposals of the Compromise of 1850?
Main Idea and Details

▶ **Many newspapers printed opinions about the new Fugitive Slave Law.**

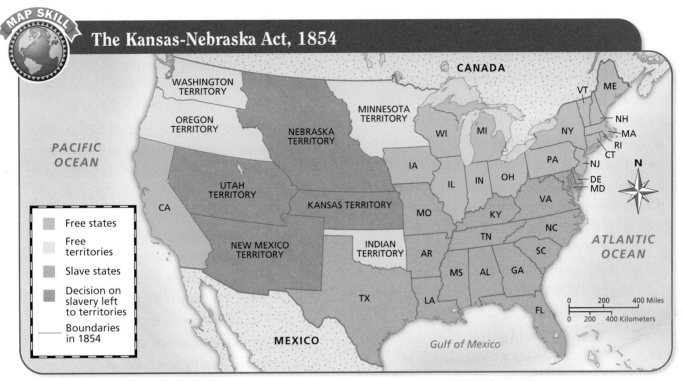

The Kansas-Nebraska Act, 1854

Free states

Free territories

Slave states

Decision on slavery left to territories

Boundaries in 1854

▶ **This map shows how the Kansas-Nebraska Act affected the United States.**

MAP SKILL Region *What was the only state in the West region in 1854?*

"Bleeding Kansas"

In 1854 Senator **Stephen Douglas** of Illinois proposed that Nebraska be split into two territories: the **Nebraska Territory** in the north and the **Kansas Territory** in the south. Because both territories were north of the Missouri Compromise line, both would be free territories. However, many Southerners insisted that slavery be allowed in both the Nebraska and the Kansas territories.

Congress again looked for a solution. Senator Douglas suggested a compromise: let the people of each territory decide whether it should be free or slave. Congress passed this law, which came to be known as the **Kansas-Nebraska Act.** Instead of solving the problem, the law created a new one in Kansas.

Because a majority vote would decide whether Kansas would be free or slave, people who favored one side or the other rushed to settle in Kansas. People against slavery

came from the North. People for slavery came from the South, especially from neighboring Missouri, a slave state.

The people of Kansas voted for slavery. But many who voted were not Kansans at all. They had crossed the border from Missouri just to vote for slavery. Northerners claimed the vote was illegal. Southerners disagreed. Although most people in Kansas just wanted to establish homes and live in peace, there were leaders on both sides of the slavery issue who were trying to cause a fight. Violence broke out in many parts of the Kansas Territory. Because of the many acts of violence, Kansas became known as "bleeding Kansas." These would not be the last drops of blood spilled between those who favored and opposed slavery.

REVIEW In what way did the Kansas-Nebraska Act change a part of the Missouri Compromise? **Compare and Contrast**

A Divided Country

In addition to the violence in "bleeding Kansas," other events deepened the split between the North and the South. One was the publication of *Uncle Tom's Cabin*, a novel by **Harriet Beecher Stowe,** in 1852. Stowe's novel described the cruelties of slavery. It sold about 300,000 copies in the first year after it was published, winning over many people to the abolitionist cause.

Another important event was the case of **Dred Scott,** an enslaved African American from Missouri. Scott's owner had taken him to Illinois, a free state, and to Wisconsin, a free territory, and then back to Missouri, a slave state. Then Scott's owner died. Scott went to court claiming he was a free man because he had lived in a free state.

Scott's case reached the United States Supreme Court. The 1857 decision written by Chief Justice Roger Taney said that Scott "had no rights" because African Americans were not citizens of the United States. Many Americans were outraged by the Supreme Court's decision. Frederick Douglass said that the decision would bring about events that would "overthrow . . . the whole slave system."

Another event that further divided the North and the South occurred in 1859. Abolitionist **John Brown,** who had led attacks on pro-slavery people in Kansas, made plans to attack slave owners in Virginia. To carry out his plan, Brown needed weapons. He planned to steal them from the army's arsenal at **Harpers Ferry, Virginia** (now West Virginia). An arsenal is a place where weapons are stored.

On October 16 Brown and 21 other men, black and white, started on their raid. But federal and state soldiers stopped them, killing some of the raiders. Brown was taken prisoner and, after being found guilty, was sentenced to death and hanged. However, his actions showed that the struggle over slavery was growing. Compromise was becoming harder to find.

REVIEW Contrast the goals of Dred Scott and John Brown. **Compare and Contrast**

Literature and Social Studies

In this excerpt from *Uncle Tom's Cabin,* Harriet Beecher Stowe describes the struggle of an enslaved mother named Eliza to keep her child from slave traders who wanted to take her child away from her.

"[Eliza's] room opened by a side door to the river. She caught her child, and sprang down the steps toward it. The [slave] trader caught a full glimpse of her, just as she was disappearing down the bank, and throwing himself from his horse . . . he was after her like a hound after a deer. In that dizzy moment her feet . . . [hardly] seemed to touch the ground, and a moment brought her to the water's edge. . . . and, nerved with strength such as God gives only to the desperate, with one wild cry and flying leap, she vaulted sheer [jumped clear] over the . . . current by the shore, on to the raft of ice beyond. It was a desperate leap,—impossible to anything but madness and despair."

The Granger Collection

▶ Abraham Lincoln spoke out against the spread of slavery while running for the Senate against Stephen Douglas.

A New Political Party

The issue of slavery led to the end of one political party and the beginning of another. The Whigs, split between a group against slavery and a group for it, ceased to exist. In 1854 some of its members who opposed slavery joined with other slavery opponents to form the Republican party. Now two major political parties, Republican and Democrat, battled over the issues of slavery and states' rights.

No election showed this conflict more clearly than the 1858 campaign for the United States Senate in Illinois. The Republicans chose **Abraham Lincoln** as their candidate. Lincoln was a lawyer from Springfield, Illinois.

Many people called him "The Rail Splitter" because when he was young, he split logs with an axe to make the rails of fences. Lincoln was opposed to the spread of slavery and spoke of the "ultimate extinction," or final end, of slavery.

Lincoln's opponent was Democratic Senator Stephen Douglas. Douglas was known as the "Little Giant" because, although he was short, he was a giant when it came to making speeches that changed people's ideas. Douglas believed in states' rights. He said, "Each state . . . has a right to do as it pleases on . . . slavery."

The candidates made speeches and debated throughout Illinois about the spread of slavery. The Lincoln-Douglas debates became well known because both candidates were such good speakers. Lincoln said:

> *"If slavery is not wrong, then nothing is wrong. . . . [But I] would not do anything to bring about a war between the free and slave states."*

Douglas stated:

> *"If each state will only agree to mind its own business . . . this republic can exist forever divided into free and slave states."*

Douglas won the election, but the debates made Lincoln the new leader of the Republican party. Within two years, he would be the Republican candidate for President. You can read more about Lincoln in the Biography on page 73.

REVIEW Summarize the views on slavery held by Lincoln and Douglas. **Summarize**

Lincoln Is Elected President

In the election of 1860, the Democratic party split. Northern Democrats chose Stephen Douglas to run for President. Southern Democrats chose John Breckinridge of Kentucky. The Republicans chose Abraham Lincoln.

Lincoln won the election, but without winning any Southern electoral votes. Southerners feared that Lincoln would attempt to end slavery not only in the western territories but in the Southern states as well. Southerners also worried that they would have no voice in the new government. Lincoln said to the South, "We must not be enemies." However, many on both sides viewed the other side as their enemy. In the North and South, the time of compromise had passed.

REVIEW Why do you think Lincoln said, "We must not be enemies" after he became President? **Draw Conclusions**

Summarize the Lesson

1820 Congress passed the Missouri Compromise.

1850 The Fugitive Slave Law was passed as part of the Compromise of 1850.

1857 In the Dred Scott case, the Supreme Court ruled that slaves were not citizens and had no rights, even in free states.

1860 Abraham Lincoln was elected President without any Southern support.

LESSON 3 ⟩ REVIEW

Check Facts and Main Ideas

1. ⟳ **Main Idea and Details** On a separate sheet of paper, complete the graphic organizer with details that support the main idea.

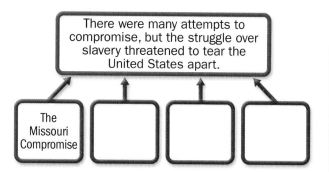

There were many attempts to compromise, but the struggle over slavery threatened to tear the United States apart.

The Missouri Compromise

2. How did the **Missouri Compromise** keep the balance of **free and slave states**?

3. How did the **Compromise of 1850** affect slavery in California and the territories gained from Mexico?

4. Who were Dred Scott and John Brown? How did their actions affect the split between the North and South?

5. **Critical Thinking: Make Inferences** What was more important to Abraham Lincoln, abolishing slavery or preserving the nation? Explain.

Link to ⚊⚊ Writing

Write a Conversation Write a conversation about the spread of slavery that might have occurred among Americans in the 1850s. You can base your conversation on the words of American leaders in this lesson, such as John C. Calhoun, Daniel Webster, Frederick Douglass, Harriet Beecher Stowe, Abraham Lincoln, and Stephen Douglas. Use the term **states' rights** in your conversation.

Abraham Lincoln *1809–1865*

Young Abraham Lincoln had to help his father on the family farm and only attended school for a total of about one year during his life. Yet Abe read anything he could get his hands on. He once said, "My best friend is the man who'll get me a book." So when a neighboring farmer, Josiah Crawford, offered to lend him a biography of George Washington, Abe was thrilled. Unfortunately, one rainy night, the book was left near the leaky cabin walls and got soaked. Abe told the truth, and Crawford was not angry. Abe paid him back by working in his fields.

The book on Washington became one of Abe's favorites, along with the autobiography of Benjamin Franklin. From these, Abe learned about the men who founded the United States and why the dream of a free country was so important to them.

BIOFACT

Lincoln grew his beard in response to a suggestion from 11-year-old Grace Bedell, who wrote him a letter.

Throughout his life, Lincoln educated himself through reading. When he decided to become a lawyer, he taught himself by studying law books. Even when he was the President, Lincoln read books to learn how to lead the war effort. After the election of 1860, President Lincoln made a speech sharing his deep belief in the future of the United States that he had read about since his childhood. With tension rising between the North and South, he said:

"If we do not make common cause to save the good old ship of the Union on this voyage, nobody will have a chance to pilot her on another voyage."

Learn from Biographies

How do you think Lincoln's reading of how Washington met the challenges of the American Revolution helped Lincoln meet the challenges of the Civil War?

For more information, go online to *Meet the People* at **www.sfsocialstudies.com**.

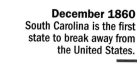

1860   1862

December 1860
South Carolina is the first state to break away from the United States.

February 1861
Seven Southern states form the Confederate States of America.

April 1861
Confederate forces fire on United States troops at Fort Sumter.

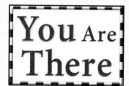
Fort Sumter

The First Shots Are Fired

You Are There Dawn is about to break in Charleston, South Carolina. The date is April 12, 1861. Mary Boykin Chesnut, the wife of a Southern officer, is staying as a guest in a house near Charleston Harbor. Troops of the Southern states begin firing on Fort Sumter, a United States fort on an island in the harbor.

Chesnut describes the event in her diary:

"I do not pretend to go to sleep. . . . How can I?" She is kept awake by the "heavy booming of a cannon." She springs out of bed and falls to her knees. "I prayed as I never prayed before." Chesnut then puts on her shawl and climbs to the top floor of the house to get a better view. "The shells were bursting." The roar of the cannons fills the air. "We watched up there, and everybody wondered that Fort Sumter did not fire a shot."

Sequence As you read, identify the events that led to the start of the Civil War.

Southern States Secede

Many Southerners believed that the South should **secede,** or break away, from the United States. In December 1860, almost two months after Abraham Lincoln was elected President, South Carolina decided to secede.

By February 1, 1861, six more states—Alabama, Florida, Mississippi, Georgia, Louisiana, and Texas—had seceded. Representatives from the seven seceding states met in Montgomery, Alabama. On February 8, they formed their own government. It was called the Confederate States of America, or the **Confederacy.**

The Confederacy adopted a constitution that supported states' rights and slavery. The Confederate constitution said that its congress could not pass laws that denied "the right of property in . . . slaves."

The Confederacy also elected **Jefferson Davis,** a former United States senator from Mississippi, as its president. Like Abraham Lincoln, Jefferson Davis was born in Kentucky, in a log cabin. But Davis grew up in Mississippi on a plantation owned by his family. Later he developed his own plantation on land given to him by his oldest brother.

After becoming president of the Confederacy, Davis said the Southern states should "look forward to success, to peace, and to prosperity." But in a letter to his wife, Varina, he wrote that the Southern states were "threatened by a powerful opposition." That opposition came from the United States and its newly elected President, Abraham Lincoln.

Lincoln was inaugurated on March 4, 1861. By then the Confederacy had taken control of most of the forts and military property of the United States in the South. The states that remained loyal to the United States government were called the **Union.** One of the forts still under Union control was **Fort Sumter,** in the harbor of Charleston, South Carolina.

REVIEW Summarize the events that occurred as the Confederacy was formed. *Summarize*

▶ **Jefferson Davis (below) was president of the Confederacy. The Confederate attack on Fort Sumter (left) was the start of the Civil War.**

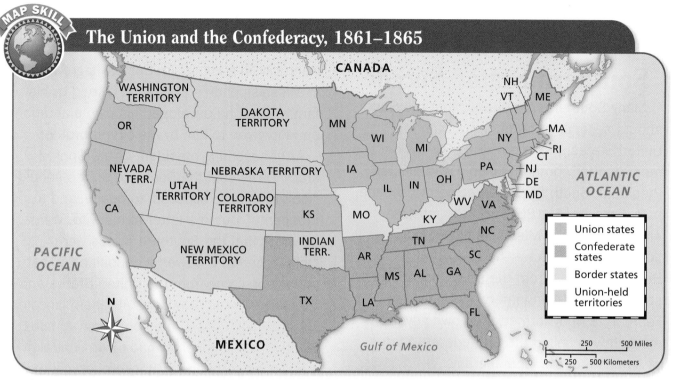

The Union and the Confederacy, 1861–1865

CANADA

WASHINGTON TERRITORY

DAKOTA TERRITORY

OR

NEVADA TERR.

UTAH TERRITORY

CA

PACIFIC OCEAN

NEW MEXICO TERRITORY

NEBRASKA TERRITORY

COLORADO TERRITORY

KS

INDIAN TERR.

TX

MEXICO

MN

WI

MI

IA

IL IN OH

MO

KY

AR

MS AL GA

LA

Gulf of Mexico

NH

VT ME

NY

MA

RI

CT

PA

NJ

DE

MD

WV VA

TN

NC

SC

FL

ATLANTIC OCEAN

Union states
Confederate states
Border states
Union-held territories

0   250   500 Miles
0   250   500 Kilometers

▶ This map shows the United States during the Civil War. Find West Virginia, which broke away from Virginia and voted to stay in the Union. West Virginia became a state in 1863.

MAP SKILL Place *Name the Confederate state that was farthest west.*

The War Begins

On April 9, 1861, Jefferson Davis met with his advisers to discuss Fort Sumter. One adviser said that making the first strike would put the Confederacy "in the wrong." Davis disagreed and decided to send officers to ask for the surrender of the fort.

A Union officer, Robert Anderson, commanded Fort Sumter. He agreed to surrender if the Confederacy would wait three more days. But the Confederate commander, Pierre G. T. Beauregard (BOH ruh gard), had given orders to fire on Fort Sumter if Anderson did not surrender in one hour.

The Confederates began firing on Fort Sumter on Friday, April 12, at 4:30 A.M. The bombing continued into Saturday. With little food and water, Major Anderson was forced to surrender. He and his troops left the fort on Sunday.

Lincoln responded to the attack on Fort Sumter and its surrender by asking Union states to supply 75,000 soldiers to put down the Confederate rebellion. Lincoln believed that this could be done quickly and said the soldiers would be needed for only 90 days.

Lincoln's call for troops so angered the states of Virginia, Arkansas, Tennessee, and North Carolina that they seceded and joined the Confederacy. There were now 11 states in the Confederacy and 23 in the Union. Four of the Union states—Delaware, Maryland, Missouri, and Kentucky—were slave states that seemed unsure whether to stay in the Union or join the Confederacy. These were called the **border states** because they were located between the Union and Confederacy. Three of these states—Delaware, Missouri, and Kentucky—said they would not provide soldiers. Maryland said it would, but only to defend Washington, D.C.

Lincoln believed it was important to keep these border states in the Union, even though they were slave states. That is why in 1861 he continued to say that his aim was to hold the United States together, not to abolish slavery.

The conflict between the states arose for a number of reasons. For Lincoln and his supporters, the main reason for fighting the war was to preserve, or keep together, the Union. However, other supporters of the North believed they were fighting to end slavery. Southerners fought the war to preserve states' rights and slavery. They also believed they were defending their homeland and their way of life.

The battle at Fort Sumter began the American Civil War. A **civil war** is a war between people of the same country. Some Northerners described the war as a rebellion and the Confederacy as a group of rebels. Many Southerners accepted the name *rebel* with pride. To them the conflict was known as the War for Southern Independence. They also called it the War of Northern Aggression. The title War Between the States is also commonly used. But no matter what it was called, the war would be longer and bloodier than anyone guessed in the spring of 1861.

REVIEW What were the main differences between the reasons the North and South fought the Civil War? *Compare and Contrast*

Summarize the Lesson

- **December 1860** South Carolina became the first state to secede from the United States.

- **February 1861** Seven Southern states formed the Confederate States of America.

- **April 1861** Confederate forces fired on United States troops at Fort Sumter, a battle that began the Civil War.

LESSON 4 REVIEW

Check Facts and Main Ideas

1. Sequence On a separate sheet of paper, complete the graphic organizer to show the events that led up to the start of the Civil War.

```
┌─────────────────────────────┐
│                             │
└─────────────────────────────┘
              ↓
┌─────────────────────────────┐
│                             │
└─────────────────────────────┘
              ↓
┌─────────────────────────────┐
│                             │
└─────────────────────────────┘
              ↓
┌─────────────────────────────┐
│    The Civil War began      │
│     on April 12, 1861       │
└─────────────────────────────┘
```

2. Why did the Southern states **secede?**

3. Critical Thinking: *Draw Conclusions* What might have been Jefferson Davis's reason for attacking Fort Sumter?

4. Describe Abraham Lincoln's main reason for fighting the Civil War.

5. Why at the beginning of the Civil War did Lincoln not say that he was fighting the war to end slavery?

Link to ⬤—⬤ Writing

Write an Article Suppose you are part of the **Union** or **Confederacy** at the start of the war in 1861. Research the man who is your president and write a brief article explaining why he is qualified for his position.

1820	1830	1840
1820 Missouri Compromise	**1831** Nat Turner leads a slave rebellion in Virginia	**1846** Congress votes to lower tariffs on imports

Chapter Summary

 Main Idea and Details

On a separate sheet of paper, fill in the main compromises made in Congress before the Civil War.

▶ **Tattered flag from the battle at Fort Sumter**

> Congress made several compromises to keep the North and South from splitting apart.

> Missouri Compromise

Vocabulary

Match each word with the correct definition or description.

1. **sectionalism** (p. 55)
2. **slave codes** (p. 61)
3. **free state** (p. 67)
4. **secede** (p. 75)
5. **Underground Railroad** (p. 63)

a. state that does not permit slavery

b. loyalty to a part of a country, not to the whole country

c. secret system to help slaves escape to freedom

d. laws controlling behavior of slaves

e. break away

People and Terms

Write a sentence explaining why each of the following people or terms was important in the events that led to the start of the Civil War. You may use two or more in a single sentence.

1. **David Walker** (p. 57)
2. **Nat Turner** (p. 62)
3. **Confederacy** (p. 75)
4. **Harriet Tubman** (p. 63)
5. **John C. Calhoun** (p. 67)
6. **Fugitive Slave Law** (p. 68)
7. **Harriet Beecher Stowe** (p. 70)
8. **Dred Scott** (p. 70)
9. **Jefferson Davis** (p. 75)
10. **Union** (p. 75)

1849
Harriet Tubman escapes slavery on the Underground Railroad

1857
Dred Scott case

1860
Abraham Lincoln is elected President

February 1861
Confederate States of America formed

April 1861
Southern forces fire on U.S. troops at Fort Sumter

Facts and Main Ideas

1 What kinds of control did slave owners have over the lives of slaves?

2 How did the issue of slavery lead to a new political party?

3 **Time Line** How many years were there between the Nat Turner revolt and the Dred Scott case?

4 **Main Idea** What were some differences between the North and South that increased tensions between the two regions?

5 **Main Idea** How did many slaves resist slavery?

6 **Main Idea** How did the differences over slavery threaten the existence of the United States?

7 **Main Idea** What effect did Lincoln's election have on the South?

8 **Critical Thinking:** *Draw Conclusions* Why did people work to keep a balance between the number of slave states and free states?

Apply Skills

Recognize Point of View
Read the two sections below from the Lincoln-Douglas debates. Then answer the questions.

"If slavery is not wrong, then nothing is wrong. . . . [But I] would not do anything to bring about a war between the free and slave states."

—Abraham Lincoln

"If each state will only agree to mind its own business . . . this republic can exist forever divided into free and slave states."

—Stephen Douglas

1 What is the subject of each section?

2 What is Lincoln's viewpoint about slavery?

3 What is Douglas's viewpoint about slavery?

Write About History

1 **Write a journal entry** as a person who observed the battle at Fort Sumter.

2 **Write a poem** about a person mentioned in this chapter whom you admire.

3 **Write a short speech** you might have given as a senator for or against the Missouri Compromise.

Internet Activity

To get help with vocabulary, people, and terms, select dictionary or encyclopedia from *Social Studies Library* at **www.sfsocialstudies.com.**

War and Reconstruction

1861

Manassas Junction, Virginia
Confederate troops win the first major battle of the Civil War.

Lesson 1

1

1863

Charleston, South Carolina
African American troops of the Union army attack Fort Wagner.

Lesson 2

2

1865

Appomattox Court House, Virginia
The South surrenders.

Lesson 3

3

1865

Washington, D.C.
President Lincoln is assassinated.

Lesson 4

4

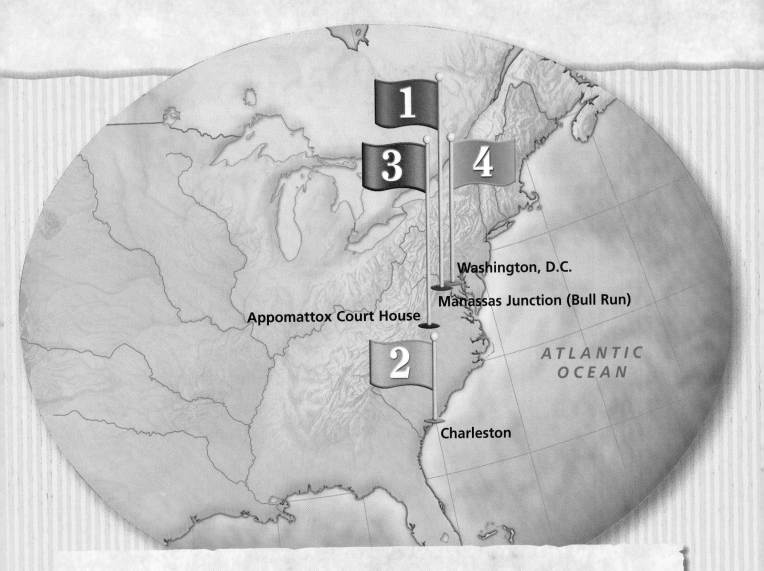

Washington, D.C.

Manassas Junction (Bull Run)

Appomattox Court House

Charleston

ATLANTIC OCEAN

Why We Remember

". . . that government of the people, by the people, for the people, shall not perish from the earth."

In 1863, in the middle of the Civil War, these words rang out over a scarred battlefield where many Union and Confederate soldiers had died a few months before. The battlefield was at Gettysburg, Pennsylvania. The speaker was President Abraham Lincoln. At the time, no one was sure who would win the war. But Lincoln was sure of his goal—to preserve the nation that had been born only 87 years earlier.

1861 **1863**

April 1861
Union begins blockade
of Southern ports.

July 1861
First Battle
of Bull Run

September 1862
Battle of Antietam

Washington, D.C.

Manassas Junction

Richmond

PREVIEW

Focus on the Main Idea
In the early years of the Civil War, the North and South formed strategies in hopes of gaining a quick victory.

PLACES
Richmond, Virginia
Manassas Junction, Virginia

PEOPLE
Winfield Scott
Thomas "Stonewall" Jackson
Robert E. Lee

VOCABULARY
blockade
Anaconda Plan
First Battle of Bull Run
Battle of Antietam

▶ This canteen was carried by a Confederate soldier in the Civil War.

The Early Stages of the War

You Are There
It is the summer of 1861. Dawn breaks over your Kentucky farm. You hear a rooster crowing. Below your attic bedroom, your mother lets out a cry. You peer down from your room and see her holding a sheet of paper. It is a letter from your oldest brother, Joshua. He left last night to join the Union army.

Joshua and your second-oldest brother, William, had been arguing about the war since spring. "The Union forever!" Joshua would say. "Down with Northern tyranny!" William would shout. You just hope the war ends soon.

You read in the newspaper that the Confederates have just won a victory in Virginia. Expecting a short war, many Southern men are rushing to join the army before the war ends. You wonder if William will leave to join the Confederate forces. If he does, could he and Joshua end up fighting against each other, brother against brother?

Main Idea and Details As you read, note how the North and South prepared for war.

Advantages and Disadvantages

Many supporters of the North believed they were fighting to preserve the Union. However, most Southern supporters thought that they were fighting to preserve their way of life. Sometimes these different opinions divided families. Some of President Lincoln's own family sided with the South. Four brothers of his wife, Mary, fought for the Confederacy.

Besides strong feelings, each side thought that it had an advantage over the other. Southerners believed that their more rural way of life would better prepare soldiers for war. Many Southerners hunted and were familiar with weapons. The South also had a history of producing military leaders. A larger share of the Mexican War veterans came from the South.

But an army needed supplies. In 1860 the Northern states produced more than 90 percent of the country's weapons, cloth, shoes, and iron. They also produced more than half of the country's corn and 80 percent of the wheat.

Moving supplies was also important to an army. The Union had far more railroads, canals, and roads than the Confederacy. In addition, the Union was able to raise far more money. By the end of the war, the Union had spent more than $2.6 billion. The Confederacy had spent only $1 billion.

REVIEW Why did each side believe that it would win the war? **Summarize**

FACT FILE

Union and Confederacy, 1861

Look at the graphs below to compare the resources each side had.

■ Union
▨ Confederacy

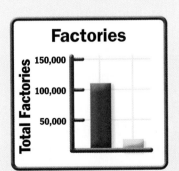
Union Flag

States

Total States

25
20
15
10
5

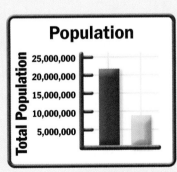

Population

Total Population

25,000,000
20,000,000
15,000,000
10,000,000
5,000,000

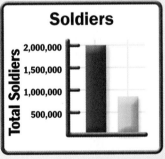

Soldiers

Total Soldiers

2,000,000
1,500,000
1,000,000
500,000

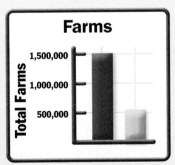

Factories

Total Factories

150,000
100,000
50,000

Farms

Total Farms

1,500,000
1,000,000
500,000

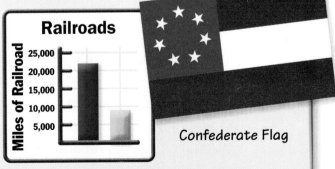

Railroads

Miles of Railroad

25,000
20,000
15,000
10,000
5,000

Confederate Flag

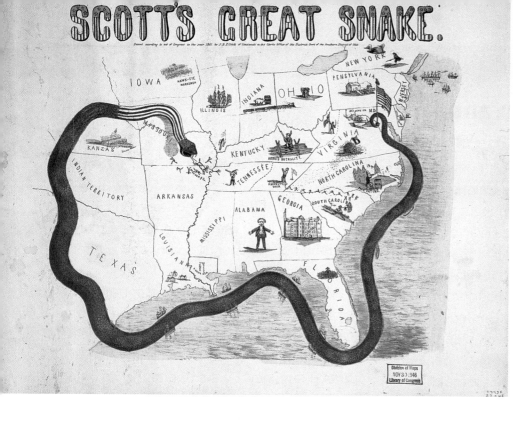

SCOTT'S GREAT SNAKE.

> ► This cartoon illustrated the Anaconda Plan by showing an anaconda snake surrounding the Confederacy.

Strategies

President Abraham Lincoln sought advice on how to win the war from General **Winfield Scott,** who had fought in the Mexican War. Scott planned a strategy with three parts. The first part was a blockade of the Atlantic and Gulf coasts of the Confederacy. A **blockade** is the shutting off of an area by troops or ships to keep people and supplies from moving in or out. With a blockade the South would not be able to ship its cotton for sale in Europe. Cotton sales were the South's main way of getting money to pay for the war.

The second stage of Scott's plan was to capture territory along the Mississippi River, the heart of the Confederacy. Gaining control of the Mississippi River would weaken the Confederacy by cutting the Southern states in two.

Third, the Union would attack the Confederacy from the east and west. Scott's strategy was called the **Anaconda Plan,** because he said that it would squeeze the Confederacy like an anaconda. An anaconda is a huge snake that kills prey by wrapping itself around an animal and suffocating it. Lincoln liked the plan. He ordered the blockade on April 19, one week after the fall of Fort Sumter.

The Confederate government had its own strategy for victory. First, it believed that the Confederacy only had to defend its territory until the Northerners got tired and gave up. Many Southerners believed that Northerners had nothing to gain from victory and would not be willing to fight for long. Southerners assumed that their soldiers would fight more fiercely for their land and their way of life.

The Confederacy also believed that Britain would assist it in the war because British clothing mills depended on Southern cotton. But Britain already had a surplus of cotton and was looking to India and Egypt for new sources of cotton. Britain allowed the South to build several warships in its shipyards, but it did not send any soldiers.

REVIEW How did Winfield Scott's Anaconda Plan attempt to weaken the Southern states?
🔄 **Main Idea and Details**

Early Battles

Early successes gave the Confederacy confidence. President Lincoln sent 35,000 troops to invade **Richmond, Virginia,** the capital of the Confederacy. On the way, on July 21, 1861, they met Confederate troops at a small stream called Bull Run near the town of **Manassas Junction, Virginia.**

The **First Battle of Bull Run** was a confusing event. Early on, the fighting went in the Union's favor. Some Confederate soldiers began to turn back, but one general from Virginia told his men to hold their place. Because the general and his men stood "like a stone wall," he became known as **Thomas "Stonewall" Jackson.**

As more Confederates arrived, the tide turned in their favor. The Union soldiers retreated. The casualties at Bull Run were about 3,000 for the Union and 2,000 for the Confederacy. Casualties include soldiers killed, wounded, captured, or missing.

Many battles took place across the South.

Union forces won some, but the Confederates seemed to be winning the war. In May 1862, "Stonewall" Jackson defeated the Union army in Virginia, and some feared that he could take over Washington, D.C.

On September 17, 1862, Union and Confederate forces met near the town of Sharpsburg, Maryland, in the **Battle of Antietam** (an TEET um). The battle involved one of the Confederacy's most capable generals, **Robert E. Lee.** He had been asked to fight for the Union but refused. Lee decided to serve the Confederacy after Virginia, the state of his birth, joined the other Southern states. You will read more about Robert E. Lee in the Biography on page 87.

The battle was an important victory for the Union. After Antietam, Great Britain ended its support for the Southern states. The Confederacy would have to fight alone.

REVIEW What effect did winning the Battle of Antietam have on the Union? *Cause and Effect*

▶ **With more than 23,000 casualties, the Battle of Antietam was the single bloodiest day of the Civil War.**

Lithograph by Kurz & Allison

85

Technology and War

Recent technologies were used and new technologies were developed during the Civil War. Soldiers used rifles that could shoot farther and more accurately than guns used in previous wars. Railroads quickly moved troops and supplies to battlefronts. The Confederacy built several submarines—ships that could travel under the water's surface—to overcome the Union's blockade. Both sides used an early version of the hand grenade.

Another new weapon was the ironclad, or iron covered ship. The Confederates built an ironclad by taking an abandoned Union ship called the *Merrimack* and covering it with iron. They renamed it the *Virginia*. In March 1862, the *Virginia* easily sank several wooden Union ships. Union cannonballs simply bounced off the *Virginia's* iron sides. Then, on March 9, a Union ironclad named the *Monitor* arrived to battle the *Virginia*. The two ships fired at each other for hours. But neither ship was able to seriously damage the other.

These new technologies made the war more deadly, resulting in huge numbers of casualties. Unfortunately, medical knowledge had not advanced as much as other technologies. Many soldiers died from disease and infection.

REVIEW What were the advantages and disadvantages of new technology in the Civil War? **Compare and Contrast**

Summarize the Lesson

April 19, 1861 The Union began a blockade of Southern ports.

July 21, 1861 Confederate forces defeated Union troops in the First Battle of Bull Run in Manassas.

September 17, 1862 Union and Confederate troops fought a bloody battle at Antietam, an important Union victory.

LESSON 1 REVIEW

Check Facts and Main Ideas

1. **Main Idea and Details** On a separate sheet of paper, fill in the details of the **Anaconda Plan.**

General Winfield Scott's Anaconda Plan attempted to weaken the Confederate states.

2. Compare advantages the Union had at the beginning of the war to those of the Confederacy.

3. How did the strategies of the North and South differ?

4. Summarize the events of the **First Battle of Bull Run.**

5. **Critical Thinking:** *Analyze Information* What effect did military technology have on Civil War soldiers?

Link to Mathematics

Analyze Graphs Look again at the graphs on page 83. How many more people lived in the Northern states than in the Southern states? How many more miles of railroad did the North have compared to the South? Why would a larger population and more miles of railroad be an advantage?

Robert E. Lee *1807–1870*

Robert E. Lee did not know his father for long. When Robert was six, his father, Harry Lee, visited a friend who published a newspaper that criticized the United States for going to war with Great Britain in 1812. Like his friend, Harry Lee opposed this war. A group of angry people attacked the newspaper offices while Harry Lee was inside, and he was badly beaten. Robert had to say goodbye as his father boarded a ship to Barbados, where he went to heal from his wounds. Harry Lee died before he could return home.

Lee rode his beloved horse, Traveller, throughout the Civil War. Traveller outlived Lee, walked behind Lee's coffin at his funeral, and was later buried near Lee's grave in Lexington, Virginia.

Many years later, at the beginning of the Civil War, Robert E. Lee was asked to make the most difficult decision of his life. Lee was a rising star in the United States Army. But Lee had been born and raised in Virginia, and, although he personally disapproved of slavery, he loved his home and his state. Perhaps he thought of his father, who had defended the things he loved at great cost to himself. Lee resigned from the United States Army and wrote:

"I have not been able to make up my mind to raise my hand against my relatives, my children, my home."

Lee hoped that Virginia would not take sides in the conflict, and he would not have to fight at all. But when Virginia seceded and joined the Confederacy, his path became clear to him. Lee accepted a position commanding Virginia's forces. Later, Lee's wife, Mary, remembered the night of his decision. She said that he "wept tears of blood."

Learn from Biographies

Why was Lee's decision so difficult to make? What do you think his wife meant when she said that he "wept tears of blood"?

For more information, go online to *Meet the People* at **www.sfsocialstudies.com.**

1863   1864

January 1863
Emancipation Proclamation takes effect.

July 1863
African American troops attack Fort Wagner.

June 1864
Congress gives black and white troops equal pay.

Fort Wagner

PREVIEW

Focus on the Main Idea
As the Civil War continued, people in the North and the South suffered many hardships, including the growing loss of life.

PLACES
Fort Wagner, South Carolina

PEOPLE
Mathew Brady
William Carney
Belle Boyd
Clara Barton

VOCABULARY
draft
Emancipation Proclamation

Life During the War

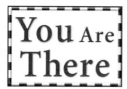 These letters are from soldiers who fought in the Battle of Fredericksburg in Virginia on December 13, 1862. They were on opposing sides, but whether fighting for the Union or the Confederacy, soldiers were horrified by the loss of life.

December 16, 1862

Gone are the proud hopes, the high aspirations [goals] that swelled our bosoms [chests] a few days ago. Once more unsuccessful, and only a bloody record to show our men were brave.

Captain William T. Lusk, Union soldier

January 11, 1863

I can inform you that I have seen the Monkey Show [battle] at last, and I don't want to see it anymore. Martha I can't tell you how many dead I did see. . . . one thing is sure, I don't want to see that sight anymore.

Private Thomas Warrick, Confederate soldier

 Main Idea and Details As you read, note the difficulties during the Civil War for both soldiers and civilians.

Life for Soldiers

Families of soldiers like Captain Lusk and Private Warrick learned about the war from soldiers' letters and newspaper articles. They could also see the horrors of war thanks to a new technology—photography. Civil War photographers like **Mathew Brady** took pictures in camps and on the war's many battlefields. Photographs showed the dead and wounded, but also showed soldiers warming themselves by campfires, or resting after a long day's march.

The average age of a Civil War soldier was about 25. However, drummer boys as young as twelve years old went to the battlefield. A soldier's life was a hard one, even when he was not in battle. Soldiers might march as many as 25 miles a day while carrying about 50 pounds of supplies in knapsacks, or backpacks. They grew thirsty marching in summer's heat and shivered through winter's cold.

Marching was especially tough for Confederate soldiers. The Union blockade prevented many supplies from reaching Southern armies. Soldiers wore out their shoes and often fought in bare feet until they could get another pair.

On both sides, soldiers were usually unhappy with the food. They were given beans, bacon, pickled beef, salt pork, and a tough flour-and-water biscuit called "hardtack." When they could, troops hunted for food in nearby forests, or even raided local farms.

As the war continued, volunteers for the war decreased. A volunteer is a person who chooses freely to join or do something. Both sides passed draft laws. A **draft** requires men of a certain age to serve in the military if they are called. However, Confederates who owned 20 or more slaves could pay substitutes to take their place. In the Union, men could pay $300 to avoid fighting in the war. The draft was unpopular, because it favored the wealthy. In July 1863, riots broke out in New York City to protest the draft. Many called the conflict "a rich man's war and a poor man's fight."

Losses on each side were terrible. A total of about 1 million Union and Confederate soldiers were killed or wounded. In comparison, only about 10,600 Patriots were killed in the Revolutionary War. Disease was the most common cause of death in the Civil War. Of the more than 360,000 soldiers that died in the Union army, only about 110,000 died in battle. In the Confederate army, 258,000 soldiers died, but only about 94,000 died in battle. As you read in Lesson 1, disease and infections killed many soldiers. This is because no one knew about germs yet, so doctors did not know how to keep wounds from getting infected.

REVIEW What were some of the challenges faced by Civil War soldiers?
🔄 **Main Idea and Details**

▶ **Life was difficult and dangerous for both Union soldiers (left) and Confederate soldiers (right).**

The Emancipation Proclamation

At first, the Civil War was not a war against slavery. Lincoln's goal was to preserve the Union, or keep the country together. By 1862, though, Lincoln began to believe that he could save the Union only by making the abolition of slavery a goal of the war.

Lincoln's advisers feared that ending slavery would hurt the war effort. Some said that it would unite the South and divide the North. But Lincoln explained, "Slavery must die that the nation might live."

On January 1, 1863, President Lincoln issued the **Emancipation Proclamation.** Emancipate means "to set free." A proclamation is a statement. The Emancipation Proclamation was a statement that freed all slaves in the Confederate states at war with the Union. Moments before signing the proclamation Lincoln said, "I never in my life felt more certain that I was doing right." The Proclamation said:

> **"Slaves within any State . . . in rebellion against the United States, shall be then . . . and forever free."**

The Emancipation Proclamation did not end slavery in the border states or in Confederate land that Union forces already controlled. It did declare an end to slavery in the rest of the Confederacy. But since Union forces did not control these areas, most African Americans remained enslaved.

Free African Americans like Frederick Douglass supported Lincoln's efforts. Douglass encouraged African Americans to assist the Union in the war. "Fly to arms," he wrote. Large numbers of African Americans responded by joining the Union army.

REVIEW What was a result of the Emancipation Proclamation? **Cause and Effect**

HERE AND THERE

Slaves and Serfs

At About the Same Time that President Lincoln was issuing the Emancipation Proclamation, people in other areas of the world were gaining liberty. In 1861 leaders in Russia began freeing people called serfs. Serfs worked on an owner's land in exchange for protection and housing. Like slaves, serfs could not marry, change their occupation, or leave the land without the owner's permission.

EUROPE RUSSIA ASIA

▶ The African American soldiers of the 54th Regiment gained fame for their brave attack on Fort Wagner.

The Granger Collection

Library of Congress

African Americans in the War

In the beginning of the war, African Americans were not allowed to join the army. But they did serve as cooks, servants, and other workers. They were first allowed to join the Union army in 1862.

African American soldiers were not treated the same as whites. They received less pay than white soldiers. They had to buy their own uniforms, while white soldiers did not.

The situation improved for African Americans before the end of the war. One reason for this change was the role played by the Massachusetts 54th Colored Regiment. A regiment is a group of 600 to 1,000 soldiers. The 54th was one of the first groups of black troops to be organized for combat in the Union army.

On July 18, 1863, the 54th Regiment led an attack on **Fort Wagner** in South Carolina.

Confederate fire was heavy, but the men of the 54th charged the fort before being forced back. The group lost more than four out of every ten men.

William Carney, a sergeant in the battle, was seriously wounded. Yet he never dropped the regiment's flag. Carney later said that he had fought "to serve my country and my oppressed brothers." He was one of 16 African Americans to win the Congressional Medal of Honor during the war.

The Union did not win the battle at Fort Wagner. But the bravery of the 54th Regiment changed the minds of many Northerners who had doubted the abilities of black soldiers to fight. Nearly 200,000 black soldiers fought for the Union in the Civil War, and 37,000 lost their lives. In June 1864, Congress voted to give black and white troops equal pay.

REVIEW What conclusion can you draw about why African American troops fought in the Civil War? **Draw Conclusions**

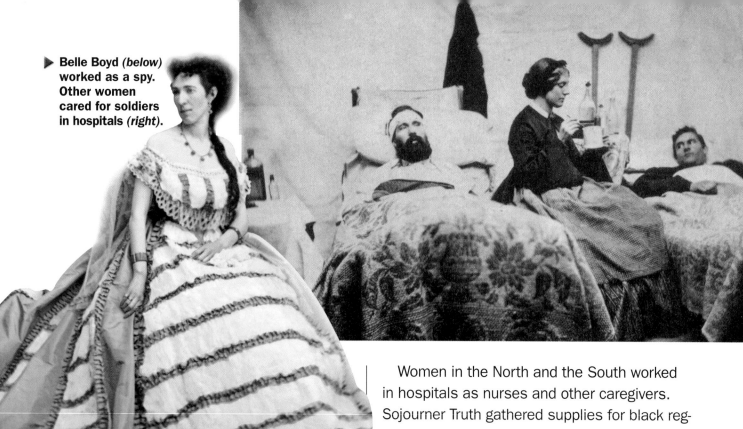

▶ Belle Boyd (below) worked as a spy. Other women cared for soldiers in hospitals (right).

Women and the War

Women contributed to the war effort in many ways. They ran farms and businesses while their husbands were fighting. They became teachers and office workers. Some even became involved in the war more directly. Frances Clalin, for example, disguised herself as a man so that she could fight in the Union army.

Some women became spies. Women were less likely to be suspected as spies and were punished less severely if they were caught. They often hid weapons and documents under their large hoop skirts to avoid being caught. **Belle Boyd,** nicknamed "La Belle Rebelle," was one of the most famous Confederate spies. She continued spying even after six arrests. She once communicated to a Confederate by hiding messages inside rubber balls and throwing them out of her cell window.

Women in the North and the South worked in hospitals as nurses and other caregivers. Sojourner Truth gathered supplies for black regiments. One Northern woman, **Clara Barton,** explained why she cared for soldiers, "While our soldiers stand and fight, I can stand and feed and nurse them." Barton earned the nickname "Angel of the Battlefield" as she cared for wounded soldiers during the First Battle of Bull Run. In 1881 Barton organized the American Association of the Red Cross to help victims of wars and natural disasters.

Women in the South also had to deal with shortages of supplies. Because demand was greater than supply, prices rose dramatically. The average Southern family's monthly food bill rose from $6.65 just before the war to $68 in 1863. In April of that year, hundreds of women rioted in Richmond to protest the rise in prices. Similar bread riots occurred in other Southern cities as well.

Despite their own difficulties, women in the North and South did all they could for the soldiers. They sewed clothing, rolled bandages, sold personal possessions, and sent any food they could spare to the armies.

REVIEW How did women help the war effort? ↻ **Main Idea and Details**

The War Goes On

In 1863 the Vice President of the Confederacy, Alexander Stephens, said, "A large majority on both sides are tired of the war." And it was true. Union and Confederate soldiers alike were singing a song called "When This Cruel War Is Over." The lack of supplies, delays in pay, sleeping uncovered in the rain, and the terrible death of friends and family members were taking their toll.

By 1863 some soldiers were refusing to go to war. Thousands of Union and Confederate men deserted, or left their military duty without permission.

Explained one Union soldier, "I'm tired of the war anyhow, and my time's up soon."

▶ **Soldiers on both sides were tired of war.**

But, as you will read, Union victories would soon lead to the war's end.

REVIEW Compare how people in the North and the South felt about the war after the first two years. **Compare and Contrast**

Summarize the Lesson

- **January 1863** President Abraham Lincoln formally issued the Emancipation Proclamation, freeing slaves in territories still fighting Union forces.

- **July 1863** The Massachusetts 54th, one of the first African American regiments to fight for the Union, attacked Fort Wagner in South Carolina.

- **June 1864** Congress gave black soldiers the same pay as white soldiers.

LESSON 2 REVIEW

Check Facts and Main Ideas

1. ⟳ **Main Idea and Details** On a separate sheet of paper, fill in the details that support the main idea.

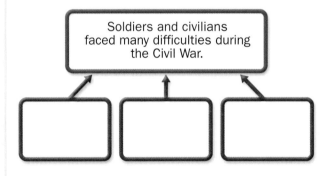

Soldiers and civilians faced many difficulties during the Civil War.

2. Why was the Civil War called a "rich man's war and a poor man's fight"?

3. **Critical Thinking:** *Problem-Solving* Suppose you had to help President Lincoln decide when to issue the **Emancipation Proclamation.** How would you solve this problem?

4. How did the Massachusetts 54th help change people's minds?

5. What role did women play in the Civil War?

Link to ⌘ Writing

Write Letters Letters written by soldiers and their families often described conditions on the battlefield or at home. Write a letter detailing life as a Civil War soldier. Write another letter in response that relates the situation at home in the city or on a farm. Use the word **draft** in your answer.

Working for Lasting Peace

Many years after the terrible bloodshed of the Civil War, new kinds of weapons, such as landmines, pose a threat to the lives of innocent people.

When Jody Williams heard schoolchildren pick on her brother, Stephen, she got angry. "I couldn't understand why people would be mean to him because he was deaf," says Williams. From that early experience of cruelty in Poultney, Vermont, came Williams's fierce desire to "stop bullies [from] being mean to . . . people, just because they are weak."

Today defending innocent people against landmines is Jody Williams's life work. Landmines have been used since the late 1800s. They are hidden in the ground and are intended to harm enemy soldiers during war by exploding when people walk over them. When the wars end, however, many landmines remain. Today millions and millions of landmines are in the ground in about 70 countries—mainly poor ones like Angola, Afghanistan, and Cambodia. Williams says:

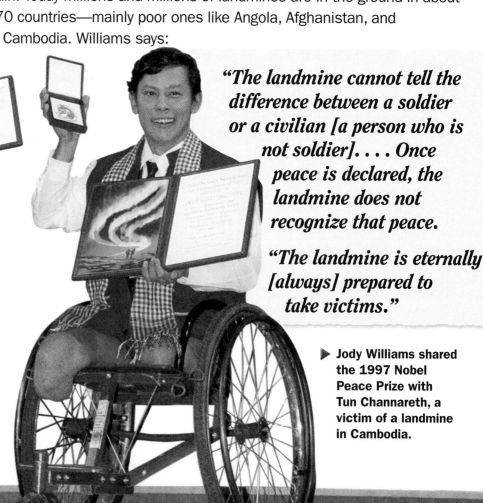

"The landmine cannot tell the difference between a soldier or a civilian [a person who is not soldier]. . . . Once peace is declared, the landmine does not recognize that peace.

"The landmine is eternally [always] prepared to take victims."

▶ **Jody Williams shared the 1997 Nobel Peace Prize with Tun Channareth, a victim of a landmine in Cambodia.**

94

BUILDING CITIZENSHIP

★ **Caring**

Respect
Responsibility
Fairness
Honesty
Courage

In the 1980s Jody Williams learned of the dangers of landmines while working for human rights in war-torn Central America. There she saw children who had lost legs or arms after stepping on buried landmines. She met families who could not farm land because there were so many landmines buried there.

In 1991 Jody Williams and others started the International Campaign to Ban Landmines (ICBL). Their goal is a landmine-free planet. Williams works tirelessly for a ban on landmines, visiting affected countries and sending e-mails and faxes to tell people around the world about the dangers of these buried killers.

In recognition of their efforts, Jody Williams and ICBL were awarded the Nobel Peace Prize in December 1997. At the end of 1997, leaders from 121 countries signed a treaty to outlaw landmine production and destroy existing landmines.

Caring in Action

Link to Current Events "When we began we were just three people sitting in a room," says Williams about ICBL's beginnings. "It's breathtaking what you can do when you set a goal and put all your energy into it." Get together with two other classmates. What caring action can you plan for your school or community? What are some steps your group could take to carry it out?

1863   **1865**

July 1863
The Union gains control of the Mississippi River.

November 1863
President Lincoln delivers the Gettysburg Address.

April 1865
The Confederacy surrenders to the Union.

PREVIEW

Focus on the Main Idea
A series of Northern victories led to the end of the Civil War by 1865.

PLACES
Gettysburg, Pennsylvania
Vicksburg, Mississippi
Atlanta, Georgia
Savannah, Georgia
Appomattox Court House, Virginia

PEOPLE
Ulysses S. Grant
William Tecumseh Sherman

VOCABULARY
Battle of Gettysburg
Gettysburg Address
Battle of Vicksburg
total war

How the North Won

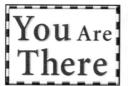 **You Are There** The date is November 19, 1863. About 15,000 people have gathered at Gettysburg, Pennsylvania. They are here for a ceremony to honor the soldiers who died in the Battle of Gettysburg just four months earlier. President Lincoln has been asked to speak.

The main speaker at the event is former Massachusetts governor Edward Everett. He delivers a speech that lasts almost two hours. Finally, President Lincoln rises and addresses the crowd for about three minutes. The speech is so short that no one realizes that Lincoln is finished. The crowd is silent for a moment. Then a few people begin to clap. Lincoln sits down before the photographer can take his picture.

One newspaper calls his speech "silly." Lincoln calls it "a flat failure." But his speech, the Gettysburg Address, will become known as one of the greatest speeches in United States history.

 Main Idea and Details As you read, keep in mind the goals of the North as the war reached an end.

The Battle of Gettysburg

One of the most important battles of the Civil War was a three-day struggle fought in **Gettysburg, Pennsylvania.** This was the farthest north that Confederate forces had advanced into Union territory.

The **Battle of Gettysburg** began on July 1, 1863. The Confederates, led by Robert E. Lee, pushed the Union soldiers back, but missed an opportunity to pursue the Northerners and follow up their attack.

By the second day of fighting, more Union soldiers had arrived. The Confederates attacked again, but the Union troops held their ground. One Confederate from Texas remembered "the balls [bullets] were whizzing so thick that it looked like a man could hold out a hat and catch it full."

On July 3, more than 150 Confederate cannons fired at Union troops. Northern cannons responded. The noise was so loud it was heard 140 miles away in Pittsburgh. Southern General George Pickett then led an attack on Union troops known as "Pickett's Charge." Thousands of Confederates marched in the open and uphill toward the well-protected Union troops. The attack was a disaster. Of the nearly 10,500 Confederates in Pickett's Charge, more than 5,000 were killed or wounded, and hundreds were captured.

The Battle of Gettysburg was an important victory for the North. Lee's advance into the North was stopped, and he retreated back into Virginia. It was also a costly battle for both sides. There were more than 23,000 Union casualties. The South suffered more than 28,000 casualties.

REVIEW Describe the events of each day in the Battle of Gettysburg. **Sequence**

Map Adventure

Battle of Gettysburg, 1863

Suppose you are visiting the battle site where the fighting at Gettysburg took place. Today it is a national military park. Answer the questions about the battle site.

1. Describe the location of the Union and Confederate headquarters.

2. In which direction was Pickett's Charge made?

3. What advantage did the location of Little Round Top give the Union forces?

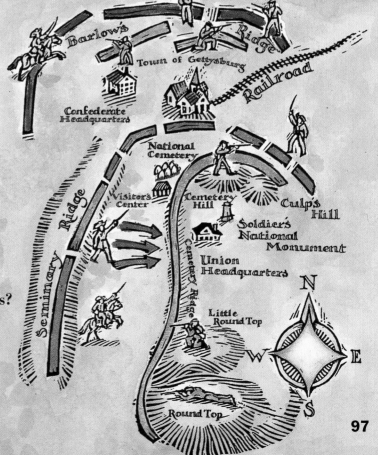

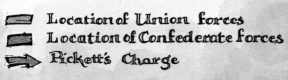

Location of Union forces
Location of Confederate forces
Pickett's Charge

97

The Gettysburg Address

In November 1863, the Gettysburg battlefield was made into a national cemetery to honor the men who died there. As you have read, President Lincoln was one of the people asked to speak at the ceremony. Read his speech, known as the **Gettysburg Address.**

The Gettysburg Address inspired the Union to keep fighting. The speech made it clear that a united nation and the end of slavery were worth fighting for.

REVIEW How did President Lincoln express his admiration for the soldiers who had died at Gettysburg? **Main Idea and Details**

The Gettysburg Address

Four score [80] and seven years ago our fathers brought forth on this continent a new nation, conceived [formed] in Liberty, and dedicated [devoted] to the proposition [idea] that all men are created equal.

Now we are engaged in a great civil war, testing whether that nation, or any nation so conceived and so dedicated, can long endure. We are met on a great battlefield of that war. We have come to dedicate a portion of that field, as a final resting place for those who here gave their lives that that nation might live. It is altogether fitting and proper that we should do this.

But, in a larger sense, we cannot dedicate—we cannot consecrate [make worthy of respect]—we cannot hallow [make holy]—this ground. The brave men, living and dead, who struggled here, have consecrated it, far above our poor power to add or detract [take away]. The world will little note, nor long remember what we say here, but it can never forget what they did here. It is for us the living, rather, to be dedicated here to the unfinished work which they who fought here have thus far so nobly advanced. It is rather for us to be here dedicated to the great task remaining before us—that from these honored dead we take increased devotion to that cause for which they gave the last full measure of devotion—that we here highly resolve [are determined] that these dead shall not have died in vain—that this nation, under God, shall have a new birth of freedom—and that government of the people, by the people, for the people, shall not perish [die out] from the earth.

Painting by J. L. G. Ferris

The Tide Turns

The Battle of Gettysburg was one of a series of battles that turned the tide of the war in favor of the Union. As you read in Lesson 1, one part of the Anaconda Plan called for Union troops to gain control of the Mississippi River to weaken the Confederacy. Capturing **Vicksburg, Mississippi,** which lay on the east bank of the river, would achieve this goal.

General **Ulysses S. Grant,** who had served with General Robert E. Lee in the Mexican War, headed the Union forces in the **Battle of Vicksburg.** In May 1863, Union forces began a blockade of the city. They bombarded Vicksburg with cannon fire by land and sea for 48 days. Many people in the town dug caves in the hillside for protection.

Confederate civilians and soldiers in Vicksburg faced starvation under the Union blockade. Butcher shops sold rats, and soldiers received one biscuit and one piece of bacon a day.

Finally, on July 4, 1863, one day after the Battle of Gettysburg ended, the Southerners surrendered Vicksburg. The Confederacy was cut in two. Study the map below to see where Vicksburg and other major battles of the Civil War took place.

REVIEW Why do you think it took so long for the Confederates to surrender at Vicksburg? **Draw Conclusions**

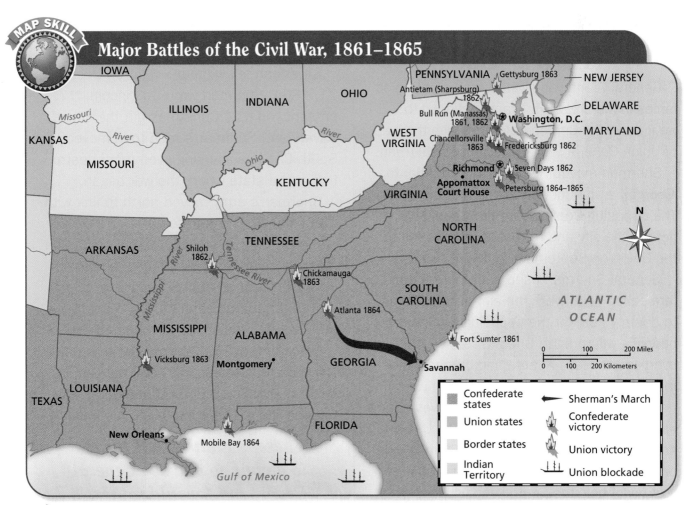

MAP SKILL

Major Battles of the Civil War, 1861–1865

▶ In July 1863, Union victories at Gettysburg and Vicksburg turned the tide of the war.

MAP SKILL Use a Map Scale *How many miles apart were the battles of Gettysburg and Vicksburg?*

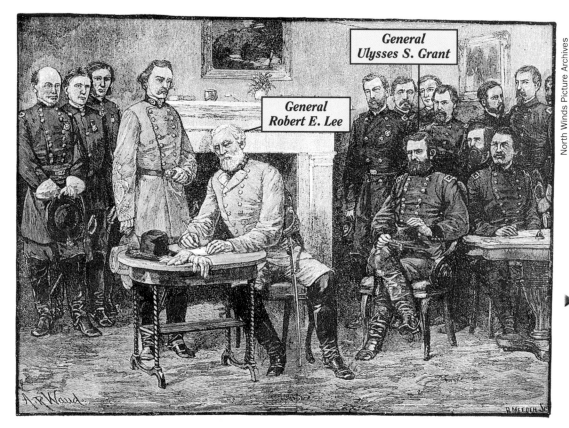

General Ulysses S. Grant

General Robert E. Lee

▶ After four years of fighting, General Lee agreed to surrender his army to General Grant.

North Winds Picture Archives

The War Ends

General Grant was given control of all Union forces in March 1864. Grant continued to wear down the Confederate army with the help of Union General **William Tecumseh Sherman.**

Sherman moved his army toward **Atlanta, Georgia,** a vital industrial and railway center. The opposing Confederate army could not defend the city and retreated. Atlanta fell to the Union on September 2, 1864.

General Sherman used a method of warfare called **total war.** The aim of total war is to destroy not just the opposing army, but the people's will to fight. Sherman's men ordered everyone to leave Atlanta and burned almost the entire city.

Starting in November, his army moved southeast toward **Savannah, Georgia.** The Union soldiers marched 300 miles in a 60 mile-wide path. As they went, they destroyed anything that might help the South keep fighting, including houses, railroads, barns, and fields. Soldiers caused $100 million dollars worth

of damage in Sherman's "March to the Sea."

Savannah fell without a fight on December 21, 1864. Sherman wrote to Lincoln, "I . . . present you as a Christmas gift the city of Savannah." Sherman's men then moved to South Carolina, causing even more destruction in the state where the war began.

Sherman's army moved north to link with Grant's army. The Northerners were closing in on Lee's army in Virginia. In April 1865 Confederate soldiers left Richmond, and Union troops entered on April 3. President Lincoln arrived to tour the captured Confederate capital. The city's former slaves cheered him.

Lee's army of 55,000 was tired and starving. The men tried to escape west, but Grant's force of about 113,000 outnumbered and trapped them. Lee admitted to his men,

"There is nothing left for me to do but go and see General Grant, and I would rather die a thousand deaths."

Generals Lee and Grant met in a farmhouse in **Appomattox Court House, Virginia,** on April 9, 1865, to discuss the terms of surrender. Grant allowed Lee's men to go free. The Southerners were allowed to keep their personal weapons and any horses they had. Grant also offered to give Lee's men food from Union supplies. Lee accepted. As Lee returned to his men, the Union soldiers began to cheer. Grant silenced them, explaining,

> *"The war is over; the rebels are our countrymen again."*

The Civil War was the most destructive war in United States history. About 620,000 soldiers died. Towns, farms, and industries—mostly in the South—were ruined. Families had been torn apart by the struggle.

Even so, Lincoln expressed sympathy for the South. After news of the Confederate surrender reached Washington, D.C., he appeared before a crowd and asked a band to play the song "Dixie," one of the battle songs of the Confederacy. "I have always thought 'Dixie' one of the best tunes I ever heard," he told the people.

Lincoln wanted the country to be rebuilt. He had a plan to heal the nation's deep divisions. But he would never see his plans carried out.

REVIEW What were the results of General Sherman's strategy of total war?
Cause and Effect

Summarize the Lesson

- **July 4, 1863** Union soldiers led by General Grant cut the Confederacy in two by capturing Vicksburg, Mississippi.

- **November 19, 1863** President Abraham Lincoln gave the Gettysburg Address honoring the men who died in battle there.

- **April 9, 1865** General Robert E. Lee surrendered to General Ulysses S. Grant at Appomattox Court House, Virginia, ending the Civil War.

LESSON 3   REVIEW

Check Facts and Main Ideas

1. **Main Idea and Details** On a separate sheet of paper, fill in the missing details that support the main idea.

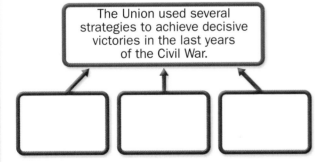

The Union used several strategies to achieve decisive victories in the last years of the Civil War.

2. What circumstances led the Union to victory on the third day in the **Battle of Gettysburg**?

3. What were Lincoln's goals as expressed in the **Gettysburg Address**?

4. **Critical Thinking:** *Interpret Maps* Look at the map on page 99. In what state did most of the major battles occur in the Civil War? Give a reason you think this would be so.

5. What was the purpose of **total war** and Sherman's "March to the Sea"?

Link to ∞ Mathematics

Analyze a Speech Reread President Lincoln's Gettysburg Address on page 98. What year was he referring to in the speech when he said "Four score and seven years ago"? Why would he have referred to that year?

Read a Road Map

What? A **road map** is a map that shows roads, cities, and places of interest. Different types of lines show large and small highways and even smaller roads. Symbols show if a road is a major **interstate highway,** a large road that connects cities in different states. Other symbols show state roads, and still others show smaller roads.

   Different sizes of color areas and dots are used to show cities and towns of various sizes. Many road maps use special symbols to show places of interest. Some road maps also show distances from one place to another.

Why? People often have to drive to places they do not know. They may be traveling for business, vacation, or other reasons. Drivers use road maps to figure out how to get from one place to another.

   Many people are interested in the history of the Civil War. Some visit Civil War sites. Our nation keeps many Civil War sites as parks or monuments. Tourists may go from one site to another during a vacation. Often they visit places they have never been before, and they find their way with road maps.

▶ Today the Gettysburg battlefield is a national military park.

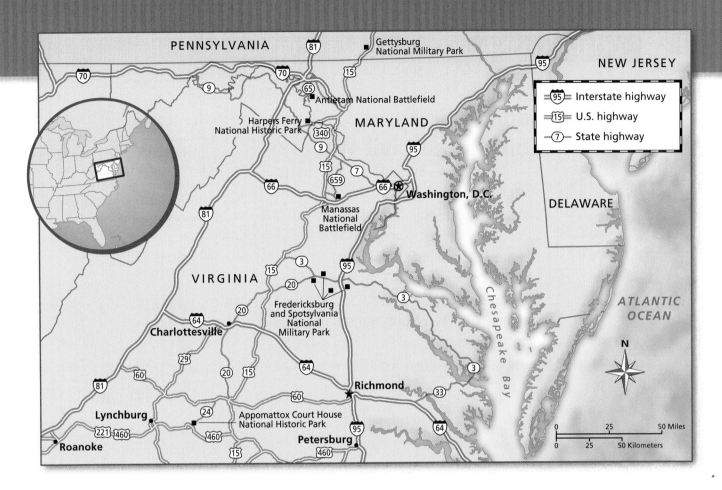

How?

To use a road map, you need to know where you are and where you want to go. Then you find these places on the map. You also have to understand what kinds of roads are shown and how they are marked on the map.

Say that you are starting at Richmond, Virginia, and want to get to Gettysburg, Pennsylvania. Look at the road map on this page, which shows many Civil War sites in Pennsylvania, Maryland, and Virginia. You notice that Gettysburg is about 180 miles north of Richmond. You see that Route 64 goes northwest from Richmond to Route 15. From there, Route 15 goes north all the way to Gettysburg.

Think and Apply

1. How would you travel from Gettysburg National Military Park to Manassas National Battlefield?

2. What interstate highway is part of the shortest route from Manassas National Battlefield Park to Washington, D.C.?

3. How would you travel from Washington, D.C., to the Fredericksburg and Spotsylvania National Military Park?

Internet Activity

For more information, go online to the *Atlas* at **www.sfsocialstudies.com.**

Communications During the Civil War

The Civil War was one of the first large conflicts in which armies could communicate instantly using the telegraph, which sent messages along wires. By 1861 every state east of the Mississippi River was linked by telegraph wires. That April, when the Confederacy attacked Fort Sumter in South Carolina, word went out immediately: "Fort Sumter is fired upon." Both Union and Confederate armies used Morse code and secret military codes to communicate.

Signal Drum

Drums and bugles were played on the field, signaling instructions for firing and troop movements. This drum was found on the Gettysburg battlefield.

Animal hide drum head

Handpainted eagle and crest

Strapping to keep drum head taut

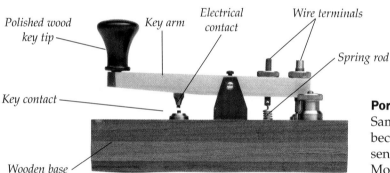

Polished wood key tip

Key arm

Electrical contact

Wire terminals

Spring rod

Key contact

Wooden base

Portable Telegraph Key

Samuel Morse, an American artist who became an inventor, developed a way to send telegraph messages using a code called Morse code.

Rolled canvas window blind

Sending and receiving telegraphic terminals

One of two telegrapher's desks

Telegrapher

Signal officer

Army Field Telegrapher's Wagon

This portable telegrapher's office had sending and receiving sets.

Hanging Military Telegraph Wires

As armies moved, telegraph wires had to be strung to areas that might not have been wired yet. Army telegraph poles were often trees from which bark and limbs had been removed.

Insulated wire hook

Bamboo field poles for temporary hook-ups to existing heavy lines

Wire spool

Field telegrapher's wagon

Sending and receiving key and letter indicator

Brass wheel with stamped letters

Receiving terminals

Sending terminals

Beardslee Telegraph

Most soldiers could not read Morse code, so the Union army adopted the Beardslee telegraph. Electric signals sent or received over the Beardslee system moved a metal arrow around a large brass wheel with the letters of the alphabet stamped on it. These letters spelled out messages in English or secret code. The Beardslee's range was limited to five miles.

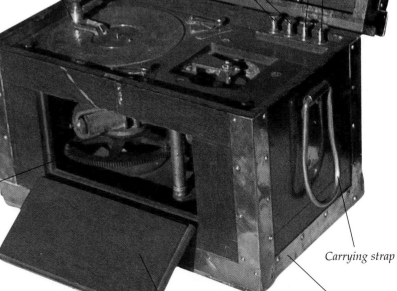

Letter wheel gear mechanism

Wire wrapping

Carrying strap

Brass fittings

Service door

1865   1867

April 1865
President Lincoln
is killed.

December 1865
The Thirteenth
Amendment
ends slavery.

March 1867
Congress
passes the first
Reconstruction Act.

Washington, D.C.

PREVIEW

Focus on the Main Idea
The country faced many difficult challenges after the Civil War ended, including rebuilding the South and protecting the rights of newly freed African Americans.

PLACES
Washington, D.C.

PEOPLE
Andrew Johnson
Hiram R. Revels
Blanche K. Bruce

VOCABULARY
assassination
Reconstruction
Thirteenth Amendment
black codes
Freedmen's Bureau
Fourteenth Amendment
Fifteenth Amendment
impeachment
Jim Crow laws
segregation
sharecropping

The End of Slavery

You Are There

It is Friday, a little after 10:00 P.M. President Abraham Lincoln and his wife, Mary, are enjoying a play. The President and his guests are seated in a box above the stage of Ford's Theater.

Suddenly, the audience hears something like an explosion. Blue-colored smoke comes from the box where the President is seated. Mary Lincoln screams. President Lincoln has been shot. The bullet has entered the back of his head near his left ear. Lincoln is still breathing but is unconscious.

A young doctor comes forward to aid the President. After checking his wound, he says, "It is impossible for him to recover."

Main Idea and Details
As you read, look for details about rebuilding the nation after the Civil War.

▶ Poster for the play President Lincoln was seeing when he was shot.

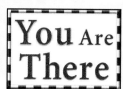

FORD'S THEATRE
TENTH STREET, ABOVE E.
SEASON II . . . WEEK XXXI . . . . NIGHT 191
WHOLE NUMBER OF NIGHTS, 400.
JOHN T. FORD . . . . PROPRIETOR AND MANAGER
(Also of Holliday's St. Theatre, Baltimore, and Academy of Music, Phila
Stage Manager . . . . J. B. WRIGHT
Treasurer . . . . H. CLAY FORD

Friday Evening, April 14th, 1865.

THIS EVENING
The Performance will be honored by the presence of
PRESIDENT LINCOLN

BENEFIT
— AND —
LAST NIGHT
OF MISS
LAURA KEENE
THE DISTINGUISHED MANAGERESS AUTHORESS, and ACTRESS
Supported by
MR. JOHN DYOTT
AND
MR. HARRY HAWK

TOM TAYLOR'S CELEBRATED ECCENTRIC COMEDY
As originally produced in America by Miss Keene, and performed by her upwards of

ONE THOUSAND NIGHTS,
ENTITLED
OUR AMERICAN
COUSIN

FLORENCE TRENCHARD . . . MISS LAURA KEENE
(Her Original Character)
Abel Murcott, Clerk to Attorney . . . . John Dyott
Asa Trenchard . . . . Harry Hawk
Sir Edward Trenchard . . . . T. C. GOURLAY
Lord Dundreary . . . . E. A. EMERSON
Mr. Coyle, Attorney . . . . J. MATTHEWS
Lieutenant Vernon, R. N. . . . . W. J. FERGUSON
Captain De Boots . . . . C. BYRNES
Binny . . . . G. G. SPEAR
Buddicomb, a Valet . . . . J. H. EVANS
John Whicker, a Gardner . . . . J. L. DeBONAY
Bilage, a Groom
Bailiffs . . . . O. A. PARKHURST and L. JOHNSON
Mary Trenchard . . . . Miss J. GOURLAY
Mrs. Mountchessington . . . . Mrs. H. MUZZY
Augusta . . . . Miss R. TRUEMAN
Georgina . . . . Miss M. HART
Sharpe . . . . Mrs. J. H. EVANS
Skillet . . . . Miss M. GOURLAY

SATURDAY EVENING, APRIL 15,
BENEFIT OF MISS JENNIE GOURLAY
When will be presented BOURCICAULT'S Great Sensational Drama,

A New President

After being shot, President Abraham Lincoln died in the early morning of April 15, 1865, in **Washington, D.C.** Until that time, no United States President had ever been assassinated. **Assassination** is the murder of a political or government leader.

Lincoln's killer was John Wilkes Booth, a 26-year-old actor who supported the Confederacy. Federal troops found Booth in a Virginia barn where he was shot and killed after he refused to surrender. Others who took part in the assassination plan were also caught and later hanged.

A funeral train carried President Lincoln's body to his hometown of Springfield, Illinois, where he was buried. People in New York City, Philadelphia, Cleveland, Chicago, and other cities paid their respects as the train passed through their communities.

▶ **People lined the streets when Lincoln's funeral train passed through New York City.**

Vice President **Andrew Johnson** became the new President. The former senator from Tennessee intended to carry out Lincoln's plan for **Reconstruction**—the rebuilding and healing of the country after the war.

One of the first steps toward reconstruction was ending slavery throughout the nation. The **Thirteenth Amendment,** which abolished slavery in the United States, took effect on December 18, 1865.

Johnson also had a plan to readmit the former Confederate states into the Union. Each state had to form a new state government. It had to pledge to obey all federal laws and deal fairly with newly freed African Americans. By the end of 1865, President Johnson believed that Reconstruction was complete.

Under Johnson's plan, though, Southern states were free to pass laws called **black codes.** These laws denied African American men the right to vote or act as jurors in a trial. Black people also could not own guns, take certain jobs, or own land. African Americans who were out of work might be fined or arrested. The laws had the effect of making an African American's life much the same as it had been under slavery.

Many in Congress were angered by the black codes. They thought Johnson's Reconstruction plan was too easy on the South. The Republicans, who had won a majority in both houses of Congress, did not trust Johnson, who was a Southerner and had been a Democrat before becoming Lincoln's Vice President. Members of Congress began developing a new plan of Reconstruction.

REVIEW What effect did black codes have on African Americans? *Cause and Effect*

Collection of the New York Historical Society

107

Reconstruction Under Congress

Congress passed the first Reconstruction Act in 1867. The former Confederate states were divided into five military districts, and about 20,000 federal troops were sent to the South. The troops, led by military governors, were responsible for maintaining order, supervising elections, and preventing discrimination against African Americans.

The Reconstruction Acts required Southern states to write new state constitutions giving African American men the right to vote. The Acts also prevented former Confederate leaders and military officers from voting or holding elected office.

The **Freedmen's Bureau** was established to help the 4 million freedmen, or former slaves, after the war. The Freedmen's Bureau built hospitals and schools for blacks in the South. The Bureau hired black and white teachers from the North and the South.

For the first time in United States history, African Americans became elected officials. In Mississippi, two African Americans were elected United States senators. In 1870 Republican **Hiram R. Revels**, a minister and teacher, was elected to the Senate seat that Jefferson Davis held before the Civil War. In 1874 **Blanche K. Bruce**, a former slave, was elected to the Senate. Twenty other African Americans from the South were also elected to the House of Representatives.

▶ During Reconstruction, African American children studied at new schools in the South.

▶ Hiram R. Revels was elected to the Senate.

Many white Southerners did not like the changes brought by Reconstruction. Some resented the new state governments, which they felt were forced on them by outsiders. Some were angered by Northerners who moved south to start businesses. These new arrivals were called carpetbaggers, because they often arrived carrying their belongings in suitcases made of carpet. Southerners who supported Reconstruction were called scalawags. Carpetbaggers and scalawags were accused of trying to profit from the hardships of the South.

New leaders raised taxes to help rebuild roads, construct railroads, and establish a free education system. Many Southerners had a hard time paying these taxes. They were trying to rebuild their own farms and businesses.

Some white Southerners also objected to the rights gained by African Americans. After the new state governments repealed black codes, a small group of white Southerners formed the Ku Klux Klan. The Klan's goal was to restore white control over the lives of African Americans. Members of the Klan burned African American schools and homes, and attacked blacks for trying to vote.

REVIEW What changes did Congress bring about in the South during Reconstruction?
↻ **Main Idea and Details**

108

New Amendments

Before being readmitted into the Union, former Confederate states had to accept two new amendments. The **Fourteenth Amendment**, ratified in July 1868, gave African Americans citizenship and said that no state could deny the equal protection of the law to all citizens.

The **Fifteenth Amendment**, ratified in February 1870, gave all male citizens the right to vote. It stated,

> "... the right of citizens of the United States to vote shall not be denied ... on account of race, color, or previous condition of servitude [slavery]."

Sojourner Truth pointed out that a woman had "a right to have just as much as a man." But the Fifteenth Amendment did not give voting rights to women. This angered many women who had fought for abolition and thought women as well as African Americans should have the right to vote.

President Johnson opposed the Fourteenth Amendment and other Reconstruction laws. He believed that the Reconstruction Acts were unlawful because they were passed without the representation of Southern states in Congress. He tried to block the passage of several laws that granted further rights to African Americans.

Angry about Johnson's actions, the Republicans in Congress tried to remove him from office by **impeachment**. Impeachment is the bringing of charges of wrongdoing against an elected official by the House of Representatives. If found guilty in a Senate trial, an impeached President is removed from office. Johnson avoided being removed from office by one vote in May 1868, but his ability to lead the nation was weakened.

REVIEW Why did Congress want to impeach President Johnson? **Summarize**

▶ After the Fifteenth Amendment became law, African American men were able to vote.

CHART SKILL *Describe the rights provided by the Thirteenth, Fourteenth, and Fifteenth Amendments.*

Reconstruction Amendments, 1865–1870

Amendment	Ratified	Description
Thirteenth	December 1865	Declares slavery illegal
Fourteenth	July 1868	Declares former slaves to be citizens and guarantees equal protection of the law to all citizens
Fifteenth	February 1870	Prevents the denial of the right to vote based on race or previous condition of enslavement

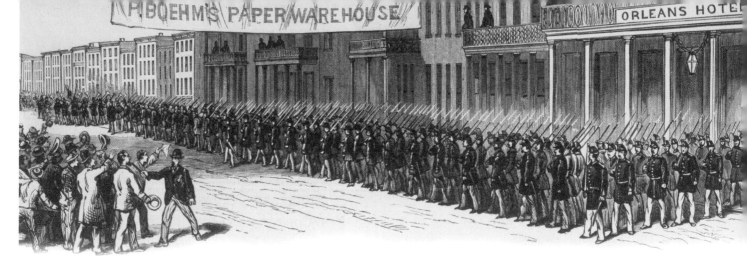

Library of Congress

Reconstruction Ends

By 1870 all of the former Confederate states had met the requirements of Reconstruction. They had written new state constitutions that accepted the Thirteenth, Fourteenth, and Fifteenth Amendments to the U.S. Constitution and extended freedom and citizenship rights to African Americans. The Southern states were then readmitted to the Union. Also, many Northerners were tired of having their taxes used to help rebuild the South. In 1877 the remaining federal troops were withdrawn from the South.

Reconstruction had some successes in the South. A public school system was established and many industries were expanded. However, many of Reconstruction's goals failed to have a lasting impact.

After Reconstruction, white Southern Democrats regained their power in state governments. Almost immediately, new laws were passed that again restricted the rights of African Americans. Whites tried to prevent blacks from voting in several ways. They set up voting booths far from African American communities, or changed the location of the booths without informing blacks. Some states required a poll tax, or a payment, in order to vote. Many African Americans could not afford the poll tax.

In some places blacks were forced to take a reading test before voting. Under slavery, many people had not been allowed to learn to read or write, and so they failed the test. A "grandfather clause" was added to some state constitutions. It said that men could only vote if their father or grandfather had voted before 1867. The "grandfather clause" kept most African Americans from voting because they had not gained the right to vote until 1870.

Jim Crow laws were also passed. These laws enforced **segregation,** or separation of blacks and whites. Under Jim Crow laws, blacks could not sit with whites on trains or stay in certain hotels. They also could not eat in certain restaurants or attend certain theaters, schools, or parks.

During Reconstruction, Congressman Thaddeus Stevens said that every African American adult should be given "40 acres and a mule." His hope was to help former slaves begin new lives. However, there was no land to be distributed.

Many African Americans had no choice but to return to the plantations where they had worked as slaves, because they could not find jobs elsewhere. Many blacks as well as whites became trapped in a system called **sharecropping.** Sharecroppers rented land from landowners. They paid for their rent with a portion of their crop. Sharecroppers sold the rest of their crop to pay for food, clothing, and farming equipment.

Usually, the costs of sharecropping were higher than the income received. Sharecropper John Mosley related, "When our crop was gathered, we would still be in debt."

The end of Reconstruction set the stage for a new phase in American history. The era of slavery was over. The federal government had established its power over individual states. The Fourteenth and Fifteenth Amendments provided a constitutional basis for equal rights, although it would take a long time for these rights to be fully recognized.

As you will read in the following units, after Reconstruction the nation continued expanding westward and building a strong economy. The South, however, continued to rely on an agricultural economy. It remained the poorest section of the country.

REVIEW What conclusions can you draw about how life changed in the South after Reconstruction ended?
Draw Conclusions

Summarize the Lesson

April 1865 President Abraham Lincoln was assassinated.

December 1865 The Thirteenth Amendment was adopted, abolishing slavery in the United States.

March 1867 Congress passed the first Reconstruction Act, sending military forces to the former Confederate states.

LESSON 4 REVIEW

Check Facts and Main Ideas

1. ⊙ **Main Idea and Details** On a separate sheet of paper, fill in the details to the main idea.

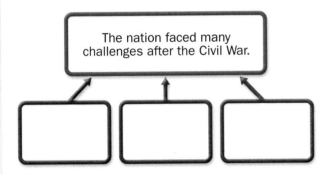

The nation faced many challenges after the Civil War.

2. Why did Republicans in Congress dislike Johnson's **Reconstruction** plan?

3. Critical Thinking: *Cause and Effect* How did the Reconstruction Acts affect the South?

4. Why were three amendments added to the Constitution during Reconstruction?

5. How were the lives of African Americans made more difficult after the end of Reconstruction? Use the word **segregation** in your answer.

Link to ⧜ Writing

Research Biographies Many African Americans became government leaders for the first time during Reconstruction. Research Hiram R. Revels, Blanche K. Bruce, or another African American member of Congress elected during Reconstruction. Were they enslaved or free before the Civil War? How did they become involved in politics? How did the end of Reconstruction affect them? Write a summary of what you learn.

CHAPTER 2
REVIEW

1861   1862   1863

April 1861
Union blockade of
Southern ports begins.

January 1863
Emancipation Proclamation
takes effect.

Chapter Summary

Main Idea and Details

On a separate sheet of paper, fill in other details that support the main idea. Find at least one detail for each lesson of the chapter.

> The Civil War and Reconstruction had many effects on the nation.

Vocabulary

Match each word with the correct definition or description.

1 blockade (p. 84)

2 draft (p. 89)

3 total war (p. 100)

4 black codes (p. 107)

5 impeachment (p. 109)

a. preventing supplies from moving in or out

b. laws denying rights to African Americans

c. charging an official with unlawful action

d. destroying an enemy's will to fight

e. law requiring people to serve in the military

People and Terms

Write a sentence explaining why each of the following people or terms was important. You may use two or more in a single sentence.

1 Anaconda Plan (p. 84)

2 Thomas "Stonewall" Jackson (p. 85)

3 Mathew Brady (p. 89)

4 Emancipation Proclamation (p. 90)

5 Clara Barton (p. 92)

6 Battle of Gettysburg (p. 97)

7 William Tecumseh Sherman (p. 100)

8 Freedmen's Bureau (p. 108)

9 Hiram R. Revels (p. 108)

10 Jim Crow laws (p. 110)

1864   1865   1866   1867

July 1863
Battle of Gettysburg is a victory for Union forces.

November 1863
President Lincoln delivers the Gettysburg Address.

April 1865
The Confederacy surrenders. President Lincoln is killed.

December 1865
The Thirteenth Amendment abolishes slavery.

Facts and Main Ideas

1 What kinds of new technology were used during the Civil War?

2 Describe the significance of the attack on Fort Wagner.

3 **Time Line** How long did the Civil War last?

4 **Main Idea** What early strategies did each side plan for quick victories?

5 **Main Idea** What hardships did people on each side suffer during the Civil War?

6 **Main Idea** How did the Union army gain key victories in the final years of the war?

7 **Main Idea** What were the goals of Reconstruction?

8 **Critical Thinking:** *Compare and Contrast* Compare the lives of African Americans living in the South before the Civil War and after Reconstruction.

Write About History

1 **Write a newspaper story** about one of the battles discussed in your text.

2 **Write a journal entry** as a soldier describing General Robert E. Lee's surrender to General Grant.

3 **Write a letter** telling a friend about the *Monitor* or the *Virginia,* how these ironclads worked, and what they were like.

Apply Skills

Use Road Maps

Study the road map below. Then answer the questions.

1 Which three interstate highways lead into and out of Atlanta?

2 How would you travel from Atlanta to Savannah?

3 Andersonville National Historic Site is the location of a Civil War prisoner of war camp. How would you travel to Andersonville from Kennesaw Mountain National Battlefield?

Internet Activity

To get help with vocabulary, people, and terms, select dictionary or encyclopedia from *Social Studies Library* at **www.sfsocialstudies.com.**

When Johnny Comes Marching Home

by Patrick S. Gilmore

The Civil War inspired many songs in the North and the South. Some songs became popular on both sides. One of these was "When Johnny Comes Marching Home," written in 1863 by Patrick Gilmore, a bandleader in the Union army. Who is "Johnny" in this song?

1. When John-ny comes march-ing home a-gain,
2. Let love __ and friend-ship on the day, Hur - rah! __ Hur - rah! __
3. Get read - y for the ju - bi - lee,

We'll give him a heart - y wel-come then,
Their choic - est trea - sure then dis - play, Hur - rah! __ Hur - rah! __
We'll give __ the he - ro three times three,

The _ men will cheer, _ the boys will shout, The la - dies they _ will all turn out,
And _ let each one _ per-form some part, To fill with joy _ the war-rior's heart,
The _ laur - el wreath _ is read - y now To place up - on _ his roy - al brow,

And we'll shout "Hur - rah" when John-ny comes march - ing home! _

Review

Test Talk

Look for the key words in the question.

Main Ideas and Vocabulary

TEST PREP

Read the passage below and use it to answer the questions that follow.

The growing nation faced problems of <u>sectionalism</u>. Northerners and Southerners disagreed about whether slavery should be allowed in new states. Northern and Southern states also had different ways of life. Many Northerners and Southerners were loyal to their region of the country.

Abraham Lincoln joined the Republican party, which opposed the spread of slavery. After he was elected President in 1860, South Carolina <u>seceded</u> from the Union. Other Southern states followed and formed the Confederacy. Confederate troops attacked Union-held Fort Sumter in April 1861, beginning the Civil War.

The Civil War dragged on for four years. New weapons of war left many soldiers dead or wounded. A lack of knowledge about disease killed many more. In the spring of

1865, the Confederacy surrendered. President Lincoln was killed shortly afterwards by a Confederate supporter.

Congress passed the Reconstruction Acts to rebuild the country and readmit the Southern states to the Union. Federal troops were sent to the South to maintain order and regulate elections. During this period, much of the damage from the war was repaired. African American men were granted the right to vote and some became members of Congress. The Freedmen's Bureau built hospitals and schools to help freed slaves.

When Reconstruction ended in 1877, many laws were passed to restrict the rights of African Americans again. Jim Crow laws segregated blacks and whites.

1 According to the passage, what was one difference between the North and South?
   A Northerners and Southerners had similar ways of life.
   B Northerners and Southerners disagreed about slavery in new states.
   C The South had more resources.
   D The North had fewer resources.

2 In the passage, the word <u>sectionalism</u> means—
   A wanting to divide the country in half
   B ending slavery in part of the country
   C loyalty to one's country
   D loyalty to one's region

3 In the passage, the word <u>seceded</u> means—
   A joined with others
   B broke away from a group
   C objected to something
   D formed a new government

4 What is the main idea of the first paragraph in passage?
   A The North won the Civil War.
   B The Civil War ended slavery.
   C Differences between North and South led to the Civil War.
   D War destroys people and places.

People and Terms

Match each person and term to its definition.

1. **Joseph Cinque** (p. 62)
2. **John Brown** (p. 70)
3. **border state** (p. 76)
4. **Catherine Coffin** (p. 63)
5. **Ulysses S. Grant** (p. 99)
6. **segregation** (p. 110)

a. abolitionist who attacked an arsenal at Harpers Ferry

b. separating people

c. helped slaves escape to freedom

d. leader of Union forces at the Battle of Vicksburg

e. leader of *Amistad* rebellion

f. allowed slavery but did not secede

Write and Share

Create a Quiz Show Work with a group of students to create a quiz show about some of the main events and people in the period just before, during, and after the Civil War. Select a quiz show host and assistants to write the questions and answers. Then select contestants and develop a scoring system. Decide on a prize for the winner, and present the show to your class.

Read on Your Own

Look for these books in the library.

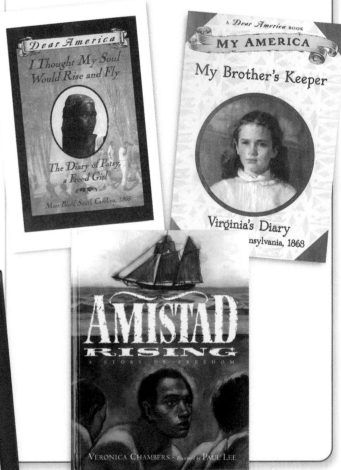

Apply Skills

Prepare a scrapbook about different points of view on a current subject. First, choose the topic. Then clip articles that present opposing points of view about the topic. Paste the articles into a scrapbook. Under each article, write a sentence that summarizes the writer's point of view.

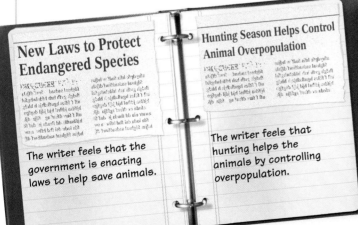

New Laws to Protect Endangered Species

The writer feels that the government is enacting laws to help save animals.

Hunting Season Helps Control Animal Overpopulation

The writer feels that hunting helps the animals by controlling overpopulation.

UNIT 1 Project

We Interrupt This Program

Participate in a "live, at the scene" news update from the past.

1 Form a group to present a special report about a historic event in this unit.

2 Present the event as breaking news. Focus on the event's significance in world history.

3 Assign jobs, including news anchors, government officials, reporters, and citizens.

4 Write a press release or a brief summary of the event and its significance.

5 Create a banner and bring in materials that help describe the event. You may choose to create a scenic background.

Internet Activity

Explore the Civil War.
Go to **www.sfsocialstudies.com/activities** and select your grade and unit.

An Expanding Nation

How do new transportation methods affect where people live?

UNIT 2

Begin with a Primary Source

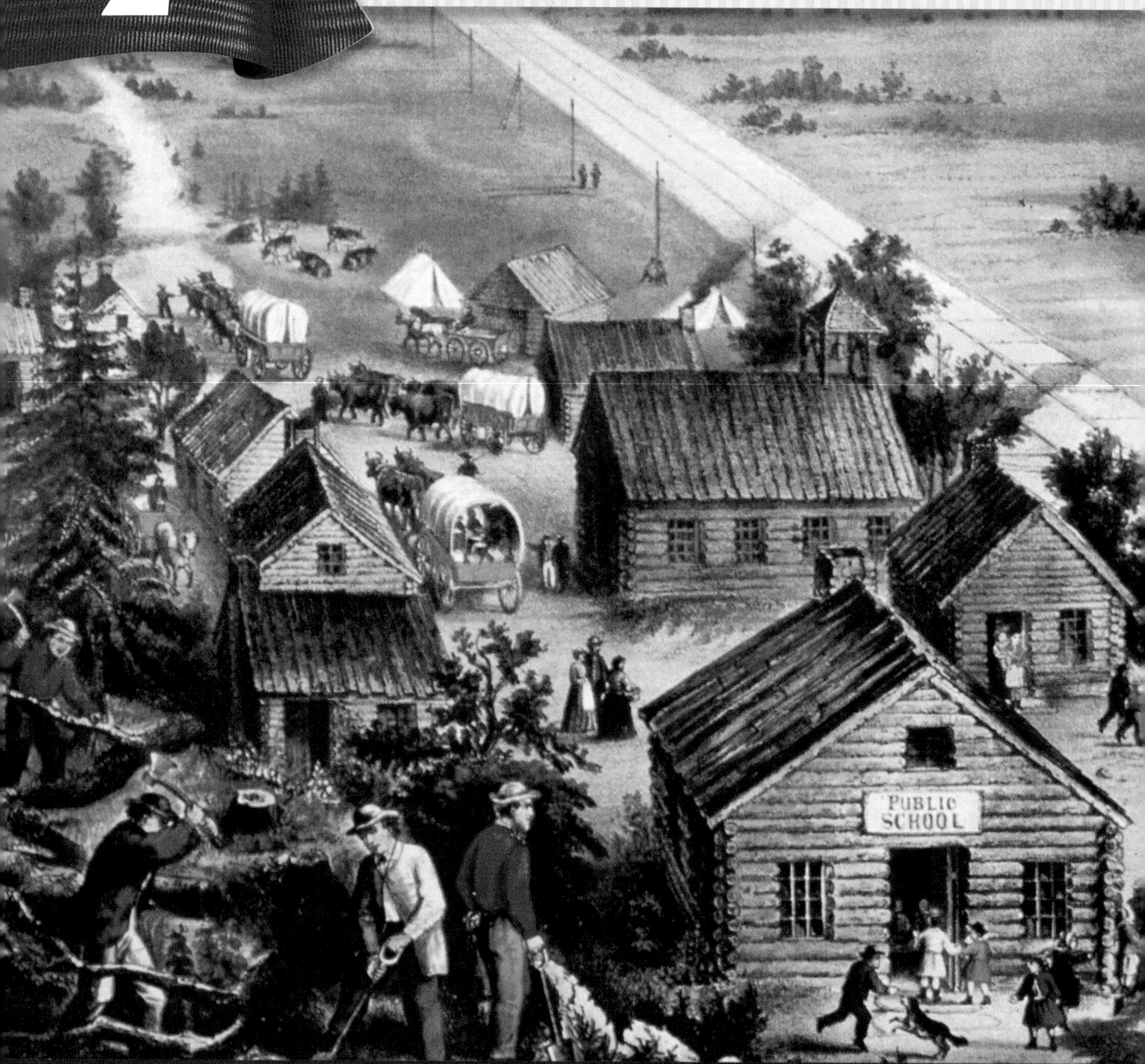

PUBLIC SCHOOL

1845 | 1855 | 1865 | 1875

1849
The California gold rush begins.

1861
The first telegraph line crosses the country.

1876
The Lakota defeat Custer at Little Bighorn.

1877
African American pioneers establish Nicodemus, Kansas.

1879
Thomas Edison invents a working light bulb.

> *"People laughed at the time [at the idea] of building a railroad across those mountains."*
>
> —Charles Crocker, an owner of the Central Pacific Railroad

This 1868 picture by Currier and Ives shows a small town in the West that was built near a railroad.

1885   1895   1905   1915   1925

1882
The first Labor Day celebration is held in New York City.

1900
The United States is the world's leading producer of manufactured goods.

1924
The United States government passes a law limiting immigration.

Meet the People

Samuel Morse

1791–1872

Birthplace: Charlestown, Massachusetts

Inventor, teacher, painter

- Established the first commercial telegraph system in the 1840s
- Donated much of his money to colleges in the United States
- President of the National Academy of Design, which encourages respect for the arts

Levi Strauss

1829–1902

Birthplace: Bavaria, Germany

Salesperson, clothing manufacturer

- Opened a dry goods store in San Francisco
- Made sturdy work pants for miners
- Founded a company to manufacture denim jeans

Andrew Carnegie

1835–1919

Birthplace: Dunfermline, Scotland

Entrepreneur

- Started work at age 12 in a cotton factory
- Founded the Carnegie Steel Company
- Donated millions of dollars to charities

Chief Joseph

1840–1904

Birthplace: Wallowa Valley, Oregon Territory

Nez Percé leader

- Became chief of the Nez Percé in 1871
- Led his followers on a 1,600-mile journey to escape from United States soldiers
- Surrendered to soldiers in 1877

1775	1800	1825	1850

1791 • Samuel Morse

1829 • Levi Strauss

1835 • Andrew Carnegie

1840

1847

1848

Alexander Graham Bell

1847–1922

Birthplace: Edinburgh, Scotland

Inventor

- Developed techniques to teach speech to the deaf
- Invented the telephone in 1876
- Became president of the National Geographic Society to teach people about distant lands

Lewis Latimer

1848–1928

Birthplace: Chelsea, Massachusetts

Inventor

- Served in the United States Navy during the Civil War
- Made improvements on Thomas Edison's electric light bulb
- Taught English and drawing to immigrants

George Shima

1863(?)–1926

Birthplace: Japan

Farmer

- Overcame poverty to become the "Potato King"
- Developed a system to pump water out of the soil
- Donated food and money to help those in need

Mary Antin

1881–1949

Birthplace: Polotsk, Russia

Writer

- Immigrated to the United States in 1894
- Wrote several books about the experiences of immigrants
- Fought against anti-immigration laws

1875	1900	1925	1950

1872

1902

1919

• Chief Joseph   1904

• Alexander Graham Bell   1922

• Lewis Latimer   1928

1863(?) • George Shima   1926

1881 • Mary Antin   1949

123

An Expanding Nation

Sequence

Learning to find the sequence of events—the order in which things happen—will help you understand many kinds of writing. Study the chart at left.

Dates help establish sequence. Clue words such as *first, once, before, later, after, then,* and *finally* also help signal the order in which events took place.

Word clue	Date	Event
First	1844	Telegraph message sent.
Then	1861	Transcontinental telegraph built.
Finally	1876	Invention of telephone.

Read the paragraph. **Words** that help signal sequence have been highlighted in blue. **Dates** are highlighted in yellow.

Many communication improvements were made in the 1800s. The Pony Express began delivering mail in 1860. After one year, though, the transcontinental telegraph line replaced it. Earlier, in 1844, Samuel Morse sent the first telegraph message. With the invention of the telephone in 1876, voices could be carried over wires.

Word Exercise

Words with Suffixes [communication, construction, invention, transportation, improvement, advancement]

Suffixes are word endings such as *-ion, -ment, -ness,* and *-tion.* When a suffix is added to a word, the new word is related in meaning to the original, or base, word.

construction = **construct** (put together) + **-ion** (act of)

The act of putting together the National Road began in 1811.

Construction on the National Road began in 1811.

improvement = **improve** (make better) + **-ment** (the result of)

The result of making equipment better made farming less difficult.

Improvements in equipment made farming less difficult.

Connecting the Country: A Sequence of Events

Throughout the 1800s, improvements in communication and transportation helped to bring people in the United States closer together. Stagecoaches drawn by horses took passengers from city to city on roads. Construction on the National Road began in 1811. The invention of the steamboat in 1807 made navigation of inland waterways easier.

The country's first railroad was built in 1830. Almost 40 years later, in 1869, the transcontinental railroad was completed. Passengers could go across the continent by train. Automobiles—or "horseless carriages"—began appearing on roads in the United States in the 1890s.

At the same time that transportation was improving, advancements in communications also were being made. In 1860 horses and riders of the Pony Express started delivering mail in only ten days from Missouri to California. Even the Pony Express seemed slow when, in the following year, a transcontinental telegraph line was completed. In moments, a message could be sent from one end of the country to the other. Samuel Morse had helped develop a way, in the 1830s, to send messages over the telegraph.

Alexander Graham Bell later improved instant communication when he invented the telephone in 1876. The telephone also used wires but allowed two people far apart to speak to each other. Then, with the invention of radio communication in 1895, it was possible for many people with radios to listen to the same message at the same time.

Use the reading strategy of sequence to answer the first two questions. Then answer the vocabulary question.

1. Was the transcontinental railroad completed before or after the telephone was invented?

2. In what sequence did the following events take place: radio communication is invented, Pony Express begins, a way of sending telegraph messages is developed, steamboat is invented, construction begins on the National Road? How many years passed between the first event and the last?

3. Find a word in the above passage that has a suffix. Use a graphic organizer like the one shown at the bottom of page 124 to explain the meanings of the base word, the suffix, and the new word. Then use each form of the word in a sentence.

CHAPTER 3

Crossing the Continent

1869

Promontory Point, Utah Territory
The first transcontinental railroad is completed.

Lesson 1

1877

Nicodemus, Kansas
African American pioneers called exodusters found a town on the Great Plains.

Lesson 2

1880s

Virginia City, Nevada
The boom town of Virginia City becomes a ghost town when the gold and silver run out.

Lesson 3

1890

Wounded Knee, South Dakota
A memorial now stands where a battle occurred between Native Americans and United States soldiers.

Lesson 4

CANADA

1

4

3

Promontory
Point

Wounded
Knee

2

Virginia City

Nicodemus

PACIFIC
OCEAN

UNITED STATES

MEXICO

Gulf of
Mexico

Why We Remember

By the late 1800s, the map of the United States would have looked familiar to you. The nation's territory stretched to the Pacific Ocean, and new states were being admitted to the Union. Telegraph wires and railroad tracks were built across the plains and mountains, linking the East and West Coasts. Soon pioneers began to settle on this land. At the same time, Native Americans, also known as American Indians, were being forced from their homes. The way of life of all Americans was being changed in ways no one could have predicted.

1860 **1870**

1861
The first telegraph line crosses the country.

1862
Construction of the transcontinental railroad begins.

1869
The transcontinental railroad is completed.

Promontory Point

Sacramento • Omaha

PREVIEW

Focus on the Main Idea
In the 1860s new railroad lines made it possible to travel and move goods across the United States much more quickly than ever before.

PLACES
Omaha, Nebraska
Sacramento, California
Promontory Point,
 Utah Territory

PEOPLE
Samuel Morse
Red Cloud

VOCABULARY
Pony Express
telegraph
transcontinental railroad

Rails Across the Nation

 You Are There

It is a scorching hot day in July 1859. You are sitting in the back of a horse-drawn wagon, bouncing across an endless plain. You feel a little sick from the constant bumping and swaying of the seat. You are covered with dust and itching all over from some kind of bug bites. The man next to you sees you scratching. "It's the sand flies," he says.

This journey began three days ago in Missouri. Now you are in either Kansas or Nebraska, but you are not exactly sure. You do know you are traveling west toward California, and you know the trip will take at least three weeks.

Do you regret your decision to cross the country by stagecoach? Not really. This is your first chance to see huge herds of buffalo and snow-covered mountains. It is going to be an adventure.

Sequence As you read, pay attention to the order of the events that linked the eastern and western parts of the United States.

▶ **Stagecoach**

Linking East and West

There was no easy way to get across the United States in the 1850s. Nearly all of the country's railroads were east of the Mississippi River. To travel from the East Coast to the West Coast, you had two choices. You could take a train west to Missouri, where the railroad tracks ended. From there you could continue traveling west by stagecoach. Stagecoaches were horse-drawn wagons that traveled in regular stages, or sections of a route.

Your second choice was to sail south to Central America, travel west across Panama by train, and then get on another boat and sail north to California. You also might sail all the way around South America. Just like traveling by stagecoach, the ocean voyage was long, expensive, and often dangerous. People began looking for faster ways to move people, mail, and goods across the United States.

In 1860 a new business called the **Pony Express** began delivering mail from Missouri to California in just 10 days. The Pony Express was like a 2,000-mile relay race.

Each express rider rode about 75 miles, then handed his bags of mail to the next rider. By changing horses every 10 or 15 miles, Pony Express riders were able to keep moving at about 10 miles per hour all day long. Most of the riders were teenagers, some as young as thirteen years old.

The Pony Express was soon put out of business by an invention called the telegraph. The **telegraph** sent messages along wires using electricity. An American inventor named **Samuel Morse** helped develop a way to send telegraph messages using a code called Morse code. He also built the first working telegraph system and sent the first telegraph message. With this technology, people could share news and information much more quickly than ever before. The first telegraph line across the country was completed in October 1861. Morse code messages could now be sent from coast to coast in just a few minutes!

REVIEW What event in 1861 brought the Pony Express to an end? ⟳ Sequence

▶ **It was expensive to send letters by Pony Express, but people were willing to pay to have their mail delivered quickly.**

The Transcontinental Railroad

The telegraph allowed news to travel quickly, but it did not help people or goods cross the country; that still took weeks, and even months. Many people believed that the best way to link East and West would be to build a **transcontinental railroad**, a railroad across the continent. A railroad engineer named Theodore Judah made a bold prediction about how the transcontinental railroad would change travel in the United States:

> *"How long will it take to go from St. Louis [Missouri] to San Francisco [California]? The answer is as short as the question. It can be run in three days, or seventy-two hours."*

▶ Most of the thousands of workers on the transcontinental railroad were immigrants from Europe and China.

President Abraham Lincoln was a strong supporter of the transcontinental railroad. As you read in Unit 1, the Civil War began soon after Lincoln took office in 1861. Lincoln looked forward to a time when new railroads would help bind the country together.

In 1862 the United States government gave two companies the job of building the transcontinental railroad. The Union Pacific began building track west from **Omaha, Nebraska.** The Central Pacific began building east from **Sacramento, California.**

REVIEW Which began first, the Civil War or construction of the transcontinental railroad?
🔄 Sequence

MAP SKILL

Transcontinental Railroads, 1869–1893

▶ By 1893 several transcontinental railroad lines had been completed.

MAP SKILL Use Routes *Which railroad line served the city of New Orleans?*

▶ Union Pacific workers laid about one to three miles of track a day across the plains.

Across the Plains

The United States government paid the Central Pacific and Union Pacific for every mile of track completed. The companies were paid in land and money. As a result, the two companies raced against each other. Each company tried to build track more quickly than the other.

Geography gave the Union Pacific an advantage in this race. The Union Pacific began building on the broad, flat plains of Nebraska. The Central Pacific had the difficult job of building in the rugged Sierra Nevada mountain range in California.

The Union Pacific did face challenges, however. One problem was finding enough workers in a region that was far from big towns and cities. This problem was solved when the Civil War ended in 1865. Thousands of Irish immigrants who had served in the Union Army moved west to work on the railroad. The Union Pacific's workers also included former Confederate Army soldiers and formerly enslaved African Americans.

A more serious challenge was conflict with Native Americans. As the railroad moved west, tracks began cutting across the traditional hunting grounds of such groups as the Lakota and Cheyenne. A Lakota chief named **Red Cloud** told Union Pacific workers, "We do not want you here, you are scaring away the buffalo."

The Union Pacific was determined to continue building, and the United States government fully supported the railroad. General William Tecumseh Sherman warned Native American leaders: "We will build iron roads, and you cannot stop the locomotive." Soldiers began guarding Union Pacific workers, and the tracks continued moving west.

REVIEW How did the Union Pacific benefit from the end of the Civil War in 1865? ⟳ Sequence

▶ Red Cloud

Over the Mountains

While the Union Pacific built track across the Great Plains, the Central Pacific was stuck in the steep slopes of the Sierra Nevada. "People laughed at the time [at the idea] of building a railroad across those mountains," recalled Charles Crocker, one of the owners of the Central Pacific.

Like the Union Pacific, the Central Pacific had a hard time finding enough workers. Many of the people in California had come there to search for gold. They were not interested in railroad jobs that paid $35 a month. But thousands of young Chinese immigrants were interested in these jobs. Like so many other people, they had come to California with dreams of finding gold. Most, however, were treated unfairly at gold mining camps, so they began looking for other opportunities.

Chinese immigrants made up about 80 percent of the Central Pacific workforce. Most of them were teenagers. These young men did the difficult work of blasting tunnels through the solid rock of the mountains. In a typical week, they used more explosives than were used during the biggest Civil War battles. Many workers were killed in accidents, but the work never stopped.

▶ **Tunneling through mountains to lay railroad tracks was difficult and often dangerous work.**

The Central Pacific finally finished building track through the mountains in 1867. Work then sped up, as tracks were built east across the Nevada desert. Almost every day, newspapers around the country printed stories about the race to build the transcontinental railroad. This project was a source of excitement and pride for many Americans. One Chicago newspaper wrote that people would soon "have an opportunity of bathing in the Atlantic one week and in the Pacific the next." This may not seem so amazing to us today, but it was a very new idea to Americans in the 1860s.

REVIEW Why was the Central Pacific able to build track more quickly after 1867?

 Sequence

The Golden Spike

On May 10, 1869, the tracks of the Union Pacific and Central Pacific met at **Promontory Point, Utah Territory.** A special golden railroad spike was made to symbolize the success of the project. Leland Stanford, president of the Central Pacific, was given the honor of hammering the golden spike into the tracks. Stanford lifted a hammer, swung at the spike—and missed. People began celebrating anyway—the railroad was finished! The message "Done" was telegraphed from Utah to cities around the country.

The transcontinental railroad changed travel in the United States. Before this railroad, traveling across the continent took months and cost about $1,000. Now the trip could be made in a week for less than $100. As you will read, these new railroads brought change and conflict to the United States.

REVIEW How many years did it take to complete the transcontinental railroad?
⟳ Sequence

Summarize the Lesson

1861 The first telegraph line across the United States was completed.

1862 The Union Pacific and Central Pacific began building the transcontinental railroad.

1869 The transcontinental railroad was completed at Promontory Point, Utah Territory.

LESSON 1   REVIEW

Check Facts and Main Ideas

1. ⟳ Sequence On a separate sheet of paper, fill in key events from this lesson in the order they happened.

> 1860: The Pony Express begins delivering mail across the West.
> ↓
> 1861:
> ↓
> 1862:
> ↓
> 1867:
> ↓
> 1869:

2. Why did new **telegraph** lines put the **Pony Express** out of business?

3. Describe two problems faced by the Union Pacific railroad.

4. What role did Chinese workers play in building the Central Pacific railroad?

5. **Critical Thinking:** *Predict* Suppose you lived in the United States in 1869. What kinds of changes would you expect the new **transcontinental railroad** to bring?

Link to 〜〜 Mathematics

Planning the Pony Express Suppose you were planning the Pony Express. You know the route is 2,000 miles. And you know each rider will ride 75 miles. What is the minimum number of riders you will need to hire?

Hawaii–Aleutian Time

Read a Time Zone Map

What? A **time zone** is an area on Earth that runs north and south in which all places have the same time. Earth is divided into 24 different time zones. **Standard time** is the time set by law for all the places in a time zone.

Why? At one time, each community decided its own time. Because of this, two communities that were close to each other might have different times. This could be confusing and was not practical. Problems increased when trains started to cross the country in the 1870s. Think of how confusing train schedules would have been if each town on a railroad line decided its own time. People needed a time system they could depend on.

United States Time Zones

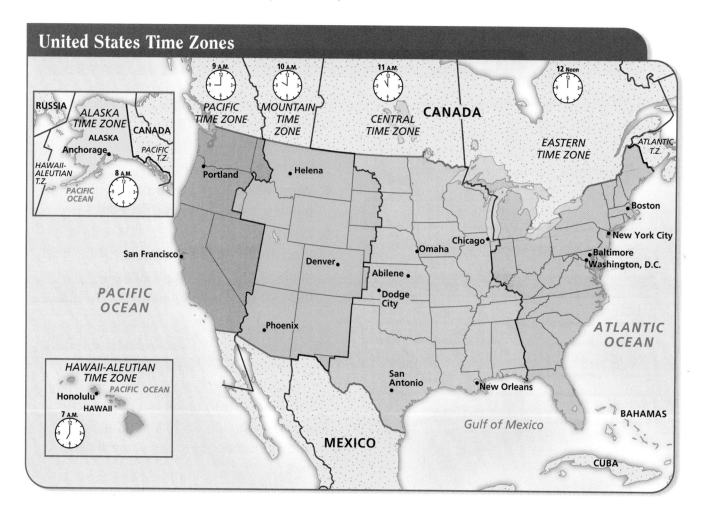

Alaska Time   **Pacific Time**   **Mountain Time**   **Central Time**   **Eastern Time**

To solve this problem, in the late 1870s, Canadian railway engineer Sandford Fleming worked out a plan for the 24 worldwide time zones that are used today.

If you drive from New York to California, you go through four of these time zones. It is important for you to know when the time changes and what time it is in the new zone. You would also need to have this information if you have promised to telephone someone at a particular time in a part of the country that is in a different time zone.

How? The map shows the six time zones of the United States. Standard time in each is one hour different from the time in the zone on either side. To help you understand how this works, look at the clocks shown with each time zone. Notice that each time zone has a name. Standard time is the same throughout each time zone.

To use a time zone map, you need to know whether you are east or west of another time zone. The time in a zone that is east of you is later than the time in your zone. The time in a zone that is west of you is earlier than the time in your zone.

If you were to travel east, you would move your watch ahead one hour for each time zone you entered. If you were to travel west, you would move your watch back one hour for each time zone you entered.

For example, say you live in San Antonio, and your watch shows that the time is 3:00 P.M. What is the time in New York City and in San Francisco? Find all three cities on the map and note the time zone of each. San Antonio is in the Central time zone. In which time zone is New York City? San Francisco? New York City is one time zone to the east of San Antonio. So the time there is one hour later than your time, or 4:00 P.M. San Francisco is two time zones to the west, so the time there is two hours earlier than your time, or 1:00 P.M.

Think and Apply

1. What time zone do you live in?

2. In what time zones are Denver and Boston? What time is it in Denver when it is 12 noon in Boston?

3. If you are in Baltimore and want to watch a ballgame that starts at 2:00 P.M. in Chicago, what time should you turn on your television set?

Internet Activity

For more information, go online to the *Atlas* at **www.sfsocialstudies.com**.

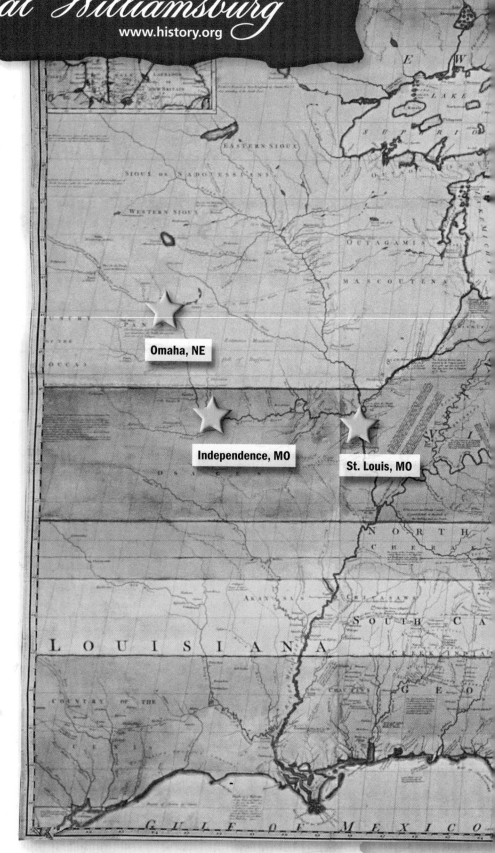

Living History from *Colonial Williamsburg*

www.history.org

Westward Growth of America, 1607-1862

John Mitchell published this map of North America in 1775. You can see from the map that Americans were looking west very early in our history. Over time, people moved west and the nation expanded. Here are some key events in the westward growth of our nation.

Omaha, NE

Independence, MO

St. Louis, MO

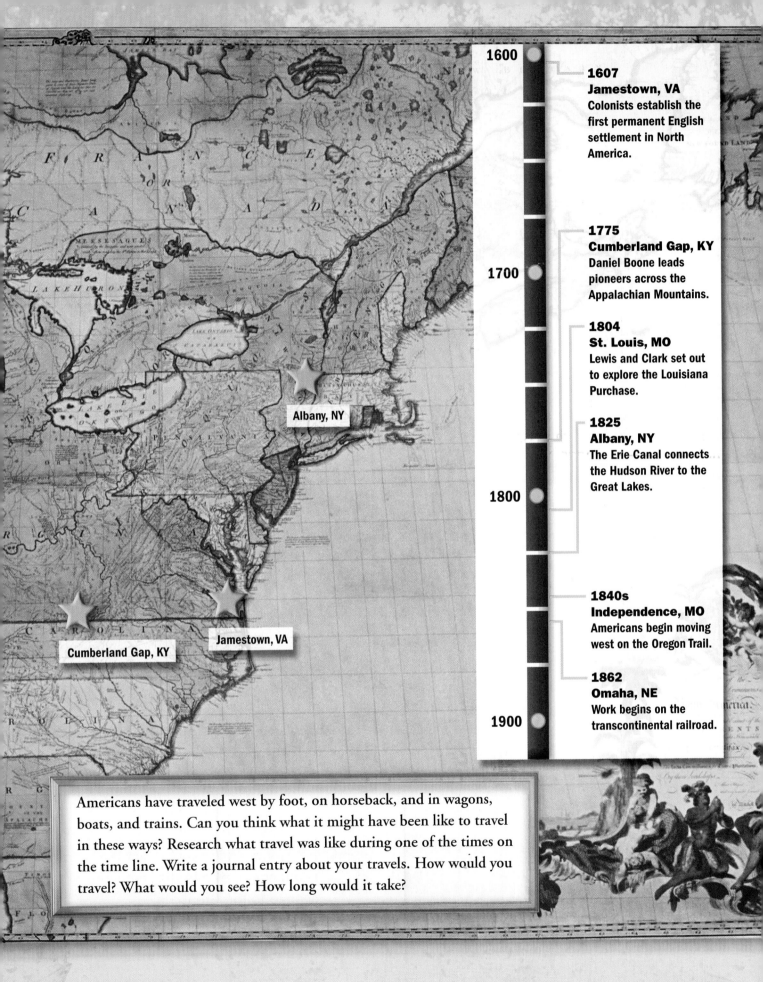

1600

1607
Jamestown, VA
Colonists establish the first permanent English settlement in North America.

1775
Cumberland Gap, KY
Daniel Boone leads pioneers across the Appalachian Mountains.

1700

1804
St. Louis, MO
Lewis and Clark set out to explore the Louisiana Purchase.

1825
Albany, NY
The Erie Canal connects the Hudson River to the Great Lakes.

1800

1840s
Independence, MO
Americans begin moving west on the Oregon Trail.

1862
Omaha, NE
Work begins on the transcontinental railroad.

1900

Albany, NY

Cumberland Gap, KY

Jamestown, VA

Americans have traveled west by foot, on horseback, and in wagons, boats, and trains. Can you think what it might have been like to travel in these ways? Research what travel was like during one of the times on the time line. Write a journal entry about your travels. How would you travel? What would you see? How long would it take?

1860

1880

1862
Lincoln signs the Homestead Act.

1874
Joseph Glidden invents barbed wire.

1877
African American pioneers establish Nicodemus, Kansas.

GREAT PLAINS

•Nicodemus

Pioneers on the Plains

PREVIEW

Focus on the Main Idea
Farmers began settling in the Great Plains in the 1860s, and they soon turned the plains into a productive farming region.

PLACES
Great Plains
Nicodemus, Kansas

PEOPLE
Willa Cather
Benjamin Singleton
George Shima

VOCABULARY
pioneer
Homestead Act
homesteader
sodbuster
exoduster
technology

You Are There
Howard Ruede (ROO day) has just finished building his new home—if you can call it a home. Actually, it is a hole in the ground, with a roof of wood. At least it will keep out the wind and some of the rain.

It is the summer of 1877, and this 23-year-old from Pennsylvania has just moved west to Kansas. He brought his entire life savings of about $50. Luckily, his underground house only cost $10 to build.

Sitting on a homemade chair in his dark, damp home, Ruede writes a letter to his family in Pennsylvania. He describes his new land and the farm he dreams of building. "The sweat runs off of me," he writes, "and some of the drops wet the paper; so if you can't read it you'll know the reason."

Sequence As you read, list the sequence of events that brought change to the Great Plains.

▶ **Railroads often used posters to advertise free land in the West.**

2,000,000 FARMS of Fertile Prairie Lands to be had Free of Cost

IN

CENTRAL DAKOTA

30 Millions of Acres

YOU NEED A FARM!

CHICAGO AND NORTH WESTERN

HOW TO GET THERE

Chicago & North-Western R'y.

The Great Plains

How would you like to move to a place nick-named the "Great American Desert"? This is what many Americans called the **Great Plains** in the mid-1800s. They looked at the plains and saw a vast region of dry grassland in the middle of the country. They saw few trees, harsh weather, and low rainfall. People did not think the Great Plains would ever make good farmland.

The United States government wanted to encourage **pioneers,** or new settlers, to move to the Great Plains. Leaders hoped that with hard work, pioneers could turn the plains into productive farmland. New railroad lines could then carry farm goods from the Great Plains to growing cities in the East.

But how do you encourage people to move to the "Great American Desert"? The government's solution was to give the land away. In 1862 President Abraham Lincoln signed the **Homestead Act.** This law offered free land to American citizens and immigrants who were willing to start new farms on the Great Plains.

If you were a man over the age of twenty-one, or a woman who was the head of a family, you could claim 160 acres of land. You had to pay a small fee—usually about $10. You had to farm your land and live on it for five years. Then the land was yours.

Now you know why Howard Ruede left his home and family in Pennsylvania to move to the Great Plains in Kansas. Ruede dreamed of owning land of his own. With a life savings of just $50, he could afford land on the Great Plains because of the Homestead Act.

Settlers who claimed land through the Homestead Act were called **homesteaders.** Like many homesteaders, Howard Ruede traveled by train to his new home. Getting there was the easy part. Building a success-ful farm on the Great Plains would take many years of hard work.

REVIEW What steps did a homesteader have to take to become a landowner?

↻ **Sequence**

▶ **Much of the Great Plains may look flat, but the land actually rises slowly from east to west. The land reaches elevations of more than 5,000 feet at the base of the Rocky Mountains.**

Settling on the Plains

Before they could plant crops on their properties, homesteaders had to rip up the grass on their land. This was not as easy as it sounds. The grasses on the Great Plains had thick, tangled roots that reached several inches down into the soil. Because they had to bust through this "sod" before planting crops, Great Plains farmers were called **sodbusters.**

After ripping up the sod from their land, most sodbusters used the sod to build houses. In a region with few trees, sod was a very useful building material. Houses built from blocks of sod stayed cool in summer and warm in winter, and they were fireproof. Unfortunately for homesteaders, the sod walls were often home to bugs, mice, and snakes.

Once homesteaders were able to plant crops, they found that the soil was very fertile. This was not the "Great American Desert" after all! Author **Willa Cather,** who grew up on the plains of Nebraska, described changing feelings about the Great Plains in her famous novel *O Pioneers!* In one scene a pioneer named Alexandra tells her friend Carl about her struggle to build a farm:

> *"We hadn't any of us much to do with it, Carl. The land did it. It had its little joke. It pretended to be poor because nobody knew how to work it right; and then, all at once, it worked itself. It woke up out of its sleep and stretched itself, and it was so big, so rich, that we suddenly found we were rich, just from sitting still."*

REVIEW Why was sod a useful building material for homesteaders?
Main Idea and Details

▶ **This pioneer family built a sod house in Nebraska.**

America Fever

Stories about the fertile soil of the Great Plains spread quickly to Europe. The desire to move to this region was so strong that it became known as "America Fever." Thousands of families from Germany, Sweden, Norway, Russia, and other European countries crossed the Atlantic Ocean to begin new lives on the Great Plains.

Many of these immigrants brought valuable farming skills to the United States. Farmers from Russia, for example, brought seeds for a hardy type of wheat they had grown at home. American farmers were having a hard time finding a type of wheat that could survive the weather on the Great Plains. The wheat brought from Russia grew well on the plains. The Great Plains soon became one of the world's most productive wheat-growing regions—and it still is today.

The Homestead Act also provided opportunities for African American homesteaders. As you have read, African Americans continued to face unfair treatment after the end of slavery. In the 1870s, a carpenter named **Benjamin Singleton** began urging his fellow African Americans to leave the South and move to the Great Plains. "We needed land for our children," he later explained.

Calling themselves **exodusters,** thousands of African American pioneers started new lives in communities on the Great Plains, such as **Nicodemus, Kansas**. The name "exodusters" came from a book of the Bible called Exodus. This book tells the story of Moses leading the Israelites out of slavery. Many southern African Americans felt that their story was similar—they too were making a journey to freedom. An exoduster named John Solomon Lewis never forgot the first thing he said when he arrived in Kansas: "This is free ground."

REVIEW How did European farmers contribute to the success of farming on the Great Plains? Draw Conclusions

Nicodemus, Kansas

The town of Nicodemus (nik uh DEE muhs), Kansas, was founded by African American pioneers in 1877. By the end of the 1880s, Nicodemus had grown into a bustling town, with stores, churches, newspapers, a school, and a baseball team. Today Nicodemus lives on as a symbol of freedom and opportunity. Visitors come from all over the country to see the town's historic buildings and celebrate the important contributions of African American pioneers.

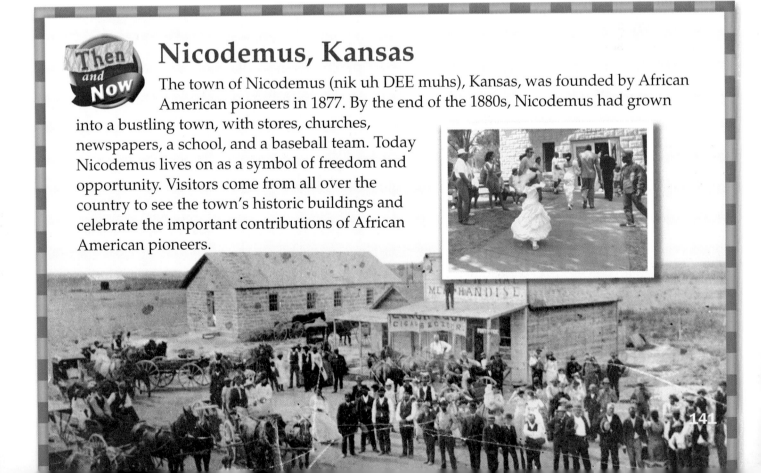

Life on the Plains

The Great Plains may have had fertile soil, but that does not mean it was easy to build a successful farm. As the Fact File on the next page shows, new technology helped make life on the Great Plains a little bit easier. **Technology** is the use of new ideas to make tools that improve people's lives. Even with technology, though, homesteaders had to work hard to survive. A pioneer from England named Percy Ebbutt put it simply: "You must make up your mind to rough it."

Roughing it included facing the harsh weather and natural disasters of the Great Plains. Bitter cold and deadly blizzards swept along the plains in winter. Spring often brought tornadoes, hailstorms, and flooding. Summer could mean blazing heat and little rain. In fall the grasses dried and settlers had to watch out for fires. A pioneer from Norway named Gro Svendsen described these fires in a letter to his family:

> *"It is a strange and terrible sight to see all the fields a sea of fire. Quite often the scorching flames sweep everything along in their path—people, cattle, hay, fences."*

▶ **A farmer hopes for rain on the Great Plains.**

If the weather was not enough to worry about, farmers also faced the dreaded grasshopper. In the mid-1870s, millions of grasshoppers swarmed across the Great Plains. Green bugs darkened the sky and covered the ground in layers up to six inches thick. Grasshoppers ate everything in their path—crops, grass, and even fences and axe handles. After seeing her crops destroyed by one of these invasions, homesteader Mattie Oblinger wrote, "Nebraska would have had a splendid crop if the grasshoppers had stayed away a while."

REVIEW What challenges made life difficult for homesteaders? **Summarize**

▶ **This painting by Winslow Homer from 1871, called *The Country School*, gives an idea what school was like for children of pioneers in the West.**

Technology on the Plains

Farming the Great Plains presented many new challenges. Here are some of the technologies that helped pioneers turn the "Great American Desert" into one of the world's richest farming regions.

Steel Plows Iron plows used in the East did not work well on the tough sod and thick soil of the Great Plains. An inventor named John Deere began building stronger steel plows in 1837. In the 1860s farmers could buy steel plows that were specially made for farming on the Great Plains.

Windmills Most of the water in the Great Plains is deep underground. New types of windmills were designed to pump this water up to the surface. Steady winds on the Great Plains made windmills a useful power source for farmers.

Barbed Wire Farmers always need fences to keep animals away from their crops. In a region with little wood, however, Great Plains farmers had a hard time finding material to build fences. Joseph Glidden solved this problem by inventing barbed wire in 1874. Barbed wire fences were cheap and easy to build.

Dry Farming The dry Great Plains climate forced farmers to find new ways to grow their crops. Farmers adapted to the lack of rain by developing a method called "dry farming." This method uses moisture stored in the soil, rather than rainfall. Dry farming allowed Great Plains farmers to grow wheat and other crops.

ILLUSTRATIONS OF SOME OF THE FORMS OF "BARBED FENCE."

Growth in the West

While pioneers were settling on the Great Plains, people were also moving farther west. New railroad lines brought thousands of people to Washington, Oregon, and California. Towns at the western end of railroad lines, such as Seattle, in Washington, and Los Angeles, in California, quickly grew into important cities.

The West also attracted farmers from other countries. In the late 1800s, thousands of Japanese immigrants began arriving in California. Many Japanese families built successful farms in the West. You will read about one successful Japanese farmer, **George Shima** (SHEE mah), in the Biography on the next page.

REVIEW How did railroads help the West to grow? *Cause and Effect*

Summarize the Lesson

1862 The Homestead Act gave Americans and immigrants free land on the Great Plains.

1874 Joseph Glidden invented barbed wire, one of many technologies that made life easier for Great Plains farmers.

1877 Nicodemus, Kansas, was founded, one of many towns built by African American pioneers.

LESSON 2 ⟨ REVIEW

Check Facts and Main Ideas

1. ↻ Sequence Redraw this diagram on a separate sheet of paper, putting the events in their correct order. Include the year of each event.

> Nicodemus, Kansas, founded
>
> ↓
>
> Homestead Act passed
>
> ↓
>
> John Deere built stronger steel plow
>
> ↓
>
> Barbed wire invented

2. What did the government hope that the **Homestead Act** would accomplish?

3. Who were the **exodusters**? What caused them to move to the Great Plains?

4. Describe two inventions that helped pioneers on the Great Plains.

5. **Critical Thinking:** *Decision Making* You know about the difficulties of living and farming on the Great Plains. Would you have wanted to be a **homesteader**? Use the Decision Making steps on page H3.

Link to ⟨⟩ Writing

Write a Letter Suppose you are a young homesteader in Kansas. Write a letter to your family in the East describing your new life. What have you accomplished? What challenges do you face? Do you expect to stay in Kansas for a long time? Why or why not?

George Shima
1863(?)–1926

George Shima, who was born in Japan, arrived in California in 1888. He was so poor that he had nothing to eat. He soon got a job harvesting potatoes and pulling up tree stumps on a farm in the San Joaquin (wah KEEN) Valley. Shima did whatever he could to learn about farming. He later remembered:

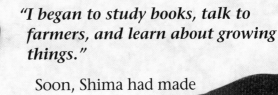

BIOFACT

Shima was the first grower to wash and classify potatoes before selling them, so that the best of his crop could be sold for more money.

"I began to study books, talk to farmers, and learn about growing things."

Soon, Shima had made enough money to rent ten acres of land, where he experimented with growing potatoes. He made farmland on the many small, marshy islands in the San Joaquin River by pumping water out of the soil, creating ideal conditions for growing potatoes. Over time, he bought and drained more land, planting potatoes everywhere. Soon, he had a quickly expanding business that made him wealthy. Shima became known as the "Potato King."

But things were not always easy. Despite his success, Shima sometimes met discrimination. When he bought a new home near a university, some white people protested. But Shima would not move. The United States was his home, he said, and his family would stay.

Shima became an important leader in his community. He was president of the Japanese Association of California for many years. Shima also donated food to those in need and paid for college educations for poor students.

Learn from Biographies

Like many immigrants, George Shima made contributions to the United States. What were some of his contributions?

For more information, go to *Meet the People* at **www.sfsocialstudies.com**.

Read Climographs

What? A **climograph** is a graph that shows two kinds of information about the climate of a place. It shows both the average temperature and the average precipitation—rain or snow—for a particular place over a period of time. You can see examples of climographs on this page and the next page.

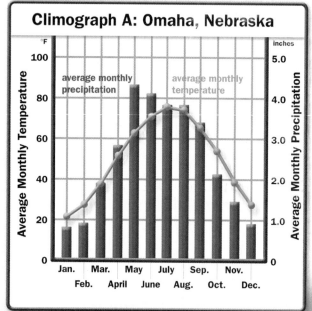

Climograph A: Omaha, Nebraska

average monthly precipitation

average monthly temperature

Average Monthly Temperature (°F): 0, 20, 40, 60, 80, 100

Average Monthly Precipitation (inches): 0, 1.0, 2.0, 3.0, 4.0, 5.0

Jan. Feb. Mar. April May June July Aug. Sep. Oct. Nov. Dec.

Why? Climographs help you understand the typical climate of a place. You have been reading about farmers of the Great Plains during the late 1800s. Some people called this region the "Great American Desert." You learned that despite harsh weather and little rain, farmers were able to successfully grow crops. To study the climate of the Great Plains today, you can use a climograph.

▶ **Omaha, Nebraska**

How? Climograph A shows the average monthly temperature and precipitation today in Omaha, Nebraska, a city in the Great Plains. Read each of the labels at the sides. The left side labels the average monthly temperatures in degrees Fahrenheit (°F). Temperature is shown on the line graph. You can see that the average January temperature for Omaha is about 21° Fahrenheit. You can see that the average temperature in July for Omaha is about 77°F.

The right side of the graph shows average monthly precipitation. Precipitation is shown on the bar graph. The average precipitation in January for Omaha is about 0.8 inches. What is the average monthly precipitation in July for Omaha?

Climograph B shows the average monthly temperatures and precipitation for Winchester, Virginia. Author Willa Cather was born near Winchester and moved with her family at age nine to Nebraska. Compare the average January temperatures for Omaha, Nebraska, and Winchester, Virginia. Which is colder? How do you know? Which receives more precipitation in November? How do you know?

▶ **Winchester, Virginia**

1. During which months in Omaha is the average daily temperature below freezing (32°F)? Are there months when the average daily temperature is at or below freezing in Winchester?

2. Which month gets the most precipitation in Omaha?

3. In Winchester, what is the warmest month? What are the two wettest months?

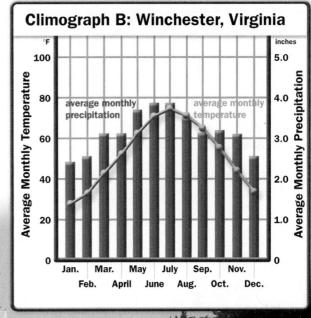

Climograph B: Winchester, Virginia

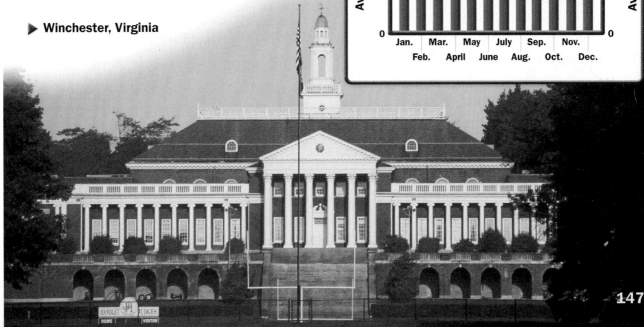

1840   1860

1849
The California gold rush begins.

1859
Gold is found in the Rocky Mountains.

1860s
Cattle drives begin.

Virginia City   Chicago
Denver   Dodge City

PREVIEW

Focus on the Main Idea
Cattle drives and the search for gold offered new opportunities and led to lasting changes in the western United States.

PLACES
Dodge City, Kansas
Chicago, Illinois
Denver, Colorado
Virginia City, Nevada

PEOPLE
Charles Goodnight
Nat Love
Luzena Stanley Wilson
Levi Strauss
Mark Twain

VOCABULARY
cattle drive
gold rush
entrepreneur

▶ Cowboys herded longhorn cattle.

Cowboys and Miners

You Are There

Nat Love wants to be a cowboy. Born into slavery in Tennessee in 1854, Love gained his freedom at the end of the Civil War. Now it is 1869 and Love is 15 years old. He has come west to Dodge City, Kansas, in search of opportunity and adventure.

Love finds a group of Texas cowboys, walks right up to the boss, and asks for a job. "He asked me if I could ride a wild horse," Love later wrote. "I said, 'Yes sir.' He said, 'If you can I will give you a job.'"

The cowboys bring Love a wild horse named Good Eye. Love jumps on, and Good Eye starts bucking and kicking. Love holds on until the horse gets tired. The cowboys are impressed. "The boss said he would give me a job and pay me $30.00 per month," Love wrote. His new life as a cowboy had begun.

Sequence As you read, follow the sequence of events that brought lasting change to the western United States.

▶ Working long days on horseback, cowboys earned about $30 a month. A group of about ten cowboys could handle a herd of more than 2,000 head of cattle.

Cowboy Life

By the end of the Civil War, there were five million head of cattle in Texas. They were a tough breed known as Texas longhorns. These longhorns sold for just $4 each in Texas, but they were worth about $40 each in the growing cities of the East, where beef was scarce. Ranchers realized that they could make huge profits if they could figure out a way to get their cattle across the country.

The solution was the **cattle drive.** On cattle drives, cowboys guided huge herds of cattle north to the new railroad lines extending across the Great Plains. The cattle drives began in Texas and ended in towns along the railroad, such as **Dodge City, Kansas.** From these towns, the cattle were taken by train to eastern cities

One of the main cattle drive trails was the Goodnight-Loving Trail, which ran from Texas to Colorado. **Charles Goodnight,** a rancher who established this trail in 1866, remembered cowboy life as the happiest time of his life:

"Most of the time we were solitary [lone] adventurers in a great land as fresh and new as a spring morning."

Cowboy life may have been an adventure, but it was also exhausting and dangerous. Cowboys worked sixteen-hour days on horseback. They worked seven days a week for the two or three months it took to drive the cattle north. At night cowboys took turns watching the herd, guarding against the constant danger of stampedes. In a stampede, entire herds of longhorns took off running wildly. They could trample horses and people, or charge into rivers and drown. Almost anything could set off a stampede—a burst of lightning, a coyote's howl, even the sound of cooking pots banging together. To try to keep the animals calm, cowboys would sing to them.

Cowboys were a varied group. About one-third of all cowboys were Mexican American or African American. Many were very young. As you read, **Nat Love** began working as a cowboy when he was just fifteen years old.

REVIEW By how much did the price of one longhorn in Texas and in eastern cities differ? Why?
Compare and Contrast

▶ Nat Love was a famous cowboy.

The End of the Drives

Cattle drives came to an end by the late 1880s. One cause was the growing conflict between cattle ranchers and farmers on the Great Plains. To keep cattle off their farm-land, homesteaders began fencing in their land with barbed wire. Expanding railroad lines also helped end the cattle drives. As new railroad lines reached into Texas, it was no longer necessary for ranchers to drive their cattle north.

The cattle drives had ended, but cattle ranching continued to be an important industry. People all over the country still wanted fresh meat at prices they could afford. To meet this demand, ranchers raised millions of cows, as well as hogs and sheep. Expanding railroad lines made it easier and cheaper to transport animals from ranches to cities such as **Chicago, Illinois.** As a major railroad center near the middle of the country, Chicago was perfectly located to become the nation's leading supplier of fresh meat. From Chicago, train cars quickly transported meat to cities around the country.

REVIEW What happened to the cattle ranching industry after the end of cattle drives? ⟳ Sequence

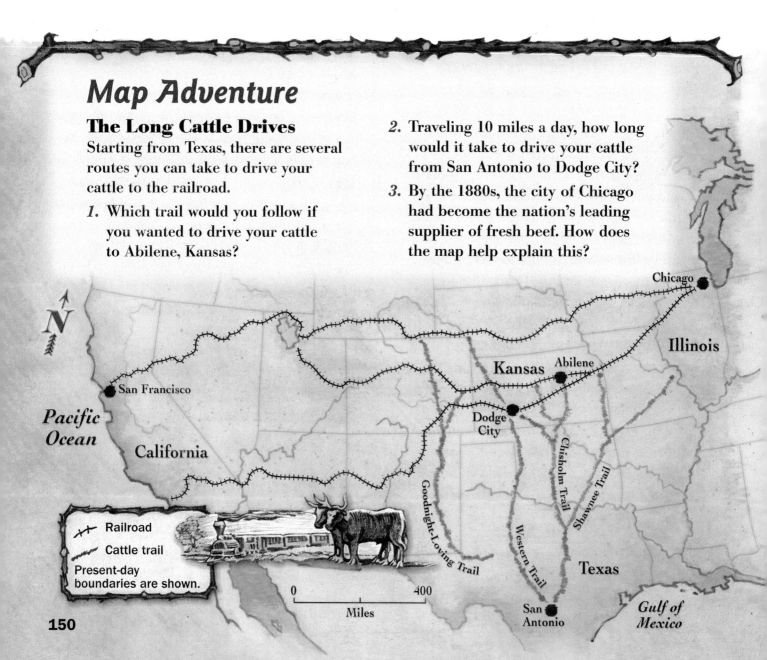

Map Adventure

The Long Cattle Drives
Starting from Texas, there are several routes you can take to drive your cattle to the railroad.

1. Which trail would you follow if you wanted to drive your cattle to Abilene, Kansas?

2. Traveling 10 miles a day, how long would it take to drive your cattle from San Antonio to Dodge City?

3. By the 1880s, the city of Chicago had become the nation's leading supplier of fresh beef. How does the map help explain this?

Chicago

Illinois

San Francisco

Kansas   Abilene

Dodge City

Pacific Ocean

California

Chisholm Trail

Shawnee Trail

Goodnight-Loving Trail

Western Trail

Texas

✦ Railroad
〜 Cattle trail
Present-day boundaries are shown.

0   400
Miles

San Antonio

Gulf of Mexico

▶ It was rare for gold miners to find large gold nuggets like this one *(right)*. **More often they just found gold dust, which they searched for in the ground near or in rivers.**

Dreams of Gold

You have read that Great Plains farmers and cattle ranchers changed the United States. People who moved to the West for gold also helped change the country.

Luzena Stanley Wilson was living with her family in Missouri when she heard the news that gold had been found in California. "The gold excitement spread like wildfire," she remembered. "And as we had almost nothing to lose, and we might gain a fortune, we early caught the fever." The year was 1849. Just like thousands of other families from all over the country, the Wilsons rushed west. They settled in Nevada City, California.

The California gold rush changed the West. During the **gold rush** thousands of people went to California to search for gold. By 1850 California had enough people to become a state. Another effect of the gold rush was that people began to wonder where else in the West gold might be found.

This explains why a hopeful miner named George Jackson was exploring the freezing Rocky Mountains in January 1859. In a creek near the small town of **Denver, Colorado,**

Jackson found a few gold flakes. "I went to bed and dreamed of riches galore," he wrote in his diary.

When Jackson and his partners took some of the gold they had found to Denver, people in town cheered. "The stuff is here after all!" one man shouted. News of gold in the Rockies quickly spread across the country, and a new gold rush was on. Thousands of miners starting searching all over the mountains and deserts of the West.

While everyone dreamed of finding big nuggets of shining gold, such discoveries were actually very rare. Gold mining required long, hard days of work and patience. Using a metal pan, miners scooped sand from the bottom of streams. Then they carefully washed out the sand, hoping to see tiny pieces of gold, known as "gold dust." If miners were lucky, they slowly filled bags with gold dust. The bags were then taken to the nearest town, where the gold could be traded for supplies or deposited in a bank.

REVIEW What was the effect of George Jackson's discovery of gold in the Rockies? **Cause and Effect**

Boomtowns and Blue Jeans

Miners were always quick to rush to any spot where gold was found. They set up camps of canvas tents, then went right to work. As more and more miners rushed in, mining camps often grew into booming towns with diverse populations.

These "boomtowns" offered exciting opportunities for entrepreneurs such as Luzena Stanley Wilson. An **entrepreneur** is a person who starts a new business, hoping to make a profit. After moving with her family to the mining town of Nevada City, California, Wilson saw a way to make money. "The miners were glad to get something to eat, and were always willing to pay for it," she wrote. She built a long table and opened a restaurant in her home. The first night, 20 hungry miners sat at her table. "Each man as he rose put a dollar in my hand and said I might count him as a permanent customer," she wrote.

An immigrant from Germany named **Levi Strauss** found opportunity in San Francisco, California. Strauss learned that miners wanted sturdy pants that would not fall apart under tough working conditions. He began making pants out of blue denim, a strong cotton material. He used rivets, or metal pins, to hold the pants together. These were the world's first blue jeans. The jeans were very popular with miners, and Strauss's business grew.

▶ **Levi Strauss**

One of the West's biggest boomtowns was **Virginia City, Nevada.** When gold and silver were discovered there, Virginia City grew from a small mining camp to a town of nearly 30,000 people in just a few years. A young writer named **Mark Twain** arrived in 1862. Years before he wrote his classic tales about

Literature and Social Studies

Roughing It

Mark Twain wrote for a Virginia City newspaper during the boom years of the early 1860s. In his book *Roughing It*, Twain described the excitement of living in a town where people dug for gold and silver right under the city streets.

"Virginia had grown to be the 'livest' town, for its age and population, that America had ever produced. The sidewalks swarmed with people. . . . So great was the pack [crowd], that buggies [wagons] frequently had to wait half an hour for an opportunity to cross the principal street. Joy sat on every countenance [face], and there was a glad, almost fierce, intensity in every eye, that told of the money-getting schemes [plans] that were seething in every brain. . . . Money was as plenty as dust; every individual considered himself wealthy."

Huckleberry Finn and Tom Sawyer, Twain wrote news reports for Virginia City's newspaper, the *Territorial Enterprise*. In Virginia City, Twain found crowded streets lined with hotels, restaurants, banks, and theaters. "Large fire-proof brick buildings were going up in the principal streets," Twain wrote, "and the wooden suburbs were spreading out in all directions."

The boom times did not last forever. When the gold and silver ran out in Virginia City in the 1880s, people left town. Like many mining towns, Virginia City became a "ghost town," or a town of empty buildings.

All over the West, however, the mining boom had a lasting effect. The hope of finding gold had drawn thousands of new settlers to the region. Towns that had once been supply stations for miners soon grew into important cities. Denver, Colorado, and San Francisco, California, are two examples. Miners had changed the West forever.

REVIEW How did Virginia City change after the gold and silver ran out? ↻ Sequence

Summarize the Lesson

- **1849** The California gold rush lured thousands of settlers to California.

- **1859** Gold was found in the Rocky Mountains, causing miners to begin searching for gold all over the West.

- **1860s** The ranching industry grew when cowboys began driving cattle from Texas to towns along the railroad.

LESSON 3 REVIEW

Check Facts and Main Ideas

1. ↻ **Sequence** On a separate sheet of paper, fill in the missing dates in this chart.

Date   Event

    : Gold is found in the Rocky Mountains.
            ↓
    : Mark Twain moves to Virginia City.
            ↓
    : The Goodnight-Loving trail is established.
            ↓
    : Nat Love becomes a cowboy.

2. Why did ranchers decide to drive their cattle from Texas to towns along the railroad?

3. What changes brought **cattle drives** to an end?

4. Summarize the lasting effects of the search for gold in the West.

5. **Critical Thinking:** *Analyze Primary Sources* You read Mark Twain's description of life in Virginia City. List three details that Twain uses to give the reader an idea of what life was like there.

Link to ⊶⊶ Art

Advertise Your Business Suppose you have just moved to a booming mining town in the 1860s. You decide to be an **entrepreneur** and start a business of your own. What kind of business would you want to open? What would you name it? Draw a poster advertising your new business.

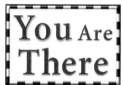

Black Hills

SOUTH DAKOTA

Black Hills

1875

1876
Lakota forces defeat Custer at Little Bighorn.

1877
The Nez Percé surrender in Montana.

1890

1890
Wars in the West come to an end.

War in the West

Focus on the Main Idea
As more and more settlers came to the western United States, Native American groups fought to maintain control of their lands.

PLACES
Black Hills

PEOPLE
Sitting Bull
George Custer
Crazy Horse
Chief Joseph
Geronimo

VOCABULARY
reservation
Battle of Little Bighorn

You Are There The Lakota chief Sitting Bull sees that the Great Plains are changing. Telegraph lines and railroads are slicing across the plains. Farmers, ranchers, and miners are arriving in growing numbers.

The vast herds of buffalo are beginning to disappear. Newcomers are killing buffalo by the thousands—for their hides, to feed railroad workers, and for sport.

For centuries the Lakota have followed buffalo herds over the open plains, relying on these animals for food, clothing, and shelter. Sitting Bull believes that most Lakota want to continue this traditional way of life. "The life my people want is a life of freedom," he says. "I have seen nothing that a white man has, houses or railways or clothing or food, that is as good as the right to move in the open country and live in our fashion."

Sequence As you read, pay attention to the order of events that led to the defeat of Native Americans in the western United States.

▶ **Lakota leader Sitting Bull**

Conflict on the Plains

As you have read, thousands of settlers began moving to the Great Plains in the 1860s. This led to conflict between new settlers and Native Americans of the Great Plains. Such American Indian groups as the Lakota, Cheyenne, and Crow could see that their traditional way of life was threatened. Battles between these groups and settlers became more and more common on the Great Plains.

The United States government was determined to support the settlers. The government wanted the region to be open for expanding railroad lines, growing farms and ranches, and new towns. At first, the government offered money and goods to Native Americans. However, as you read, Sitting Bull did not value the white man's goods. So government leaders decided that Native Americans should move onto reservations. A **reservation** is an area of land set aside for Native Americans. The government was ready to use military force to move Native Americans onto reservations.

Realizing that they could not defeat the United States army, many Native Americans agreed to move to reservations. In 1868 Lakota leaders signed a treaty with the United States creating the Great Lakota Reservation. This large reservation included the **Black Hills,** a region of rugged cliffs and dark green valleys in what is now South Dakota and Wyoming. According to the treaty, this land was to belong to the Lakota people forever.

Then gold was found in the Black Hills in 1874. As always, the news spread quickly. About 15,000 gold miners illegally rushed onto the Lakota reservation.

The United States government now hoped that the Lakota would be willing to sell the Black Hills. A government representative told Lakota leaders, "Gold is useless to you, and there will be fighting unless you give it up." But Lakota leaders refused to move again. "I do not want to sell any land to the government," **Sitting Bull** declared. He picked up a tiny bit of dirt between two fingers. "Not even as much as this."

REVIEW What key events took place after gold was found in the Black Hills?
⟳ Sequence

▶ **Trains often slowed down to allow railroad workers and passengers to shoot buffalo. There were once about 30 million buffalo on the Great Plains. By the late 1880s, there were fewer than 1,000.**

The Battle of Little Bighorn

In March 1876 an American soldier named Thomas Eagan wrote a letter to his sister. "I think we will have some hard times this summer," Eagan wrote. "The old chief Sitting Bull says that he will not make peace with the whites as long as he has a man to fight." Eagan was part of the Seventh Cavalry. Led by Colonel **George Custer,** the Seventh Cavalry's mission was to defeat the Lakota and force them onto a new reservation.

Sitting Bull and the Lakota were camped on the banks of the Little Bighorn River in Montana. **Crazy Horse,** one of the Lakota's most successful young war leaders, was in camp along with many Cheyenne fighters. The Cheyenne were ready to battle alongside the Lakota.

Custer found the Lakota camp on June 25. The American soldiers were badly outnumbered, but Custer decided to attack anyway. "The soldiers charged so quickly we could not talk," said a Lakota chief named Red Horse. Lakota fighters grabbed their guns and the battle began.

Crazy Horse helped lead the Lakota to victory at the **Battle of Little Bighorn**. This battle is also known as "Custer's Last Stand," because George Custer was killed along with his entire force of more than 200 soldiers.

Little Bighorn is remembered as an important battle for two reasons. First, it was the biggest victory Native Americans ever won over United States forces. Second, it soon led to the end of freedom for Native Americans of the Great Plains. Custer's defeat convinced the United States government to take stronger action against the Lakota and other Native American groups.

▶ **Colonel George Custer**

More soldiers were sent to the Great Plains. By the end of 1877, Crazy Horse and most Lakota had been forced onto reservations. Sitting Bull had escaped to Canada. The Black Hills were now open to gold miners and settlers from the United States.

REVIEW How did the United States government react to the Battle of Little Bighorn? **Cause and Effect**

▶ **This is part of the land in the Black Hills that the Lakota fought for.**

Chief Joseph

West of the Great Plains, other Native American groups were also struggling to hold on to their land. The Nez Percé (nez per SAY) lived in the Wallowa Valley of Oregon. In 1877 the United States government decided to move the Nez Percé to a reservation in Idaho Territory. The government wanted the Wallowa Valley to be open to settlers. Many Nez Percé, however, did not want to leave their traditional land. "It has always belonged to our people," said Nez Percé leader **Chief Joseph.**

In June 1877 United States soldiers were sent to capture the Nez Percé and take them to a reservation. The Nez Percé refused to be taken. For the next three months, the army chased Chief Joseph and about 700 Nez Percé across Oregon, Idaho, and Montana. Several fierce battles were fought along this 1,600-mile chase.

Running short of food and supplies, the Nez Percé tried to escape across the Canadian border. They hoped to get help at Sitting Bull's camp in Canada. They were just 40 miles from the border when they were surrounded by American soldiers.

General Nelson Miles promised Chief Joseph that if the Nez Percé surrendered they would be allowed to return to Oregon. This convinced Chief Joseph to stop fighting. He told the American soldiers,

> *"I am tired of fighting. Our chiefs are killed. . . . The little children are freezing to death. . . . I am tired; my heart is sick and sad. From where the sun now stands I will fight no more forever."*

General Miles's promise was not kept, however. The Nez Percé soon learned they were to be taken to a reservation in Oklahoma. This came as a shock to Chief Joseph. "I believed General Miles, or I never would have surrendered," he said. You will read more about Chief Joseph in the Citizen Heroes following this lesson.

REVIEW What reasons did Chief Joseph give when he agreed to stop fighting? Summarize

▶ **Chief Joseph surrendering**

▶ **Chief Joseph**

After the Wars

The Lakota and Nez Percé were just two of many American Indian groups that fought for their land. In the southwestern United States, the Apache continued fighting well into the 1880s. An Apache leader named **Geronimo** (je RON ih moh) resisted capture by leading a small group into the mountains of northern Mexico. When Geronimo was finally forced to surrender in 1886, he told American soldiers, "Once I moved about like the wind. Now I surrender to you and that is all."

The last major conflict between United States soldiers and Native Americans took place in 1890. A group of Lakota families decided to leave their reservation. They were soon surrounded by United States soldiers at Wounded Knee, South Dakota. While the Lakota were giving up their weapons, someone fired a shot. United States soldiers began firing their guns, and about 300 Lakota were killed.

The fighting at Wounded Knee marked the end of the wars between United States forces and Native Americans. Native Americans all over the western half of the United States had been moved onto reservations. The map on this page shows the locations of the major reservations in 1890.

Native Americans now had to adjust to life on reservations. A Hidatsa woman named Buffalo Bird Woman said, "Our Indian life, I know, is gone forever." Even on the reservation, however, Buffalo Bird Woman continued speaking the Hidatsa language and farming in the traditional way of her people. Buffalo Bird Woman's brother, Wolf Chief, chose a different way of adjusting to life on a reservation. Wolf Chief learned English and started his own store. "I want to be strong and go forward," he said.

In 1900 there were about 230,000 Native Americans living in the United States. This was fewer than at any time since the arrival of Columbus more than 400 years before.

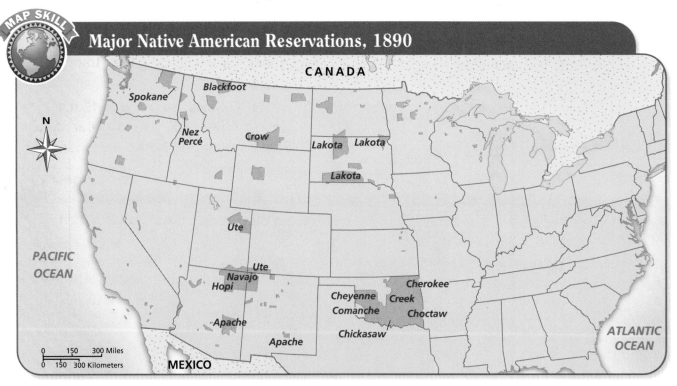

Major Native American Reservations, 1890

MAP SKILL

Many Native Americans were forced to live on reservations, which were often far from their original homes.

MAP SKILL Location *Which two groups lived near the Navajo reservation?*

Today the Native American population has grown to more than 2.5 million. About half of the Native Americans in the United States live on or near reservations. By winning court cases and helping to pass new laws, Native Americans have gained more control over reservation land.

► After his surrender, Apache leader Geronimo became a farmer in Oklahoma.

Both on and off reservations, a wide variety of American Indian groups are keeping their traditional cultures alive. Young people are learning the languages of their ancestors. About 200 tribal languages are still spoken in the United States today. Native American writers and filmmakers continue to tell stories about their people's history and way of life.

REVIEW How did life change for Native Americans after 1890? Compare and Contrast

Summarize the Lesson

1876 The Lakota won a major victory over United States forces at the Battle of Little Bighorn.

1877 Chief Joseph and the Nez Percé surrendered after a long chase across the West.

1890 The wars between United States forces and Native Americans ended.

LESSON 4 **REVIEW**

Check Facts and Main Ideas

1. **Sequence** On a separate sheet of paper, create a chart of the struggle of Native Americans for their land. Fill in one key event for each year shown.

| 1868: |

↓

| 1874: |

↓

| 1876: |

↓

| 1877: |

2. What changes threatened the way of life for Native Americans of the Great Plains in the 1860s?

3. Why was the **Battle of Little Bighorn** important?

4. What are some ways in which Native Americans are keeping their traditions alive today?

5. **Critical Thinking: Summarize** Summarize the outcome of the wars between United States forces and Native Americans.

Link to **Language Arts**

Tell a Story One of the ways in which Native Americans keep their traditions alive is by telling stories. Find a book of Native American stories in the library. Choose one story you like and tell the story to your class.

Fighting for a Homeland

The Nez Percé lived in the Wallowa Valley of Oregon. As more and more new settlers arrived, the Nez Percé lost their land and were forced to move onto reservations. Chief Joseph spent his life fighting for the right of his people to be treated fairly.

▶ **The Nez Percé National Forest is in Idaho.**

The Nez Percé had always had friendly relations with settlers, ever since Lewis and Clark passed through their land in the early 1800s. Chief Joseph's father, Joseph the Elder, was a Nez Percé chief who had worked with the United States government on an agreement that gave lands in Oregon and Idaho to his people. In 1863, gold was found on Nez Percé land, however, and more settlers arrived in the region. The United States government took back six million acres of land promised to the Nez Percé and told them they would have to move to a reservation in Idaho. Joseph the Elder refused to move his people there.

When Joseph the Elder died in 1871, his son became chief and soon had to deal with the same problems his father had. In 1877 General Oliver Otis Howard threatened to attack the Nez Percé if they would not move to the Idaho reservation. Chief Joseph was a peaceful man who did not want to see his people killed so he agreed to move. A group of Nez Percé fighters did not agree and attacked nearby settlers. Fearing punishment for the attack, Chief Joseph decided to take his people to Canada.

For three months, United States soldiers chased 700 Nez Percé 1,600 miles across Oregon, Idaho, and Montana. Finally, the army surrounded the Nez Percé in the Bear Paw

▶ **Chief Joseph**

BUILDING CITIZENSHIP

Caring
Respect
Responsibility
★ Fairness
Honesty
Courage

Mountains, just 40 miles from the Canadian border. With escape cut off, Chief Joseph surrendered on October 5, 1877. The Nez Percé were taken to a reservation in Oklahoma, where many became sick and died. In 1885 the Nez Percé were allowed to return to reservations in the Northwest. Some were sent to Idaho, others to Washington. However, no reservations were set aside in their original homelands.

Chief Joseph spent the rest of his life working and speaking for the fair and equal treatment of Native Americans. He traveled to Washington, D.C., to speak with President Rutherford B. Hayes and, later, President Theodore Roosevelt. During his visit to see President Hayes in 1879, Chief Joseph said,

"Treat all men alike. Give them the same laws. Give them all an even chance to live and grow. . . . You might as well expect all rivers to run backward as that any man who was born a free man should be contented [satisfied] penned up and denied liberty to go where he pleases. . . . Let me be a free man, free to travel, free to stop, free to work, free to trade where I choose, free to choose my own teachers, free to follow the religion of my fathers, free to talk, think and act for myself— and I will obey every law."

▶ A group of Nez Percé from the early 1900s

Fairness in Action

Do Chief Joseph's words describe your understanding of the term *fairness*? Write a paragraph called "What Fairness Means to Me." Give examples from the story of the Nez Percé, other examples from history, or even present-day examples.

Chapter Summary

Sequence

On a separate sheet of paper, copy the chart and place the following events in the sequence in which they happened. Include the date for each one.

▶ **Ad for barbed wire**

_____ The last major Native American conflict ends in Wounded Knee, South Dakota.

↓

_____ The Goodnight-Loving Trail is established.

↓

_____ Barbed wire is invented.

↓

_____ The Pony Express begins.

↓

_____ Gold is discovered near Denver.

Vocabulary

Match each word with the correct definition or description.

1 telegraph (p. 129)

2 exoduster (p. 141)

3 technology (p. 142)

4 cattle drive (p. 149)

5 Battle of Little Bighorn (p. 156)

a. use of new ideas to make tools that improve people's lives

b. sends messages along wires

c. Lakota defeat of George Custer

d. African American pioneer

e. cowboys guiding cattle to railroad lines

People and Places

Write a sentence explaining why each of the following people or places was important in the United States in the middle and late 1800s.

1 Samuel Morse (p. 129)

2 Sacramento, California (p. 130)

3 Benjamin Singleton (p. 141)

4 George Shima (p. 144)

5 Chicago, Illinois (p. 150)

6 Denver, Colorado (p. 151)

7 Levi Strauss (p. 152)

8 Black Hills (p. 155)

9 George Custer (p. 156)

10 Chief Joseph (p. 157)

1870	1880	1890

1862
President Lincoln signs the Homestead Act.

1869
The transcontinental railroad is completed.

1876
Lakota defeat Custer at Little Bighorn.

1877
African American pioneers establish Nicodemus, Kansas.

1877
Nez Percé surrender in Montana.

Late 1880s
Cattle drives come to an end.

Facts and Main Ideas

1 Why did the telegraph replace the Pony Express?

2 How did the gold rush help California become a state?

3 **Time Line** How many years after the first telegraph line crossed the country was the transcontinental railroad completed?

4 **Main Idea** What challenges did companies building the transcontinental railroad face?

5 **Main Idea** Why did many African Americans move to the Great Plains?

6 **Main Idea** Why did cattle drives come to an end by the late 1800s?

7 **Main Idea** How and why were Native American lands threatened by newcomers?

8 **Critical Thinking:** *Compare and Contrast* Contrast the ways in which Buffalo Bird Woman and Wolf Chief adjusted to life on a reservation. Explain why both made good choices.

Write About History

1 **Write a brief news message** describing events at Promontory Point, Utah Territory, on May 10, 1869.

2 **Write a letter** home about your experience as a homesteader.

3 **Write a help-wanted ad** for a cowboy. Describe the responsibilities and benefits of the job.

Apply Skills

Study the climograph of Houston, Texas, below. Then use the climograph to answer the questions that follow.

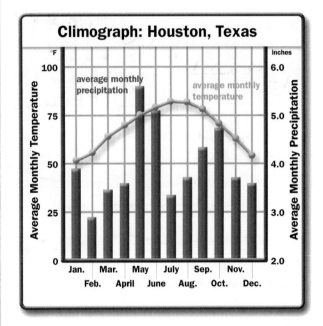

Climograph: Houston, Texas

1 In which month is the average precipitation highest?

2 Which month is usually coldest?

3 Describe the climate during an average day in July in Houston.

Internet Activity

To get help with vocabulary, people, and terms, select dictionary or encyclopedia from *Social Studies Library* at **www.sfsocialstudies.com**.

CHAPTER 4

Industry and Immigration

1879

Menlo Park, New Jersey
Thomas Edison invents a useful light bulb.

Lesson 1

1

1870s

Pittsburgh, Pennsylvania
Andrew Carnegie begins making steel at affordable prices.

Lesson 2

2

1894

Boston, Massachusetts
Mary Antin, one of millions of new immigrants, settles in Boston with her family.

Lesson 3

3

1899

New York, New York
New York "newsies" go on strike to protest the rise in the price of newspapers.

Lesson 4

4

CANADA

4

1

3

2

Boston

New York City
Menlo Park

UNITED STATES

Pittsburgh

ATLANTIC
OCEAN

Why We Remember

"Give me your tired, your poor,
Your huddled masses yearning to breathe free. . ."

These words are part of a poem by Emma Lazarus that was written for the Statue of Liberty in New York Harbor. "Lady Liberty" has been a symbol of hope and freedom for the millions of immigrants who have come to the United States from all over the world. In this unit you will see how Americans—both newcomers and those born here—contributed to the remarkable growth and change that altered our nation forever.

1875　　　　　　　　　　　　　　　　　　1900

1876
Alexander Graham Bell invents the telephone.

1879
Thomas Edison develops a working light bulb.

1903
The Wright Brothers make the world's first airplane flight.

Menlo Park

Richmond

Kitty Hawk

PREVIEW

Focus on the Main Idea
In the late 1800s and early 1900s, new inventions changed the way people lived and led to the rise of new industries.

PLACES
Menlo Park, New Jersey
Richmond, Virginia
Kitty Hawk, North Carolina

PEOPLE
Alexander Graham Bell
Thomas Edison
Lewis Latimer
Frank Sprague
Frank Duryea
Charles Duryea
Wilbur Wright
Orville Wright
Blanche Stuart Scott

VOCABULARY
investor

▶ The world's first telephone

Inventors Change the World

You Are There

The year is 1863. The place is Edinburgh, Scotland. A 16-year-old boy named Alexander has just finished building a very strange machine out of tin, rubber, and wood. He calls it a "talking-machine," because it is designed to imitate the human voice. He built it with the help of his brother Melville, who is 18.

The brothers have set up their machine to say the word *Mamma*. But will anyone think it sounds like a real person? They decide to find out. They bring the machine out into the street. The brothers hide while the machine calls out, "Mamma, mamma."

And sure enough, people come outside to see who is calling. "Good gracious," cries one neighbor, "what can be the matter with that baby?"

The brothers congratulate each other on a successful experiment.

Sequence As you read, keep track of the sequence of important events that changed the way Americans lived.

The First Telephone

Alexander Graham Bell was always interested in sound and speech. As a very young boy in Scotland, he tried to teach his dog, Mr. Perd, how to speak. It did not work. But he learned a valuable lesson about being an inventor—you have to learn from your failures, and you have to keep trying.

As you just read, Bell built a talking-machine when he was 16. By the time he was in his twenties, he had a new idea. He believed it was possible to make a machine that would allow people to talk to each other across wires. He called this idea the "talking telegraph."

In 1871 Bell moved to Boston, Massachusetts. He worked at the Boston School for the Deaf, teaching deaf students to speak. Developing better ways to teach deaf children was another of Bell's main interests.

At night Bell continued working on his talking telegraph, or telephone. He hired Thomas Watson to help him design and build models of his invention. Bell and Watson knew they had to work quickly if they wanted to invent the first working telephone. Other inventors were also trying to develop a telephone.

On March 10, 1876, Bell and Watson were ready to test their invention. They stood in separate rooms, with the doors closed. Into one end of the telephone, Bell shouted,

> *"Mr. Watson, come here, I want to see you."*

Watson raced into Bell's room and announced that he had heard the sentence clearly.

Bell predicted that the telephone would soon change the way people communicated with each other. He was right. By the time Bell died in 1922, there were millions of telephones in use in the United States.

REVIEW What events in Alexander Graham Bell's life led up to his invention of the telephone? ⟳ **Sequence**

▶ Bell's invention helped change the way Americans communicate (*above*).

▶ Alexander Graham Bell is seen here (*left*) placing the first long-distance telephone call, between New York and Chicago.

167

Edison's Light Bulb

Another inventor who helped change the world was **Thomas Edison.** A year after Bell built the first telephone, Edison used some of the same scientific ideas to invent the phonograph. Edison's phonograph was the first machine that could record a voice and then play it back. This technology would soon allow musicians to record music and sell records.

After the phonograph, Edison turned to a different idea. He wanted to build a safe and dependable electric light bulb. At that time, people used gas lamps or candles for indoor lighting. Scientists already knew how to build light bulbs, but they could not build one that lasted long enough to be used in homes. Edison began working on this problem with a team of young scientists in his laboratory in **Menlo Park, New Jersey.** Many inventors like Edison did not have enough money of their own to pay for experiments. They relied on investors. **Investors** are people who give money to a business or project, hoping to gain a profit.

▶ **Thomas Edison, with his light bulb above, made more than 1,000 inventions.**

The hardest part about building the light bulb was finding the right material to use for the filament. The filament is the thin wire inside a light bulb that glows when electricity passes through it. Every filament that Edison tried either burned out quickly or exploded. "I've tried everything," Edison wrote. "I have not failed. I've just found 10,000 ways that won't work." In 1879 Edison and his team solved the problem. They built a bulb with a carbon filament that glowed for two days.

This was a great start, but would you want to replace your light bulbs every two days? An inventor named **Lewis Latimer** helped improve the light bulb. Latimer developed a method of making carbon filaments that lasted much longer. This invention helped make electric light practical for everyday use.

REVIEW How did Thomas Edison and Lewis Latimer each contribute to the effort to make a working light bulb? **Summarize**

▶ **Lewis Latimer was also an artist. Alexander Graham Bell hired him to draw up plans for his new invention, the telephone.**

168

Electricity Brings Change

Thomas Edison knew that electric light could change life in the United States. First, however, there would have to be some way to get electricity into people's homes and businesses. Edison decided to build an electrical power station in New York City. From this station, wires could carry electricity to buildings in the city.

Edison knew that it would be risky to build his first power station in the country's biggest city. If he failed, everyone would know about it. However, like many inventors, Edison was also an entrepreneur. He wanted to show the world that his power station really worked. Then people would pay his company to bring them electricity.

Edison began testing his power station in the summer of 1882. "It was a terrifying experience as I didn't know what was going to happen," he said. After a few failures, Edison got the system working. When he turned the power station on, lights in 40 different buildings began glowing. Soon other cities began building power stations of their own. Stores, offices, newspapers, factories, and theaters began installing electric lights.

Change came more slowly to people's homes. At first only wealthy families could afford to have electric lighting at home. As the graph on this page shows, only eight percent of all U.S. homes had electric service in 1907. The number of homes with electricity began rising quickly after that.

REVIEW Why did Edison decide to build a power station in New York City?
Main Idea and Details

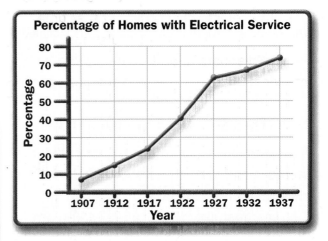

Percentage of Homes with Electrical Service

▶ Home use of electricity increased quickly.

GRAPH SKILL *By what year did 40 percent of homes have electricity?*

▶ **Electricity lit up this Coney Island amusement park in New York City.**

169

▶ **The traffic in New York City in the 1890s included both horse-drawn carriages and electric streetcars.**

Streetcars and Horseless Carriages

American cities began building streetcar systems in the 1830s. Horses pulled these early streetcars along steel tracks laid in the street. Just like buses today, streetcars would pick up and drop off passengers at different stops around the city. With the rise of electricity and power stations in the 1880s, people started thinking of ways to improve the streetcar.

An electrical engineer named **Frank Sprague** was the first to succeed. He designed the world's first system of electric streetcars in **Richmond, Virginia,** in 1888. Electric streetcars traveled more quickly and held more people than horse-drawn streetcars. Within a few years, electric streetcar systems were built in cities all over the world.

At the same time, other inventors were working on the world's first cars. People called this invention the "horseless carriage," because it was like a carriage that did not need horses to pull it. The first cars with gasoline-powered engines were built in Germany in the late 1880s.

Two brothers named **Frank Duryea** and **Charles Duryea** were the first to build a working automobile in the United States. In their workshop in Springfield, Massachusetts, the Duryea brothers built the first American car in 1893. A newspaper announced the news with the headline, "No Use for Horses: Springfield Mechanics Devise a New Mode of Travel."

This was the beginning of a new American industry. Companies all over the country began designing and selling cars. Still, it would be many years before companies built cars that most people could afford.

REVIEW What advantages did electric streetcars have over horse-drawn streetcars? **Compare and Contrast**

▶ **These men are riding in one of the earliest automobiles.**

Invention Time Line

Here are some inventions that changed life in the United States and around the world. Can you picture what life would be like today without some of these inventions?

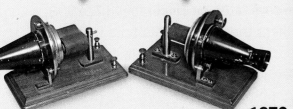

1850

1850 Sewing Machine
Isaac Singer's machine makes it possible to make clothing much more quickly.

1873 Typewriter
American inventor Christopher Latham Sholes builds the first typewriter.

1876 Telephone
The first long-distance phone line connects New York and Philadelphia in 1887.

1870

1879 Electric light bulb
Electric lights begin lighting city streets in 1880.

1885 Automobile
The earliest cars can only go eight miles per hour.

1890

1895 Radio
Italy's Guglielmo Marconi invents the radio at the age of 20.

1903 Airplane
Orville and Wilbur Wright build *Flyer*, the world's first successful airplane.

1910

The Wright Brothers

In Dayton, Ohio, **Wilbur Wright** and **Orville Wright** were working on another invention that would change the world. The Wright brothers built and repaired bicycles for a living. In their free time, they thought about building a flying machine.

The first challenge they faced was that they knew almost nothing about flying. They would have to begin experimenting. In 1899 the Wright brothers built a glider, or a plane with no engine that can glide on the wind. They traveled to the small fishing village of **Kitty Hawk, North Carolina,** to test their glider. The beach at Kitty Hawk was a good location because it had strong winds and soft sand for landing. Because it was far from any big towns, the brothers could do their experiments in secret.

After two years of failures, the Wright brothers were discouraged. Wilbur Wright remembered, "At this time I made the prediction that man would sometime fly, but that it would not be in our lifetime."

But they kept trying. They built a new plane, called *Flyer.* They designed a special lightweight motor for *Flyer,* with a propeller to pull the plane forward. They took *Flyer* to Kitty Hawk to test it. When the plane was ready, the brothers tossed a coin to see who would get to fly first. Wilbur won. He tried to fly, but *Flyer* would not take off.

Three days later, on December 17, 1903, the brothers tried again. This time it was Orville's turn—and *Flyer* actually took off! The plane flew just 120 feet before landing, but the Wright brothers knew they had made history. "This flight lasted only 12 seconds," Orville wrote, "but it was nevertheless the first in the history of the world in which a machine carrying a man had raised itself by its own power into the air in full flight."

REVIEW After deciding to build a plane, what steps did the Wright brothers take to achieve their goal? ↻ Sequence

▶ **The first airplane flight lasted only 12 seconds. This historic flight is pictured below. Today the Wright brothers' airplane, *Flyer* (*above*), is in the National Air and Space Museum in Washington, D.C.**

Inventions and Industry

The inventions you have read about in this lesson all led to new industries. People started businesses to offer telephone service and electrical service. They started companies to make streetcars, automobiles, and airplanes. Many of these new companies began competing with each other for business.

This kind of competition was good news for a young woman named **Blanche Stuart Scott.** Scott helped advertise a new car company by driving one of its cars across the country in 1910. This trip made her famous, but she soon got an even more exciting opportunity. She joined a team of pilots who worked for the Curtiss Airplane and Motor Company. Her job was to fly Curtiss airplanes at fairs and air shows. Scott was the first American woman to fly an airplane. "I soared to the dizzying height of 25 feet," she said of her first flight. "It seemed like a hundred!"

REVIEW What was one effect of the inventions you read about in this lesson?
Cause and Effect

Summarize the Lesson

1876 Alexander Graham Bell invented the telephone.

1879 Thomas Edison developed the first working light bulb.

1903 The Wright brothers made the world's first airplane flight.

LESSON 1 REVIEW

Check Facts and Main Ideas

1. **Sequence** Redraw this chart on a separate sheet of paper, putting the events in their correct order. Include the year of each event.

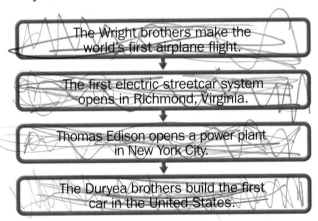

The Wright brothers make the world's first airplane flight.

↓

The first electric streetcar system opens in Richmond, Virginia.

↓

Thomas Edison opens a power plant in New York City.

↓

The Duryea brothers build the first car in the United States.

2. How did Alexander Graham Bell's invention affect communication in the United States?

3. What are two important inventions for which Thomas Edison is remembered?

4. Describe three inventions that changed the way people traveled.

5. **Critical Thinking:** *Cause and Effect* How did inventions such as the telephone, electric light, and car lead to the rise of new industries?

Link to ⚭ Science

Study Inventors Many inventors have changed the way people live. Choose one inventor and find out more about him or her, including whether the inventor relied on **investors** for help. Write a one-page report about the inventor. Explain how the inventor's work changed the way people lived.

Research and Writing Skills

Write an Outline

What? An **outline** is a written plan for organizing information about a subject. An outline can be used as a study guide or as a summary of a reading selection. It is made up of main ideas and details that support the main ideas.

Outlines are often made up of three parts. First are the main ideas. These statements usually have Roman numerals (I, II, III, IV . . .) in front of them. Next are the subtopics, which support the main ideas. They are often labeled with capital letters. Third are the details of the topic. The details may have Arabic numerals (1, 2, 3, 4 . . .) in front of them. Below is a selection about an inventor in the early 1900s. An outline of this selection is shown on the following page.

Inventor of the Windshield Wiper

Mary Anderson was inspired to invent the windshield wiper when she took a trip from her home in Alabama to New York City in the winter of 1903. While she was riding on a streetcar, a snowstorm started. Anderson noticed that the shivering streetcar operator had to keep leaning out of the window to wipe off the snow from his windshield so he could see. This was inconvenient and dangerous!

Anderson had an idea to improve visibility for drivers during stormy weather. She quickly drew a picture of the idea in her sketchbook. Her invention was a sort of swinging arm with a rubber blade that swept off ice and snow. The driver could move the arm with a handle inside the car. During warmer weather, the arm could easily be removed.

Anderson believed the public could use her invention. A few months after her trip, she applied for and received a patent for the mechanical windshield wiper. A patent is a grant given by the government to an inventor. It gives the inventor the sole right to make and sell the invention for a set period of time. Anderson's invention was very popular. By 1913 the windshield wiper was standard equipment in most American cars. Her invention helped save lives by allowing drivers to see clearly in snow, rain, and sleet.

Why? Writing an outline will help you better organize your thoughts and remember what you read. When you study for an exam, you will be able to see the main ideas at a glance. Outlines also help you write a clear report or speech. They allow you to organize the information you find before you start writing. This can make your writing better and help you remember all the points you want to cover.

I. Mary Anderson's trip, 1903
   A. Inspiration
      1. Streetcar operator had to lean out of window to wipe away snow
      2. Inconvenient and dangerous
   B. Invention to improve visibility for drivers
      1. Swinging arm with rubber blade to sweep away snow, ice, or rain
      2. _____
      3. Arm can be removed in warm weather

II. Ready for the public
   A. _____
      1. A grant given by the government
      2. She had the right to make and sell her invention
   B. Standard equipment in cars by 1913
      1. Allowed drivers to see clearly in snow, rain, and sleet
      2. Saved lives

How? Follow these steps to write an outline:

- As you read, think about what the main ideas are. Write the headings next to Roman numerals. Read the passage on the previous page. If you were to write an outline based on this selection, one heading might be *Mary Anderson's trip, 1903*.
- Next, divide the text you read into subtopics under the headings. Write these subtopics next to capital letters. A possible subtopic for this passage could be *Inspiration*.
- Using your own words, write important details below the subtopics. List the details next to numbers. One detail you might include in your outline for the passage is *Streetcar operator had to lean out of window to wipe away snow.*

Think and Apply

1. In the outline on this page, what detail can go next to 2, under Roman numeral *I*, letter *B*?

2. What subtopic can go next to *A* under Roman numeral *II*?

3. How can writing outlines help you study or write a report?

1850   1900

1859
Oil is found
in Pennsylvania.

1893
The United States has
more than 160,000 miles
of railroad track.

1900
The U.S. is the
leading producer
of manufactured
goods.

Cleveland
Pittsburgh

PREVIEW

Focus on the Main Idea
In the late 1800s and early 1900s, big businesses helped the United States economy grow quickly.

PLACES
Pittsburgh, Pennsylvania
Cleveland, Ohio

PEOPLE
Andrew Carnegie
John D. Rockefeller
George Westinghouse
William Randolph Hearst
Madame C. J. Walker
J. P. Morgan

VOCABULARY
corporation
stock
monopoly
free enterprise
consumer
human resource
capital resource

The Rise of Big Business

You Are There

The year is 1894. All over the nation, steel is being used to build new bridges, railroads, and buildings. But who is making the steel? A writer named Hamlin Garland wants to find out. He is visiting a huge steel mill near Pittsburgh, Pennsylvania.

Garland stands in one of the mill's massive buildings, amazed by all the action and noise. Everywhere engines are roaring, cranes are swinging, and workers are pouring red-hot liquid steel out of giant pots. A young man walks past Garland, panting and sweating.

"That looks like hard work," Garland says.

"Hard! I guess it's hard," the man says. "I often drink two buckets of water during twelve hours; the sweat drips through my sleeves, and runs down my legs and fills my shoes."

Main Idea and Details As you read, pay attention to the important industrial leaders and the businesses they started.

▶ **Steel was used to build the Empire State Building, once the tallest building in the world at 1,250 feet.**

Building with Steel

Human beings have been making steel for more than 2,000 years. Steel is made by heating iron until it melts and then adding carbon. The advantage of steel is that it is a stronger material than iron. Steel can hold more weight than iron, and it can bend without cracking.

Until the middle 1800s, however, steel was very expensive to produce. An English inventor named Henry Bessemer helped change this. In 1856 Bessemer developed the Bessemer process, a new way of making steel. Bessemer's furnaces produced strong steel at affordable prices. Now it was possible to produce steel in massive quantities.

An entrepreneur named **Andrew Carnegie** saw that there could be a huge market for steel in the rapidly growing United States. In the 1870s, Carnegie began using the Bessemer process to make steel in **Pittsburgh, Pennsylvania.**

Carnegie's goal was to produce steel at the lowest possible cost. He accomplished this by controlling all the steps of the steel-making process. He bought iron and coal mines to provide his steel mills with these necessary resources. He bought ships and railroads to bring the resources to his mills, and to deliver the finished steel all over the country. Carnegie helped steel become a "big business," or a major industry, in the United States. By 1900 the United States was producing more steel than any other country in the world. Carnegie's mills alone were producing more steel than the entire nation of Great Britain.

Steel was strong and now it was widely available. People used it to build buildings, bridges, automobiles, trains, and railroads. With so much steel being used, Carnegie became one of the richest men in the world. You will read more about how he spent his money in the Biography on page 183.

REVIEW How did the steel industry change after 1856? ↺ Sequence

▶ **Andrew Carnegie produced steel for bridges, buildings, automobiles, and railroads.**

Railroads Link Markets

Railroad companies needed steel to build tracks and trains. You read that the first transcontinental railroad was completed in 1869. By 1893 four more railroad lines crossed the country. The United States now had more than 160,000 miles of railroad track!

Railroad companies became one of the nation's first large corporations. A **corporation** is a business that is owned by investors. Corporations sell shares of the company, called **stocks**, to investors. A corporation can use the money from selling stocks to buy equipment for the company. By becoming corporations, railroad companies were able to raise enough money to buy the equipment they needed.

Railroads were the fastest and cheapest way to transport goods. Railroads linked cities, farms, factories, and mines all over the United States. A farmer on the Great Plains could grow more wheat and corn, because trains transported crops to cities where the food could be sold. A factory owner in the East could produce more tools because trains could take the tools to stores all over the country.

By providing these links, railroads helped the United States economy grow. Cities that were major railroad centers also grew. Railroad centers such as Chicago were soon among the biggest cities in the country.

REVIEW Why did many railroad companies form corporations? **Main Idea and Details**

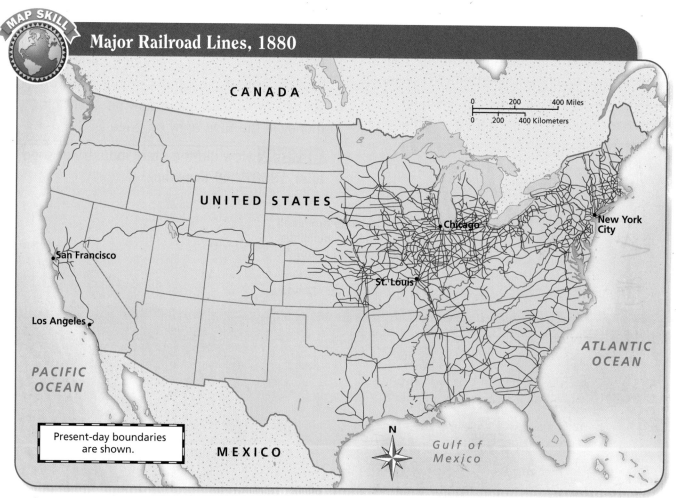

MAP SKILL

Major Railroad Lines, 1880

CANADA

0   200   400 Miles
0   200   400 Kilometers

UNITED STATES

Chicago

New York City

San Francisco

St. Louis

Los Angeles

ATLANTIC OCEAN

PACIFIC OCEAN

Present-day boundaries are shown.

MEXICO

N

Gulf of Mexico

▶ The populations of cities such as Chicago and St. Louis grew as the cities became railroad centers.

MAP SKILL Use a Transportation Map *In which parts of the United States do you think most people lived in 1880? How did you reach this conclusion?*

The Oil Industry

On August 27, 1859, a former railroad conductor named Edwin Drake drilled a hole in the ground in western Pennsylvania. When he reached a depth of 69 feet, a thick, black liquid came up from the ground. This was oil—exactly what Drake had been hoping to find. People rushed to the region to drill for oil, or "black gold," as it was sometimes called. The young oil industry was suddenly big business.

This discovery was big news to a teenager named **John D. Rockefeller.** Rockefeller saw a great opportunity to start a business of his own. "I want to make a hundred thousand dollars," he told his friends. He realized that he could earn money in the oil business by refining oil, or turning it into useful products such as kerosene. At that time, kerosene lamps were the main source of lighting in the United States.

Rockefeller built his first oil refinery in **Cleveland, Ohio,** in 1863. Using the profits from this business, he bought other refineries. Rockefeller's company, Standard Oil, slowly gained control of the nation's oil industry.

By the early 1880s, Standard Oil controlled about 90 percent of the oil business in the United States. Standard Oil had become a monopoly (muh NOP uh lee). A **monopoly** is a company that has control of an entire industry. Monopolies have little or no competition, so they can charge any price they want for their products. As you will read in the next unit, some people began arguing that monopolies were bad for the country.

By the early 1900s, electric lights were replacing kerosene lamps as the most important source of lighting. But this did not mean the end of the oil industry. Americans were beginning to buy cars in large numbers. This created a huge demand for other products made from oil, such as gasoline and motor oil. People started searching for oil all over the country. Major oil discoveries were made in Texas, Oklahoma, and California. The oil industry continued to grow, and it remains one of the biggest industries in the country today.

REVIEW What effect did the rise of the car industry have on the oil industry?
Cause and Effect

► The 1901 Spindletop gusher in Texas (*left*) was the biggest oil strike so far in the country. John D. Rockefeller (*right*) built refineries to make oil into useful products.

Free Enterprise

Andrew Carnegie, John D. Rockefeller, and others were able to start their own businesses because the United States economy is based on the system of free enterprise. In a **free enterprise** system, people are free to start their own businesses and own their own property. Business owners are free to decide what to produce, and how much to charge for their products or services. Consumers are free to make choices about how to spend their money. A **consumer** is a person who buys or uses goods and services.

Since consumers are free to decide what to buy, companies must compete with each other to sell their products. Competition between companies is an important part of the free enterprise system. For example, a major competition took place in the electricity industry in the late 1800s. An inventor and entrepreneur named **George Westinghouse** formed the Westinghouse Electric Company in 1886. Westinghouse used a new technology called alternating current, or AC, to deliver electricity to homes and businesses. Thomas Edison's electric company used a system called direct current, or DC. Both Westinghouse and Edison argued that they had the better system.

This competition grew so fierce, it became known as the "War of the Currents." Westinghouse won the war for one simple reason. He had the better product. When consumers had a chance to see both systems in action, they saw that Westinghouse's AC worked better than Edison's DC. The Westinghouse Electric Company quickly grew into a large corporation with thousands of employees.

A newspaper owner named **William Randolph Hearst** thought of new ways to compete in the newspaper business. Hearst used big, eye-catching headlines in his newspapers. He added illustrations and color sections. These changes helped Hearst sell more newspapers than anyone else in the early 1900s.

Madame C. J. Walker took a different road to success. In 1906 Walker began bottling shampoo and other products in her attic. She could not afford employees or a store, so she sold her products door-to-door. "I got my start by giving myself a start," she often said. Ten years later, she had thousands of employees. Walker was the first African American woman to become a millionaire.

REVIEW Why did Westinghouse win the "War of the Currents"? Summarize

▶ **William Randolph Hearst's newspaper the New York Journal reported the death of President William McKinley in 1901.**

Resources and Big Business

You have read about many of the reasons for the rise of big business. Inventions led to new industries. Railroads linked markets around the country. Entrepreneurs and their new ideas helped businesses grow. Another reason business grew was that the United States is rich in important resources.

Economists, people who study the economy, divide resources into three categories: natural resources, human resources, and capital resources. Each type of resource was, and still is, important to American industries.

Natural resources are things found in nature that people can use. You read that Carnegie used railroads to bring natural resources such as iron and coal to his steel mills. Rockefeller used oil pumped from the ground to make valuable products.

Human resources are people who work to produce goods and services. The United States had a rapidly growing population in the late 1800s and early 1900s. Millions of people had valuable knowledge and skills. This meant that there were plenty of human resources to run the country's businesses.

Capital resources are the tools and machines that companies use to produce goods and services. The money used to buy this equipment is also a capital resource. Think about a steel company, for example. A furnace that is used to make steel is a capital resource. So is the money that is used to buy the furnace.

During the rise of big business, banks helped companies get the capital resources they needed. **J. P. Morgan** was the country's richest and most powerful banker. Morgan's banks invested hundreds of millions of dollars in railroads, steel mills, and other companies. This helped American industries keep growing.

▶ **J. P. Morgan**

REVIEW Define the three types of resources discussed on this page. *Main Idea and Details*

▶ **These women made detachable shirt collars in a factory in Troy, New York, in 1890.**

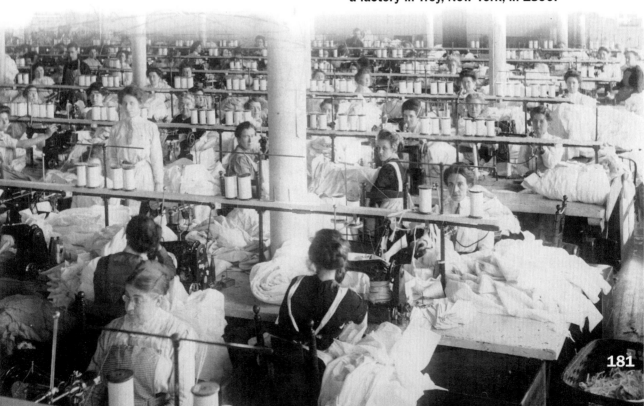

Help Wanted

The rise of big business in the late 1800s changed the United States. Before the Civil War, most Americans lived and worked on farms. By 1900 more Americans worked in industries than on farms. The United States had become the world's biggest producer of manufactured goods. By the early 1900s, businesses in the United States were producing about 35 percent of all the manufactured goods in the world. The United States economy was one of the strongest and fastest growing economies in the world.

Growing industries created millions of new jobs in American cities. Many people moved from rural areas to cities to take these jobs. The jobs also attracted people from other countries. Immigrants came from all over the world to find new opportunities in the United States. You will read about this "job rush," along with some of the immigrants' stories, in the next lesson.

REVIEW How did growing businesses lead to the growth of cities?
Draw Conclusions

Summarize the Lesson

1859 Oil was found in Pennsylvania, leading to the rise of a huge new industry.

1893 The United States had five transcontinental railroad lines and more than 160,000 miles of railroad track.

1900 The rise of big business made the United States the world's leading producer of manufactured goods.

LESSON 2   REVIEW

Check Facts and Main Ideas

1. Main Idea and Details Complete the chart below by filling in three details about the rise of big business in the United States.

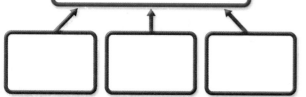

Entrepreneurs built big businesses in many industries during the late 1800s and early 1900s.

2. How was Andrew Carnegie able to produce huge amounts of steel at low prices?

3. How did railroads help the United States economy grow?

4. What freedoms do business owners and **consumers** have in a **free enterprise** system?

5. Critical Thinking: Cause and Effect What are some ways that the rise of big business changed the United States?

Link to ⚭ Mathematics

Measure the Railroad In 1865 the United States had 35,000 miles of railroad track. By 1890 the United States had 167,000 miles of track. How many miles of track were built in this 25-year period? What was the average number of miles of track built each year?

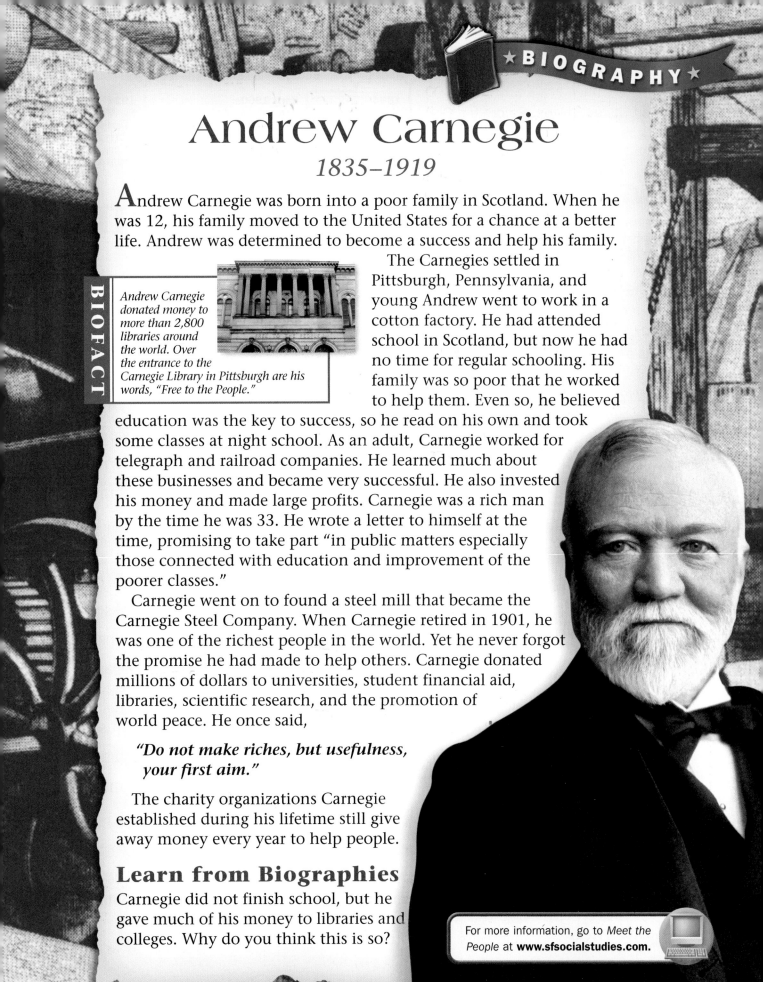

Andrew Carnegie
1835–1919

Andrew Carnegie was born into a poor family in Scotland. When he was 12, his family moved to the United States for a chance at a better life. Andrew was determined to become a success and help his family.

The Carnegies settled in Pittsburgh, Pennsylvania, and young Andrew went to work in a cotton factory. He had attended school in Scotland, but now he had no time for regular schooling. His family was so poor that he worked to help them. Even so, he believed education was the key to success, so he read on his own and took some classes at night school. As an adult, Carnegie worked for telegraph and railroad companies. He learned much about these businesses and became very successful. He also invested his money and made large profits. Carnegie was a rich man by the time he was 33. He wrote a letter to himself at the time, promising to take part "in public matters especially those connected with education and improvement of the poorer classes."

Carnegie went on to found a steel mill that became the Carnegie Steel Company. When Carnegie retired in 1901, he was one of the richest people in the world. Yet he never forgot the promise he had made to help others. Carnegie donated millions of dollars to universities, student financial aid, libraries, scientific research, and the promotion of world peace. He once said,

> *"Do not make riches, but usefulness, your first aim."*

The charity organizations Carnegie established during his lifetime still give away money every year to help people.

Learn from Biographies
Carnegie did not finish school, but he gave much of his money to libraries and colleges. Why do you think this is so?

For more information, go to *Meet the People* at **www.sfsocialstudies.com.**

Angel Island
Ellis Island

1890

1894
Mary Antin arrives in the United States.

Early 1900s
More than half of the people in most big Americans cities are immigrants or children of immigrants.

1924
The United States government passes a law limiting immigration.

1925

PREVIEW

Focus on the Main Idea
During the late 1800s and early 1900s, millions of immigrants arrived in the United States in search of freedom and opportunity.

PLACES
Ellis Island
Angel Island

PEOPLE
Mary Antin

VOCABULARY
prejudice
diversity

New Americans

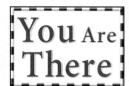

You Are There

Nathan Nussenbaum stands on a crowded New York City street. He stares at the tall buildings and rushing crowds of people.

The year is 1896. Nathan, a Jewish teenager from Austria, has just arrived in the United States. He has a total of nine dollars in his pocket. He speaks German and Yiddish—a language spoken by many Jews in Europe—but knows almost no English. He knows no one in this country.

He walks through the busy streets. Every time he hears the word *listen* he turns around. He thinks people are saying "Nisn," which is how you say the name Nathan in Yiddish. He soon realizes that people are not talking to him.

Nathan knows that it will be difficult to adjust to life in the United States. But he is not discouraged. "I was determined to try my luck in this country," he later said.

Summarize As you read, keep track of the different reasons that immigrants came to the United States.

New Immigrants

Nathan Nussenbaum was one of more than 23 million immigrants who arrived in the United States between 1880 and 1920. The entire population of the United States in 1880 was about 50 million, so this meant there was one new immigrant for every two people already in the country!

Before 1890 most immigrants came from the countries of northern Europe, including Ireland, Great Britain, Germany, and Sweden. After 1890 most came from southern and eastern European countries, such as Italy, Austria-Hungary, and Russia. However, not all immigrants who arrived at this time were European. People moved south from Canada and north from Mexico, Cuba, and Puerto Rico. Others came to the United States from China, Japan, and the Philippines.

Immigrants came for different reasons. Many were escaping poverty, hunger, or lack of jobs. For them, the farms and factories of the United States offered the hope of an income, food, and work. Others were escaping violence, war, or injustice.

Many Jewish immigrants left Europe to escape mistreatment because of their religion. A young immigrant named **Mary Antin** wrote that she had not been allowed to attend school in Russia because she was Jewish. In 1894 Antin and her family moved to Boston, Massachusetts, in search of a better life. You will read Antin's story in the Biography on page 191.

Most immigrants did not expect to find easy riches in the United States. They did expect to find jobs, political and religious freedom, and even some adventure. They came hoping for opportunities to make better lives for themselves and their families. Often that is just what they found.

REVIEW What opportunities did immigrants hope to find in the United States?
Main Idea and Details

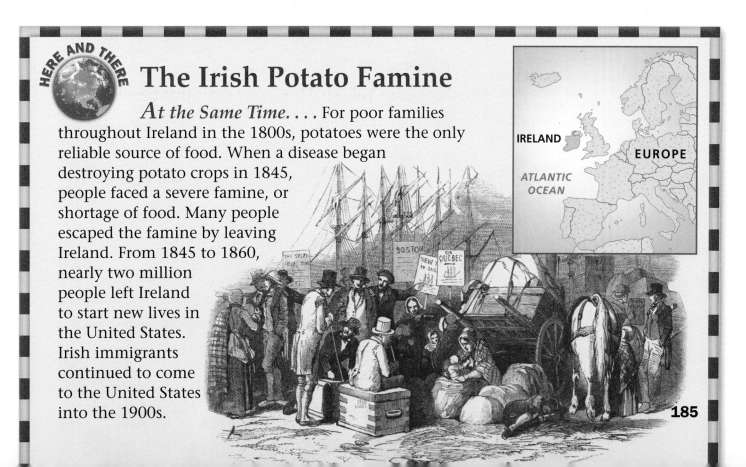

HERE AND THERE The Irish Potato Famine

At the Same Time. . . . For poor families throughout Ireland in the 1800s, potatoes were the only reliable source of food. When a disease began destroying potato crops in 1845, people faced a severe famine, or shortage of food. Many people escaped the famine by leaving Ireland. From 1845 to 1860, nearly two million people left Ireland to start new lives in the United States. Irish immigrants continued to come to the United States into the 1900s.

IRELAND

EUROPE

ATLANTIC OCEAN

185

Ellis Island

When he was 15 years old, Abraham Hyman (HEYE min) left his home in Russia and sailed to the United States. Like millions of immigrants from Europe in the late 1800s and early 1900s, Hyman and his family were poor. He could only afford a steerage class boat ticket. Steerage passengers were packed into crowded rooms beneath the deck of the ship. "The boat [ride] was about fifteen, sixteen days [long]," Hyman remembered. "It was bad. You wouldn't want to put pigs in it."

Most ships carrying immigrants from Europe landed in New York City. As the ships sailed into New York Harbor, passengers rushed to the deck to see the Statue of Liberty, a famous symbol of the United States. A young immigrant from Italy named Edward Corsi never forgot this moment:

> *"Mothers and fathers lifted up babies so that they too could see, off to the left, the Statue of Liberty."*

When their ships landed in New York, most immigrants were taken by ferry boat to **Ellis Island**. This small island in New York Harbor was an immigration station—a place immigrants had to go before getting permission to enter the country. At Ellis Island, doctors checked immigrants for dangerous diseases. Government officials asked immigrants questions about where they were from, what kind of work they did, and where they planned to live.

Immigrants often spent an entire day waiting in the long lines at Ellis Island. Once the examinations were over, they took a ferry back to New York City. Now they could begin their new lives in the United States.

REVIEW After leaving Europe, what steps did immigrants have to take before entering the United States? ⟳ Sequence

▶ Immigrants being checked at Ellis Island often ate at the huge dining hall (*above right*). Today visitors can tour the old immigration station, which is now a museum of immigration history on Ellis Island.

Angel Island

For immigrants from China in the early 1900s, the first stop was **Angel Island** in San Francisco Bay. At that time, a law limited the number of Chinese immigrants who could enter the United States. To get permission to enter, most Chinese immigrants had to prove that they had family members already living in the United States. Until they could prove this, they were held at Angel Island.

Inspectors questioned immigrants before they allowed them to leave the island. For example, if a young man said his father lived in San Francisco, inspectors would ask him many questions about his family life in China. Inspectors asked simple questions such as "How many people are in your family?" They also asked very detailed questions such as "How many windows did your house have?" or "Where do all your family members sleep?" Then the inspectors would ask the young man's father the same questions and compare the answers.

▶ **Most immigrants at Angel Island were Chinese, but some came from other countries in Asia, as did these immigrants from Japan.**

While waiting on Angel Island, some people expressed their frustration and anger by carving poems on the wooden walls. One person wrote,

> *"Counting on my fingers, several months have elapsed [passed].*
> *Still I am at the beginning of the road."*

Many Chinese immigrants spent weeks or months on Angel Island. One immigrant, who was there for about a month, he summed up the feelings of many immigrants when he said, "All of us—all we wanted was to stay in this country."

REVIEW Why did it take a long time for some people to leave Angel Island?
Main Idea and Details

▶ **This monument honors the immigrants who came through Angel Island. It says in Chinese, "Leaving their homes and villages, they crossed the ocean, only to endure confinement in these barracks [buildings]. Conquering frontiers and barriers, they pioneered a new life by the Golden Gate."**

A New World

What was it like for immigrants to arrive in a big American city in the late 1800s or early 1900s? For many, it was like stepping into a different world. Immigrants often came from small farming villages. Now they were suddenly surrounded by skyscrapers, electric streetcars, automobiles, and crowds of people rushing in all directions. An immigrant from Poland named Walter Mrozowski (mroh ZOW skee) felt very far from home when he first saw New York City. "I was in a new world," he said.

Like most recent arrivals, Mrozowski needed to do two things right away—find a place to live and find a job. Some immigrants could go to friends or relatives for help. Those who did not know anyone usually headed to a neighborhood where there were other people from their homeland. Living in a community where the language and traditions were familiar made it a little easier to adjust to life in a new country.

After finding a place to live, most immigrants began looking for work. Many found jobs in the country's busy railroads, factories, and mines. Others started their own small businesses. If families did not have enough money to open a store, they could sell goods from pushcarts. Pushcarts were used to sell everything from food and clothing, to tools and eyeglasses. Streets in

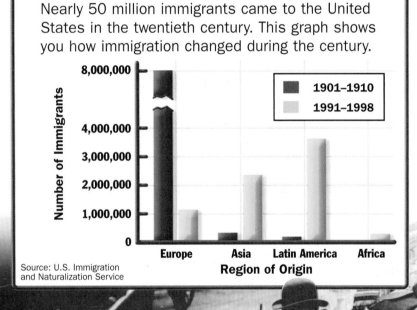

Immigration in the Twentieth Century

Nearly 50 million immigrants came to the United States in the twentieth century. This graph shows you how immigration changed during the century.

Number of Immigrants

8,000,000
4,000,000
3,000,000
2,000,000
1,000,000
0

■ 1901–1910
▨ 1991–1998

Europe   Asia   Latin America   Africa
Region of Origin

Source: U.S. Immigration and Naturalization Service

GRAPH SKILL *About how many Europeans came to the United States between 1901 and 1910?*

▶ Busy street markets were common in immigrant neighborhoods.

▶ These immigrants ran a grocery store in San Francisco, California, in 1877.

immigrant neighborhoods were often lined with pushcarts and crowded with shoppers shouting to be heard in many different languages.

After finding a place to live and a job, immigrants could start thinking about how to improve their lives. Like so many people, 17-year-old Howard Ellis came to the United States with a dream. "I wanted to be a medical man," he said. Ellis came here from the West Indies in 1911. First he found a job as an elevator operator. Then he began studying. At the age of 26, he graduated from medical school. At first, Ellis had a hard time finding a job as a doctor. "They weren't hiring black doctors," he said. "I went back to work as an elevator operator. With a medical license!" Ellis never quit, though, and he finally got a job in a hospital.

Howard Ellis was not alone. Many immigrants faced the hardship of prejudice. **Prejudice** is an unfair negative opinion about a group of people. For example, job advertisements sometimes included phrases like "No Irish need apply." Immigrants from many different countries faced prejudice.

Like everyone else who was trying to get ahead in the growing cities, immigrants had to work long hours to make a living. Many worked 12 hours a day. Often, they would also go to school at night. It was hard to do well in school after such a long day of work, but these workers realized that an education was one key to a better life. Hard work was the other key. Though life remained hard for many, a large number of immigrants found great success in their new country.

REVIEW After arriving in New York, what two things did most recent arrivals need to do right away? ⟳ Sequence

▶ This man sold potatoes from a pushcart in an immigrant neighborhood in New York City.

189

Immigration and Diversity

From the 1880s through the 1920s, more immigrants arrived in the United States than at any other time in American history. Immigrants knew that life in a new country would be difficult. But they also knew that the United States offered freedoms and opportunities that they would not have found anywhere else in the world.

By the early 1900s, more than half of the people in most big American cities were immigrants or children of immigrants. More people of Irish background lived in New York City than in Dublin, Ireland's biggest city. Los Angeles, California, had the world's second-largest Mexican population—second only to Mexico City, Mexico. These examples show how immigrants contributed to the **diversity,** or variety, of the American population.

This period of largely unregulated immigration came to an end in 1924. The United States government passed new laws that put a limit on the number of immigrants who could enter the country each year.

REVIEW How did immigration affect the population of big American cities?
Cause and Effect

Summarize the Lesson

1894 Mary Antin was one of 23 million immigrants to arrive in the United States in the late 1800s and early 1900s.

Early 1900s More than half of the people in most big Americans cities were immigrants or children of immigrants.

1924 The period of largely unregulated immigration ended when the United States government passed a law limiting immigration.

LESSON 3 ⟩ REVIEW

Check Facts and Main Ideas

1. Summarize Complete the chart below by filling in reasons that immigrants came to the United States.

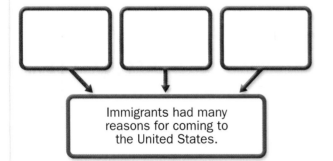

Immigrants had many reasons for coming to the United States.

2. How were Ellis Island and Angel Island similar? How were they different?

3. How did **prejudice** create problems for some immigrants in the late 1800s and early 1900s?

4. Why did the period of largely unregulated immigration come to an end in the 1920s?

5. Critical Thinking: *Express Ideas* Why do you think so many people were willing to face the challenge of starting new lives in the United States?

Link to ⟶ Writing

Write a Letter Suppose the year is 1896 and you are a new immigrant in the United States. Write a letter home explaining why you decided to come to the United States. Describe what you have seen so far and how you feel about it. Explain what your plans are for the future.

Mary Antin
1881–1949

Thirteen-year-old Mary Antin could not believe her eyes. After the Antins spent years waiting and hoping, her mother finally had ship tickets to take the whole family to the United States. Mary's father had sent the tickets. He had gone to Boston, Massachusetts, to find work three years earlier. Mary's family was Jewish, and because of their religion they were denied many rights in their homeland of Russia. There was always the danger of pogroms, or organized attacks against Jews. Mary's father believed that they would all have better lives in the United States.

BIOFACT

Mary Antin's autobiography, The Promised Land, *sold more than 80,000 copies.*

Before Mary left for the United States, her uncle made her promise that she would write down everything about her journey. Just to reach the ship was difficult, and Mary was often scared. She and her family sometimes traveled in trains so crowded that there was no room to move.

Finally, the Antins boarded a ship to cross the Atlantic Ocean. Mary later described the end of their journey:

> *"And so suffering, fearing, brooding, rejoicing, we crept nearer and nearer to the coveted [desired] shore, until, on a glorious May morning, six weeks after our departure from [Russia], our eyes beheld the Promised Land, and my father received us in his arms."*

Mary kept her promise to her uncle and wrote a long letter about the trip that brought her to a new land. Later she would use a copy of this letter as a basis for several successful books about her experiences.

Learn from Biographies

What did Mary mean when she said, "Our eyes beheld the Promised Land"?

For more information, go to *Meet the People* at **www.sfsocialstudies.com.**

1880   1890

1882
The first Labor Day celebration is held in New York City.

1886
Samuel Gompers forms the American Federation of Labor.

1892
Homestead Strike at Carnegie's Homestead Steel Works

New York City

• Homestead

PREVIEW

Focus on the Main Idea
Workers formed labor unions to fight for better wages and working conditions.

PLACES
Homestead, Pennsylvania
New York, New York

PEOPLE
Lewis Hine
Samuel Gompers
Mary Harris Jones

VOCABULARY
sweatshop
labor union
strike

The Labor Movement

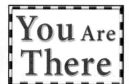 The place is New York City. The time is the early 1900s. A teenager named Rose Cohen walks into a busy, noisy clothing factory. She sees a man standing at a table, folding coats. He looks up at her and demands, "Yes? What do you want?"

Rose explains that she is here for her first day of work. The man hands her pieces of a coat that need to be sewn together. "Let's see what you can do," he says.

Rose sits down at a crowded table and begins working. When she finishes sewing the coat, the man inspects her work. Then he gives her two more coats to sew. After twelve hours at the work table, Rose begins to wonder if the day will ever end. "My neck felt stiff and my back ached," she later said. "From this hour a hard life began for me."

Draw Conclusions As you read, think about the reasons why some people formed unions and went on strike.

▶ **These women worked in a sweatshop in New York City. The front page headline** (right) **describes the fire at the Triangle Shirtwaist Company.**

Factories and Sweatshops

As you have read, big businesses created millions of new jobs in the late 1800s and early 1900s. Both immigrants and people born in the United States found work in factories and mines. However, it was a difficult time for many workers.

You know about the success of Andrew Carnegie's steel mills. Workers at Carnegie's mills, however, barely earned enough money to survive. At Carnegie's Homestead Steel Works in **Homestead, Pennsylvania,** steelworkers put in 12-hour days, seven days a week. The average salary was only about $10 a week.

Many women worked in clothing factories, where they earned even less. Women operated sewing machines in hot, cramped workshops known as **sweatshops.** A teenager named Sadie Frowne worked in a sweatshop in **New York, New York.** Frowne hoped to be able to sew fast enough to earn $7 a week. She described her experience,

"The machines go like mad all day because the faster you work the more money you can get. Sometimes in my haste I get a finger caught and the needle goes right through it. . . . I bind the finger up with a piece of cotton and go on working."

Sweatshops could be very dangerous places to work. At a sweatshop run by the Triangle Shirtwaist Company in New York City, workers were worried about the danger of fires. They asked the owners to build fire escapes and keep the workshop doors unlocked. The owners refused. On a Saturday afternoon in March 1911, a fire started. Workers were trapped inside. The fire killed almost 150 people, mostly young women.

REVIEW Why were the late 1800s and early 1900s a difficult time for workers?
Summarize

Children at Work

Because wages were so low, children often had to work to help support their families. In 1900 about two million children under the age of 16 were working in the United States. Children were paid even less money than adults.

Children did all kinds of jobs. Many worked in textile mills, where machines were used to weave thread into cloth for clothing. Others worked canning fruits and vegetables, opening oyster shells, or picking crops on farms. In coal mining towns, young children worked as "breaker boys." After coal was brought up from the mines, it was broken up into small pieces. Breaker boys sat on benches and sorted through the coal. Their job was to pick out the rocks and keep only the clean coal.

At most of these jobs, children worked 12 or more hours a day for just 10 to 20 cents a day. There was no time for school. The working conditions were often unhealthy or dangerous. Breaker boys, for example, breathed in coal dust all day, often damaging their lungs. Children in textile mills could get their fingers caught in the spinning machines.

▶ Some people protested against child labor.

▶ Lewis Hine photographed these boys working in a cotton mill in Georgia.

Some people began speaking out against child labor. A New York City schoolteacher named **Lewis Hine** was a leader in this movement. Hine believed that more people would oppose child labor if they knew how terrible children's working conditions really were. "I wanted to show the things that had to be corrected," he said. Hine spent 12 years traveling around the United States, taking pictures of children at work. His powerful photographs helped convince many people to demand an end to child labor. You will read more about the struggle to end child labor in Issues and Viewpoints following this lesson.

REVIEW What did Lewis Hine hope to accomplish with his photographs? **Draw Conclusions**

Labor Unions

Low wages, long workdays, and disasters like the Triangle Shirtwaist Company fire encouraged many workers to join labor unions. *Labor* is another word for "work." In **labor unions,** people worked to gain improved working conditions and better wages. Labor unions also worked to end child labor.

One of the early union leaders in the United States was **Samuel Gompers.** As a teenager, Gompers worked in a cigar factory in New York City. He helped form a union of cigar factory workers. When owners lowered cigar makers' wages in 1877, Gompers led his union on a strike. In a **strike,** workers refuse to work to try to force business owners to meet their demands.

This strike was not successful. Factory owners ignored the union's demand for better wages. Gompers realized that unions would have more power if they joined together. In 1886 Gompers brought many workers' unions together to form the American

▶ **Samuel Gompers (***below***) and Mary Harris Jones (***above right***) helped workers join labor unions.**

▶ **Mary Harris Jones**

Federation of Labor, or AFL. The AFL fought for better wages, an 8-hour work day, safer working conditions, and an end to child labor.

At the same time, a union called the United Mine Workers was struggling to improve working conditions for coal miners. A woman named **Mary Harris Jones** helped lead this effort. When she was in her 50s, Jones began traveling to coal mining towns in the Appalachian Mountains. "Join the union, boys," she urged the miners. Miners started calling her "Mother Jones."

Managers of coal mining companies did not usually welcome the sight of Mother Jones. They did not want their workers forming unions or going on strike. At one mining camp, Jones was warned that the manager did not want to see her around his mine. Jones refused to leave. "I am not coming to see him anyway," she replied. "I am coming to see the miners." Even when she was in her 90s, Jones continued organizing unions and speaking out in support of better treatment for workers.

REVIEW Why did Samuel Gompers want many labor unions to join together?
Main Idea and Details

Going on Strike

Tensions between striking workers and business owners sometimes led to violence. This happened at Andrew Carnegie's Homestead Steel Works in 1892. The Homestead Strike is remembered as one of the most famous strikes in American history.

The price of steel was falling in the early 1890s. Carnegie and his partner, Henry Frick, decided to lower wages at Homestead. Union workers did not think this wage cut was fair. They voted to go on strike. Carnegie was out of the country, so Henry Frick handled the strike. He refused to talk with striking workers. Instead, he hired armed guards to break up the strike. When the guards arrived at night, thousands of striking workers were waiting for them. The guards and workers fought, and people on both sides were killed.

The Homestead Strike lasted several months. Finally, the workers decided to give up the strike. Many years passed before a new union was formed at the Homestead plant.

Unlike the Homestead Strike, most strikes were settled peacefully. One example is the "newsies" strike of 1899. Newsies were children who sold newspapers on the street. In New York City, newsies could buy 100 newspapers for 50 cents. Then they sold as many as they could for one cent each.

Trouble started when the *New York World* and *New York Journal* decided to raise the price they charged to newsies. The newspaper owners said that 100 newspapers would now cost newsies 60 cents. Angry newsies gathered in a city park and voted to go on strike. They gained public support by handing out flyers that said, "Help us in our struggle to get fair play by not buying the *Journal* or the *World*."

After two weeks, sales of the two newspapers had fallen sharply. The newspaper owners decided to offer a deal. One hundred newspapers would still cost 60 cents, but the newspaper companies would now buy back any papers the newsies were not able to sell. Newsies thought this was fair, and they went back to work.

REVIEW How were the Homestead Strike and newsies strike similar? How were they different? **Compare and Contrast**

▶ **The diversity of workers is reflected in the signs they carried during this 1913 strike.**

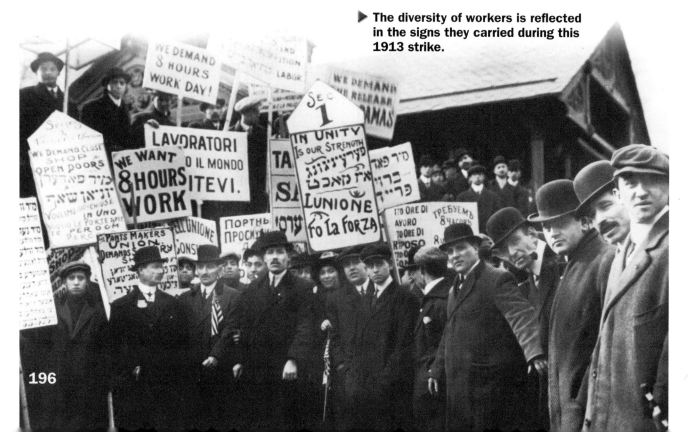

Improving Conditions

Unions continued to gain members in the early 1900s. Many business owners, religious organizations, and political leaders also helped improve life for workers. New laws shortened hours and improved safety in the workplace.

Unions also created a new holiday—Labor Day. The first Labor Day celebration was held in New York City in September 1882. Thousands of workers paraded through the streets carrying signs saying "Shorter Hours, Fairer Pay" and "Stop Child Labor." Within a few years, workers were holding Labor Day celebrations in many cities. In 1894 Congress declared Labor Day to be an official national holiday. We still celebrate Labor Day on the first Monday in September.

REVIEW Explain how Labor Day became a national holiday. **Summarize**

▶ **The first Labor Day celebration was held in New York City in 1882.**

Summarize the Lesson

1882 The first Labor Day celebration was held in New York City.

1886 Under the leadership of Samuel Gompers, many unions joined together to form the American Federation of Labor.

1892 The Homestead Strike at Carnegie's Homestead Steel Works led to violence between workers and guards.

LESSON 4 REVIEW

Check Facts and Main Ideas

1. Draw Conclusions Complete the chart below on a separate sheet of paper. Fill in a conclusion that could be drawn from the information given.

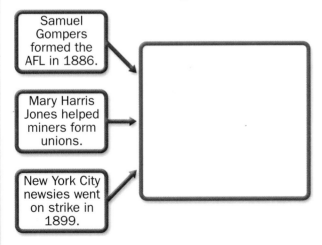

Samuel Gompers formed the AFL in 1886.

Mary Harris Jones helped miners form unions.

New York City newsies went on strike in 1899.

2. What conditions led to the rise of **labor unions**?

3. What were the main goals of labor unions such as the AFL?

4. In what ways did conditions begin to improve for workers in the early 1900s?

5. Critical Thinking: *Evaluate* Why do you think a disaster like the Triangle Shirtwaist Factory fire might have encouraged people to join unions?

Link to 🔗 Citizenship

Research Changing Laws Citizens worked hard to change child labor laws in the early 1900s. Do research to find out about a national law called the Fair Labor Standards Act. What year was this law passed? What did it do?

Working Against Child Labor

People around the world continue to work to end child labor.

In 1871, when she was only 12 years old, Florence Kelley saw something that would change her life. Her father took her to a glassmaking factory. While the adults admired the huge furnaces, Florence's eyes saw something else. She saw boys no bigger than herself doing hard and dangerous work.

By 1900 two million children under the age of 16 were working in the fields, factories, mills, and mines of the United States. Florence Kelley became one of the first people in the nation to fight against child labor. She wrote a report about child labor in her neighborhood in Chicago. Kelley's report pushed the state of Illinois to pass the first law forbidding child labor.

However, businesses in other states did not have that law, and some businesses in Illinois did not obey the law. So Florence Kelley urged people to boycott products made with child labor.

Child labor is rare in the United States today, but it still occurs in poorer countries. Following in Florence Kelley's footsteps, however, many people are fighting to put an end to child labor wherever it is happening.

"The children make our shoes in the shoe factories; they knit our stockings . . . in the knitting factories. . . . They carry bundles of garments from the factories to the tenements . . . robbed of school life that they may work for us."

Florence Kelley, *1905*

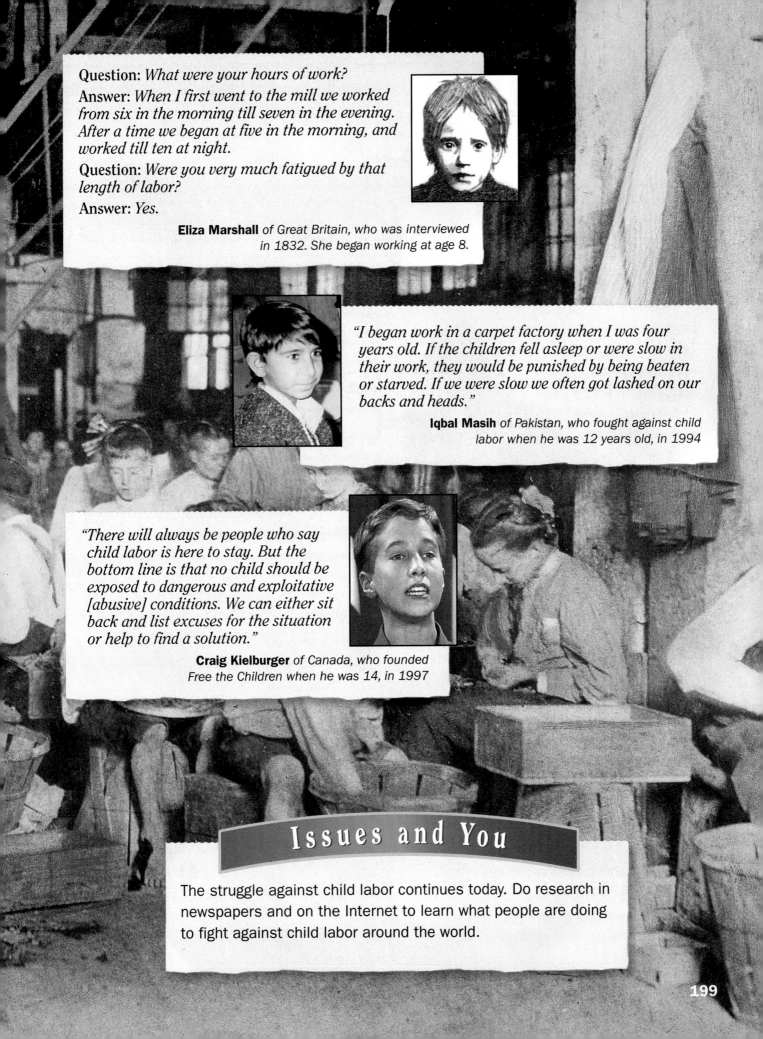

Question: *What were your hours of work?*

Answer: *When I first went to the mill we worked from six in the morning till seven in the evening. After a time we began at five in the morning, and worked till ten at night.*

Question: *Were you very much fatigued by that length of labor?*

Answer: *Yes.*

Eliza Marshall *of Great Britain, who was interviewed in 1832. She began working at age 8.*

"I began work in a carpet factory when I was four years old. If the children fell asleep or were slow in their work, they would be punished by being beaten or starved. If we were slow we often got lashed on our backs and heads."

Iqbal Masih *of Pakistan, who fought against child labor when he was 12 years old, in 1994*

"There will always be people who say child labor is here to stay. But the bottom line is that no child should be exposed to dangerous and exploitative [abusive] conditions. We can either sit back and list excuses for the situation or help to find a solution."

Craig Kielburger *of Canada, who founded Free the Children when he was 14, in 1997*

Issues and You

The struggle against child labor continues today. Do research in newspapers and on the Internet to learn what people are doing to fight against child labor around the world.

1855   1865   1875

1856
Henry Bessemer develops a new way to make steel.

1876
Alexander Graham Bell invents the telephone.

1879
Thomas Edison invents a working light bulb.

Chapter Summary

Sequence

On a separate sheet of paper, copy the chart and place the following events in the sequence in which they happened. Include the date for each one.

▶ **An early radio**

- Thomas Edison begins testing his power station in New York City.
- Guglielmo Marconi invents the radio.
- John D. Rockefeller builds his first oil refinery in Cleveland, Ohio.
- The United States government passes a law limiting immigration.
- Samuel Gompers forms the American Federation of Labor.
- Congress declares Labor Day an official holiday.

Vocabulary

On a separate sheet of paper, write **T** for each sentence that correctly defines the underlined word and **F** for each definition that is false. If false, rewrite the definition so it is correct.

1 A <u>monopoly</u> is when several companies have control of one industry.

2 A <u>consumer</u> is a person who buys or uses goods and services.

3 <u>Diversity</u> is an unfair negative opinion about a group of people.

4 <u>Sweatshops</u> are crowded and often unsafe workshops.

5 When workers go on <u>strike</u>, they work longer hours than usual.

People and Places

Write a sentence explaining the role of each of the following people or places in the changing United States of the late 1800s and early 1900s. You may use two or more in a single sentence.

1 Alexander Graham Bell (p. 167)

2 Menlo Park, New Jersey (p. 168)

3 Orville Wright (p. 172)

4 Pittsburgh, Pennsylvania (p. 177)

5 William Randolph Hearst (p. 180)

6 Ellis Island (p. 186)

7 Angel Island (p. 187)

8 Lewis Hine (p. 194)

1885	1895	1905	1915

1882
The first Labor Day celebration is held in New York City.

1892
The Homestead Strike occurs.

1900
About 2 million children under age 16 are working in the United States.

1903
The Wright Brothers build the world's first successful airplane.

1906
Madame C. J. Walker begins bottling shampoo and other products in her attic.

Facts and Main Ideas

1 What steps did Andrew Carnegie take to produce steel at the lowest possible cost?

2 How were the experiences of immigrants at Ellis Island and Angel Island alike and different?

3 **Time Line** How many years after the first Labor Day celebration did the Homestead Strike occur?

4 **Main Idea** What were some inventions that brought about major changes in the way people lived in the late 1800s and early 1900s?

5 **Main Idea** What industries did large business owners help build in the late 1800s?

6 **Main Idea** What challenges did many immigrants face when they arrived in the United States?

7 **Main Idea** Why did some workers form labor unions in the late 1800s?

8 **Critical Thinking:** *Draw Conclusions* Why do you think Lewis Hine's photographs of children at work helped convince people to put an end to child labor?

Apply Skills

Reread page 180 about free enterprise. Then answer the questions based on the outline.

I. George Westinghouse
  A. Westinghouse Electric Company
    1. Formed in 1886
    2. Developed alternating current to deliver electricity to homes
  B. "War of the Currents"
    1. _____
    2. Consumers chose Westinghouse's better product

II. Madame C. J. Walker
  A. _____
    1. Began bottling shampoo in her attic in 1906
    2. Sold her products door-to-door
  B. Success
    1. Ten years later she had thousands of employees
    2. First African American woman to become a millionaire

1 What detail would you write next to *1*?

2 What main idea belongs next to *A*?

3 How did Madame C. J. Walker start her business?

Write About History

1 **Write a short story** describing what it would have been like to see the first successful airplane flight.

2 **Write a letter to a friend** back home describing your experience as an immigrant at Ellis Island or Angel Island.

3 **Write an editorial** trying to convince workers either to join or not to join a labor union.

Internet Activity

To get help with vocabulary, people, and terms, select dictionary or encyclopedia from *Social Studies Library* at **www.sfsocialstudies.com.**

End with a Song

Red River Valley

If you had worked on the cattle drives of the 1800s, you would probably have known lots of cowboy songs. Cowboys sang these songs to keep their cattle calm. And they sang to pass the time during the long, lonely days and nights on the trail. What does the cowboy song "Red River Valley" tell you about what life was like for cowboys?

VERSE

1. From this val - ley they say you are go - ing, — We will
2. Won't you think of the val - ley you're leav - ing? — Oh, how

miss your bright eyes and sweet smile; For they say you are tak - ing the
lone - ly, how sad it will be. Oh, — think of the fond heart you're

sun - shine, — That bright - ens our path - way a - while.
break - ing, — And the grief you are causing me to see.

REFRAIN

Come and sit by my side if you love me, — Do not

has - ten to bid me a - dieu; But re - mem - ber the Red Riv - er

Val - ley — And the girl that has loved you so true.

203

Main Ideas and Vocabulary

TEST PREP

Read the passage below and use it to answer the questions that follow.

From the middle to late 1800s, changes in technology helped people in the United States stay connected. The Pony Express began in 1860, but was replaced by the transcontinental telegraph only one year later. By 1869 the transcontinental railroad stretched from one coast of the country to the other.

As the West became easier to reach, more people decided to settle there. Pioneers moved to the Great Plains to farm, and miners rushed to the West to find gold. For Native Americans, these changes led to the loss of their traditional lands. When the government forced Native Americans to move to <u>reservations</u>, many fought to keep their homelands.

Inventors and business leaders also changed how people lived. In 1876 Alexander Graham Bell invented the telephone. Automobiles and electric streetcars moved people around faster than before. <u>Entrepreneurs</u> such as Andrew Carnegie and John D. Rockefeller made millions of dollars in the steel and oil businesses. Millions of people worked in new and growing industries.

Many of the workers in growing industries were immigrants. In the late 1800s and early 1900s, millions of immigrants came to the United States in search of opportunities. They often faced prejudice. In 1924 the United States passed a law limiting immigration.

Workers formed labor unions in the late 1800s to fight for better working conditions, shorter hours, and higher pay. Labor Day, made an official holiday in 1894, recognizes the contributions of workers across the country.

1 According to the passage, why did workers start labor unions?
  A to get new jobs
  B to fight for better working conditions
  C to protest against Labor Day
  D to work on new inventions

2 In the passage, the word <u>reservation</u> means—
  A land in the mountains
  B land on the Great Plains
  C farms
  D land set aside for Native Americans

3 In the passage, the word <u>entrepreneurs</u> means—
  A railroad workers
  B immigrants
  C people who start new businesses, hoping to make a profit
  D people who move to the Great Plains

4 According to the passage, technology
  A caused changes in the United States
  B helped the Native Americans keep their homelands
  C was not important in the late 1800s
  D caused people to leave the country

People and Places

Match each person and place to its definition.

1. **Promontory Point, Utah Territory** (p. 133)

2. **Virginia City, Nevada** (p. 152)

3. **Crazy Horse** (p. 156)

4. **Lewis Latimer** (p. 168)

5. **Kitty Hawk, North Carolina** (p. 172)

6. **Mary Antin** (p. 185)

a. location of the first airplane flight

b. inventor of a long-lasting filament for light bulbs

c. large boom town

d. place where the transcontinental railroad was completed

e. immigrant from Russia

f. leader of the Lakota at the Battle of Little Bighorn

Apply Skills

Write an Outline Choose a page from a lesson in this unit. Reread the page and make note of the main ideas and the facts that support the main ideas. On a sheet of paper, use your notes to write an outline of the page you chose. Use Roman numerals to identify the main ideas, capital letters for subtopics, and numbers for important details.

The First Telephone
I. Alexander Graham Bell's childhood
   A. Tried to teach dog to speak
   B. Learned from failures, kept trying

II. _____
   A. _____
     1. _____
     2. _____
   B. _____
     1. _____
     2. _____

Write and Share

Write a Class Newspaper Suppose you were a newspaper reporter in the late 1800s. Work with a group in your class to write an article about a business leader you read about in the unit. Conduct research to find out about how the leader's business affected the industry and its workers. When all the articles are finished, work together as a class to paste the articles into a newspaper. Remember to include headlines with your article, and decide together as a class what to call the newspaper. You can include pictures, drawings, and captions to help bring the stories to life.

Read on Your Own

Look for books like these in the library.

Vision of Beauty: The Story of Sarah Breedlove Walker

Ten Mile Day and the Building of the Transcontinental Railroad by Mary Ann Fraser

Alexander Graham Bell: An Inventive Life Elizabeth MacLeod

UNIT 2 Project

Inventions Change the Country

Advertise a product from the past.

1 Form a group and choose an invention from the late 1800s or early 1900s that you read about in this unit.

2 Research the invention and describe what made the invention popular or revolutionary. Write who invented it and why, how it helped people, if it saved time or money, and if it changed the world.

3 Make a poster or large advertisement for this invention. Include a picture of the product.

4 Present your advertisement to the class. You may make the presentation as if you were the inventor.

The First Typewriter

Internet Activity

Explore immigration to the United States. Go to **www.sfsocialstudies.com/activities** and select your grade and unit.

Expansion and Change

What kinds of changes do nations face?

UNIT 3

Begin with a Primary Source

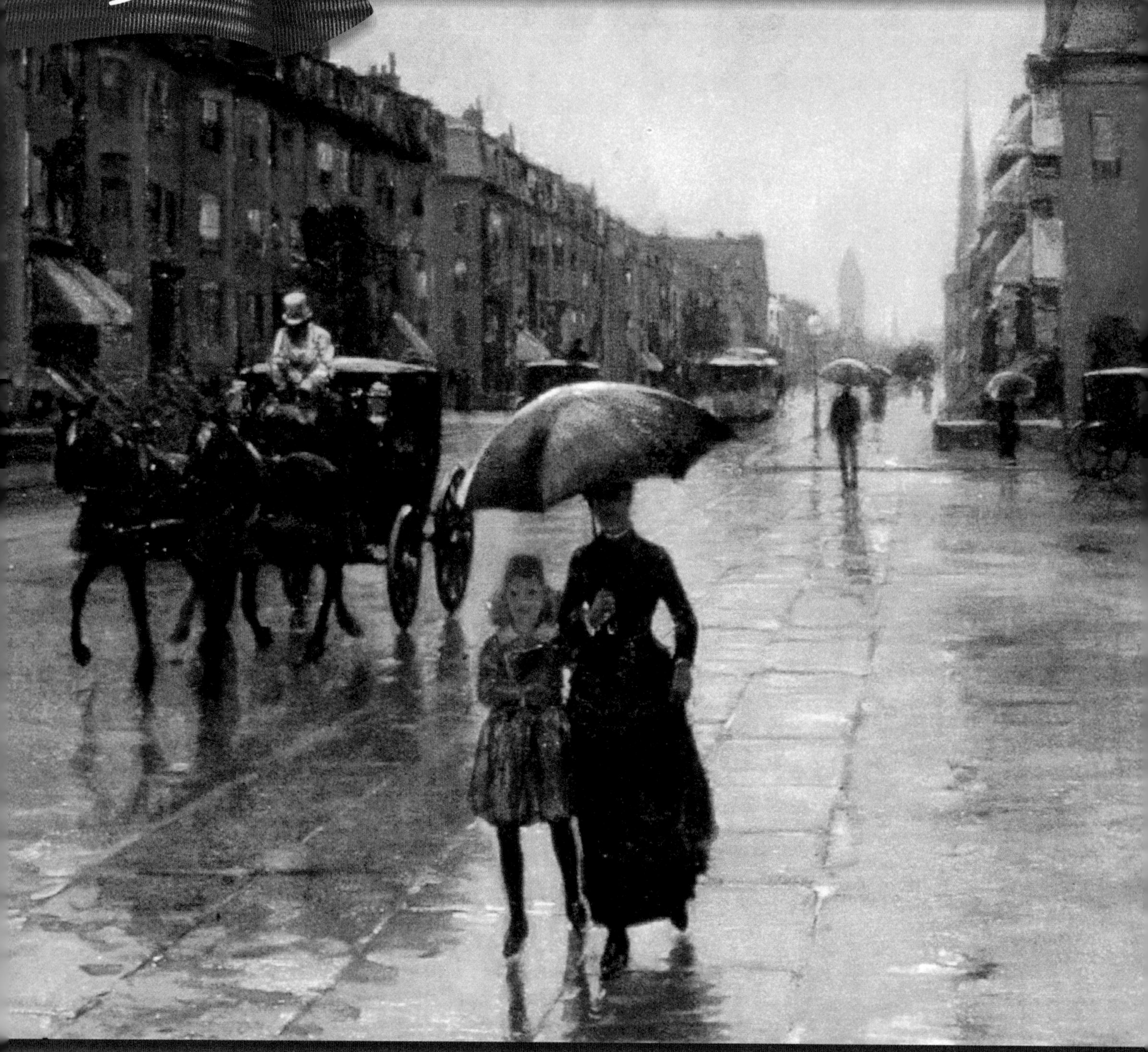

1835 | 1855 | 1875

1834
Cyrus McCormick invents mechanical reaper.

1867
United States buys Alaska from Russia.

1885
First skyscraper is built in Chicago.

Artist Childe Hassam's painting *Rainy Day in Boston* shows the growing city of Boston, Massachusetts, in 1885.

1895

1915

1935

1898
Spanish-American War

1906
Upton Sinclair publishes *The Jungle.*

1914
The Panama Canal opens.

1917
United States enters World War I.

1919
Treaty of Versailles ends World War I.

Nineteenth Amendment passes.

209

Meet the People

Elizabeth Cady Stanton

1815–1902

Birthplace: Johnstown, New York

Abolitionist, women's rights leader

- Helped organize the first women's rights convention
- Called for equal rights for women
- Leader of movement to give women the right to vote

Susan B. Anthony

1820–1906

Birthplace: Adams, Massachusetts

Women's rights leader

- Leader in the struggle for women's suffrage
- Worked for the abolition of slavery
- First woman to appear on a U.S. coin, the Susan B. Anthony dollar

John Muir

1838–1914

Birthplace: Dunbar, Scotland

Writer, naturalist

- Wrote hundreds of newspaper and magazine articles about protecting nature and wilderness areas
- Worked to establish several national parks
- Helped found the Sierra Club

Liliuokalani

1838–1917

Birthplace: Honolulu, Hawaii

Hawaiian leader

- Organized schools for Hawaiian children
- Became the first queen of Hawaii in 1891
- Opposed the annexation of Hawaii by the United States in 1898

1800	1820	1840	1860

1815 • Elizabeth Cady Stanton

1820 • Susan B. Anthony

1838 • John Muir

1838 • Liliuokalani

1856

1856

1858

1862

Booker T. Washington

1856–1915

Birthplace: Hardy, Virginia

Educator, leader for African American rights

- Founded Tuskegee Institute in 1881
- Gave "Atlanta Compromise" speech, in which he stated that hard work and economic security would eventually bring equality to African Americans
- Wrote autobiography, *Up From Slavery*

Woodrow Wilson

1856–1924

Birthplace: Staunton, Virginia

Governor, President

- Passed federal act to stop unfair business practices in 1914
- Brought the United States into World War I in 1917
- Developed the League of Nations in an attempt to prevent future wars

Theodore Roosevelt

1858–1919

Birthplace: New York, New York

Soldier, President

- Led troops in the Spanish-American War
- Became the youngest President of the United States in 1901 at age 42
- Won the Nobel Prize for Peace for his help in ending the Russo-Japanese War

Ida Wells-Barnett

1862–1931

Birthplace: Holly Springs, Mississippi

Journalist

- Wrote and spoke about unjust treatment of African Americans
- Worked to help women get the right to vote
- Wrote an autobiography called *Crusade for Justice*

1880	1900	1920	1940	

1902

1906

1914

1917

Booker T. Washington — 1915

Woodrow Wilson — 1924

Theodore Roosevelt — 1919

Ida Wells-Barnett — 1931

Reading Social Studies

Expansion and Change

Compare and Contrast

Using graphic organizers can help you compare and contrast as you read. A Venn diagram, shown at far left, can help you show how two things or events are different and similar. The graphic organizer on the right shows differences only.

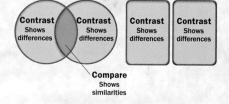

- To compare, writers may use clue words or phrases such as *both, like, as,* and *also.* To contrast, writers may use clue words such as *unlike, different,* and *in contrast.* Other clues can be *before* and *after.*

- When there are no clue words, ask yourself, *How are these events or things similar? How are they different?*

Read the following paragraph. **Comparisons** and **contrasts** have been highlighted.

In Unit 2 you learned how the United States grew as a nation. It gained land across the continent. Stagecoaches moved settlers and goods across the new land. However, stagecoaches were limited in the amount they could carry. In contrast, the new railroads could carry larger numbers of people and goods. Both forms of transportation were important to the growth of the West.

Word Exercise

Use Context Clues As you read a sentence, you may have to use clues from the text and what you already know to figure out the meaning of new words. How can you figure out the meaning of *appliances* in this passage?

Taking care of the home was once difficult and time-consuming. There were few, if any, machines to make the job go more quickly. But this would soon change. Inventors were hard at work. They created new electrical appliances to make housework easier.

Compare and Contrast Events in a Changing Nation

Following Reconstruction, the United States was again a united country. More settlers moved west. Unlike travelers of the early 1800s, who walked or rode in wagons, travelers of the late 1800s could cross the country more quickly by railroad.

Inventors produced useful new technologies that became more widely available by the late 1800s. New farming tools made it possible for a farmer to farm more land. Electric lines supplied electricity to homes, and new electrical appliances made housework easier. As telephone lines spread across the country, communication became easier.

Industry continued to grow. More and more factories were built in or near cities. People who needed jobs moved into the cities. Some workers came from farms, while others were immigrants who moved to the United States from other countries.

Cities across the country grew rapidly.

The rapid growth of cities created many problems. Cities became overcrowded and dirty. There were more violence and more disease. Many men and women worked to improve the difficult city conditions and to make the lives of immigrants better.

Life changed for many in the United States, but some changes came slowly. Slavery was outlawed, but laws in many states made it legal to continue treating African Americans unfairly. African American leaders fought discrimination and worked hard for equality.

The United States had always had a policy of letting other countries handle their own problems. As the United States entered the 1900s, the government found it necessary to go to war to protect itself and its allies in Cuba and Europe.

Use the reading strategy of comparing and contrasting to answer questions 1 and 2. Then answer the vocabulary question.

1 How did inventions in the 1800s change farming?

2 Compare and contrast cities before the growth of industry and after.

3 What clues can help you figure out the meaning of the word *industry* in the third paragraph above? Read the paragraph carefully. What does it tell you about industry? When you think you know the meaning, check a dictionary to see if you are correct.

Changing Ways of Life

1834

Walnut Grove, Virginia
Cyrus McCormick perfects the mechanical reaper.

Lesson 1

1885

Chicago, Illinois
The first skyscraper is built.

Lesson 2

1881

Tuskegee, Alabama
Booker T. Washington founds the Tuskegee Institute, a school for African Americans.

Lesson 3

1887

Argonia, Kansas
Susannah Medora Salter is the first woman elected mayor in the United States.

Lesson 4

CANADA

2

4

1

UNITED STATES

3

Chicago

ILLINOIS

KANSAS

VIRGINIA

Walnut Grove

Argonia

PACIFIC OCEAN

ALABAMA

ATLANTIC OCEAN

Tuskegee

Gulf of Mexico

MEXICO

Why We Remember

As the 1800s came to an end, the United States saw changes that solved some problems and created others. New tools and technologies made life easier for many people. Factories made goods more widely available. However, as people moved to the cities to work in factories, the cities grew too quickly. Also, people were not always treated equally. Many immigrants had trouble finding jobs. Women still could not vote in national elections. African American men could vote but were kept separate from whites. But for every problem, there were people who worked to find solutions. The United States continued its work of building a country that offered equality and hope to all of its citizens.

1830 .... **1900**

1834
Cyrus McCormick invents a mechanical reaper.

1879
First electric power station opens in San Francisco.

1893
New telephone companies form.

Rural Life Changes

PREVIEW

Focus on the Main Idea
During the Industrial Revolution of the 1800s, new machines and technologies affected the lives of people in the rural areas of the United States.

PLACES
Walnut Grove, Virginia
Ahwahnee Valley, California
Appleton, Wisconsin

PEOPLE
Cyrus McCormick
L. O. Colvin
Gustav de Laval
Ellen Eglui
Aaron Montgomery Ward
Richard Sears
Alvah C. Roebuck

VOCABULARY
manual labor
mechanization
reaper
threshing
   machine

You Are There
"Wake up," Father says. "Time for work."

You roll out of bed, dress quickly, and join him on the front porch of your farmhouse. It is still dark outside, and the Kansas air is cool. In the dim light of the moon, you can see the field of wheat waving in the wind. You follow your father to the barn.

"We have a lot to do today," Father says. "The wheat is ripe, and it is time to harvest."

You smile and your father smiles too. Harvesting has always been hard work, but this year it will be easier and faster! You have been reading for months about the new machine that cuts wheat. At last, your father was able to buy one. Your family used to pay laborers to help you cut the wheat by hand, but with this machine, you can do it all yourselves.

You get the horses, Molly and Millie, out of the barn and head for the wheat fields. The sun is coming up, and you are happy for this exciting, new day!

Compare and Contrast As you read, compare and contrast the life of a rural farmer before and after the invention of farm machines.

Mechanization on the Farm

Farming in the early 1800s was difficult and tiring. Manual labor was the only way to get tasks done. **Manual labor** means the jobs done by hand, without the help of machines. The larger the farm, the more laborers it took to do the work.

Inventors in the 1800s, some of whom were farmers themselves, created new machines to help make farming easier. Using machines to do work is called **mechanization.** Mechanization dramatically changed farming in the United States.

A farmer was no longer limited to a "walking plow" but could buy a wheeled one that was pulled by horses. It had a seat, so the farmer could ride rather than walk. In 1834 **Cyrus McCormick,** a farmer and inventor from **Walnut Grove, Virginia,** perfected the mechanical reaper. A **reaper** is a machine that cuts grain. One reaper could cut as much wheat as 16 men with hand-held blades. Steam engines were put to use running **threshing machines** that separated the grain from the plant stalks. New binding machines made the farmer's chore of tying up hay into bundles or bales much easier.

Farmers who raised milk cows also benefited from mechanization. In 1862 **L. O. Colvin** developed the first milking machine. Farmers could now milk more than one cow at a time. The cream separator was another useful tool. Cream takes about 24 hours to rise to the top of the milk on its own. The cream separator invented by **Gustav de Laval** in 1879 spun the milk and separated the cream in minutes.

Machines worked faster than people could. Because of this, farmers with new machines were able to get more work done in less time. This meant they could farm more land, and farms increased in size. In the time it once took to plant or harvest a small plot of land, farmers could now plant and harvest many acres.

Once farmers provided food mainly for their families. As farms increased in size, farmers could sow fields with crops they grew only to sell. These were called "cash crops," because farmers grew them for cash. Cash crops brought in more money, so farmers could buy more land.

REVIEW Contrast how farmers worked before and after mechanization.

⤵ **Compare and Contrast**

▶ **The first McCormick reaper required two workers, one to drive and one to move the cut wheat away from the machine. Later reapers needed only one worker.**

217

Industry's Impact

Industry was growing in cities such as New York and Chicago. Factories produced all kinds of goods. There were dresses and buckets, tractors and birdcages. A shopper could buy a washing machine with the new clothes wringer invented by **Ellen Eglui.** More goods were being produced, and they were less expensive to buy. Stores increased in number and size to sell these affordable goods to people in the cities.

However, not everyone lived in or near cities. In the late 1800s, many Americans lived on farms and ranches. Almost everything they needed was made by hand, including clothes, soap, and furniture. People's homes were often far from the nearest town. Getting supplies was a challenge.

How could farmers hope to buy new, factory-made items if they lived far from a city? **Aaron Montgomery Ward** had an answer: mail order. In 1872 in Chicago, Ward established the first mail-order business. A customer could just flip through the pages of a Montgomery Ward catalog, select an item, and then write an order. Whether a customer lived in the city of Boston or on a homestead in Texas, the goods were available. Ordered goods were carried across the country by train.

In 1893 **Richard Sears** and **Alvah C. Roebuck** formed a mail-order company that soon grew to be larger than Montgomery Ward's. Even houses could be bought from Sears and Roebuck. They promised that their prices were cheapest. They also said:

> *"Tell us what you want in your own way, written in any language, no matter whether good or poor writing, and the goods will be promptly sent to you."*

REVIEW Compare and contrast the shopping experiences of a farmer far from the city and a worker in Chicago.

> **Compare and Contrast**

Mail-Order Catalogs

Mail-order catalogs became popular with people in big cities, small towns, and farms. Catalogs are still popular today. They arrive in mailboxes across the country on a regular basis.

Many catalogs are now online. Shoppers don't have to write their orders on paper like people did in the 1800s. They can choose what they want and press a key.

► Early pages from Montgomery Ward and Sears, Roebuck catalogs reflect the styles and products of their day.

Getting Connected

In Unit 2, you read about the invention of the telephone by Alexander Graham Bell in 1876. Before this time, if people wanted to stay in touch, the only choices they had were to write letters, send telegrams, or go for a visit. With the telephone's invention, people had a new way to communicate.

Telephone poles and lines quickly spread west across the country. Phones were installed in homes and businesses. A Chicago factory owner could now talk about business with a supplier in St. Louis without having to travel. Families who lived far apart could hear each other's voices again. An emergency was less frightening when you could call a doctor or firefighter. Until the 1890s, however, telephone rates were very high. Some rural areas and small towns had no service at all.

Alexander Graham Bell owned the first telephone company, because he owned the patent on the equipment. Bell's company had to install all the telephone poles and lines his system needed. In cities, each mile of telephone line Bell put up could serve 40 customers. In rural areas, that same mile of line only served two customers. Because of this, Bell's company did not serve many people in rural areas. It was too expensive.

▶ **Telephones were available in many rural areas by the early 1900s.**

In 1893 Bell's patent expired. Small telephone companies began to form in rural areas. Sometimes when there were no local phone companies, farmers banded together and put up their own poles and lines. One of the first places where this happened was in **Ahwahnee Valley, California.** Farmers in this valley, which is now part of Yosemite National Park, each contributed money and labor to create their own phone system. The building materials could be ordered from mail-order catalogs, so could the telephones.

REVIEW Contrast the ways people could communicate before and after telephones were available. ↻ **Compare and Contrast**

▶ **Before computers existed, all telephone connections had to be made by hand. Notice the plugs and cords these operators from 1900 used to make the connections.**

Electric Appliances Change Work

New electric appliances began to appear in the late 1800s. Rugs no longer had to be taken outside and beaten. Irons stayed hot without a nearby stove. Scrubbing clothes by hand was a thing of the past. Appliances run by electricity made work easier and faster.

▶ **Electric upright vacuum cleaner, 1907**

▶ **Electric sewing machine, 1880s**

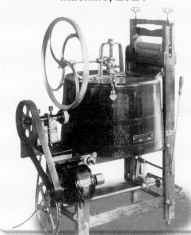

▶ **Electric washing machine, 1914**

▶ **Electric iron, 1893**

Electrifying the Countryside

People had known about electricity for a long time. The first electric battery was made in 1800. The first electric motor was built in 1821. However, it took the building of electric power stations to make electricity widely available.

The first power station in the United States opened in San Francisco, California, in 1879. But the first hydroelectric power plant, which opened in 1882, was built in the town of **Appleton, Wisconsin.** Hydroelectric power plants use running water to generate electricity.

Power stations made electricity available for more than just lighting homes. The power plant in Appleton helped run paper mills. It also supplied power for an electric streetcar system that was opened in 1886.

Although some rural towns had electricity early, it was difficult to set up electrical lines over long distances. People who lived far from power plants had to wait to get electricity, sometimes for years. Farmers in these areas continued to rely on wind power, water-power, machine power, and their own power to get work done.

In 1936 the Rural Electrification Act was passed. This act gave the government the right to lend money to states to use for creating and improving electric service to rural areas. Slowly, electricity came to the country. Farmers' lives changed for the better.

New electric appliances helped farmers and their families with daily chores. An electric iron made ironing faster, because an iron no longer had to be heated on a stove. The electric stove didn't need coal or wood to create heat. Electric vacuum cleaners helped keep floors clean. A family with enough money could buy an electric washing machine. This machine cleaned clothes faster and better, and was easier to use than doing laundry by hand.

Electricity also came in handy outside the farmhouse. Electric pumps brought water from the ground. Farmers didn't have to wait for the wind as they had when using windmills. Electric lights helped the farmer see inside the barn without a lantern, and they were safer than lanterns, which could

cause fires. Feed for animals could be prepared with an electric feed grinder.

Mechanical reapers and threshers had helped farmers and their families years earlier. Electricity brought additional changes to work and life in rural areas.

REVIEW Compare and contrast housework before and after the invention of electric appliances. ⟳ Compare and Contrast

Summarize the Lesson

- **1834** Cyrus McCormick invented a mechanical reaper.
- **1879** First electric power station opened in San Francisco.
- **1893** New telephone companies formed when Bell's patent expired.

▶ Edison's "electric lamp"

LESSON 1 REVIEW

Check Facts and Main Ideas

1. ⟳ **Compare and Contrast** On a separate sheet of paper, fill in the boxes to contrast rural people's lives before and after the arrival of electricity.

Before electricity	After electricity

2. How did advances in **mechanization** affect farm life in the late 1800s? Use the highlighted word in your answer.

3. How did the growth of industry make it easier for farmers to get goods?

4. Why did big cities have new services such as telephone systems and electricity before rural areas did?

5. **Critical Thinking:** *Draw Conclusions* Why do you think people in the 1880s were so eager to have telephones?

Link to ○-○ Writing

Create an Advertisement Suppose you are **Cyrus McCormick.** Write a newspaper advertisement about your **reaper,** to be placed in a rural 1800s newspaper. How can you excite farmers about this new invention? Use the term **manual labor** in your advertisement.

1880   1900

1885
First skyscraper
is built in
Chicago.

1889
Jane Addams
opens Hull House
for the poor.

1900
New York City's
population nears
3.5 million.

New York
City Boston
Chicago
St. Louis Philadelphia

Life in the Growing Cities

PREVIEW

Focus on the Main Idea
During the late 1800s and the early 1900s, people in American cities found that life was changing as populations grew larger.

PLACES
New York, New York
Chicago, Illinois
Philadelphia, Pennsylvania
St. Louis, Missouri
Boston, Massachusetts

PEOPLE
Jane Addams
Jacob Riis
"Boss" William M. Tweed
Elisha Graves Otis
James Buchanan Eads
John Roebling

VOCABULARY
urbanization
tenement
settlement house
political machine
suspension
  bridge

You Are There

It is 1895, and you and your family have just moved to Philadelphia. You had thought you knew what to expect. You had been to the town near your farm at least once a month. You had gone to the fair, where you saw almost everyone in the county. But that didn't prepare you for this. Your whole town could fit in one street here. And the whole county could probably fit in one of the city's tall buildings.

The size of the city and the crowds are not the only differences. The air is not as fresh as it was back on the farm. And there is so much noise. Cars, horses, wagons, and people fill the streets. Horns are honking and people are shouting. You know how to read, but you can't read many of the signs. Your mother tells you that it is because they are in different languages. There is so much that is new. It is a little bit scary, but exciting too.

Cause and Effect As you read, pay attention to the changes that occurred in big cities as their populations grew.

Growing Cities

In the late 1800s and early 1900s, the United States was changing. It was transforming from a largely rural, agricultural nation into a nation of city dwellers.

New York City, Chicago, and **Philadelphia,** the country's three largest cities at this time, grew rapidly. So did other cities. Cities near good transportation grew fastest. Access to both trains and water contributed to the growth of San Francisco, California; Buffalo, New York; Toledo, Ohio; and Chicago, Illinois. Other cities grew dramatically because they were on major railroad lines. The railroad cities included Atlanta, Georgia; Indianapolis, Indiana; Minneapolis, Minnesota; Fort Worth, Texas; and Tacoma, Washington.

REVIEW What factor determined which cities grew fastest during the late 1800s? **Cause and Effect**

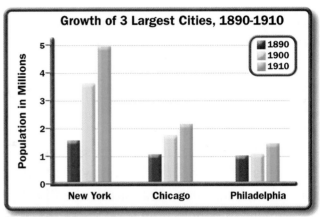

Growth of 3 Largest Cities, 1890-1910

▶ Some cities saw dramatic growth.

GRAPH SKILL Use a Bar Graph *How much did the population of New York increase between 1890 and 1900?*

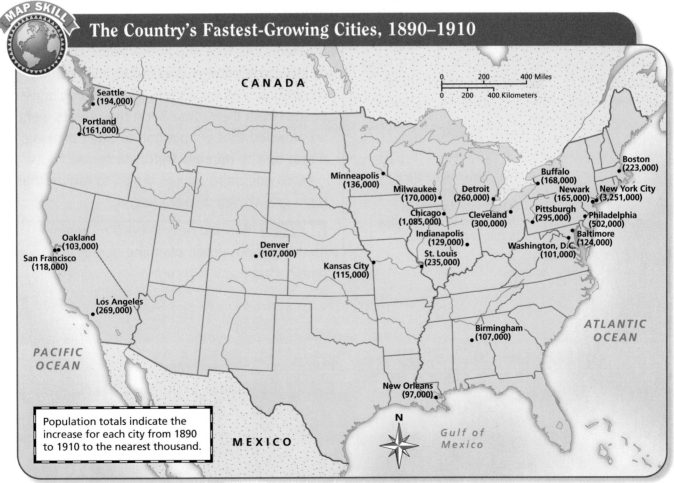

The Country's Fastest-Growing Cities, 1890–1910

Seattle (194,000)
Portland (161,000)
Oakland (103,000)
San Francisco (118,000)
Los Angeles (269,000)
Denver (107,000)
Kansas City (115,000)
Minneapolis (136,000)
Milwaukee (170,000)
Chicago (1,085,000)
Indianapolis (129,000)
St. Louis (235,000)
Detroit (260,000)
Cleveland (300,000)
Buffalo (168,000)
Pittsburgh (295,000)
Newark (165,000)
New York City (3,251,000)
Philadelphia (502,000)
Baltimore (124,000)
Washington, D.C. (101,000)
Boston (223,000)
Birmingham (107,000)
New Orleans (97,000)

CANADA

MEXICO

PACIFIC OCEAN

ATLANTIC OCEAN

Gulf of Mexico

N

0 200 400 Miles
0 200 400 Kilometers

Population totals indicate the increase for each city from 1890 to 1910 to the nearest thousand.

▶ During this time, existing cities grew and new cities were born.

MAP SKILL Using a Map Key *What do the numbers below each city's name tell you about the city?*

223

Immigration and Urbanization

Between 1890 and 1910, the population of the United States grew from about 63 million to more than 92 million people. Of this 29-million-person increase, nearly two-thirds were immigrants. This was the largest number of arrivals the United States had ever experienced in such a short time span.

Industrialization had created millions of new jobs. The flood of immigrants had come to the United States to fill these jobs, most of which were in cities.

But it was not just immigrants swelling the country's urban population. This was a time of rapid urbanization. **Urbanization** is the movement of people from rural areas to cities. With new machines making farm work easier, fewer farm workers were needed. People who had always worked the land now moved to the city to find factory jobs.

With so many people moving to the cities, there was a shortage of housing. New arrivals crowded into **tenements,** or buildings that are divided into small apartments. Factories

▶ City children often had nowhere to play except the sidewalk.

began to move into residential areas. Tenements were built between houses. No one had ever thought about urban planning, so there were no rules about where it was appropriate to build.

The "city beautiful" movement started in the 1890s. This represented the earliest efforts to fight what was seen as the ugliness and disorder of uncontrolled industrial growth. People also built parks and playgrounds for city dwellers. But the cities grew so fast that these facilities were soon not enough.

Transportation both solved and created problems. As foot and horse traffic changed to streetcar, subway, and automobile traffic, city boundaries expanded. Workers could live farther from their jobs. Soon the streets were so crowded that people had to start thinking about how to improve traffic patterns.

More and more people began to realize that rapid growth had disadvantages.

REVIEW Why did people have to begin thinking about urban planning during this time? *Cause and Effect*

▶ The crowding on New York City's Mulberry Street was typical of that found in many cities in the early 1900s.

Many immigrant families lived and worked in small tenement apartments like this one in New York City.

Urban Woes

In 1880 a report in the *Chicago Times* read: "The river stinks. The air stinks. People's clothing . . . stinks. No other word expresses it so well as stink."

This report reflected the conditions in many of the cities around the country. Urban growth had brought about some good changes. Record numbers of people had jobs, and many people were making more money than they had ever dreamed of making. However, the uncontrolled growth had also created many problems.

Overcrowding was one of the biggest problems. As people continued to arrive, housing became increasingly difficult to find. Families of eight or more often lived together in one tiny tenement apartment. Family members often shared beds, because there was so little space.

In addition to being crowded, many tenements were often unsafe or uncomfortable. Some apartments lacked heat. Others had no windows, making it hard to get fresh air.

With so many people living close together, diseases spread quickly. In southern states, thousands died from yellow fever. Across the country, epidemics of polio, tuberculosis, smallpox, and scarlet fever killed tens of thousands of people. In 1918 an outbreak of influenza killed more than 500,000 Americans. Also, because milk was rarely refrigerated, it could spoil in hot weather. As a result, thousands of babies died every summer. Doctors, researchers, and concerned citizens realized that, with so many people living together, they had to think about caring for whole cities, not just individuals. This idea became known as public health.

The cities were becoming dirtier. Many factories spouted smoke and soot into the air. Traffic increased on the roads. There was more garbage and waste, some of it dumped in the streets, much of it dumped into rivers. Dirt and noise became the constants of city life.

As you read in Unit 2, immigrants sometimes faced prejudice when looking for work. Some people thought immigrants were taking jobs away from local people. Some feared people who were "different." Sometimes the prejudice was an old grudge that one group of immigrants still carried against another group. Prejudice contributed to making life in the city harder.

REVIEW What were some of the troubles that people faced in cities as the populations grew? **Main Idea and Details**

Seeking Solutions

Many organizations were already hard at work trying to solve the problems created by the rapid growth of cities. Still active today are the YMCA, YMHA, and Salvation Army, all of which started during the 1800s. In fact, it was in 1891 at the YMCA in Springfield, Massachusetts, that Dr. James Naismith invented the game of basketball, in order to give city children a sport they could play indoors during the winter. Dwight L. Moody started schools in Chicago for underprivileged city children, and he mobilized people across the country to address the problems of the inner cities. There were groups of successful immigrants who aided struggling newcomers, as well as groups who banded together to help each other. But the cities grew too fast, and more help was needed.

In 1889 **Jane Addams** rented a house in a poor neighborhood in Chicago. She fixed it up and opened it as a settlement house called Hull House. A **settlement house** is a center that provides help for those who have little money. At Hull House, immigrants could take free English classes and get help in finding work. There was day care for the children of families in which both parents worked.

▶ **Hull House was designed to make people feel comfortable and at home.**

▶ **Jane Addams, at right, opened Hull House, one of the country's first settlement houses.**

The idea of settlement houses spread across the country. Following the example of Hull House, hundreds opened in other cities.

Jacob Riis was an immigrant from Denmark. He settled in New York City in 1870. Like many other immigrants, he was poor when he arrived, and he struggled to get ahead. Then he got a job as a police reporter for the *New York Tribune.* He began writing articles about the hardships faced by immigrants at home and at work.

In 1890 Riis published a book called *How the Other Half Lives.* In words and photographs, he revealed the terrible conditions faced by poor urban immigrants. Some wealthy New Yorkers were saddened by what Riis wrote. They donated money to build parks and medical centers for the poor. City officials tore down several of the worst tenements. Theodore Roosevelt, who became President of the United States in 1901, called Riis "the most useful citizen of New York."

REVIEW Why do you think Riis was interested in helping poor immigrants?
Draw Conclusions

Rise of Political Machines

Growing cities needed better streets, more housing, and better sewage disposal. Plans were needed to control building and traffic. Immigrants needed help finding jobs and fighting prejudice.

Because city governments were having trouble handling the problems, people were unhappy. Political machines formed to take advantage of this unhappiness. A **political machine** is an organization of people who control votes to gain political power. Many of the votes controlled by political machines were those of immigrants.

Here is how a political machine would work. Members of the machine wanted to get certain candidates elected to city offices. They told immigrants that they would help them get homes and jobs if the immigrants voted for the candidates selected by the machine. Sometimes they did help, but most were more interested in power than kindness. The candidates that the machines put in city offices did what the political machines told them to do.

A powerful political machine in New York City was called Tammany Hall. Tammany Hall did improve sewer, water, police, and other services. However, it was best known for its dishonesty. A Tammany leader named **"Boss" William M. Tweed** was known for bribing leaders and cheating people out of money. He also stole millions of dollars from the city.

► **"Boss" Tweed was sent to jail for his crimes. This poster was published when he escaped.**

George W. Plunkitt, another Tammany leader, grew wealthy from the "deals" he made but liked the power more than the money. He said, "If a family is burned out, I don't ask whether they are Republicans or Democrats. I just . . . fix them up till they are runnin' again. Who can tell how many votes these fires will bring me?"

Political machines also could be found in Boston, Philadelphia, Pittsburgh, Chicago, and other cities. Although most political machines were dishonest and influenced by bribes, many immigrants wanted their help. They were glad that someone seemed to be taking their side.

REVIEW What was a cause of the formation of political machines? **Cause and Effect**

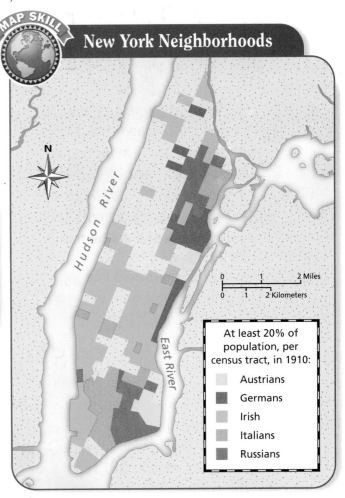

MAP SKILL

New York Neighborhoods

At least 20% of population, per census tract, in 1910:

- Austrians
- Germans
- Irish
- Italians
- Russians

► **The 1910 census showed that ethnic groups often settled together. This helped machine politicians gain power, because they could appeal to ethnic pride.**

MAP SKILL Place *What can you determine about the speckled, tan areas of the map?*

Up, Over, and Under

A city can expand by moving its limits outward, but that makes it harder to reach people with the services they need. So rather than build out, a city can build up. In the late 1800s, two things came together that made taller buildings possible.

As you have read, the process for creating affordable steel was developed in England in the mid-1800s. With the rise of industrialization in the United States, steel was suddenly widely available. Steel is strong enough to support the weight of buildings with many floors.

▶ Otis demonstrated his safety elevator to New Yorkers in 1854.

In 1852 inventor **Elisha Graves Otis** created the first safety elevator. This elevator had brakes that would keep it from falling. He installed the first passenger elevator in a five-story department store in New York City in 1857. The stage was set. Steel and elevators would make very tall buildings, or skyscrapers, possible.

The Great Chicago Fire had destroyed all of Chicago's downtown area in 1871, so Chicago was the perfect place to experiment with new types of buildings. The first skyscraper was built in 1885. This skyscraper, the Home Insurance Building in Chicago, was the tallest building in the country. It was ten stories tall!

Some people doubted that tall buildings were a good idea, but people wanted and needed more space for apartments, offices, and stores. Skyscrapers soon appeared in St. Louis, New York, and Buffalo.

Steel also helped create stronger bridges. The first steel bridge was built in 1874 by **James Buchanan Eads.** It spanned the Mississippi River from Illinois to **St. Louis, Missouri.** To test the bridge for strength, fourteen trains weighing a total of 700 tons were sent across the center span. The bridge passed the test.

The world's first suspension bridge was built in Cincinnati, Ohio, in 1866. A **suspension bridge** is one that is suspended, or hung, from steel cables. The designer of this bridge, a German immigrant named **John Roebling**, was hired by leaders of New York City to create a larger version of this new type of bridge. John

▶ This building, shown being constructed in Chicago in 1894, is made strong by its steel frame.

Roebling died before construction began, but his son, Washington Roebling, took over the project. When he was injured during construction, Washington's wife, Emily Roebling, completed the construction of the great bridge. The Brooklyn Bridge crossed the East River, connecting Brooklyn to the island of Manhattan. When the bridge opened in 1883, it was the longest bridge in the world.

If builders could go up, could they also go down? As the streets became more crowded, city planners and engineers began to consider underground transportation. Many cities were experimenting with ideas, but it was **Boston, Massachusetts** that built the country's first successful underground train system, or subway. Boston's electric subway system opened in 1897.

REVIEW Why was steel so important to the continued growth of cities? Main Idea and Details

Summarize the Lesson

- **1885** The first skyscraper was built in Chicago.
- **1889** Jane Addams opened Hull House for the poor.
- **1900** New York City's population neared 3.5 million.

LESSON 2 REVIEW

Check Facts and Main Ideas

1. Cause and Effect Complete this chart by filling in one effect of each event listed below.

Cause	Effect
The population grew so fast that housing couldn't keep up with it.	
Immigrants were offered help from political machines.	
Jane Addams wanted to help immigrants.	
Steel was strong enough to support great weight.	

2. How did **urbanization** bring about the need for **settlement houses**? Write two or three sentences to answer the question. Be sure to use the highlighted words.

3. List three problems faced by some immigrants who moved to big cities in the late 1800s.

4. Why did political machines want to control the votes of immigrants?

5. Critical Thinking: *Draw Conclusions* You have read that immigrants faced many hardships in the big cities of the United States. Why do you think so many people continued to immigrate?

Link to Writing

Write a Profile As you read on page 226, many people in the 1800s wanted to make life better for people in the cities. Research a social reformer or organization that worked to improve the lives of others during this era. What problems did they try to solve? What actions did they take to make improvements? Write a profile of the reformer or organization you chose.

Chart and Graph Skills

Read Line and Circle Graphs

What? Graphs show information in a visual way. A **line graph** can show change over time. The line graph below compares the growth of the urban population, or people living in the cities, in the United States with the country's rural population, or people living out in the country, in farming areas or small towns. The graph gives information for the years 1790 to 2000. A **circle graph** shows how a whole is divided into parts. It can show how different groups compare to each other in size. The circle graphs on page 231 show the percentage of people who worked in rural professions such as farming in 1900 and in 2000, as well as the percentage of those who performed jobs more likely to be found in urban areas.

Why? As you read in Lesson 2, cities in the United States grew because of immigration and urbanization. Of course people still moved to rural areas too, but by the early 1900s, urban growth was greater. A line graph like the one on this page makes it possible to see, at a glance, how the population grew in both the urban and rural areas. It lets you compare their growth rates.

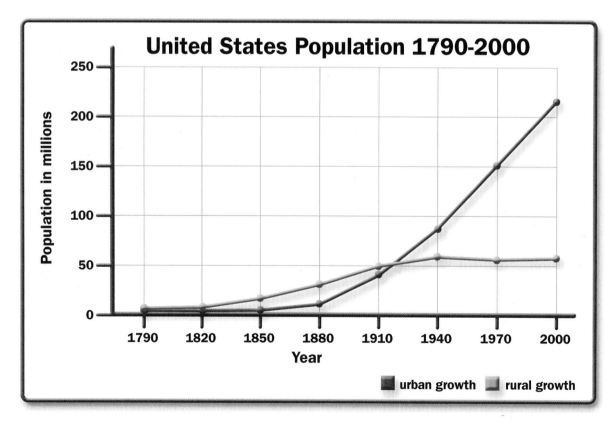

Unlike a line graph, a circle graph does not show change over time. Instead, it gives a certain view of the subject being studied at one moment in time. For example, when you look at the circle graph on the left on this page, you get a picture of how many workers in the United States in 1900 were employed in such rural occupations as farming compared with those who were employed in occupations more likely to be found in or near cities, such as manufacturing and service industries.

The circle graph on the right makes the same comparison of occupations for the year 2000.

How? When you use a line graph, look first at the title. Notice that the title of the line graph on page 230 tells you what it is about. It shows the growth in both rural and urban areas in the United States from 1790 to 2000. After you have read the title, look at the words along the axes, the lines at the edge of the graph, to see what the graph is showing. This line graph, for example, shows years along the bottom and population along the side. The dots in the middle of the graph show population in a certain year. When you connect those dots with a line, you have a line graph showing how the population has changed over time. This graph has a line showing growth of the urban population and another line showing growth of the rural population. Each is a different color to make the differences easier to identify. The graph shows that the country's urban population reached about 42 million in 1910. When did the rural population reach 55 million?

To use a circle graph, first look at the title. Then read the words in the graph to learn what each section represents. In these circle graphs, each section represents a percentage of the workforce in the United States in 1900 and in 2000. You can see that the largest percentage of the labor force in 1900 worked in farming.

What occupation represented the smallest percentage of the workforce in the year 2000?

Think and Apply

❶ Which type of graph shows change over time? Which type shows information for only a single year?

❷ How many more people lived in rural areas than in urban areas in 1850?

❸ How does each graph reflect the increase in improved farming technology and the rise of urbanization?

1875   1915

1877
Remaining federal troops leave the South after Reconstruction ends.

1909
NAACP is founded.

1915
Great Migration of African Americans begins.

Tuskegee

PREVIEW

Focus on the Main Idea
In the late 1800s and well into the 1900s, African Americans, along with other racial and ethnic groups, faced lives that were affected by prejudice, segregation, and unequal opportunities.

PLACES
Chicago, Illinois
Tuskegee, Alabama

PEOPLE
Jack L. Cooper
W. E. B. Du Bois
Booker T. Washington
George Washington Carver
Ida Wells-Barnett

VOCABULARY
tenant
enfranchise
Great Migration

▶ The people known as carpetbaggers often carried large traveling bags like these, which were made of carpet.

Unequal Opportunities

You Are There
You stand with your uncle at the edge of town. The Union soldiers are leaving, and you watch the troops march by. "They're heading north," your uncle says. "They think their work is finished, but I'm not so sure."

"Well, at least those greedy carpetbaggers are leaving too," you note. "They did no one any good."

"Yes, everyone is glad to see them leave," your uncle agrees.

You watch the soldiers, wondering what will happen next. "Lots of our friends have moved away. If we stay, how will we get by?" you ask.

"Mr. Johnson has offered me a deal that sounds pretty good," your uncle tells you. "He will give us a piece of land to farm, and we just have to pay him with some of the crops."

Your family has farmed for generations, so you feel hopeful about this news. Still, you wonder how sharing crops with an owner will work.

Main Idea and Details As you read, keep in mind the main idea and supporting details that tell you more about life after Reconstruction.

The South After Reconstruction

After Reconstruction, the South remained the poorest section of the country. It was to remain impoverished until the 1930s. Many blacks and poor whites became tenant farmers. A **tenant** is someone who pays rent to use land or buildings that belong to someone else. Most tenants make monthly payments with cash. But not everyone had cash in the 1870s. As you read in Unit 1, when a tenant pays rent with crops he or she has grown, the tenant is called a sharecropper. Sharecropping began during Reconstruction, and it lasted well into the 1940s.

At first, sharecropping had seemed to be a great bargain. It offered people a degree of independence and the ability to work for themselves, and they got to keep as much as half of the crop. But falling crop prices often meant too little income. Also, in order to buy seed and tools, sharecroppers often borrowed against future crops. People usually have to pay interest when they borrow money. Interest is a type of fee that gets paid to the lender. If interest rates were high and crops didn't get good prices, sharecroppers could be in debt after the harvest. Sharecroppers often felt trapped by debt.

The South's poverty was rooted largely in the destruction caused by the Civil War. It was worsened by the carpetbaggers of the Reconstruction era. Though many of the so-called carpetbaggers were truly concerned about the welfare of African Americans, the many dishonest ones gave a bad name to everyone who had come to help. They exploited the region and supported corrupt financial schemes.

Three institutions grew up in the South in reaction to the poverty and the involvement of the federal government. One was sharecropping. Growing cotton, tobacco, and rice required a lot of work, so there were millions of farm jobs available. In many southern states, nearly half of the population was sharecroppers.

Another institution was one-party politics. Southern Democrats soon controlled all the southern states, even states that did not have white majorities. Much as the big-city political machines had turned to immigrants for votes, Southern Democrats turned to the newly enfranchised African Americans. **Enfranchised** means having the right to vote. Once again, promises turned into election victories.

The third institution was racial segregation, which you will read about in the next section.

REVIEW What contributed to the poverty of the South after Reconstruction?
Main Idea and Details

Library of Congress

▶ The departure of Federal troops from the South marked the end of Reconstruction.

233

Prejudice and Segregation

As you read in Unit 1, Jim Crow laws passed in the 1880s made racial segregation legal in the South. Although the laws required that facilities be equal, they enforced the separation of races. Schools, train cars, buses, and even cemeteries were segregated.

In 1892 Homer Plessy was chosen by a group of influential African American leaders to challenge the Jim Crow laws. He entered the whites-only section of a train car in

Louisiana. Plessy was of mixed race, but he was considered black by southern law. Blacks could not be in the whites-only car, so he was arrested. Plessy sued the state. By 1896 his case had reached the United States Supreme Court. Plessy was found guilty of breaking the law. This court case made it clear that, as long as facilities for blacks and whites were equal, it was legal to keep the races separate.

African Americans were not the only group to face prejudice and segregation. In some areas, Hispanics experienced discrimination. This happened even in areas where Hispanic communities had been in place for several generations.

▶ In the West, Chinese immigrants often faced prejudice and anger.

▶ Segregation laws required that equal facilities be available for blacks and whites, but that they be separate.

Chinese immigrants in the West faced years of prejudice and violence. In the 1870s, a group of Chinese businessmen wrote to President Ulysses S. Grant, relating how badly they were being treated. They also wrote:

"Many charges are made against our people . . . [that are] calculated to mislead honest minds, and create unjust prejudice against us."

In spite of this appeal, Congress passed the Chinese Exclusion Act in 1882. This law prevented immigration on the basis of race. In 1905 San Francisco established a segregated school for Chinese children, including those who were born in the United States.

Different racial or ethnic groups were segregated well into the 1900s. Often the segregation was limited to housing. For example, residential areas were sometimes closed to Jews, although these same people might be welcomed into the business community. While not everyone agreed with these policies, fear and prejudice caused many people to demand laws to protect their jobs or separate them from those who were "different."

REVIEW How did Homer Plessy challenge the Jim Crow laws? **Main Idea and Details**

Great Migration

Some African Americans living in the South during the late 1800s and early 1900s began to wonder if there might be a better place to live. Was there a place with greater rights, better jobs, and good schools? Many believed this place was the North. Newspapers from northern cities told of homes and jobs for African Americans. Friends who had already moved north shared stories of greater freedom and new-found success.

A **Chicago, Illinois,** newspaper, *The Chicago Defender,* encouraged African Americans to come to its city. This paper often listed black churches and other organizations that offered help to African Americans when they arrived. Thousands of African Americans wrote anxious letters to the churches, asking for assistance.

Between 1915 and the 1940s, more than a million African Americans moved north. This came to be called the **Great Migration.** There were many jobs available in factories in the North, especially when the United States entered World War I in 1917. You will read more about this war in the next chapter. The military needed tanks, ships, and weapons. Factories that made these items offered jobs with higher pay. African Americans hoped to fill these jobs. As northern workers left to fight the war, more and more jobs became available. Some of the open jobs went to women, but most of them went to the arriving African Americans.

REVIEW What issues led to the Great Migration? **Cause and Effect**

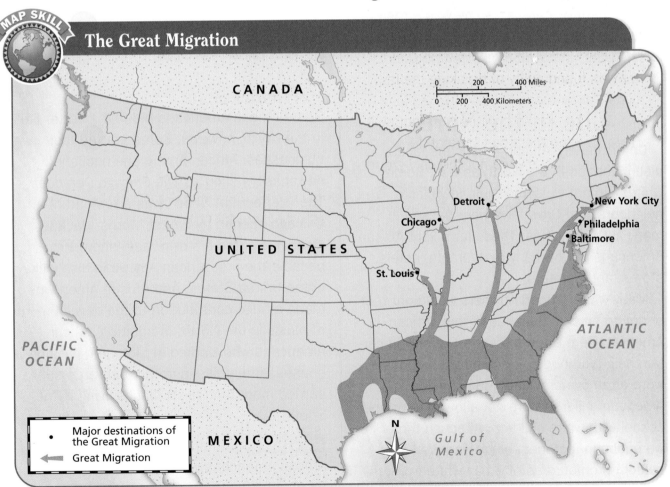

The Great Migration

CANADA

UNITED STATES

Detroit
Chicago
New York City
Philadelphia
Baltimore
St. Louis

PACIFIC OCEAN

ATLANTIC OCEAN

MEXICO

Gulf of Mexico

0   200   400 Miles
0   200   400 Kilometers

• Major destinations of the Great Migration
← Great Migration

▶ **During the early 1900s, many African Americans moved to the North.**

MAP SKILL Movement *In the South, African Americans lived mainly in rural areas. To what types of areas did they migrate?*

▶ This painting by Jacob Lawrence is titled *The Migrants Arrived in Great Numbers*. It shows families on the move during the Great Migration. You will read more about Lawrence in Unit 4.

The Museum of Modern Art, New York. Gift of Mrs. David M. Levy. Tempera on gesso on composition board, 12" x 18".

Life in the North

Unfortunately, African Americans faced discrimination in the North as well. Some whites did not welcome their new black neighbors. Jim Crow laws were passed in many northern cities. These laws kept African Americans out of many restaurants, hotels, stores, and theaters.

Many white property owners would not rent or sell to blacks. Because of this, African American were often forced to live only in certain neighborhoods. These neighborhoods were often overcrowded. Many African American children were not allowed to attend school with white children. Although there were jobs in factories, black workers were seldom promoted as often as white workers.

Some African Americans did find a better life in the North, however. Some started their own businesses. African Americans published newspapers such as *The Chicago Defender*. The "Perfect Eat Shop" was a restaurant in Chicago opened by Ernest Morris. **Jack L. Cooper** created his own radio show. He became the first African American disc jockey in the United States. And African Americans made a huge contribution to the development of music in the North. In addition, African Americans who worked in factories, packing-houses, steel mills, and railroad yards still earned more than most blacks living in the South.

REVIEW Summarize the experience of African Americans who moved north with the Great Migration. **Summarize**

New Leaders Arise

As had happened since before the Civil War, African American leaders spoke out against discrimination. **W. E. B. Du Bois** (doo BOYZ) was born in Massachusetts in 1868. His family had not been enslaved, and he attended school with white students. As a young man, he went to Fisk University, an African American college in Nashville. He saw how African Americans were affected by discrimination outside the college campus. He believed discrimination had to be challenged. He said, "We refuse to allow the impression to remain that African Americans assent to inferiority."

▶ **W. E. B. Du Bois**

Du Bois became a successful writer and editor. In 1909 he helped to start the National Association for the Advancement of Colored People, or NAACP. The association's main goal was to bring an immediate end to racial discrimination.

Unlike Du Bois, **Booker T. Washington** had been enslaved. Washington's ideas and work for the rights of African Americans were different from those of Du Bois too. Washington did not push for a quick fix. He thought education and training for jobs were keys to equality. With education and income, he believed, African Americans would eventually overcome racial discrimination. In 1881 he founded the Tuskegee Institute, a college for African Americans, in **Tuskegee, Alabama.** In his autobiography *Up from Slavery,* Washington wrote:

> *"It is important and right that all privileges of the law be ours, but it is vastly more important that we be prepared for . . . these privileges."*

Noted African American scientist **George Washington Carver** joined him in 1896. Carver, who had also been enslaved, shared Washington's vision. He organized the school's agriculture department, and then taught and did research there for the rest of his life.

The institute changed many lives, and it soon rose to national prominence. Washington remained its president until his death in 1915. You will read more about Washington in the biography on p. 239.

REVIEW Compare and contrast the ideas of Du Bois and Washington concerning African Americans. ↻ **Compare and Contrast**

▶ **In the Tuskegee Institute printing shop, students could prepare for careers in publishing. This photograph of students at work is from 1902.**

Others Join the Fight

Men and women of many races and backgrounds joined the fight for equality. There was much at stake for many groups. **Ida Wells-Barnett** was born in 1862 in Mississippi, the daughter of slaves. Wells-Barnett went to Chicago in 1893, where she helped start an African American newspaper. She also started one of the first organizations to seek voting

▶ **Ida Wells-Barnett told her story in an autobiography called *Crusade for Justice.***

rights for African American women. She fought—and won—a battle against the passage of a state law that would have segregated blacks and whites on trains and buses in Illinois.

REVIEW What actions taken by Ida Wells-Barnett support the main idea that she was a fighter against discrimination? **Main Idea and Details**

Summarize the Lesson

1877 The remaining federal troops left the South after Reconstruction.

1909 The National Association for the Advancement of Colored People was founded.

1915 The Great Migration of African Americans began.

LESSON 3   REVIEW

Check Facts and Main Ideas

1. Main Idea and Details Complete the chart below by filling in three details that support the main idea that Jim Crow laws led to segregation.

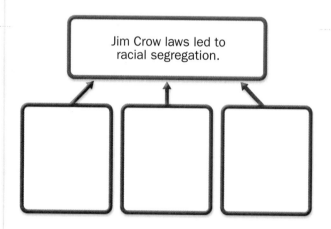

Jim Crow laws led to racial segregation.

2. Why did most sharecroppers stay in debt?

3. What issues did African Americans face in the North?

4. What are some of the ways in which African American leaders responded to discrimination?

5. Critical Thinking: *Make Generalizations* Describe some of the hopes African Americans might have had when they moved North during the **Great Migration.** Use the highlighted term in your answer.

Link to 🔗 Mathematics

Plan a Trip Suppose a family from Atlanta moves to Chicago during the Great Migration. The distance is 752 miles. They travel by wagon at 16 miles a day. How many days will it take?

Booker T. Washington
1856–1915

Booker T. Washington was born into slavery on a Virginia plantation. Because he was enslaved, he did not go to school, but he remembered carrying the schoolbooks of the young white mistress of the plantation when she went. Going to school, he thought, must be like going to paradise.

After emancipation, Washington's family moved to West Virginia to work in the coal mines. Washington never lost his desire for an education, and in 1872 he attended Hampton Institute, a school for former slaves. Going to school simply increased his love of education and his belief that education and character building were the keys to equality.

BIOFACT

Booker T. Washington was the first African-American to ever dine at the White House with the President.

Top Hat, TUIN 888
National Park Service, Museum
Managent Program and Tuskegee
Institute National Historic Site

In 1881 he moved to Tuskegee, Alabama, and founded the Tuskegee Institute. The institute started as a teacher's college. It offered the state's first nursing program. Soon it added instruction in other trades. Students not only studied, they also built their own buildings and grew their own food. They sold their products to the white community nearby.

Washington became a well-respected African American leader. He started educational institutions throughout the South, encouraged African American businesses, and advised American Presidents. He taught that equal rights could be gained through education, hard work, and understanding. He said:

> *"Success is to be measured not so much by the position that one has reached in life as by the obstacles which he has overcome."*

Learn from Biographies

How did Booker T. Washington's early life affect his feelings about the way equal rights should be gained?

For more information, go to *Meet the People* at **www.sfsocialstudies.com**.

1840   1920

1848
Seneca Falls Convention is held.

1869
The Territory of Wyoming leads the nation in giving women the vote.

1887
First woman mayor is elected in Argonia, Kansas.

1919
Nineteenth Amendment is passed.

Seneca Falls

Argonia

Women's Rights

PREVIEW

Focus on the Main Idea
Women hoped to benefit from the spirit of reform that began in the mid-1800s.

PLACES
Seneca Falls, New York
Argonia, Kansas

PEOPLE
Lucretia Mott
Elizabeth Cady Stanton
Lucy Stone
Susannah Medora Salter
Susan B. Anthony
Carrie Chapman Catt

VOCABULARY
suffrage
suffragist
Nineteenth
  Amendment

| You Are There |

The city street is crowded with men and women. All eyes are focused on a speaker who is standing in the back of a wagon. You look up at your mother as she speaks to the crowd. It is spring 1912.

"We only demand what is rightfully ours!" your mother shouts. She wears a long white skirt, a white blouse, and a hat covered in bows. She also wears a banner reading "Votes for Women!"

Around the wagon are other women. Some wave American flags. Some have babies with them. The baby carriages are covered in red, white, and blue.

"Aren't you proud of your mother?" asks a woman near you. You nod. You are very proud. You have come with her to this rally to demand the right for women to vote. Many women out West already have this right. Surely, someday soon, all American women will be able to vote!

Sequence As you read, be aware of the sequence of events that led to increased rights for women.

Women's Roles in the 1800s

Why were women rallying for the right to vote in 1912? Though other rights for women were increasing, most women still could not vote.

Women's roles changed dramatically during the 1800s. Women were still expected to care for the house and children. Before the rise of industrialization, women spun yarn, wove cloth, hand made all clothes, and produced necessities such as butter and soap. As more goods became available, much of this work became unnecessary. In rural areas, life changed more slowly. But as you have read, mail-order catalogs soon made goods available there too.

Some women worked outside the home as teachers or factory workers, and many in the cities worked as maids or housekeepers. But few women were allowed to pursue the same careers as men.

This was less true in rural areas. Pioneer couples had to work together to survive.

Almost nothing was considered purely "men's work." Women helped work the crops, tended livestock, and chopped wood. Some hunted. Pioneer women had fewer comforts than city women, but they were more nearly equal to men in work and rights.

▶ **In rural areas, women often had equal rights and equal work.**

As new inventions for both housework and farm work became available, people's lives changed even more. Many city women had free time for visiting and shopping. As a result, the first department stores were opened, often with tea rooms. Some women who had been housekeepers now found jobs in these new stores.

REVIEW During the 1800s, why were rural women more nearly equal to men in work and rights? **Draw Conclusions**

▶ **Because of new inventions, women gained time for leisure activities, often for the first time in their lives. In urban areas, women might use this time to shop or have tea with friends.**

Women Work for More Rights

Women in the United States enjoyed the freedom and protection offered by citizenship. But in the 1800s their opportunities and rights did not equal those of men. Colleges were closed to women. Married women did not have the right to own property. The social and legal status of women was not equal to that of men. Many women wanted to participate in the reform movements of the day, including abolition and temperance. The temperance movement was trying to stop the widespread abuse of alcohol. But involvement in reforms was off limits for women.

In 1848 women's rights leaders **Lucretia Mott** and **Elizabeth Cady Stanton** invited interested women and men to gather in **Seneca Falls, New York,** to discuss women's rights. At the Seneca Falls Convention, Stanton stated, "Woman is man's equal, was intended to be so by the Creator, and . . . she should be recognized as such."

Issues discussed at the convention included education and jobs. The most controversial issue was whether women should be able to vote. Almost half of the people at the convention were against this idea. Stanton and abolitionist Frederick Douglass were determined that it be included as a goal. Much of the press criticized the convention. Stanton thought the reports would at least get people thinking about the issues.

After the Civil War, the passage of the Fifteenth Amendment gave newly freed African American men the right to vote. Women were amazed that the new law had not included them. Women's rights leaders now felt that gaining the right to vote was their most important goal. Another term for the right to vote is **suffrage,** which is why people working for women's voting rights were called **suffragists.** Suffragist **Lucy Stone** founded the American Woman Suffrage Association at this time. This organization supported the Fifteenth Amendment and worked for women's suffrage as well.

As you read, women came closer to having equality in rural areas, and it was in rural areas that they first got the vote. In 1869, the Territory of Wyoming led the nation in giving women the vote. Kansas allowed women to vote in local elections, and in 1887 the small town of **Argonia, Kansas,** elected **Susannah Medora Salter** mayor. She was the first woman mayor in the United States.

Susan B. Anthony's fight for women's rights began in the mid-1800s and continued until her death in 1906. As you will read in her biography on page 245, Anthony traveled and lectured on women's suffrage. Anthony said:

> *"There will never be complete equality until women themselves help to make laws and elect lawmakers."*

▶ **Elizabeth Cady Stanton (left) and Lucretia Mott called a convention to discuss women's rights.**

Another suffragist leader in the early 1900s was **Carrie Chapman Catt.** Catt was a teacher in Iowa when she became involved in the suffrage movement. At first she worked locally in her home state. She then began traveling, writing, and speaking to promote women's suffrage.

Catt's goal was to get Congress and the states to pass an amendment to the Constitution that would give women the right to vote. Catt felt certain of victory. She said:

"When a just cause reaches its flood tide . . . whatever stands in its way must fall before its overwhelming power."

REVIEW When did women's suffrage become the most important goal for women's rights leaders? Sequence

▶ **Women lined up to vote after the passage of the Nineteenth Amendment.**

The Nineteenth Amendment

By 1912 many states had approved a woman's right to vote. These included Colorado, Idaho, Kansas, Utah, Oregon, and Arizona. However, it would take the Congress of the United States to make voting legal for women throughout the country.

World War I helped strengthen the cause of women's suffrage. As men went into the armed forces, women replaced them in the workforce. Women performed jobs they had never done before, such as repairing automobiles and driving buses. Women worked in factories producing weapons. About 11,000 women joined the women's branch of the United States Navy, which had never before allowed women to serve in its ranks. If women could do all this, they argued, they should be allowed to vote!

Even though Congress was made up entirely of men, women had successfully made their case. In 1919 Congress passed the **Nineteenth Amendment** to the Constitution. It stated:

"The right of citizens to vote shall not be denied or abridged [limited] by the United States or by any state on account of [the] sex [of a person.]"

In August 1920, the states ratified the amendment, and it became law.

REVIEW How did World War I help the suffragists' cause? Cause and Effect

Other Opportunities

In the late 1800s, many colleges opened to women students. Soon women worked as professors too. Women pursued new careers, including politics.

Some women wanted even greater adventures. Annie Smith Peck was a university professor before she became a mountain climber. She climbed mountains all over the world. In 1906 she reached the top of Peru's Mount Huascaran, the tallest peak in the Western Hemisphere. She was 60 years old!

▶ By the late 1800s, women were graduating from colleges.

Delia Akeley was an African explorer. Marguerite Harrison, a journalist, became a spy during World War I. Louise Arner Boyd was an Arctic explorer. The whole world was now open to women.

REVIEW What new opportunities opened for women in the late 1800s and early 1900s? **Main Idea and Details**

Summarize the Lesson

1848 The Seneca Falls Convention was held.

1869 The Territory of Wyoming led the nation in giving women the right to vote.

1887 The first woman mayor was elected in Argonia, Kansas.

1919 The Nineteenth Amendment was passed.

LESSON 4 REVIEW

Check Facts and Main Ideas

1. Sequence Redraw this chart on a separate sheet of paper, putting the events in their correct order.

> Congress approves the right to vote for all American women.

↓

> African American men get the right to vote.

↓

> The Seneca Falls Convention proposes equality for women.

↓

> Susannah Medora Salter is the first woman in the United States to be elected mayor.

2. What was the goal of the **suffragists**? Why did **suffrage** become more important to women's rights leaders after the passage of the Fifteenth Amendment?

3. How did **Susan B. Anthony** contribute to the cause of women's rights?

4. What rights and opportunities did women gain during the late 1800s and early 1900s?

5. Critical Thinking: _Evaluate_ How do you think the work-saving tools mentioned at the beginning of this lesson, along with the way they changed people's lives, might have contributed to women having greater interest in equal rights?

Link to ⛓ Art

Create a Poster Illustrate a poster to show how women's lives changed during the late 1800s and early 1900s.

244

Susan B. Anthony

1820–1906

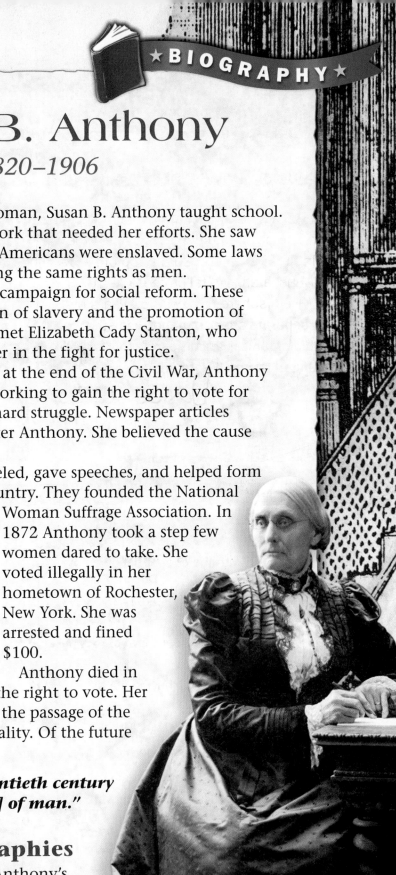

As a teenager and young woman, Susan B. Anthony taught school. Yet she felt there was other work that needed her efforts. She saw injustice around her. African Americans were enslaved. Some laws prevented women from having the same rights as men.

In 1849 Anthony began to campaign for social reform. These reforms included the abolition of slavery and the promotion of women's rights. In 1850 she met Elizabeth Cady Stanton, who became her friend and partner in the fight for justice.

After slavery was abolished at the end of the Civil War, Anthony turned her energies toward working to gain the right to vote for women. It was to be a long, hard struggle. Newspaper articles attacked her. This did not deter Anthony. She believed the cause could not fail.

Anthony and Stanton traveled, gave speeches, and helped form suffrage groups across the country. They founded the National Woman Suffrage Association. In 1872 Anthony took a step few women dared to take. She voted illegally in her hometown of Rochester, New York. She was arrested and fined $100.

Anthony died in 1906, before women gained the right to vote. Her work, however, helped make the passage of the Nineteenth Amendment a reality. Of the future of women's rights, she said:

> *"The woman of the twentieth century will be the peer [equal] of man."*

BIOFACT

Anthony was the first woman to appear on United States currency. The Susan B. Anthony dollar coin first appeared in 1979.

Learn from Biographies

How do you think Susan B. Anthony's voting, arrest, and fine might have affected the cause of women's suffrage?

For more information, go to *Meet the People* at **www.sfsocialstudies.com**.

1830   1850   1870

1834
Cyrus McCormick
invents a
mechanical reaper.

1848
Seneca Falls
Convention
is held.

1869
Territory of Wyoming
leads the nation in
giving women the vote.

Chapter Summary

Target Skill

Compare and Contrast

On a separate sheet of paper, copy the graphic organizer to compare and contrast the United States before and after the beginning of the Industrial Revolution of the 1800s.

Before Industrial Revolution began	After Industrial Revolution began

Vocabulary

Match each word with the correct definition or description.

1 mechanization (p.217)

2 urbanization (p. 224)

3 settlement house (p. 226)

4 enfranchised (p. 233)

5 suffragist (p. 242)

a. person working for women's voting rights

b. having the right to vote

c. use of machines to do work

d. movement of people from rural to urban areas

e. a center that provides help for the poor

People and Terms

Write a sentence explaining the importance of each of the following people or terms in the changing United States. You may use two or more in a single sentence.

1 threshing machine (p. 217)

2 Cyrus McCormick (p. 217)

3 Richard Sears (p. 218)

4 Jane Addams (p. 226)

5 Jacob Riis (p. 226)

6 political machine (p. 227)

7 John Roebling (p. 228)

8 Booker T. Washington (p. 237)

9 Susan B. Anthony (p. 242)

10 Nineteenth Amendment (p. 243)

1890	1910	1930

1879
First electric power station opens in San Francisco.

1885
First skyscraper is built in Chicago.

1889
Jane Addams opens Hull House for the poor.

1915
Great Migration of African Americans begins.

1919
Nineteenth Amendment is passed.

Facts and Main Ideas

1 How did the inventions of L. O. Colvin and Gustav de Laval help farmers?

2 What was the Great Migration?

3 How did industrialization contribute to changes in women's roles?

4 **Time Line** How many years were there between the time Wyoming gave women the vote and the passage of the Nineteenth Amendment?

5 **Main Idea** Name two or three inventions from the late 1800s and describe how they changed the way people lived.

6 **Main Idea** What were the main problems faced by big cities in the late 1800s?

7 **Main Idea** Identify two or three of the difficulties African Americans faced in the late 1800s and into the 1900s?

8 **Main Idea** What were some of the ways women worked to gain suffrage?

9 **Critical Thinking:** *Draw Conclusions* In 1916, many African Americans moved from the South to the North. In what ways was their experience similar to that of immigrants from other countries? In what ways do you think their experience was different?

Apply Skills

Read Line and Circle Graphs

Look back at the graphs on pages 230 and 231. Use them to answer the following questions.

1 How many more people lived in urban areas than in rural areas in 1970?

2 Which careers did most workers hold in the year 1900? in the year 2000?

3 If you were to make a graph comparing the kinds of jobs people in different areas of the United States held in the present year, which type of graph would you use and why?

Write About History

1 **Write a letter** to a friend describing a new invention from the late 1800s. Explain how it will change the way people live.

2 **Write an editorial** trying to convince people that women should have the right to vote.

3 **Write a story** about an immigrant family who has just arrived in the United States. Describe their home, workplace, and other experiences.

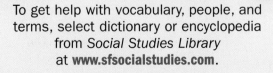

Internet Activity

To get help with vocabulary, people, and terms, select dictionary or encyclopedia from *Social Studies Library* at **www.sfsocialstudies.com**.

Becoming a World Power

1914
Panama Canal
The Panama Canal connects the Atlantic and Pacific oceans.

Lesson 1

1

1908
Grand Canyon National Monument
President Theodore Roosevelt protects the Grand Canyon from developers.

Lesson 2

2

1919
Versailles, France
Allied leaders meet in Versailles, France, to draw up a peace treaty to end World War I.

Lesson 3

3

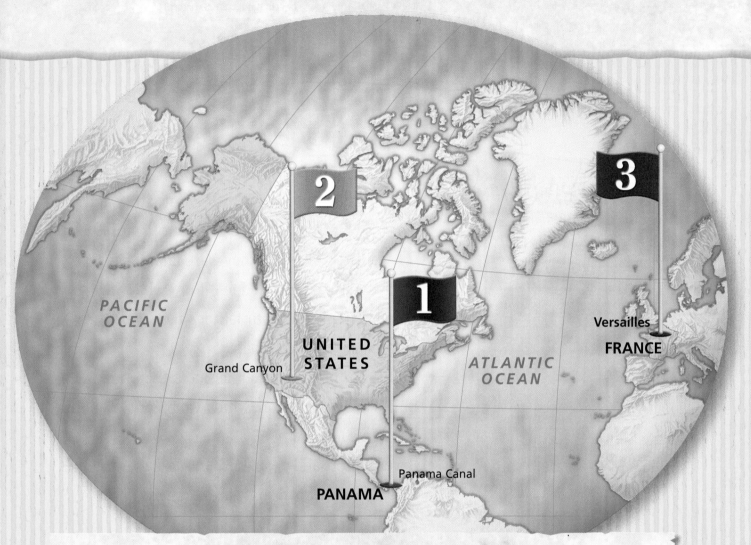

Why We Remember

The United States continued to expand, gaining new lands and becoming involved outside its borders. As the country grew, so did its challenges. In the late 1800s, the rapid growth of industry created problems for people and cities. Some industries were dirty or unsafe, and sometimes both. A few businesses were not fair to other companies. Many people worked to stop these abuses. With problems to solve at home, most Americans felt that the United States did not need to get involved in the problems of other countries. Attacks on U.S. ships and citizens changed that, however. The United States found it could no longer remain isolated. In the early 1900s, the nation was drawn into war overseas.

1865   1915

1867
The United States buys Alaska from Russia.

July 1898
Hawaii is annexed by the United States.

August 1898
Spanish-American War ends with U.S. victory.

1914
Panama Canal opens.

Panama Canal

PREVIEW

Focus on the Main Idea
By the end of the 1800s, the United States had gained new territory and became a world power.

PLACES
Hawaii
Puerto Rico
Cuba
Panama Canal

PEOPLE
William Seward
Liliuokalani
Theodore Roosevelt
Walter Reed
John Stevens

VOCABULARY
yellow journalism
Spanish-American War
Rough Riders
Buffalo Soldiers
isthmus

▶ Alaska is beautiful, rugged, and cold. It is also bigger than Texas, California, and Montana combined.

Expanding Overseas

You Are There

It is March 1867. Your father and mother have gone out to dinner. As they left, they were talking about a place called Alaska, but you don't know what they are discussing. You pick up your father's newspaper to learn more, and you read that:

- Russia has offered to sell Alaska to the United States for $7.2 million, which works out to about two cents an acre.

- Several thousand people live in Alaska—most are native Inuit people; some are Russian.

- There are reports that the land is rich in resources such as timber, coal, and fish.

You think it sounds like a good deal. But how will Congress vote on this sale?

Cause and Effect As you read, note the causes of the actions of individuals or countries.

Alaska

It seemed an incredible bargain—land for two cents an acre! Why was it for sale? Russia had claimed Alaska since 1741. As Canadian and American settlement closed in around Alaska, Russians worried that they might lose the land, so they offered to sell it. But many Americans opposed the deal. Hadn't the Civil War cost the country too much?

William Seward had been interested in Alaska since before the Civil War. He was the secretary of state for Abraham Lincoln and had continued in that job with President Andrew Johnson. Seward wanted to see the United States grow. Alaska was so large that it would increase the size of the United States by nearly 20 percent. Seward also believed that Alaska's fishing, fur trade, and mining were valuable.

The Civil War had interrupted Seward's plans. In 1866 the Russians began dis-

▶ **William Seward**

cussions again. The terms of the sale were approved by Russia on March 30, 1867. The United States would buy Alaska for $7.2 million in gold. The United States Senate approved the purchase in April 1867 and the House of Representatives approved it the next year.

At first, newspapers attacked Seward. They called the new territory "Seward's Icebox" and "Seward's Folly" (foolish act or silly idea). But Alaska's value would soon be recognized.

Gold had been discovered in Alaska as early as 1861, but new discoveries at Juneau (1880), Nome (1898), and Fairbanks (1903) brought fortune seekers north. Fishing became increasingly important to Alaska's economy. In 1878 Alaska's first salmon cannery was built. This was the beginning of what has become the largest salmon industry in the world.

In 1906 Alaska sent its first elected representative to Congress, though this delegate could not vote on laws. Alaska had an elected legislature by 1912. This was the beginning of the road to statehood.

REVIEW Contrast people's feelings about the purchase of Alaska before and after the discovery of gold.

↻ **Compare and Contrast**

Literature and Social Studies

To Build a Fire

A young American writer named Jack London traveled to Alaska in 1897. In a story called "To Build a Fire," a gold miner falls into a stream on a bitter cold Alaska day. He must build a fire quickly, or he will freeze to death.

"He worked slowly and carefully, keenly aware of his danger. Gradually, as the flame grew stronger, he increased the size of the twigs with which he fed it. He squatted in the snow, pulling the twigs out from their entanglement in the brush and feeding directly to the flame. He knew there must be no failure. When it is seventy-five below zero, a man must not fail in his first attempt to build a fire...."

Hawaii

Thousands of miles southwest of Alaska lies **Hawaii,** a group of islands in the Pacific Ocean. Europeans discovered these islands in 1778. The Hawaiian people were impressed with the Europeans and their tools. In the early 1800s, one Hawaiian leader used European weapons to take control of the islands. He became Hawaii's first king.

People soon came to Hawaii from many countries. Houses, schools, and stores were built. Cows and horses were introduced. New ideas were also introduced. Even Hawaii's king took an interest in the idea of constitutional government.

American planters began moving to Hawaii in the mid-1800s. The islands' warm climate was perfect for growing sugarcane and pineapples. The planters established large plantations for these valuable cash crops. The Hawaiian king signed an agreement that gave Americans special trading rights and the port of Pearl Harbor for shipping.

Liliuokalani (li lee uh who kuh LAH nee) became Hawaii's queen in 1891—the first woman to rule Hawaii. She was well educated, had traveled in Europe, and was married to an American. However, she did not want foreigners having so much control. She thought that the previous king should not have agreed to work with the Americans. She would not renew the agreement.

The many foreigners in Hawaii were not ready to be sent home. In 1893 they asked Liliuokalani to give up the throne, and then declared that she was no longer queen and took control of the government. President Grover Cleveland told the American planters that Liliuokalani must be queen. They ignored his order, because the islands were not under U.S. authority.

A group of Hawaiians gathered weapons and planned a revolt, but they were discovered. Queen Liliuokalani was arrested and forced to stay in her palace. The queen realized she could not win this battle. She said:

> *"I yielded [gave up] my authority to the forces of the United States in order to avoid bloodshed."*

The American planters, who had gained greater power than other groups living in the islands, wanted Hawaii to be annexed, or added to the United States. Hawaii was annexed in July 1898.

REVIEW What led up to the annexing of Hawaii to the United States? *Sequence*

▶ Queen Liliuokalani, pictured here, wrote many songs about Hawaii that are still sung today.

▶ Hawaii is famous for its warm climate and great beauty. The Hawaiian islands have many lovely beaches like this one.

▶ The explosion of the *Maine* shocked Americans.

NEW YORK JOURNAL
AND ADVERTISER.

DESTRUCTION OF THE WAR SHIP MAINE WAS THE WORK OF AN ENEMY

$50,000!
$50,000 REWARD!
For the Detection of the
Perpetrator of
the Maine Outrage!

Assistant Secretary Roosevelt
Convinced the Explosion of
the War Ship Was Not
an Accident.

The Journal Offers $50,000 Reward for the
Conviction of the Criminals Who Sent
258 American Sailors to Their Death.
Naval Officers Unanimous That
Ship Was Destroyed
on Purpose.

$50,000!
$50,000 REWARD!
For the Detection of the
Perpetrator of
the Maine Outrage!

Causes of the Spanish-American War

Islands closer to the United States than Hawaii were also demanding attention at this time. By the late 1800s, Spain's empire in the Western Hemisphere had been reduced to just two Caribbean islands: **Puerto Rico** and **Cuba.** In 1895 the Cuban people revolted against Spanish rule. The Spanish army reacted harshly. To keep people from joining the revolution, Spanish soldiers imprisoned hundreds of thousands of Cubans.

Many people in the United States were angered by Spain's treatment of the Cuban people. They were also upset because businesses in Cuba owned by American citizens were being destroyed. They worried that Americans living in Cuba might be in danger too. The United States government decided to act. In January 1898 President William McKinley sent the battleship USS *Maine* to Cuba's Havana harbor. The *Maine's* goal was to protect the lives and property of Americans in Cuba.

On the night of February 15, a huge explosion destroyed the *Maine,* killing 260 Americans. Several United States newspa-pers reported that Spain had caused the explosion. In the years since, studies have shown that an accident aboard the ship probably caused the explosion, although we may never know the true cause. However, newspaper reporters of the day were convinced that it must be Spain's fault. One even stated that a torpedo hole had been discovered. Such false or exaggerated reporting is called **yellow journalism.** The newspaper publishers knew that these types of reports sold more papers. Yellow journalism also gave them greater political power, because they could control voters' opinions.

United States citizens already believed bad things about Spain. Newspapers had published many biased and exaggerated articles on how the Spaniards treated the Cubans. Also, Cuban refugees living in the United States were urging Americans to help free their country. People called for action, crying,

"Remember the **Maine***!"*

Congress declared war on April 25, 1898, and the **Spanish-American War** began.

REVIEW Why were Americans willing to go to war against Spain? **Summarize**

253

War with Spain

In addition to Cuba and Puerto Rico, Spain had colonies in the Philippines and Guam, groups of islands in the Pacific Ocean. The United States Navy's first goal was to destroy the powerful Spanish fleet in the Philippines. The Navy's Pacific fleet had been stationed in Hong Kong since January 1898. When war was declared in April, battleships sailed to the Philippines under the command of Commodore George Dewey. When Dewey spotted the Spanish ships in Manila Bay, he gave Captain Charles Gridley the order, "You may fire when you are ready, Gridley." The Spanish fleet was completely destroyed.

In the United States, people prepared for battle. Nearly one million Americans volunteered to fight in the Spanish-American War. **Theodore Roosevelt,** the assistant secretary of the navy, left his job to organize a group of volunteer soldiers. He put together a fighting force of cowboys, Native Americans, college athletes, and wealthy New Yorkers. Newspapers began calling Roosevelt's soldiers the **Rough Riders.**

Also chosen to go to Cuba to fight were several units of experienced African American soldiers. These soldiers were known as **Buffalo Soldiers,** a nickname they got while serving in the wars against Native Americans on the Great Plains.

American soldiers fought their way across Cuba through dense, tropical forest. On July 1, 1898, they reached Spain's main force on Cuba's San Juan Hill. Rough Riders, Buffalo Soldiers, and other American soldiers charged the Spanish troops.

The Spanish were defeated at the Battle of San Juan Hill. Two days later, American ships destroyed the Spanish fleet in Cuba. In August 1898 the United States and Spain agreed to a treaty ending the war.

REVIEW Who were the Buffalo Soldiers?
Main Idea and Details

▶ This statue honors the Buffalo Soldiers, a group of African Americans who had fought out west. They also went into battle alongside the Rough Riders.

▶ Theodore Roosevelt led the Rough Riders up San Juan Hill.

254

Results of War

On the map below, you can see some effects of the United States victory over Spain in the Spanish-American War. The United States gained control of several Spanish territories, including Puerto Rico, the Philippines, and Guam. Cuba gained independence from Spain, but remained under U.S. protection for a few years, while it set up a new government. The Philippines remained an American territory until 1946, when it became an independent nation. Puerto Rico and Guam are still part of the United States, and their people are United States citizens.

With its swift victory over Spain, the United States showed that it had become a powerful nation. The United States was now a world power, or one of the most powerful nations in the world.

Theodore Roosevelt became a national hero. As he stepped off the boat from Cuba, the crowds shouted, "Hurrah for Teddy and the Rough Riders!" Roosevelt was soon elected governor of New York and later became President of the United States. In the Biography on page 259, you will find out how childhood experiences helped prepare Roosevelt for leadership.

Victory in the Spanish-American War, however, was costly. More than 5,000 American soldiers died. Of these, fewer than 400 were killed in battle. The rest died from diseases such as malaria and yellow fever.

REVIEW How did the Spanish-American War change the role of the United States in the world? **Cause and Effect**

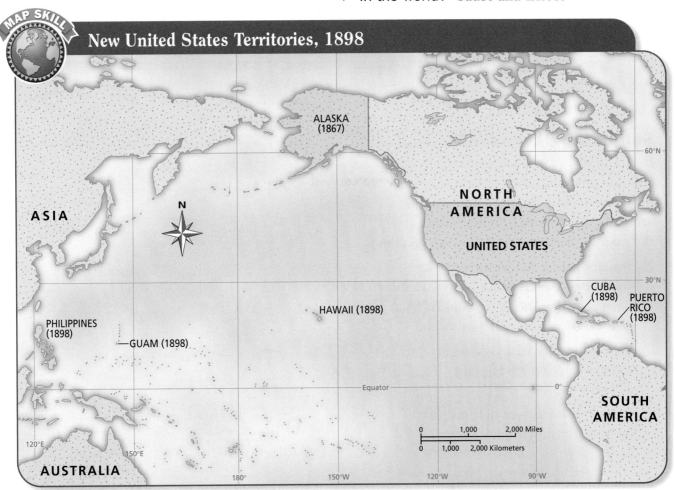

MAP SKILL

New United States Territories, 1898

▶ By 1898 the United States controlled territories throughout the Pacific Ocean.

MAP SKILL Use Latitude and Longitude *Estimate the location of Guam using latitude and longitude.*

Panama Canal

To sail from one coast of the United States to the other, ships had to sail around Cape Horn at the southern tip of South America. The trip took more than two months! The trip was not simply long; the cape's strong current and fierce storms could make it dangerous too. Like many other Americans, Theodore Roosevelt wanted U.S. ships to be able to travel between the Atlantic and Pacific Oceans quickly, for both trading and military purposes. After the Spanish-American War, this seemed even more important, because the navy had played such a big part in the war.

The trip could be shortened from months to days if a canal could be cut across the Isthmus of Panama. An **isthmus** is a narrow strip of land that connects two larger areas. The Isthmus of Panama connects North and South America. Roosevelt set out to build such a canal. But first, he had to solve a number of problems.

First, the United States had to get control of the land. Panama at that time belonged to the South American nation of Colombia. Colombia refused to give it up. But backed by the United States, Panama declared independence in 1903. Panama then agreed to let the United States build a canal through its land. (In 1921, the United States repaid Colombia for the loss of Panama.)

Second, deadly diseases such as yellow fever and malaria were common in hot, wet areas such as Panama. These diseases killed thousands every year. Army doctor **Walter Reed,** considered one of the world's great doctors and medical researchers, discovered that these diseases were carried by mosquitoes. He even tested his theory on himself.

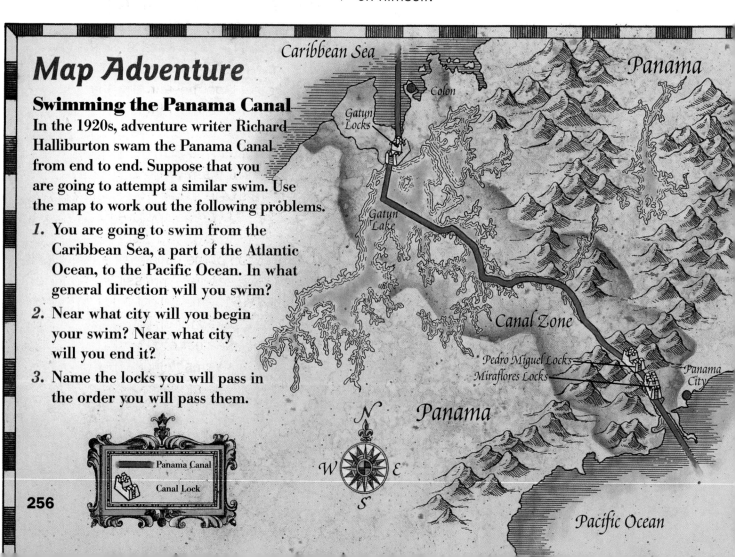

Map Adventure

Swimming the Panama Canal

In the 1920s, adventure writer Richard Halliburton swam the Panama Canal from end to end. Suppose that you are going to attempt a similar swim. Use the map to work out the following problems.

1. You are going to swim from the Caribbean Sea, a part of the Atlantic Ocean, to the Pacific Ocean. In what general direction will you swim?

2. Near what city will you begin your swim? Near what city will you end it?

3. Name the locks you will pass in the order you will pass them.

Panama Canal

Canal Lock

Disease-carrying mosquitoes swarmed in the dense rainforest through which the canal would be built. Another Army doctor, W. C. Gorgas, led the effort to drain the areas of standing water where mosquitoes laid their eggs. The mosquito population shrank, and so did the number of cases of yellow fever and malaria.

Third, the mountains, swamps, and mud of Panama would make the job of digging a canal very difficult. But in 1904, more than 40,000 people and lines of steam shovels set to work.

At first the digging was slow. Then in 1905 **John Stevens** was appointed chief engineer for the project. It was Stevens who approved and funded Gorgas's efforts to eliminate mosquitoes. He then dramatically increased the workforce, hiring Americans, Panamanians, and people from the Caribbean islands. He paved the streets of Panama's main cities and built new towns, with hospitals, hotels, and schools, to house the workers. He then created an efficient system of railroad tracks for moving equipment and carrying dirt away

▶ **President Roosevelt, in the white suit, takes a turn at the controls of a steam shovel in Panama.**

from the digging sites.

Among the many important contributions Stevens made was convincing Theodore Roosevelt and Congress of the wisdom of building a system of locks. Others had wanted a sea-level canal, where the canal was dug so deep that ships could simply sail through. Several factors made the use of locks important. The tides in the Pacific are much greater than those in the Atlantic. This would make navigation difficult. The land was high above sea level, and the deeper digging would cost vastly more, in dollars and lives, and would take many years longer. It was likely that a sea-level canal would be a complete failure. Congress approved Stevens's plan, but only by a narrow margin.

The creation of the canal was a huge task. Sometimes it seemed impossible. But on August 15, 1914, the 50-mile long **Panama Canal** was opened for shipping. Roosevelt called it "the greatest engineering feat of the ages." Now a steamship could move from one end of the canal to the other in just nine hours!

REVIEW What problems did the United States have to solve in order to build the Panama Canal? **Summarize**

▶ **A huge ship cruises through the Panama Canal.**

Panama Today

The treaty signed in 1903 gave the United States the right to control the Panama Canal "in perpetuity," or forever. In exchange, the United States would pay Panama millions of dollars and guarantee the country's independence. The United States managed the canal without challenge until 1964. Some of Panama's citizens felt that they should control the canal, because it was in their country.

In 1977 a new treaty was signed between the two countries. In the year 2000 the

▶ **U.S. President Jimmy Carter turns over control of the canal to Panamanian President Mireya Moscoso.**

treaty went into effect. It gave Panama full control of the canal. Today, most of the ships passing through the canal are from the United States and Asia. Petroleum is the main product transported through the canal.

REVIEW What caused the United States to sign a new treaty with Panama? **Cause and Effect**

Summarize the Lesson

1867 The United States bought Alaska from Russia.

July 1898 Hawaii was annexed by the United States.

August 1898 Spanish-American War ended with a United States victory.

1914 Panama Canal opened.

LESSON 1 REVIEW

Check Facts and Main Ideas

1. Cause and Effect On a separate sheet of paper, fill in an effect of each major event from this lesson.

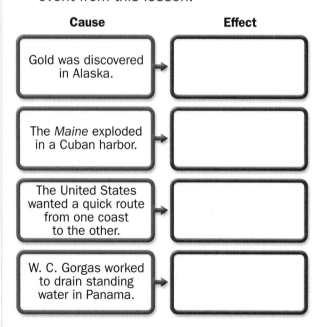

Cause	Effect
Gold was discovered in Alaska.	
The *Maine* exploded in a Cuban harbor.	
The United States wanted a quick route from one coast to the other.	
W. C. Gorgas worked to drain standing water in Panama.	

2. Why did **William Seward** want to buy **Alaska**?

3. Why did American planters move to **Hawaii**?

4. How did **yellow journalism** help bring about the **Spanish-American War**? Answer in two or more sentences. Use the highlighted terms.

5. Critical Thinking: *Draw Conclusions* By 1900 the United States was seen as a world power. How do you think the events described in this lesson helped the United States become a world power?

Link to ∞ Geography

Research United States Territories Look back at the map of the new United States territories on page 255. Choose one of these places and find out more about it. Write a short oral report describing the land and people of this place. Share your report.

Theodore Roosevelt
1858–1919

As a child, Teddy Roosevelt was often sick, and this left him very weak. One day, when he was 13, Teddy was alone on a train when two boys started to tease him. They made fun of his glasses, his clothes, and his skinniness. Right then and there Teddy decided that he would build up his body so no one would ever tease him again.

Back at home, he started exercising with weights and taking boxing lessons. Soon he was winning track and field events such as foot races and the broad jump. In his twenties, Roosevelt went out west to the Dakota Territory. There he became an expert horseback rider, roping cattle and building fences as well as most cowboys. But he never forgot the lesson he had learned as a child. Roosevelt was determined that he would do everything he could to protect the weak.

Between 1898 and 1900, as governor of New York, Roosevelt backed laws to protect women and children from unhealthy conditions where they worked and from long hours of work. Roosevelt became known as a person who stood up for the poor.

Roosevelt also loved nature and fought to protect it. As President, he told Congress that,

"To waste, to destroy our natural resources, to skin and exhaust [use up] the land instead of using it so as to increase its usefulness, will result in undermining [weakening] . . . the very prosperity [good life] . . . which we ought . . . to hand down to [our children] . . ."

BIOFACT

Named in honor of Teddy Roosevelt, the teddy bear became a popular toy in the early 1900s.

Learn from Biographies

Describe how Roosevelt's experience with childhood illness affected his ideas as an adult.

For more information, go to *Meet the People* at **www.sfsocialstudies.com**.

Thinking Skills

Credibility of a Source

What? A **source** is any written or oral account that may provide information. Some sources are **credible,** or reliable. Other sources are not credible, or not reliable. When you decide whether a source is credible or not credible, you are determining whether or not to believe the information the source is giving you.

Why? Do you sometimes read or hear about things you find difficult to believe? Perhaps you should believe them.

▶ **This painting shows one artist's view of the explosion of the *Maine.***

Source A

I was...so quiet that Lieutenant J. Hood came up and asked laughingly if I was asleep. I said "No, I am on watch." Scarcely had I spoken when there came a dull, sullen roar. Would to God that I could blot out the sound and the scenes that followed. Then came a sharp explosion—some say numerous detonations [blasts]. I remember only one....I have no theories as to the cause of the explosion. I cannot form any. I, with others, had heard the Havana harbor was full of torpedoes [mines], but the officers whose duty it was to examine into that reported that they found no signs of any. Personally, I do not believe that the Spanish had anything to do with the disaster.

—Lieutenant John J. Blandin

Or perhaps you should not. You need to know how to determine the credibility of any source of information.

In 1898 the U.S. battleship *Maine* exploded in Havana Harbor. Americans and others wondered what caused the explosion. The ship's officers and sailors who survived wrote reports.

At the same time, some newspaper publishers decided that they could sell many newspapers if they printed sensational stories, or stories that would make people excited or interested. They also knew that they could affect public opinion.

Source A is from a report by Lieutenant John J. Blandin, who was on board the *Maine* when it exploded. Source B is from a front-page article published in the *New York Journal* on February 17, 1898.

How? To determine whether a source is credible, the first step is to consider the author of the source. Decide whether the author has first-hand or expert knowledge about the event. Decide whether the author has any reason to exaggerate, change the facts, or describe events in a particular way. It also helps to find out whether the author does or does not have a reputation for being truthful and accurate. You can also check another source.

Source B

Think and Apply

1. What is Source A? What is Source B?

2. What did Lieutenant Blandin say about the probable cause of the explosion? What did the newspaper say about the probable cause of the explosion?

3. Which report do you think has more credibility? Why?

1900 ———————————————————————— 1915

1901
Theodore
Roosevelt
becomes
President.

1906
Upton Sinclair
publishes *The
Jungle.*

1913
The Sixteenth
Amendment creates a
national income tax.

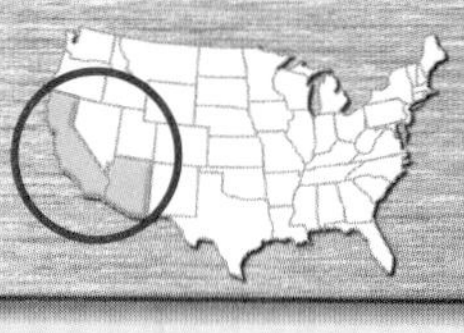

Yosemite
National
Park

Grand
Canyon

The Progressive Movement

PREVIEW

Focus on the Main Idea
Reformers worked to improve
conditions in the United States
during the early years of the
industrial age.

PLACES
Yosemite National Park
Grand Canyon National
Monument

PEOPLE
Ida Tarbell
Upton Sinclair
John Muir

VOCABULARY
trust
Progressives
muckraker
Blue Laws
conservation

You Are There
You and your family have just
settled into your new tenement
apartment. The apartment is not
really new, however. It is old.

Your family has moved to the city to work in a
cotton mill. Both your mother and father work at the
mill, and so do all of your neighbors. The mill seems
to provide most of the jobs in this part of town.

When your parents think you have fallen asleep,
your father reads aloud from the newspaper. You can
hear him say, "Yesterday there was an accident at the
cotton mill. A floor collapsed under the weight of the
spinning machines. Several people were hurt." He
stops reading and adds, "You know, it is not just the
floors that have me worried. Those machines move so
fast. I don't know if the bosses care about what happens, but I worry about it sometimes."

As you lie in the dark, you wonder, *Does anyone care about workers like my Mom and Dad?*

Compare and Contrast As you read, think
about how life changed because of the work
of reformers.

Problems of an Industrial Society

Cotton mills were not the only source of worry for Americans during the early 1900s. As industry grew in the United States, the problems created by industry grew too.

As you read in Unit 2, factories at this time could be dangerous places, both for adults and for the children that many industries hired. Workers operating dangerous machines were sometimes poorly trained. Many factories were not healthful places in which to work. Factories were often fire hazards too.

Children were small enough to climb in and out of the machinery to repair it, which could be dangerous. Also, children who worked often could not attend school.

Some industries filled the air with smoke. Some dumped waste into rivers or lakes. Forests were cut down for mines, ships, and buildings, but few companies planted new trees. There were frequent explosions and accidents in coal mines.

▶ In 1908 in this Indiana factory, young boys were still at work at midnight.

As industry became more important to everyone, some companies joined together to form groups that could control whole industries. These groups, often called **trusts,** had the power to drive out any competition. Companies usually compete with one another, which leads to better products and fairer prices. Without competition, trusts could act like monopolies. They could charge higher prices for their products.

REVIEW What problems arose because of the increase in industry during the early 1900s? **Summarize**

▶ Like many other cities in the early 1900s, Chicago suffered from problems caused by the rapid growth of industry.

263

Theodore Roosevelt and the Progressives

As problems related to industry increased, people came forward who wanted to solve the problems. Theodore Roosevelt helped lead the way to reform.

The Spanish-American War had made Roosevelt a national hero. In 1900 he was elected Vice-President under President McKinley. When McKinley was assassinated in 1901, Roosevelt became President. He was elected for a full term in 1904.

Roosevelt agreed with the goals of a group of reformers known as Progressives. **Progressives** were reformers who worked to stop unfair practices by businesses and to improve the way in which government worked.

One group of Progressives was made up of writers. They were called **muckrakers,** because they uncovered what some people saw as "muck"—shameful conditions in business and other areas of American life.

In 1902 muckraker **Ida Tarbell** wrote a series of magazine articles about Standard Oil, the company founded by John D. Rockefeller. She wrote about the dangers of trusts such as Standard Oil, which controlled the oil industry. Other trusts were

formed in the railroad and steel industries. Trusts could hurt smaller businesses, she argued, and they could hurt the reputations of large companies that did not form trusts. Tarbell's work helped convince Roosevelt that he should be an active "trust-buster." He used the Sherman Antitrust Act, passed in 1890, to attack trusts. This law allowed the government to force trusts to break up into smaller companies.

In 1906 muckraker **Upton Sinclair** wrote a novel called *The Jungle.* This book tells about conditions in the meat-packing plants of Chicago. Roosevelt had barely finished reading the book when he told his secretary of agriculture, James Wilson, to investigate the lack of cleanliness in food processing.

Soon Roosevelt supported and signed two reform acts—the Meat Inspection Act and the Pure Food and Drug Act. The Meat Inspection Act allowed government inspectors to check meat to make sure it was safe to eat. The Pure Food and Drug Act helped make food and medicine safer by requiring companies to tell the truth about their products.

Progressives did not limit their concern to business and government. Wherever they saw a problem, Progressives went to work, trying to improve education, health, and more. They also tried to solve social, moral, and family problems, although this was not always as welcome as other reforms.

REVIEW What were muckrakers?
Main Idea and Details

▶ **This famous political cartoon shows the cartoonist's impression of President Roosevelt's response to problems in the meat industry.**

North Wind Picture Archives

Growing Concern for Worker Safety

The factories being built across the United States were filled with machinery and workers. Before industrialization, safety equipment was not very important. But now there were big machines and new problems. Everything happened faster, and many jobs were dangerous.

In the late 1800s, safety laws were passed to make the machines safer and to protect workers. Goggles and helmets are now required in many industries. Can you think of other safety equipment used in factories today to protect workers?

Impact of Reforms

Progressives believed that change could come through laws. They had been working for change for many years, but their efforts gained strength with Theodore Roosevelt in the White House. As you have read, Roosevelt broke up the big trusts and passed laws to make food and medicine safer.

Progressives were responsible for the passing of many new laws. Building codes made tenements and factories safer. Coal mines were inspected. Young children were kept from working in factories. Children were now required to attend school. And schools were required to hire nurses to protect children's health. In Chapter 5 you read about two other important concerns of the Progressives: civil rights and women's rights.

Progressives also helped pass **Blue Laws** in many towns. These were laws designed to solve some of the social problems of the day. A very serious problem was that many people abused alcohol. One Blue Law said that people could not buy alcohol on Sundays. In some areas, this law did help reduce abuses. However, some people did not want the government to force morals on them.

One long-lasting change introduced by the Progressives was the income tax. Before the late 1800s, the United States had few taxes. The country needed money to pay for reforms and other projects. In 1913 the Sixteenth Amendment gave Congress the legal right to tax income, or money earned from work or investing.

REVIEW What was the goal of the laws passed because of the Progressive Movement? Summarize

Caring for Nature

As interest in the West increased, some people became concerned that wilderness areas might be damaged. A movement to save western lands started shortly after the Civil War. Yellowstone National Park became the world's first national park in 1872. The Progressives continued this work.

John Muir, a naturalist and writer, had a great impact on the conservation of some of the country's most beautiful areas. **Conservation** is protecting something from being destroyed or used up.

Muir traveled across the United States, visiting the great wilderness areas. He wrote magazine articles that described the beauty of these places. He helped establish **Yosemite National Park** (yoh SEM it ee) in California in 1890 and helped found the Sierra Club in 1892. The club was named for the Sierra Nevada, the mountain range where Yosemite is located. Muir hoped that the club would contribute to the preservation of the environment.

Theodore Roosevelt had always loved being outdoors. He and Muir were good friends. They shared an appreciation of America's natural beauty. "I want to drop politics absolutely for four days and just be in the open with you," President Roosevelt wrote to Muir in 1903. Soon afterward, Roosevelt joined Muir on a camping trip in Yosemite.

For the next three days, the two men rode Yosemite's trails on horseback. They rested by rushing streams. They admired the magnificent mountains, trees, and waterfalls. The trip convinced Roosevelt that he must do more to conserve the nation's natural resources. Of the sights he had seen on the trip, he said,

> *"It would be a shame to our civilization to let them disappear . . . . We are not building this country of ours for a day. It is to last through the ages."*

▶ **This postcard from 1912 shows visitors enjoying a view of the Grand Canyon, which Theodore Roosevelt had set aside as a National Monument in 1908.**

Roosevelt wanted the country's many natural wonders protected—and he did something about it. He created the National Wildlife Refuge Program and organized the U.S. Forestry Service. He stopped the sale of 235 million acres of timberland and made them into national forests. In 1908 he set aside 800,000 acres in Arizona as the **Grand Canyon National Monument.** This protected the canyon from developers until Congress decided, eleven years later, to make it a national park. Roosevelt also

▶ **John Muir and Teddy Roosevelt shared a love of the wilderness.**

preserved Crater Lake in Oregon and the Anasazi ruins of Mesa Verde, Colorado. By the time he left office in 1909, Roosevelt had created 16 national monuments, 51 wildlife refuges, and 5 new national parks.

REVIEW How did Muir's work promote conservation? *Main Idea and Details*

Summarize the Lesson

1901 Theodore Roosevelt became President.

1906 Upton Sinclair published *The Jungle,* a book that exposed unsafe conditions in Chicago's meatpacking plants.

1913 The Sixteenth Amendment created a national income tax.

LESSON 2   REVIEW

Check Facts and Main Ideas

1. ⊙ **Compare and Contrast** Pick three or four problems the **Progressives** tried to solve. On a separate sheet of paper, complete this diagram by comparing life before Progressives tried to solve the problems to life after they acted.

Before	After

2. What were the **Blue Laws**? Why did some people not like them?

3. Why did **Progressives** want to see **trusts** broken up?

4. Describe some of the work that **John Muir** did to promote **conservation.** Use the highlighted terms in your answer.

5. **Critical Thinking:** *Draw Conclusions* Why do you think writers such as **Ida Tarbell** and **Upton Sinclair** were so important to the Progressive Movement?

Link to ⚭ **Art**

Create a Brochure Look for information about the United States National Parks. Combine information and pictures to create a brochure that could be used to interest people in visiting one or more of the national parks. Use the word **conservation** in your brochure.

Research and Writing Skills

Interpret Political Cartoons

What? A **political cartoon** is a drawing that shows people or events in the news in a way that makes you smile or laugh. The goal of political cartoons is to make you think about events. Political cartoons often have a point of view.

Why? You can find political cartoons in newspapers and magazines. Often the cartoonist wants to express an opinion about people or events. You may or may not agree with the opinion, but a good political cartoon should make you think about the issue.

How? To understand a political cartoon, you need to understand the symbols that the cartoonist uses. For example, a drawing of a character called Uncle Sam is often a symbol for the United States. A drawing of a donkey is a symbol for the Democratic Party, and a drawing of an elephant is a symbol for the Republican Party. Political cartoonists first created these symbols.

Republican Party

Democratic Party

Uncle Sam

In Lesson 2, you read about President Theodore Roosevelt's reforms. Look at the political cartoon on this page. Do you recognize the lion tamer? He is President Roosevelt. The cartoonist made the face look like Roosevelt's. Just in case you did not recognize the face, he wrote "San Juan" on the chest medal to show that the lion tamer is the hero of the Battle of San Juan Hill, during the Spanish-American War.

In the cartoon, Roosevelt is holding a whip to tame the lions. Each lion has a label to show what it stands for. For example, the lion closest to the reader is labeled "BEEF TRUST." The lions are walking out of a door labeled "WALL ST." The stocks of many large companies are traded in the New York Stock Exchange, located on Wall Street in New York City.

The cartoonist is saying something about Theodore Roosevelt and the trusts. If you have ever seen a lion tamer, you probably can figure out what the cartoonist intended.

Think and Apply

1. What labels are shown on the other lions?

2. What is the label on the door from which another lion appears? Why do you think the door has that label?

3. What do you think the cartoonist intends to say about Theodore Roosevelt and the trusts?

Investigating and Sharing the Truth

Ida Tarbell investigated problems in United States businesses. She used her pen to share her findings in order to bring about change.

Ida Tarbell did not follow the traditional role of women in the late 1800s. She attended Allegheny College in Pennsylvania and was the only woman in her class. She wanted to be a journalist, or news reporter and writer, which was unusual for women of the time.

As a girl, Tarbell had seen how some people who ran businesses, when not regulated, could cause harm to others. Her father owned an independent oil company. John D. Rockefeller's Standard Oil Company gained control over most of the country's oil companies, forming a powerful trust. Ida's father could not compete. He went bankrupt and lost his business. This event would later lead to Tarbell's most famous and important writings.

Tarbell went to Paris, France, to study. While there, she wrote articles for several American magazines, which she mailed back to the United States for publication. She came to know that a good reporter must do research and work hard to write well. While other magazines and newspapers exaggerated stories to make them more exciting, Tarbell wrote responsible stories that got the facts straight.

When back in the United States, Tarbell decided to write about the Standard Oil Company. She took her responsibility as a reporter seriously. She closely examined the trust that the Standard Oil Company had formed. She collected documents from government investigations. She interviewed a Standard Oil executive. She found that Standard Oil used illegal methods, such as bribes, to take control of the oil industry.

In 1904 she wrote a series of articles for *McClure's Magazine* about Standard Oil. John D. Rockefeller claimed that Tarbell did not tell the

BUILDING
CITIZENSHIP
Caring
Respect
★ Responsibility
Fairness
Honesty
Courage

truth. But she had done her work too well, and he could not prove her wrong. Tarbell's investigation and reporting helped lead to new government acts. President Theodore Roosevelt read her reports and worked to end the Standard Oil Company trust. The company was broken into several smaller companies.

Ida Tarbell realized that it was her education that had put her in a position to make a difference. She believed that a good education would help make better citizens. When speaking about the responsibility of college graduates, she said,

> "[College graduates] recognize that their education is not merely a personal matter, it is a community matter."

Today, we are protected from trusts because responsible people such as Ida Tarbell worked to correct a problem. Others have learned from her example and continue to strive to change things that need changing.

Responsibility in Action

Discuss with your class ways that students can act responsibly. Have you ever stood up for something you felt was right? Have you ever stood up for another student even when others have not? Have you ever tried to change something that was wrong? How can you best share your views with others?

LESSON 3

1910   1920

1914
World War I
begins in Europe.

1917
United States
enters World
War I.

1919
Treaty of
Versailles ends
World War I.

Versailles
FRANCE   AUSTRIA-
          HUNGARY

SERBIA

World War I

PREVIEW

Focus on the Main Idea
When it appeared the United States might be in danger, the country became involved in World War I.

PLACES
Austria-Hungary
Serbia
Versailles, France

PEOPLE
Woodrow Wilson
John J. Pershing
Eddie Rickenbacker
Alvin C. York

VOCABULARY
World War I
nationalism
alliance
isolationism
League of Nations
Treaty of Versailles

You Are There

It is 1916. One of the bloodiest battles in history has just ended at Verdun in France. A young American, Samuel Benson, is there to help wounded French soldiers. Benson is a volunteer in the American Ambulance Service. For months he has been transporting wounded soldiers to medical aid stations. Now he sits down to write himself a letter:

"My dear sir, self: . . . You may sometimes think you have it pretty hard staying out here in France away from home and loved ones . . . laboring without pay, and often getting little rest or sleep. But listen . . . you are at this hour in the midst of the biggest crisis of history. The world has never seen such a moment . . . and [you are] living for others."

That "moment" is World War I. It is being fought mainly in Europe, but also in Africa and Asia. Soon the United States will enter the war.

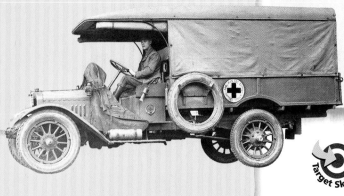

Compare and Contrast As you read, compare and contrast the United States before and during World War I.

A Gathering Storm

What brought on this war, which would one day be called **World War I**? Fierce rivalries had developed among European nations. Countries competed for military power and ownership of European lands. Strong feelings of nationalism existed. **Nationalism** is a love of one's country and the desire to have that country free from the control of others. Tensions grew because many lands were under the control of other nations. European nations also competed for new land in Africa, Asia, and the Middle East. New land meant new trading opportunities, greater wealth, and more power.

Fearing attack from their rivals, several European nations formed alliances. An **alliance** is an agreement among nations to defend one another. If one ally, or member of an alliance, is attacked, the other members promise to come to its aid. The two major alliances were the Allied Powers and the Central Powers. The Allied Powers included Great Britain, France, Russia, Serbia, and Belgium. The Central Powers included Germany, Austria-Hungary, Bulgaria, and Turkey.

In 1914 **Austria-Hungary**, a country in south central Europe, was in control of land that another country, **Serbia**, believed it owned. On June 28, 1914, a Serbian nationalist assassinated Archduke Franz Ferdinand, heir to the Austria-Hungarian throne. Austria-Hungary declared war on Serbia.

REVIEW How did nationalism help bring about war in 1914? *Draw Conclusions*

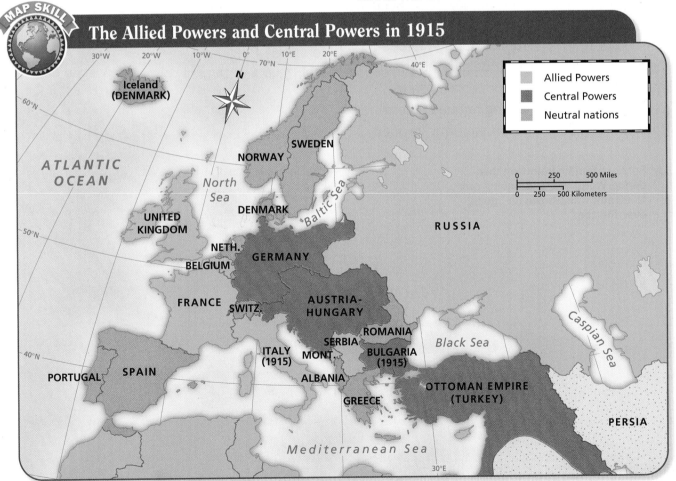

MAP SKILL

The Allied Powers and Central Powers in 1915

Allied Powers
Central Powers
Neutral nations

► The Allied and Central Powers fought during World War I. Some alliances changed after the war began.

MAP SKILL **Use a Map Key** *In 1914 Italy was a member of the Central Powers. What happened in 1915?*

Fighting Begins in Europe

When Austria-Hungary declared war on Serbia, Russia worried that the fighting would threaten the trade route it had from the Black Sea to the Mediterranean Sea. On July 30, 1914, Russia prepared for war to protect its trade route and to help Serbia defeat Austria-Hungary.

Germany, allied with Austria-Hungary, demanded that Russia demobilize, or dismiss its army, and not fight. Russia did not listen to Germany's demands. On August 1, 1914, Germany declared war on Russia.

Germany was afraid that it would have to fight in two different places. Russia was to Germany's east. France, Russia's ally, was to the west. Germany asked France if it planned to fight on the side of Russia. France did not give a clear answer, so Germany declared war on France on August 3.

In order to reach France, German forces needed to march through Belgium. Germany asked the Belgian king for permission to cross his country. The king refused. Therefore, on August 4 the German army invaded Belgium. Great Britain, an ally of Belgium, declared war on Germany. Soon every major European country was involved in the war.

The fighting was fierce. Soldiers on each side dug a system of trenches that faced each other and could extend hundreds of miles. Barbed-wire fences protected the front of each trench. A "no-man's land"—the land between trenches that neither side controlled—spread out between the opposing armies. Soldiers ate and slept in the trenches, which were often flooded or filled with rats.

Each side shot at the other's trenches or sent poison gases into them. Occasionally, troops on one side would go "over the top." They climbed out, crawled through the barbed wire, and raced across no-man's land to attack the enemy. As casualties climbed month after month, it seemed that the killing would never end.

REVIEW What caused Germany to invade Belgium?
Main Idea and Details

▶ Soldiers fought from trenches during World War I. Climbing out to attack was known as "going over the top."

The United States Enters the War

At first, the United States stayed out of World War I. The country had not become involved in European wars in the past. There was a policy of **isolationism.** This meant that the United States preferred to remain neutral and let other countries handle their own affairs. With an ocean between the United States and Europe, it was easy to stay isolated. Also, many European immigrants living in the United States did not want the country to take sides. They feared that they might have to fight the countries from which they had come.

On May 7, 1915, a German submarine torpedoed and sank the British steamship *Lusitania.* More than 100 U.S. citizens were killed. President **Woodrow Wilson** wrote a letter to the German government stating that the United States objected to attacks on non-military ships. Some Americans called for war.

Early in 1917 other events caused the United States to turn firmly against the Central Powers. In January the United States learned that a telegram had been sent from Germany to Mexico asking Mexico to enter the war on the side of the Central Powers. In return, Germany promised to help Mexico get back lands it had lost to the United States.

Then in February 1917, Germany ordered its submarines

▶ **President Wilson asked Congress to declare war in 1917.**

to attack any ships suspected of carrying weapons to the Allied Powers. German submarines sank three American-owned trade ships in March. The deaths of American sailors angered many in the United States.

On April 2 President Wilson asked Congress to declare war on the Central Powers. He stated,

> *"It is a fearful thing to lead this great peaceful people into war, into the most terrible and disastrous of all wars. . . . But the right is more precious than the peace."*

President Wilson hoped that by entering the war, the United States would make the world "safe for democracy." On April 6, 1917, Congress declared war on Germany.

REVIEW Why did the United States enter World War I? Summarize

▶ **American officer's uniform from World War I**

275

America at War

American forces began landing in France in June 1917, with General **John J. Pershing** in command. Pershing was an experienced soldier and had fought in many battles, including at San Juan Hill. On July 4, 1917, Pershing led a parade through Paris to the tomb of the Marquis de Lafayette, who had aided George Washington during the American Revolution. Standing in front of the tomb, Pershing's aide, Colonel Charles Stanton, said,

"Lafayette, we are here!"

These words gave hope to the allies. They showed that Americans were ready to help.

The arrival of American troops in Europe dramatically increased the fighting strength of the Allied Powers, who had already been fighting for three years. More than four million American soldiers, sailors, and marines fought in World War I. Skilled leaders and fierce battles soon molded them into a powerful fighting force. The American presence began to turn the war around—it was one of the deciding factors in the Allied Powers' eventual victory.

The war produced many heroes. **Eddie Rickenbacker** was one of the first U.S. fighter pilots. He was considered an "ace" because he shot down 22 German planes and 4 observation balloons. When World War I planes fought each other in the air, it was called a "dog fight."

One of the most famous heroes of the war was Sergeant **Alvin C. York.** Raised in the mountains of Tennessee, York had needed to learn to use a rifle to hunt food for his family. Even before the war, he was well known for his "sharp shooting." But he was also known as a man of peace. What happened when he went to war?

In October 1918, York was among a patrol of 17 men sent out to stop the German machine guns that were keeping American soldiers from moving forward. The patrol was behind enemy lines, and they came under heavy attack. Six men were killed and three were wounded. Alone, York traded fire with the Germans, a rifle against German machine guns. He shot quickly and accurately. He knocked out 35 machine guns. At last the German major said in English, "Don't shoot anymore!" York and the ten other American soldiers returned to the American lines with 132 German prisoners. York was given the Medal of Honor and was promoted to rank of sergeant.

REVIEW Why was Alvin York promoted to the rank of sergeant? **Main Idea and Details**

▶ Soldiers were taught how to use gas masks to protect themselves during poison gas attacks.

New Technologies

When you read about the American Civil War, you learned that technology changed the way war was fought. By 1915, fifty years later, new technology had once again created weapons that were more powerful and deadly than older ones. For example, in April 1915 Germany began using poison gas as a weapon. The gas burned lungs and blinded eyes. Soon, both sides were using gas against each other. The Germans continued to develop deadlier gases.

Gas masks were developed to protect soldiers from the fumes.

Engineers turned the airplane, a new invention, into a weapon of war. Airplanes dropped bombs on enemy targets and fired machine guns, another new technology, at troops on the ground or enemy planes in the air.

Tanks were used for the first time by the British during World War I. Submarines, which had been in development for many years, were now put to use on a large scale to destroy enemy ships.

REVIEW How did new technologies affect the fighting in World War I? *Summarize*

▶ **Tanks were used for the first time in World War I.**

ANZACs at Gallipoli

HERE AND THERE

Anyone fighting Britain faced all the countries of the British Commonwealth. In April 1915 the Australian and New Zealand Army Corps, or ANZACs, landed on the Gallipoli Peninsula in western Turkey. The ANZACs had been told they would land on flat beaches. What they found were steep cliffs. At the top of the cliffs were heavily armed Turkish forces. Gallipoli overlooks the Dardanelles, the narrow waterway connecting the Mediterranean and Black Seas. Controlling the Dardanelles could help the Allies win the war.

The ANZACs were the first soldiers to arrive at Gallipoli. They were attacked from the cliffs above by artillery and gunfire. Many were killed in the first hours and thousands more in the weeks to follow. The battle raged for eight months. The ANZACs did not get the supplies or medical care they needed, but they fought on. In January 1916 the ANZACs and other Allied soldiers were ordered to withdraw. The battle was a failure, but the ANZACs earned great respect for their valor and sacrifices.

▶ **ANZACs dug into the cliffs for shelter between battles.**

▶ **Gallipoli's steep cliffs made fighting difficult.**

War's Impact at Home

While machine-gun fire and cannon shot blazed through Europe, people in the United States were busy doing what they could to help win the war. Americans sang the new patriotic song "Over There." They gave money to the Red Cross. Uncle Sam pointed out from posters, saying "I Want You" to young men who had not yet joined the army.

There were fewer hands to work the farms with the men off at war. Because of this, less food was being produced. In spite of the shortages, a lot of food was needed for the soldiers fighting overseas. People started raising vegetables in "war gardens." Town squares and parks across the country were dug up and planted with food crops, to help feed people at home and overseas.

The government set up a Food Administration. It still looked like there might not be enough food. The administration encouraged people to eat less, using posters and slogans such as "Food Will Win the War!" Extra food was sent to soldiers and Allied civilians overseas.

Some women went to work in factories, taking over jobs men had done. Women helped produce weapons, tanks, and ammunition. African Americans who had moved North also took over many of the jobs now available.

REVIEW What caused the government to set up the Food Administration? *Cause and Effect*

▶ This poster used the symbol of Uncle Sam to encourage young men to volunteer for the army.

Poster by James Montgomery Flagg, 1918

I WANT YOU FOR U.S. ARMY

NEAREST RECRUITING STATION

▶ These children are harvesting cabbage in a New York City "War Garden."

▶ Children and adults across the United States worked in "war gardens" like this one. The food they grew helped the war effort, feeding workers and their families at home and soldiers overseas.

The War Ends

The war raged into 1918. In September 1918 more than one million United States troops fought in a huge battle in the Meuse-Argonne (MUZ ahr GOHN), a region of northeastern France. More Americans fought in this battle than in any other single battle in United States history. The Allied Powers won the battle, which led to the final defeat of the Central Powers. The United States had helped turn the tide of the war.

On November 11, 1918, the Central Powers surrendered. Today, November 11 is celebrated as Veterans Day, to remember the Americans who fought in World War I and our nation's other wars.

In World War I, losses were huge for both sides. The Central Powers lost more than 3 million soldiers and nearly 3.5 million civilians. The Allied Powers lost nearly 5 million soldiers and more than 3 million civilians. The United States alone lost about 120,000 individuals. Many more were wounded. The war had been devastating and costly. Everyone hoped there would never be another war like that again. They called it "The War to End All Wars," because no one could imagine it happening again.

REVIEW Why did people hope there would never again be another war like World World I? **Draw Conclusions**

In Flanders Fields

Flanders in Belgium is the site of a cemetery and monument for Americans who died fighting to free Belgium. In 1919 Lieutenant Colonel John McCrae, a Canadian soldier and physician, wrote a poem about those who had lost their lives and the cause for which they died.

....

In Flanders fields the poppies blow
Between the crosses, row on row,
That mark our place; and in the sky
The larks, still bravely singing, fly
Scarce heard amid the guns below.

We are the Dead. Short days ago
We lived, felt dawn, saw sunset glow,
Loved, and were loved, and now we lie
In Flanders fields.

Take up our quarrel with the foe:
To you from failing hands we throw
The torch; be yours to hold it high.
If ye break faith with us who die
We shall not sleep, though poppies
  grow
In Flanders fields.

▶ Poppies grow where the dirt has been recently dug. The poem reflects the time when all the graves were new. Here you see the graves of Flanders fields as they appear today. Veterans groups still use paper poppies, like the one at left, to honor the war dead.

The United States and the Peace Process

In January 1919, President Wilson and the other Allied leaders met in **Versailles, France** (vair SIGH), outside Paris, to draw up a peace treaty. Wilson hoped the treaty would not punish the Central Powers and would make sure there would be a lasting peace. He suggested an international organization be formed to prevent wars—a **League of Nations.**

The **Treaty of Versailles** officially ended World War I. Against Wilson's wishes, the treaty did punish the Central Powers. It demanded that Germany pay heavy fines and not rebuild its army. However, the treaty also created the League of Nations, which Wilson had wanted.

The United States Senate did not approve the treaty. They disagreed with the harsh treatment of Germany. Also, many Americans feared that joining the League of Nations might force the United States into future wars. People wanted to return to a policy of isolationism. Peace and isolation would last only about 20 years.

REVIEW Why did President Wilson want a League of Nations? *Draw Conclusions*

Summarize the Lesson

- **1914** World War I began in Europe.
- **1917** United States entered World War I.
- **1919** Treaty of Versailles ended World War I.

LESSON 3 — REVIEW

Check Facts and Main Ideas

1. **Compare and Contrast** On a separate sheet of paper, fill in the boxes to describe what life was like in the United States before and during **World War I.**

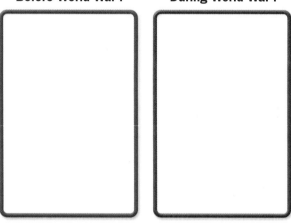

Before World War I | During World War I

2. Identify the two **alliances** that fought each other in **World War I** and the nations that belonged to each. Answer in one or two sentences. Use the highlighted terms.

3. Why did the United States have a policy of isolationism, and what happened to change the policy?

4. Describe new technologies that were developed and used during **World War I** and how these technologies affected the way people fought.

5. **Critical Thinking:** *Draw Conclusions* Why did so many people at home get involved in the effort to help win the war?

Link to ⊸⊸ **Science**

Study Technology Look at the new technologies that were used in **World War I.** Choose one, such as tanks, airplanes, or submarines. Research the technology to find out how it has changed with time. Write a short report to share with the class.

Leather hood and mask

Leather face mask and anti-splinter glass goggles

War in the Air

When World War I started in 1914, the history of powered flight was barely 10 years old. The first warplanes flew as observation craft. They scouted enemy lines from the air and helped direct artillery fire. Soon planes were carrying bombs to drop on enemy targets. By the end of the war, the role of military aircraft had changed from being a minor help to a major force in their own right.

Raised collar to keep neck warm

Sheepskin lined leather gloves to protect against frostbite

Air "Aces"

To qualify as an air "ace", a pilot had to bring down at least 10 enemy aircraft. Captain Eddie Rickenbacker, an American "ace" and war hero, had 24 1/3 hits.

Flying Gear

Pilots flew in open cockpits, so they wore special clothing to keep out the cold.

Sheepskin boots

Thick sole to give a good grip

Wooden box-structure wings covered with canvas

wooden struts

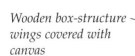

26 ft. 11 in. wingspan

Symbol of British Royal Flying Corps, later the Royal Air Force

Sopwith Camel

The Sopwith F1 Camel first flew in battle in June 1917. It became the most successful Allied fighter in shooting down German aircraft. Pilots enjoyed flying the Camel because it was easy to steer and could make sharp turns at high speed.

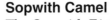

CHAPTER 6
REVIEW

1890   1900

July 1898
Hawaii is annexed by the United States.

August 1898
Spanish-American War ends with United States victory.

1901
Theodore Roosevelt becomes President.

Chapter Summary

Target Skill

Compare and Contrast

On a separate sheet of paper, copy the graphic organizer. Use it to contrast the gaining of Alaska with the gaining of Hawaii. Write several points in each box.

Gaining Alaska	Gaining Hawaii
	• was valuable for growing sugarcane and pineapples

Vocabulary

Match each word with the correct definition or description.

1 yellow journalism (p. 253)

2 isthmus (p. 256)

3 muckraker (p. 264)

4 conservation (p. 266)

5 alliance (p. 273)

a. an agreement among nations to defend one another

b. the protection of forests, rivers, and other natural resources

c. a narrow strip of land that connects two larger areas

d. false or exaggerated reporting

e. person who uncovered shameful conditions in businesses

People and Terms

Write a sentence explaining why each of the following people or terms was important to the United States becoming a world power. You may use two or more in a single sentence.

1 William Seward (p. 251)

2 Spanish-American War (p. 253)

3 Walter Reed (p. 256)

4 Progressives (p. 264)

5 Ida Tarbell (p. 264)

6 Blue Laws (p. 265)

7 John Muir (p. 266)

8 General John J. Pershing (p. 276)

9 Sergeant Alvin C. York (p. 276)

10 Treaty of Versailles (p. 280)

Facts and Main Ideas

1 Who were the Buffalo Soldiers? What did they accomplish?

2 Why did John Stevens prove to be a good choice for chief engineer in building the Panama Canal?

3 What did Woodrow Wilson suggest be formed to prevent war in the future?

4 **Time Line** How many years were there between the end of the Spanish-American War and the United States, entering of World War I?

5 **Main Idea** How did the Spanish-American War help expand the power of the United States abroad?

6 **Main Idea** What major changes did the Progressives bring about in the United States?

7 **Main Idea** Identify two reasons for tensions in Europe before World War I.

8 **Critical Thinking:** *Make Inferences* Before World War I, the United States had a policy of isolationism. What might have happened if the United States had kept that policy and not fought in World War I?

Internet Activity

To get help with vocabulary, people, and terms, select dictionary or encyclopedia from *Social Studies Library* at **www.sfsocialstudies.com**.

Apply Skills

Interpret Political Cartoons
Answer the questions about this cartoon.

1 What is this cartoon about?

2 What is the man throwing? What does it stand for?

3 What do you think is the cartoonist's point of view?

Write About History

1 **Write a brief news story** describing the building of the Panama Canal.

2 **Write an editorial** trying to convince Americans of the importance of conservation.

3 **Draw a political cartoon** about one of the Progressives' issues of the time, such as unsafe work conditions, powerful trusts hurting competition, the need to conserve nature, or alcohol abuse.

"Over There"

by George M. Cohan

By the time the United States decided to enter World War I, there was a feeling of patriotism and responsibility in joining the fight. Songwriters created thousands of new songs in support of American soldiers. George M. Cohan's "Over There" was optimistic and energetic. It was also one of the most popular songs during the war.

Words and Music by George M. Cohan

O - ver there, o - ver there,

Send the word, send the word o - ver there

That the Yanks are com - ing, the Yanks are com - ing, The

drums rum tum - ming ev - 'ry - where.

So pre - pare, say a pray'r,

Send the word, send the word to be - ware

We'll be o - ver, we're com - ing o - ver, And we

won't come back 'till it's o - ver o - ver there.

Main Ideas and Vocabulary

Read the passage below and use it to answer the questions that follow.

In the late 1800s and early 1900s, major changes occurred in the United States. New technologies improved the lives of many Americans. Telephones became widely available. Electric appliances saved time and energy. By the late 1800s, farmers no longer had to rely on manual labor alone. Mechanical reapers and threshing machines made harvesting faster and easier.

Goods of all kinds were produced in factories and mills. People moved from farms to the cities to fill the new jobs. Immigrants came to American cities to work in the factories. Cities became overcrowded and unsafe.

Women and African Americans worked to gain equal rights as citizens. Progressives pushed for laws to protect workers in the workplace. They wrote about the dangers of trusts. They also worked to conserve the wilderness.

Events outside the United States created changes too. To help Cubans gain independence from Spain, the United States fought the Spanish-American War. The United States became a world power.

The United States entered World War I in 1917. Americans helped the Allied Powers defeat the Central Powers.

Life for Americans was very different at the end of World War I from what it had been at the end of the Civil War.

1 According to the passage, what changed farm work in the late 1800s?
A New machines made harvesting faster.
B New laws made farmers hire more workers.
C More people became farmers.
D Americans bought less food.

2 In the passage, the term manual labor means—
A work done with machines
B work done slowly
C work done by hand
D work done quickly and easily

3 In the passage, the word trusts means—
A relies or counts on
B companies that have joined together to control an industry
C industries that make farm machines
D factories with unsafe working conditions

4 What is the main idea of the passage?
A Progressives exposed shameful conditions.
B African Americans and women worked for equal rights.
C The United States fought in two wars.
D Many events in the late 1800s and early 1900s changed life in the United States.

Test Talk

Narrow the answer choices. Rule out answers you know are wrong.

People and Places

Match each person and event to its definition.

1. **Walnut Grove, Virginia** (p. 217)

2. **James Buchanan Eads** (p. 228)

3. **Hawaii** (p. 252)

4. **Rough Riders** (p. 254)

5. **Upton Sinclair** (p. 264)

6. **Austria-Hungary** (p. 273)

a. chain of islands annexed by the United States in 1898

b. home of inventor Cyrus McCormick

c. wrote the muckraking book *The Jungle*

d. country in south central Europe where World War I began

e. Roosevelt's soldiers during the Spanish-American War

f. built the first steel bridge in 1874

Write and Share

Create a Brochure Work in a group to create a brochure to advertise one of the important technologies developed or improved during the 1800s or early 1900s. Possible technologies include the milking machine, mechanical reaper, elevator, subway, and electric stove. Use the textbook or other resources to fill in details about the chosen technology. Create pictures, graphs, or diagrams to help illustrate the technology. Share the brochure with the class, explaining the technology's uses and benefits.

Read on Your Own

Look for books like these in the library.

Apply Skills

Create a Political Cartoon Display Make a poster of political cartoons you have found in newspapers or magazines. You can add cartoons that you draw yourself. Under each cartoon, write a sentence or two explaining what the cartoon is about and what point of view it shows about the subject.

Political Cartoons

President Roosevelt is upset about the meat scandal.

The cartoonist believes that recycling is important.

Arts and Letters

Create an infomercial about an important invention.

1 **Form** a group and choose an invention studied in this unit.

2 **Research** the invention. Write about the inventor and the time during which he or she lived. Explain why he or she made the invention. Describe how the invention has helped people.

3 **Make** a poster or backdrop to advertise your invention.

4 **Present** your infomercial to your class. You may want to dress in the clothing of the time and add sound effects.

Internet Activity

Find more about women's rights. Go to **www.sfsocialstudies.com/activities** and select your grade and unit.

Prosperity, Depression, and War

How do people deal with changing economies?

UNIT 4

Begin with a Primary Source

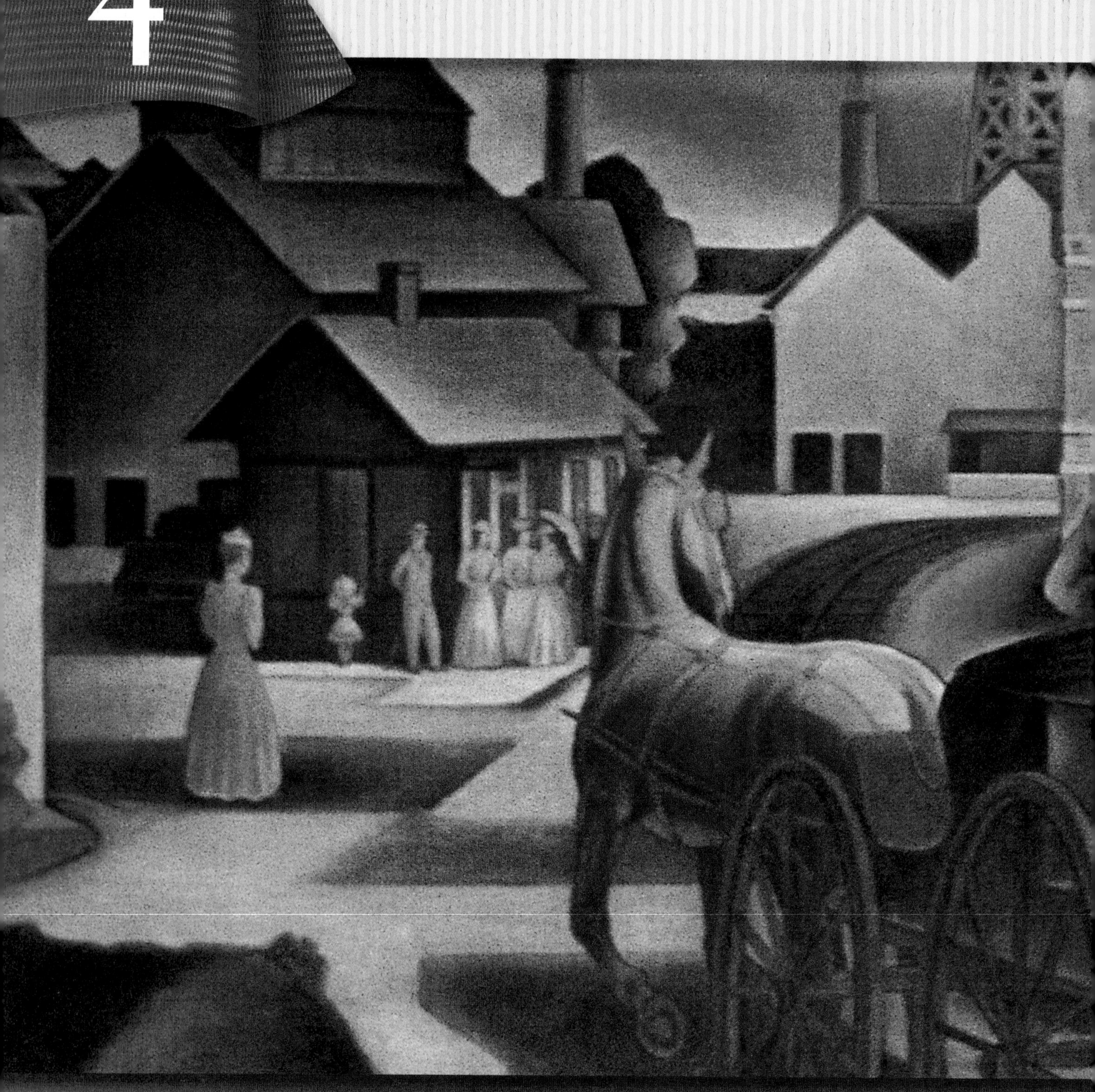

1905 1910 1915 1920 1925

1908
Henry Ford introduces the Model T car.

1919
The Eighteenth Amendment begins Prohibition.

1920
The country's first professional radio station begins broadcasting.

William A. Dolwick created this mural, *Gas City in Boom Days*, in the 1930s as part of a Works Progress Administration (WPA) project. The WPA was a government agency set up to create jobs during the hard times of the Great Depression.

1930   1935   1940   1945

1927 Charles Lindbergh flies alone across the Atlantic Ocean.

1929 The stock market crashes.

1933 President Roosevelt begins the New Deal.

1933 The Twenty-first Amendment ends Prohibition.

1939 World War II begins.

1941 Japan bombs Pearl Harbor.

1942 Japanese Americans are moved to relocation camps.

1945 World War II ends.

Meet the People

Henry Ford

1863–1947

Birthplace: Wayne County, Michigan

Entrepreneur, inventor

- Founded the Ford Motor Company
- Developed the Model T automobile
- Manufactured his cars using an assembly line

Franklin D. Roosevelt

1882–1945

Birthplace: Hyde Park, New York

Governor, President

- Governor of New York State from 1929 to 1932
- President of the United States from 1933 to 1945
- Led the United States during the Great Depression and World War II

Georgia O'Keeffe

1887–1986

Birthplace: near Sun Prairie, Wisconsin

Artist

- Best known for her paintings of large, colorful flowers and desert landscapes
- Received the Presidential Medal of Freedom in 1977
- Taught art at schools in Texas, South Carolina, and Virginia

Dwight D. Eisenhower

1890–1969

Birthplace: Denison, Texas

Army officer, President

- Commanded a tank training center during World War I
- Supreme commander of Allied forces in Europe during World War II
- President of the United States from 1953 to 1961

1860   1880   1900   1920

1863 • Henry Ford

1882 • Franklin D. Roosevelt

1887 • Georgia O'Keeffe

1890 • Dwight D. Eisenhower

1895 • Dorothea Lange

1903 • Zora Neale Hurston

1912 • Benjamin O. Davis, Jr.

1917

For more information, go online to *Meet the People* at **www.sfsocialstudies.com.**

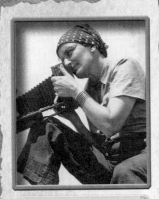

Dorothea Lange

1895–1965

Birthplace: Hoboken, New Jersey

Photographer

- Took photographs of people during the Great Depression
- Photographer for the Farm Security Administration
- Known as one of the greatest documentary photographers of the United States

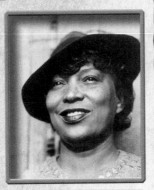

Zora Neale Hurston

1903–1960

Birthplace: Eatonville, Florida

Writer

- Major writer of the Harlem Renaissance
- Wrote about the experiences of African American women
- Studied the folklore of African Americans in the South

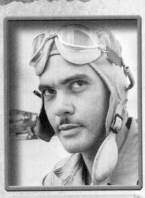

Benjamin O. Davis, Jr.

1912–2002

Birthplace: Washington, D.C.

Pilot, Air Force officer

- Commanded the Tuskegee Airmen during World War II
- Became the first African American general in the United States Air Force
- Wrote an autobiography called *Benjamin O. Davis, Jr., American*

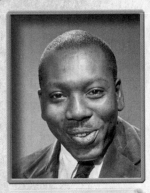

Jacob Lawrence

1917–2000

Birthplace: Atlantic City, New Jersey

Artist

- Created several series of paintings on African American history
- Designed a mural that was installed in 2001 in a New York City subway station
- Professor of art at the University of Washington in Seattle

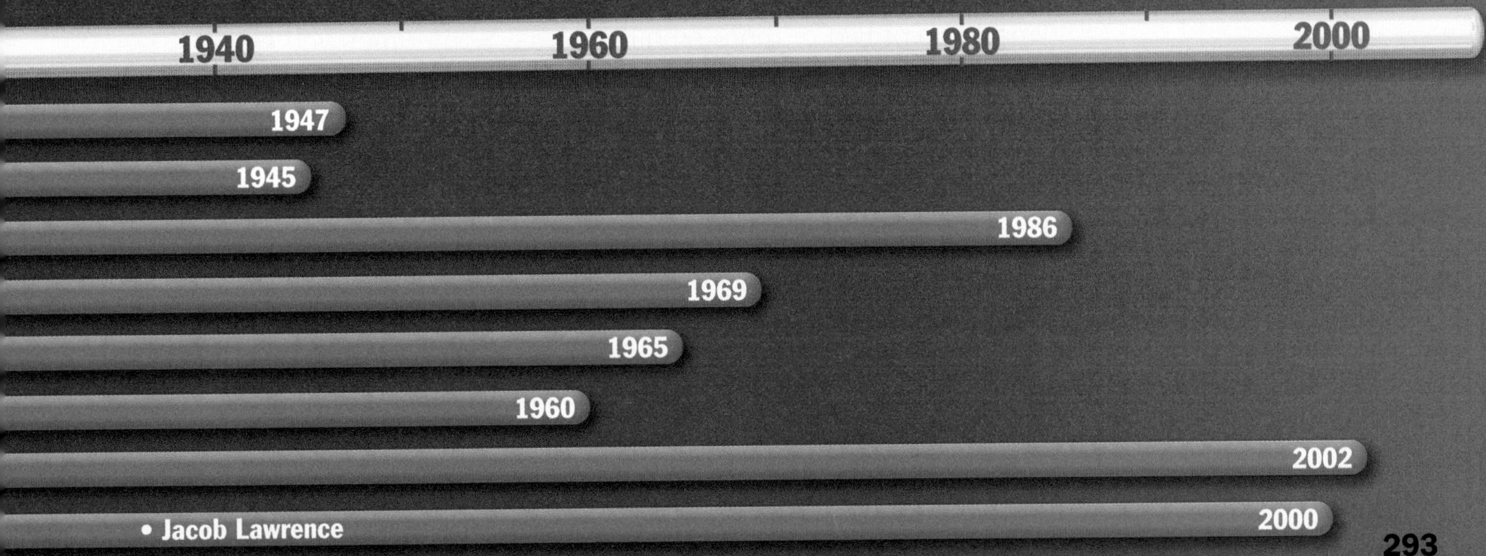

1940
1960
1980
2000
1947
1945
1986
1969
1965
1960
2002
• Jacob Lawrence
2000

Reading Social Studies

Prosperity, Depression, and War

Draw Conclusions

- A conclusion is a judgment based on facts or details.
- Sometimes readers must draw their own conclusions based on the facts and details presented.
- Draw conclusions after you have read a passage. Think about the facts and ideas as a whole. You can also use what you already know.

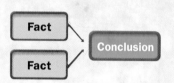

Read the following paragraph. The **facts and details** are highlighted in yellow. The **conclusion** is highlighted in blue.

World War I lasted about 4 years and involved 28 countries. It led to the loss of more than 14 million lives. No war before this had involved more countries or more casualties, making World War I the most devastating of its time.

Word Exercise

Compound Words Compound words are words that are made up of two or more smaller words. Sometimes you can figure out the meaning of a compound word by looking at the words that form it. Compound words can be two or more separate words, words joined by a hyphen, or words that have been combined.

Compound Words		
Separate Words	Hyphenated Words	Combined Words
African American Harlem Renaissance	well-known	everything

Draw Conclusions About the Roaring Twenties

After World War I, the United States entered a time of economic growth that improved the lives of many Americans. Businesses grew in the 1920s, providing people with new jobs and higher pay. Many Americans were able to buy new products such as automobiles and radios.

People had more money and more leisure time. In the cities especially, people looked for more entertainment. Jazz and dance clubs became popular. The search for fun in the cities, combined with illegal alcohol, earned this era the name the "Roaring Twenties."

Many more Americans were going to movies and buying books, magazines, and music. F. Scott Fitzgerald became famous for his novels and short stories about the Roaring Twenties. Fitzgerald's best-known novel, *The Great Gatsby,* is about a rich young man named Jay Gatsby. He has everything that money can buy, but he is not completely happy. Many people saw *The Great Gatsby* as a description of the feelings of many Americans in the 1920s.

Another famous writer of the 1920s was Langston Hughes. Hughes was an important figure in the Harlem Renaissance (REN uh sahns). This was a movement of African American artists centered in Harlem, a neighborhood of New York City. Many artists of the Harlem Renaissance used their writings, paintings, and music to explain how it felt to be an African American at the time. The Harlem Renaissance marked the first time African American artists in the United States gained national attention for their work.

Hughes wrote many novels and children's books, but he is known mostly for his poetry. In his poem, "I, Too," Hughes expresses his hope for better treatment of African Americans.

Apply it!

Use the reading strategy of drawing conclusions to answer the first two questions, then answer the vocabulary question.

1 What can you conclude about how the United States changed after World War I?

2 What facts support the conclusion that the 1920s were a time of change?

3 Look for one example of each kind of compound word described on page 294. Determine the meanings of the two words that make up each compound word. Then define each compound word.

CHAPTER 7

Times of Plenty, Times of Hardship

1908

Detroit, Michigan
Henry Ford builds the first Model T car.

Lesson 1

1

1920s

New Orleans, Louisiana
Jazz music develops in New Orleans and becomes popular during the Roaring Twenties.

Lesson 2

2

1929

New York City, New York
The stock market crashes, beginning the Great Depression.

Lesson 3

3

1933

Washington, D.C.
President Franklin D. Roosevelt begins the New Deal.

Lesson 4

4

1 Detroit

4 Washington, D.C.

3 New York City

2 New Orleans

UNITED STATES

ATLANTIC OCEAN

Why We Remember

The early 1900s were years of great changes in the United States. Inventions such as the automobile, radio, and movies began changing American culture. The 1920s were a period of good times for much of the country. However, these good years were followed in the 1930s by severe economic hardships for many Americans. What was the country like during both good and bad times? Let's find out.

Detroit
Los Angeles

1900   1920

1901
Marconi sends the first radio message across the Atlantic Ocean.

1908
Ford introduces the Model T car.

1920
The world's first radio station begins broadcasting.

An Industrial Nation

PREVIEW

Focus on the Main Idea
The automobile, radio, and movies changed American culture in the early 1900s.

PLACES
Detroit, Michigan
Los Angeles, California

PEOPLE
Henry Ford
Guglielmo Marconi
David Sarnoff
Frank Conrad

VOCABULARY
assembly line
mass production
mass media

You Are There
It is a beautiful autumn afternoon in 1909. Your whole family has gone to take a look at a Model T automobile. Everyone is talking about this car. Some people have nicknamed it the "Tin Lizzie." Your brother complains that it "looks like a bathtub on wheels," but you disagree. The sun sparkles on the black-painted metal. You are pleased to see that there is room for the whole family.

Your family gets in the car for a test drive. The salesman starts the engine with a hand crank. At first the motor gives off a strong smell of gasoline. The ride is a bit bouncy, but you have never been able to go this fast with your family's horses and wagon. As the car moves along at 25 miles an hour, you think about all the exciting places you would be able to drive to in it.

Draw Conclusions As you read, see what conclusions you can draw about how new technology of the early 1900s connected Americans to one another.

Ford's Model T

Few inventions had a greater effect on American life than the Model T, a car built by **Henry Ford,** an entrepreneur and inventor. Before Ford built his first Model T in 1908, few cars could be found on the country's roads. Cars were very expensive to build and to buy. Some of the earliest cars were so loud and unsafe that many people feared riding in them. Ford dreamed of making a car that was sturdy and safe, yet affordable for most people. He said,

> *"I will build a motor car for the great multitude [large number of people]. It will be large enough for the family but small enough for the individual to run and care for. . . . But it will be so low in price that no man making a good salary will be unable to own one."*

Ford could sell his car at a low price because all Model Ts were exactly alike. This was possible because the Model Ts were built using an assembly line. Workers on an **assembly line** stood in one place and put parts of the cars together as the pieces went by on a moving belt. This system allowed Ford's workers to build an entire car in only an hour and a half. Without the assembly line, it would have taken more than 12 hours! This system also allowed Ford to sell his cars for under $500 each, less than half the cost of other cars. He still made enough money to pay his workers $5 a day at a time when the average automobile factory worker made only $2.34 a day.

Ford built his first assembly line in a factory in **Detroit, Michigan.** The Model T was produced from 1908 to 1927. By 1913, 40 percent of the cars sold in the United States were Model Ts. By 1920 half of the cars in the world were Model Ts. In all, 15 million Model Ts were built. For most of the time that the Model T was produced, it came in only one color—black. Some people made fun of the simple style of the Model T. "Why is a Model T like a bathtub?" some joked. "Because you hate to be seen in one." However, the Model T remained the country's most popular car for many years.

REVIEW Why was the Model T the most popular car in the United States?
↻ Draw Conclusions

▶ **Assembly lines decreased the time it took to make automobiles.**

A Nation of Drivers

By 1929 there were about 26 million cars on roads in the United States. The huge increase in car ownership changed the entire nation. For example, farmers who had to carry their crops to markets now had faster and more reliable transportation than their old horses and wagons. One farmer asked that his family bury him with his Model T after his death. "I've never been in a hole yet where my Ford didn't get me out," he explained.

Soon the growing number of cars led to a demand for better roads. Local and state governments used tax money to improve the conditions of roads. Some governments raised money for road improvements by issuing traffic tickets to bad drivers.

The increase in automobiles also helped create many new jobs. Factories needed workers to build cars. Construction workers were needed to improve the roads. Some people opened auto repair shops to fix cars that broke down. Others opened hotels, gas stations, and restaurants for travelers.

Cars gave Americans a kind of freedom they had never had before. Now people could live farther from their jobs. Some people moved to new communities on the edges of cities. Here they could live away from the noise and crowds of the city yet still drive into the city to work. On weekends, many American families who lived in cities drove to the country for sightseeing trips. The Sunday drive became a weekly custom for many American families.

REVIEW How did the automobile change life in the United States?
◑ Draw Conclusions

▶ This postcard from 1923 shows people who used automobiles to travel long distances on vacation.

▶ Trucks helped farmers to deliver goods, such as these ducks, to markets quickly.

Map Adventure

Natural Resources for Detroit's Automobile Industry, 1920

Henry Ford needed many natural resources to make automobiles. However, not all of the necessary resources were in Detroit, Michigan. Suppose you were in charge of ordering natural resources for an automobile factory in Detroit. Use the map to answer the questions below.

1. In what states on the map are oil and gas found? Which state with oil and gas is closest to Detroit?

2. What is the most direct way for a company in Cleveland to transport coal to your automobile factory in Detroit?

3. A manager in your factory suggests that you might be able to save shipping costs by combining shipments, such as buying iron, oil, and coal from the same area and using one shipping company. What is the closest state that has all the major natural resources you need?

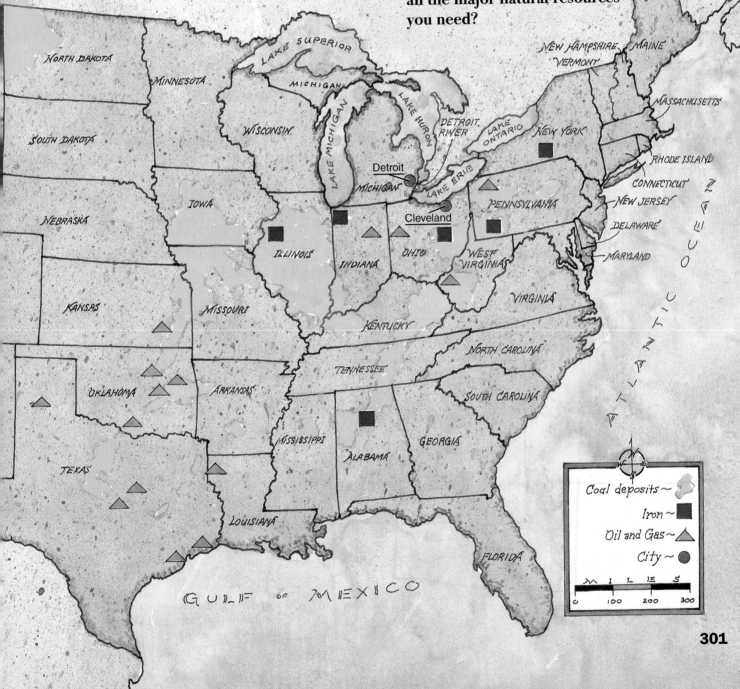

Coal deposits ~
Iron ~ ■
Oil and Gas ~ ▲
City ~ ●

MILES
0   100   200   300

The Age of Radio

Ford's assembly line system soon spread to many other businesses. **Mass production,** the making of large numbers of goods that are exactly alike, was used to manufacture many different products. One of the most popular mass-produced items was the radio.

Originally the inventors of radio technology did not plan on it being used in homes. In 1901 Italian inventor **Guglielmo Marconi** (gool YELL moh mar COH nee) sent the first radio message across the Atlantic Ocean. He set up a business selling radios for communication between ships.

In 1916 one of Marconi's employees, **David Sarnoff,** suggested that Marconi could make money by selling radios for entertainment. Sarnoff talked about making "radio music boxes" to broadcast music, news, entertainment, and sports to people in their homes. Marconi's company rejected this idea.

Other people also saw radio's potential. **Frank Conrad,** an engineer at Westinghouse Electric, developed the technology that would make commercial radio possible. He began making amateur broadcasts, and Westinghouse was soon selling radios to Conrad's

listeners. The company applied for a license, and on November 2, 1920, radio station KDKA began broadcasting from Pittsburgh, Pennsylvania. It was the first professional radio station in the world! The station's first broadcast reported the results of the presidential race between Warren Harding and James Cox.

About this same time, David Sarnoff presented his ideas to the newly formed Radio Corporation of America (RCA). RCA had been founded to compete with Marconi's company. As RCA began to make radios for home use, Sarnoff planned programming to attract listeners. On July 2, 1921, RCA presented a live broadcast of a championship boxing match. Hundreds of thousands of people heard the action on radios set up in public places. Radio sales soared.

Radio listeners began tuning in to more and more new programs. Comedies, dramas, and music programs were popular. By the 1930s, young listeners especially liked action adventures such as *Captain Midnight, Little Orphan Annie,* and *The Lone Ranger.*

REVIEW Why do you think Marconi's company rejected David Sarnoff's ideas about the future of radio?
⟳ **Draw Conclusions**

▶ *(Below)* **The comedy team of Stan Laurel *(left)* and Oliver Hardy *(right)* are shown making a radio broadcast.**

▶ *(Above)* **Radio inventor Guglielmo Marconi *(left)* and radio broadcaster David Sarnoff *(right)*.**

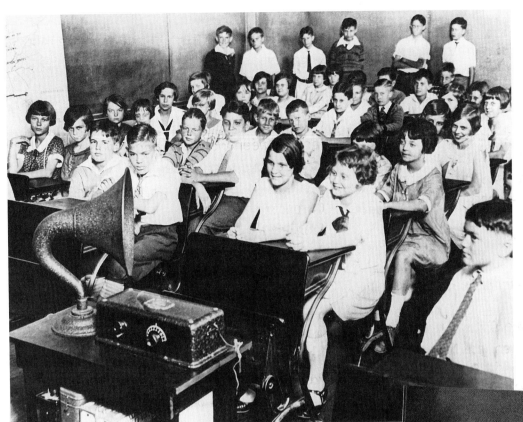

▶ These students from Atlanta, Georgia, listened to a radio broadcast during a lesson on current events in 1926.

▶ Mass media made it possible for millions of readers to see this magazine ad for talcum powder.

VIVAUDOU'S
MAVIS
TALC

Paris VIVAUDOU New York

Mass Media

At first radio makers saw broadcasting as a way to sell their radios. Once many people already owned radios, however, sales slowed. In 1922 radio companies began to raise money for their shows by selling time on the air to companies who wanted to advertise products. In this way the first commercials were born.

The first radio commercials were usually much longer than the 30-second commercials you see on television today. Companies often bought 15 full minutes of airtime for a program about its product. Sometimes a company paid all the expenses of producing an entertainment program, and the show became closely tied to its product. So many soap companies paid for romantic dramas that these shows were nicknamed "soap operas."

Radio joined newspapers as a form of mass media that helped advertisers attract a large audience. **Mass media** are public forms of communication that reach large audiences. As families gathered around their radios to listen to their favorite shows, they joined millions of other Americans doing the same thing. People throughout the country started buying the same products that were advertised on radio. Songs instantly became popular across the entire nation. Through the power of mass media, a common American culture began to take shape.

REVIEW How did radio bring changes to life in the United States? 🔁 Draw Conclusions

303

Going to the Movies

Radio was not the only form of entertainment changing the country. The movie industry also grew during this time. You read in Unit 2 about Thomas Edison's invention of the light bulb. Edison and other inventors also developed the movie camera and projector in the late 1800s. These inventions made possible the motion-picture—or movie—industry.

Beginning in the early 1900s, movies became a popular form of inexpensive entertainment. People went to theaters called nickelodeons, where people paid a nickel to watch a movie. Early movies were short—usually only a few minutes long. Today they are known as silent movies, because they had no sound. Popular subjects included re-creations of news events and well-known stories.

Edison also developed the first motion-picture studio, a place to make movies, in New Jersey. Soon, though, most movies were being made in Hollywood, a part of **Los Angeles, California.** Hollywood became the center of movie making mainly because it had a warm climate most of the year. Also, it was close to a variety of outdoor settings, including mountains, seashores, forests, and deserts. This allowed the movie makers to film outdoor scenes year-round at a low cost.

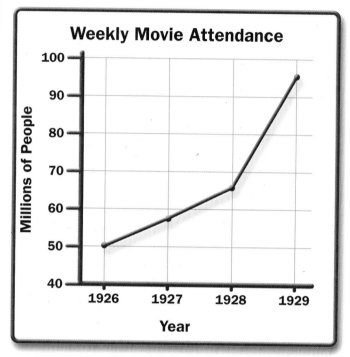

Weekly Movie Attendance

▶ Movies with sound began to appear in theaters in 1927. Do you think sound had a positive or negative effect on attendance?

GRAPH SKILL *About how many more people attended movies each week in 1929 compared with 1926?*

▶ People line up to see a movie.

Like radio, movies encouraged a common culture. Many people copied the hairstyles and clothing of their favorite stars. Actress Mary Pickford's curls inspired women all over the country to curl their hair. When movie star Rudolph Valentino died suddenly in 1926, about 100,000 people gathered outside his funeral in New York City.

American movie attendance grew throughout the early 1900s. In 1916 about 10 million people went to the movies every week. By 1920 that number rose to 35 million. In 1927 new technology allowed the once silent movies to include sound. These new movies were called "talkies."

REVIEW Why do you think many moviegoers copied the hairstyles and clothing of movie stars? ⟳ Draw Conclusions

Summarize the Lesson

1901 Guglielmo Marconi sent the first radio message across the Atlantic Ocean.

1908 Henry Ford introduced the Model T automobile.

1920 The world's first licensed radio station, KDKA in Pittsburgh, Pennsylvania, began broadcasting.

▶ **Posters advertised upcoming movies**

LESSON 1   REVIEW

Check Facts and Main Ideas

1. ⟳ **Draw Conclusions** On a separate sheet of paper, fill in the diagram with a conclusion supported by the facts given.

Facts

The automobile made long-distance travel easier than before.

Radio listeners bought many of the same products.

Moviegoers often copied the hairstyles and clothes of movie stars.

Conclusion

2. What effect did Henry Ford's **assembly line** have on American industry?

3. List some of the major events that led to the Age of Radio.

4. How did **mass media** affect businesses and audiences?

5. Critical Thinking: *Compare and Contrast* Compare and contrast the effects of new technologies on life in the 1920s.

Link to ⟨⟩ Writing

Write an Advertisement Write a script for a radio advertisement for the Model T. Be sure to include the advantages the automobile has over the horse and carriage. Perform your advertisement for the class.

305

Fact and Opinion

What? One of our most important records of the past is the words of the people who participated in events. But words can be misleading, because they can express both facts and opinions. A **fact** is a statement that can be checked. It can be proved to be true. An **opinion** is a personal view. It cannot be proved to be true or false.

Why? You read and hear both facts and opinions every day. For example, you read about World War I in Unit 3. The statement that "the United States declared war on Germany in April 1917" is a fact. You can check it by looking in an encyclopedia or other source. The statement that "the day on which the Central Powers surrendered to the Allied Powers was the best day in all of history" is an opinion. You cannot prove it to be true or false.

▶ **People waited in long lines to see new movies in the 1920s.**

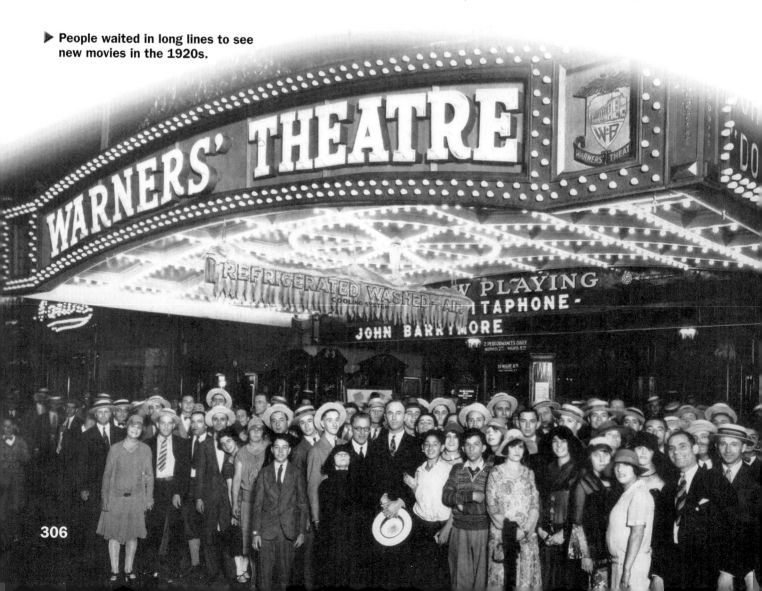

How? To separate fact from opinion, first read the passage. Then determine the subject matter. Finally, look for clue words.

To determine which statements are facts, look for clues such as dates, numbers, and specific information that you know can be checked by looking at other sources. Ask yourself: *Can I prove this statement to be either true or false?*

To determine which statements are opinions, look for clues such as the words *think, believe, feel, best,* and *worst.* Ask yourself: *Is this someone's personal view? Can it be proved true or false?*

It is not always easy to identify facts and opinions. Sometimes a writer may express an opinion with such confidence that it sounds like a fact. At other times a writer may state a fact as if it were an opinion. Learning to think about facts and opinions as you read will help you understand many different types of writing.

Read the passage below about early motion pictures in the United States. It is written from the point of view of a movie fan living in 1930. As you read, think about which statements are facts and which are opinions.

1. What is the topic of this passage?

2. Give one example of a fact in this passage. What clue tells you that it is a fact?

3. Give one example of an opinion in this passage. What clue tells you that it is an opinion?

4. When did the movie *Easy Street* open? How can you check this fact?

"*Movies are the best form of entertainment in the world. When I was young, I used to go to nickelodeons. In these theaters, you paid five cents to see a silent movie. My favorite silent movies are those starring Charlie Chaplin. In 1917 I saw the Charlie Chaplin movie* Easy Street *when it opened. It was the funniest movie ever.*"

"*Today I saw the movie* All Quiet on the Western Front. *This movie is a 'talkie,' which means you can actually listen to the actors speaking to each other! The story is about a group of soldiers fighting in World War I. I believe this is the best movie ever made. I even prefer it to* The Hunchback of Notre Dame, *a silent movie that opened in 1923. All movies should be talkies. They are much better than silent movies.*"

Inventions of the Early 1900s

Televisions. Hair dryers. Crayons. Movies. It is hard to imagine life without many of the things that were invented in the early 1900s. Many of today's inventions are improvements on original ideas from the past and look much different from the originals. The first telephone, for example, was a metal tube. It did not have a ringer or buttons for numbers as telephones do today. Other products look almost identical to the way they did in the past. The stapler has kept the same basic design as earlier models—although the first staplers were made to fasten shoe parts together, not paper! Look at the pictures of inventions from the early 1900s. How does each compare with its present-day version?

Staying Dry
The first hair dryers were boxes that stood on the table. Handheld dryers were introduced in 1920.

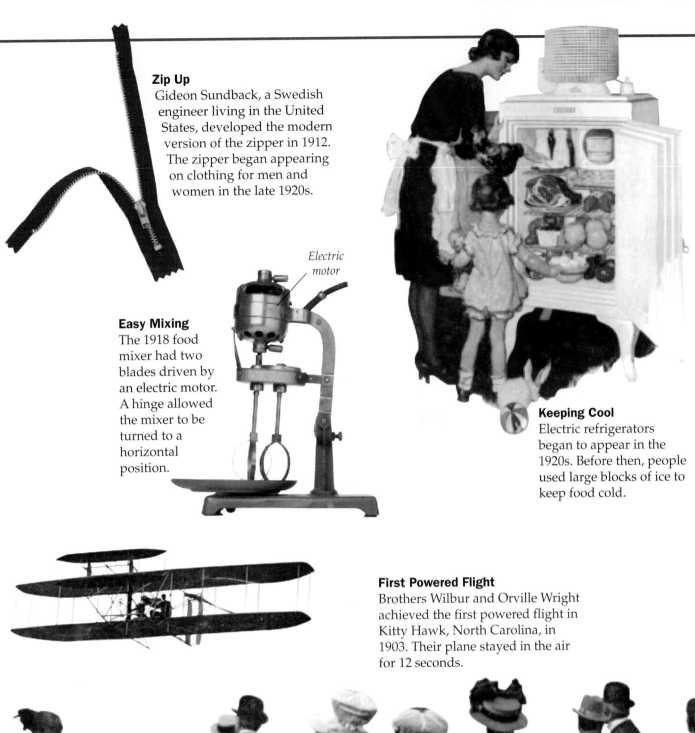

Zip Up
Gideon Sundback, a Swedish engineer living in the United States, developed the modern version of the zipper in 1912. The zipper began appearing on clothing for men and women in the late 1920s.

Electric motor

Easy Mixing
The 1918 food mixer had two blades driven by an electric motor. A hinge allowed the mixer to be turned to a horizontal position.

Keeping Cool
Electric refrigerators began to appear in the 1920s. Before then, people used large blocks of ice to keep food cold.

First Powered Flight
Brothers Wilbur and Orville Wright achieved the first powered flight in Kitty Hawk, North Carolina, in 1903. Their plane stayed in the air for 12 seconds.

1915 — 1930

1919
The Eighteenth Amendment begins Prohibition.

1925
The Great Gatsby by F. Scott Fitzgerald is published.

1927
Charles Lindbergh flies alone across the Atlantic Ocean.

Harlem

New Orleans

PREVIEW

Focus on the Main Idea
Changes in culture and the roles of women in the 1920s had a major effect on life in the United States.

PLACES
New Orleans, Louisiana
Harlem, New York

PEOPLE
Duke Ellington
Louis Armstrong
Bessie Smith
F. Scott Fitzgerald
Langston Hughes
Zora Neale Hurston
Jacob Lawrence
Charles Lindbergh
Amelia Earhart
Georgia O'Keeffe

VOCABULARY
Prohibition
Eighteenth Amendment
Twenty-first Amendment
jazz
Harlem Renaissance

The Roaring Twenties

You Are There
It is 1928, nearly the end of the decade known as the "Roaring Twenties." This has been a great year for you. You often read about your favorite heroes. Baseball player Babe Ruth always seems to be hitting home runs. Airplane pilot Amelia Earhart has just become the first woman to fly across the Atlantic Ocean.

Sometimes you and your friends listen to the new styles of music on the radio. Jazz is your favorite kind of music. It has so much energy. Sometimes you listen to the blues too. You enjoy new dances such as the Charleston.

There is always something new to learn or do. It's a great time to be young.

Draw Conclusions As you read, draw conclusions about why the 1920s were nicknamed the "Roaring Twenties."

Prohibition

The decade of the 1920s was a time of change—new fashions, home products, and music. There were even major changes to the law. In Unit 3 you read about Progressive reformers who helped pass Blue Laws to limit the sale of alcoholic beverages. People who supported these laws were concerned that some people abused alcohol and spent their money on alcohol instead of on their families. Some reformers encouraged temperance, or moderation, in the use of alcoholic beverages. Others called for **Prohibition,** a complete ban on the sale of alcohol.

▶ **During Prohibition, law enforcement officers destroyed barrels of illegal alcohol.**

Carry Nation was one person who became famous for speaking out against the sale of alcohol in the late 1800s. Her home state of Kansas had Blue Laws, but some people operated illegal taverns. Nation often used a hatchet to destroy furniture and bottles of alcohol in illegal bars. She was jailed many times for doing this. Most Prohibition supporters protested against alcohol in peaceful ways.

Reformers who supported Prohibition helped pass the **Eighteenth Amendment** to the United States Constitution in 1919. It is also called the Prohibition Amendment. The amendment outlawed the manufacture, sale, and transportation of alcoholic beverages throughout the United States.

Many Americans supported Prohibition. In some areas there were improvements, and levels of abuse declined. However, some people opposed the law. They argued that the government should not try to control how people behaved. Some people simply ignored the law and found ways to buy alcohol.

Criminals known as bootleggers took over the alcohol business. Bootleggers brought alcohol made in other countries into the United States, or they made their own alcohol. Sometimes they sold alcohol that was dangerous. Wood alcohol could make people go blind, and even killed people. Bootleggers often sold the alcohol to speakeasies, illegal places where people drank alcohol. Competition for business with the speakeasies sometimes led to violent clashes among bootleggers.

Police had little success in stopping bootleggers. There were too many bootleggers and too few officers. Even many people who followed the law were opposed to Prohibition. Finally, in 1933 the **Twenty-first Amendment** to the Constitution was adopted, ending Prohibition.

REVIEW Why was Prohibition ended?
🔄 Draw Conclusions

311

The Jazz Age

In Lesson 1, you read about how mass media brought entertainment to people throughout the country. Radio and movies brought new styles of music to a wide audience. No musical form was more popular in the 1920s than **jazz**, which was influenced by African American musical traditions. Jazz began among African American musicians in **New Orleans, Louisiana.**

Many of the most popular performers and composers of jazz music were African Americans. A composer is someone who writes music. **Duke Ellington** was one of the best-known jazz composers and bandleaders.

Louis Armstrong was another famous jazz musician. His nickname was Satchmo, short for "Satchel [bag] Mouth," which referred to the way his cheeks puffed out when he played the trumpet. Armstrong sang, played, and wrote many kinds of jazz, from fast dance music to slow blues music. The blues is a style of jazz music that expresses feelings of sadness. Armstrong made several recordings with blues singer **Bessie Smith,** including a recording of the song "St. Louis Blues."

Jazz music led to new kinds of dances throughout the nation. Young people loved to move their feet to fast, energetic dances with names like the Charleston and the Lindy Hop. The Charleston could be performed by one person, with a partner, or in a group. Two people usually performed the Lindy Hop, which was also known as the Jitterbug. This dance was done to the jazz style of music known as swing. Swing was often more energetic in beat and rhythm than other jazz styles. Many dance halls held competitions to judge the best performers of the new dance styles.

REVIEW Who were some of the important musicians of the early days of jazz music?
Main Idea and Details

▶ Duke Ellington *(at piano),* Louis Armstrong *(right),* and Bessie Smith *(top)* were popular jazz musicians during the 1920s. Irving Berlin *(far right)* wrote sheet music for jazz musicians to play.

IRVING BERLIN'S
REMEMBER

▶ Actor and dancer Fred Astaire *(left)* plays the piano with composers George and Ira Gershwin.

Changing Culture

Jazz influenced many other parts of American culture, such as theater, dance, and literature. Jazz was such an important part of the 1920s that writer **F. Scott Fitzgerald** nicknamed the decade "The Jazz Age." Fitzgerald's books, such as *The Great Gatsby,* tell stories about the way some city people lived during this period. The characters in his books and short stories moved through a world filled with jazz, popular dances, speakeasies, bootleg alcohol, and the fashions and ideas of the 1920s.

Composer George Gershwin wrote some of the country's most popular songs. He also wrote concert music, such as the famous, jazz-influenced *Rhapsody in Blue.* His work *An American in Paris,* which was later used as the soundtrack for a movie of the same name, brought another feature of American life into music. It re-creates the sounds of traffic and car horns honking. With his

brother, Ira Gershwin, George Gershwin wrote music for the play *Porgy and Bess,* an opera that used jazz-influenced music to tell the story of an African American community.

Composer Aaron Copland used jazz in his music for several ballets and symphonies based on the country's history. The ballet *Rodeo,* for example, is about American frontier life. Copland also used other American forms in his compositions, including traditional folk tunes. One of his best-loved works is *Appalachian Spring,* which adapted folk songs from rural America. Dancer Martha Graham helped develop a new dance style, known as modern dance, for this ballet. Modern dance used freer movements than traditional ballet.

Isadora Duncan was another leader in modern dance. She often danced barefoot in free-flowing costumes. Duncan wrote, "Imagine then a dancer . . . whose body dances in accordance [agreement] with a music heard inwardly . . . This is the truly creative dancer."

REVIEW How did jazz influence modern culture?
Cause and Effect

▶ **Isadora Duncan founded dance schools in Germany, Russia, and the United States.**

The Harlem Renaissance

In Unit 3 you read about the Great Migration, a movement of African Americans from the South to the North. In the 1920s many African American artists moved to **Harlem, New York,** a neighborhood in New York City. They used writing, music, and painting to share their ideas and feelings about life. The period when these works were created is known as the **Harlem Renaissance** (REN uh sahns). A renaissance is a time of great achievements in art and learning. In his 1933 autobiography, writer James Weldon Johnson described the Harlem Renaissance,

> *"Harlem was made known as the scene of laughter, singing, dancing. . . . Writers flocked [gathered] there; many came from far, and depicted [showed] it in many ways and in many languages. They still come; the Harlem of story and song still fascinates them."*

Writers such as Johnson used their work to call for an end to discrimination, or unfair treatment, of African Americans. Writer

▶ **Many popular performers appeared at the Lafayette Theater in Harlem in the 1920s.**

Langston Hughes, for example, wrote poems, books, and plays about the lives of African Americans. You can read one of Hughes's poems on this page. **Zora Neale Hurston** often wrote about the experiences of African American women. Her novel *Their Eyes Were Watching God* tells of a young African American living in Florida in the early 1900s.

Painter **Jacob Lawrence** created several series, or groups, of paintings that showed African American life and history. You will read more about Lawrence in the Citizen Heroes feature on pages 318 and 319.

REVIEW How did the period known as the Harlem Renaissance get its name?
↻ **Draw Conclusions**

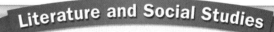
Literature and Social Studies

Langston Hughes wrote this poem, "I, Too," in 1925. What did he mean when he wrote, "I, too, am America"?

I, too, sing America.

I am the darker brother.
They send me to eat in the kitchen
When company comes,
But I laugh,
And eat well,
And grow strong.

Tomorrow,
I'll be at the table
When company comes.
Nobody'll dare
Say to me,
"Eat in the kitchen,"
Then.

Besides,
They'll see how beautiful I am
And be ashamed—

I, too, am America.

Athletes and Pilots

The 1920s was also a time when sports became more popular than ever before. Mass media, which you read about in Lesson 1, helped make many athletes famous.

Sports fans listened to baseball and other sports on the radio. Athletes such as swimmer Gertrude Ederle and baseball player Babe Ruth became as well known as movie stars. Ederle became the first woman to swim across the English Channel, from France to Great Britain, in 1926. Ruth set a record in 1927, when he became the first player to hit 60 home runs in one season. His record was unbroken for more than 30 years.

Radio and newspapers quickly spread the news of historic accomplishments. Pilots were making daring flights that expanded the horizons of airplane travel.

▶ **Baseball star Babe Ruth (right) helped make his sport popular around the country.**

In 1927 pilot **Charles Lindbergh** became the first person to fly alone across the Atlantic Ocean. Lindbergh left New York City on May 20, 1927, in his plane, *The Spirit of St. Louis.* He landed in Paris, France, 33½ hours later. He had fought hard not to fall asleep during the flight. When he landed, Lindbergh announced to the crowd, "I'm Charles A. Lindbergh." But the 100,000 people surrounding his plane already knew who he was. The press nicknamed him "Lucky Lindy," and he became a worldwide hero.

▶ **Charles Lindbergh (left) after his famous flight, and Amelia Earhart (below) in her plane**

In 1928 **Amelia Earhart** also captured the public's imagination. As a passenger, she became the first woman to fly across the Atlantic Ocean. In 1932 Earhart as a pilot, became the first woman to make this journey alone. Three years later she became the first person to fly alone across the Pacific Ocean from Hawaii to California.

REVIEW Why do you think people were so interested in the achievements of athletes and pilots? ⟳ Draw Conclusions

Women at Work

Life for many women changed greatly after they got the right to vote in 1920. The booming economy and changing culture opened up many new job opportunities. The percentage of women who worked remained about the same throughout the 1920s—about 25 percent of adult women. However, the types of work they did changed greatly. Many moved from difficult factory work into jobs in offices.

Several women, such as Amelia Earhart, became leaders in their fields. Painter **Georgia O'Keeffe** became famous for her colorful scenes from nature. You will read more about O'Keeffe in the Biography on page 317.

▶ The subjects of Georgia O'Keeffe's paintings often included flowers such as red poppies.

REVIEW How did working life for women change in the 1920s? Summarize

Summarize the Lesson

1919 The Eighteenth Amendment began Prohibition.

1925 *The Great Gatsby* by F. Scott Fitzgerald is published.

1927 Charles Lindbergh made the first solo flight across the Atlantic Ocean.

LESSON 2 REVIEW

Check Facts and Main Ideas

1. ⟳ Draw Conclusions On a separate sheet of paper, fill in facts that lead to the given conclusion.

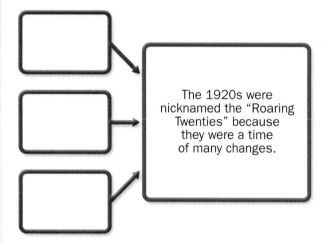

The 1920s were nicknamed the "Roaring Twenties" because they were a time of many changes.

2. What led to the adoption of the **Eighteenth** and **Twenty-first Amendments**?

3. What was the purpose of the work of **Harlem Renaissance** artists?

4. How did mass media help make athletes and pilots famous?

5. Critical Thinking: *Analyze* What changes occurred for working women in the 1920s?

Link to ⟷ **Writing**

Write Poetry Write a poem about the experiences of women in the 1920s. The poem should show how life changed for working women. Mention the experiences of at least one woman discussed in this lesson.

Georgia O'Keeffe

1887–1986

Growing up on a wheat farm near Sun Prairie, Wisconsin, Georgia O'Keeffe was never like other girls she knew. While her sisters wore ribbons in their hair and sashes on their dresses, Georgia disliked frills. By the eighth grade, she knew exactly what she wanted to do—be an artist.

At seventeen, Georgia attended the School of the Art Institute in Chicago. Urged by her teachers to copy other people's paintings, she struggled to find her own style. She wanted to paint what she saw and felt. However, making a living as an artist was an especially difficult goal for a woman at that time. She studied in New York, Virginia, and Texas over the next ten years. She began exhibiting her paintings in New York City in 1916 and soon became known as one of the country's most important and successful artists.

BIOFACT

Georgia O'Keeffe often tiptoed in her stockings across huge canvasses to add final touches before the paint dried.

O'Keeffe's paintings show the beauty in simple, everyday things—especially in nature. Her subjects include New York skyscrapers and desert landscapes of the Southwest. O'Keeffe once said about her success as a painter,

> *"It's mostly a lot of nerve and a lot of very, very hard work."*

Learn from Biographies

Why do you think Georgia O'Keeffe said it took "a lot of nerve" for her to become a successful painter?

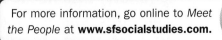

For more information, go online to *Meet the People* at **www.sfsocialstudies.com.**

A Different Kind of Story

There are different ways to tell a story. Most stories are written. Artist Jacob Lawrence told stories in paintings. He wanted to create paintings that told the truth about events in African American history.

Jacob Lawrence was 13 years old when he went to Harlem, in New York City, in 1930. His family was one of many African American families who moved from the South to Harlem during the Great Migration, seeking job opportunities and a better life in northern cities. Lawrence's mother enrolled him in an after-school arts-and-crafts program, and it was there that he decided he wanted to become an artist. The crowded streets of Harlem were a new experience for Lawrence. He recorded what he saw in his paintings. "When I first started painting, I was just making designs. . . . Later I started painting street scenes. I painted peddlers [sellers], parades, fire escapes, apartment houses—all that was new to me."

In 1940 Lawrence began work on a series of 60 paintings known as *The Great Migration.* Lawrence spent many hours reading books from that time period, taking notes, and making drawings. He completed the series of paintings one year later.

In his paintings, Lawrence shows what life was like for African Americans who left their homes in the South and moved to the North. He wanted to show what the Great Migration was like for African Americans, but he wanted to make sure that his "story" was truthful. He made sure to show both sides of the Great Migration—the positive and the negative. Lawrence said,

"The choices made were hard ones, so I wanted to show what made the people get on those northbound trains. I also wanted to show just what it cost to ride them. Uprooting yourself from one way of life to make your way in another involves conflict and struggle. But out of the struggle comes a kind of power, and even beauty. I tried to convey [show] this in the rhythm of the pictures, and in the repetition of certain images."

▶ Jacob Lawrence

BUILDING CITIZENSHIP

Caring

Respect

Responsibility

Fairness

★ Honesty

Courage

Jacob Lawrence, courtesy of the Jacob and Gwendolyn Lawrence Foundation/Digital Image (c) The Museum of Modern Art/Licensed by SCALA/Art Resource, NY

▶ One of Jacob Lawrence's paintings from his series called *The Great Migration* shows the better education opportunities African Americans had in the North.

The paintings show the challenges that many African Americans faced when they arrived in northern cities. Yet the paintings are also full of hope. With the help of his wife, Gwendolyn Knight, also an artist, Lawrence wrote captions for each of the paintings. In these captions, he tried to be as honest as he could. The caption for a painting that shows three African American girls writing on a chalkboard (above) explains that African Americans had better opportunities for a good education in the North than they did in the South.

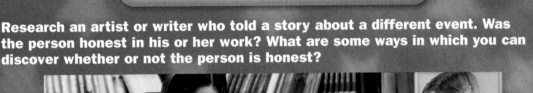

Honesty in Action

Research an artist or writer who told a story about a different event. Was the person honest in his or her work? What are some ways in which you can discover whether or not the person is honest?

New York City

1925 — 1935

1928
Herbert Hoover is elected President.

1929
The stock market crashes.

1932
More than 25 percent of American workers are unemployed.

1932
Franklin D. Roosevelt is elected President.

PREVIEW

Focus on the Main Idea
The Great Depression began with the stock market crash of 1929 and became the worst period of economic hardship in United States history.

PLACES
New York, New York

PEOPLE
Herbert Hoover

VOCABULARY
unemployment
stock market
Great Depression
credit

► Stock tickers like this one printed out the changes in stock prices throughout the day.

The Good Times End

You Are There
It is Thursday morning, October 24, 1929. You are at the New York Stock Exchange on Wall Street, where you run errands for the stock traders. They buy and sell stocks, which are shares in a company. The 1920s have been a boom time for many traders and investors. Many people have grown rich.

The trading will begin in a few minutes. Normally the Stock Exchange is a busy and exciting place, but today the Exchange seems too quiet. Something is wrong. Yesterday's trading ended with an unusually large amount of stocks being sold. Traders are worried that the selling trend will continue. "Ding!" You hear the opening bell that starts the day of trading. Almost immediately the "sell" orders outnumber the "buy" orders. You realize that it will not be a good day on Wall Street.

Cause and Effect As you read, note the main causes and effects of the Great Depression.

Beneath the Surface

As late as September 1929, stock prices continued to rise higher than they ever had before. A year earlier, Presidential candidate **Herbert Hoover** had talked about how well the economy was doing,

> *"We are nearer today to . . . the abolition [end] of poverty and fear from the lives of men and women than ever before in any land."*

Most people agreed with Hoover, and he won the election. However, there were some serious weaknesses in the economy. To help feed the Allied Powers in World War I, farmers had borrowed money from banks to buy additional land and tools to produce more food. After the war, farmers had a surplus—an extra amount—of crops. As crop production increased, crop prices fell. Farmers had difficulty paying off their debts.

Factory workers who made the popular goods of the 1920s also faced problems.

▶ **Coal miners suffered in the 1920s as oil from oil wells** (below left) **replaced coal** (below right) **as a source of fuel.**

▶ **Herbert Hoover was elected President in 1928.**

Just like farmers, factories were producing more goods than they could sell. With not enough buyers for their products, many factories began to lay off workers by the late 1920s. **Unemployment,** or the condition of being out of work, began to grow. Rising unemployment meant fewer people could afford to buy new products.

There were also several industries that had problems even during the economic boom of the 1920s. The mining industry suffered as oil replaced coal for fuel. The lumber industry lost customers who switched to new building materials such as concrete. Not everyone was able to enjoy the good times of the 1920s.

REVIEW What were some weaknesses in the economy during the 1920s?
Main Idea and Details

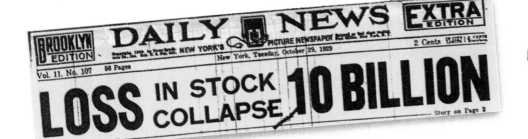

This headline announced the 1929 stock market crash that helped lead to the Great Depression.

The Stock Market Crash

The economic good times ended for many more people after the **stock market** crash of October 1929. A stock market is a place where stocks are bought and sold. If a company needs to raise money, it often sells stocks, or shares of the company, to investors called stockholders. If the company makes money, the price of the stock usually rises and stockholders make a profit when they sell their stocks. The center of the stock market is the New York Stock Exchange on Wall Street in **New York, New York.**

In September 1929, prices began to fall slowly, causing many stockholders to sell their stocks. This caused stock prices to drop further. In October a crash occurred—stock prices fell quickly, causing many investors to panic and sell their stocks. On October 29— known as "Black Tuesday"—a record 16 million shares were traded.

As the stock market fell, billions of dollars were lost. Many people lost all of their money. Banker Sidney J. Weinberg described "Black Tuesday": "It was like a thunderclap. Everybody was stunned. Nobody knew what it was all about . . . [Wall] Street had general confusion."

People panicked as they realized that stocks they owned were worthless. At one point no one would buy the stock of a sewing machine company even after the asking price fell from $48 to $11 per share. A young messenger offered $1 per share and became a leading owner of the company!

Stock prices continued to fall steadily after the crash. By November investors had lost about $26 billion on the stock market. Still, many economic and political leaders expressed little concern about the crash. They saw it as a natural part of the ups and downs of the economy.

REVIEW List the events that occurred during the stock market crash of 1929. Sequence

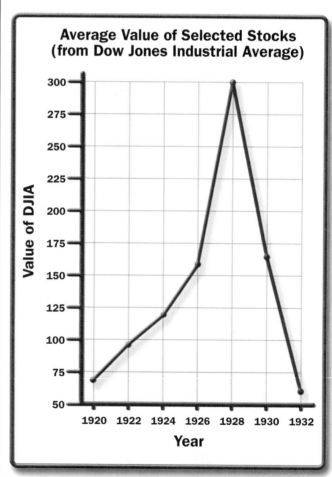

Average Value of Selected Stocks (from Dow Jones Industrial Average)

Value of DJIA / Year

The Dow Jones Industrial Average (DJIA) is used to measure the average value of selected stocks. This graph shows the DJIA value for the last trading day of each year shown.

GRAPH SKILL *About how much did the DJIA value drop from 1928 to 1932?*

▶ Hungry people waited in line to receive food during the Great Depression. These bread lines were often so long that sometimes there was no food left for people at the back of the line. Many people standing in bread lines had well-paid jobs until the Great Depression.

Causes of the Depression

Within weeks of the stock market crash, the country entered the worst period of economic hardship in its history—the **Great Depression.** The stock market crash of 1929 was only one of many causes of the depression, but it exposed the weaknesses in the country's economy.

One reason why the crash had caused panic among investors was that many of them had bought their stocks on **credit,** or borrowed money. They planned to pay back the money lent to them by banks after the prices of the stocks rose. This system was fine as long as prices kept rising. When the crash came, however, many people owed more money than their stocks were worth.

The credit problem hurt many banks. When people could not pay back their loans, banks went broke as well. Many banks had to close. Customers of other banks became frightened and rushed to take all of their money out before their bank closed. The banks did not have enough cash for every customer and even more banks closed. By 1933, 11,000 of the country's 25,000 banks had closed. Many people had lost their savings.

Another economic problem was caused by high tariffs. A tariff is a tax on goods that are produced in other countries and sold in the United States. To help farmers, Congress passed a record-high tariff in 1930. The tariff was meant to reduce competition for American farmers from crops from other countries. In response, many countries also passed high tariffs on goods from the United States. Many American companies and farmers could not sell their goods overseas. Between 1929 and 1934, world trade dropped by 66 percent.

REVIEW How did high tariffs affect the economy? *Cause and Effect*

Hard Times

As the economy worsened, people cut back on their spending. Because they were buying fewer products, many factories closed and others cut back on production. By 1932 factories were making about half of the goods they had made in 1929.

With less production, companies needed fewer workers. By 1932 about 25 percent of the workers in the United States were unemployed. In the three years after the crash, an average of 100,000 people lost their jobs every week. Even people who still had jobs often had to accept pay cuts. Many people lost their homes and faced poverty and hunger for the first time in their lives.

Fewer people working meant less tax money for local governments. To save money, school boards cut teachers' pay. Some schools even had to close.

The effects of high tariffs and crop surpluses continued to hurt farmers. Crop prices declined even further. For example, between 1929 and 1932, the price of cotton fell from 17 cents to 6 cents a pound. Farmers' incomes continued to fall.

President Hoover took several actions to try to improve the economy. He asked business leaders not to lay off workers or cut wages. He asked local and state governments to create jobs by constructing roads and public buildings. He supported the Reconstruction Finance Corporation (RFC), which Congress established in 1932 to lend money to banks and industries. However, the depression continued.

REVIEW How did the economy change between 1929 and 1932?
Compare and Contrast

▶ **Some people who lost their homes built shelters called shanties. Shantytowns became known as "Hoovervilles."**

Surviving the Depression

The Great Depression changed life for most people in the United States. Young people graduating from high school and college could not find jobs. Many young adults put off getting married or having children. In 1932 there were 250,000 fewer weddings than in 1929.

Families struggled during the depression. Women and children could sometimes find work more easily than men because companies paid them less. Many women went to work outside the home for the first time.

Some children quit school to help the family earn money. Others left home to try to find work. "Everyone in America was looking for work," said Langston Hughes.

Charity groups and local governments struggled to help those in need. Hungry people stood for hours in breadlines waiting for free soup and a piece of bread. Homeless people built shelters called shanties out of cardboard or other materials. Groups of these shelters became known as shantytowns.

▶ **Many unemployed men sold apples on the sidewalk to make money.**

Despite his efforts, many people blamed President Hoover for the continuing depression. Shantytowns became known as "Hoovervilles." Empty pockets turned inside out were called "Hoover flags." Newspapers used by homeless people to keep warm were called "Hoover blankets."

REVIEW How did the depression affect the lives of families? **Cause and Effect**

▶ **Unemployment remained high during the Great Depression.**

325

The Election of 1932

As the Great Depression dragged on, many people began to demand that the United States government do more to help. President Hoover believed that the economy would eventually improve with little help from the government. By the time Hoover faced reelection in 1932, many voters wanted a change.

The Democrats nominated New York Governor Franklin D. Roosevelt. He believed that the government needed to take bold action to fight the depression. When Roosevelt won the presidential election, many hoped that he would be able to

▶ **Campaign buttons for Franklin D. Roosevelt and Herbert Hoover**

fulfill his promise to help those in need. You'll read more about Franklin D. Roosevelt in the Biography on page 327.

REVIEW How did Hoover's and Roosevelt's views of the role of government in the depression differ? **Compare and Contrast**

Summarize the Lesson

- **1928** Herbert Hoover was elected President.
- **1929** Many people lost all of their money when the stock market crashed.
- **1932** More than 25 percent of the workers in the United States were unemployed.
- **1932** Franklin D. Roosevelt was elected President after he promised bold action to fight the Great Depression.

LESSON 3 ⟩ REVIEW

Check Facts and Main Ideas

1. Cause and Effect On a separate sheet of paper, complete the chart below by filling in the effects of each cause of the Great Depression.

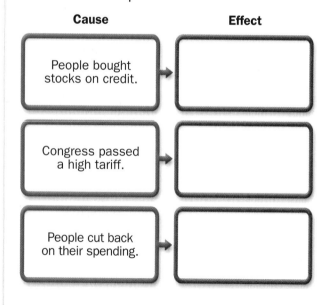

Cause		Effect
People bought stocks on credit.	→	
Congress passed a high tariff.	→	
People cut back on their spending.	→	

2. What were some weaknesses in the economy of the 1920s?

3. What were the main events of the **stock market** crash?

4. What were some causes of the **Great Depression**?

5. Critical Thinking: *Cause and Effect* How did the Great Depression change the lives of Americans?

Link to ⟨∞⟩ Mathematics

Compare Stock Prices Suppose that you are an investor who bought 10 shares of a company's stock for $300 per share in September 1929. After the crash, the price dropped to a low of $100 per share in November 1929. How much money did you lose between September and November?

Franklin Delano Roosevelt
1882–1945

As a young man, most things came easily to Franklin D. Roosevelt. Born into a wealthy family, he had the best of everything. So when Roosevelt went on vacation with his wife and children in 1921, he could not imagine that anything would go wrong. But one morning, when Roosevelt tried to get up, his legs did not work. He had a disease called polio, and for the rest of his life, he would not be able to walk without help.

Franklin Roosevelt never gave up. When he was allowed out of bed, he pulled himself up staircases and tried to go farther each day using crutches. Three years later, Roosevelt was asked to make a speech in support of the Democratic candidate for President. On the night of the speech, wearing heavy braces on his legs, Roosevelt leaned one arm on a cane and the other on his son, James. Breathing hard and straining with each step, Roosevelt made it to the podium. He leaned there to catch his breath, then looked up and smiled. The crowd cheered.

BIOFACT

The Franklin Delano Roosevelt Memorial was dedicated on May 1, 1997, in Washington, D.C.

In 1932 during the Great Depression, Roosevelt was elected President. He worked to help others facing difficult situations. Roosevelt was usually photographed sitting behind his desk, and many Americans did not realize that he could not walk. After his illness, he began to see the world differently. He once said,

"If you have spent two years in bed trying to wiggle your big toe, everything else seems easy."

Learn from Biographies

One of Roosevelt's close friends said that after he got polio, he "began to see the other fellow's point of view." Why should leaders be able to see more than one point of view?

For more information, go online to *Meet the People* at **www.sfsocialstudies.com**.

1930

1933
President Roosevelt begins the New Deal.

1935
The worst dust storm of the decade strikes the Dust Bowl.

1940

1939
John Steinbeck publishes *The Grapes of Wrath*.

Queens
Dodge City

PREVIEW

Focus on the Main Idea
The New Deal helped ease some problems of the Great Depression, but hard times continued throughout the 1930s.

PLACES
Dodge City, Kansas
Queens, New York

PEOPLE
Franklin D. Roosevelt
Eleanor Roosevelt
Dorothea Lange
John Steinbeck

VOCABULARY
New Deal
Social Security
drought
Dust Bowl
migrant worker
inflation

The New Deal

You Are There
It is March 4, 1933. You and your family are listening on the radio to Franklin D. Roosevelt's speech at his inauguration—or swearing-in ceremony—as President of the United States, in Washington, D.C. You will hear many more radio speeches by President Roosevelt over the next few years. They are called "fireside chats." In his speeches he explains his plans to try to help end the Great Depression. He assures everyone that the United States can overcome these hardships. You hope he is right. He sounds confident as he says, "This great nation will endure [carry on] as it has endured, will revive and prosper . . . the only thing we have to fear is fear itself."

Main Idea and Details As you read, identify and describe the major programs of the New Deal.

Goals of the New Deal

When **Franklin D. Roosevelt** became President in March 1933, he immediately urged Congress to do more to try to help the country out of the Great Depression. The programs started at this time came to be called the **New Deal.** The term was taken from one of Roosevelt's campaign speeches,

> *"I pledge to you, I pledge myself, to a new deal for the American people."*

Many of the programs became law in the first 100 days of Roosevelt's term.

The New Deal focused on three major goals: relief, recovery, and reform. The relief efforts helped people right away. One program spent $500 million to feed and house the poorest people in the country. Recovery programs tried to help the economy. Several of these programs helped farmers. One job of the Farm Security Administration (FSA) was to help farmers buy needed equipment.

Reform programs tried to make sure that conditions that led to the Great Depression never happened again. The new Securities and Exchange Commission (SEC) was set up to protect investors in the stock market. Another new reform law gave workers greater rights to organize unions.

Despite all of the New Deal programs, the Great Depression continued. Unemployment remained high. There were still ten million unemployed workers in 1939. In 1937 President Roosevelt recognized that times were still hard. He said,

> *"I see one-third of a nation ill-housed, ill-clad, ill-nourished [poorly fed]."*

However, the New Deal and many private groups did help many people survive the Great Depression until the economy improved. Some programs, such as **Social Security,** are still in effect today.

With Roosevelt's reforms, the government became larger and more powerful. Many people today disagree about how big a role the government should play in people's lives.

REVIEW What were the three main goals of the New Deal? **Main Idea and Details**

▶ Franklin D. Roosevelt and his wife, Eleanor, greeted supporters in 1941, on the day he began his third term as President.

FACT FILE

New Deal Programs

The New Deal created a so-called "alphabet soup" of new government agencies known mainly by their initials.

AAA

The Agricultural Adjustment Administration's goal was to help farmers decrease production, therefore raising the price of crops. Farmers were paid to grow less of certain crops, such as wheat, corn, cotton, tobacco, and rice.

▶ A poster for the CCC in 1935

CCC

The Civilian Conservation Corps set up work camps for more than two million unemployed young men between the ages of 18 and 25. The men received housing, food, and $30 a month, $25 of which was sent home to their families. The CCC is best known for its work planting trees on public lands.

WPA

The Works Progress Administration employed more than eight million people to build roads, schools, bridges, parks, and airports. The Federal Art Project (FAP) was part of the WPA. It employed thousands of artists to create works of art, such as murals on post office buildings. Murals are wall paintings that often take up the entire wall. Painter Jacob Lawrence was one of the artists hired by the FAP to create murals.

▶ The WPA produced posters such as this one in 1935.

TVA

The Tennessee Valley Authority built about 50 dams along rivers in the South to prevent flooding. Workers also built 13 power plants to provide electricity to many homes in the region for the first time.

▶ Norris Dam in Tennessee is one of the first great dams built by the TVA.

SSB

The Social Security Board, one of the New Deal programs that still exists, is now called the Social Security Administration. It provides monthly payments to the elderly, the disabled, and unemployed. Payments are paid for by taxes on employers and employees. Every citizen of the United States is issued a social security card with his or her own identification number.

▶ This poster, issued in 1935 by the Social Security Board, urged citizens to take advantage of the recently passed Social Security Act.

The Dust Bowl

Just as the New Deal programs were beginning to help some farmers, a severe **drought**, or long period without rain, hit the Great Plains in the 1930s. Farmers watched their soil turn to dust in the hot sun. High winds that scattered the soil, called dust storms, left some farmland unusable. Much of the Great Plains became known as the **Dust Bowl**.

The worst single dust storm of the Dust Bowl, called "Black Sunday," occurred in April 1935. It affected parts of Kansas, Colorado, Texas, and Oklahoma. A huge dust cloud blew across the plains, making the sky as dark as night in the middle of the day. Harley Holladay was thirteen years old when this storm hit his family's farm near **Dodge City, Kansas**.

"I happened to look up and noticed this long gray line on the horizon. It looked like a thunderhead, but it was too long and flat and it was rolling toward me way too fast. I sprinted to the house to tell my parents that the dust was coming. . . . The cloud caught me outside . . . I couldn't see anything at all. It was black as night. I got down on my hands and knees and tried to crawl toward the house. I finally felt the porch, and reached up and opened the screen door and crawled inside. . . . Some families strung clothesline between the house and the barn so that they could always find their way back to the house."

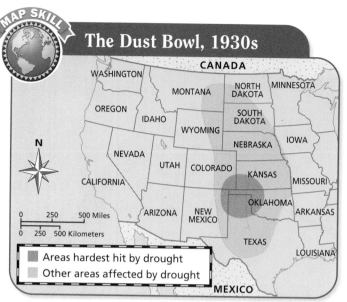

MAP SKILL

The Dust Bowl, 1930s

Areas hardest hit by drought
Other areas affected by drought

▶ Drought turned parts of the Great Plains into a "Dust Bowl."

MAP SKILL Place *Which states were hardest hit by drought?*

More than three million people in the area affected by the drought left their farms. They packed up their belongings and headed west, hoping to find work and new lives in California. Many found only disappointment in California, where there were few jobs. Some became **migrant workers,** moving from place to place to harvest crops.

REVIEW What caused the Dust Bowl?
Cause and Effect

▶ Photographer Dorothea Lange took this picture of a family standing on their farmland in the Dust Bowl.

This photograph of a family moving west from the Dust Bowl was taken by Dorothea Lange, shown below with her camera. Her pictures showed the hardships people faced during the Great Depression.

Photograph by Dorothea Lange

Making a Difference

During the Great Depression, many people helped those in need. One of the busiest people in the White House was First Lady **Eleanor Roosevelt.** As you read in the Biography on page 327, Franklin Roosevelt had been crippled by polio. Because of this, it was hard for him to get around. His wife, Eleanor, became his "eyes and ears." She helped him by traveling across the country to see if New Deal programs were improving conditions.

Eleanor Roosevelt said, "These trips gave me a wonderful opportunity to visit all kinds of places and to see and get to know a good cross section of people. Always during my free time I visited as many government projects as possible, often managing to arrive without advance notice, so that they could not be polished up for my inspection." She was especially concerned about whether children, women, and African Americans were being treated fairly.

During the early part of the depression, photographer **Dorothea Lange** (LANG) took photographs of people standing in breadlines and farm families in the Dust Bowl. Later, a New Deal agency, the Farm Security Administration (FSA), hired her to travel the country and take photographs showing how the Great Depression affected people. Some of her most famous photographs were of migrant workers in the West. The FSA used Lange's photographs to bring the conditions of the poor to the public's attention.

Author **John Steinbeck** used words to describe the hardships faced by migrant workers and their strengths in overcoming them. His novel *The Grapes of Wrath,* published in 1939, tells the story of a family that leaves the Dust Bowl of Oklahoma to find work in California. The book was very successful, and many people learned for the first time what life was like for many of the migrant workers who escaped the Dust Bowl. You will read a passage from *The Grapes of Wrath* on pages 370 to 371.

REVIEW How did some people help those in need during the Great Depression? **Main Idea and Details**

Entertainment During Hard Times

Although the New Deal programs helped many people, they did not end the depression. By 1939 unemployment remained at about 17 percent. People looked for ways to forget their troubles and have fun without spending a lot of money.

A new form of entertainment in the 1930s was the comic book, with characters that included Superman and Batman. People also enjoyed activities at home. Many families played *Monopoly®,* a board game about buying and selling land.

People also went to the movies. A new kind of movie theater appeared in the 1930s—the drive-in. Often whole families sat in their parked cars to watch movies on a large screen. Movies filled with music, dancing, and beautiful costumes were particularly popular. Sometimes people had fun watching scary movies such as *King Kong,* about a giant gorilla that frightens the people of New York City. Adults and children enjoyed cartoon movies such as Walt Disney's *Snow White and the Seven Dwarfs.*

Many people looked to the World's Fairs of 1933 and 1939 as symbols of hope for the future. These fairs were large public displays of the latest technologies. The 1933 fair was held in Chicago. Millions attended the 1939 fair in **Queens, New York,** a part of New York City. The theme of the fair was "Building the World of Tomorrow." Many got their first look at a new invention called television. President Roosevelt declared the fair "open to all mankind."

▶ **A poster advertising the 1933 Chicago World's Fair**

REVIEW What were some ways that people tried to entertain themselves during the Great Depression? Summarize

▶ Some people went to the movies to see musicals such as this one with Ginger Rogers and Fred Astaire *(left).*

Global Depression

The Great Depression had begun in the United States, but it quickly spread to other parts of the world. Millions of people around the world were unemployed and feeling helpless. Some countries in Europe, such as Germany, were especially hard hit.

Germany had not experienced the good times of the Roaring Twenties. It had huge debts to repay to other countries after losing World War I. **Inflation**—a rapid rise in prices—was out of control, and German money became worthless. A lifetime of savings could not buy even a subway ticket. In the next chapter, you will read about how these hardships led to another conflict in Europe that eventually involved the United States.

REVIEW How did the Great Depression affect Europe? *Cause and Effect*

Summarize the Lesson

1933 President Roosevelt began many of his New Deal programs in the first 100 days of his term.

1935 The worst dust storm of the decade struck the Dust Bowl of the Great Plains.

1939 John Steinbeck published his novel about migrant workers, *The Grapes of Wrath.*

LESSON 4 REVIEW

Check Facts and Main Ideas

1. Main Idea and Details On a sheet of paper, complete the graphic organizer to show details supporting the main idea.

> New Deal programs were an "alphabet soup" of government agencies that tried to help people during the Great Depression.

2. What caused the **Dust Bowl**? How did it affect farmers of the Great Plains?

3. How did artists such as Dorothea Lange and John Steinbeck make people aware of the hardships of the Great Depression?

4. Why were forms of entertainment such as movies and board games popular in the 1930s?

5. Critical Thinking: *Draw Conclusions* Why do you think the Great Depression spread around the world?

Link to Art

Design a Mural Choose a topic from the lesson. Draw a design for a mural about that topic that might have appeared on a public building built by a New Deal program.

1900

1901
Marconi sends the first radio message across the Atlantic Ocean.

1908
Ford introduces the Model T car.

Chapter Summary

 Draw Conclusions

On a separate sheet of paper, fill in the diagram to supply three facts on which the given conclusion could be based.

Facts

Conclusion

Americans experienced a drastic change from the good times of the early 1900s to the economic hardships of the 1930s.

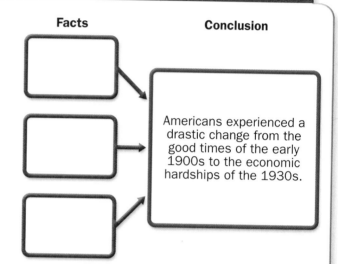

Vocabulary

Match each word with the correct definition or description.

1 mass production (p. 302)

2 Prohibition (p. 311)

3 jazz (p. 312)

4 stock market (p. 322)

5 credit (p. 323)

6 drought (p. 332)

a. place where stocks are bought and sold

b. musical form influenced by African American music traditions

c. long period without rain

d. making a large number of goods that are exactly alike

e. borrowed money

f. complete ban on the sale of alcohol

People and Places

Write a sentence explaining the role of the following people or places in the period between 1900 and 1939. You may use two or more terms in a single sentence.

1 Guglielmo Marconi (p. 302)

2 Los Angeles, California (p. 304)

3 Duke Ellington (p. 312)

4 Harlem, New York (p. 314)

5 Herbert Hoover (p. 321)

6 New York, New York (p. 322)

7 Dorothea Lange (p. 333)

8 Queens, New York (p. 334)

1919
The Eighteenth Amendment begins Prohibition.

1920
The country's first successful radio station begins broadcasting.

1927
Charles Lindbergh flies alone across the Atlantic Ocean.

1935
The worst dust storm of the decade strikes the Dust Bowl.

1939
John Steinbeck publishes *The Grapes of Wrath*.

Facts and Main Ideas

1 How did Henry Ford's assembly line change life in the United States?

2 Why did Prohibition end?

3 **Time Line** In what year was *The Grapes of Wrath* published?

4 **Main Idea** Describe changes in American culture in the early 1900s.

5 **Main Idea** In what ways did life change for Americans during the Roaring Twenties?

6 **Main Idea** Identify the major causes and effects of the Great Depression.

7 **Main Idea** Identify the three major goals of the New Deal.

8 **Critical Thinking:** *Compare and Contrast* Compare the economy of the United States in the 1920s and the 1930s.

Apply Skills

Read the passage below about a child who saw a baseball game in 1928. Decide what information is fact and what is opinion. Then answer the questions.

On Friday my family and I went to see a baseball game at Yankee Stadium in New York City. We saw Babe Ruth, who plays for the New York Yankees. He is the best baseball player in the country. Last year Ruth set a record for most home runs in one season—60! I know that no other baseball player will ever be able to beat that record. My sister likes Ruth's teammate, Lou Gehrig, but in my opinion he is not as good a baseball player as Babe Ruth.

1 Which statements about Babe Ruth are facts?

2 Which statements about Babe Ruth are opinions?

3 Is the statement about Lou Gehrig fact or opinion?

Internet Activity

To get help with vocabulary, people, and terms, select dictionary or encyclopedia from *Social Studies Library* at **www.sfsocialstudies.com.**

Write About History

1 **Write a newspaper article** explaining the benefits and problems of the Prohibition Amendment.

2 **Write a biography** of one of the artists of the Harlem Renaissance.

3 **Write a journal entry** about the new technologies you saw while visiting the 1939 World's Fair in Queens, New York.

World War II

1941

Pearl Harbor, Hawaii
After Japan attacks Pearl Harbor, the United States enters World War II.

Lesson 1

1

1941

Tuskegee, Alabama
The first African American fighter pilots begin training.

Lesson 2

2

1945

Tokyo Bay, Japan
Japan surrenders, ending World War II.

Lesson 3

3

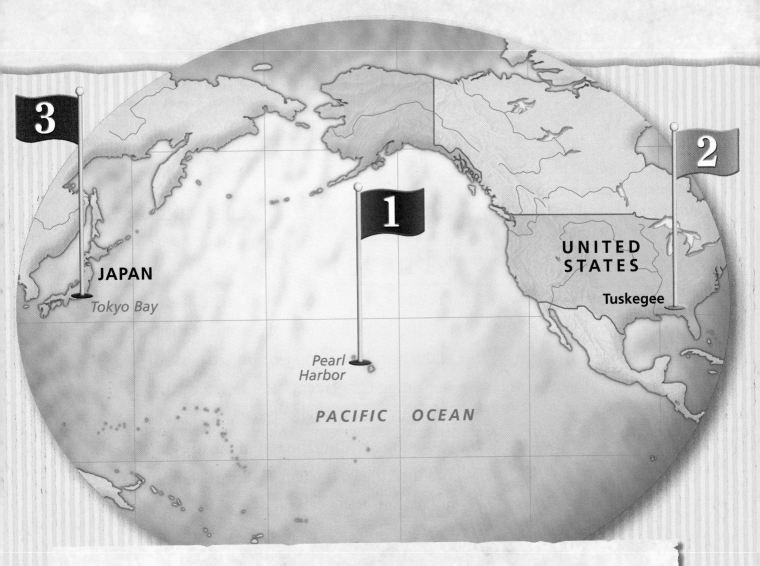

Why We Remember

In 1936 President Franklin D. Roosevelt declared, "This generation of Americans has a rendezvous [meeting] with destiny [the future]." He could not have realized how true his words would be. Americans faced one of their greatest challenges under his presidency—World War II. All Americans participated in the war effort. Millions of men fought on battlefields around the world. At home, women worked in factories making weapons. Children collected scrap metal that was recycled to make war supplies. It was a difficult time, but American efforts paid off. The United States and its allies won World War II, and the United States went on to become one of the most powerful nations in the world.

Pearl Harbor

| 1930 | | | 1945 |

1933 Adolf Hitler takes power in Germany.

1939 World War II begins.

1941 Japan bombs Pearl Harbor.

PREVIEW

Focus on the Main Idea
The United States entered World War II when Japan attacked Pearl Harbor in 1941.

PLACES
Pearl Harbor, Hawaii

PEOPLE
Franklin D. Roosevelt
Adolf Hitler
Benito Mussolini
Winston Churchill
Hideki Tojo
Joseph Stalin

VOCABULARY
dictator
fascism
Axis
Allies
World War II
Lend-Lease

▶ **An early radio**

World War II Begins

You Are There It is the evening of October 5, 1937. You turn on the radio and hear a voice that sounds familiar—it's President Franklin Roosevelt. "The peace, the freedom and the security of ninety percent of the population of the world are being jeopardized [risked] by the remaining ten percent," Roosevelt says.

You think about what the President is saying. A few nations are putting the rest of the world in danger. You turn the volume up. "We are determined to keep out of war," Roosevelt says, "yet we cannot insure [protect] ourselves against the disastrous effects of war and the dangers of involvement."

That sounds bad. He's saying that the United States may be forced to go to war. You listen to the rest of the speech, and you start to wonder how this news will affect your future.

Draw Conclusions As you read, see what conclusions you can draw about the early years of World War II.

Target Skill

The Rise of Dictators

Suppose you had just listened to that speech by President **Franklin D. Roosevelt** in 1937. You had been so focused on the hard times at home that you had not been paying much attention to problems around the world. Now you decided to find out what was happening.

Here is what you found out. As in the United States, most of the world had been stuck in an economic depression for years. People in some countries had lost confidence in their governments. They did not believe that their governments could ever make things better. They turned to new leaders who promised to make their troubles disappear. Some people were so desperate for change, they were even willing to sacrifice their freedom. This led to the rise of dictators in several countries. A **dictator** is a leader who gains complete control of a country's government.

Why did this make the world a more dangerous place? The story of **Adolf Hitler** helps make this clear. Hitler became the dictator of Germany in 1933. Hitler and his political party, called the Nazi party, believed in **fascism.** This is a form of government in which individual freedoms are denied and complete power is given to the government.

Hitler believed that Germans were superior to other people. He spoke of hatred for many groups. He particularly attacked Jewish people, who had lived in Germany for more than 1,000 years. He promised to expand Germany's borders, using force when necessary. He said, "Someday, when I order war, I shall not . . . hesitate because of the ten million young men I shall be sending to their death."

Hitler was not the only dangerous dictator to rise to power. **Benito Mussolini** took power in Italy in the early 1920s. Like Hitler, Mussolini promised to attack and conquer other countries. In Japan, a small group of military leaders came to power. They planned to use military force to build a massive empire in East Asia. Now you can see why the rise of dictators was a cause for concern in the 1930s.

REVIEW Why was Hitler's rise to power dangerous for countries bordering Germany?
 Draw Conclusions

▶ **Adolf Hitler (right) watched German troops march through Poland in 1939.**

341

The Axis Powers

In 1936 Hitler and Mussolini signed a treaty agreeing to support each other. Japan later joined this alliance. Germany, Italy, and Japan became known as the **Axis.**

The world watched as Germany, Italy, and Japan went on the attack in the mid-1930s. Italy invaded the African nation of Ethiopia and made it an Italian colony. Japan invaded China. Germany took control of Austria and Czechoslovakia.

In 1939 German forces prepared to invade the neighboring country of Poland. The leaders of Britain and France decided it was time to try to stop Hitler. Britain and France, known as the Allied Powers, or **Allies,** promised to protect Poland. They warned Hitler that if he attacked Poland, it would mean war with the Allies.

Hitler ignored this threat. On September 1, 1939, German troops rushed into Poland. In response, Britain and France declared war on Germany. For the second time in just 25 years, a major war had begun. It would soon be known as **World War II.**

▶ **During German bombings on London, Britain's capital, people took shelter in subways.**

The German military was very successful in the early years of World War II. After defeating the Polish army, the German army moved west. Hitler's massive force of soldiers, tanks, and airplanes quickly conquered nearly all of Western Europe. France fell to the Germans in June 1940. Now Britain stood alone in Europe in the fight against the Axis.

REVIEW List three events that led to the start of World War II. **Sequence**

▶ **Great Britain used posters to recruit people to join the Royal Air Force, or RAF.**

The Debate at Home

In the United States, Americans read news of the war in their newspapers. During the summer and fall of 1940, the big story was the Battle of Britain. German planes were pounding London and other British cities with bombs every night. The British air force was fighting for its country's survival.

The leader of the British government, **Winston Churchill,** had to move his offices into an underground bomb shelter. He often came out in the mornings to inspect the terrible damage done by German bombs. "We can take it," he told the people of London.

Churchill urged President Roosevelt to help Great Britain. Most Americans, however, wanted to stay out of the fighting. Americans remembered the horrors of World War I. Also, the country was still suffering through the Great Depression. Many Americans wanted their government to focus on troubles at home. This led to strong support for the policy of isolationism.

▶ **Members of the America First Committee (*above*) opposed American involvement in World War II.**

President Roosevelt decided to help Britain without joining in the actual fighting of the war. Roosevelt and Congress declared that the United States would let Britain borrow all the military supplies it needed to fight the Axis. This policy was known as **Lend-Lease.** The United States did not ask for payment for the military supplies sent to Britain.

Isolationists protested against Lend-Lease. They thought Roosevelt was leading the country into war. Roosevelt responded by saying that if the Axis Powers were not stopped, they would soon attack the United States. He warned, "Frankly and definitely there is danger ahead—danger against which we must prepare."

REVIEW Why did many Americans support isolationism when World War II began?

⟲ **Draw Conclusions**

▶ **Prime Minister Winston Churchill showed the "V for Victory" sign to encourage the British people during World War II.**

Declaring War

By the spring of 1941, the British air force had won the Battle of Britain. Britain was safe from German invasion. However, events on the other side of the world soon pulled the United States into war.

Like Germany, Japan had great military success in the early years of World War II. By 1941 Japanese forces controlled much of China and Southeast Asia. Leaders in the United States spoke out against Japanese expansion. This caused tensions to rise between Japan and the United Sates. The military leader of Japan, **Hideki Tojo,** believed the United States was standing in the way of Japan's goals. Tojo and the other top Japanese generals decided to attack.

In the morning on December 7, 1941, Japanese planes bombed the United States naval base at **Pearl Harbor, Hawaii.** Japanese

▶ **In December 1941 the Japanese attacked Pearl Harbor in Hawaii. The terrible destruction included the sinking of many American ships.**

bombs sank many American warships and destroyed hundreds of American airplanes. More than 2,300 American soldiers, sailors, and civilians were killed.

Americans reacted with fury to the surprise attack on Pearl Harbor. People who had been isolationists on December 6 were suddenly calling for war against Japan.

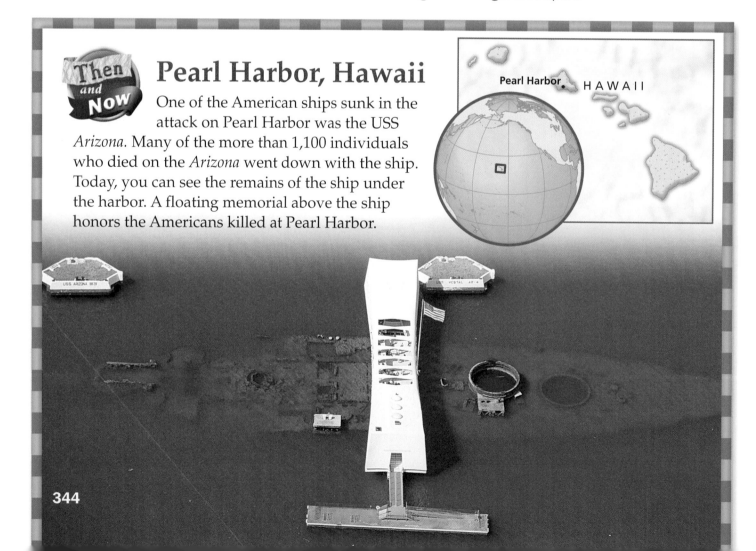

Then and Now

Pearl Harbor, Hawaii

One of the American ships sunk in the attack on Pearl Harbor was the USS *Arizona.* Many of the more than 1,100 individuals who died on the *Arizona* went down with the ship. Today, you can see the remains of the ship under the harbor. A floating memorial above the ship honors the Americans killed at Pearl Harbor.

Pearl Harbor · HAWAII

When the news reached Winston Churchill in London, he immediately called President Roosevelt. "Mr. President, what's this about Japan?" he asked. "It's quite true," Roosevelt replied. "They have attacked us at Pearl Harbor. We are all in the same boat now." Roosevelt meant that, like Britain, the United States would soon be at war with the Axis.

On December 8, Roosevelt spoke to the members of Congress:

> *"Yesterday, December 7, 1941—a date which will live in infamy—the United States was suddenly and deliberately attacked by naval and air forces of the Empire of Japan."*

At Roosevelt's request, the House of Representatives and Senate voted to declare war on Japan. Germany and Italy quickly declared war on the United States. The United States was now one of the Allies.

A navy surgeon named Paul Spangler was at Pearl Harbor at the time of the surprise attack. After the attack, he began thinking about what entry into World War II would mean for him and his country. "It is not going to be an easy job in my opinion," he wrote to his friends. "We have the ability and skill, but it is going to mean many sacrifices for all and a long hard pull."

REVIEW How did the United States government respond to the attack on Pearl Harbor? **Cause and Effect**

FACT FILE

Major Powers of the Axis and Allies

The Allies were led by the world's leading democratic nations and the Soviet Union. Around the world, more than 50 countries fought in World War II. These were the flags of the Allies and the Axis countries during the war.

Axis

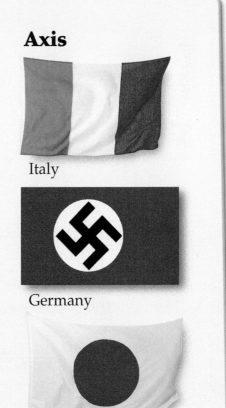

Italy

Germany

Japan

Allies

Great Britain

Soviet Union

United States

Canada

Axis Advances

As the United States entered World War II, things did not look good for the Allies. The map below shows that the Axis Powers held nearly all of Europe and North Africa, as well as much of East Asia and the Pacific Ocean.

Now find the Soviet Union, a huge nation in Europe and Asia. The Soviet Union was also known as the Union of Soviet Socialist Republics, or U.S.S.R. It was ruled by a dictator named **Joseph Stalin.** Before World War II began, Stalin and Hitler made an agreement not to attack each other. Like Hitler, Stalin had dreams of expanding his nation's borders. When Germany invaded Poland from the west in 1939, the Soviet Union invaded from the east. The two powers split Poland and other nations in Eastern Europe between them.

So how did the Soviet Union become an Allied Power? In June 1941, Hitler broke his agreement with Stalin. German forces invaded the Soviet Union. Stalin had no choice—he had to join the Allies and fight against Germany and the Axis Powers.

The leaders of the United States and the Soviet Union had not been friendly with each other before the war. Now that they were allies, however, the United States decided to help the Soviet Union. Under the Lend-Lease program, the United States sent the Soviet Union badly needed supplies, such as trucks, radios, and boots. Millions of pounds of American canned meat helped feed the hungry Soviet army.

REVIEW Why did the United States send military supplies to the Soviet Union? *Summarize*

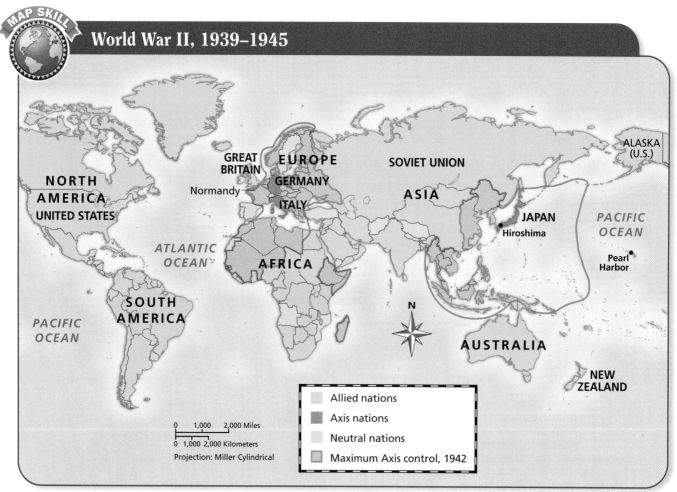

World War II, 1939–1945

MAP SKILL

ALASKA (U.S.)

GREAT BRITAIN

EUROPE

SOVIET UNION

NORTH AMERICA

UNITED STATES

Normandy

GERMANY

ITALY

ASIA

JAPAN

Hiroshima

PACIFIC OCEAN

ATLANTIC OCEAN

AFRICA

Pearl Harbor

PACIFIC OCEAN

SOUTH AMERICA

N

AUSTRALIA

NEW ZEALAND

Allied nations
Axis nations
Neutral nations
Maximum Axis control, 1942

0   1,000   2,000 Miles
0 1,000 2,000 Kilometers
Projection: Miller Cylindrical

▶ By 1942 German armies had captured nearly all of Europe and North Africa.

MAP SKILL Location *Which major Axis nation was in Asia?*

The Draft

When the United States entered World War II, the country was not prepared for a major war. The armed forces did not have nearly enough men to fight battles around the world. The draft helped solve this problem. Before the war was over, more than 10 million men were drafted into the military.

The government informed young men that they had been drafted by sending out short letters saying, "You have been selected for training and service in the Army." Charlie Miller

▶ **This soldier said goodbye to his family before leaving for the war.**

was 21 years old when he got one of these letters. He remembered, "I was young and going about my daily life and all of a sudden the sky opens and there we are: World War II."

REVIEW Why did the United States need to draft millions of soldiers? *Main Idea and Details*

Summarize the Lesson

- **1933** Adolf Hitler became the dictator of Germany.
- **1939** World War II began when the German army invaded Poland.
- **1941** The United States entered World War II after Japan bombed Pearl Harbor.

LESSON 1 REVIEW

Check Facts and Main Ideas

1. ⟳ **Draw Conclusions** On a separate sheet of paper, fill in a conclusion that could be drawn from the facts given below.

By 1942 Germany had conquered most of Europe.

By 1942 Japan had built a huge empire in east Asia.

2. What actions by Adolf Hitler led to the start of **World War II**?

3. How did Japan's attack on Pearl Harbor affect feelings of isolationism in the United States?

4. List the major powers of the **Axis** and the **Allies.**

5. **Critical Thinking:** *Express Ideas* Do you think it took courage for President Roosevelt to decide to lend Britain supplies?

Link to ⟷ Writing

Write to Your Newspaper Suppose you are living in the United States in 1940. Do you think the United States should get involved in World War II? Do you believe we should send military supplies to Great Britain? Write a letter to your local newspaper expressing your views.

1940 | 1945

1942
Japanese Americans are moved to internment camps.

1942
The Manhattan Project begins.

1944
Millions of American women work in weapons factories.

• Los Alamos

The Home Front

PREVIEW

Focus on the Main Idea
After the United States entered World War II, the Great Depression came to an end and many Americans found new opportunities.

PLACES
Los Alamos, New Mexico

PEOPLE
Benjamin O. Davis, Jr.
Albert Einstein

VOCABULARY
rationing
Tuskegee Airmen
atomic bomb
Manhattan Project

▶ A World War II tank

> **You Are There** What is going on in Elkton, Maryland? The year is 1943, and the population of this small city has doubled in the past year. The stores, restaurants, and movie theaters are packed, and almost every room in every house has been rented.
>
> Like so many places in the United States, Elkton is being changed by the war. A local factory is now making supplies for the military. The factory keeps expanding, hiring all the workers it can get. About 80 percent of the new workers are women.
>
> Some of these women have left other jobs to help with the war effort. Some are taking time off from college. Some have come straight from high school. Many have husbands, fathers, or brothers who are fighting overseas. "My husband is in the Navy," one young woman says. "I felt nearer to him, working like this."

Main Idea and Details As you read, think about how life changed during World War II for different groups of people in the United States.

The Depression Ends

In December 1940, President Franklin Roosevelt described the vital role that American industry would play in World War II. "We must have more ships, more guns, more planes—more of everything," Roosevelt urged. "We must be the great arsenal of democracy." An arsenal is a building where weapons are made or stored.

The United States was not yet in the war in 1940, but Roosevelt knew that the United States was the only democratic nation in the world that could produce enough weapons to defeat the Axis Powers. He called on factory owners and workers to pour their energy into making military equipment.

The country responded to Roosevelt's call. Automobile companies stopped making cars and started making tanks and military trucks. Shipyards operated 24 hours a day, building ships more quickly than Japan or Germany. The United States airplane industry grew so quickly, it became the single biggest industry in the world by 1945. The massive industrial strength of the United States gave the Allies a major advantage in World War II.

All this production had another very important effect. Factories had to expand to produce all the military equipment the Allies needed. This created millions of new jobs. As a result, the Great Depression finally came to an end. The chart on this page shows you how quickly unemployment fell during World War II.

People poured into cities where factories were located. Cities with busy shipyards, such as Mobile, Alabama, and Norfolk, Virginia, became boom

▶ **Millions of women went to work in factories making supplies for the war.**

towns. In 1944 President Roosevelt congratulated Americans on their energy and teamwork. He announced, "The production which has flowed from this country to all the battlefronts of the world has been due to the efforts of American business, American labor, and American farmers working together as a patriotic team."

REVIEW Why was American industry important to the Allied war effort?
◑ Draw Conclusions

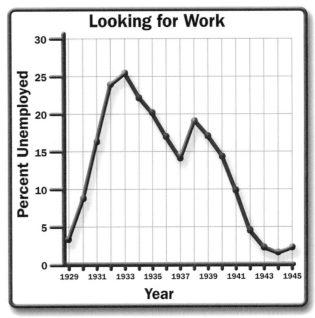

Looking for Work

▶ **When the war began, many unemployed people found work making war supplies.**

GRAPH SKILL *In what year did unemployment reach its lowest point?*

▶ "Rosie the Riveter" *(far right)* became a symbol of women who kept American factories running during the war.

We Can Do It!

New Jobs for Women

When she was 21 years old, Gertrude Pearson joined the Women's Army Corps, or WAC. She learned how to send military codes. Then she was sent to France. Pearson's job often took her very close to the fighting. "We could clearly hear the artillery guns ahead of us," she said. Some military leaders thought women could not handle working so close to combat. Pearson was proud to prove them wrong:

> *"They felt that women were incapable of enduring the hardships and rough conditions of a combat area. However, our success and outstanding work changed many attitudes."*

Gertrude Pearson was one of more than 350,000 women who served in the United States military during World War II. Women worked as nurses, airplane pilots, radio operators, and mechanics. They served all over the world.

At the same time, the United States was facing a shortage of workers. Millions of men had left their jobs to serve in the military. Since industry was booming, factories needed more workers than ever. Women helped solve this problem by going to work to make weapons and other war-related products. Seven million women war workers joined the workforce. Grocery stores started staying open late so working mothers could buy food for their children on their way home.

The war even created new opportunities for female athletes. With so many baseball players off fighting the war, team owners started looking for new ways to entertain baseball fans. The result was a new baseball league—the All American Girl's Baseball League. One of the league's top stars was "Dottie" Schroeder, a shortstop for a team called the South Bend Blue Sox. Schroeder was thrilled to be one of the country's first women to play professional baseball. "All I wanted to do was play ball," she said.

REVIEW What new opportunities did women have during World War II? *Summarize*

"Do Your Part"

During World War II, posters and radio commercials urged Americans to "Do Your Part." There were many things people of all ages could do to help the war effort. For example, children knew that the country's factories faced constant shortages of metals such as tin and aluminum. Many children organized "scrap drives." They knocked on doors in their neighborhood, collecting tin cans and old cooking pots. Some children even turned in their toy cars and trucks so the metal could be recycled.

With millions of soldiers to feed, the country also faced food shortages. As a result, the government decided to limit the amount of food each person in the United States could buy. This is called **rationing.** The government gave families ration stamps every month. Everyone got a certain number of stamps for meat, dairy, canned vegetables, and other kinds of foods. When you bought an item, you had to turn in some of your stamps. When you ran out of stamps for a certain item—butter, for example—you could not buy any more of it until the next month. You can see why this forced families to plan their meals very carefully.

Another way Americans helped the war effort was by planting "Victory Gardens." These were small vegetable gardens that helped increase the amount of food available in the country. Millions of people who had never grown food before planted Victory Gardens in their backyards or on the rooftops of their apartment buildings.

REVIEW How did Americans respond to food shortages during the war?
Main Idea and Details

HERE AND THERE The Home Front in Great Britain

At the Same Time . . . The children of Great Britain also did everything they could to help their country win the war. Ann Stalcup, who was a young girl when the war began, remembers, "We would go from house to house, asking for things like old saucepans that could be melted down and used to make plane or tank parts." British children also donated their coins to the "Spitfire Funds." This money was used to build British fighter planes called Spitfires.

GREAT BRITAIN

EUROPE

ATLANTIC OCEAN

▶ Due to shortages caused by the war, people in Britain, like those in the United States, recycled their newspapers, tins, and glass.

PAPER PAPER TINS BOTTLES JARS

351

New Opportunities

Before World War II began, many factories did not welcome African Americans workers. During the war, however, factory owners could not afford to practice this kind of discrimination. They needed all the workers they could get. This created new job opportunities for African American men and women.

Hundreds of thousands of African Americans left the South to find work in the cities of the North and West. Many were able to earn more money than they ever had before. However, they often earned lower wages than white workers. Discrimination was still a problem in many places.

Discrimination also existed in the United States military. Black and white soldiers served in segregated units. African American soldiers were helping to fight for democracy and freedom around the world, yet they were denied equality themselves.

In spite of this discrimination, some African Americans did find new opportunities in the military. **Benjamin O. Davis, Jr.,** graduated from West Point Military Academy in 1936. He wanted to be a fighter pilot. But the Air Corps, which later became the Air Force, did not accept black pilots. African American leaders protested this unfair policy. In 1941

▶ **Captain Benjamin O. Davis, Jr., (right) led the Tuskegee Airmen, the first African American Air Force pilots.**

Davis and 12 other young African Americans began fighter pilot training.

The pilots trained at an army base in Tuskegee, Alabama. Lemuel Custis was one of the first **Tuskegee Airmen.** "It was a proud feeling," he remembered. "We were focused on the task—didn't feel like pioneers or anything. Later, looking back, we realized our trail-breaking role."

The Tuskegee Airmen were sent to join the fighting in 1943, with Benjamin O. Davis, Jr., in command. They flew thousands of combat missions in North Africa and Europe. Davis later became the first African American general in the United States Air Force.

More than one million African Americans served in the military during World War II. By the end of the war, some were serving in integrated units, meaning both black and white soldiers served together.

REVIEW How did World War II change life for many African Americans?
Cause and Effect

Japanese Americans

Henry Ebihara was a high school student when he heard that Japan had attacked Pearl Harbor. "My family's life turned into a living nightmare," he later wrote. As a Japanese American, he suddenly found that other Americans suspected him of being an enemy of the United States. "We became identified as one and the same with our hated enemy who bombed Pearl Harbor!"

About 125,000 Japanese Americans lived in the United States in 1941. Most lived on the West Coast. When the war began, many Americans worried that Japan might soon attack the West Coast. They feared that Japanese Americans would help with this attack.

In February 1942, President Roosevelt signed Executive Order #9066. This order allowed the military to remove from the West Coast anyone seen as a threat. Japanese Americans were forced to leave their homes. They were moved into relocation camps—also called internment camps—around the country. A writer named Yoshiko Uchida never forgot the day the military came to take the people of her community away. She said,

▶ Japanese American soldiers were honored for their bravery during World War II.

> *"Before long, we were told to board the buses that lined the street outside, and the people living nearby came out of their houses to watch."*

By the summer of 1942, more than 110,000 Japanese Americans were held in relocation camps. Still, many of these young men and women wanted to serve their country. Henry Ebihara wrote to the secretary of war, asking for permission to join the military. "I only ask that I be given a chance to fight to preserve [protect] the principles that I have been brought up on," he wrote. Ebihara was one of thousands of Japanese Americans who served in the United States military.

REVIEW What happened to Japanese Americans after Japan attacked Pearl Harbor? **Main Idea and Details**

▶ Japanese Americans had to line up for meals at an internment camp in Puyallup, Washington.

Technology and War

The race to find new technologies was a very important part of World War II. Scientists in Axis and Allied countries competed to invent new tools that could help their side win the war.

When World War II began, **Albert Einstein** was one of the most famous scientists in the world. Einstein was a Jew who had escaped from Germany after Hitler rose to power. Now he was living in the United States. In 1939 Einstein told President Roosevelt that it might be possible to build "extremely powerful bombs of a new type." These **atomic bombs** would create massive explosive energy by splitting atoms, the basic unit of matter. They would be far more powerful than anything ever built before. Einstein warned that German scientists were probably working on atomic bombs.

Roosevelt knew that the United States could not afford to lose the race to build an

▶ **This machine was used by American code breakers to figure out Japanese codes.**

atomic bomb. In 1942 the government started the **Manhattan Project.** This was the code name given to the effort to build an atomic bomb. Thousands of scientists went to work at top-secret laboratories around the country. Philip Morrison was a young scientist who worked at a secret lab in **Los Alamos, New Mexico.** "We knew the idea was to make the most destructive of all possible bombs," he later said. "We believed Hitler was well ahead of us." By July 1945 scientists at Los Alamos were ready to test the world's first atomic bomb.

Scientists on both sides also raced to develop more and more complicated secret codes. Codes were vital during the war. Suppose a general in Hawaii wanted to send a message to an American ship 2,000 miles away in the Pacific Ocean. He had to send the message by radio. The problem is that anyone can listen to a radio message. So the message had to be sent using a secret code.

Each side also worked to figure out—or "break"—the enemies' codes. By breaking Japanese and German codes, the Allies

▶ **After leaving Germany, Albert Einstein taught at Princeton University in New Jersey.**

354

would know what their next move would be. The German military used an extremely complicated code machine called Enigma. They were sure Enigma's codes could never be broken. They were wrong. A team of British mathematicians built what is considered to be the world's first computer. They used it to break the Enigma code. As a result, Allied generals were often able to read German military plans. Historians think this

▶ The Allies could track the movements of a ship or plane by watching a radar screen.

helped shorten the war by at least one year.

The Allies gained another advantage with the use of radar. Radar uses radio beams to determine the location of objects such as airplanes or ships. During the Battle of Britain, for example, the British used radar to find German planes at night. This helped British fighter pilots shoot down hundreds of German planes.

REVIEW Why was technology an important tool in World War II? ⟳ Draw Conclusions

Summarize the Lesson

1942 More than 100,000 Japanese Americans were removed from their homes on the West Coast.

1942 The United States government began the Manhattan Project, a secret effort to build an atomic bomb.

1944 Millions of American women worked in the country's weapons factories.

LESSON 2 ⟩ REVIEW

Check Facts and Main Ideas

1. Main Idea and Details Redraw this chart on a separate sheet of paper and fill in details that support the main idea.

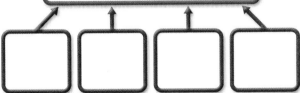

During World War II, many people in the United States found new opportunities and faced new challenges.

2. How did World War II affect the American economy?

3. How did children contribute to the war effort in the United States and Britain?

4. What was the goal of the **Manhattan Project**?

5. Critical Thinking: *Decision Making* Do you think the military draft was a good idea? Explain your answer. Use the decision-making steps on page H5.

Link to 🔗 **Art**

Design a Poster During World War II, the government used posters to encourage Americans to help the war effort. Design a poster that asks people to collect scrap metal, conserve fuel, or grow Victory Gardens. Give your poster a title.

355

1944   1946

June 1944
The Allies invade France.

May 1945
Germany surrenders.

August 1945
Japan surrenders, ending World War II.

Normandy • Hiroshima • Iwo Jima

The World at War

PREVIEW

Focus on the Main Idea
The United States helped lead the Allies to victory in World War II, the deadliest war in human history.

PLACES
Normandy, France
Iwo Jima, Japan
Hiroshima, Japan

PEOPLE
Chester Nimitz
Dwight D. Eisenhower
George S. Patton
Douglas MacArthur
Harry S. Truman
Anne Frank

VOCABULARY
Battle of Midway
Battle of Stalingrad
Battle of the Bulge
concentration camp
Holocaust

▶ Sometimes soldiers and family members sent photographs to each other along with letters.

You Are There
It is May 1944. Allied forces have invaded Italy, and they are battling their way north. The fighting is brutal and progress is slow. When he finally has a free moment, American soldier Paul Curtis sits down to write a letter to his younger brother back in Tennessee. His brother had asked him what it was like to be in combat. Now Curtis tries to put this experience into words:

"I have seen some action—a few hard, hard days in which I saw more than I imagined I ever would. I don't think any man can exactly explain combat. It's beyond words. Take a combination of fear, anger, thirst, exhaustion, disgust, loneliness, homesickness, and wrap that all up in one reaction and you might approach the feelings a fellow has."

Sequence As you read, make a list of the major events that led to the end of World War II in 1945.

American Soldiers

Robert Rasmus joined the army when he was 19 years old. "When I went in the army, I'd never been outside the states of Wisconsin, Indiana, and Michigan," he said. After two months of training, Rasmus boarded a troop ship, sailed to Europe, and joined the fighting. He remembered being shocked at how quickly his life had changed:

> *"It seemed unreal. All of a sudden, there you were right in the thick of it and people were dying and you were scared out of your wits."*

More than 16 million Americans served in the military during World War II. Like Robert Rasmus, many of them had never been far from home before. Now they found themselves on battlefields in Europe, Africa, and Asia, and on islands in the Pacific Ocean. The only way to keep in touch with their families was by writing letters. Soldiers wrote home describing their friends, the places they had seen, and the battles in which they had fought.

Millions of American soldiers were the children of immigrants. This turned out to be a great advantage. In any large group of soldiers, there was often at least one person who spoke German, Italian, French, Russian, Spanish, or Japanese.

This was helpful for an army that was fighting all over the world.

American soldiers gained another advantage with language—this time from a language very few people knew. A group of Navajo soldiers known as "Code Talkers" used their language to create an unbreakable secret code. The Navajo language was perfect for codes because, aside from Navajo people, only about 30 people in the world knew the language. Because the language does not have a written alphabet, there was no way to study it. "In Navajo everything is in memory," explained Code Talker William McCabe.

Navajo Code Talkers took part in many of the major battles against Japanese forces. Often working under heavy fire, Code Talkers could send coded messages much more quickly than code machines could. This saved lives and helped win battles.

REVIEW How did Navajo Code Talkers use language to save lives? ↻ **Draw Conclusions**

► **The Navajo Code Talkers helped the United States to victory in World War II.**

357

Major Turning Points

As 1942 began, the Axis Powers continued gaining ground around the world. In Asia, Japanese forces captured the Philippines and many other islands in the Pacific Ocean. In Europe, the German army advanced hundreds of miles into the Soviet Union. Over the next year, however, the Allies were able to win several major victories. These victories became turning points in the war.

The **Battle of Midway** was a major turning point in the war against Japan. Japan had destroyed many American ships at Pearl Harbor. Now it hoped to destroy the rest of the American ships in the Pacific in one major battle. They chose to attack Midway Island, a small island located northwest of Hawaii.

In May 1942 a fleet of Japanese ships began to move east in the Pacific Ocean. Admiral **Chester Nimitz**, commander of American naval forces in the Pacific, knew that Japan was planning a major attack. But he did not know where the attack would be.

American code-breakers told him it would happen at Midway. Working from a base at Pearl Harbor, the code-breakers cracked Japanese codes and read secret messages sent by Japan's war planners. An expert code-breaker named Joe Rochefort was in charge of this effort. Rochefort was able to tell American naval commanders what Japan was planning:

> *"We could tell them what was going to happen, such things as where the Japanese aircraft carriers would be."*

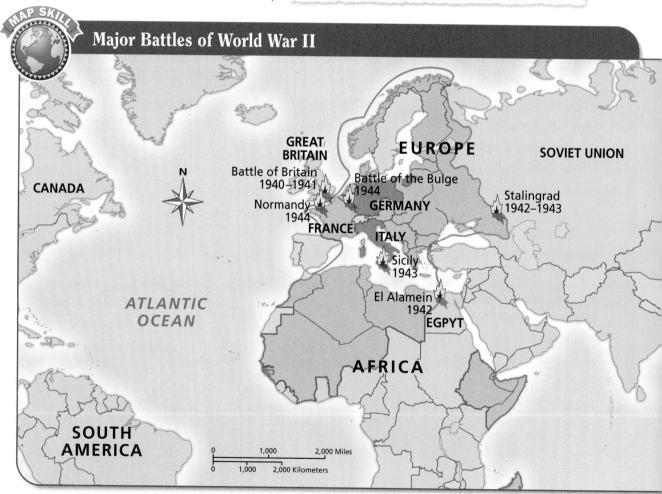

MAP SKILL

Major Battles of World War II

- CANADA
- GREAT BRITAIN
  - Battle of Britain 1940–1941
  - Normandy 1944
- EUROPE
- SOVIET UNION
- Battle of the Bulge 1944
- GERMANY
- Stalingrad 1942–1943
- FRANCE
- ITALY
- Sicily 1943
- ATLANTIC OCEAN
- El Alamein 1942
- EGPYT
- AFRICA
- SOUTH AMERICA

N

0   1,000   2,000 Miles
0   1,000   2,000 Kilometers

▶ World War II battles were fought at many places in the world.

MAP SKILL Use a Map Key *Which battles of the Pacific Ocean occurred outside of the Axis-controlled area?*

358

This knowledge was very useful, but American sailors and pilots still had to fight the battle. On June 3 American fighter pilots spotted the Japanese fleet. Flying planes called "dive bombers," the navy pilots destroyed four Japanese aircraft carriers and many other ships and planes. After the Battle of Midway, Japan's navy was no longer strong enough to continue capturing islands in the Pacific. The United States slowly began to win territory back from Japan.

A second major turning point came in the Soviet Union. You read that Germany invaded the Soviet Union in 1941. This was the largest invasion of one country by another in the history of the world. German forces quickly fought their way toward the major cities of the Soviet Union. One of Hitler's main goals was to capture the industrial city of Stalingrad.

The Soviet army fought desperately to hold on to Stalingrad. By the summer of 1942, the city had been completely destroyed by guns and bombs. General Vasily Chuikov, commander of Soviet troops in Stalingrad, said, "The streets of the city are dead. There is not a single green twig left on the trees."

Fighting from behind piles of crumbled stones and bricks, Soviet soldiers battled for every inch of ground. In January 1943, the German soldiers at Stalingrad were finally forced to surrender. The **Battle of Stalingrad** was a major turning point in World War II. After Stalingrad, the Soviet army started forcing the Germans to retreat.

REVIEW Why was the Battle of Midway a major turning point in World War II?
⟳ Draw Conclusions

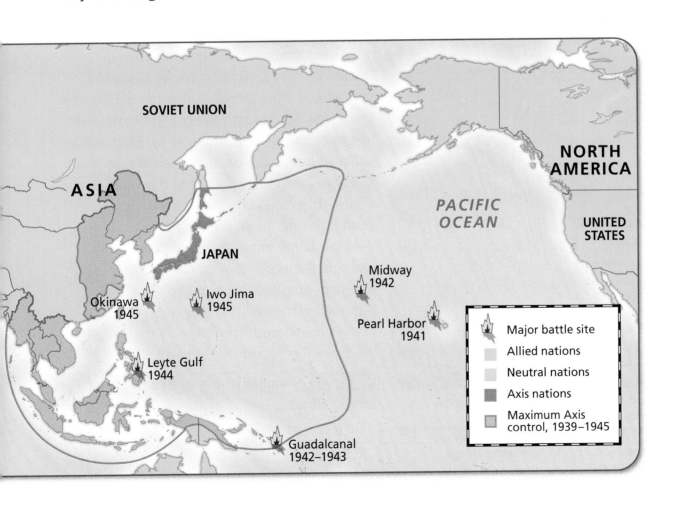

Victory in Europe

By the spring of 1944, the Soviet army had pushed the Germans out of the Soviet Union. The Allies had also defeated Axis forces in North Africa and Italy. The war was far from over, however. The Allies knew they would have to invade German-controlled Western Europe. The Germans knew it too, and they were preparing.

American General **Dwight D. Eisenhower** was in command of Allied forces. You will read more about him in the Biography on page 365. Eisenhower chose the coastal region of **Normandy, France,** as the location for the Allied invasion. On the night of June 5, 1944, an invasion force of 175,000 soldiers and 6,000 ships sailed from Great Britain toward the coast of France. The date of the invasion, or D-Day, would be June 6. It would be the largest invasion by sea in world history.

The Allied forces reached Normandy early on the morning of June 6. American, British, and Canadian soldiers jumped from boats and began wading up to the land. Facing deadly blasts from German guns, Allied soldiers fought their way onto the beach. The invasion cost many lives, but it was a success. By the night of June 6, the Allies had captured the beaches of Normandy. "Right here was history in the making," wrote an American soldier named Eugene Lawton. "Events taking place that kids will be reading about in future at school."

Allied troops began battling their way toward Germany. The Allies liberated town after town from German control. Then in December 1944, German forces made one final attack. This attack, called the **Battle of the Bulge,** turned into the biggest battle ever fought by the United States Army. Both sides suffered heavy losses, but American General **George S. Patton** helped lead the Allies to victory. The Allies continued their march, soon crossing the border into Germany.

At the same time, the Soviet Union was invading Germany from the east. When Soviet troops neared the German capital of Berlin, Hitler killed himself. On May 8, 1945, Germany surrendered. The Allies named May 8 V-E Day—for "Victory in Europe."

REVIEW Summarize the events of June 6, 1944. **Summarize**

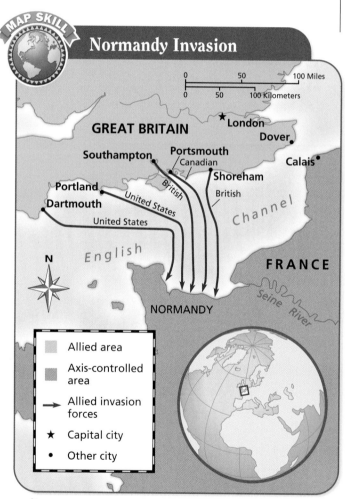

MAP SKILL

Normandy Invasion

0   50   100 Miles
0   50   100 Kilometers

GREAT BRITAIN
★ London
Dover
Southampton
Portsmouth
Canadian
Calais
Shoreham
Portland
British
British
Dartmouth
United States
United States
Channel
English
N
FRANCE
NORMANDY
Seine River

Allied area
Axis-controlled area
→ Allied invasion forces
★ Capital city
• Other city

▶ The Allies landed on five beaches along the Normandy coast in France.

MAP SKILL Understand Map Symbols *From which port cities did the United States troops leave Great Britain?*

Victory in Asia

Americans celebrated the victory in Europe, but the United States was still battling a very determined Japanese army. American General **Douglas MacArthur** planned to fight his way to Japan using a strategy called "island hopping." The goal of this strategy was to capture the most important islands from the Japanese. Islands farther out would be captured first and then these islands could be used as bases for attacks on islands located closer to Japan.

In February 1945 the United States Marines invaded the small Pacific island of **Iwo Jima, Japan.** General Holland Smith called the fighting on Iwo Jima "the toughest the Marines ran across in 168 years." After taking Iwo Jima, American forces attacked the Japanese island of Okinawa. Nearly 50,000 Americans were killed or wounded before the Japanese were defeated on Okinawa. Japanese losses were much higher. Now the United States forces were just 350 miles from the Japanese mainland. Military leaders began planning an invasion of Japan. However, they feared it might cost as many as one million American lives.

On April 12, 1945, President Roosevelt suddenly died. While Americans mourned,

▶ **This image of American soldiers raising the American flag on Iwo Jima is one of the most famous photographs from World War II.**

▶ **The Japanese surrender was signed on a ship in Tokyo Bay, Japan.**

Vice-President **Harry S. Truman** took the oath of office. What was it like to step into the presidency at a time like this? "I felt like the moon, the stars, and all the planets had fallen on me," he later said.

Truman soon faced the biggest decision of his life. In July 1945 he was told that American scientists had successfully tested the world's first atomic bomb in the New Mexico desert. Two more atomic bombs were ready for use. Truman had to decide whether or not to use them against Japan. He decided they should be used, hoping they would force Japan to surrender. This would make an invasion unnecessary and save many American lives.

On August 6, 1945, an Air Force bomber named *Enola Gay* dropped an atomic bomb on the city of **Hiroshima, Japan.** The bomb completely destroyed the city and killed more than 80,000 people in just a few seconds. Three days later, a second atomic bomb was dropped on the city of Nagasaki, killing nearly 60,000 people. Japan surrendered on August 14. This was called V-J day—for "Victory in Japan." World War II was finally over.

REVIEW What major decision did President Truman face in 1945? What did he decide? *Main Idea and Details*

The Holocaust

You have read that Adolf Hitler came to power in Germany in 1933. Hitler's Nazi party had a strict policy of anti-Semitism, or hatred of Jews. The Nazis passed new laws to limit the rights of Jews in Germany. Jews were no longer allowed in many public places, such as movie theaters or sports stadiums. Signs saying "Jews Unwelcome" were hung in store windows. Jewish-owned stores were boycotted by non-Jewish Germans.

The Nazis took their anti-Semitism to a violent extreme during World War II. Hitler and other Nazi leaders decided to destroy the entire Jewish population of Europe. When German forces captured a country, they arrested all the Jews who lived there. Jews were put on trains and taken to **concentration camps.** People who were imprisoned in concentration camps had very little chance of surviving. Many were murdered right away. Others were forced to work as slave laborers until they died of hunger or disease.

▶ **The Nazis forced Jewish people to wear yellow stars identifying them as Jews.**

Allied soldiers found these concentration camps as they liberated Europe in 1945. Many could not believe their eyes. An American officer named William Cowling described the condition of prisoners at one camp:

"They were dirty, starved skeletons with torn tattered clothes . . . . It is unbelievable how any human can treat others as they were treated."

The Nazis murdered about six million Jews during World War II. Historians call this the **Holocaust,** a word meaning "widespread destruction." Jews were not the only victims of Nazi crimes. About six million non-Jewish people were also murdered in concentration camps.

A Jewish girl named **Anne Frank** was living in the Netherlands when World War II began. In 1942 German soldiers began arresting Jews in the Netherlands and sending them to concentration camps. Anne and her family

▶ **Anne Frank**
(right)

"Believe me, if you have been shut up for a year and a half, it can get too much for you some days. . . . Cycling, dancing, whistling, looking out into the world, feeling young, to know that I'm free— that's what I long for."

were prepared, however. They had built a secret hiding place above Anne's father's office.

Anne was 13 years old when she and her family moved into their hiding place. In her diary, she described what it was like to share this small space with seven other people. She wrote about Christian friends who risked their lives to bring food to the hiding place. She wrote about her fears and her hopes for the future.

German police found Anne's hiding place in 1944. Anne and her family were arrested. She died in a concentration camp in Germany, just two months before the end of the war. Anne Frank's diary was later found in the family's hiding place. It has become one of the most famous accounts of life under Nazi rule.

REVIEW Why did Anne Frank have to go into hiding in 1942? **Cause and Effect**

▶ **The Nazis forced millions of people** *(above left)*, **including most of Europe's Jews, into concentration camps. Signs like this one** *(left)*, **which reads, "Jews are not admitted here," were placed in many public places in Nazi Germany.**

The Costs of War

World War II was the bloodiest war in the history of the world. Between 40 and 50 million soldiers and civilians died in the conflict. Many of the major cities of Europe and Asia were left in ruins. More than 400,000 American soldiers died in World War II. The only war in which more Americans died was the Civil War.

The world now faced a massive rebuilding job. The United States took the lead in this effort. The world also faced the threat of a new kind of weapon—the atomic bomb. People saw that it was now possible to build weapons more powerful and deadly than anyone had dreamed of in the past. In the next chapter, you will read about how atomic weapons changed the world.

REVIEW How did World War II compare with other wars in history? **Compare and Contrast**

Summarize the Lesson

June 1944 Allied forces began liberating Western Europe.

May 1945 Under attack from east and west, Germany surrendered.

August 1945 After atomic bombs destroyed Hiroshima and Nagasaki, Japan surrendered.

LESSON 3 ⟩ REVIEW

Check Facts and Main Ideas

1. Sequence On a separate sheet of paper, fill in major events that led to the end of World War II. Include the month and year of each event.

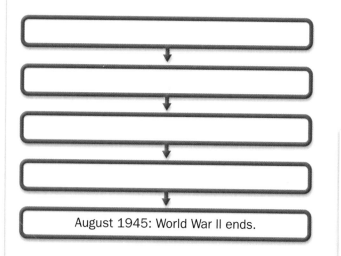

August 1945: World War II ends.

2. Identify one major turning point in World War II and explain its importance.

3. What effect did the use of atomic bombs have on the outcome of World War II?

4. Summarize the events of the **Holocaust.**

5. Critical Thinking: *Analyze Primary Sources* You read that when Truman became President he said, "I felt like the moon, the stars, and all the planets had fallen on me." What do you think he meant by this?

> **Link to** ⟨co⟩ **Writing**
>
> **Investigate World War II** Which part of World War II do you find the most interesting? Choose one topic, such as the Tuskegee Airmen, D-Day, the All American Girl's Baseball League, the Manhattan Project, or anything else from the chapter. Research this topic. Summarize the topic in a one-page report.

Dwight David Eisenhower
1890–1969

Dwight David Eisenhower, nicknamed "Ike," was where he most loved to be—on the football field. Ike had the ball on a running play in the next-to-last game of the season. As he rushed past his opponents, someone grabbed his foot. Ike finished the play, but he knew something was wrong. His knee had been severely injured. A few days later, doctors told Ike the bad news: he would never play football again.

The injury saddened Ike. At first, he thought about leaving West Point Military Academy. But he stayed on. Soon he started exercising again, adjusting to a weak knee by concentrating on strengthening his arms.

Right before he graduated, a doctor at West Point told Ike that his damaged knee might prevent him from being a good soldier and that he should consider giving up his army career. But Ike succeeded in becoming an officer in the United States Army.

It was a good thing too. Eisenhower went on to become a very successful army officer. During World War II, he commanded the Allied troops that landed in Europe on D-Day, June 6, 1944. This was the greatest invasion from the sea in history. It began the effort that would help defeat Germany. In 1953 Eisenhower became President of the United States. In his first speech as President, he said,

BIOFACT

In 1943 Eisenhower helped design a short jacket for United States Army troops. The jacket came to be known as the "Eisenhower Jacket," or "Ike Jacket."

"We must be willing, individually and as a nation, to accept whatever sacrifices may be required of us. A people that values its privileges above its principles soon loses both."

Learn from Biographies

Why do you think Eisenhower did not quit West Point after his injury? How do you think this experience affected his later decisions as a soldier and as President?

For more information, go online to *Meet the People* at **www.sfsocialstudies.com.**

365

Map and Globe Skills

Understand Key Lines of Latitude and Longitude

MAP A: Latitude

MAP B: Longitude

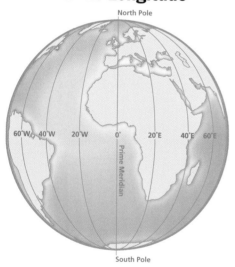

What? Keeping track of battles won and lost was important to the Allies during World War II. In order to record these locations on maps as accurately as possible, they relied on the system of **latitude** and **longitude.** Lines of latitude—also called parallels—circle the globe in an east-west direction. They measure distances north and south of the equator. Lines of longitude—also called meridians—run in a north-south direction. They measure distances east and west of the prime meridian. Some lines of latitude and longitude have been given names to help define their location. These lines divide Earth into different zones.

Why? Lines of latitude and longitude form a **grid,** a set of crossing lines. We can describe every location on Earth by naming the latitude and longitude lines that cross there.

How? Find latitude 0° on Map A. This line of latitude, which divides Earth in half, is called the equator. Now find the Tropic of Cancer, a parallel at latitude 23° 27'N. The symbol ° means "degree." A degree is a unit that measures latitude and longitude. The symbol ' means "minute." Every degree of latitude and longitude is divided into 60 minutes. Therefore, each minute is one-sixtieth of a degree. Everything north of the equator is north latitude, which is labeled *N.* Everything south of the equator is south latitude, which is labeled *S.* Find the Tropic of Capricorn, a parallel at latitude 23° 27'S. The area between this line of latitude and the line for the Tropic of Cancer is known as the tropical zone.

Now find the Arctic and Antarctic Circles on Map A. The Arctic Circle is at latitude 66° 30'N. The Antarctic Circle is found at latitude 66° 30'S. The areas between these lines and the Poles are called polar zones, because they are near the North and South Poles.

Map C: Major World War II Battles of the Pacific

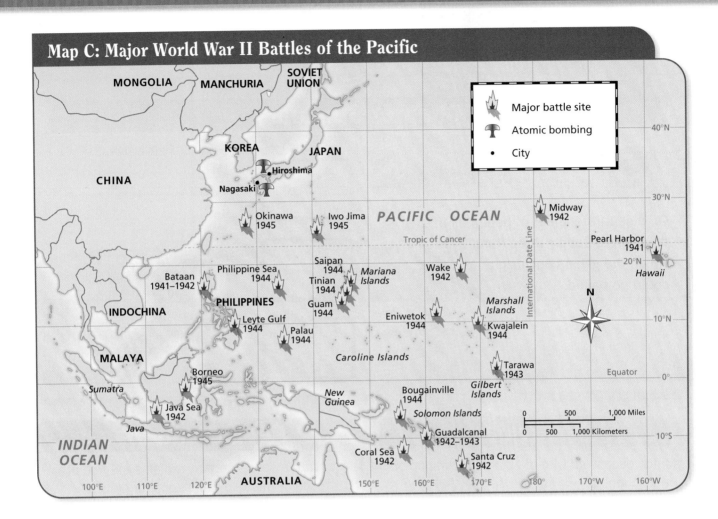

Look at Map B. The line of longitude at 0° is known as the prime meridian. Longitude is measured 180° east and west of the prime meridian. The line of longitude at 180° forms part of the **International Date Line.** This line is part of the system of world time zones. Find the International Date Line on Map C. If you cross the date line from east to west, you move ahead one day. If you cross the line from west to east, you go back one day.

For more information, go online to the *Atlas* at **www.sfsocialstudies.com**.

Think and Apply

1. What two battles occurred east of the International Date Line?

2. What two battles occurred closest to the Tropic of Cancer?

3. Find the location of the battle of Eniwetok. At approximately what latitude and longitude was the battle fought?

1930

1933
Hitler takes power in Germany.

1939
World War II begins.

Chapter Summary

Draw Conclusions

On a separate sheet of paper, fill in the diagram to supply three facts upon which the given conclusion could be based.

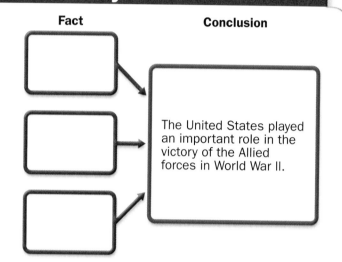

Fact

Conclusion

The United States played an important role in the victory of the Allied forces in World War II.

Vocabulary

Match each word with the correct definition or description.

1. **dictator** (p. 341)

2. **fascism** (p. 341)

3. **atomic bomb** (p. 354)

4. **concentration camp** (p. 362)

5. **Holocaust** (p. 362)

a. place where people were imprisoned and killed by the Nazis

b. widespread murder by the Nazis

c. leader who gains complete control of a country and its people

d. form of government in which a dictator has complete power

e. extremely powerful weapon

People and Places

Write a sentence that explains the role of each of the following people or places in World War II. You may use two or more in a single sentence.

1. **Franklin D. Roosevelt** (p. 341)

2. **Adolf Hitler** (p. 341)

3. **Winston Churchill** (p. 343)

4. **Pearl Harbor, Hawaii** (p. 344)

5. **Benjamin O. Davis, Jr.** (p. 352)

6. **Normandy, France** (p. 360)

7. **George S. Patton** (p. 360)

8. **Harry S. Truman** (p. 361)

9. **Hiroshima, Japan** (p. 361)

10. **Anne Frank** (p. 362)

1940   1950

1941
Japan
bombs
Pearl
Harbor.

1942
Japanese Ameri-
cans are moved
into internment
camps.

1942
The Man-
hattan Pro-
ject begins.

1944
Millions of
American women
work in weapons
factories.

**June
1944**
Allies
invade
France.

**May
1945**
Germany
surrenders.

August 1945
Japan surrenders,
ending World
War II.

Facts and Main Ideas

1 How did World War II help to end the Great Depression in the United States?

2 Why did Nazis create concentration camps, and what occurred in them?

3 **Time Line** How many years passed between the beginning and end of World War II?

4 **Main Idea** What were some of the events that led to the start of World War II?

5 **Main Idea** What were some of the things Americans did at home to help the war effort?

6 **Main Idea** Describe two major turning points in World War II that led to the Allied victory.

7 **Critical Thinking:** *Cause and Effect* What effect did the attack on Pearl Harbor have on the United States' role in the war?

Write About History

1 **Write a short newspaper article** about the Allied invasion of Normandy, France.

2 **Write a paragraph analyzing** the race to develop new technologies during World War II.

3 **Write a journal entry** as a player or fan of the All American Girl's Baseball League, including the reasons the league was formed.

Apply Skills

Understand Key Lines of Latitude and Longitude

Use the map on page 367 to answer the following questions.

1 Is the country of Japan north or south of the Equator?

2 At approximately what latitude and longitude was the battle of Guadalcanal fought?

3 What was the farthest west line of longitude that Japanese forces reached during World War II? What battle occurred at this longitude?

Internet Activity

To get help with vocabulary, people, and terms, select dictionary or encyclopedia from *Social Studies Library* at **www.sfsocialstudies.com**.

The Grapes of Wrath

by John Steinbeck

By the mid-1930s, parts of the Great Plains were known as the Dust Bowl. Strong winds caused terrible dust storms that sometimes made day as dark as night. This excerpt from John Steinbeck's 1939 novel *The Grapes of Wrath* describes the effects of a dust storm. How did people try to protect themselves from the dust?

The dawn came, but no day. In the gray sky a red sun appeared, a dim red circle that gave a little light, like dusk; and as that day advanced, the dusk slipped back toward darkness, and the wind cried and whimpered over the fallen corn.

Men and women huddled in their houses, and they tied handkerchiefs over their noses when they went out, and wore goggles to protect their eyes.

When the night came again it was black night, for the stars could not pierce the dust to get down, and the window lights could not even spread beyond their own yards. Now the dust was evenly mixed with the air, an emulsion [a mixture that does not blend together] of dust and air. Houses were shut tight, and cloth wedged around doors and windows, but the dust

came in so thinly that it could not be seen in the air, and it settled like pollen on the chairs and tables, on the dishes. The people brushed it from their shoulders. Little lines of dust lay at the door sills.

In the middle of that night the wind passed on and left the land quiet. The dust-filled air muffled sound more completely than fog does. The people, lying in their beds, heard the wind stop. They awakened when the rushing wind was gone. They lay quietly and listened deep into the stillness. Then the roosters crowed, and their voices were muffled, and the people stirred restlessly in their beds and wanted the morning. They knew it would take a long time for the dust to settle out of the air. In the morning the dust hung like fog, and the sun was as red as ripe new blood. All day the dust sifted down from the sky, and the next day it sifted down. An even blanket covered the earth. It settled on the corn, piled up on the tops of the fence posts, piled up on the wires; it settled on roofs, blanketed [covered] the weeds and trees.

The people came out of their houses and smelled the hot stinging air and covered their noses from it. And the children came out of the houses, but they did not run or shout as they would have done after a rain. Men stood by their fences and looked at the ruined corn, drying fast now, only a little green showing through the film of dust. The men were silent and they did not move often.

UNIT 4

Review

Test Talk

Look for details to support your answer.

Main Ideas and Vocabulary

Read the passage below and use it to answer the questions that follow.

The early 1900s were years of great change for many Americans. The growing mass media—newspapers, radio programs, and movies—helped a common American culture develop. In 1919 the Eighteenth Amendment began <u>Prohibition</u>. Many people opposed Prohibition, and it was ended in 1933 by the Twenty-first Amendment.

In 1929 the stock market crashed, beginning a period of economic hardship called the Great Depression. Many businesses failed and unemployment rose. President Franklin D. Roosevelt began New Deal programs to help the economy recover.

In 1933 Adolf Hitler became dictator of Germany. Germany, Italy, and Japan formed an alliance known as the Axis. In 1939 Germany invaded Poland, beginning World War II. The Allies—Britain and France—fought against the Axis. They were later

joined by the Soviet Union. On December 7, 1941, Japan attacked Pearl Harbor, Hawaii, and the United States joined the Allies.

American industries expanded to produce war supplies. This meant more jobs and an end to the Great Depression. Women found new jobs in factories and joined the Women's Army Corps. The Tuskegee Airmen became the first African American fighter pilots in the United States Air Corps.

By mid-1944, the Allies were fighting their way toward Germany from both the east and the west. On May 8, 1945, Germany surrendered. Allied soldiers found <u>concentration camps</u> as they liberated Europe.

In order to defeat Japan and save American lives, President Harry Truman ordered that the world's first atomic bombs be dropped on the Japanese cities of Hiroshima and Nagasaki. Japan surrendered to the Allies on August 14, 1945, ending World War II.

1 In the passage, the word <u>Prohibition</u> means a
 - **A** popular type of literature
 - **B** ban on jazz music
 - **C** ban on the sale and use of alcohol
 - **D** ban on the use of assembly lines

2 According to the passage, what effect did World War II have in the United States?
 - **A** Women were banned from working in factories.
 - **B** War industries ended the Great Depression.
 - **C** Alcohol was made illegal.
 - **D** African Americans were forced to move to relocation camps.

3 In the passage, the term <u>concentration camps</u> means
 - **A** places where Jews and non-Jewish people were imprisoned and murdered
 - **B** places where Germany and Japan surrendered
 - **C** the name of a battle in Germany
 - **D** the name of a battle in Japan

4 According to the passage, what caused the United States to join the Allies?
 - **A** The Soviet Union refused to join the Allies unless the United States did.
 - **B** Germany attacked Pearl Harbor.
 - **C** Japan attacked Pearl Harbor.
 - **D** Italy attacked Japan.

People and Places

Match each person and place to its definition.

1 **Detroit, Michigan** (p. 299)

2 **Bessie Smith** (p. 312)

3 **Benito Mussolini** (p. 341)

4 **Los Alamos, New Mexico** (p. 354)

5 **Dwight D. Eisenhower** (p. 360)

6 **Iwo Jima** (p. 361)

a. island where the United States won a major battle

b. blues singer

c. American general in command of Allied forces

d. site of Henry Ford's first assembly-line factory

e. site of a secret laboratory working on the atomic bomb

f. dictator of Italy

Apply Skills

Write a Letter Using Facts and Opinions Suppose you lived during the Harlem Renaissance or the Great Depression. Write a letter to a friend describing what it is like. Use as many facts as you can, and add some of your opinions. When you are finished, pair up with a classmate. Exchange your letters, and then write replies to each other.

Dear Jessica,
How are you? I haven't written in a long time, and I have so much to tell you.

Write and Share

Create a Poster Encourage Americans during World War II to help their country by creating a "Do Your Part" poster. Include examples you read about in Unit 4, such as collecting scrap metal and planting Victory Gardens. Be creative. Include drawings and a brief explanation of why each activity is helpful.

Read on Your Own

Look for books like these in the library.

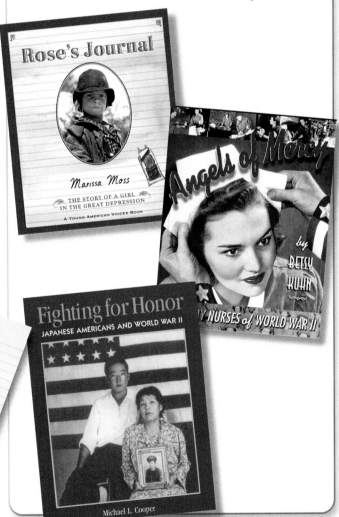

Feature Movie

Bring an athlete or pilot to the screen.

1 Form a group to choose an athlete or pilot from this unit. Research the person's life and achievements.

2 Write a screenplay or script for a short movie based on the person's accomplishments. Write dialogue for the characters and instructions for camera operators. Write about the location and setting of your movie.

3 Make a backdrop for your screenplay. You may want to include a recording of music and sounds.

4 Perform your movie for the class.

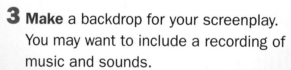

Internet Activity

Learn more about World War II.
Go to **www.sfsocialstudies.com/activities** and select your grade and unit.

Challenges at Home and Abroad

What changes have you seen in the United States during your lifetime?

1945 ─────────── 1955 ─────────── 1965

1945
The United
Nations is
formed.

1950
The Korean
War begins.

1954
Supreme Court
declares
segregation in
public schools
is illegal.

1962
Cuban
Missile
Crisis

1964
Civil Rights
Act of
1964 is
passed.

"I have a dream…."

—from a speech by Martin Luther King, Jr., 1963

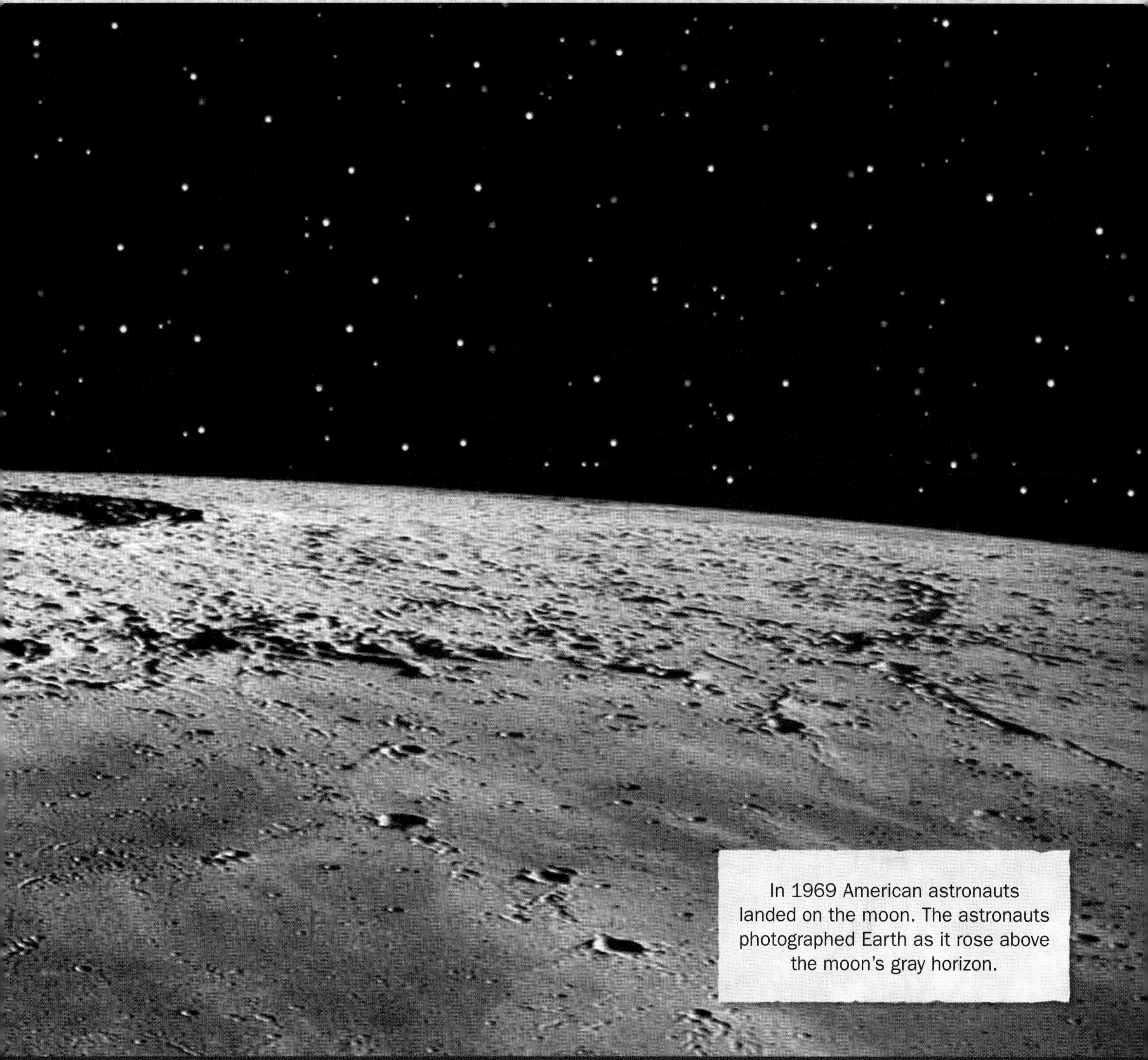

In 1969 American astronauts landed on the moon. The astronauts photographed Earth as it rose above the moon's gray horizon.

1975 | 1985 | 1995

1969
American astronauts are first to land on the moon.

1981
Sandra Day O'Connor becomes the first woman Supreme Court justice.

1991
The Soviet Union breaks up.

Meet the People

Thurgood Marshall

1908–1993

Birthplace: Baltimore, Maryland

Lawyer, Supreme Court justice

- Served as legal director for the NAACP from 1940 to 1961
- Won 1954 Supreme Court case that made segregation in public schools illegal
- First African American to be named a Supreme Court justice

Ronald Reagan

1911–2004

Birthplace: Tampico, Illinois

Governor, President

- Became a movie actor in his twenties
- Served as governor of California for eight years
- Elected President of the United States in 1980 and 1984

Rosa Parks

1913–2005

Birthplace: Tuskegee, Alabama

Civil rights leader

- Member of the NAACP
- Her actions led to the Montgomery Bus Boycott
- Founded the Rosa and Raymond Parks Institute for Self-Development

John F. Kennedy

1917–1963

Birthplace: Brookline, Massachusetts

Senator, President

- Served as senator from Massachusetts
- Elected President of the United States in 1960
- Led United States through difficult struggle with the Soviet Union

| 1900 | 1910 | 1920 | 1930 |

1908 • Thurgood Marshall

1911 • Ronald Reagan

1913 • Rosa Parks

1917 • John F. Kennedy

1929

1930

1930

For more information, go online to *Meet the People* at **www.sfsocialstudies.com**.

Martin Luther King, Jr.

1929–1968

Birthplace: Atlanta, Georgia

Minister, civil rights leader

- Gained fame as a civil rights leader who believed in nonviolent protest
- Delivered "I Have a Dream" speech before more than 200,000 people in Washington, D.C., in 1963
- Awarded Nobel Peace Prize in 1964

Neil Armstrong

1930–

Birthplace: Wapakoneta, Ohio

Navy pilot, astronaut

- Served as a Navy pilot from 1949 to 1952
- Helped perform the first successful in-orbit docking between two space vehicles in 1966
- On July 20, 1969, became the first person to walk on the moon's surface

Dolores Huerta

1930–

Birthplace: Dawson, New Mexico

Labor union leader

- Worked to improve life for migrant farm workers
- Joined with César Chávez to form the United Farm Workers labor union
- Began a radio station to speak for farm workers and immigrants

Maya Ying Lin

1959–

Birthplace: Athens, Ohio

Architect, artist

- Designed the Vietnam Veterans Memorial in Washington, D.C.
- Designed the Civil Rights Memorial in Montgomery, Alabama
- Wrote *Boundaries*, a book about her life and work

1940	1950	1960	1970

1963

- Martin Luther King, Jr.   1968
- Neil Armstrong
- Dolores Huerta

1959 • Maya Ying Lin

379

Reading Social Studies

Challenges at Home and Abroad

Cause and Effect

Learning to identify causes and effects can help you understand what you read. Look at the diagram at left.

| Cause
A cause is why something happens. | → | Effect
An effect is what happens. |

- Writers sometimes use clue words such as *because, so, as a result,* or *since* to signal cause and effect.

- A cause may have more than one effect. An effect may have more than one cause.

- An effect may become a cause of something else.

Read the following paragraph. **Cause** and **effect** have been highlighted.

In Chapter 8 you learned how the United States became involved in World War II. On December 7, 1941, Japan bombed Pearl Harbor, an American base in Hawaii. Germany then declared war on the United States. Because of these aggressive actions, the United States declared war on both Japan and Germany.

Word Exercise

Precise Words Writers often choose a specific word because it best describes what they are trying to say. For example, there are many different verbs to describe water falling from the sky. They include *raining, pouring, drizzling, teeming, showering,* and *falling.* Yet only one of these words describes very light and sporadic rain—*drizzling.*

- Read the following sentence: "The country was in the middle of a struggle to protect the constitutional rights of African Americans."

- Why use *struggle* instead of *challenge, battle,* or *combat?* The word *challenge* does not relay the seriousness of the situation. The remaining words suggest that the country was in a military fight. The word *struggle* best describes what African Americans and the United States were going through at the time.

Causes and Effects of Challenges at Home and Abroad

Following World War II, Europe and Asia were in ruins. The United States made plans to help them recover from the war and sent food, supplies, and money.

The Soviet Union gained control of Eastern and Central Europe after the war. The Soviet Union forced its own form of government, communism, on these countries. This worried many in the United States, because communist governments do not allow personal freedoms that Americans value. The United States and the Soviet Union, the two most powerful nations in the world, became enemies.

The years following World War II were a time of prosperity in the United States. The government helped veterans buy houses, gain educations, and get jobs. The home-building industry had come to a near standstill because of World War II. After the war, people saw buying a house as a priority, and many new houses were built to meet the demand.

During the last half of the 1900s, many Americans struggled to gain equal opportunities as citizens. African Americans, women, disabled Americans, migrant workers, and Native Americans were some of the groups who increased their opportunities or improved their lives.

Through the 1960s, 1970s, and 1980s the United States and the Soviet Union continued to be enemies. Although they never fought each other directly, the United States fought communism and Soviet allies in Korea and Vietnam. The two nations also raced to be the first to explore space.

In 1991 the Soviet Union broke up into fifteen countries. The United States was now the world's only superpower. The United States realized that because it had such an important position in the world, it also had an important responsibility to assist other nations in their own struggles for freedom.

Apply it!

Use the reading strategy of finding causes and effects to answer the first two questions, then answer the vocabulary question.

1. What caused the United States to worry about the Soviet Union?

2. What caused the home-building industry to start up again after World War II?

3. Find the word *demand* in the selection. Why do you think the author chose to use this word instead of *interest, need,* or *requests*?

CHAPTER 9

The Postwar World

1946

Moscow, Soviet Union
The "Iron Curtain" falls, isolating the communist world from the free world.

Lesson 1

1

1950s

Detroit, Michigan
More Americans are able to afford new automobiles produced in Detroit, Michigan.

Lesson 2

2

1952

South Korea
The United States helps South Korea defeat the invading communist armies of North Korea and China.

Lesson 3

3

Why We Remember

The world faced many changes after World War II. The United States and the Soviet Union, two nations that had fought on the same side during the war, became bitter enemies. Each distrusted the other. The Soviet Union increased its military strength and built weapons. The United States built more powerful weapons to make sure the nation would be safe and strong. In spite of this distrust, many Americans at home enjoyed good jobs, better housing, and more free time. Feelings of optimism and feelings of concern were both a part of life for citizens of the United States, one of the two most powerful nations on Earth.

1945
The United Nations is formed.

1946
The Iron Curtain "falls."

1948
The Marshall Plan goes into effect.

Moscow •
SOVIET UNION
Berlin (East & West)
EAST GERMANY
WEST GERMANY

The World is Divided

PREVIEW

Focus on the Main Idea
The Cold War was a worldwide struggle between free Western nations, including the United States, and the communist countries of the Soviet Union.

PLACES
East Berlin
West Berlin
Moscow

PEOPLE
George C. Marshall

VOCABULARY
aggressor
Marshall Plan
United Nations
communism
ideology
NATO
Berlin Airlift
Cold War
propaganda

You Are There
It is a cold autumn day in 1947. You stand in the kitchen, pouring a glass of milk. Looking out the window, you watch the wind blow dead leaves across the vegetable garden. The vegetables your family raised are now in the cellar. There will be plenty of food to feed your family through the winter.

Your mother sits at the kitchen table and reads aloud an article from the newspaper. It tells about a plan to help people in Europe who suffered during World War II. Many families in France, England, and other countries don't have enough food. The United States government wants to send money, food, and other goods, so these countries can rebuild.

It makes you sad to think about people who need food, houses, and clothing. You hope the new plan to help these people will work. You ask your mother if there is any way you can help.

Cause and Effect As you read, look for events in Europe and their effects on the relationship between the United States and the Soviet Union.

PROSPERITY

THE FRUIT OF COOPERATION

EUROPEAN RECOVERY PROGRAMME

Europe and Japan After the War

World War II caused a terrible amount of damage. Many European cities were left in ruins. Places in Asia and the Pacific where fighting had taken place were devastated. Industries, farms, and homes had been bombed during battles or burned by invading armies. The Europeans and Asians who survived the war faced serious, immediate challenges. Many people found themselves without adequate food or clothing. Many had no place to live. There was little money for rebuilding.

The United States wanted to help people recover from the war. However, Americans did not limit their aid to the Allied countries. Although Germany and Japan had been the **aggressors,** or people who started the war, the United States wanted to help them recover too. Not long after the war, Japan adopted a democratic form of government and became an ally of the United States.

In February 1945, Stalin, Roosevelt, and Churchill held a meeting in the Soviet Union to decide what to do for Europe. Stalin demanded that the Soviet Union have control over the countries on its borders, so that the country could not be attacked again. The United States did not like this demand. They wanted these countries to have independence. They also knew that this would expand communist power. However, Roosevelt was willing to give control of these countries to Stalin to keep negotiations moving. The leaders agreed that the Allies would remain in Europe to help with recovery and peace-keeping. The United States and the Soviet Union also agreed to divide Korea to rid it of Japanese forces.

The Soviet Union now controlled much of Eastern and Central Europe, including eastern Germany, Finland, and Poland. The United States stationed advisors in western Germany and Japan to help with their recovery.

Victory, military strength, and resources made the Soviet Union and the United States the world's most powerful nations. They were now superpowers.

REVIEW What made the Soviet Union demand control over the countries that bordered it? ⟳ **Cause and Effect**

▶ **Coventry Cathedral in Great Britain was in ruins after World War II. The Germans, who wanted to invade and control Great Britain, bombed the country heavily during the war.**

Continuing Aid

The United States wanted to help Europeans recover for several reasons. One reason was to show kindness to those who were suffering and in need. A second reason was to assist western European countries in becoming strong against a new threat in the east, the Soviet Union. The United States feared that with so much of Europe in ruin, the Soviets would attempt to take over even more territory. President Truman wanted a plan to strengthen Western Europe.

George C. Marshall, the United States secretary of state and a former World War II general, had an idea for making Western Europe stronger. He suggested that the European nations set up a program for reconstruction with assistance from the United States. The United States would provide funds, food, and materials to help the countries rebuild. Sixteen European countries met in 1947 and came up with a program for recovery. The plan went into effect the following year. The program became known as the **Marshall Plan.**
During the four years of the Marshall Plan, Congress gave more than $13

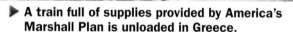

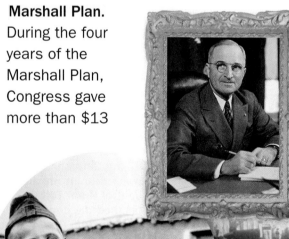

▶ A train full of supplies provided by America's Marshall Plan is unloaded in Greece.

billion for European recovery. The plan helped promote democracy in Europe and formed strong friendships between European countries and the United States.

The United States helped Asian countries rebuild too. With United States assistance, Japan and other Asian countries were able to repair farms in order to produce food again. Aid was sent for rebuilding industries, and American economic advisors helped people create new businesses and jobs.

REVIEW What caused George Marshall to suggest that the United States help Europe with its war recovery? ⟳ **Cause and Effect**

▶ President Truman (*left*) wanted to strengthen Europe. A young boy in Poland (*far left*) and crowds in Italy (*below*) happily receive American aid.

The United Nations

In April 1945, as World War II was coming to an end, representatives of 50 different countries met in San Francisco, California. These representatives had seen the devastation caused by war. They wanted to promote global cooperation, to try to avoid such terrible wars in the future. They formed a new organization called the **United Nations,** or U.N. Members of the United Nations promised to work together to try to find peaceful solutions to international problems.

Franklin D. Roosevelt was considered one of the main designers of the United Nations. He died in April 1945, just weeks before the United Nations became official. As you have read, Harry S. Truman became President after Roosevelt's death. Truman appointed Roosevelt's widow, Eleanor, to be one of the representatives in the U.N.

Eleanor Roosevelt shared many of her husband's dreams for peace. She helped the United Nations write and then adopt the Universal Declaration of Human Rights. The goal of the declaration was to establish that every person has certain rights. These rights include freedom of opinion, freedom of religion, freedom from slavery, fair trials, equality before the law, and more. While some countries deny people these rights, the U.N. hoped to influence these countries to change.

The United Nations headquarters is located in New York City. The goals of the U.N. are to keep the peace, encourage respect for human rights, and promote justice and better standards of living. The opening statement of the Charter of the United Nations says:

> *"We the peoples of the United Nations determined to save succeeding generations from the scourge [that which causes pain] of war, which twice in our lifetime has brought untold sorrow to mankind . . . do hereby establish an international organization to be known as the United Nations."*

REVIEW What brought about the formation of the United Nations? **Summarize**

▶ Flags of the countries that are members of the United Nations are displayed in front of U.N. headquarters in New York City.

▶ The United Nations flag, created in 1945, pictures the world's continents surrounded by olive branches, a symbol of peace.

387

Troubling Differences

Although the Soviet Union and the United States had been allies during World War II, the superpowers had little in common. A communist government controlled the Soviet Union. **Communism** is a political and economic system in which the government owns all of the businesses and land. Individuals have little personal freedom. The United States and the nations of Western Europe had democratic governments that promoted personal freedoms and free enterprise. You may remember that free enterprise is a system in which people are free to start their own businesses and own their own property.

There were other important differences between the Soviet Union and the West. The West valued human rights and wanted to work for peace. The Soviet Union did not share these ideals. The differences in **ideology,** or beliefs, between the Soviets and the West caused problems from the beginning.

REVIEW How is the ideology of capitalism different from that of communism?

Compare and Contrast

The Iron Curtain

As you read, the Soviet Union controlled the nations of Eastern and Central Europe after World War II. Stalin made sure that each country established a communist government. These countries were no longer free to make their own laws or elect their own governments. They were controlled by the government in **Moscow,** capital of the Soviet Union. Most citizens who lived in these countries were not allowed to travel beyond their own borders or to communicate with anyone who lived on the "outside."

Soviet actions alarmed leaders in the West. Winston Churchill, who had led Great Britain during World War II, declared in 1946:

> *"An iron curtain has descended (fallen) across the continent."*

The term *Iron Curtain* described the closing off of the Soviet Union. It was as if a curtain of iron shut out the West. Look at the map on the next page and you will see the line that divided the continent of Europe into communist and noncommunist countries. This was the line that was called the Iron Curtain.

▶ **Soviet troops take control of Bulgaria in Eastern Europe.**

The Iron Curtain in Europe, 1945–1989

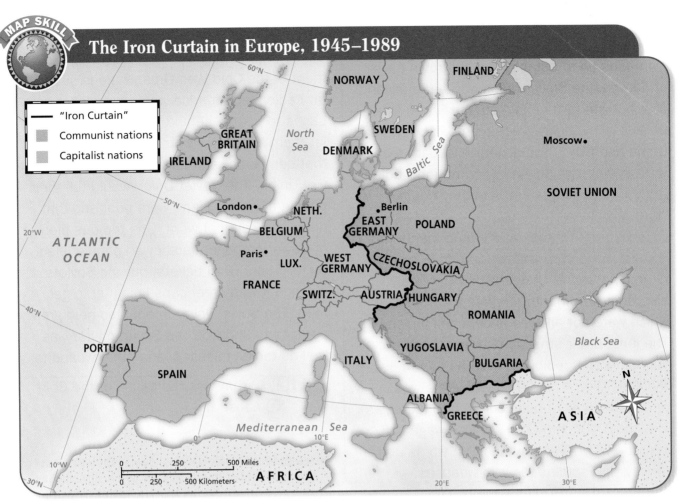

Legend:
- — "Iron Curtain"
- ▨ Communist nations
- ▨ Capitalist nations

▶ The Iron Curtain separated Eastern and Western Europe.

MAP SKILL Place *Which four free countries bordered the Iron Curtain?*

In response to the closing off of Eastern Europe, President Truman worked to strengthen the nations of Western Europe. You will remember that one response was the Marshall Plan. The plan was designed to help re-build countries after the war, to make them better able to stand up against communism. Another response was the formation of a military alliance with the nations of Western Europe. This alliance was called the North Atlantic Treaty Organization, or **NATO.** The countries of NATO promised to help each other if there was an attack by the Soviet Union.

REVIEW Why do you think Churchill used the term "iron curtain" to describe the line between communist and noncommunist countries? **Draw Conclusions**

The Berlin Airlift

Berlin, Germany's capital, had also been divided. However, Berlin was inside Soviet-controlled East Germany. In June 1948 the Soviets stopped all traffic into western Berlin. No food was allowed in. The Soviets even cut electricity to the city. Stalin hoped this would break the will of Berliners and bring the whole city under communist control.

The Americans and British would not leave the West Berliners to starve or freeze. They organized the **Berlin Airlift.** Airplanes flew in with food and fuel. The blockade was lifted in May 1949, but the Soviets kept **East Berlin** closed off from **West Berlin.**

REVIEW Why did Stalin stop traffic into Berlin? **Main Idea and Details**

A New Kind of War

In addition to establishing control in parts of Europe, the Soviet Union wanted to expand communism farther. In Asia, the Soviet Union backed communist governments in both China and North Korea. Soviet leaders made it clear that they hoped to control the whole world. In speeches they said they would "bury the West."

The United States, on the other hand, was committed to stopping the spread of communism. The United States supported freely elected governments and free enterprise, which were not allowed under communism. The long, bitter struggle between these two very different ideologies became known as the **Cold War.** In the Cold War, there was no direct attacking of one country by another, as in a "hot" war. The Cold War was waged all over the world—sometimes with words and money, and sometimes with weapons.

Propaganda, or a systematic effort to spread opinions or beliefs, was a key element of the Cold War. Organizations such as Radio Free America would broadcast messages to people behind the Iron Curtain, to let them know they were not forgotten and that democracy still existed outside the Soviet Union. The Soviet Union would tell their people that Americans were poor and that democracy did not work. One famous piece of Soviet propaganda showed people lined up for Super Bowl tickets, but the Soviets claimed it was Americans lining up to get food. The Soviet government also held great parades to show off the Soviet military, as well as tanks, missiles, and other weapons.

REVIEW What was the cause of the Cold War? **Cause and Effect**

▶ **Nikita Khrushchev was the Soviet Union's most powerful leader from 1958 to 1964. Khrushchev was well known for his threats against the West—and for pounding on the table with his shoe when he disagreed with speakers during diplomatic discussions.**

▶ **Every year, the Soviets held a parade (below) to display their huge army and many weapons. Citizens were required to attend these parades.**

A World Divided

The world became defined by the split between the West, or Free World, and the Communist World. Nations that did not fit into one of these two groups were often called Third World countries. The Cold War often focused on these countries, because the Soviet Union knew it would be easier to capture them than to take over a Free World nation.

Ideology continued to separate the West from the Soviet Union. In Soviet countries, the wants and needs of the state were put above the freedoms and rights of individuals. If citizens expressed their ideas openly, they risked arrest, imprisonment, and even death. In fact, Stalin was responsible for more deaths than Hitler was. The government decided what could be printed in newspapers. Soviet leaders declared that war would end only when the whole world was communist.

In the United States and other democratic nations, personal rights and freedoms were protected by constitutions and law. Citizens were free to speak their minds and share their ideas through the press. They could vote for the candidates of their choice. However, they had one great fear—if communism were allowed to spread to the entire world, personal freedoms would no longer exist.

REVIEW What did the term "Third World" describe? **Main Idea and Details**

Summarize the Lesson

- **1945** The United Nations was formed.
- **1946** The Iron Curtain "fell."
- **1948** The Marshall Plan went into effect.

LESSON 1   REVIEW

Check Facts and Main Ideas

1. **Cause and Effect** On a separate sheet of paper, complete this chart by filling in one cause for each effect.

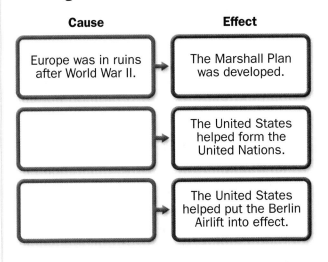

Cause		Effect
Europe was in ruins after World War II.	→	The Marshall Plan was developed.
	→	The United States helped form the United Nations.
	→	The United States helped put the Berlin Airlift into effect.

2. Describe the conditions Europe and Asia faced following World War II.

3. How did the **ideologies** of the United States and the Soviet Union bring about the **Cold War** between the Soviet Union and the United States? Write two or more sentences to answer the question. Be sure to use the highlighted words in your answer.

4. **Critical Thinking:** *Draw Conclusions* In what ways might the **Marshall Plan** have helped stop the spread of communism?

5. What role did the United States play in the development of the **United Nations**?

Link to ⚭ Geography

Work with Maps Look at the map on page 389. Of the communist nations in Europe, which is the farthest south?

Compare Primary and Secondary Sources

What? **Primary sources** are eyewitness accounts or observations. They are created by people who participated in or watched the events being described. Primary sources can be diaries, letters, documents, speeches, interviews, and even paintings or photographs.

The primary source shown on this page is part of an interview with Retired Colonel Gail Halvorsen. Colonel Halvorsen was a U.S. Air Force pilot who flew food and goods to the people of Berlin as part of the Berlin Airlift from 1948 to 1949. The interview was conducted by newscasters from CNN in 1995.

Secondary sources are secondhand accounts of history. Writers of secondary sources are not eyewitnesses of the events they report. They collect information about events from different sources, including primary and secondary sources. Then they organize that information and present it in a way that suits their purposes. History textbooks and articles in encyclopedias and newspapers are examples of secondary sources.

"I volunteered to fly the airlift. . . . The worst cargo I ever flew was 50-gallon drums of gasoline. These were miserable to handle. . . . The best load we ever had was a load of bottled milk: fresh whole milk for the kids in Berlin, and that was great. . . . We flew everything: medical supplies, newsprint—but the coal was the biggest thing, and it was the biggest problem, too, for the control columns in the airplane. Of course they had it in bags. . . . The coal dust could seep in on the floor and control cables [and] make it difficult to control the airplane. [After we landed] we came out of the cockpit and watched them [Berliners] unload. And before they unloaded they came up to us. . . . and looked at us like we're angels from heaven. It was a [feeling] that I guess it's hard to explain. It's one that you don't often receive: feeling good about a really rough situation. . . . Working for a common goal, day and night, through thunderstorms and bad weather, whatever. . . . I didn't hear any pilot complain about flying all night or the storms. . . ."

Why? As you study, you will use both primary and secondary sources.

Primary sources can give firsthand accounts about the experiences people had during a certain event. Primary sources can offer emotion, vivid descriptions, and insight into an event. However, a primary source gives a limited viewpoint, because it comes from one person in one place and time.

"NEAR TEMPLEHOF (TEM-PUL-HOF) AIRPORT [IN BERLIN], YOUNG AND OLD GERMANS CROWD A ROOFTOP TO WATCH A UNITED STATES AIR FORCE C-54 ROAR IN WITH VITAL SUPPLIES FOR 2,100,000 PEOPLE OF THE BLOCKADED WESTERN ZONES. EVERY THREE MINUTES AROUND THE CLOCK, IN FAIR WEATHER AND FOUL, AN OPERATION VITTLES TRANSPORT LANDS TO DISGORGE [UNLOAD] FOOD, FUEL, CLOTHING, MEDICINE, BUILDING MATERIALS. WITHIN 17 MINUTES IT IS EMPTY AND READY FOR ANOTHER FLIGHT. . . . OPERATION VITTLES STARTED ON JUNE 16, 1948, FIVE DAYS AFTER RUSSIA CUT OFF RAIL, HIGHWAY, AND BARGE SHIPMENTS INTO SHATTERED, HUNGRY BERLIN. BY LATE FEBRUARY 1949, THE USAF [UNITED STATES AIR FORCE] AND RAF [BRITAIN'S ROYAL AIR FORCE] WERE DELIVERING NEARLY 8,000 TONS SOME DAYS."

▶ **This secondary source comes from the article "Airlift to Berlin," published in May 1949 in *National Geographic.***

Secondary sources can report broader perspectives and more precise details about a certain event. This is because a secondary source can draw on multiple sources for its information. Secondary sources, however, don't share individual experiences. This might make the reports seem less personal.

How? To compare primary and secondary sources, consider the following:

In a primary source, there will be words or phrases that describe personal emotions, observations, and thoughts as well as actions. It is clear that the person sharing the information was part of the event. In the interview on page 392, Colonel Halvorsen describes how he felt about carrying cargo to Berlin. He described how the Berliners looked at the pilots after they landed with the goods. He gave the details as he, himself, experienced them.

In a secondary source, personal emotions are less likely to appear, unless the article or report includes an eyewitness quote. Secondary sources present secondhand accounts that often include facts, figures, names, dates, and actions. The writer of a secondary source is not part of the event described. He or she is sharing information gathered from other sources. Because many sources are used, a secondary source often has more perspective. The portion of the article on this page shares broader details about the Berlin Airlift as a whole.

Both primary and secondary sources are useful. They can provide a different point of view of the same information.

Think and Apply

1. Suppose you wanted to understand what it was like to be a near-starving Berliner receiving goods during the Berlin Airlift. Which kind of source would you look for? Explain your answer.

2. How might you use the interview given by Colonel Halvorsen?

3. If you needed a single source to learn about all the action that took place during the Berlin Airlift, do you think a secondary or primary source would be more helpful? Explain your answer.

1940   1960

1944
G.I. Bill of
Rights is
signed.

1955
AFL and CIO
labor unions join
to form AFL-CIO.

1956
Interstate
highway system
is created.

Boom Years at Home

PREVIEW

Focus on the Main Idea
Following World War II, the
United States entered a time
of economic growth and
technological advancement.

PLACES
Anaheim, California
Detroit, Michigan

PEOPLE
Walter Cronkite
Edward R. Murrow

VOCABULARY
suburb
AFL-CIO
G.I. Bill of Rights
consumer credit
credit card
commute

You Are There

"Come on," your father calls from the front door. "Let's go for a drive!" You jump up from your chair in the living room and race outside. Your mother and two sisters join you. Everyone stares at the new car parked at the street curb. Your father just brought the car home from the dealership. It's a bright, shiny blue convertible with lots of chrome and white-walled tires!

Your sisters want to sit by the windows. You want to sit there too, but agree to let them go first.

Your family drives out of the city to an area where new houses are being built. Most of the houses have fenced yards, driveways, and garages. There are trees, grass, and flower gardens. You wonder if your family might be able to move to an area like this soon. Now that your father has gotten a raise at work, it just might be possible!

Cause and Effect As you read, think about some of the factors that brought about economic growth and prosperity in the United States.

▶ A strong economy made it possible for many Americans to buy homes in rapidly growing suburbs.

A Growing Economy

When World War II ended, Americans hoped for security, peace, and comfort at home. They were happy that the war was over and that the Allies had won. Many felt confident about the future in spite of concerns about the Cold War.

Americans had sacrificed a great deal during the war. Many had struggled while the family's chief wage earner was overseas. Americans had given up many goods and foods for the war effort. After the war, families were reunited. Rationing was over. Americans could once again purchase as much meat, sugar, gasoline, milk, and clothing as they could afford.

In the late 1940s and 1950s, industries that had produced war materials now turned their resources into producing consumer goods. Shiny new cars appealed to adult consumers. Families wanted televisions and barbecue grills. New toys caught children's attention. Teenagers listened to portable radios with their friends. Americans couldn't get enough of American products, and the economy became strong. As consumers bought more goods, businesses and industries grew. This created new jobs—jobs that often offered good wages and benefits such as insurance and paid vacations. Good wages meant workers could buy more.

The Great Depression and World War II had slowed down the home-building industry. When soldiers returned from overseas in the mid-1940s, however, they wanted to buy homes for their families. A new idea sprang up on the East Coast. Builders bought parcels of land on the outskirts of cities. They put up hundreds of individual family houses on the land and then sold them at affordable prices. It wasn't long before **suburbs,** or communities near the edge of a city, could be found all over the country. Between 1948 and 1958, 11 million houses were built in the suburbs.

REVIEW How did consumers' desire for new goods help the economy grow?
↻ **Cause and Effect**

395

The Changing Workplace

The American workplace changed after World War II. Many women who had taken over factory jobs during the war resumed their traditional responsibilities with families and households. Returning war veterans were given their jobs once more.

Other workplace changes came about because of labor unions. As you read in Unit 2, labor unions got started in the late 1800s. By the early 1950s, many occupations were represented by unions. These included miners, telephone workers, automobile manufacturers, steel workers, and farmers. Union leaders used negotiations, or meetings with business owners, to try to improve conditions for workers. Improvements might include health care, retirement plans, and shorter working hours. In fact, by 1950 the standard workweek consisted of 40.5 work hours, compared to 59 hours in 1900. If negotiations failed, union leaders would often call a strike, to try to force business owners to make changes.

In the 1950s union memberships increased as more jobs were created. Many workers saw the advantages of belonging. However, some industries forced workers to join their unions. This caused serious conflicts, because not everyone agreed with what

▶ Labor meetings in the 1950s showed the growing size and power of the unions.

the unions were doing. Some unions became wealthy and powerful. They used their power to convince politicians to pass laws that benefited them and their members.

Some labor unions merged, or joined together, to become even more powerful. In 1955 the American Federation of Labor, or AFL, and the Congress of Industrial Organizations, or CIO, merged to form the **AFL-CIO**. With this merger, the AFL-CIO brought together nearly 85 percent of all American union members and became the largest labor organization in the nation.

REVIEW Why did many workers join labor unions? **Main Idea and Details**

▶ Unions often used strikes to try to force businesses to meet their demands.

▶ Veterans crowd Veterans Administration offices to sign up for schooling under the G.I. Bill.

The G.I. Bill

During the war, whatever Americans fighting overseas needed was issued by the government, including uniforms, vehicles, equipment, and food. Soon they began to joke that they too were government issue, or G.I.'s. When veterans returned home, the name G.I. came home with them.

The United States government wanted to help the men and women who had served in the military, because of all they had done. On June 22, 1944, President Franklin D. Roosevelt signed the **G.I. Bill of Rights.** This law provided benefits to help veterans succeed in civilian society. The idea of taking care of veterans was not new. In 1636 Pilgrims in New England declared: "If any person shall be sent forth as a soldier and shall return maimed [injured] he shall be maintained competently by the Colony during his life."

The G.I. Bill offered the following benefits to veterans:

- education and training
- a loan guaranty for a home, farm, or business
- unemployment pay of $20 a week for up to 52 weeks

- job-finding assistance

As Roosevelt signed the G.I. Bill, he said:

> "...*the members of our armed forces ... have been compelled to make greater economic sacrifice and every other kind of sacrifice than the rest of us, and they are entitled to definite action to help take care of their special problems.*"

Out of 15,440,000 World War II veterans, nearly 8 million took advantage of the G.I. Bill's education benefits. These benefits helped G.I.'s pay for tuition, books, and fees at colleges and other schools, as well as on-the-job training. When these veterans did enter the workforce, they were better prepared to support their families and contribute to society.

REVIEW Why did so many veterans take advantage of the G.I. Bill's education benefits? Draw Conclusions

The Rise of Credit Society

When World War II ended, there were suddenly several million veterans coming home, all wanting to start up their lives again. However, most returning veterans had no savings accounts or work histories. They needed someone to help them get loans so they could buy houses and cars. The government stepped in and offered to guarantee commercial loans for veterans.

For the first time in history, the government was using tax dollars to support private lending. At first, only veterans could get the government-supported loans. Soon everyone wanted to borrow, and the government expanded its programs.

With the economy growing and credit readily available, a new concept was born: consumer credit. **Consumer credit** is credit that is used to buy goods that are consumed, or used up, such as food and clothing, rather than for investments, such as farm equipment or businesses. Consumer credit is usually paid back with monthly payments.

With the government backing loans for both veterans and non-veterans, spending increased. With greater demand for goods, prices began to go up. With this inflation of prices, more people needed credit to buy the things they wanted.

Department stores, oil companies, and other businesses had offered charge cards to regular customers since the early 1900s. These allowed a person to buy merchandise and pay the total at the end of the month. After World War II, with the rise in consumer credit, credit cards became available. A **credit card** allows the card owner to charge

► The increased use of credit kept banks busy *(above)*. The Diners' Club card *(left)* was the first charge card that could be used in many different places.

goods and services and then pay off the charge, along with an extra fee, over a period of time. In 1950 Diners' Club issued the first charge card that could be used at many different locations, rather than at one store or gas station. It was designed for business travelers. It allowed customers 60 days to pay. The BankAmericard was the first credit card to give cardholders the option to pay the entire debt or to pay over time with an interest charge.

There was a downside to readily available credit, however. Many people spent too much. From 1950 until 1960, total consumer debt in the United States more than doubled. It rose from $73 billion to $196 billion in just ten years. Consumer credit, and credit cards in particular, continued to be both a benefit and a danger, and consumer debt continued to rise into the next century.

REVIEW Why did consumer debt in the United States go up in the 1950s?
↻ Cause and Effect

Evolving Role of Women

After the war, most women returned to their roles as homemakers. However, women found many things changing around them. New or improved appliances gave women more leisure time than ever before. Television programs and new magazines were created for women. New stores opened, and women became an important part of the new credit society.

Not all women returned to being homemakers, however. Women who had taken wartime jobs had developed new skills. Others had earned their own money for the first time. Some of these women decided that they preferred having careers to staying at home. Economic prosperity and growth in technology led to large numbers of women entering the workforce.

Life was not always easy for women who worked outside the home. They were still expected to take the lead role in housework and child raising. The government provided help by offering earlier schooling. Public kindergartens became common. With a

▶ Eleanor Roosevelt, an advocate for women's rights, made regular radio broadcasts to share her ideas.

place to send younger children during the day, still more women could enter the workforce. By 1950, 30 percent of American women worked outside the home. By 1960 the number had risen to 38 percent.

Women who were accepted into professions such as business, law, and medicine were not promoted as often as men. They were usually paid less too. This was largely because people assumed that women would work only until they had families. While this was true of many women, it was not true of all.

Eleanor Roosevelt was a respected advocate for women's rights. She had long worked to improve wages for women and to give them a place in politics. In 1945 she pressured the Army Nurse Corps to accept African American women into their ranks. In 1952 she spoke at the United Nations on the importance of women's rights. In 1961 she served as chairperson of the President's Commission on the Status of Women.

REVIEW How did women's roles change in the 1950s? Summarize

▶ In the 1950s most women worked at home, caring for their homes and families. New appliances helped make their work easier.

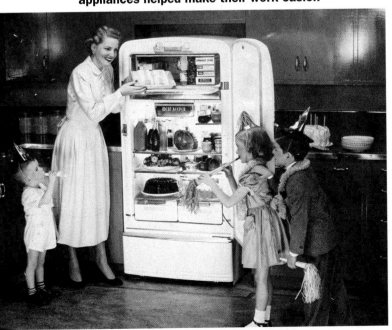

Changing Life

Families of the 1950s were making more money than families had in the past. Better jobs, shorter working hours, credit, and modern appliances created more leisure time for Americans. Now life for many was changing for the better.

Families moved to the suburbs to begin new lives. These new lives included lawns, backyard barbecues, new stores and churches, and air that was cleaner than that found in the big cities. Children didn't have to look far to find other children with whom to play. The suburbs were filled with children. From 1950 to 1960, the number of children in the United States under the age of 18 increased from 47.3 million to 64.2 million.

Parents who had lived through the Great Depression and World War II wanted their children to have advantages that they, themselves, had not had. Children played sports, took music lessons, or joined local clubs. Education, so recently made available to veterans, was seen as the key that had opened the door to this new prosperity, so the emphasis on education increased. Sales of encyclopedias jumped from $72 million in 1950 to $300 million in 1960.

Taxes in the suburbs went up in order to pay for new schools needed to educate suburban children. Many city residents had moved to the suburbs, taking their tax dollars with them. Because of this, inner-city children found themselves attending schools that the cities could not always afford to repair. The federal government helped by offering educational funds to areas in need.

FACT FILE

Baby Boomers

From 1946 until 1964, the number of babies born in the United States increased rapidly, or "boomed." This population growth was called the "Baby Boom." People born during this time came to be known as Baby Boomers, or just Boomers. Many parents during this time had confidence in their ability to take good care of their children. They bought their children whatever they needed. In many cases, they bought far more than they or their children needed. Baby Boomers were raised in a world of consumerism and credit cards.

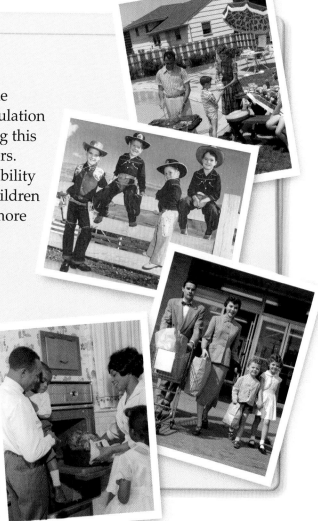

Birth Rate by Year, 1945-1965

Number of Births in Millions / Year

Men and women who lived in the suburbs and worked in the city had a new challenge to face—the **commute,** or trip to work. New highways built with tax money were crowded with automobiles going into and out of the cities on a daily basis.

Highways offered not only a way to get to work, but also a way to reach faraway destinations. Families packed their cars to go camping in the many National Parks. They also traveled to **Anaheim, California,** to visit a new place called Disneyland, which Walt Disney opened on July 18, 1955. Disneyland was the first theme park in the world!

One of the most popular American high-ways was Route 66, also called the "Mother Road." It covered 2,400 miles, reaching from Chicago, Illinois, all the way to Santa Monica, California. Many people traveled along this road in order to move their families to the West. Others took Route 66 to go on vacation. A family could have a lot of fun along the way. Route 66 was lined with billboards, trading posts, diners, tourist camps, motels, historic sites, and natural attractions such as the Petrified Forest.

REVIEW Why did the sale of encyclopedias increase in the 1950s?
Draw Conclusions

Map Adventure

Family Vacation Along Route 66, 1955

You and your family are traveling from Chicago to Los Angeles, taking Route 66 all the way. Use the map and its scale of miles to answer the following questions:

Choose three sites you would like to visit along the way. About how many miles is it between each of the three sites?

1. If your family can drive 60 miles an hour along Route 66, how long would it take to get from Kellyville, OK, to Tucumcari, NM, with no stops? from Stanton, MO, to Amarillo, TX?

2. In which direction would you drive to get from Chicago to St. Louis? from Los Angeles to Flagstaff? from Oklahoma City to Amarillo?

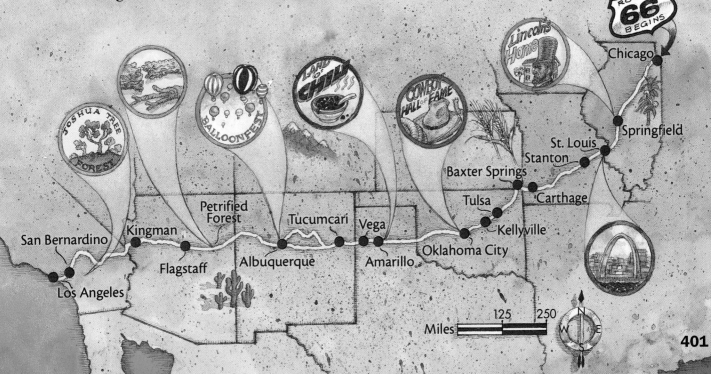

The Technology Explosion

Much of the good life in the 1950s was made possible by new and amazing technologies. After World War II, many engineers turned their energies toward developing peacetime technologies to benefit civilians.

People living in the suburbs needed cars, because there was not always public transportation nearby. The automotive industry produced more cars to fill the demand. Designers in **Detroit, Michigan,** created large, flashy new vehicles to appeal to buyers. Some car designs were based on the look of sleek World War II fighter planes. New technologies such as automatic transmission, radial tires, and power steering made the American automobile an exciting, comfortable vehicle to drive.

The Federal Aid Highway Act of 1956 created the first interstate highway system. This system linked states and major cities with direct, well-planned routes. Air travel increased in the 1950s as well. The "jet age" began in 1952 with the introduction of the de Havilland Comet jet airplane. Other commercial jets such as the Boeing 707, DC-8, and Boeing 727 followed. Travelers could go from state to state or overseas faster than ever before. Many of the first pilots on commercial airlines had been military pilots during the war.

▶ **Watching television became a popular activity for families.**

Entertainment became an important industry in the 1950s. The television became a standard appliance in American homes. By 1950 there were 1.5 million TV sets in the United States. Viewers enjoyed shows such as "I Love Lucy" and "Father Knows Best." Television was not only used for entertainment, but also as a source of news. Viewers watched nightly news broadcasts with popular commentators such as **Walter Cronkite** and **Edward R. Murrow,** to learn about national and world events.

Homes became more comfortable with better heating systems and new air-conditioning systems. And if homes didn't have air conditioners, people could still escape the heat by going to theaters and stores, where cool air became another way to attract customers.

▶ **The Boeing 727 became the biggest success story of the new "jet age."**

Coast-to-coast, direct-dial telephone service became available in 1952. This made it possible to call from one end of the country to the other without the help of a telephone operator. It also made telephone service less expensive.

▶ **This theater offered customers air-conditioned comfort.**

Room-sized computers were used to solve mathematical problems. This helped increase the speed of research and led to the development of more new technologies.

The United States was a country rich in technology. By 1954 the United States had just 6 percent of the world's population. However, it had 60 percent of the cars, 58 percent of the telephones, and 45 percent of the radios.

REVIEW What technologies helped make automobile travel easier in the 1950s? Main Idea and Details

Summarize the Lesson

- **1944** G.I. Bill of Rights was signed.
- **1955** AFL and CIO labor unions joined to form AFL-CIO.
- **1956** Interstate highway system was created.

LESSON 2 ▶ REVIEW

Check Facts and Main Ideas

1. **Cause and Effect** On a separate sheet of paper, fill in the missing effects of the major events from this lesson.

Cause	Effect
Industries began producing consumer goods.	→ The economy grew as people spent money on things they wanted.
Veterans needed financial help with education and homes.	→
More people were commuting to jobs in cities.	→

2. What is **consumer credit**?

3. Describe how the **G.I. Bill** helped returning war veterans. Answer in two or more sentences. Use the highlighted term in your answer.

4. In your own words, summarize the positive changes many American families experienced in the 1950s. Answer in two or more sentences.

5. **Critical Thinking: *Evaluate*** Which 1950s technology—television, air conditioning, or interstate highways—do you think has the biggest impact on your life today? Explain your answer.

Link to ⬦⬦ Mathematics

Calculate the Cost A family in the 1950s has a monthly income of $450. The family's house payment is $85 a month. They spend $50 on groceries, $40 for electricity, $30 on music lessons, $90 on transportation, and $100 on other bills. The family wants a new game table that costs $60, a television that costs $100, and a portable radio that costs $49. How much does the family have at the end of the month, after their bills are paid? What can the family buy without going into debt?

The Roots of Rock and Roll

Most people agree that the term *rock and roll* was first used to describe a type of music in 1954. Disc jockey Alan Freed used the term in that year to promote a "rock and roll" concert. However, the music form had already been popular for several years, and had been evolving for decades.

Rock and roll was originally a purely American form of music. It grew up largely out of such African American music forms as jazz, rhythm, blues, and gospel, but was also influenced by country and folk music.

The acoustic guitar remains important to both blues and folk music.

Brass instruments were popular among jazz musicians and were a key part of the big band sound.

The colored bar indicating music styles shows the approximate times when each style was at its most poplar. In reality, each form developed during the previous time period and carried over into the next. Music forms also changed over time, with jazz evolving into Big Band and swing. Rock and roll continues to change, and all the earlier styles remain popular.

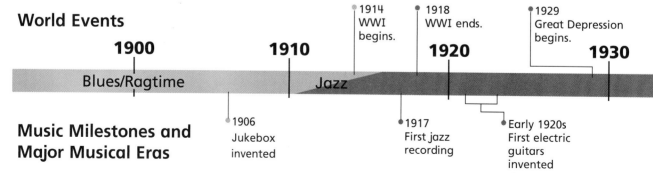

World Events

1900   **1910**   1914 WWI begins.   1918 WWI ends.   **1920**   1929 Great Depression begins.   **1930**

Blues/Ragtime   Jazz

Music Milestones and Major Musical Eras

1906 Jukebox invented

1917 First jazz recording

Early 1920s First electric guitars invented

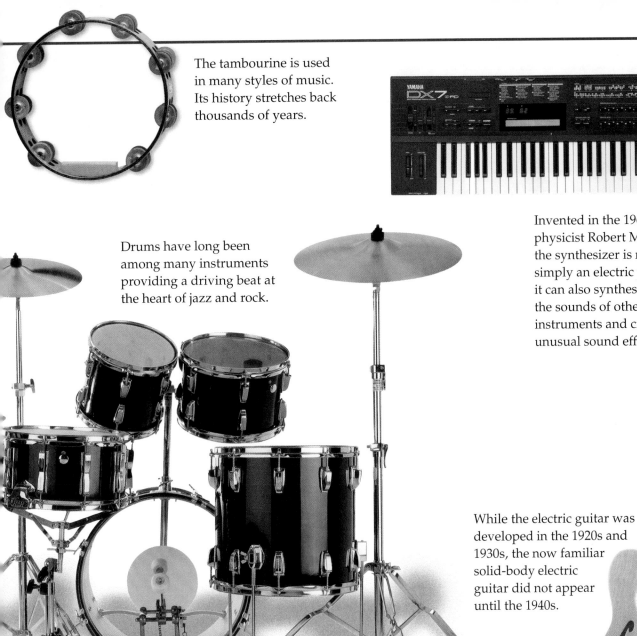

The tambourine is used in many styles of music. Its history stretches back thousands of years.

Drums have long been among many instruments providing a driving beat at the heart of jazz and rock.

Invented in the 1960s by physicist Robert Moog, the synthesizer is not simply an electric piano; it can also synthesize the sounds of other instruments and create unusual sound effects.

While the electric guitar was developed in the 1920s and 1930s, the now familiar solid-body electric guitar did not appear until the 1940s.

YAMAHA DX7 IIFD

1939
Hitler invades Poland; WWII begins.

1941
Japanese bomb Pearl Harbor.

1945
WWII ends.

1953
Korean War ends.

1969
American astronauts land on the Moon.

1940

1950

1960

1970

Big Band/Swing   Pop   Rock

1935
First tape recorder is demonstrated

1948
Long-play record album (LP) invented

1951
Top 40 radio begins.

1955
"Rock Around the Clock" becomes the first rock and roll song to hit the #1 spot on music charts.

1956
Elvis Presley has his first #1 rock and roll hit.

1959
Motown Records is founded.

1964
The Beatles come to the U.S., starting the "invasion" of British musicians influenced by American blues and rock.

405

1950   1960

February 1950
Senator McCarthy
starts anti-communist
trials.

June 1950
The Korean
War begins.

1962
Cuban
Missile
Crisis

NORTH
KOREA

SOUTH
KOREA

Cold War Conflicts

PREVIEW

Focus on the Main Idea
As the United States and the Soviet Union moved into the second half of the 1900s, Cold War conflicts intensified.

PLACES
North Korea
South Korea

PEOPLE
Joseph McCarthy
John F. Kennedy

VOCABULARY
Korean War
Red Scare
arms race
Cuban Missile Crisis
Berlin Wall

▶ Signs like this marked public bomb shelters.

CAPACITY

FALLOUT SHELTER

> **You Are There** You are walking home from school on a spring day in 1954. You notice that your neighbor is digging in his backyard. Curious, you ask him what he is doing.
>
> "Building a bomb shelter," he says.
>
> You have heard a lot about bombs lately. At school, your teachers showed students how to duck under their desks in case of a Soviet attack. You have heard that your town has put a community bomb shelter beneath the post office.
>
> "Do you think there will be a war here?" you ask your neighbor.
>
> He says, "The Soviet Union could attack us at any time. I want to protect my family. We could live here until the danger was over. We'll have enough food and water for months."
>
> You continue home. The idea of war is frightening. The communists have already taken over other countries. You wonder if your family should build a shelter too.

Summarize As you read, note ideas that will help you summarize the Cold War conflicts between the United States and the Soviet Union.

The Korean War

As you have read, a new kind of war, a Cold War, started at the end of World War II. Though the superpowers involved in the Cold War did not fight each other directly, it was not a time of peace. In 1950 the Cold War turned violent in Korea.

Following World War II, Korea had been divided into **North Korea** and **South Korea**. North Korea established a communist government with the support of the Soviet Union. On June 25, 1950, North Korean forces invaded South Korea. They hoped to unite the country under a communist government. However, the South Koreans did not want to be communists. The United Nations told North Korea to withdraw its troops, but the invasion continued. President Truman decided to send United States forces to protect South Korea. He did not want another country to fall under Soviet control. The **Korean War** had begun.

In the Korean War, soldiers from 15 other countries in the United Nations joined American soldiers. U.N. forces drove the North Koreans back. Then, in October 1950, Chinese soldiers joined the North Koreans. China had become a communist nation in 1949. Fighting continued for more than two years. Neither side was able to take control of the entire country.

In 1952 Dwight D. Eisenhower was elected President. He worked to end the Korean War. The fighting ended in 1953, with Korea still divided into two nations. The United States had helped stop communist forces from taking over South Korea. This achievement had a high price, however. More than 33,000 American soldiers died in the Korean War.

REVIEW What did the North Korean troops do that led to the Korean War?

◑ **Cause and Effect**

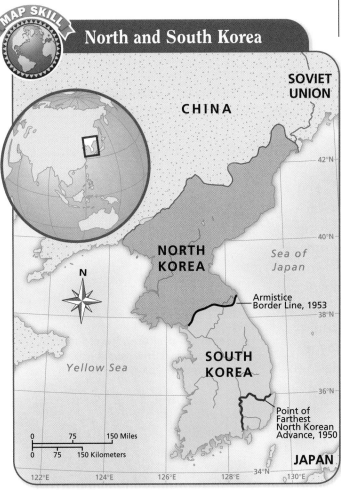

North and South Korea

MAP SKILL

► Soviet-backed North Korean forces invaded South Korea in 1950.

MAP SKILL Using Map Scale *About how much farther south would the communists have needed to advance to have controlled all of South Korea.*

► Dwight D. Eisenhower *(center)* visited American troops in Korea in December 1952, soon after he won the presidential election.

407

Divided Korea

The Korean War was over in 1953. The United States had seen the aggression of the North Koreans against South Korea. Americans had seen the Chinese come to the aid of the North Koreans in their attempt to take over South Korea. In 1954 the United States promised South Koreans that they would do all they could to prevent future invasions. American soldiers were stationed in South Korea. They helped guard the border zone between North Korea and South Korea. The need to guard this border would last into the next century.

REVIEW What caused the United States to station soldiers in South Korea after the war?

Cause and Effect

Continuing Tensions

Leaders of free nations feared communism would spread in Southeast Asia. They developed an alliance to protect countries such as South Vietnam, Laos, and Cambodia. The alliance was called the South East Asia Treaty Organization, or SEATO. Members included the United States, Britain, France, Australia, New Zealand, Pakistan, Thailand, and the Philippines. The plan was for SEATO to work much as NATO did in Europe.

SEATO never developed unity or real power because of disagreements between the members. However, some hoped the alliance at least sent a strong message to communist countries that they should stay out.

REVIEW What was the purpose of SEATO?

Main Idea and Details

Then and Now

South Korea

In the early 1950s, South Korea was one of poorest countries in the world. The Korean War had left the country in ruins. The farmers and laborers who made up much of the workforce did not have the skills needed to rebuild their country.

After the war, South Korea adopted plans for nation-wide education and rapid economic development. Under a democratic government, South Korea's average income per person rose to nearly 20 times that of North Korea's. South Korea's government encouraged the development of new industries. It also encouraged its citizens to save and invest. Today, South Korea's capital, Seoul, is a busy, prosperous, modern city. There are cell phones, cars, television stations, tall buildings, and other modern conveniences. In one generation, South Korea went from being one of the poorest to one of the richest countries in the world.

▶ Seoul, South Korea looked much different in 1951 (above) than it does today (below).

The Red Scare at Home

Cold War was new, but the fear of communism was not. The communists came to power in Russia in 1917, and the stories told by refugees fleeing the Communist Revolution were terrifying. However, some of the ideas of communism sounded positive. Even in democratic countries, some people found the ideas appealing. By 1919 the American Communist Party had 70,000 members. This caused many Americans to panic.

Red was the official color of the Communist Party, and the communists were often called "reds." So the term **Red Scare** began to be used to describe this panic. Laws were passed that made it illegal to plan the overthrow of the United States government. Many communists were arrested.

At the end of World War II, people became concerned again. Communist revolutions were violent. Millions had been killed. Many Americans feared that such a revolution might take place in the United States. When China fell to communism in 1949, concern turned to worry.

People worried about spies too. War meant spies, and the Cold War was no exception. In February 1950 everyone's worst fears seemed to be confirmed. Wisconsin Senator **Joseph McCarthy** announced that there were hundreds of communists inside the United States government.

The news media fed people's fears. Reports warned of spies and focused attention on Senator McCarthy. The country wanted him to find those communists. The Red Scare was back. Though innocent people got

▶ Newspapers kept people informed—and scared—during trials of communists held by Senator McCarthy (*above left*).

investigated, enough real spies were found to keep the public calling for more investigations.

The search soon grew to include all communists, not just those in the government. At first, taking an oath of loyalty to the government was enough to clear one's name. But as media attention and public fear grew, the investigations turned ugly. People were bullied. Lists of names were demanded from those under investigation. Some people refused to cooperate. They said the government had no right to ask about their political beliefs. Those who refused to cooperate often lost their jobs.

After the Korean War, the public began to lose interest in the hunt for communists. Their fears were calmed by the successful defense of South Korea. The U.S. Senate said that McCarthy's activities had become irresponsible and inappropriate for a senator. The Red Scare was over, and so was McCarthy's career.

REVIEW What part did the media play in the Red Scare of the 1950s? *Summarize*

The Arms Race

The Cold War continued, and so did the arms race between the United States and the Soviet Union. An **arms race** is a race to build more and better weapons than your enemy.

Both the United States and the Soviet Union built atomic bombs. These bombs were also known as nuclear (NU-klee-er) weapons. The Soviet Union had exploded its first nuclear weapon in 1949. Then, in the 1950s, scientists in both countries developed hydrogen bombs, or H-bombs. Each H-bomb was 1,000 times more powerful than the atomic bombs that had been used to end World War II.

In preparation for a Soviet nuclear attack, Americans built underground shelters. Students of the 1950s and 1960s were taught how to "duck and cover" beneath their desks in case of a bombing. Local governments stored up medicine, food, and supplies for their citizens should a war break out on American soil.

Many Americans worried about the race to build such powerful weapons. "Where will it lead us?" asked President Eisenhower. Still, American leaders felt that it was important to stay ahead of the Soviet Union in the arms race. A great deal of government money went to defense contractors who provided the weapons to the military. The United States Navy and Army grew rapidly. The strategy was simple—if the United States had more powerful weapons than the Soviets, the Soviets would be afraid to attack. Therefore, the United States continued building nuclear weapons, hoping they would never be used.

REVIEW Why did the leaders of the United States feel it was important to stay ahead in the arms race? Summarize

The Cuban Missile Crisis

In 1959 Fidel Castro led a successful revolution in Cuba. With the support of the Soviet Union, Castro formed a communist government. Cuba became the first communist nation in the Western Hemisphere. This alarmed many Americans, including **John F. Kennedy,** who was elected President in 1960. You will read more about Kennedy in the Biography on page 413. Like Truman and Eisenhower before him, Kennedy spent much of his time dealing with Cold War conflicts.

▶ During the 1950s schools held "duck and cover" drills *(left)* and some families built bomb shelters *(below).*

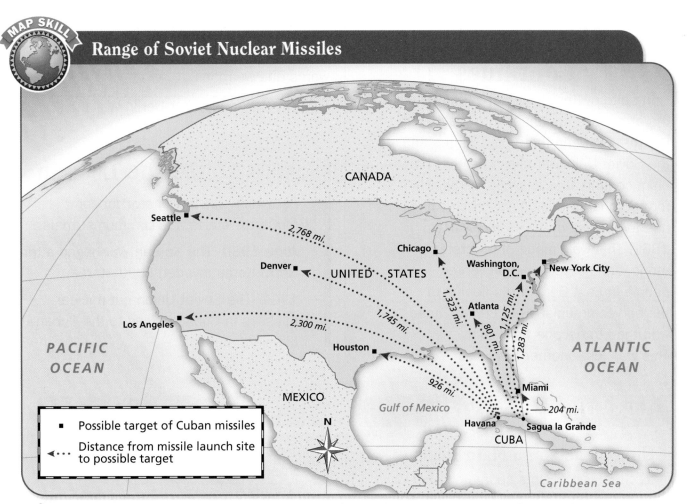

CANADA

Seattle ◄····· 2,768 mi.

Denver ◄···

UNITED STATES

Chicago

Washington, D.C.

New York City

Atlanta

1,323 mi.

1,125 mi.

Los Angeles ◄·····

2,300 mi.

1,745 mi.

801 mi.

1,283 mi.

PACIFIC OCEAN

Houston

ATLANTIC OCEAN

926 mi.

Miami

MEXICO

Gulf of Mexico

204 mi.

Havana

Sagua la Grande

CUBA

N

Caribbean Sea

- ■ Possible target of Cuban missiles
- ◄··· Distance from missile launch site to possible target

▶ The Soviet Union set up several nuclear missile sites in Cuba. The two largest sites are shown.

MAP SKILL Use a Map *The range of the nuclear missiles set up in Cuba was 300–3,400 miles. Which important United States cities could be reached by the missiles?*

The most dangerous of these conflicts was the **Cuban Missile Crisis.** In October 1962 American spy planes discovered that the Soviets were setting up nuclear missiles in Cuba—just 90 miles from the coast of Florida. On the night of October 22, Kennedy went on television to tell Americans the frightening news. He insisted that the Soviets must remove their missiles from Cuba. He declared that the United States Navy was going to block Soviet ships from bringing any more weapons to Cuba.

For the next few days, people all over the world watched the news with increasing fear. As Soviet ships approached Cuba, it looked like the world's two superpowers were moving closer and closer to nuclear war. Finally, the Soviet ships turned back. The Soviets agreed to remove their missiles from Cuba.

The crisis was over. However, both American and Soviet leaders realized how close they had come to fighting a disastrous war. In a speech in Washington, D.C., Kennedy spoke of the importance of working toward peace. Of the Americans and Soviets he said:

> *"Our most basic common link is that we all inhabit this small planet. We all breathe the same air. We all cherish our children's future."*

REVIEW Why did people watch the news with fear during the Cuban Missile Crisis?
Main Idea and Details

The Arms Race Continues

In spite of Kennedy's appeal for peace, the arms race continued into the 1960s. Distrust between the United States and the Soviet Union remained fierce. Communism continued to show its disregard for personal freedoms with such actions as the building of the **Berlin Wall** in 1961. This wall, made of concrete, stone, and barbed wire, prevented people in East Berlin from fleeing to the non-communist West Berlin. Those who tried to escape were shot. This was just another example of the tyranny of communism. Americans knew they had to remain strong with both words and weapons.

REVIEW Why was the Berlin Wall built? *Main Idea and Details*

Summarize the Lesson

February 1950 Senator Joseph McCarthy starts anti-communist trials.

June 1950 The Korean War began after North Korea invaded South Korea.

1962 The Soviet Union put nuclear missiles in Cuba, leading to the Cuban Missile Crisis.

LESSON 3   REVIEW

Check Facts and Main Ideas

1. **Summarize** On a separate sheet of paper, complete the graph, summarizing the results in the United States Cold War conflicts. Answer in a complete sentence or two.

Events

| The Korean War | The Cuban Missile Crisis | The Red Scare |

↓

Summary

2. Why did Truman believe the United States should fight in the **Korean War**?

3. Describe Senator **Joseph McCarthy's** role in the **Red Scare** of the 1950s.

Answer in one or more complete sentences. Use the highlighted terms in your answer.

4. What actions did Kennedy take after Soviet missiles were discovered in Cuba? Answer in two or more sentences.

5. **Critical Thinking: *Express Ideas*** Do you believe it was important for the United States to stay ahead of the Soviet Union in the arms race? Explain.

Link to ∞ Writing

Research Headlines Newspapers and magazines reporting on Cold War conflicts often used bold headlines to capture readers' attention. Research headlines from the 1950s and early 1960s that deal with the Red Scare, the Korean War, or the Cuban Missile Crisis. Then write your own headline for each event, making it as "catchy" as possible.

John F. Kennedy

1917–1963

On January 20, 1961, John F. Kennedy promised to faithfully fulfill the office of the President of the United States. During his Inaugural Address, the speech made after a President is sworn into office, Kennedy challenged other Americans to do all they could to help their country. He said:

> *"Ask not what your country can do for you—ask what you can do for your country."*

Kennedy knew he had difficult challenges ahead of him. The United States was in the middle of a Cold War. The country was also in the middle of the struggle for protecting the civil rights of African Americans.

Kennedy had already shown that he could handle challenges. He had served in the Navy during World War II. In 1943 Kennedy's boat was sunk by a Japanese ship. Even though he was seriously wounded, Kennedy helped get the other survivors through dangerous waters to safety.

Kennedy believed that all citizens were equal and should have equal rights. During his brief term as President, he worked to help African Americans obtain the full rights of citizenship. Kennedy also had to deal with one of the most frightening incidents in the Cold War, the Cuban Missile Crisis. Kennedy's actions prevented a possible nuclear war.

 **BIOFACT**

John F. Kennedy was the youngest man to be elected President at age 43, and he was the youngest to die in office at age 46.

On November 22, 1963, President Kennedy was assassinated in Dallas, Texas. The nation was stunned. Vice-President Lyndon B. Johnson was sworn in as the new President. During his first speech to Congress, Johnson expressed the grief of millions of Americans, saying, "All I have I would gladly give not to be standing here today."

Learn from Biographies

Why do you think John F. Kennedy worked to help African Americans obtain equality?

For more information, go to *Meet the People* at **www.sfsocialstudies.com**.

1940

1944
The G.I. Bill
of Rights
was signed.

1945
The United
Nations was
formed.

1946
The Iron
Curtain
"fell."

1948
The Marshall
Plan went
into effect.

1950

1950
The Korean
War began.

Chapter Summary

 Cause and Effect

On a separate sheet of paper, fill in three effects that came about as a result of the cause given here.

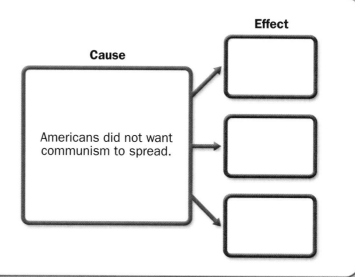

Cause

Americans did not want communism to spread.

Effect

Vocabulary

Match each word with the correct definition or description.

1 **aggressor**
(p. 385)

2 **communism**
(p. 388)

3 **ideology**
(p. 388)

4 **suburb**
(p. 395)

5 **commute**
(p. 401)

a. beliefs

b. community near the edge of a city

c. political and economic system in which all businesses and land are owned by the government

d. trip to work

e. the one who starts a fight or a war

People and Terms

Write a sentence explaining the importance each person or term. You may use two or more in a single sentence.

1 **George C. Marshall**
(p. 386)

2 **Marshall Plan**
(p. 386)

3 **Berlin Airlift**
(p. 389)

4 **NATO**
(p. 389)

5 **G.I. Bill of Rights**
(p. 397)

6 **Walter Cronkite**
(p. 402)

7 **Korean War**
(p. 407)

8 **Red Scare**
(p. 409)

9 **Joseph McCarthy**
(p. 409)

10 **John F. Kennedy**
(p. 410)

1955
The AFL and CIO labor unions joined to form the AFL-CIO.

1962
Cuban Missile Crisis

Facts and Main Ideas

1 Why did the United States want to help rebuild Europe after World War II?

2 Why was the United Nations formed?

3 What caused the Cuban Missile Crisis of 1962?

4 **Time Line** How many years after the United Nations was formed did the Korean War begin?

5 **Main Idea** Why did the Cold War develop between the United States and the Soviet Union after World War II?

6 **Main Idea** What were two or three technologies that were developed or improved upon following World War II?

7 **Main Idea** How did the United States become involved in the Korean War?

8 **Critical Thinking:** *Draw Conclusions* What do you think Americans feared would happen if communists did take over the government of the United States?

Write About History

1 **Write a journal entry** describing what the Berlin Airlift might have been like for a person in West Berlin in 1948.

2 **Write a letter** to a friend in the city about your new life in the suburbs.

3 **Write a TV news story** about the Cuban Missile Crisis.

Apply Skills

Compare Primary and Secondary Sources

Read the information below about American Red Cross canteens (coffeehouses) during the Korean War. Then answer the questions.

Two pilots just in from a jet mission came into the canteen and both burst into tears because half an hour before their buddy had been shot down. We listened to them pour it out when one of them with tears rolling down his face asked [why we had come].

Letter from Helen Stevenson, with the Red Cross in Korea, October 1951.

By the spring of 1951, there were 24 Red Cross operational locations servicing Korea, including the stationary centers at Pusan, five airfields, and 17 [other] installations.

Website: "The American Red Cross in the Korean War."

1 Which source is a primary source? How do you know?

2 In which source do you learn how many Red Cross stations were serving the military by the spring of 1951? Is this a primary or secondary source?

3 How do the two sources show the importance of the canteens?

Internet Activity

To get help with vocabulary, people, and terms, select dictionary or encyclopedia from *Social Studies Library* at **www.sfsocialstudies.com**.

A Changing Nation

1955

Montgomery, Alabama
African Americans boycott
buses after Rosa Parks
is arrested.

Lesson 1

1

1969

South Vietnam
Thousands of American
soldiers fight in the
Vietnam Conflict.

Lesson 2

2

1970

New York, New York
Americans celebrate the
first Earth Day to
bring awareness to
environmental concerns.

Lesson 3

3

1991

Kuwait
The United States armed
forces help drive Iraqi
forces out of Kuwait.

Lesson 4

4

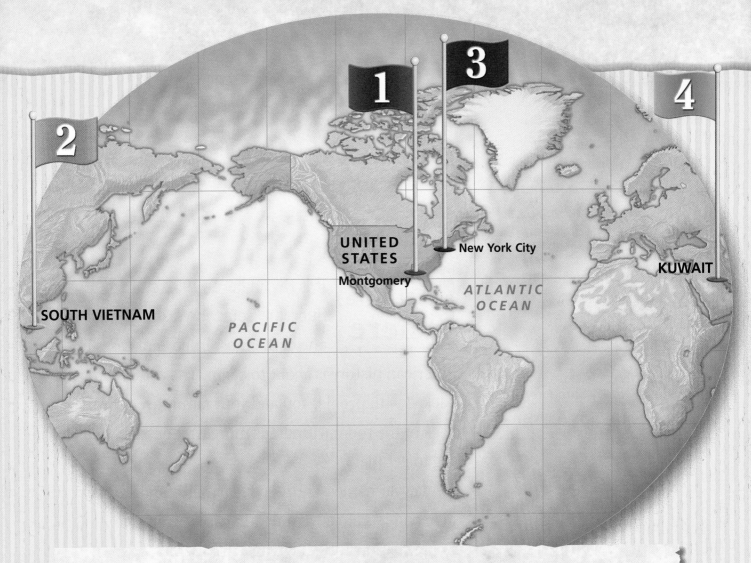

Why We Remember

The late 1900s were a time of remarkable changes, both in the United States and around the world. The Cold War came to an end. The United States continued to move toward fair treatment for all. Protecting the environment became a priority. Some countries, such as the Soviet Union, were broken up into smaller countries. With the Cold War over, the United States put its efforts into helping other countries with their struggles against aggressive invaders in order to maintain democracy and freedom.

1950   1965

1954
The Supreme Court declares segregation in public schools is illegal.

1963
Martin Luther King, Jr. leads a civil rights march.

1964
Civil Rights Act of 1964 is passed.

African Americans and Civil Rights

PREVIEW

Focus on the Main Idea
In the 1950s and 1960s, the continued efforts of African Americans to gain civil rights began to be successful.

PLACES
Montgomery, Alabama
Greensboro, North Carolina

PEOPLE
Jackie Robinson
Thurgood Marshall
Rosa Parks
Martin Luther King, Jr.
Malcolm X

VOCABULARY
civil rights
passive resistance

▶ Thurgood Marshall

You Are There
It is December 9, 1952. At the Supreme Court in Washington, D.C., one of the most important cases in American history is about to begin. The courtroom is packed with people. You and your family are near the back of the room. Hundreds more wait outside, hoping to get in.

A lawyer named Thurgood Marshall stands to speak. Marshall has already argued 15 cases before the Supreme Court. He has won 13 of them.

This case is about segregation in public schools. Many states have laws saying that black children and white children must attend separate schools. Marshall argues that these laws are wrong. He insists that segregation takes away rights guaranteed to African American children by the Constitution. You wonder what the final court decision will be.

Cause and Effect As you read, pay attention to the causes and effects of the Civil Rights movement.

Segregation

Laws had separated the races in the United States since the late 1800s. In response to segregation, African American communities developed across the nation. In these neighborhoods and towns, blacks lived, ran businesses, and built churches, colleges, and theaters. Within these "parallel worlds," a strong African American culture flourished beyond the direct effects of discrimination. It might have seemed like the system was working, but the social isolation created by segregation was a serious problem. The problem became more evident as African Americans became more successful.

▶ African Americans started businesses to meet the needs of their communities.

By the mid-1900s, African American entertainment was popular outside black communities. Entertainers such as Ethel Waters, Duke Ellington, Mahalia Jackson, and Dinah Washington were international stars, performing for royalty, winning awards, and making fortunes. Nat King Cole was the first African American to have his own radio show (1946) and his own TV show (1956). But none of these stars could walk in the front door of most hotels, even if they were performing there. It was even harder for African Americans who were not famous, or who were less educated or poor.

The issue of social isolation became increasingly important as many African Americans became more educated and more successful. It was no longer good enough to have equal facilities. African Americans wanted equality.

▶ The number of African American colleges increased.

MAP SKILL

Segregation in 1952

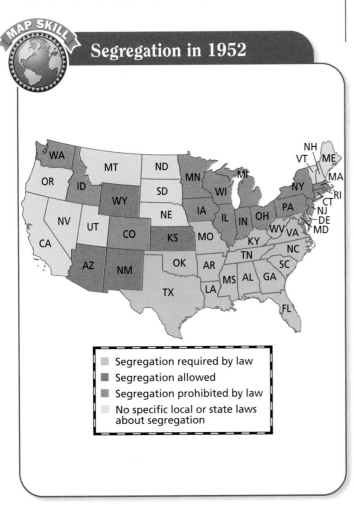

- ☐ Segregation required by law
- ☐ Segregation allowed
- ☐ Segregation prohibited by law
- ☐ No specific local or state laws about segregation

▶ In the 1950s, each state could decide what to do about segregation.

MAP SKILL Use a Map Key *Which states allowed segregation?*

REVIEW Why do you think increased success made the social isolation of African Americans more evident? *Draw Conclusions*

The Struggle Continues

As you have read, even after enslaved African Americans gained freedom in the late 1800s, they were often denied equal rights. Individuals had personal successes. For example, Bessie Coleman became the first licensed African American aviator in 1926. In 1940 Richard Wright published a successful novel, and Benjamin O. Davis became the first African American Brigadier General. There were numerous successes like these, but there was still much injustice.

In 1941 Franklin D. Roosevelt had ordered an end to discrimination in all defense industries, which opened more jobs for African Americans. After World War II, even more people joined the struggle for civil rights. **Civil rights** are the rights that are guaranteed to all citizens by the Constitution.

In 1948 President Truman ordered an end to segregation in the United States military. He stated that there must be "equality of treatment and opportunity in the armed forces without regard to race, color, religion, or national origin." This was a big step forward. However, there was still a long way to go.

Jackie Robinson was the first African American to "break the color line" in major league baseball. Robinson was a talented athlete who excelled in baseball, football, basketball, and track. In 1944 he joined the Kansas City Monarchs baseball team, part of baseball's Negro Leagues. He was a very

▶ **Jackie Robinson played for the Brooklyn Dodgers.**

successful player. The Brooklyn Dodgers, a team of white players in the major leagues, asked him to join them. Robinson agreed, even though he knew he would face insults and hostility from some players and fans. Robinson led the Dodgers to six National League titles and one World Series. He helped break down racial barriers in the United States. Soon, other white teams were hiring players away from the Negro Leagues. In a little more than a decade, all the major league teams had African American players.

REVIEW How did Jackie Robinson help "break the color line" in baseball?
Main Idea and Details

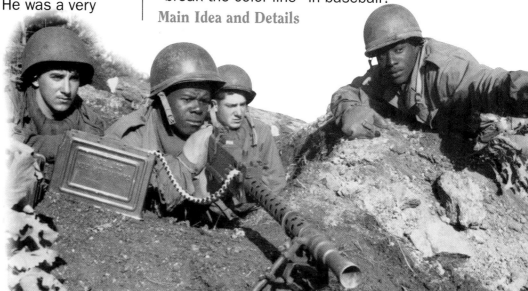

▶ **Segregation in the military ended in 1948.**

420

Ending School Segregation

Education was another area in American life where blacks and whites were kept apart. Some states spent much less money on school buildings, teachers, and books for African American children. But even in areas where education was equal, there was growing dissatisfaction with the continued social isolation. By the 1950s many states prohibited segregation, but little was being done to bring black and white students together.

The NAACP decided to end segregation in public schools. The organization's head lawyer, **Thurgood Marshall,** knew that he would have to get the Supreme Court to declare that segregation was illegal under the Constitution.

Marshall got his chance with a case based on the experience of a seven-year-old African American girl named Linda Brown. Linda Brown was not allowed to attend the public school a few blocks from her home in Topeka, Kansas. It was for white children only. She had to take a bus to a school for African American children. Linda's parents insisted that this school was of lower quality than the school near their home. The Browns took their case to court. This important case was called *Brown v. the Board of Education.* (The *v.* is short for *versus,* which means "against.")

On May 17, 1954, the Supreme Court announced its decision in this case. The Court ruled that segregation of public schools was illegal under the Constitution. A Chicago newspaper, *The Chicago Defender,* declared that the Court's ruling was a "second Emancipation Proclamation." The cause of civil rights, which was becoming a mass movement in the United States, had won a major victory.

REVIEW What caused Linda Brown's parents to take their case to court?
Cause and Effect

▶ **Segregated schools (below) were declared illegal in the Supreme Court case based on the experience of Linda Brown (left).**

The Montgomery Bus Boycott

On December 1, 1955, an African American woman named **Rosa Parks** got on a bus in **Montgomery, Alabama.** She sat down in a seat in the middle of the bus. Under state law, African Americans were supposed to sit in the back of the bus. They could sit in the middle of the bus only if no white passengers wanted those seats.

As the bus continued along its route, more people got on. The driver told Parks to move so that a white passenger could have her seat. Parks refused. The driver threatened to have her arrested. "You may do that," Parks said. She was arrested and taken to jail. She did not argue or fight.

News of the arrest angered many African Americans in Montgomery. "People were fed

▶ **During the Montgomery bus boycott, African Americans carpooled or walked to work, leaving the city's buses empty.**

up," said a local leader named Jo Ann Robinson. Robinson and other leaders decided to organize a boycott.

The Montgomery bus boycott began the following Monday. Refusing to ride the buses, African Americans carpooled or walked to work. A 26-year-old minister named **Martin Luther King, Jr.,** watched as empty buses passed his home. "I could hardly believe what I saw," he said. King was one of the leaders of the boycott. You will read more about King in the Biography on page 427.

The boycott continued for more than a year. It ended with a 1956 Supreme Court decision declaring that segregation on public buses was illegal.

REVIEW Why was Rosa Parks arrested in 1955? **Main Idea and Details**

▶ **Civil rights leader Rosa Parks sat in the front of the bus after the successful end of the Montgomery bus boycott.**

The Movement Grows

The Supreme Court had said that segregating schools and public buses was illegal. These victories were encouraging. However, Martin Luther King, Jr., the NAACP, and others wanted fairness in all areas of life. King promoted the idea of nonviolent protest, or passive resistance, to gain civil rights. **Passive resistance** means to oppose something without using violence. Three forms of passive resistance used at the time were sit-ins, freedom rides, and marches.

In 1960 four black students in **Greensboro, North Carolina,** sat down at a lunch counter for white customers only and ordered coffee. They were not served. However, they stayed seated until the store closed. Word got around about the students' protest. Sit-ins began to be held at lunch counters, on park benches, in theaters, museums, and other public places across the South and in some areas in the North. Some of the protesters were arrested. Newspapers and television reported these events across the country.

Freedom rides were organized to see if public transportation was obeying the law and

▶ African American students hold a "sit-in" at a whites-only lunch counter.

not segregating customers. African Americans and white supporters rode buses through the South. Along the way, many of the riders were threatened, and some were beaten or arrested.

Marches were also held in the South, to draw attention to the cause of civil rights. Sometimes local police attacked marchers with dogs and sticks. The protesters did not give up.

REVIEW Why do you think Martin Luther King, Jr. promoted passive resistance? Draw Conclusions

▶ African Americans and white supporters rode through the South on "freedom rides."

END SEGREGATION AND terror in the Sou... THE LAW OF THE LAND IS OUR DEMAND

Gains and Losses

Martin Luther King, Jr. and other civil rights leaders planned a massive march in Washington, D.C. They wanted to help convince Congress to pass a civil rights bill that had been proposed by President John F. Kennedy. On August 28, 1963, more than 200,000 Americans of different races gathered together in the nation's capital to show their support for civil rights. Standing before the Lincoln Memorial, King called for an end to prejudice in the United States. He spoke of his hopes for the future, saying,

"I have a dream that my four little children will one day live in a nation where they will not be judged by the color of their skin but by the content of their character..."

As you have read, President Kennedy was killed in November 1963. President Lyndon Johnson urged Congress to "honor President Kennedy's memory" by passing the civil rights bill. The following year, Congress passed the Civil Rights Act of 1964. This law banned segregation in all public places in the United States. A year later, Congress passed the Voting Rights Act of 1965. African Americans already had the right to vote, but they were often prevented from voting in some parts of the South. The Voting Rights Act protected the rights of all Americans to vote. As a result, hundreds of thousands of African Americans were able to vote for the first time.

▶ After passage of the Voting Rights Act, African Americans were eager to exercise their right to vote.

▶ In Washington, D.C., Martin Luther King, Jr., called for an end to prejudice.

One civil rights leader, **Malcolm X,** feared that new civil rights laws would not bring change quickly enough. At first, he believed that white Americans would never fully support equal rights for black citizens. Malcolm X urged African Americans to rely on themselves. He said, "The American black man should be focusing his every effort toward building his own businesses and decent homes for himself." Later in his life, Malcolm X felt differently, and he talked more of blacks and whites working together to bring change.

"Black men and white men truly could become brothers."

By the end of the 1960s, the number of African Americans winning elections to Congress and other government offices was growing quickly. However, neither Malcolm X

▶ **Malcolm X urged African Americans to rely on themselves.**

nor Martin Luther King, Jr., lived to see these changes. Malcolm X was shot and killed while speaking in New York City in February 1965. King was assassinated in Memphis, Tennessee, in April 1968.

The successes of African Americans in their struggle for civil rights inspired other groups. You will read more about these groups in Lesson 3.

REVIEW What was one effect of the Voting Rights Act of 1965? ⟳ **Cause and Effect**

FACT FILE

African American Voters Before and After the Voting Rights Act of 1965

Before the Voting Rights Act of 1965, only an estimated 23 percent of African Americans were registered to vote in the United States. Some southern states discouraged blacks from voting. The Voting Rights Act protected the rights of all Americans to vote.

The graphs below show the percentage of African Americans registered to vote in 1964, one year before the Voting Rights Act, and in 1969, four years after the act was passed. One of the biggest changes occurred in Mississippi. With more African Americans voting, more African Americans were elected to public office.

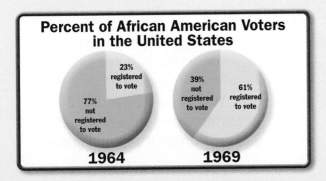

Percent of African American Voters in the United States

1964: 23% registered to vote / 77% not registered to vote
1969: 39% not registered to vote / 61% registered to vote

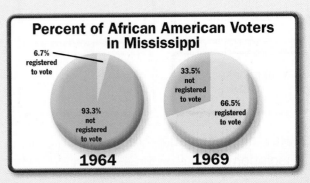

Percent of African American Voters in Mississippi

1964: 6.7% registered to vote / 93.3% not registered to vote
1969: 33.5% not registered to vote / 66.5% registered to vote

Continued Successes

The Civil Rights movement continued as the United States put its new laws into effect. Other African American leaders rose up to keep the cause of civil rights alive.

As you read in Unit 1, states were electing African Americans to Congress by 1870. There were many other African American firsts during the 1900s, and the number increased as more opportunities became available. In 1949 Ralph Bunche became the first African American to win the Nobel Peace Prize. In 1952 baseball great Jackie Robinson became the first black executive of a major TV network. Clifton R. Wharton, Sr., was the first black to head a U.S. embassy in Europe in 1958. In 1964 Arthur Ashe was the first African American man to play on the U.S. Davis Cup tennis team. Thurgood Marshall became the first black Supreme Court justice in 1967. In 1971 Samuel Lee Gravely, Jr., was the first African American admiral in the U.S. Navy. In Virginia in 1989, L. Douglas Wilder became the first African American elected governor of a state. These and many other African Americans have broken new ground and continue to encourage others.

REVIEW Who was the first African American Supreme Court justice?
Main Idea and Details

Summarize the Lesson

1954 The Supreme Court declared segregation in public schools was illegal.

1963 Martin Luther King, Jr., led a civil rights march in Washington, D.C.

1964 The Civil Rights Act of 1964 was passed.

LESSON 1 **REVIEW**

Check Facts and Main Ideas

1. ↻ **Cause and Effect** On a separate sheet of paper, complete the chart by filling in the effects of these major events of the Civil Rights movement.

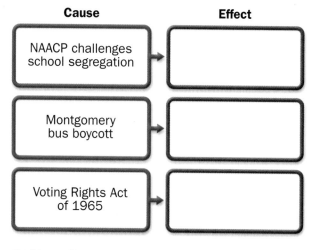

Cause	Effect
NAACP challenges school segregation	
Montgomery bus boycott	
Voting Rights Act of 1965	

2. How did segregation create social isolation?

3. How did **Rosa Parks** use **passive resistance** to help change bus segregation laws? Answer in two or more sentences. Use the highlighted terms in your answer.

4. List four events that contributed to the success of the Civil Rights movement.

5. **Critical Thinking:** *Evaluate* What was the importance of the Civil Rights Act of 1964 to all Americans?

Link to ☐☐ Writing

Learn About African American Leaders
In the library or on the Internet, read more about one of the African Americans in this lesson. Why do we remember this individual? Write a one-page report about this person and share it with the class.

Martin Luther King, Jr. *1929–1968*

Fourteen-year-old Martin Luther King, Jr., was having an exciting night. He and his teacher had traveled from their hometown of Atlanta, Georgia, to Dublin, a town farther south. Martin was competing in a speech-making contest. In his speech, he stated that under the United States Constitution, black people should have the same rights as whites. Martin said:

> *"Today thirteen million black sons and daughters of our forefathers [ancestors] continue the fight. . . . We believe with them that if freedom is good for any it is good for all."*

BIOFACT

In 1964, in honor of his nonviolent work for equal rights, Martin Luther King, Jr., was awarded the Nobel Peace Prize.

Martin won the contest and left feeling great. He and his teacher got on a bus back to Atlanta and settled into their seats. A few stops further on, white travelers came onto the crowded bus. The driver told Martin and his teacher that they would have to stand up so that the whites could sit—this was the law. Martin did not want to move, and the driver got angry. Martin's teacher finally convinced Martin to stand. The trip back to Atlanta was ninety miles. Martin later said that standing during that trip made him angrier than he would ever be again.

The ideals Martin Luther King, Jr., spoke of as a teenager became the foundation of his life's work. He became a minister and a leader in the Civil Rights movement. He spent his adult years speaking and organizing for the right of African Americans to vote, to go to good schools, to get decent jobs, and to have all the opportunities and freedoms enjoyed by other Americans. King preached nonviolence, which means resisting peacefully. He helped to accomplish enormous changes in the United States. In 1968, he was assassinated at the age of 39.

Learn from Biographies

How did the speech young Martin gave at the contest contrast with his experience later that same night?

For more information, go to *Meet the People* at **www.sfsocialstudies.com.**

427

NORTH VIETNAM

SOUTH VIETNAM

1950

1957
Soviet Union launches *Sputnik*.

1969
American astronauts are first to land on the moon.

1973
United States signs cease-fire with North Vietnam.

1975

The Cold War Continues

PREVIEW

Focus on the Main Idea
The United States continued to oppose the spread of communism and Soviet power in the 1960s and 1970s.

PLACES
North Vietnam
South Vietnam

PEOPLE
John Glenn
Neil Armstrong
Edwin "Buzz" Aldrin
Michael Collins
Richard Nixon
William Westmoreland
Maya Ying Lin

VOCABULARY
space race
Vietnam Conflict
guerrilla warfare

▶ The *Eagle* was specially designed to land on the moon.

You Are There

The date is July 20, 1969. The American spacecraft *Eagle* drifts down toward the surface of the moon.

Inside are American astronauts Neil Armstrong and Edwin Aldrin. They set the craft down gently on the moon's gray, dusty surface. "The *Eagle* has landed," Armstrong reports.

A small hatch in the craft opens. Wearing a puffy white spacesuit and a giant helmet, Armstrong backs carefully down a ladder. As he becomes the first human being to step on the moon, he says, "That's one small step for man, one giant leap for mankind."

A television camera on *Eagle* beams these incredible images back to Earth. All over the world, millions of people stare with wonder at their television screens. No one has ever before seen anything like this on TV.

Summarize As you read, summarize key Cold War events of the 1960s and 1970s.

The Space Race

On October 4, 1957, the Soviet Union launched a satellite named *Sputnik* into outer space. A satellite is an object that revolves around a planet. *Sputnik* was the first artificial satellite. It was sent into space to circle Earth.

Americans were shocked when they heard the news. The United States was clearly behind in the **space race**—a race to explore outer space. Many Americans felt that it would be dangerous to lose this race. They realized that if the Soviets could work or travel in space, they could easily spy on or attack the United States.

▶ *Sputnik,* the first artificial satellite, made history in 1957.

The United States launched its first satellite in January 1958. Then in October 1958, the National Aeronautics and Space Administration, or NASA, was founded to promote United States space exploration projects. The first successful weather satellite was launched by NASA in April 1960.

The Soviets took another step forward in April 1961, when Yuri Gagarin became the first person to orbit, or circle, Earth in space.

The United States was behind in the race, but it began to catch up. In

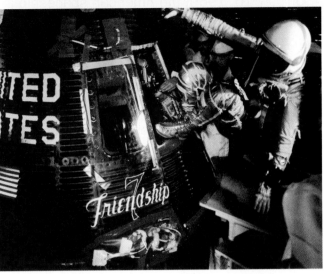

▶ **Astronaut John Glenn is shown climbing into the** *Friendship 7* **capsule before his historic flight.**

February 1962, **John Glenn** became the first American to orbit Earth. His Mercury spacecraft was named *Friendship 7.* More than 60 million Americans viewed the launch on television. Some parents let their children stay home from school to watch this historic event. The rocket lifted off from Cape Canaveral, Florida, at 9:47 in the morning. The space capsule carrying Glenn was in space for 4 hours and 48 minutes. The capsule then returned to Earth, landing in the ocean 800 miles southeast of Bermuda.

The United States and the Soviet Union continued to build and test new rockets and satellites. It was discovered that satellites could be used for communication. The United States satellite *Telstar 1* relayed the first transatlantic telecast in 1962.

REVIEW Why were many Americans worried when the Soviet Union launched *Sputnik?* Main Idea and Details

▶ **The huge Mercury-Atlas rocket blasted off, carrying the small** *Friendship 7* **capsule into space. The capsule is the top half of the dark tip of the rocket.**

Apollo 11 and Beyond

On July 16, 1969, the American spaceship *Apollo 11* blasted off, carrying astronauts **Neil Armstrong, Edwin "Buzz" Aldrin,** and **Michael Collins.** They reached the moon four days later. While Collins circled the moon in *Apollo 11,* Armstrong and Aldrin guided the *Eagle,* a small, specially designed spacecraft, down to the moon's surface. As the world watched on television, Armstrong and Aldrin became the first people to walk on the moon. They collected rocks and did some experiments. They also spoke to President **Richard Nixon.** Nixon said:

> *"Neil and Buzz, I am talking to you by telephone from the Oval Office at the White House, and this certainly has to be the most historic telephone call ever made."*

Before leaving the moon, Armstrong and Aldrin planted an American flag and plaque stating, "We came in peace for all mankind."

They left the Moon and rejoined Collins for the return to Earth. With the success of *Apollo 11,* the United States had taken the lead in the space race.

The space race continued until the collapse of the Soviet Union in 1990, but space exploration continues to the present day. Today satellites take photographs from space to show weather patterns, they relay phone calls and television programs, and they help with further research of space.

The first American space shuttle was launched in April 1981. Unlike rockets that came before, the space shuttle is a reusable craft. It can be used to recover or repair damaged satellites. It can take people or supplies to the International Space Station. The International Space Station is an orbiting station on which American and astronauts from former Soviet countries now explore space as friends.

REVIEW What are four things that Armstrong and Aldrin did while they were on the moon in 1969? **Main Idea and Details**

▶ **The world watched American astronauts walk on the moon in 1969.**

Trouble in Southeast Asia

Since the late 1800s, much of Vietnam, a country in Southeast Asia, had been a colony of France. During World War II, communist fighters under the leadership of Ho Chi Minh began to resist the French. When Ho Chi Minh declared Vietnam's independence in 1945, the conflict became more violent. In 1954 the French suffered a bad defeat at the hands of the communists. The French did not want to fight any longer. But if they withdrew, who would stop the communist forces?

An international conference was held in Geneva, Switzerland, to try to solve the problem. The Geneva Accords, the agreements made at the conference, stated that Vietnam should become independent. Elections were to be held in two years, but the country would be split into two parts, **North Vietnam** and **South Vietnam,** until that time. You can see this region of Asia on the map at right. All the Vietminh soldiers, the communists fighting with Ho Chi Minh, were to go north. All the Vietnamese soldiers who had fought for the French were to go to the south. Civilians were also allowed to move, and hundreds of thousands of Vietnamese fled to the south to escape the communists.

▶ **Ho Chi Minh**

With the support of the Soviet Union and Red China, North Vietnamese leader Ho Chi Minh began fighting to unite all of Vietnam under one communist government. The South Vietnamese did not want communism. They resisted the communists, and a long war began.

The United States was dedicated to stopping the spread of communism. Presidents Eisenhower and Kennedy sent money and weapons to the government of South Vietnam. American soldiers were sent to help train the South Vietnamese army. In spite of this aid, the communists were winning the war. Lyndon Johnson, who became President after Kennedy's assassination in 1963, was determined not to allow the communist forces to win. "I'm not going to lose Vietnam," he said. In 1964 Johnson sent more American soldiers to Vietnam. Over the next few years, the American involvement in Vietnam grew quickly.

REVIEW What caused the United States to send money and aid to South Vietnam?
↻ **Cause and Effect**

MAP SKILL **North and South Vietnam**

▶ Vietnam was divided in 1954.

MAP SKILL Location *Which country bordered both North Vietnam and South Vietnam?*

431

The Vietnam Conflict

By the year 1968, there were more than 500,000 American soldiers in Vietnam. They fought alongside the South Vietnamese to push back the North Vietnamese. The United States government wanted to aid South Vietnam but was not willing to declare war against North Vietnam. For that reason, the fighting was officially called the **Vietnam Conflict,** although it differed from full war in name alone.

The Vietnam Conflict would be one of the most difficult wars ever fought by Americans. Much of the land was covered with mountains and thick jungles. American soldiers often had to cut their way through the vegetation to get from place to place. Helicopters were frequently needed to drop soldiers into heavily forested areas and to evacuate the wounded. Sometimes a new chemical called Agent Orange was sprayed from planes to make the plants wither and die. This made it easier for American soldiers to see where they were going and to find the enemy.

▶ **American soldiers were sent to Vietnam to fight for the independence of South Vietnam.**

The North Vietnamese Army, often called the NVA, was unlike other enemies fought by Americans in past wars. North Vietnamese soldiers often used guerrilla warfare tactics. **Guerrilla warfare** includes random, surprise attacks that come from any direction at any time, day or night. NVA soldiers sometimes did not wear uniforms, so they could be difficult to identify. They often used women and children in their attacks. These civilians sometimes delivered explosives to kill American soldiers.

Not only did American soldiers fight the North Vietnamese army, they also fought civilians who were loyal to Ho Chi Minh. These civilians, called the Vietcong, fought against the Americans and the South Vietnamese government. They were aided and armed by the North Vietnamese. The Vietcong also used guerrilla warfare tactics.

During the Vietnam Conflict, American soldiers were better armed than any soldiers had been before. A squad of ten had as much firepower as thirty soldiers in World War II. When needed, a squad could call for air support using a mobile radio.

General **William Westmoreland** was the leader of the American troops from 1964 until 1968. Westmoreland had served with honor during World War II and the Korean War. Even with his well-armed troops and his knowledge of war, Westmoreland found the tactics of the enemy to be a very difficult challenge. He ordered supply routes and other areas bombed. He asked President Johnson to send more soldiers to help with the fighting. Yet it seemed as if the communists could not be stopped.

REVIEW What contributed to making the Vietnam Conflict so difficult?
Main Idea and Details

The Conflict at Home

At home in the United States, people watched film of the fighting on television. This was the first time that Americans could watch scenes from a war on the evening news. Battles filmed in the Vietnamese jungles and rice fields one day would come into American living rooms through televisions within twenty-four hours. The fighting seemed more real and harsh than any other war before.

Some people began to question what was happening in Vietnam. Many soldiers were dying. Vietnam civilians were being killed. Yet it was becoming clear that the United States and South Vietnam were not winning. Should the United States continue fighting? In the late 1960s, this question began to divide Americans.

People who opposed the war were called "doves." They believed the conflict in Vietnam was a civil war that should be settled by the Vietnamese people. Some doves protested peacefully by marching with signs and holding vigils. Anti-war protesters staged sit-ins and sang protest songs. On October 15, 1969, about one million Americans held a candle-light vigil in cities across the country, calling for an end to the conflict. Others protested less peacefully. Some protesters tore up the offices of a company that produced chemicals used in the war. Many destroyed or burned the American flag. More radical protesters

▶ The difficulty of finding the right "road" to peace in Vietnam is reflected in this political cartoon.

▶ This political cartoon reflects the anger and disagreement of the time.

bombed buildings. Some young men who did not want to join the army burned their draft cards or moved to Canada. These men were called "draft dodgers."

People who supported the war were known as "hawks." They believed that the war was necessary to stop the spread of communism. They knew that South Vietnam alone could not win against the Soviet-supported North. Some hawks accused doves of encouraging the enemy. On Veterans Day 1969, hawks staged demonstrations across the country in support of United States war policy. Richard Nixon, who was elected President in 1968, believed that most Americans agreed with the need to fight. Since most Americans did not protest for the war, however, he called these people the "silent majority."

The issue of the Vietnam Conflict was very controversial. Even the leaders of the United States began to question the wisdom of continuing the fight.

REVIEW How did hawks and doves differ in their views on the Vietnam Conflict?
Compare and Contrast

433

The War Ends

In 1968 President Johnson ordered the bombing of North Vietnam stopped. He tried to organize peace talks with North Vietnam to end the war, but the talks failed. The following year, President Nixon sent National Security Advisor Henry Kissinger to meet with North Vietnamese and Vietcong leaders in Paris. These talks failed too.

President Nixon wanted to remove American soldiers from Vietnam, but he did not want the communists to win the war. From 1969 to 1972, the number of American soldiers in Vietnam fell from 540,000 to 50,000. At the same time, American planes increased their bombing of North Vietnam. Nixon hoped this would convince the North Vietnamese to stop fighting. The fighting continued.

In January 1973 the United States signed a cease-fire, or an agreement to stop fighting, with North Vietnam. In March of that year, the last American troops left Vietnam, and South Vietnam continued fighting the communists. In April 1975 South Vietnam surrendered to North Vietnam. The war was over, and Vietnam was united under a communist government.

The Vietnam Conflict had done much damage. About 2 million Vietnamese had been killed. More than 57,000 Americans had been killed, and many were wounded. Nearly 2,000 were still missing. Other soldiers came to believe that their health had been seriously harmed by the Agent Orange used to destroy Vietnamese jungles.

In 1980 a memorial was designed to honor the American men and women who served in Vietnam. On page 436 you will read about citizen hero Jan Scruggs, the Vietnam veteran who planned and raised money for the memorial, and about 21-year-old **Maya Ying Lin,** who designed the memorial. Today you can visit the Vietnam Veterans Memorial in Washington, D.C.

REVIEW What was the effect of the surrender of South Vietnam to North Vietnam? **Cause and Effect**

▶ **The Vietnam Veterans Memorial lists the names of those who died or were missing in action during the Vietnam Conflict. Friends and family members look for the names of loved ones and often make rubbings of their names, as shown at left.**

Mending Relations

Throughout the 1990s and into the 2000s, the United States has worked toward creating better relations with Vietnam. One goal is to establish normal trade with Vietnam. Another is to share information on science and technology.

One thing that remains a high priority for the United States, however, is for Vietnam to give a full account of the American soldiers who are still considered prisoners of war

▶ **At a 1995 meeting, Robert McNamara *(left)*, who helped direct America's fighting in Vietnam, shake hands with General Giap, who commanded the NVA during the conflict.**

(POWs) or missing in action (MIA.) Many families still do not know what happened to loved ones, and they hope to learn their fates.

REVIEW What are the goals of the United States in their relations with Vietnam today?
Summarize

Summarize the Lesson

— **1957** The Soviet Union launched the satellite *Sputnik*.

— **1969** American astronauts were the first to land on the moon.

— **1973** The United States signed a cease-fire agreement with North Vietnam, ending American involvement in the Vietnam Conflict.

LESSON 2 ▶ REVIEW

Check Facts and Main Ideas

1. Summarize On a separate sheet of paper, complete the chart below by summarizing these events.

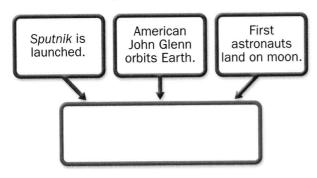

Sputnik is launched. → American John Glenn orbits Earth. → First astronauts land on moon.

2. What caused the United States to send soldiers to fight in Vietnam?

3. How did the Vietcong's use of **guerrilla warfare** make the **Vietnam Conflict** a difficult assignment for American soldiers? Answer in one or more sentences. Use the highlighted terms.

4. Describe the different reactions of the doves and hawks to the Vietnam Conflict. Explain why each felt the way they did. Answer in two or more sentences.

5. Critical Thinking: *Point of View* Do you think President Johnson was more of a hawk or a dove? Explain how you reached your answer.

Link to ⛓ Science

Research Space Today the United States and Russia work together on the International Space Station. Do some research in books or on the Internet about the space station, and then write a one-page paper about what you discover. How was the space station built? What kinds of experiments are being done on the space station today?

Honoring the Veteran

Many Americans were against United States involvement in the Vietnam Conflict. When the conflict was over, nothing was done to honor the memories of those who gave their lives during this controversial war. One man, a Vietnam veteran himself, decided to change this.

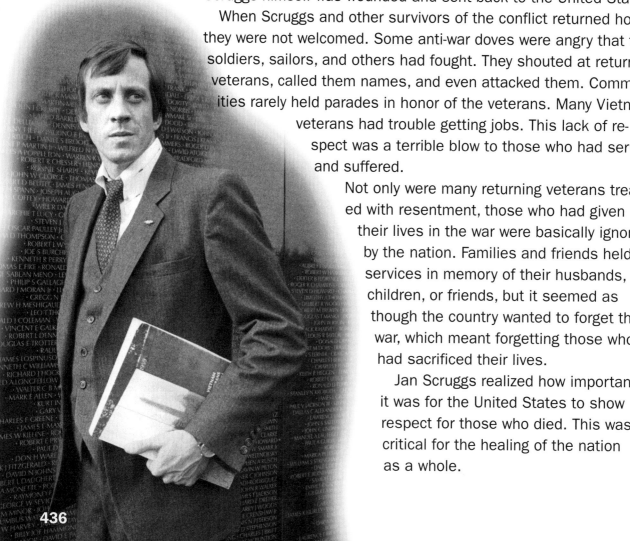

Jan C. Scruggs came home alive from his tour of duty in Vietnam. Many of those with whom he fought did not. Scruggs had served bravely for a year in the jungles and mountains of South Vietnam. He had seen his fellow soldiers injured and killed. Then Scruggs himself was wounded and sent back to the United States.

When Scruggs and other survivors of the conflict returned home, they were not welcomed. Some anti-war doves were angry that the soldiers, sailors, and others had fought. They shouted at returning veterans, called them names, and even attacked them. Communities rarely held parades in honor of the veterans. Many Vietnam veterans had trouble getting jobs. This lack of respect was a terrible blow to those who had served and suffered.

Not only were many returning veterans treated with resentment, those who had given their lives in the war were basically ignored by the nation. Families and friends held services in memory of their husbands, children, or friends, but it seemed as though the country wanted to forget the war, which meant forgetting those who had sacrificed their lives.

Jan Scruggs realized how important it was for the United States to show respect for those who died. This was critical for the healing of the nation as a whole.

BUILDING
CITIZENSHIP
Caring
Respect
Responsibility
Fairness
Honesty
Courage

Scruggs decided there should be a memorial in Washington, D.C., to recognize those who had died in the war. In 1979 Scruggs and a group of other veterans formed the Vietnam Veterans Memorial Fund (VVMF) to raise money to build the memorial. At first, some people made fun of the idea of Vietnam veterans trying to raise money for a monument. However, Scruggs and the other members of the VVMF did not give up. Donations began to come in from citizens across the country. By the time the fundraising ended, the VVMF had more than $8.4 million for the memorial. At last, Congress agreed to allow the memorial to be built.

A competition was held for the memorial's design. Maya Ying Lin, a Chinese-American architecture student, came up with a simple concept—a black granite wall in the shape of a "V" on which the names of all who had died or were missing in action would be inscribed. Her design was chosen out of 1,400 entries.

In 1982 the Vietnam Veterans Memorial was completed. It has become one of the most visited sites in Washington, D.C. Visitors often leave flowers and photos at the wall. Most people touch the names on the wall. Jan Scruggs saw that the memorial was helping the nation recover from its war wounds. He wrote a book about the building of the memorial titled *To Heal a Nation.* Scruggs said,

▶ **Veterans of the conflict and families of those who died in Vietnam look for the names of friends and loved ones at the completed Vietnam Veterans Memorial.**

> *"The Wall helped us find a home in our hearts for those who served in Vietnam."*

Respect in Action

Link to Current Events There are times when people do not show respect to other people, out of anger, fear, or misunderstandings. This may happen in a school, a community, or a country. Have you ever seen people in your school being treated disrespectfully? Write down your observations and share them with your class. Why is there disrespect? What can be done to change disrespect into respect?

1965 ———————————————————————— 1995

1966
National Organization for Women forms.

1981
Sandra Day O'Connor becomes the first woman Supreme Court justice.

1990
The Americans with Disabilities Act passes.

New York City •

PREVIEW

Focus on the Main Idea
From the 1950s through the 1990s, many Americans worked toward equal rights for women, minorities, and the disabled, and gained new interest in protecting the environment.

PLACES
New York, New York

PEOPLE
Sandra Day O'Connor
Phyllis Schlafly
César Chávez
Dolores Huerta
Rachel Carson

VOCABULARY
National Organization for Women
United Farm Workers of America
Americans with Disabilities Act
Equal Employment Opportunity Commission
Earth Day
Environmental Protection

Years of Change

You Are There

It is September 1965. Your mother waves to you as she steers the car out of the driveway. She quit college when she and your father got married, and now she is going back to school. She plans to get her degree in medicine and become a doctor.

"Good luck!" you call to her. You know things will be different for your family now. You and your brother are going to have to do more to help around the house. Your dad will cook meals every other night.

You really miss having your mother at home, but you are proud of her and what she is doing. You know she will be successful in school and will get the job she wants. However, you have heard her say that women usually are paid less than men are paid. You wonder if your mother's future employer will treat her fairly and equally. You hope so.

Cause and Effect As you read, pay attention to the causes and effects of the struggle for citizens' rights and a cleaner environment.

Unequal Opportunities for Women

Women in the United States had the same legal rights as men, but they did not always have the same opportunities. You have read that many women began working outside the home during the two World Wars. During the 1950s, the number of women in the workplace continued to grow.

A young woman named **Sandra Day O'Connor** graduated from Stanford Law School in 1952. She was one of the top students in her class, but when she began looking for work, she found that many law firms did not want to hire female lawyers. She remembered,

> *"I interviewed with law firms in Los Angeles and San Francisco, but none had ever hired a woman before as a lawyer, and they were not prepared to do so."*

O'Connor did not give up. She opened her own private law practice, served as a State Senator from Arizona, and became a judge in 1975.

Labor force participation of women by age, 1950 and 1998

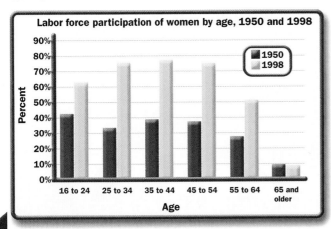

▶ The number of women in the workforce increased after 1950.

GRAPH SKILL Use a Bar Graph *Which age group saw the greatest change?*

▶ Women were generally expected to care for their homes and families. Many women still enjoyed this traditional role, but after the mid-1900s, many looked for work outside the home.

As O'Connor discovered, some jobs were generally seen as being men's work. Even after more women had college degrees, more men than women were hired to fill these jobs. Women were also not allowed to officially participate in certain sports, because it was feared that some sports were unhealthy or dangerous for women. In 1959 NASA allowed women to begin testing to become astronauts. However, NASA stopped the testing, because it was feared that women might be injured by space flight. Some people wanted to protect women, but not all women wanted to be protected.

REVIEW Why did Sandra Day O'Connor have trouble getting a job as a lawyer?
🔁 **Cause and Effect**

▶ Working for business executives was seen as appropriate employment for women, but some women wanted the top jobs themselves.

439

Making Progress

In the 1960s and 1970s, many people got involved in the Women's Rights Movement, a struggle for equal opportunities for women. In 1966 the **National Organization for Women**, or NOW, was formed and became an important player in this struggle. However, many women disagreed with some of NOW's goals. Lawyer, political leader, and author **Phyllis Schlafly** wrote books and articles supporting women who wanted to focus on more traditional roles and values.

One goal of the movement was passing the Equal Rights Amendment, or ERA. The proposed amendment stated that everyone must be treated exactly the same. Many women feared that this would remove important laws that protect them from being forced into dangerous situations. The ERA passed in Congress in 1972. Thirty-eight states were needed to ratify, or accept, the amendment for it to become part of the Constitution. Only thirty-five states ratified the ERA, and some of these later rescinded, or cancelled, their ratification.

Despite its failure to pass, the ERA focused attention on women's issues and created more opportunities for women in business and public service. A 1972 law called Title 9 stated that public schools and colleges that receive federal tax dollars must offer equal opportunities to male and female students, including equal opportunities in sports.

▶ **Title 9 guaranteed women opportunities in school sports.**

In 1981 Sandra Day O'Connor became the first woman named to the Supreme Court. Dr. Sally Ride became the first American woman in space in 1983. Many women still choose traditional roles, but for those who choose other careers, there are more opportunities than ever.

REVIEW What were the goals of the Women's Rights Movement? *Summarize*

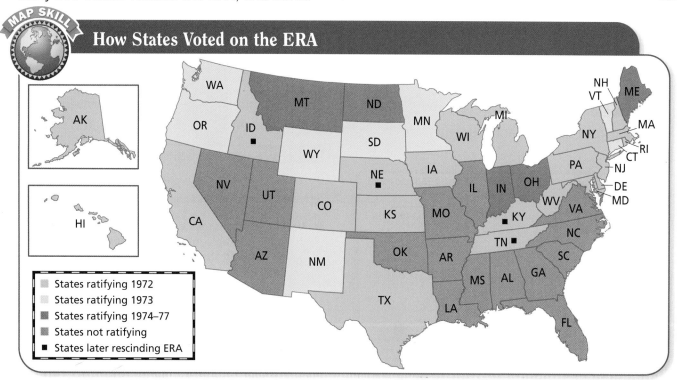

MAP SKILL

How States Voted on the ERA

- States ratifying 1972
- States ratifying 1973
- States ratifying 1974–77
- States not ratifying
- ■ States later rescinding ERA

▶ **The country was divided on the issue of the Equal Rights Amendment.**

MAP SKILL Use the Map Key *Which states rescinded their original vote? In what year had these states ratified the ERA?*

Working for Change

The successes of the Civil Rights Movement inspired others to work for change during the 1960s and 1970s. One group that wanted change was migrant workers. Migrant workers worked seasonally, moving from farm to farm harvesting fruit and vegetables. In addition to long days of work for low pay, the workers, many of whom were Hispanic, also faced discrimination. Two Mexican American leaders, **César Chávez** and **Dolores Huerta,** wanted to help these workers gain equal rights and protection. Chávez, a veteran of World War II, formed the National Farm Workers Association, in an effort to gain rights for migrant workers. He worked hard and made many personal sacrifices. Chávez said:

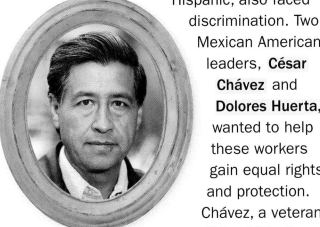

▶ **César Chávez worked for the rights of farm workers.**

> *"You can't change anything if you . . . avoid sacrifice."*

Later, Chávez and Huerta, one of the first women involved in union leadership, formed the **United Farm Workers of America** (UFW). They used the passive resistance they had seen work for Martin Luther King, Jr., which led to many improvements. In the Biography on page 445, you will read more about Huerta and the struggle of migrant workers.

American Indian leaders worked to improve life and create opportunities for Native Americans. Some American Indian groups have

▶ **Americans with disabilities worked to bring attention to the difficulties they faced.**

regained the right to fish in waters that had been taken from them and to use traditional methods such as spear fishing. Others have been given access to sacred lands once more. In some areas, business opportunities have improved dramatically.

Another group determined to gain equal opportunities were Americans with disabilities. Before the 1990s, many Americans with disabilities faced discrimination in the job market and difficulty accessing classrooms and other facilities. In 1990 people working for change helped pass the **Americans with Disabilities Act,** or ADA. This law makes it illegal for businesses to refuse to hire a qualified person just because that person has a disability. Public schools are now required to provide equal access to education to disabled students. Public buildings must be accessible to those in wheelchairs. Public facilities that provide emergency 911 telephone service are required to have a system in place to allow hearing-impaired individuals to place direct calls. In public elevators, safety information and floor numbers are written in Braille to accommodate visually impaired riders.

REVIEW What are some of the successes of the Americans with Disabilities Act?
Main Idea and Details

▶ Clarence Thomas became the second African American Supreme Court Justice in 1991, and Ruth Bader Ginsburg (*back row*) joined Sandra Day O'Connor (*front row*) on the Supreme Court in 1993.

Opportunities and Recognition

By the late 1900s, Americans found themselves with more opportunities than ever before. Those who had written, spoken out, and created new laws had helped make life better for many citizens.

The **Equal Employment Opportunity Commission,** which was formed in 1965, enforces civil rights laws that have to do with the workplace. It ensures that no one is denied employment based on a person's sex or race. Because of this, the workplace changed dramatically in the late 1900s.

Norman Mineta, a Japanese American who had been in an internment camp with his family during World War II, served as a Congressman for 20 years. He was the force behind the passage of the Civil Liberties Act of 1988, which officially apologized for the injustice endured by Japanese Americans during the war. In 2001 Mineta was appointed to President George W. Bush's Cabinet.

Native American soldiers who served during World War II as "code talkers" at last gained recognition in 2001. These Native Americans had transmitted important radio messages during the war. They used their native Navajo language, which the Japanese could not translate. President George W. Bush presented 29 Navajo marines with Congressional Gold Medals in July 2001 and presented more than 400 other code talkers with Silver Medals in November 2001.

Opportunities continued to open up for the disabled, both in work and in sports. Individuals of all backgrounds have taken on new challenges. The growing population and increasing diversity of the United States continues to offer both challenges and opportunities, but the laws are in place to ensure that everyone has an equal chance for "life, liberty, and the pursuit of happiness."

REVIEW What is the purpose of the Equal Employment Opportunity Commission? Summarize

▶ Minority groups and people with disabilities now have more opportunities in business and sports.

A Cleaner World

Throughout history, people have dumped garbage wherever they wished. As population levels grew, this became a serious problem. With the Industrial Revolution, pollution increased dramatically. Some countries, including the United States, realized that this had to change. As you read, the Progressives began protecting the environment in the late 1800s. America's efforts at conservation and clean up increased after World War II.

Rachel Carson was a biologist who worked for the Fish and Wildlife Service. She became worried about the effects of pesticides on the environment. Pesticides are poisons used to kill insects that damage crops or carry disease. In 1962 Carson wrote *Silent Spring*.

▶ In 1952 Cleveland's Cuyahoga River was so polluted, it actually caught fire.

▶ Today, the Cuyahoga River is clean, safe, and beautiful.

This book warned that some pesticides could also kill birds, fish, and mammals. Carson's book encouraged Congress to ban the use of a common pesticide. It also made more people aware of environmental problems.

In 1970 the first **Earth Day** was held. Earth Day was designed to make people aware of ways they could help the environment. It was celebrated across the country. **New York, New York,** held one of the largest Earth Day events that year.

People learned that recycling and not littering were things anyone could do to help. Some people protested industries that polluted the air or water. In 1970 the **Environmental Protection Agency,** or EPA, was created to enforce environmental laws. Many communities now have "Clean Up" days in which citizens help pick up litter from parks and other sites.

REVIEW What caused Rachel Carson to write *Silent Spring*? ⟳ **Cause and Effect**

Literature and Social Studies

Silent Spring

Rachel Carson's 1962 book *Silent Spring* told about the dangers unregulated use of pesticides can have on the environment. Her book helped awaken a new generation to the need to protect the earth.

". . . chemicals sprayed on croplands or forest or gardens lie long in the soil, entering into living organisms, passing from one to another in a chain of poisoning and death. Or they pass mysteriously by underground streams until they emerge and . . . combine into new forms that kill vegetation, sicken cattle, and work unknown harm on those who drink from once pure wells."

Looking to the Future

Today students help plant trees, clean the school grounds, and study the environment in science classes. Many people recycle paper, plastics, glass, and aluminum. Today the United States is cleaner and healthier than ever before. The efforts to protect the environment are working. For example, the United States now has more trees than it did in 1950. But people need to stay involved.

Scientists and researchers are hard at work looking for ways to improve current technologies and tools. They are also working on new technologies that will help make the world cleaner and healthier. However, the future of the environment is in the hands of today's students, as they learn to participate as citizens.

▶ **Students contribute to clean up efforts.**

REVIEW How are some students helping the environment? *Main Idea and Details*

Summarize the Lesson

1966 The National Organization for Women was formed.

1981 Sandra Day O'Connor became the first woman Supreme Court justice.

1990 The Americans with Disabilities Act was passed.

LESSON 3 · REVIEW

Check Facts and Main Ideas

1. 🔄 **Cause and Effect** On a separate sheet of paper, complete the chart below by filling in the effects of these issues during the late 1900s.

Cause		Effect
Navajo "code talkers" had made important contributions during World War II.	→	
Americans with disabilities wanted fair treatment.	→	
Migrant workers had hard lives.	→	

2. How did the Civil Rights movement influence the **United Farm Workers of America**? Answer in two or more sentences. Use the highlighted term in your answer.

3. What are some difficulties women faced in the mid-1900s? How did the situation change during the 1960s–1980s?

4. What are two ways in which Americans worked to improve the environment in the late 1900s?

5. Critical Thinking: *Draw Conclusions* What conclusion can you draw about your role in the future of the environment? Explain your answer.

Link to ∞ Art

Create an Environmental Comic Strip Draw a comic strip showing an environmental issue in your community that needs attention. Some ideas are an area covered in litter, a place with too much noise, or a park that needs new trees or flowers. As you create your comic strip, show the problem and how citizens might make improvements. Share your comic strip with the class.

Dolores Huerta

1930–

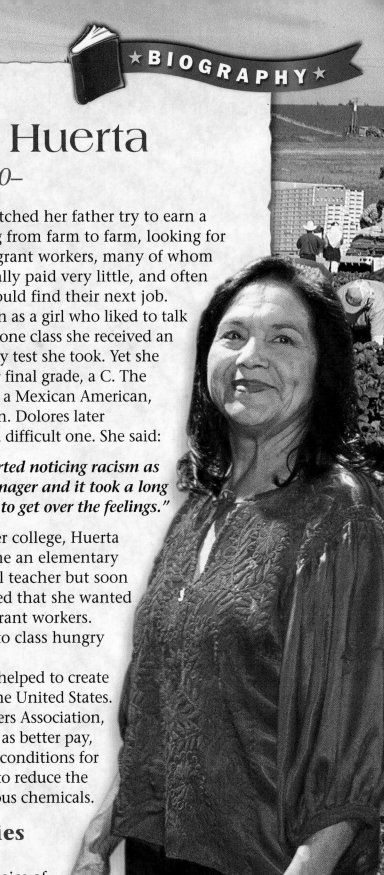

As a child, Dolores Huerta had watched her father try to earn a living as a migrant worker—moving from farm to farm, looking for enough work to feed his family. Migrant workers, many of whom were Mexican Americans, were usually paid very little, and often had no idea when or where they would find their next job.

In high school, Dolores was known as a girl who liked to talk a lot and always did well in class. In one class she received an A for every paper she wrote and every test she took. Yet she was very surprised when she saw her final grade, a C. The teacher did not believe that Dolores, a Mexican American, could do such good work on her own. Dolores later remembered this time in her life as a difficult one. She said:

BIOFACT

To support a farm worker's strike, Dolores Huerta helped organize a boycott of table grapes in the 1960s.

"I started noticing racism as a teenager and it took a long time to get over the feelings."

After college, Huerta became an elementary school teacher but soon decided that she wanted to work to improve the lives of migrant workers. "I couldn't stand seeing kids come to class hungry and needing shoes," she said.

Along with César Chávez, Huerta helped to create the first union for farm workers in the United States. The union, the National Farm Workers Association, successfully fought for such benefits as better pay, health insurance, and safer working conditions for farm workers. Today they also fight to reduce the exposure of farm workers to dangerous chemicals.

Learn from Biographies

How do you think Dolores Huerta's experiences as a child affected her choice of work? What caused her to change careers from teaching to union organizing?

For more information, go to *Meet the People* at **www.sfsocialstudies.com.**

1970 **1995**

1972
Nixon visits
China and the
Soviet Union.

1979
Egypt and Israel
sign a peace treaty
with US help.

1991
The Soviet Union
breaks up.

PREVIEW

Focus on the Main Idea
In the late 1900s, events occurred that brought the Cold War to an end and put the United States on new courses for the future.

PLACES
Middle East
Afghanistan
Kuwait

PEOPLE
Gerald Ford
Jimmy Carter
Ronald Reagan
Mikhail Gorbachev
George Bush
Condoleezza Rice
Colin Powell
Bill Clinton
Madeleine Albright
George W. Bush

VOCABULARY
arms control
Persian Gulf War
Internet

▶ A piece of the Berlin Wall.

Changing World, Changing Roles

You Are There The date is November 9, 1989, and something shocking is happening in the German city of Berlin. Since 1961, the Berlin Wall has divided this city. East Berlin is part of communist East Germany. West Berlin is part of West Germany and has a free government and a free market economy.

But all that is now changing. Crowds of people from both East and West Berlin have jumped onto the Berlin Wall. On top of the wall, people are dancing and singing. Some take hammers or axes and smash off pieces of the hated wall.

People all over the world have good reason to celebrate. For 28 years, the Berlin Wall has stood as a reminder of the Cold War. And now the wall is coming down. The Cold War is finally coming to an end.

Cause and Effect As you read, notice what led to the end of the Cold War and what occurred after it ended.

▶ **President Nixon walked along the Great Wall of China during his historic visit in 1972.**

Steps Toward Peace

Since a communist government came to power in China in 1949, the United States and China had been bitter Cold War rivals. President Nixon wanted to change this. He began working to improve relations with China. "If there is anything I want to do before I die, it is to go to China," Nixon said. No American president had ever been to China.

Nixon's work paid off in 1972 when the Chinese government invited him to visit. Nixon went to China and met with Mao Zedong (MOW ze DOONG), the Chinese communist leader. This was an important step toward friendlier relations with China.

Later that year, Nixon traveled to the Soviet Union. He met with Soviet leaders and signed an **arms control** agreement—a deal to limit the production of weapons. This agreement limited the number of nuclear weapons each side could have and helped ease tensions between the United States and the Soviet Union. Nixon and the Soviets also signed an agreement to cooperate in space exploration and to use space for peaceful purposes only.

Nixon's success in China and the Soviet Union helped him win reelection in November 1972, but the Watergate scandal soon brought an end to his second term. A scandal is an action that leads to shame or disgrace.

Why was the scandal named Watergate? While Nixon was running for reelection, five men were caught breaking into an office in the Watergate Hotel in Washington, D.C. The men confessed that they were there to collect information on Nixon's political opponents. Nixon said he had not helped plan the break-in. Over the next year, however, evidence showed that Nixon had taken some illegal steps to hide information about the break-in.

Congress prepared to impeach Nixon, or accuse him of wrongdoing. On August 9, 1974, Nixon resigned. He was the only U.S. President ever to resign from office. Vice-President **Gerald Ford** became the President.

REVIEW Why did Nixon visit China and the Soviet Union? **Main Idea and Details**

Tensions Rise Again

Jimmy Carter was elected President in 1976. One of Carter's goals was to try to help bring peace between Egypt and Israel. These nations are among the countries in Southwest Asia that make up the region known as the **Middle East.** Egypt and Israel had been enemies for a long time and had fought several wars. Carter invited the leaders of both nations to the United States. They worked out a peace treaty, which was signed in March 1979.

Carter also hoped to continue lowering Cold War tensions with the Soviet Union. Those hopes were crushed in December 1979, when Soviet troops invaded **Afghanistan,** a nation in Asia bordering the Soviet Union. Carter spoke out against this attempt to expand Soviet power. The United States refused to send athletes to the 1980 Summer Olympics, held in the Soviet capital of Moscow. As the 1980s began, Cold War tensions were on the rise again.

REVIEW Carter helped which two Middle Eastern nations reach a peace agreement in 1979? **Main Idea and Details**

The Cold War Ends

When the 1980s began, no end was in sight for the Cold War. The new President, **Ronald Reagan,** believed the United States needed to strengthen its military in order to block continued Soviet efforts to expand communism around the world. The United States increased spending on weapons and defense systems.

The Soviet Union was also spending large amounts of money on weapons, but the Soviet economy was not as strong as the American economy. The high cost of the arms race was weakening the Soviet Union. So much money was spent on weapons and other Cold War strategies that people in the Soviet Union often didn't have enough food or other necessities. Also, people in Soviet-controlled countries were tired of having no rights and so few freedoms.

In 1985 a new leader named **Mikhail Gorbachev** (mi KAYL GOR bah chahv) came to power in the Soviet Union. Gorbachev began allowing more political and economic freedom.

Relations between the Soviet Union and the United States began to improve. In 1987

▶ In 1987 President Reagan stood at the Berlin Wall and challenged: "Mr. Gorbachev, tear down this wall!" Three years later, Reagan himself helped destroy the wall *(right).* Berliners celebrated—and contributed to the wall's destruction *(below).*

Reagan and Gorbachev signed a new arms control agreement. For the first time, the United States and the Soviet Union agreed to destroy some of their nuclear weapons. The arms race was over.

After serving as Reagan's Vice-President for eight years, **George Bush** was elected President in 1989. Bush continued working with Gorbachev to ease Cold War tensions.

Meanwhile, people in Eastern Europe gained more freedom. They began working to overthrow their communist governments. In 1989 communist governments fell in several Eastern European nations. People began replacing communist governments with elected governments and free enterprise economies. The Berlin Wall, a visible example of the harshness of communist control, was destroyed. Then, in 1991 the Soviet Union itself broke up into 15 independent republics. "The Cold War is now behind us," Gorbachev announced.

The Cold War was over. President Bush said:

> ***"The end of the Cold War was clearly a victory for the forces of freedom and democracy."***

An African American woman named **Condoleezza Rice** was one of the advisors who helped Bush during this time. She helped bring democratic reform to Poland and played a role in forming many of Bush's policies with the former Soviet Union.

REVIEW What helped bring about the collapse of communist governments in Eastern Europe? ⟳ **Cause and Effect**

MAP SKILL

The End of Soviet Control

Countries that overthrew communist governments

Present-day country names and borders are used.

ARCTIC OCEAN

ATLANTIC OCEAN

NORWAY
SWEDEN
FINLAND
UNITED KINGDOM   *North Sea*
ESTONIA
Baltic Sea
LATVIA
LITHUANIA
NETH.
BELG.   GERMANY   POLAND   BELARUS
FRANCE
CZECH REP.
SWITZ.   AUSTRIA   SLOVAKIA   UKRAINE
ITALY   HUNGARY
SLOVENIA
CROATIA   ROMANIA   MOLDOVA
BOSNIA AND HERZEGOVINA   SERBIA-MONT.
ALBANIA   BULGARIA   *Black Sea*
MACEDONIA
GREECE   TURKEY
TUNISIA
Mediterranean Sea
CYPRUS   SYRIA
LEBANON   IRAQ
ISRAEL
LIBYA

RUSSIA

KAZAKHSTAN
Aral Sea
Caspian Sea
GEORGIA
ARMENIA
AZERBAIJAN
UZBEKISTAN   KYRGYZSTAN
TURKMENISTAN   TAJIKISTAN   CHINA
IRAN   AFGHANISTAN
PAKISTAN   INDIA

N

0   300   600 Miles
0   300   600 Kilometers

▶ By 1991 Eastern Europe was free of Soviet control, and the Soviet Union itself had broken up.

MAP SKILL Use a Compass Rose *Which of the countries once controlled by the Soviet Union is farthest north? farthest south?*

▶ Colin Powell met with American troops in Saudi Arabia before Operation Desert Storm.

A New Role in the World

The United States was now the world's only superpower. This position brought many new challenges. For example, how should the United States use its power? Should the American government and military play a leading role in trying to end conflicts around the world?

The United States faced these questions in the **Persian Gulf War.** In 1990 the Middle Eastern nation of Iraq invaded its neighbor, **Kuwait.** Iraq's dictator, Saddam Hussein, (sah DAHM hoo SAYN) wanted to take control of Kuwait's rich oil supply.

President Bush decided to work with other nations to force Iraq out of Kuwait. The United Nations demanded that Iraq leave Kuwait, but Hussein refused. American troops were sent to the Middle East. There was hope that the United States military would encourage the Iraqis to leave Kuwait and also prevent the Iraqis from invading Kuwait's neighbor, Saudi Arabia. Saudi Arabia also has a large oil supply. The presence of the American troops in the Middle East was called Operation Desert Shield.

Hussein was ordered to withdraw his troops from Kuwait by January 15, 1991, but he refused. The United States led an alliance of more than 20 nations in Operation Desert Storm, an attack on Iraqi forces in Kuwait. General **Colin Powell,** the highest-ranking officer in the United States armed forces, was one of the planners of Desert Storm. The fighting lasted only six weeks. Iraq was driven from Kuwait.

Elected in 1992, President **Bill Clinton** continued working with other nations to settle conflicts around the world. One such conflict took place in Eastern Europe. The communist country of Yugoslavia was made up of six regions populated by people of different religious and ethnic backgrounds. The people of Yugoslavia overthrew their communist government in 1990 and held their first free elections in nearly 50 years. But then the regions of Slovenia (slow-VEE-nee-uh) and Croatia (krow-AY-shuh) declared themselves independent republics. Soon, the regions of Serbia (SUR-bee-uh), Macedonia (ma-see-DOH-nee-uh) and Bosnia-Herzegovina (BAHZ-nee-uh her-see-go-VEE-nuh) did the same.

With demands for independence, there came violent struggles for control of the new republics. Old tensions between the different ethnic and religious groups broke out in savage fighting.

The United States joined the United Nations in condemning this fighting. President Clinton sent American soldiers to the region to help restore peace. In 1994 former President Jimmy Carter flew to Eastern Europe to negotiate a cease-fire. In 1995 the armed conflict in this region officially ended.

One of the people who helped President Clinton make decisions during the 1990s was **Madeleine Albright.** Albright became the secretary of state in 1997. She was the first woman to hold that office. Albright believed that cooperation between nations was the key to peace. She said,

> *"We must maintain strong alliances, for there is no better way to prevent war."*

During Clinton's presidency, the United States also witnessed an increase in terrorism, including the bombing of the World Trade Center in 1993 and attacks on United States embassies in 1998. Clinton continued to send the military where needed.

Like President Nixon, Clinton faced a serious scandal during his second term as President. During an investigation on his actions, Clinton lied while under oath. In 1998 the House of Representatives voted to impeach Clinton. He was only the second President to be impeached. After a trial in the Senate, senators voted not to remove Clinton from office.

REVIEW What led up to the Persian Gulf War and how did it end? *Sequence*

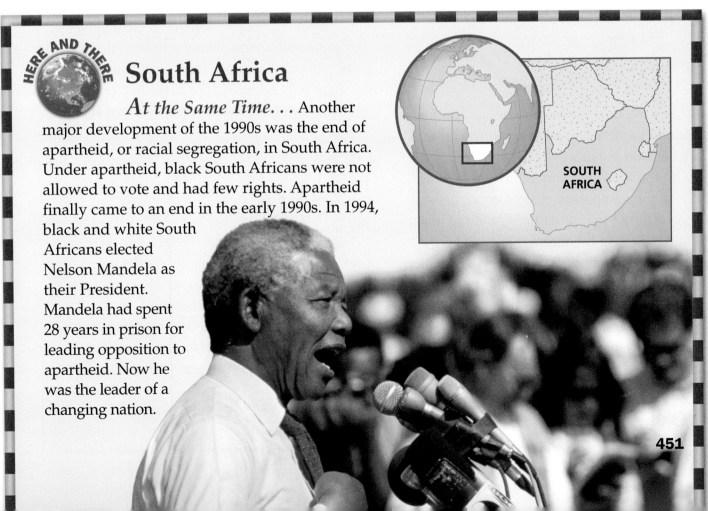

HERE AND THERE
South Africa

At the Same Time... Another major development of the 1990s was the end of apartheid, or racial segregation, in South Africa. Under apartheid, black South Africans were not allowed to vote and had few rights. Apartheid finally came to an end in the early 1990s. In 1994, black and white South Africans elected Nelson Mandela as their President. Mandela had spent 28 years in prison for leading opposition to apartheid. Now he was the leader of a changing nation.

SOUTH AFRICA

The Internet

One of the most important developments of the 1990s was the rise of the Internet. You may know that the **Internet** is a worldwide network of computers. But did you know that the Internet started as a result of the Cold War?

During the 1960s, the United States government wanted to build a communications system that would continue working even after a nuclear attack. American scientists came up with the idea of linking computers together.

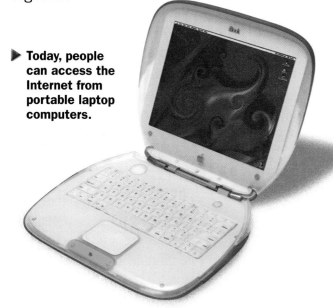

▶ **Today, people can access the Internet from portable laptop computers.**

At first, only the military and universities used this network. As the Internet grew, it became important to businesses. Soon, with the invention and rapid increase of desk-top computers, people could access the Internet from their homes. Today, millions of people use the Internet every day. The Internet still delivers news and information, but now enables people to shop online, play games, do research, send e-mails, and more. It has dramatically changed the way people communicate.

REVIEW How was the Cold War responsible for the creation of the Internet?

⟲ **Cause and Effect**

The End of the Century

As the century came to an end, the United States continued to focus on issues such as health and the environment. The nation sponsored World Health Day in 1999. Most of the issues during World Health Day had to do with the health of older Americans, as many of the Baby Boom Generation had already turned 50. NASA kept track of the world's temperature to see if air pollutants were making Earth warmer. Managing land and water properly remained a priority for many Americans.

In 2000 **George W. Bush,** son of former President George Bush, faced Al Gore. Gore had served as Bill Clinton's Vice-President. Gore received 50.9 million votes and Bush received 50.4 million. Bush, however, won the vote in the electoral college 271–266. Bush became the forty-third President in 2001.

This presidential election was among the closest in American history. Only four other presidential elections have been so close. Thomas Jefferson's election was a tie that was decided in the House of Representatives,

▶ **Elections give political cartoonists a lot of ideas.**

"I think it was an election year."

and in three other elections, electoral votes won over popular vote. You will read more about the electoral college in Unit 6.

President Bush put together a team that included Condoleezza Rice as the National Security Advisor and Colin Powell as secretary of state to help him make decisions for our country. Powell was the first African American to head the State Department.

George W. Bush was reelected to his second term as President

▶ **George W. Bush**

in 2004, defeating John Kerry. When Colin Powell stepped down from his position in 2004, Condoleezza Rice became the new secretary of state. She was the first African American woman to hold the position.

REVIEW Who were the two main candidates in the presidential election of 2004?
Main Idea and Details

Summarize the Lesson

1972 Nixon visited China and the Soviet Union.

1979 Egypt and Israel signed a peace treaty with U.S. help.

1991 The Soviet Union broke up into 15 independent republics.

LESSON 4 REVIEW

Check Facts and Main Ideas

1. ⟳ **Cause and Effect** On a separate sheet of paper, complete the chart below by listing three effects of the end of the Cold War.

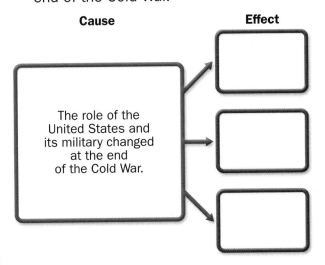

Cause

The role of the United States and its military changed at the end of the Cold War.

Effect

2. How did Nixon's visit to China affect relations between the United States and China?

3. Why did Jimmy Carter invite the leaders of Egypt and Israel to the United States in 1979?

4. How did **Mikhail Gorbachev's** actions help lead to the collapse of communism in Europe during the 1990s? Answer in two or more sentences. Use the highlighted name in your answer.

5. **Critical Thinking: *Predict*** In what ways do you think the **Internet** could be used to help people solve conflicts in the future? Answer in one or more sentences. Use the highlighted word in your answer.

Link to 🔗 Geography

Work with Maps Find a map created before 1990 that shows the Soviet Union. Compare it with a current map of the same region. Identify the differences between the maps, including new country names, new borders, and new capitals.

453

Map and Globe Skills

Understand Map Projections

What? You have seen many maps of the world in this book, including the map on page 346. Each map is really a map projection. A **map projection** is a way of showing the round Earth on a flat surface, such as a piece of paper.

Like Earth, a globe is a sphere and therefore can show places accurately in size and shape. Globes also show accurate distances between places. But all flat maps, or map projections, have errors in size, shape, distance, or direction. These errors are called distortions. They occur because it is not possible to show a round Earth as a flat surface without changing something. Each map projection has advantages and disadvantages.

Why? A globe is the most accurate way of showing the world, but no one takes globes along when they travel. We use maps because they can be folded and carried easily. It is important to understand the kind of map we see and the kind of distortion it has. Then we know which features may be accurate on the map and which ones may be distorted.

Map A

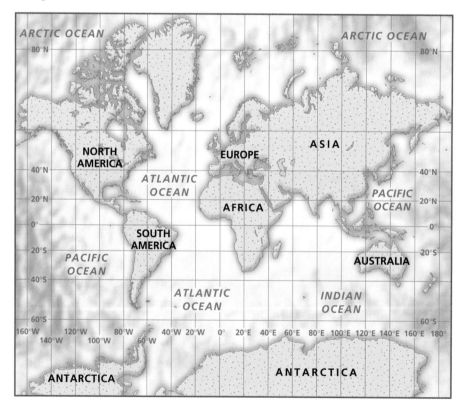

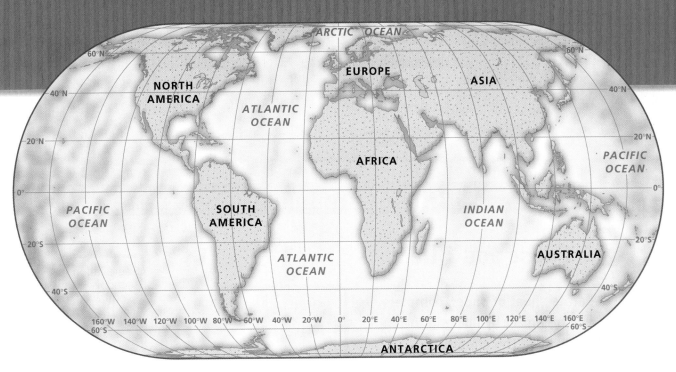

Map B

How? Look at Map A. It uses a Mercator (mer KAY ter) projection. Gerardus Mercator first introduced this kind of map in 1569. If you study the map, you will see that the lines of latitude are all parallel to one another, as they are on a globe. But the lines of longitude are also shown parallel. On a globe, lines of longitude all meet at the North and South Poles.

On a Mercator projection, the distances and the shapes and sizes of the land are fairly accurate near the equator. But places farther north and south on the map appear larger and farther apart than they really are. For example, Greenland seems to be larger than Africa, but Africa is really fourteen times larger than Greenland.

This kind of map was useful for sailors who sailed east or west from Europe. They were interested in locating places by latitude.

Another type of projection is the equal-area projection, seen in Map B. It tries to correct the distortions by showing the lines of longitude—except for the prime meridian—

curving in toward the poles. As a result, the sizes of land are closer to their actual sizes than they are on a Mercator projection. Compare the sizes of Africa and Greenland on this map. Compare the shapes of the continents on the two maps.

Think and Apply

1 What is a map projection?

2 On which map do the continents of South America and Africa appear more equal in size?

3 Which map would you use to compare the actual sizes of North and South America?

Internet Activity

For more information, go online to the Atlas at
www.sfsocialstudies.com.

1950   1960   1970

1954
Supreme Court declares segregation in public schools is illegal.

1957
Soviet Union launches *Sputnik*.

1964
Civil Rights Act of 1964 is passed.

1969
American astronauts are the first to land on the moon.

Chapter Summary

 Cause and Effect

On a separate sheet of paper, complete the graphic organizer by filling in the cause that created the effects.

Cause   **Effect**

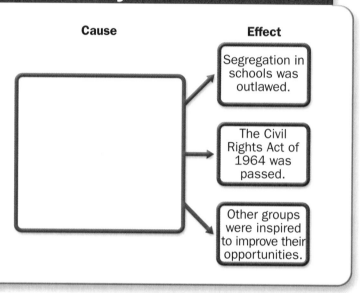

Effects:
- Segregation in schools was outlawed.
- The Civil Rights Act of 1964 was passed.
- Other groups were inspired to improve their opportunities.

Vocabulary

Match each word with the correct definition or description.

1 civil rights (p. 420)

2 passive resistance (p. 423)

3 space race (p. 429)

4 arms control (p. 447)

5 Internet (p. 452)

a. a deal to limit the production of weapons

b. a worldwide network of computers

c. rights guaranteed to all citizens by the Constitution

d. a race to explore outer space

e. the opposing of something without using violence

People and Terms

Write a sentence explaining why each of the following people or terms was important to the United States in the late 1900s. You may use two or more in a single sentence.

1 Jackie Robinson (p. 420)

2 Rosa Parks (p. 422)

3 Vietnam Conflict (p. 432)

4 General William Westmoreland (p. 432)

5 Americans with Disabilities Act (p. 441)

6 Environmental Protection Agency (p. 443)

7 Ronald Reagan (p. 448)

8 Mikhail Gorbachev (p. 448)

9 Condoleezza Rice (p. 449)

10 Persian Gulf War (p. 450)

1980   1990   2000

1973
United States signs
ceasefire with North
Vietnam.

1979
Egypt and
Israel sign a
peace treaty.

1981
Sandra Day O'Connor
becomes the first woman
Supreme Court Justice.

1991
The Soviet
Union breaks
apart.

Facts and Main Ideas

1 What did the Voting Rights Act of 1965 accomplish?

2 Why was the Internet first developed?

3 **Time Line** How many years were there between the Soviet launching of Sputnik and the landing of American astronauts on the moon?

4 **Main Idea** How did Martin Luther King, Jr. help African Americans gain civil rights?

5 **Main Idea** Why did the United States become involved in the Vietnam Conflict?

6 **Main Idea** Identify two or three groups that were inspired by the successes of the Civil Rights movement. List one or more success for each group you identify.

7 **Main Idea** Describe America's involvement in the Persian Gulf War.

8 **Critical Thinking:** *Evaluate* Why do you think meetings like the ones President Nixon had with leaders in China and the Soviet Union helped the United States?

Apply Skills

Understand Map Projections
Study the map below. Then answer the questions.

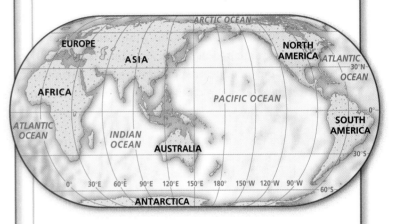

1 Is this a Mercator projection or an equal-area projection? Explain.

2 Compare this map with Map B on page 455. How are they similar? How are they different?

3 Which map do you think is better for measuring the distance between North America and Asia? Why?

Write About History

1 **Write a letter** to a friend as if you had witnessed part of the Montgomery bus boycott.

2 **Write a TV news story** about the American astronauts landing on the moon in 1969.

3 **Write a brochure** about how students can help take care of the environment.

Internet Activity

To get help with vocabulary, people, and terms, select dictionary or encyclopedia from *Social Studies Library* at **www.sfsocialstudies.com**.

End with a Transcript

Apollo 11

On July 20, 1969, Neil Armstrong became the first human ever to step onto the surface of the moon. Armstrong and Edwin "Buzz" Aldrin, Armstrong's partner in the *Eagle* lunar module, spent several hours exploring and setting up experiments. In the moon's orbit above, Command Module *Columbia* pilot Michael Collins listened to what was going on and awaited their return.

During the mission, the astronauts communicated with Charles Duke and Bruce McCandless at the command center in Houston, Texas. Below are excerpts from the transcript, or written copy, of the conversation between the astronauts and the Houston Command Center. Tranquility Base is the place on the moon where the astronauts landed.

As the Eagle *lunar module [LM] descends to the moon's surface:*

Aldrin: 40 feet, down 2 1/2. Picking up some dust.

Aldrin: 30 feet, 2 1/2 down.

Aldrin: Contact Light.

Armstrong (**on-board**): Shutdown.

Aldrin: Okay. Engine Stop.

Duke: We copy you down, *Eagle*.

Armstrong (**on-board**): Engine arm is off. (**Pause**) Houston, Tranquility Base here. The *Eagle* has landed.

After turning on the TV camera, Neil Armstrong leaves the Eagle *LM and steps out onto the moon:*

McCandless: We're getting a picture on the TV!

Aldrin: You got a good picture, huh?

McCandless: Okay. Neil, we can see you (on the TV) coming down the ladder now. (**Pause**)

Armstrong: I'm at the foot of the ladder. The LM footpads are only depressed in the surface about 1 or 2 inches, although the surface appears to be very, very fine grained, as you get close to it. It's almost like a powder. (The) ground mass is very fine. (**Pause**)

Armstrong: I'm going to step off the LM now.

[Neil puts his right hand on the ladder and steps down with his left foot.]

Armstrong: That's one small step for (a) man; one giant leap for mankind. (**Long Pause**)

Armstrong: Yes, the surface is fine and powdery. I can kick it up loosely with my toe. It does adhere [stick] in fine layers, like powdered charcoal, to the sole and sides of my boots. I only go in a small fraction of an inch, maybe an eighth of an inch, but I can see the footprints of my boots and the treads in the fine, sandy particles.

After Aldrin joins Armstrong outside the LM, they prepare to plant the American flag on the surface of the Moon:

McCandless: Columbia, this is Houston. Reading you loud and clear. Over.

Collins: Yeah. Reading you loud and clear. How's it going?

McCandless: Roger. The [Moonwalk] is progressing beautifully. I believe they are setting up the flag now.

Collins: Great!

McCandless: I guess you're about the only person around that doesn't have TV coverage of the scene.

Collins: That's all right. I don't mind a bit. (**Pause**) How is the quality of the TV?

McCandless: Oh, it's beautiful, Mike. It really is.

Collins: Oh, gee, that's great! Is the lighting halfway decent?

McCandless: Yes, indeed. They've got the flag up now and you can see the stars and stripes on the lunar surface.

Collins: Beautiful. Just beautiful. (**Long Pause**)

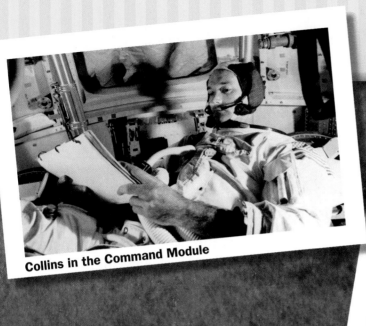

Collins in the Command Module

Aldrin descends to the moon's surface.

Main Ideas and Vocabulary

TEST PREP

Read the passage below and use it to answer the questions that follow.

When World War II ended, the United States worked to help rebuild Europe and Asia. Americans also enjoyed a time of growing prosperity.

The Soviet Union posed a new threat. It wanted to spread communism around the globe. Because the United States did not want this to happen, the two nations were involved in an <u>arms race.</u>

The United States and the Soviet Union never fought each other directly. However, the United States did fight in several areas of the world to help stop the spread of communism.

The United States helped prevent communist North Korea from taking over democratic South Korea.

During the Vietnam Conflict, American troops faced <u>guerrilla warfare</u> and an enemy that was often hard to identify. This conflict ended with a withdrawal of U.S. troops and the eventual uniting of South Vietnam and North Vietnam under communist control.

African Americans, women, disabled Americans, migrant workers, and people of various ethnic backgrounds worked through the end of the century for greater opportunities and to improve their lives.

At the end of the 1900s, the Soviet Union broke up. The United States was the only remaining superpower. The nation took on a role as peacekeeper.

1 According to the passage, why was the Soviet Union a threat?
   A The Soviet Union lost World War II.
   B The Soviet Union wanted communism to spread everywhere.
   C The Soviet Union had two presidents.
   D The Soviet Union was weak.

2 In the passage the term <u>arms race</u> means—
   A a test to see which weapons fire more quickly
   B a war between two superpowers
   C nations building powerful weapons
   D nuclear weapons

3 In the passage the word <u>guerrilla warfare</u> means—
   A a deadly battle
   B fighting in Asia
   C using nuclear weapons in war
   D fighting that includes sneak and surprise attacks

4 What is the main idea of the passage?
   A The United States fought to keep communism out of South Korea.
   B The late 1900s brought changes in the world and the United States.
   C Citizens in the United States gained new opportunities in the 1950s.
   D The Soviet Union was an enemy of the United States.

Test Talk

Use sources to help you find the answer.

People and Places

Match each person and place to its definition.

1 **Thurgood Marshall** (p. 421)

2 **Greensboro, North Carolina** (p. 423)

3 **Neil Armstrong** (p. 430)

4 **Dolores Huerta** (p. 441)

5 **Middle East** (p. 448)

6 **Kuwait** (p. 450)

a. helped form the United Farm Workers of America.

b. first person to walk on the moon's surface

c. area in Southwest Asia that includes Israel and Egypt

d. invaded by Iraq in 1990

e. African American students staged the first lunch counter sit-in here

f. first African American to become a Supreme Court justice

Apply Skills

Compare primary and secondary sources on current events, community issues, or something from the unit. Find primary and secondary sources that relate to the topic. Make copies of pages or clip out articles and paste them in a notebook. Underline important points or write a brief summary. Which of the two articles below is the primary source?

Why I Enjoy Volunteering

Writer has helped clean up parks and plant trees. He is happy he is making a difference.

Volunteering Increases Across the U.S.

Statistics show that more people are volunteering in every state. The environment and poverty are top concerns.

Write and Share

Present a Time Line With a partner or in a small group, prepare a time line showing the main events from a decade in the last half of the 1900s: 1941–1950, 1951–1960, 1961–1970, and so on. Use the textbook or other resources to identify important events from the decade. Prepare illustrations about the selected events. Be prepared to give a short presentation about the events selected that includes your illustrations.

Read on Your Own

Look for books such as these in the library.

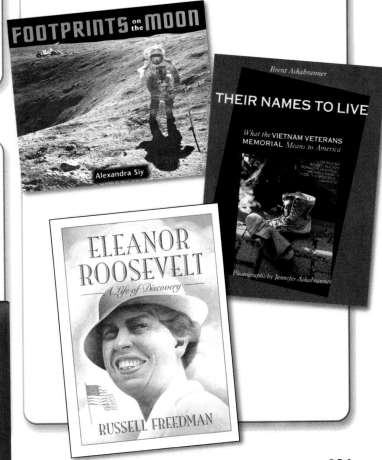

FOOTPRINTS on the MOON
Alexandra Siy

Brent Ashabranner
THEIR NAMES TO LIVE
What the VIETNAM VETERANS MEMORIAL Means to America
Photographs by Jennifer Ashabranner

ELEANOR ROOSEVELT
A Life of Discovery
RUSSELL FREEDMAN

UNIT 5 Project

Then and Now

Bring the past to life in a documentary.

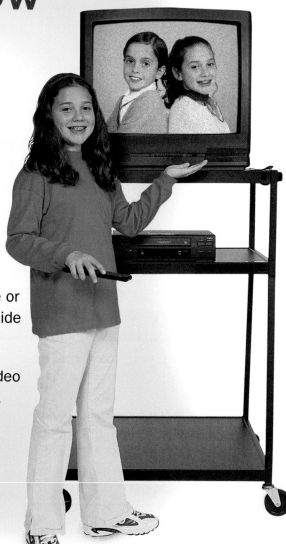

1 **Form** a group and choose a decade from the 1900s.

2 **Research** historic events, advances in technology, and changes in everyday life that occurred during the decade.

3 **Have** each person in the group take on the role of a person living in the decade. Write what each person would say, as if he or she were speaking for a documentary. Decide who will speak first, second, and so on.

4 **Give** your presentation to the class. If a video camera is available, tape the presentation.

Internet Activity

Learn more about civil rights. Go to **www.sfsocialstudies.com/activities** and select your grade and unit.

Moving into the Twenty-first Century

What challenges and changes do Americans face in the future?

Begin with a Primary Source

1970   1975   1980   1985   1990

1971
The Twenty-sixth Amendment gives all citizens 18 years old and older the right to vote.

1981
Sandra Day O'Connor becomes the first female Supreme Court justice.

1992
The United States, Canada, and Mexico sign the North American Free Trade Agreement.

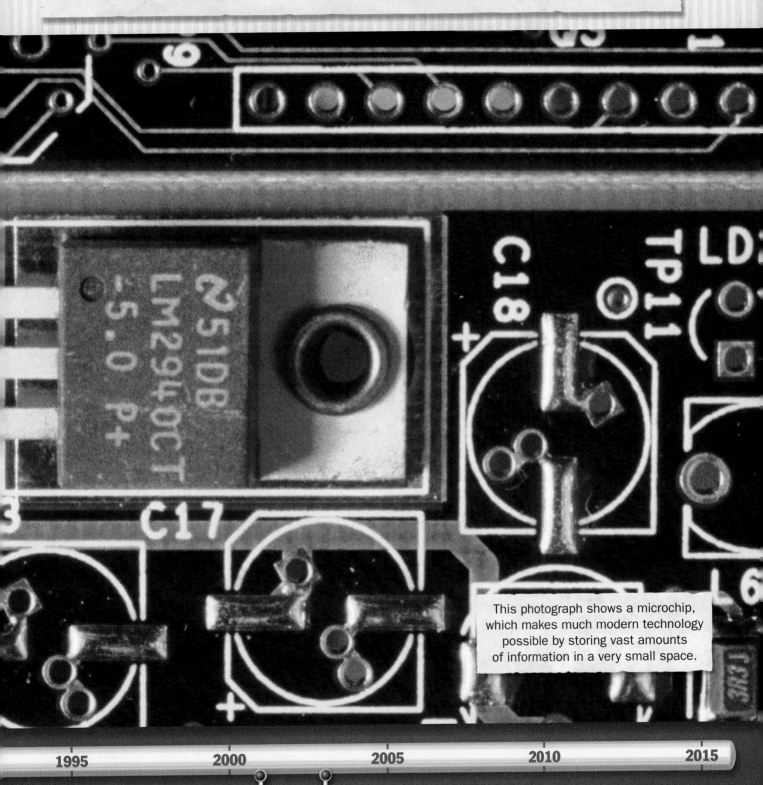

> *"The next century will witness an even more far-reaching scientific revolution."*
>
> —Michio Kaku, professor and scientist

This photograph shows a microchip, which makes much modern technology possible by storing vast amounts of information in a very small space.

1995 2000 2005 2010 2015

September 11, 2001
Terrorists attack the United States.

October 2001
The United States attacks terrorist bases in Afghanistan.

March 2003
The war in Iraq begins.

20??
What does the future hold?

Meet the People

An Wang

1920–1990
Birthplace: Shanghai, China
Engineer, inventor
- Founded a successful electronics company in 1951 with only $600
- Invented new technology that improved computer memory
- Wang Center for the Performing Arts in Boston was named for him

Jimmy Carter

1924–
Birthplace: Plains, Georgia
Naval officer, President
- Naval officer on nuclear-powered submarines
- Served as President of the United States from 1977 to 1981
- Won the Nobel Prize for Peace in 2002

Sandra Day O'Connor

1930–
Birthplace: El Paso, Texas
Lawyer, Supreme Court justice
- Became the first woman to serve as a Supreme Court justice in 1981
- Inducted into the National Women's Hall of Fame in 1995
- Co-wrote a memoir with her brother about her childhood on a ranch in Arizona

Rudolph Giuliani

1944–
Birthplace: New York, New York
Lawyer, political leader
- As United States Attorney for the Southern District of New York, he convicted thousands of criminals
- Mayor of New York City from 1993 to 2002
- Led New York City's recovery after terrorist attack on the World Trade Center on September 11, 2001

1920	1930	1940	1950	1960

1920 • An Wang

1924 • Jimmy Carter

1930 • Sandra Day O'Connor

1944 • Rudolph Giuliani

1946 • George W. Bush

1946 • Daniel Libeskind

1948 • Esmeralda Santiago

1954

For more information, go online to *Meet the People* at **www.sfsocialstudies.com**.

George W. Bush

1946–

Birthplace: New Haven, Connecticut

Governor, President

- Was an owner of the Texas Rangers baseball team
- Served as governor of Texas from 1995 to 2000
- Became President of the United States in 2001

Daniel Libeskind

1946–

Birthplace: Lodz, Poland

Architect

- Designed the Jewish Museum in Berlin, Germany
- Designed the new plan for the World Trade Center site in New York City
- In 2001 was awarded the Hiroshima Art Prize, given to an artist whose work encourages international understanding and peace

Esmeralda Santiago

1948–

Birthplace: San Juan, Puerto Rico

Writer

- In 1993 wrote her first book—*When I Was Puerto Rican*—about moving to New York City
- Founded an award-winning documentary film company
- Her novel *Almost a Woman* was made into an award-winning television movie

Condoleezza Rice

1954–

Birthplace: Birmingham, Alabama

Educator, diplomat

- Taught political science at Stanford University
- Advised President George Bush on foreign policy and military issues from 1989 to 1991
- Became the first woman to head the National Security Council in 2001

1970   1980   1990   2000   2010

1990

- Condoleezza Rice

Moving into the Twenty-first Century

Summarize

Summarizing means telling the main idea of a paragraph, section, or story. Being able to write a summary helps you to be sure that you understand the meaning of the passage and helps you remember the important ideas.

● A summary is short. It tells the most important ideas.

Sometimes a paragraph's **topic sentence** provides a summary. **Details** can be found in other parts of the paragraph.

> **The Bill of Rights guarantees important freedoms to all citizens of the United States.** The Bill of Rights is the name used for the first ten amendments to the United States Constitution. **It includes freedom of speech, freedom of religion, and the right to a jury trial.**

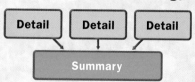

Words with Multiple Meanings Many words have more than one meaning. Some words have dozens of meanings.

States are examples of political regions—areas *run* by separate state governments.		
• to go	• to operate	• to be in charge of

Which meaning of the word *run* applies to the sentence? Look first at the context. The sentence is about politics and government. Next, pick a definition and use it in context. For example, you can say *The government is in charge of this area.*

This definition of *run* makes sense in context. It is the correct choice.

Summarizing the Rights and Responsibilities of American Citizens

All United States citizens are guaranteed certain rights by the Constitution, and with those rights come responsibilities. Theodore Roosevelt, the twenty-fifth President of the United States, once said this about our rights and responsibilities: "You can no more have freedom without striving and suffering for it than you can win success as a banker or a lawyer without labor and effort. . . . The people who say that they have not time to attend to politics are simply saying that they are unfit to live in a free community."

It is indeed important to understand that some rights had to be fought for. One such right is the right to vote. Those who fought in the American Revolution in 1776 wanted a government in which they could have a say. Voting is now a right. It is also a responsibility. It is the responsibility of all American citizens age eighteen and over to help choose their leaders. If citizens do not vote, democracy cannot work.

Another right that comes with responsibility is the right to a jury trial. This right is guaranteed by the Sixth Amendment. The amendment states that any citizen accused of a crime will get a fair trial. A group of fellow citizens will determine the guilt or innocence of the person on trial. In order to ensure this right, all adult citizens of the United States must participate in jury duty. This means that a citizen is called upon to serve on a jury to help determine the outcome of a trial.

The different branches of government all have a part in making certain that our freedoms and rights are kept safe. This works best when we remember our responsibilities.

Apply it!

Use the reading strategy of summarizing to answer the first two questions. Then answer the vocabulary question.

1 Which sentence summarizes the entire passage?

2 Write a sentence summarizing the ideas in the second paragraph.

3 The word *trial* has several meanings. It can mean "trying something out," "a hardship," or "a formal examination of a case in court." In the context of the above passage, what does *trial* mean?

The United States Today

Atlanta, Georgia
The Sunbelt's population is the fastest-growing of any region in the United States.

Lesson 1

1

Washington, D.C.
The Legislative Branch of the United States government meets in the Capitol.

Lesson 2

2

Seattle, Washington
As a result of growing trade with other countries, many ports in the United States have become busier.

Lesson 3

3

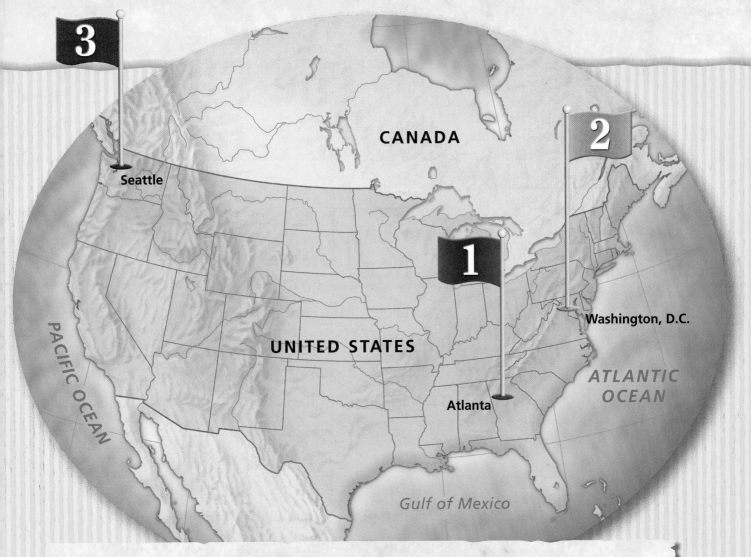

Why We Remember

The United States is a modern country with large cities and growing industries. The free enterprise system has made our economy the largest in the world. Our republican system of government has been in place for more than 200 years. When you are 18 years old, you will be able to vote for the people you want to represent you in government. But you can make a difference in your community, state, and country now. The United States is also about the many kinds of people who live here. You are part of our country's history. You will be part of its future. You will become part of our country's proud tradition of diversity, involvement, and change.

PREVIEW

Focus on the Main Idea
The United States is a land of varied geography and has a diverse population that is united by common ideals.

PLACES
Northeast
Southeast
Midwest
Southwest
West

PEOPLE
Esmeralda Santiago

VOCABULARY
region
Sunbelt
ideals
ethnic group

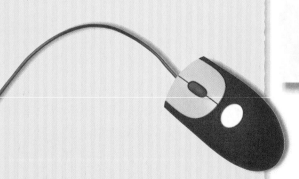

The Fifty States

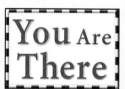

How would you describe your home state to someone who has never even been to the United States? Your Internet pen pal from China wants to know what your home state of Virginia is like. One description just won't do! Where do you begin? In the west, Virginia has the beautiful Blue Ridge Mountains. To the east is the Chesapeake Bay, leading to the Atlantic Ocean. There are big cities, small farms, fishing ports, and forest trails. There are also colonial homes and historic battlefields. One of Virginia's nicknames is "Mother of Presidents." That's because eight United States Presidents were born here! Today people from all over the world live here. Like the rest of the country, Virginia is a land of great variety.

Summarize As you read, look for details that summarize the ways that Americans are both the same and different.

States and Regions

Look at the map below. It shows the 50 states of the United States. The states are often divided into regions to make it easier to study them. A **region** is a large area that has common features that set it apart from other areas. Different kinds of features define regions. For example, regions can be defined by political features, by geography, by economics, or by culture. States are examples of political regions—areas run by separate state governments.

The United States can also be divided into larger regions based on geography. The map shows the five main geographic regions of the country: the **Northeast, Southeast, Midwest, Southwest,** and **West.** The states of Alaska and Hawaii are not contiguous. This means that they do not border any of the other states.

The culture of a region can be influenced by geography. For example, in the snow-capped mountains of Colorado, many children grow up learning how to snow ski. In the warm island state of Hawaii, many children grow up learning how to surf on the ocean's waves.

REVIEW What are the five main regions of the United States? ↻ Summarize

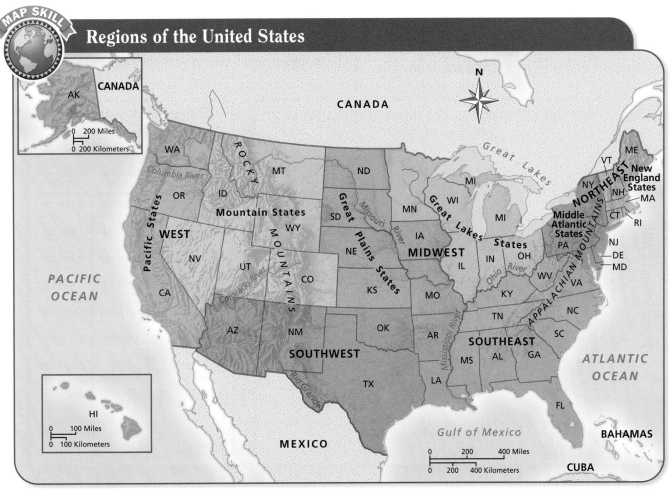

MAP SKILL

Regions of the United States

▶ The Midwest, West, and Northeast each are divided into two subregions. Identify these subregions.

MAP SKILL Understand Borders *Which states are in the Great Lakes subregion? Why do you think this region has this name?*

Americans on the Move

The culture of different regions of the country changes over time as people migrate from place to place. Until the mid-1900s, many Americans lived their entire lives in one area. Now more people move often and over greater distances. Between 1995 and 2000, nearly half of the people in the United States over the age of five moved at least once.

Today improved transportation and communication make it much easier to move. Most people move to get better jobs. As a result, some areas have seen dramatic changes in the number of people living there.

The population of the Southeast and Southwest—an area known as the **Sunbelt**—began to increase after World War II. Many businesses moved to the Sunbelt to take advantage of its warm climate, natural resources, and lower wages. The populations of Sunbelt cities such as Atlanta, Georgia,

have grown over the years. The invention of air conditioning made it more comfortable for people to live and work in the often hot climate of the Sunbelt.

Changing social and political conditions also encouraged this migration. As you have read, during the early 1900s many African Americans left the South for better opportunities in the North and West. Today there is a reverse migration. Many African Americans are moving to the Sunbelt. They go there for the job opportunities made possible by the Civil Rights movement.

As the population of the Sunbelt has grown, the population of many older cities in the Northeast and Midwest has declined. For example, between 1950 and 2000 the population of Detroit, Michigan, declined by nearly 50 percent.

REVIEW Why did more people move to the Sunbelt after World War II? ➲ Summarize

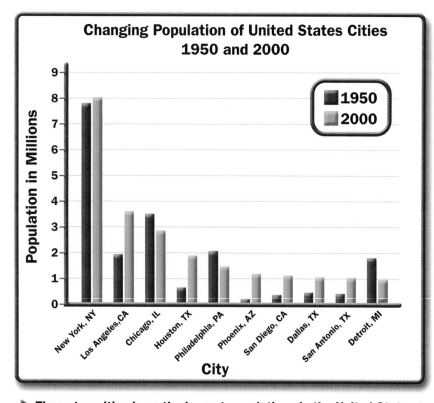

Changing Population of United States Cities 1950 and 2000

Legend: ■ 1950　■ 2000

City	Population 1950	Population 2000
New York, NY	7,891,957	8,008,278
Los Angeles, CA	1,970,358	3,694,820
Chicago, IL	3,620,962	2,896,016
Houston, TX	596,163	1,953,631
Philadelphia, PA	2,071,605	1,517,550
Phoenix, AZ	106,818	1,321,045
San Diego, CA	334,387	1,223,400
Dallas, TX	434,462	1,188,580
San Antonio, TX	408,442	1,144,646
Detroit, MI	1,849,568	951,270

2003 World Almanac

▶ These ten cities have the largest populations in the United States today.

GRAPH SKILL *Which cities had a decline in population?*

A United Country

People in the United States have many different cultures and live in different regions. Yet the citizens of this large, diverse country are united as Americans.

This unity is expressed in the motto *e pluribus unum,* which is Latin for "out of many, one." It originally referred to the 13 different colonies that came together to form one nation. You can find this motto on the Great Seal of the United States. You can also find it on United States coins and the one dollar bill.

In a way, this motto fits the country even better today than when the nation was first formed. The population of the United States is very diverse, but Americans share certain basic **ideals,** or important beliefs. These ideals include freedom of speech and freedom of religion.

Read the excerpt below from an 1882 poem by Margaret B. Peeke. What does she think about the shared ideals of the American people?

From East and West, from North and South,
All Nations here are joining
Their varied gifts, and out of this
A higher life is coining [created]
All hail, America, the blessed!
All lands in one combining,
Whose star so bright, through future years,
Shall evermore be shining.

REVIEW What does the motto *E Pluribus Unum* say about the United States today?

↻ **Summarize**

HERE AND THERE

Immigration to Brazil

Like the United States, the South American country of Brazil has a very diverse population. Enslaved people from Africa, as well as immigrants from many countries in Europe and Asia, helped build the country. Today Brazilians share a culture that mixes elements from all of these groups.

BRAZIL
SOUTH AMERICA

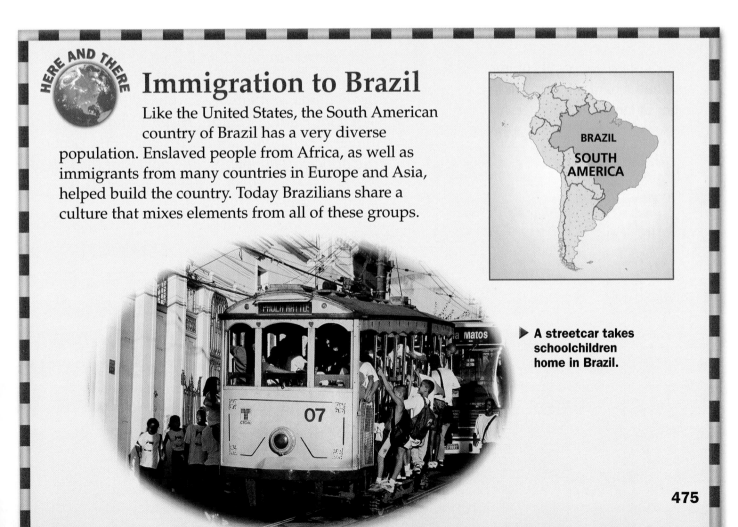

▶ A streetcar takes schoolchildren home in Brazil.

A Diverse Country

Part of the rich diversity in the United States comes from its mixture of ethnic groups. An **ethnic group** is a group of people who share the same customs and language. For example, Americans whose families originally came from Italy are part of the ethnic group of Italian Americans. People of the country's many different ethnic groups have contributed to making the United States the world's richest and most powerful nation.

Today the United States has a greater diversity of ethnic groups than ever before. This is partly because of a growing diversity of immigrants coming to the country. Until the early 1900s, most immigrants to the United States came from Europe. Since the late 1900s, however, most immigrants have come from Asia, Latin America, and Africa.

The increasing diversity of immigrants has meant an increase in the number of languages spoken here.

When I Was Puerto Rican

In 1961 writer Esmeralda Santiago moved from Puerto Rico to New York City with her mother, "Mami," and her brothers and sisters. She was thirteen years old. She wrote about her experiences, including how she learned English, in her autobiography.

Every day after school I went to the library and took out as many children's books as I was allowed. I figured that if American children learned English through books, so could I, even if I was starting later. I studied the bright illustrations and learned the words for the unfamiliar objects of our new life in the United States: A for Apple, B for Bear, C for Cabbage. As my vocabulary grew, I moved to large-print chapter books. Mami bought me an English-English dictionary [a dictionary that defines English words in the English language] because that way, when I looked up a word I would be learning others.

By my fourth month in Brooklyn, I could read and write English much better than I could speak it, and at midterms I stunned the teachers by scoring high in English, History, and Social Studies. During the January assembly, Mr. Grant [the principal] announced the names of the kids who had received high marks in each class. My name was called out three times.

It has also created an increase in the variety of customs and religions. As you read in Unit 2, immigrants sometimes face difficulties, but they also have many new opportunities.

Many people who move to the United States from other places must learn a new language—English. Writer **Esmeralda Santiago** moved from Puerto Rico to New York City. One of the hardest things for her to get used to was the English language. However, she learned English so well that she later became a successful writer of books in English.

REVIEW Why are there so many different ethnic groups in the United States?
🔄 Summarize

Hello   Hola   Jambo   здравствулте   لَاهْ   你好

▶ This sign says *hello* in six different languages: English, Spanish, Swahili, Russian, Arabic, and Chinese.

Summarize the Lesson

- The 50 states of the United States are divided into five main regions that vary in geography and culture.

- The population of the Sunbelt grew rapidly after World War II.

- The motto *E Pluribus Unum*—"Out of many, one"—explains that the diverse people of the United States share important ideals.

- Today most immigrants to the United States come from Asia, Latin America, and Africa.

LESSON 1 ▸ REVIEW

Check Facts and Main Ideas

1. 🔄 Summarize On a separate sheet of paper, complete the following chart to summarize the meaning of the motto *e pluribus unum.*

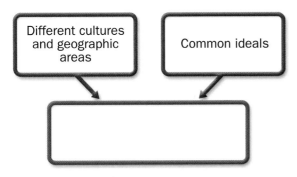

```
┌──────────────────┐    ┌──────────────────┐
│ Different cultures│    │  Common ideals   │
│  and geographic  │    │                  │
│      areas       │    │                  │
└──────────────────┘    └──────────────────┘
          │                      │
          ▼                      ▼
     ┌─────────────────────────────┐
     │                             │
     │                             │
     └─────────────────────────────┘
```

2. Describe each of the five main geographic **regions** of the United States.

3. Explain why people moved to the **Sunbelt** after World War II.

4. How has immigration to the United States changed since the late 1900s?

5. Critical Thinking: *Cause and Effect* What are some of the effects of immigration to the United States?

Link to ⌒⌒ Writing

Make a Brochure Suppose you are a business owner trying to encourage people to move to your region. Make a brochure to help attract people to the region. Be sure to include reasons why your region is a good place to live and work.

477

Map and Globe Skills

Compare Population Density Maps

What? **Distribution maps** show patterns of how things such as population or natural resources are spread out over an area. A **population density map** is one type of map that shows the distribution of population. *Density* here refers to the number of people living in an area. For example, the population density of a city is greater than that of a rural area.

Why? You have been reading about the five major regions of the United States and how the population in these regions changes. You know that Americans today move more than ever, and that new immigrants continue to come to seek better opportunities. Comparing population density maps of two regions in the United States can help you to see how different areas are being affected by these changes.

How? Map A shows the population density of the Midwest in 2000. This information is based on the 2000 census, or count of Americans. Each color on the map represents the number of people living in one square mile or kilometer. How large is a square mile? Picture a large square drawn on land in which each side measures one mile. For a square kilometer, each side measures one kilometer. A square kilometer is smaller than a square mile.

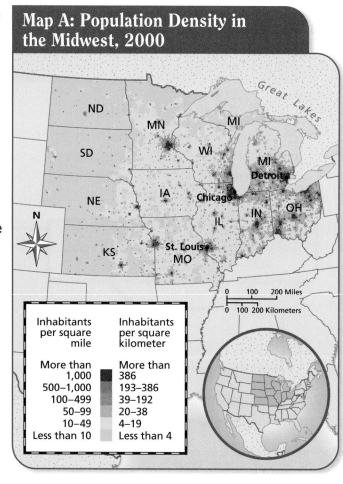

Map A: Population Density in the Midwest, 2000

Inhabitants per square mile	Inhabitants per square kilometer
More than 1,000	More than 386
500–1,000	193–386
100–499	39–192
50–99	20–38
10–49	4–19
Less than 10	Less than 4

Look again at Map A. You can see that the most densely populated areas are those in which more than 1,000 people live within one square mile of land, or more than 400 people live within one square kilometer of land. What color represents these areas on the map?

Now look at Map B, which shows the population of the Southeast region of the United States in 2000. By comparing the two maps, you can see that the Southeast has areas that are more densely populated than some areas in the Midwest.

What did you learn about the two regions that might help to explain this? Remember that more people began moving to the Southeast from other regions after World War II. As the Southeast's population grew, the population of the Midwest decreased.

Think and Apply

1. What is a population density map?

2. How would you compare the population densities in the Midwest and Southeast regions?

3. Which state is more densely populated, Florida or Kansas? How do you know?

Internet Activity

For more information, go online to the Atlas at www.sfsocialstudies.com.

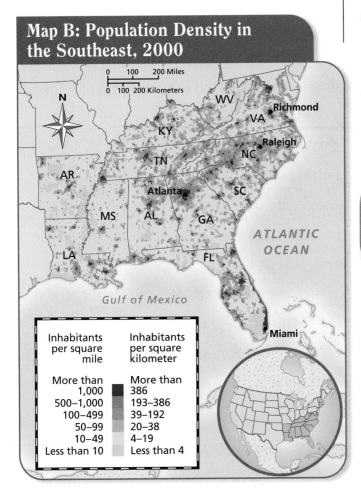

Map B: Population Density in the Southeast, 2000

Inhabitants per square mile	Inhabitants per square kilometer
More than 1,000	More than 386
500–1,000	193–386
100–499	39–192
50–99	20–38
10–49	4–19
Less than 10	Less than 4

Washington, D.C.

Government of the People

PREVIEW

Focus on the Main Idea
The United States is a republic in which the people elect representatives to run the government.

PLACES
Washington, D.C.

PEOPLE
Sandra Day O'Connor

VOCABULARY
democracy
popular sovereignty
citizen
electoral college
Legislative Branch
Executive Branch
Judicial Branch

You Are There One of your friends is running for president of the student council at your school. The two of you are trying to decide what to put on her campaign posters.

You think about why your friend decided to run for student council. The main job of your student council is to set up student activities at your school. She wants to have an effect on what those activities are and how they are carried out. You also think about why you would vote for her. You think she would make a good student council leader because she is honest, listens to other people, and has good ideas. Are these good traits for a student council leader? Are they good traits for a leader of our country? What would you write on the campaign posters?

Summarize As you read, pay attention to the basic principles of the United States government.

We the People

Have you ever run for an elected position at school or in another organization? If you were in charge, what kind of leader do you think you might be? Who would you ask for advice in making your decisions?

The leaders of the United States listen to many different people to help them make decisions. President Abraham Lincoln once said our government was "of the people, by the people, and for the people." In a **democracy** like the United States, all people have a say in how the government is run. This idea is also called **popular sovereignty.** The word *sovereignty* means "rule." Popular sovereignty does not exist in every country.

There are different types of democracies. In a direct democracy, each individual has the opportunity to vote on every decision the group makes. You may have done this in a school club or in your class. However, this type of democracy does not work well for a large country such as the United States. It would be very difficult to get anything done if every person voted on every decision.

The United States is a representative democracy, also called a republic. You read earlier that in a republic people elect representatives to make laws and run the government for them. Representatives, such as members of Congress, then make decisions on behalf of the American people.

The United States is also a constitutional democracy. This means that it follows a written plan of government, or constitution. The United States Constitution was written in 1787.

REVIEW Why is the United States a republic instead of a direct democracy?
⟳ **Summarize**

▶ **The Senate and the House of Representatives meet in the United States Capitol in Washington, D.C.**

481

▶ Most voters in the United States go to a designated place to vote, such as a fire station or school. Whether voting is done electronically or with paper, voters choose from a list of candidates. Some places are working on developing Internet voting, so people can vote on computers.

Citizens at Work

The first three words of the United States Constitution are "We the People." No one is more important in the political process of this country than the citizens. A **citizen** is a member of a country. Being a citizen includes both rights and responsibilities.

The United States Constitution protects many of our basic rights. These rights include the right to freedom of speech, freedom of religion, and a fair trial if accused of a crime. All citizens 18 years old and older have the right to vote.

In addition to rights, there are many responsibilities of citizenship. All citizens must obey the laws of our country. Adult citizens must serve on juries to ensure the right of a fair trial. As you read in the Overview, people must pay money to the government in the form of taxes. Federal, state, and local governments use taxes to provide services. These services include education, protection, and roads and bridges.

The right to vote is also an important responsibility. Citizens must vote in order to make sure the government does what the people want it to do. Although you are too young to vote, there are many other ways that you can be an active citizen. Getting involved is an important part of citizenship. For example, you can help political candidates you like or take part in a community project, such as planting trees at a park.

You can also write or call the office of a political leader to express your opinion about an issue. The views of the majority of people have an important role in a democracy, but the United States Constitution also protects the rights of the minority. Even if most other people disagree with your opinion or beliefs, you have a right to express your own views in a peaceful way.

REVIEW How is voting both a right and a responsibility? ↻ Summarize

▶ At city council meetings, people can voice their opinions about matters affecting their community.

The Electoral College

The process of electing the President of the United States involves a special system of voting called the **electoral college.** In this system, all voters cast a vote for President. The total of these votes is called the popular vote. Within each state, these votes actually count toward electors—people whose votes determine who becomes President. The number of electors in each state is based on population. The states with larger populations have a larger number of electors. The number of electors in each state is the same as the number of representatives and senators each state has in Congress. This system ensures that states with smaller populations are fairly represented. For example, New York City alone has a larger population than most states. It would be difficult for people living in a big city to know everything that affects people in rural areas or in other regions, but the city would have the most votes. The electoral college allows smaller states and rural areas to have a say in the government.

In most states the presidential candidate who receives a majority of the popular vote receives all of that state's electoral votes. For this reason, it is possible for a candidate to get a majority of the popular vote but still lose the election. As you read in Unit 5, this happened in the 2000 presidential election. George W. Bush became President because he received the majority of electoral college votes.

REVIEW Explain how the electoral college system works. ↻ **Summarize**

Map Adventure

"Counting the Votes"

In the 2000 presidential election, Al Gore received 50.9 million votes, and George W. Bush received 50.4 million votes. Yet Bush became President. The map below shows the number of electoral votes each candidate received in each state. Use the map to see how Bush became President.

1. Which state has the most electoral votes available? Which candidate won this state?

2. How many electoral votes did each candidate get?

3. How many states did each candidate win in the electoral college?

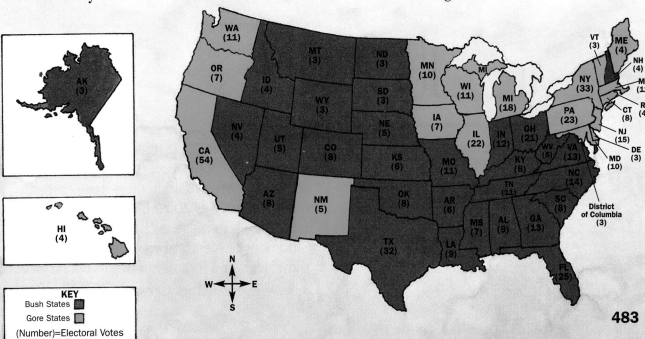

KEY
Bush States ▪
Gore States ▫
(Number)=Electoral Votes

The Living Constitution

The Constitution has often been called a "living document." This means that it can be changed over time. The Constitution can be changed by adding amendments to it. For example, until 1971 citizens had to be twenty-one years old to vote. The Twenty-sixth Amendment gives all citizens eighteen years old and older the right to vote.

The Constitution set up three branches, or parts, of the federal government. The **Legislative Branch,** led by Congress, makes the laws. The **Executive Branch,** led by the President, makes sure these laws are carried out. The **Judicial Branch,** made up of the court system, interprets the laws. The three branches of government meet in the nation's capital, **Washington, D.C.**

The highest court in the land is the Supreme Court. The justices, or judges, of the Supreme Court must determine if laws follow the Constitution. The President appoints the Supreme Court's judges, with the approval of the Senate. You read in Unit 5 that in 1981, President Ronald Reagan appointed **Sandra Day O'Connor** as the first female Supreme Court justice. You'll read more about O'Connor in the Biography on the next page.

REVIEW Why is the United States Constitution often called a "living document"? ⟳ Summarize

Summarize the Lesson

- The United States is a republic in which the people elect representatives to run the government.

- United States citizenship includes many rights as well as many responsibilities.

- The President of the United States is elected through a system called the electoral college.

- The United States Constitution is a "living document" that can be changed by amendments.

LESSON 2 REVIEW

Check Facts and Main Ideas

1. ⟳ Summarize On a separate sheet of paper, fill in the details for the summary about the United States government.

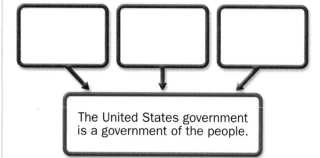

The United States government is a government of the people.

2. List some of the rights and responsibilities of United States citizenship.

3. How is the winner of a presidential election determined?

4. **Critical Thinking:** *Decision Making* Do you think the **electoral college** system is an effective way to choose a President? Why or why not?

5. What makes the Constitution a "living document"?

Link to ⟐ Geography

Analyze Regions Compare the map of United States regions on page 473 with the map of the 2000 electoral vote. Use the maps to make a chart listing the number of electoral votes each candidate received in each region of the country.

Sandra Day O'Connor
1930–

Sandra Day O'Connor grew up on a large ranch in southeastern Arizona. At an early age she started doing things that girls did not usually do—driving a truck, fixing fences, and riding horses. Later she attended law school, which was something else girls usually did not do at the time. O'Connor graduated with excellent grades when she was only twenty-two years old. However, because she was a woman, no law firm wanted to hire her. "I was surprised," she later said. "I had always assumed that, sure, there'd be jobs. But I should have known better." O'Connor didn't let this stop her. She eventually found work in a prosecutor's office. She served as an Arizona state senator from 1969 to 1974, and in 1974 she became a judge.

In 1981 President Ronald Reagan appointed O'Connor as the first female United States Supreme Court justice. She knew that this was important not only for herself but for women everywhere. "It's fine to be the first," she said, "but you really don't want to be the last. I felt a responsibility that if I took the job and did not do it adequately [well enough], it would have been a step backward for women."

BIOFACT

On June 7, 2002, Sandra Day O'Connor was inducted into the National Cowgirl Museum's Hall of Fame.

O'Connor had served on the Supreme Court for more than 20 years when she announced her retirement in 2005. She believes that the same determination and hard work that helped her as a child on the ranch have helped in her job as one of the country's most important judges. Her advice is:

"Do the best you can in every task, no matter how unimportant it may seem at the time. No one learns more about a problem than the person at the bottom."

Learning from Biographies

Why do you think Sandra Day O'Connor believed it was important to do a good job as the first woman on the Supreme Court?

For more information, go online to *Meet the People* at **www.sfsocialstudies.com**.

Becoming a United States Citizen

Alexander Graham Bell, inventor of the telephone. Madeleine Albright, the first woman named secretary of state. Actor Arnold Schwarzenegger. What do all of these people have in common? They all became naturalized United States citizens.

Throughout American history, immigrants have come to the United States in search of new and better opportunities. Suppose you are a legal immigrant to the United States. You have lived here for five years and decide that you want to become a citizen. In order to become a naturalized citizen you have to go through several steps.

First, if you don't already know English, you have to learn to read, write, and speak it. You also have to pass a test showing your knowledge of the government and history of the United States. Some of the questions you might be asked are "Who is the current chief justice of the United States Supreme Court?" or "What is the Legislative Branch of our government?"

Once you have passed the test, met the requirements, and completed the paperwork, it's time for the naturalization ceremony. The ceremony can take place in a courtroom, at a historic monument, in a sports arena, or in someone's home. You might be surrounded by 20 or 2,000 people. A federal judge leads the event. At the most important moment of the ceremony, you will be asked to raise your right hand and swear an oath of allegiance to the United States. After that, you will officially be a United States citizen, with all of its rights and responsibilities.

Oath of Allegiance
"I hereby declare, on oath, that . . . I will support and defend the Constitution and laws of the United States of America against all enemies . . . that I will bear true faith and allegiance to the same . . . and that I take this obligation freely . . . so help me God."

"I remember being very excited, but also a little scared. Because I did not know whether I would be accepted in this new land . . . I should not have worried. . . . We were . . . provided the chance to make new friends and build new lives in freedom. . . . I will forever be grateful."

Madeleine Albright, former secretary of state, speaking about her experience moving to the United States, at a naturalization ceremony, 2000

"The cheer that went up when all of us became U.S. citizens reverberated [echoed] around the hall. When I looked at the flag, it seemed much red, white, and bluer than before. . . . I cried."

Lorraine Toussaint, actress, on becoming a United States citizen, 2000

"Being an immigrant, the opportunity of serving in Congress . . . I really felt I had an opportunity to do my . . . best, not only on behalf of my constituents [people I represent], but for the millions of people who have been allowed to come to this country, to repay the freedom and opportunity we gained by becoming American citizens."

Tom Lantos, congressman from California, who became a naturalized citizen in 1953 and was later elected to the House of Representatives, 2000

Issues and You

Interview a naturalized citizen or research stories about naturalized citizens in the library or on the Internet. Using what you learn, write a paragraph explaining why people want to become citizens of the United States. What would you want to say to those who are becoming new citizens?

Boston

Economy and Trade

PREVIEW

Focus on the Main Idea
Technology has changed the ways people work, study, and play.

PLACES
Boston, Massachusetts

PEOPLE
An Wang

VOCABULARY
supply
demand
producer
opportunity cost
export
import
North American Free Trade
  Agreement
globalization
interdependence

Lemonade 25¢
Hot Chocolate 50¢

You Are There

Your after-school club is planning its annual fall fundraiser. You are all hoping for a good profit this year, so that your group can take an out-of-town trip. Last year your club raised money by selling drinks at ballgames. You noticed, however, that some drinks sold better than others. For example, early in the season when the weather was still warm, cold lemonade was the most popular drink. As the weather got cooler, hot chocolate became the most popular drink. You always ran out of lemonade in warm weather and hot chocolate in cool weather.

One of the members of your club suggests a way that the group can raise more money than last year. She suggests making more lemonade and charging more for it during warm weather. In cooler weather, she says, you should make more hot chocolate and charge more for it. How would this plan help the group make more money?

Cause and Effect As you read, look for causes and effects of recent changes in the United States economy.

Supply and Demand

Making and charging more for lemonade and hot chocolate at the times when they are most popular is an example of the rule of supply and demand. **Supply** is the amount of a product that is available. **Demand** is the amount of that product that people are willing to buy.

Producers, or people who make goods, usually set the prices that people pay for goods. People who buy goods are consumers. Producers can usually charge more for an item if there is a high demand for it. They can charge an even higher price if demand for the item is high, but the supply is limited.

This is what the cattle ranchers were able to do in the 1800s. As you learned in Chapter 3, people in the East wanted beef. Cattle was scarce there, so Southwestern ranchers were able to charge people in the East higher prices for beef.

When the rule of supply and demand affects one business, it can also help other businesses. For example, an increased demand for automobiles led to an increased demand for oil in the early 1900s. People who discovered oil during this time became rich. Why? The oil producers were meeting the demands created by the demand for automobiles. Oil producers would then create a demand for drilling equipment, and so on.

Supply and demand is one part of a free enterprise economy. However, running a successful business involves more than supply and demand. Business owners must also make smart decisions based on opportunity cost. The **opportunity cost** is the value of what must be given up in order to produce a certain good.

Suppose you hear that people really enjoy raspberry lemonade and there is a great demand for it. You decide to buy raspberries as well as lemons. Therefore, it will cost more to make the raspberry lemonade than it will to make the regular lemonade. This might mean you have to cut back on the amount of other drinks you supply, such as iced tea. This is the opportunity cost of making the raspberry lemonade.

REVIEW How does the system of supply and demand affect prices? **Cause and Effect**

▶ **Clearance signs are common when the supply of a product is higher than demand.**

Twenty-first Century Jobs

Have you thought about what kind of job you might want to have someday? The types of jobs that will be needed in the future might change for many reasons. That is why it is important to have a variety of skills that will help you in almost any job.

The free enterprise system has encouraged many new and exciting businesses to grow in the United States. In many cases new inventions have changed the job market. For example, in the late 1800s, the introduction of electricity led to growth in a variety of new businesses and jobs, from lighting manufacturers to electricians.

Computers had the same effect in the late 1900s and early 2000s. The fastest-growing jobs in the early twenty-first century are related to the computer industry. Such jobs include software engineers and computer help specialists. Computers are such an important part of life today that many jobs involve at least some computer skills.

Changes in the population can also affect what kinds of jobs will be needed in the future and who will fill those jobs. For example,

Five Fastest-Growing Job Types

1. Computer technology
2. Human health care
3. Social services
4. Veterinary medicine
5. Education

U.S. Bureau of Labor Statistics

▶ Computer technology is such a large industry partly because it affects almost every other industry.

CHART SKILL *Which of the industries listed in the table affect your daily life?*

thanks to improved health care, people are living longer than ever before. One of the fastest-growing groups of people in the country are those over the age of 65. Many of these people are not only continuing to work, but are also starting second and third careers after finishing their first. Former government official Donna Shalala described this change:

> *"We have transformed [changed] what it means to grow old in America. . . . The fact is: older Americans are now living not only longer but also better."*

With this change comes new job opportunities. After computers, the health care field is the fastest-growing area for jobs. Many of these jobs are focused on helping older Americans live better lives. The fastest-growing career not related to computers is personal and home care aides for people who have special physical needs.

REVIEW How have new inventions changed the types of jobs available to Americans? **Cause and Effect**

▶ These workers manufacturing computers are part of the country's fastest-growing industry.

Technology and Life

How many times have you used a type of technology today? Have you called someone on the telephone, ridden in a car or bus, watched television, or used the Internet? Electronic and computer technologies are important parts of daily life. Different kinds of technology have helped improve communication, transportation, medicine, and even sports.

Computer technology has not only changed the way we work, it has also changed how we learn and play. The Internet allows people quick access to all kinds of information, such as news and research. By 2001 more than half the people in the country were using the Internet. More than 90 percent of students between the ages of 5 and 17 were using computers.

Medical technology is developing rapidly as well. Tiny cameras can take pictures inside a person's heart. New machines can detect injuries or disease better than ever before. Disabled individuals have new tools to help them move, work, and communicate.

Space technology is also affecting our lives. The diagram below shows many different ways that space satellites help with communication. Satellites allow cellular telephones and pagers to work. Satellites take pictures of Earth to track weather changes. They also make satellite television and wireless Internet service possible. Satellites can even help you determine your location anywhere in the world with a Global Positioning System, or GPS. A GPS in a car can help you find your way on a trip.

In Chapter 7 you read how the radio helped create a common culture across the country. Recent technology has led to even more similarities among people in different regions. People from Alaska to Florida watch many of the same television programs, view the same Internet materials, and play the same computer games.

REVIEW How has technology caused a change in American culture?
Cause and Effect

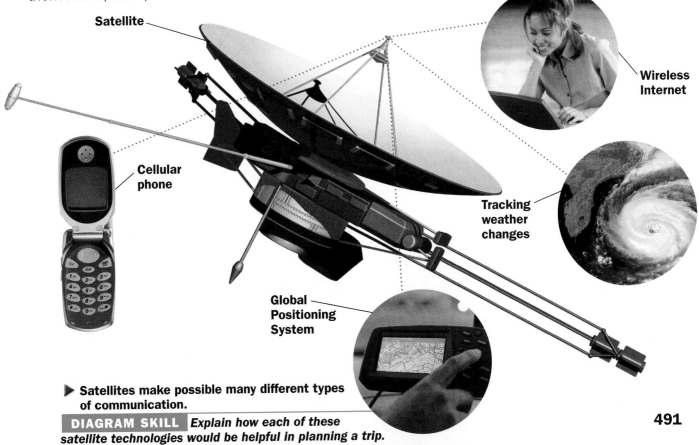

Satellite

Wireless Internet

Cellular phone

Tracking weather changes

Global Positioning System

▶ Satellites make possible many different types of communication.

DIAGRAM SKILL *Explain how each of these satellite technologies would be helpful in planning a trip.*

International Trade

Communication technology not only connects Americans to one another, but also to people around the world. In addition, international trade connects our economy to the economies of other countries. We are connected through the buying and selling of imports and exports. Goods that are sold to other countries are called **exports.** For example, the United States exports a lot of food to other countries. At the same time, the United States buys more cars from other countries than any other product. Goods that one country buys from another are called **imports.** Because of increased international trade, the populations of some port cities in the United States, such as Seattle, Washington, have increased. Imports and exports are shipped in and out of such cities.

As you read earlier, the United States and other countries have sometimes limited trade by placing tariffs on imports. At different times, some people have worried that too much trade could hurt businesses at home. Today the United States and most other countries encourage trade. This has led the United States to sign several trade agreements with other countries. For example, in 1992 the United States, Canada, and Mexico signed the **North American Free Trade Agreement** (NAFTA). This agreement allows the three countries to import and export with each other without having to pay taxes or fees.

REVIEW How have views on trade changed over the years? ◑ Summarize

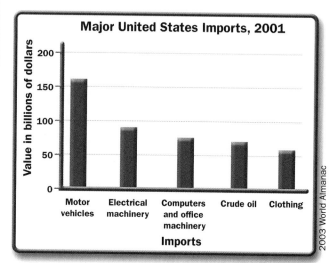

The United States receives most of its imports from Canada, Mexico, Japan, China, and Germany.

GRAPH SKILL *Does the United States import more electrical machinery or crude oil?*

A ship brings imported computer parts. The parts are loaded onto a truck.

The parts are delivered to the factory.

Globalization

Better transportation, new communication technology, and increased trade among countries have led to globalization. **Globalization** is the development of a world economic system in which people and goods move freely from one country to another. As a result of globalization, what happens to the economy in one country can affect the economies of other countries. This interaction is called **interdependence.**

One example of the effects of interdependence is what happened after the Cold War ended in 1991. China began to adopt a free enterprise system. Many new businesses were started. Companies in the United States began to make goods in China because wages are lower there. Companies and consumers in both China and the United States benefited, but many American workers lost their jobs when the factories moved.

Globalization affects culture as well. You have read that technology has spread a common culture across the United States. People all over the world also share more things than ever before. People often see the same movies, listen to the same music, and even dress alike. Places that once seemed far away to Americans are now visited for both business and vacations.

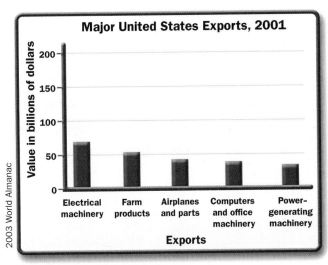

Major United States Exports, 2001

2003 World Almanac

▶ The United States sends most of its exports to Canada, Mexico, Japan, the United Kingdom, and Germany.

GRAPH SKILL *What is the major United States export?*

REVIEW What are some effects of interdependence and globalization? **Cause and Effect**

The completed computers leave the factory.

The computers are loaded onto a ship to be exported. The ship leaves with computers.

Technology and Change

What do you expect to be doing 50 years from now? The twenty-first century holds many possibilities. Sometimes all it takes is the effort of one person to develop new technology and create many new jobs.

In Chapter 4 you read how inventor Thomas Edison changed the United States with his inventions in the late 1800s. The same thing has happened during the computer age. In the 1950s inventor **An Wang** set up a laboratory in **Boston, Massachusetts.** Wang invented more than 35 items that were essential to the development of computer technology. You will read more about Wang in the Biography that follows this lesson.

What kind of inventions would you like to see that would change the world during your lifetime? Perhaps you could become the Thomas Edison or An Wang of the twenty-first century!

REVIEW What kinds of inventions do you think might cause changes in daily life in the twenty-first century? **Cause and Effect**

Summarize the Lesson

- Supply and demand determine prices in the free enterprise system.
- New technology has changed the way people work, communicate, learn, and play.
- International trade continues to grow.
- Interdependence and globalization make countries more connected than ever before.

LESSON 3 ⟨ REVIEW

Check Facts and Main Ideas

1. Cause and Effect On a separate sheet of paper, fill in the effect that you could expect based on the rule of **supply** and **demand.**

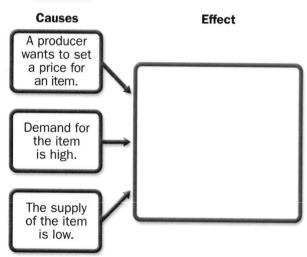

Causes

- A producer wants to set a price for an item.
- Demand for the item is high.
- The supply of the item is low.

Effect

2. What job fields are expected to grow the most during the early 2000s?

3. How does technology affect the way Americans live and work?

4. How has the United States government's policy on trade changed?

5. Critical Thinking: *Draw Conclusions* **Globalization** and international trade have created worldwide **interdependence.** Consider the advantages and disadvantages of this, and then write whether or not you think this is a positive trend and why.

Link to 〜∞〜 Mathematics

Analyze Graphs When a country imports more of a product than it exports, it has a trade deficit, or shortage, for that product. When it exports more of a product than it imports, it has a trade surplus. Look at the **import** and **export** graphs on pages 492 and 493. Which items appear on both graphs? About how much of a deficit or surplus does the United States have for these items?

An Wang
1920–1990

When An Wang immigrated to the United States from China in 1945, he was only twenty-five years old. Yet he had already experienced great tragedy. His parents and his sister had been killed during the Japanese invasion of China during World War II. Wang was working as an engineer for the Chinese government when it sent him to the United States to learn more about electronics. His journey to the United States seemed like the opportunity for a fresh start.

Within three years, Wang earned a doctorate degree in physics from Harvard University in Massachusetts. He decided to use his knowledge of electronics to start a business. In 1951, with only $600, Wang started a small company. His business grew as it became one of the first companies to develop and market calculators.

In the 1970s his company began developing computers and word processors. Wang invented technology that improved computer memory. His company became one of the biggest producers of word processors in the world. By 1986 Wang's business employed 30,000 people and sold more than $3 billion worth of products. When asked about his success, Wang talked about the importance of simplifying problems in order to find solutions.

BIOFACT

An Wang received the U.S. Medal of Liberty on July 3, 1986, at the relighting of the Statue of Liberty's torch. This award was given to 12 naturalized citizens who achieved great things.

> *"No matter how complicated a problem is, it usually can be reduced to a simple, comprehensible [understandable] form, which is often the best solution."*

Wang believed that it was very important to use his wealth to help others. He gave money to schools, art centers, and hospitals.

Learning from Biographies

An Wang started a business in electronics, an area that interested him. Based on your interests, what type of business might you like to start?

For more information, go online to *Meet the People* at **www.sfsocialstudies.com.**

Research and Writing Skills

Internet Research

What? Research is a way of gathering information to learn more about a subject. An increasingly useful tool for research is the Internet. The Internet is a worldwide network of computers linked together. Information on the Internet can be viewed and shared in onscreen pages called Web sites. A Web site can be set up by a company, school, government, or individual.

Why? Doing research on the Internet is often the way to find the most up-to-date information about a subject. Reference books and nonfiction books in the library also have useful information, but the Internet may have more information, or information that was updated after a book was printed.

Another reason to use the Internet is that most libraries cannot keep books on every subject. When you need to research a topic for which your library has little information, the Internet lets you use a larger computer-based library. It can also connect you to other students who may be researching the same topic or to homework-help programs.

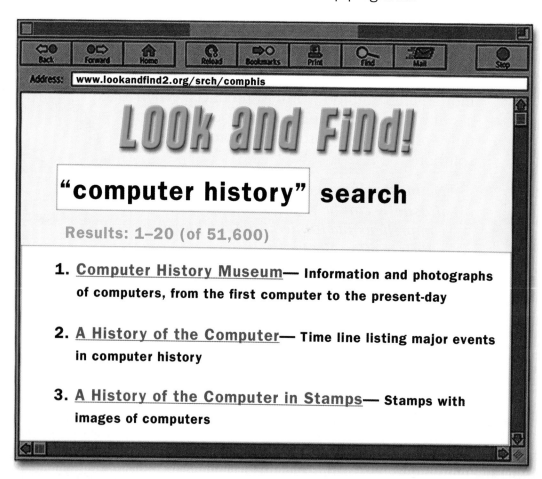

How? One of the quickest ways to find information on the Internet is to use a search engine. A search engine is a special Web site that locates other Web sites that can provide information about the topic you are researching.

You begin a search by typing in a word or phrase. Suppose you want to find out more about the history of computers. Type "computer history" in quotation marks in the search box. The quotation marks tell the search engine that the topic you want is a complete phrase. Look at page 496 to see some of the results that appeared in a search for "computer history."

Underlined words in color are links to other sites. If you click on a link, you can get more information about a specific topic. Because the search resulted in more than 50,000 sites, it is obvious that you are going to have to narrow down your choices. You may want to start with the Computer History Museum. Click on the link. It will bring up more

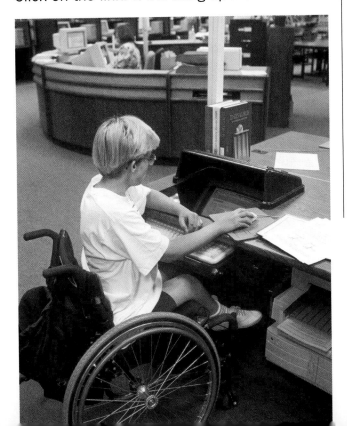

information on your topic. Look also for study information and school sites.

You can often print out information that you find on the Internet. Remember to keep the name of the Web site. It usually appears at the bottom of the page or in the address box at the top.

Keep in mind that not all Web sites offer reliable information. Encyclopedia Web sites are reliable. Nonprofit organizations have Web sites that end with *.org,* and their sites are usually reliable. Government sites, which end in *.gov,* have dependable information. School Web sites end with *.edu,* but you have to be careful with *.edu* sites, because often students can put reports on their school's Web site, and these may not be reliable. Also, remember what you've learned about telling fact from opinion when judging how dependable a Web site is.

Think and Apply

1. Look at the Web site list on page 496. Why are some words shown in color? What is special about them?

2. Which of the Web sites on the list is least likely to help you in you1r research? Why?

3. How would you find out more information about computer technology?

Internet Activity

For more practice in using the Internet, go online and explore **www.sfsocialstudies.com.**

CHAPTER 11
REVIEW

Chapter Summary

Summarize

On a separate sheet of paper, complete the graphic organizer by filling in three details from the chapter that support the summary.

There have been many important changes in the United States in recent years.

Vocabulary

Choose a word to complete each of the sentences that follow.

regions (p. 473)   **citizen** (p. 482)

ideals (p. 475)   **globalization** (p. 493)

democracy (p. 481)

1 In a ___, all people have a say in how the government is run.

2 People from many cultures live in the United States, but they share ___, or basic beliefs.

3 A ___ has both rights and responsibilities.

4 The United States is made up of five main geographic ___.

5 ___ means people and goods move freely from one country to another.

People and Terms

Write a sentence explaining why each of the following people or terms is important in the United States today. You may use two or more in a single sentence.

1 Sunbelt (p. 474)

2 ethnic group (p. 476)

3 electoral college (p. 483)

4 Executive Branch (p. 484)

5 Sandra Day O'Connor (p. 484)

6 supply (p. 489)

7 import (p. 492)

8 An Wang (p. 494)

Facts and Main Ideas

1 Why do more people move to other regions of the country today than ever before?

2 What is popular sovereignty?

3 **Main Idea** What are some ways people in the United States are different from one another? How are they the same?

4 **Main Idea** What is the role of each branch of the federal government?

5 **Main Idea** How has modern technology changed the kinds of jobs that people do?

6 **Critical Thinking:** *Compare and Contrast* How is a direct democracy different from a republic? What are the advantages and disadvantages of each system?

Write About History

1 **Write a letter** that a recent immigrant to the United States might write to his or her family back home.

2 **Write a commercial** encouraging people to vote in the next election.

3 **Write a paragraph** about an invention you would like to see in the twenty-first century. What would it do?

Apply Skills

Use the Internet for Research

Read the following paragraphs, written in the style of an Internet encyclopedia Web site. Then answer the questions.

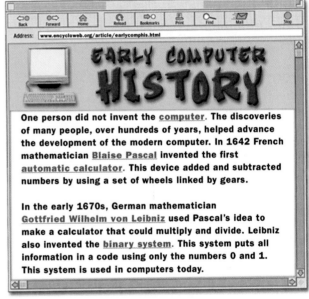

EARLY COMPUTER HISTORY

One person did not invent the underlined computer. The discoveries of many people, over hundreds of years, helped advance the development of the modern computer. In 1642 French mathematician Blaise Pascal invented the first automatic calculator. This device added and subtracted numbers by using a set of wheels linked by gears.

In the early 1670s, German mathematician Gottfried Wilhelm von Leibniz used Pascal's idea to make a calculator that could multiply and divide. Leibniz also invented the binary system. This system puts all information in a code using only the numbers 0 and 1. This system is used in computers today.

1 Why are some words shown in color and underlined?

2 What would happen if you clicked on the underlined words?

3 What other search words could you use to find more information about this topic?

Internet Activity

To get help with vocabulary, people, and terms, select dictionary or encyclopedia from *Social Studies Library* at **www.sfsocialstudies.com**.

499

Global Challenges

2001

New York, New York
Americans unite after
terrorists attack the
United States.

Lesson 1

1

200?

United States
What does the future hold?

Lesson 2

2

Why We Remember

Every day, history is being made all around us. New technologies and medical discoveries are improving the lives of people in all parts of the world. Spacecraft are being sent farther and farther from Earth to help us learn more about other planets. New challenges faced by the United States and other countries will change our lives in ways we can't predict. What does the future hold for the United States and the rest of the world? What will your role be in the twenty-first century?

AFGHANISTAN

IRAQ

2000　　　　　　　　　　　　　　　2005

September 11, 2001
Terrorists attack the United States.

October 2001
The United States attacks terrorist bases in Afghanistan.

March 2003
The war in Iraq begins.

December 2004
A tsunami devastate Southeast Asia.

New Dangers

PREVIEW

Focus on the Main Idea
Americans united in response to the terrorist attacks of September 11, 2001.

PLACES
Afghanistan
Iraq

PEOPLE
Rudolph Giuliani
George W. Bush
Osama bin Laden
Saddam Hussein
Condoleezza Rice
Daniel Libeskind

VOCABULARY
terrorist
weapons of mass destruction

▶ Proceeds from the sale of these buttons were used to aid students affected by the September 11, 2001, attacks.

United We Stand

You Are There
You used to think of history as something that happened a long time ago. Most of the events you have read about in history class took place many years before you were born. Now you know that major historical events can take place in your lifetime. The date is September 12, 2001.

Yesterday the United States was attacked by terrorists. Today people all over the country are responding. You and other students from school are collecting donations of food, clothing, and money to help victims of the attacks. Adults are standing in line at the hospital waiting to give blood. Everywhere you look you see American flags hanging in the windows of stores and homes. This is a frightening time. But it feels good to see how people are pulling together.

Summarize As you read, think about ways to summarize the events of September 11, 2001, and the ways Americans responded to these events.

September 11, 2001

Think about the most famous dates in American history. You know that members of the Continental Congress approved the Declaration of Independence on July 4, 1776. You know that Japan attacked Pearl Harbor on December 7, 1941, drawing the United States into World War II. Do you also think of September 11, 2001, as a famous date? On that day, terrorists carried out a massive attack against the United States. **Terrorists** are people who use violence and fear to try to achieve their goals.

Early in the morning on September 11, a group of terrorists hijacked, or used force to take over, four airplanes. The airplanes were on their way from the Northeast to cities in California, and were carrying a total of 264 people. After they took over the airplanes, the terrorists flew two of the airplanes to New York City. They crashed these two planes into the twin towers of the World Trade Center, New York's two tallest buildings. These two 110-story buildings were completely destroyed.

The terrorists crashed a third plane into the Pentagon, a huge office building that is the headquarters of the Department of Defense. The Pentagon is located in Virginia, just outside of Washington, D.C. The fourth hijacked plane crashed in a field in Pennsylvania. It is believed that the passengers tried to retake control of the plane from the terrorists. This action probably prevented the terrorists from crashing the plane into another important building, perhaps the White House or the United States Capitol.

More than 3,000 people were killed in the attacks of September 11. The victims included people from more than 90 different countries. Most of the deaths occurred at the World Trade Center in New York City, where more than 2,800 people were killed.

REVIEW Why is September 11, 2001, one of the most famous dates in American history? ↻ Summarize

▶ **Before the terrorist attacks (*below left*), the twin towers of the World Trade Center rose high above New York City. After the attacks (*below right*), the city's skyline was changed forever.**

Before

After

Americans United

The American people responded to the attacks of September 11 with courage and caring. Moments after the attacks, New York City firefighters, police officers, and rescue workers raced to the World Trade Center. These heroes rushed into the burning buildings and guided thousands of people to safety. Many of them died saving the lives of others.

All over the country, people lined up to give blood to help those injured in the attacks. Millions of people of all ages donated food,

clothing, and money. Firefighters from cities and towns all over the United States jumped into their trucks and drove to New York City to help with the rescue effort.

Rudolph Giuliani (joo lee AH nee) was the mayor of New York City in 2001. He praised Americans for pulling together, saying,

"New Yorkers, and all Americans, have united as never before. Inspired by countless examples of courage and generosity, we have met the worst of humanity with the best of humanity. The darkest day in our long history has led to our finest hour."

▶ **New York City Mayor Rudolph Giuliani, New York Governor George Pataki, President George W. Bush, New York Senator Charles Schumer, and New York City Fire Commissioner Thomas Van Essen toured ruins of the World Trade Center on September 14, 2001.**

President **George W. Bush** also expressed hope for the future. In a speech on September 20, he said, "As long as the United States of America is determined and strong, this will not be an age of terror. This will be an age of liberty here and across the world." By standing together, Americans made it clear that they were determined and strong.

Another unfortunate event brought Americans together to help those in need. On December 26, 2004, an undersea earthquake in the Indian Ocean created a tsunami that devastated countries in Southeast Asia. In response, the American people gave more than one billion dollars to help victims and their families.

Americans also helped victims of Hurricanes Katrina and Rita, which devastated the Gulf Coast from Alabama to Louisiana in 2005. The hurricanes caused extensive flooding and property damage and forced many people to leave the area. Many Americans helped rebuild the area after the storm.

REVIEW How did Americans respond to the terrorist attacks of September 11, 2001? **Main Idea and Details**

FACT FILE

Heroes Help Others

After the events of September 11, 2001, the Asian tsunami disaster, and Hurricanes Katrina and Rita, Americans showed their concern by helping those in need.

Rescue workers carried people injured by Hurricane Katrina to nearby hospitals and treatment facilities for help.

This search dog, named Porkchop, needed medical care after helping find victims at the World Trade Center.

These students performed at the Kids of Hope Tsunami Relief Gala on April 21, 2005, in California. The event helped raise money for tsunami victims.

505

The Struggle Against Terrorism

The United States determined that the attacks of September 11 were planned by a terrorist group called al Qaeda (al KEYE dah). Headed by **Osama bin Laden,** a terrorist from Saudi Arabia, al Qaeda had carried out many deadly attacks in the past. Several of the attacks were aimed at American targets, such as United States embassies and ships. Al Qaeda opposed American influence in Southwest and Central Asia.

Since 1997 al Qaeda had been based in the Asian nation of **Afghanistan.** The United States demanded that the government of Afghanistan capture bin Laden and other al Qaeda leaders. But the group controlling the government of Afghanistan, the Taliban (TAH le bahn), refused. The Taliban was a group that denied many rights to its people, especially to women. President Bush and Congress decided to take military action.

On October 7, 2001, United States forces began attacking Taliban troops and al Qaeda training bases in Afghanistan. Afghanis who opposed the Taliban also joined the fight. In December 2001 the Taliban government surrendered. Some al Qaeda terrorists were captured. Others, including Osama bin Laden, escaped. Working with the United Nations, the United States began helping Afghanistan rebuild and establish a new, democratic government.

REVIEW Why did the United States use force against the Taliban? *Cause and Effect*

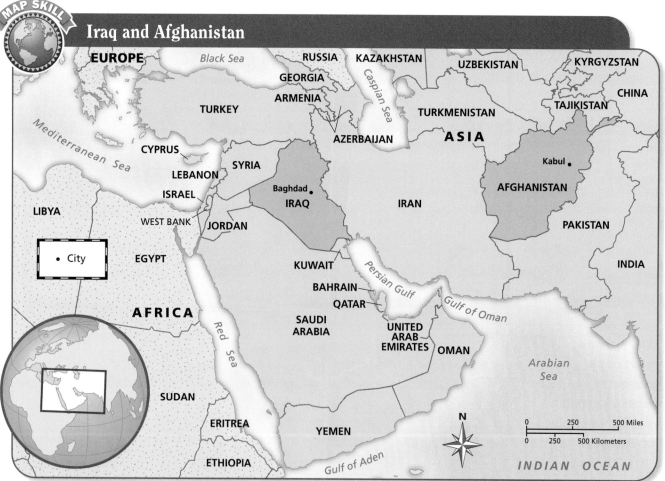

MAP SKILL

Iraq and Afghanistan

EUROPE

Black Sea

RUSSIA

KAZAKHSTAN

UZBEKISTAN

KYRGYZSTAN

GEORGIA

Caspian Sea

CHINA

ARMENIA

TURKMENISTAN

TAJIKISTAN

TURKEY

AZERBAIJAN

ASIA

Mediterranean Sea

CYPRUS

SYRIA

Kabul

LEBANON

Baghdad

AFGHANISTAN

ISRAEL

IRAQ

IRAN

LIBYA

WEST BANK

JORDAN

PAKISTAN

• City

EGYPT

KUWAIT

Persian Gulf

INDIA

BAHRAIN

Gulf of Oman

QATAR

AFRICA

Red Sea

SAUDI ARABIA

UNITED ARAB EMIRATES

OMAN

Arabian Sea

SUDAN

N

ERITREA

YEMEN

0   250   500 Miles

0   250   500 Kilometers

ETHIOPIA

Gulf of Aden

INDIAN OCEAN

▶ The United States military became involved in conflicts in the Asian countries of Iraq and Afghanistan in the early 2000s.

MAP SKILL Location *What country lies between Iraq and Afghanistan?*

War in Iraq

President Bush told the American people that the fighting in Afghanistan was just the beginning of a long, difficult war against terrorists around the world. The United States continued trying to find and capture members of al Qaeda.

President Bush also considered taking military action against **Saddam Hussein,** the dictator of **Iraq.** You read that Iraq invaded Kuwait in 1990, leading to the Persian Gulf War. As part of the agreement that ended this war, Saddam Hussein promised to destroy Iraq's weapons of mass destruction. **Weapons of mass destruction** include nuclear weapons and weapons that spread poison chemicals or deadly diseases. Hussein agreed to let experts from the United Nations inspect Iraq to make sure these weapons were destroyed.

Hussein did not continue to cooperate with the United Nations. For many years, he refused to allow inspectors into Iraq. When he was forced to admit inspectors, they could not determine if Iraq still had weapons of mass destruction. Leaders in the Bush administration argued that military force should be used to remove Hussein from power. National Security Advisor **Condoleezza Rice** said, "Saddam Hussein with nuclear, chemical, or biological weapons will be a threat to his people, his neighbors, and to us."

▶ **American troops attacked Iraq in March 2003.**

Leaders of many countries agreed that Hussein should be stopped, but leaders in some countries did not believe war was necessary. They wanted to give United Nations inspectors more time.

Seventy countries believed that it was necessary to remove Saddam Hussein from power, and 30 of these countries offered to help. The United States and Great Britain led a coalition force, or united group of military troops, from many of these countries into Iraq. On March 20, 2003, American forces began bombing Baghdad, the capital of Iraq. Coalition forces quickly defeated the Iraqi army. As in Afghanistan, after war, rebuilding began.

REVIEW Describe the two sides of the argument over going to war in Iraq.
Compare and Contrast

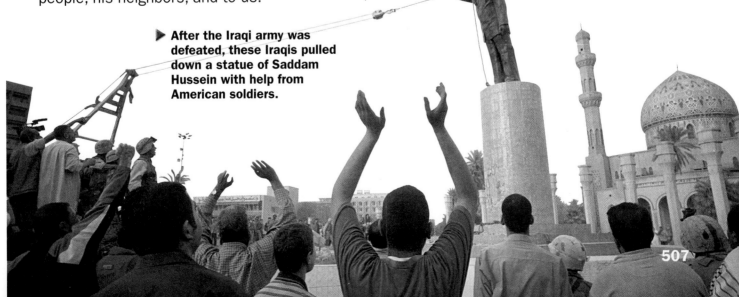

▶ **After the Iraqi army was defeated, these Iraqis pulled down a statue of Saddam Hussein with help from American soldiers.**

507

Rebuilding at Home

As the war on terrorism continued overseas, Americans worked to recover from the 2001 attacks. After September 11, 2001, New York City Mayor Rudolph Giuliani said, "This terrorist attack was intended to break our spirit. It has utterly [completely] failed." Americans immediately began to repair the damage done by the attacks. By September 2002, workers had repaired the damaged section of the Pentagon.

At the World Trade Center, workers removed more than 100,000 truckloads of broken steel and concrete. People started thinking about what should be built at the World Trade Center site. In the Biography, you will read about **Daniel Libeskind** (LEE bes kind) and his design for the new buildings.

The U.S. government also changed in response to September 11, 2001. In 2003

Tom Ridge became the first head of a new government department called the Department of Homeland Security. One of this department's main jobs is to protect the United States from the threat of terrorism. He stepped down from the position in 2004. Michael Chertoff became the second head of the department in 2005.

REVIEW What steps did Americans take to rebuild the damage done by the September 11 attacks? ⟳ Summarize

Summarize the Lesson

- **September 11, 2001** Terrorists attacked the United States, killing more than 3,000 people.
- **October 2001** United States forces attacked terrorist bases in Afghanistan.
- **March 2003** The war in Iraq begins.

LESSON 1 REVIEW

Check Facts and Main Ideas

1. ⟳ Summarize Complete this chart on a separate sheet of paper. Fill in the most important details from this lesson and then fill in a summary of the details.

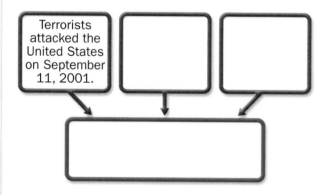

2. Summarize the **terrorist** attacks of September 11, 2001.

3. In what ways did Americans unite in response to the attacks?

4. What military actions did the United States take after September 11, 2001?

5. **Critical Thinking: *Analyze Primary Sources*** You read that New York City Mayor Rudolph Giuliani said of the September 11 attack: "This terrorist attack was intended to break our spirit. It has utterly failed." What evidence could be used to support this statement?

Link to ⟨∞⟩ Art

Design New Skyscrapers Architects created many different designs for the new buildings at the site of the World Trade Center in New York City. What do you think the new buildings should look like? Create your own drawing of the new buildings.

Daniel Libeskind
1946–

Daniel Libeskind was born in Poland in 1946. His parents had survived World War II but were still afraid of the continuing anti-Semitism in Poland. When Daniel was 11, his family left Poland and moved to Israel for two years, and then to New York City. He never forgot how arriving in the United States made him feel. "Our greatest feeling here was a total feeling of liberation from oppression [unjust power] and difficulties," he said.

Later, Libeskind became an architect. He has designed many buildings around the world, including the Jewish Museum in Berlin, Germany. Libeskind always felt a connection to New York City. After terrorists attacked the twin towers of the World Trade Center on September 11, 2001, he wanted to help rebuild the city. He said, "I was determined to do something. I felt personally attacked." In 2003 Libeskind's plan was chosen as part of the new design for the World Trade Center site.

His design includes a tower that is 1,776 feet tall, honoring the year the United States declared independence. It will be the tallest building in the world. The site will also have a memorial park set below street level, exposing some of the original building's walls that survived the attacks. He says of his design:

BIOFACT

The first television program ever shown in Poland included Daniel Libeskind, at the age of 6, playing the accordion!

"It's the story of New York. The story of the tragedy which happened, how, from the depths of what befell [happened to] New York, a city rises into a pinnacle [high point] of optimism and reaffirms [says again] what it is, what it always was, what it will be."

Learn from Biographies

Why do you think Libeskind felt such a connection to New York City?

For more information, go online to *Meet the People* at **www.sfsocialstudies.com.**

CITIZEN HEROES

Racing to the Rescue

On a day of terrifying attacks, the heroic actions of New York City firefighters saved thousands of lives.

New York City's Ladder Company 21 has a long history of fighting fires and saving lives. When the company was first formed in 1890, firefighters rushed to fires on a truck pulled by three horses. Today Ladder Company 21 uses computers and modern trucks. But some things have not changed. Firefighting is still a dangerous job that requires great courage. This is why New Yorkers have nicknamed the city's firefighters "New York's Bravest."

On the morning of September 11, 2001, terrorists crashed two planes into New York's World Trade Center. The call for help went out to fire stations all over the city. At Ladder Company 21, Benjamin Suarez was one of many firefighters who were just finishing a 24-hour shift. But Suarez did not even think about leaving the job. He called his wife and said,

"I have to help the people."

Then he and his fellow firefighters jumped on their trucks and raced to the scene of the attacks.

As firefighters arrived from around the city, they saw that the twin towers of the World Trade Center were on fire. They rushed into the buildings and up the stairs. "We saw them going up the stairs as we were going down," said a woman who escaped from one of the towers. The firefighters helped people who were injured or lost in the smoke. With the firefighters' help, thousands of people escaped to safety.

BUILDING CITIZENSHIP

Caring
Respect
Responsibility
Fairness
Honesty
⭐ Courage

Not everyone survived, however. About 3,000 people were trapped in the buildings when they collapsed. More than 300 firefighters, including Benjamin Suarez, died while saving the lives of others. Like so many heroes on that terrible day, Suarez put the desire to help other people ahead of his own safety. "That's what Benny was about," said Captain Michael Farrell of Ladder Company 21.

In the days following the terrorist attacks, neighbors visited Ladder Company 21 to show their sympathy for the firefighters who had lost their lives. Many people left flowers and made donations to the firefighters' families. Children wrote letters in which they thanked firefighters for saving lives. Some children drew pictures showing firefighters performing brave actions. The firefighters hung these letters and pictures on the wall of the fire station. Similar scenes took place at fire stations all over the city.

Rudolph Giuliani, the mayor of New York City, thanked firefighters for their incredible courage:

> *"Without courage, nothing else can really happen. And there is no better example, none, than the courage of the Fire Department of the City of New York."*

New York's firefighters not only saved thousands of lives, their actions inspired the entire nation. In a time of fear and danger, firefighters helped Americans have the courage to face the difficult times ahead.

Courage in Action

Link to Current Events Every day, firefighters, police officers, and other rescue workers perform heroic acts in communities all over the nation. Read a newspaper from your community to find out about the recent actions of your local firefighters or other emergency workers. What actions did they take? How did these actions show courage?

2020 — 2100

2020
Will hydrogen-powered cars become common?

2050
Will computers be able to think like humans?

2100
Will humans build colonies on Mars?

PREVIEW

Focus on the Main Idea
In the United States and around the world, people are working to develop new technologies and find new solutions to the challenges facing our world.

PEOPLE
Jimmy Carter

VOCABULARY
atmosphere
global warming
artificial intelligence

Looking Ahead

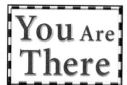
You Are There

"We have spent most of the year learning about the past," your social studies teacher tells the class. "Now let's think about the future. Suppose someone from the year 2055 came to visit our classroom. And suppose you could each ask her just one question about life in 2055. What question would you ask?"

A bunch of questions quickly come to your mind. What kinds of cars will people drive in the future? Will we build computers that are able to think like human beings? Will scientists figure out how to cure most diseases? Will humans build a colony on the moon or on Mars? These are all good questions. It is going to be hard to pick just one!

▶ This rover was designed by NASA to explore Mars.

Main Idea and Details As you read this lesson, form your own list of questions about the future.

Protecting the Environment

Over the past 100 years, people have learned more and more about how human activities affect our environment. Think about why this is very important knowledge. We need to use natural resources for everything from powering cars and computers to growing food and building homes. At the same time, we rely on clean air, water, and soil to live healthy lives. So it makes sense to use resources in ways that do not harm the environment. Finding new ways to do this will be one of the main challenges of the future.

The way we produce and use energy helps make this issue more clear. Look at the graph on this page, which shows the sources of energy people use in the United States today. Each source of energy affects the environment in a different way. Nuclear power, for example, produces waste that must be stored very carefully for centuries. Burning gasoline and coal produces gases, including carbon dioxide.

Scientists are now investigating the long-term effects of the increase of carbon dioxide in our atmosphere. An **atmosphere** is the mass of gases that surround a planet. Some scientists think that the increase of carbon dioxide is leading to a slow warming

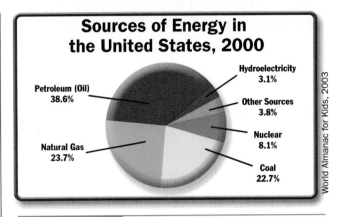

Sources of Energy in the United States, 2000

Petroleum (Oil) 38.6%
Hydroelectricity 3.1%
Other Sources 3.8%
Nuclear 8.1%
Coal 22.7%
Natural Gas 23.7%

World Almanac for Kids, 2003

GRAPH SKILL *What is the largest energy source used in the United States?*

of the global climate. This is known as **global warming.** Global warming might cause environmental problems around the world.

Will new sources of energy help us avoid problems such as global warming? In 2003 President George W. Bush watched a demonstration of cars that are designed to run on hydrogen. Cars that run on hydrogen fuel would not produce air pollution. This technology is too expensive for everyday use right now, but you will be hearing more about this story in the coming years. As President Bush told the audience at the hydrogen car demonstration, "I don't know if you and I are going to be driving one of these cars, but our grandkids will."

REVIEW Why are some scientists concerned about rising levels of carbon dioxide in our atmosphere? ⟳ Summarize

▶ **This car runs on hydrogen fuel, which is safer for the environment than gasoline.**

513

Global Solutions

Did you know that in the year 2000 there were more than one billion people in the world who were living on less than $1 a day? This is a problem known as extreme poverty. It is one of several global challenges—problems facing people around the world.

Other global challenges include hunger, war, and the lack of freedom. Disease is also a problem that harms people all over the world. Malaria, which is spread by mosquitoes, causes more than two million deaths each year. Most malaria cases occur in poor countries in Africa. Acquired Immunodeficiency Syndrome, or AIDS, also affects millions of people. AIDS is a deadly disease that attacks people's immune systems. Scientists are working on new medicines to fight diseases such as malaria and AIDS.

Citizens, organizations, and governments are all working to find solutions to global challenges. Members of the United Nations have made a list of "Development Goals." These are goals that the countries of the world hope to achieve by the year 2015.

One of these goals is to end extreme poverty and hunger. Another goal is to end the spread of malaria, AIDS, and other diseases. The United States has pledged billions of dollars to help in the fight against AIDS, hunger, and other global challenges.

Former United States President **Jimmy Carter** is one of many people working to help make these goals a reality. In 2002 Carter was awarded the Nobel Peace Prize for his work fighting disease and supporting free elections around the world. When he accepted the Nobel Prize, Carter said, "I am not here as a public official, but as a citizen of a troubled world who finds hope in a growing consensus [agreement] that the generally accepted goals of society are peace, freedom, human rights, environmental quality, the alleviation [relief] of suffering, and the rule of law."

REVIEW Describe the "Development Goals" of the United Nations. 🔄 Summarize

▶ **Volunteers like this doctor *(below left)* in the African country of Ethiopia and this teacher *(below right)* in the Central American country of Costa Rica help children from poor countries all over the world.**

FACT FILE

Challenges of the Twenty-first Century

You have read about many of the challenges the United States has faced in its history. What challenges will Americans face in the future?

▶ The United States and Russia were enemies during the Cold War, but now we cooperate in exploring space. What discoveries will be made in outer space?

▶ Computers have made it easier to share information and keep in touch with people all over the world. How will computers and the Internet continue to change our lives?

▶ Scientists have given new hope to people with serious injuries or life-threatening diseases. What medical discoveries will improve lives in the future?

▶ As the world changes, the United States and its allies prepare to face new kinds of threats. Do you think nations will fight different kinds of wars than they have in the past?

▶ Because of over-hunting, the blue whale population has decreased. Will future generations be able to save this and other animals from dying out completely?

Looking Forward

Think about some of the ways that life changed during the past 100 years. Jet airplanes made it possible to travel across oceans in just hours instead of weeks. New medicines improved our health and even increased people's life spans. Computers and the Internet changed the way people work and communicate. At the end of the twentieth century, Michio Kaku made this bold prediction about the next 100 years:

> *"The next century will witness an even more far-reaching scientific revolution."*

Kaku is a scientist and professor at the City University of New York. He based his prediction on the work that he and other scientists are doing right now. For example, scientists at the University of Southern California are working on computer chips that may be able to help people with brain damage.

At the Massachusetts Institute of Technology and other universities, scientists are working to build machines with artificial intelligence. A machine with **artificial intelligence** would have the ability to learn and to imitate human thought.

Scientists at the National Aeronautics and Space Administration, or NASA, are working on new types of space vehicles that can be used to explore Mars. By the year 2014, NASA hopes to have a spacecraft that can travel to Mars to collect samples of Martian rocks and soil and bring them back to Earth!

Then and Now

Visions of the Future

For many centuries, people have tried to predict what life in the future would be like. Here is one artist's vision of a city of the future. What kinds of buildings do you think we will see in the future?

Do you have your own ideas about life in the future? For example, what do you think will be the most important invention of this century? Will new medicines allow most people to live more than 100 years? Will we find new ways to conserve resources and protect our environment? Do you think we will succeed in ending terrorism and stopping war?

In the future, you will do more than think about these questions. You and your classmates will be the ones who will help answer them. And the answers you find may well be in the history books studied by students in the future.

REVIEW What is one question you have about the future? Add a question of your own to the questions above.
Main Idea and Details

Summarize the Lesson

- Finding ways to meet our needs while protecting the environment will continue to be an important challenge in the future.

- The effort to solve global problems such as poverty, disease, and lack of freedom continues.

- Scientists are working on new technologies that will change life in the future.

LESSON 2   REVIEW

Check Facts and Main Ideas

1. **Main Idea and Details** Complete this chart on a separate sheet of paper. Fill in details that support the main idea shown below.

> Individuals, organizations, and countries are working to solve global problems and improve life in the future.

2. If hydrogen cars become practical, how could they help prevent **global warming?**

3. Describe three global problems that people are working to solve.

4. What are three projects that scientists are working on today?

5. **Critical Thinking:** *Predict* Reread the list of questions in the text at the top of the page. Pick one of these questions, or write a question of your own about the future. Then write a one-page essay in which you answer this question with your own predictions about the future.

Link to ⌘⌘ **Writing**

Look Toward the Future What do you think is the most important challenge facing the United States today? Write a one-page essay describing this challenge. Explain what you can do to help meet this challenge.

Make Generalizations

What? The United States is taking steps to protect Earth's environment. This statement is a generalization of facts you read in Lesson 2. It is based on specific examples such as the search for new sources of energy and the effort to try and reduce global warming. A **generalization** is a broad statement or idea about a subject. It explains the way different facts might share an important idea in common.

Why? Generalizations are useful because they help you see similarities between ideas and facts that may seem unrelated at first. Generalizations let you take many facts and ideas and put them into an easy-to-remember statement. They can also help you understand new information about a topic. For example, learning about how the United States is protecting the environment can help you understand some of the future goals of the country that you might read about in other sources.

▶ **This public bus in California is powered by clean-burning fuel, including hydrogen fuel cells.**

How? To make a generalization, you need to identify the topic and gather facts about the topic. Next, determine what all the different information has in common. Finally, come up with one general statement that is true for all, or nearly all, of the information. Be sure that you test your generalization, and list facts that support it.

To practice making generalizations, read the passage below about the use of hydrogen fuel cells to power cars. Make a list of the facts. Then compare all of the information you have gathered and write a one-sentence statement describing what all of the facts have in common.

Think and Apply

1 What are the advantages of using hydrogen fuel cells?

2 What are the disadvantages of using hydrogen fuel cells?

3 Write a sentence that is a generalization of the information in this passage.

The United States and other countries are working on an invention that could change the way you travel to places in the future and protect the environment at the same time—the hydrogen-powered car. This is how it works. Hydrogen fuel cells power cars by turning hydrogen and oxygen into electricity, which in turn powers the motor of a car. Instead of filling a car with gasoline, you would fill the fuel tank with hydrogen.

There are many advantages in using hydrogen to power cars. For one, there is no pollution from exhaust or fumes. The only thing hydrogen-powered cars produce is water. You could even drink the water, if you really wanted to!

Another advantage is a reduction in the amount of oil countries would need. For example, 55 percent of the oil used in the United States comes from other countries. Today Americans use about 20 million barrels of oil a day. In 2003 President Bush said, "If we develop hydrogen power to its full potential, we can reduce our demand for oil by over 11 million barrels per day." This would mean a cleaner environment and less dependence on other countries for oil.

However, there are also disadvantages to using hydrogen fuel cells. Hydrogen is four times more expensive to produce than gasoline. This makes hydrogen cars more expensive to run. Car manufacturers and scientists are working on ways to make hydrogen fuel cells in cars and buses less expensive.

Internet Activity

For more information, go online to Current Events at **www.sfsocialstudies.com.** Select the *Science* link and look for *Environment*.

The Future and Technology

The technology of tiny microprocessors has made possible a computer industry that only a few years ago was unimaginable. For example, powerful hand-held computers can be linked to satellites to provide e-mail and Internet access. In the future, computer parts will get even smaller.

Magnetic Travel

This High-Speed Surface Transport uses magnets instead of wheels to travel. A high-strength magnetic field enables it to glide over the monorail track at speeds over 125 miles per hour.

Cutting out the Middleman

The need for film processing is now a thing of the past. Digital cameras record images directly onto a special card, which is downloaded onto a computer for viewing.

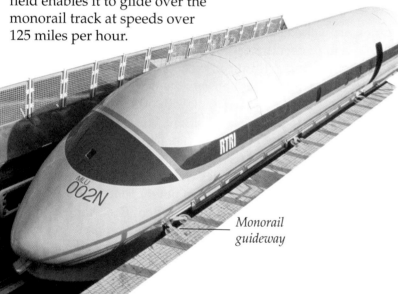

Monorail guideway

Alarm clock

Touch-pad controls

Foldaway screen

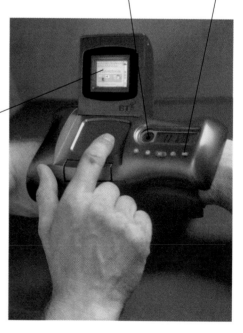

Office on the Arm

This technological advance, called the "office on the arm," will allow people to work at any time in any location. It will be powered by plugging it in to an outlet, by batteries, or by a special vest worn by the user that converts body heat into electricity to run the system.

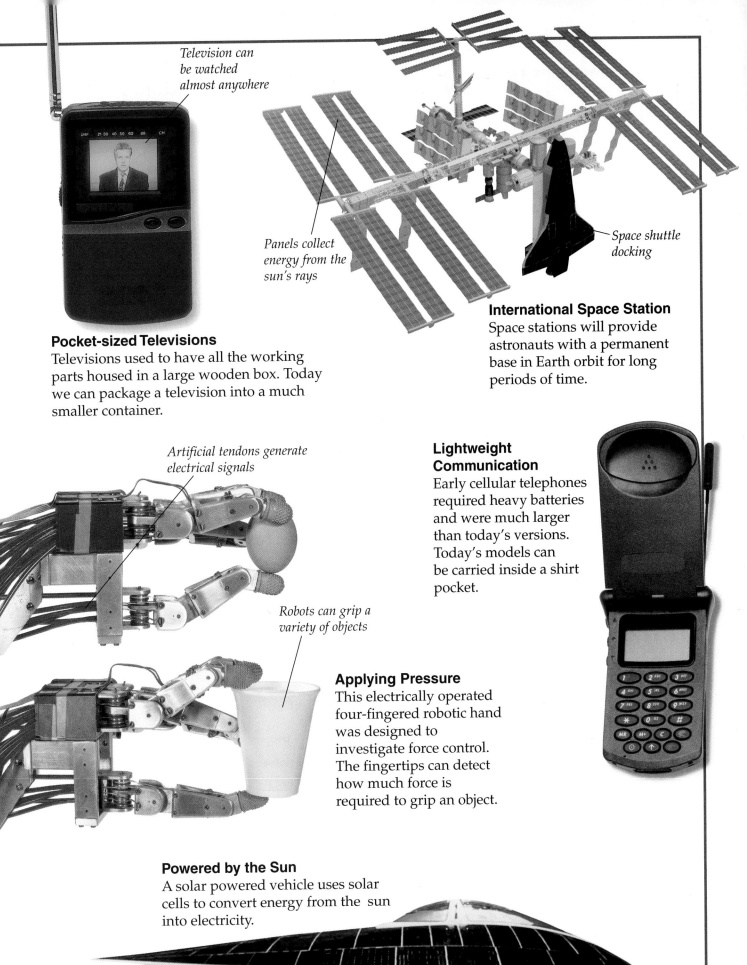

Television can be watched almost anywhere

Pocket-sized Televisions

Televisions used to have all the working parts housed in a large wooden box. Today we can package a television into a much smaller container.

Panels collect energy from the sun's rays

Space shuttle docking

International Space Station

Space stations will provide astronauts with a permanent base in Earth orbit for long periods of time.

Artificial tendons generate electrical signals

Lightweight Communication

Early cellular telephones required heavy batteries and were much larger than today's versions. Today's models can be carried inside a shirt pocket.

Robots can grip a variety of objects

Applying Pressure

This electrically operated four-fingered robotic hand was designed to investigate force control. The fingertips can detect how much force is required to grip an object.

Powered by the Sun

A solar powered vehicle uses solar cells to convert energy from the sun into electricity.

2001

September 11, 2001
Terrorists attack
the United States.

October 2001
The United States
attacks terrorist
bases in
Afghanistan.

Chapter Summary

Summarize

On a separate sheet of paper, complete the graphic organizer by filling in three details from the chapter that support the summary.

The United States has already faced major challenges in the early 2000s, and there will be new ones in the future.

Vocabulary

On a separate sheet of paper, write **T** for each sentence that correctly defines the underlined term and **F** for each definition that is false. If false, rewrite the definition so it is correct.

1 <u>Terrorists</u> try to achieve their goals by using violence and fear. (p. 503)

2 Tanks and land mines are examples of <u>weapons of mass destruction</u>. (p. 507)

3 The <u>atmosphere</u> is the mass of gases that surround a planet. (p. 513)

4 Some scientists think <u>global warming</u> is caused by the spread of mosquitoes. (p. 513)

5 A machine with <u>artificial intelligence</u> can imitate human thought but cannot learn. (p. 516)

People and Places

Match each person or place with the correct description.

1 **Rudolph Giuliani** (p. 504)

2 **George W. Bush** (p. 505)

3 **Afghanistan** (p. 506)

4 **Iraq** (p. 507)

5 **Condoleezza Rice** (p. 507)

6 **Jimmy Carter** (p. 514)

a. won the Nobel Peace Prize in 2002

b. President during September 11, 2001, attacks

c. country that would not cooperate with weapons inspectors

d. country in which the United States forced the Taliban to surrender

e. national security advisor

f. mayor of New York City

September 2002
Repairs completed on
section of Pentagon
destroyed by terrorists

March 2003
The war in Iraq
begins.

Facts and Main Ideas

1 How did Americans respond to the September 11 attacks on the United States?

2 What is al Qaeda?

3 What are some inventions scientists are working on for the twenty-first century?

4 **Time Line** How long did it take to repair the Pentagon after the terrorist attacks?

5 **Main Idea** Why did the United States take military action against Iraq in 2003?

6 **Main Idea** How can hydrogen cars help conserve the environment?

7 **Critical Thinking:** *Draw Conclusions* Why is it important for the United States to help meet global challenges such as hunger and disease?

Write About History

1 **Write a diary entry** that you would have written on September 12, 2001. How did you feel about the terrorist attacks? What would you like to do to help?

2 **Write an advertisement** encouraging people to donate canned foods to the food drive your school has organized to help people who are hungry.

3 **Write a news story** about the United States attack on Afghanistan in 2001.

Apply Skills

Make Generalizations

Read the following newspaper article about collecting samples from Mars. Then answer the questions that follow.

Preparing for Mars Samples
By Suzy Smith

Scientists believe the first samples from the rocks and soil of Mars could be brought to Earth as early as 2014. They hope that the samples will help us learn more about the environments of distant planets and could even help us learn more about our own planet. But they urge the United States government to start preparing for the arrival of the samples now. They say it will take a lot of time and money to create a special laboratory where the samples will not be affected by our environment and will not harm our environment. Scientists are excited about the possibility of finding living organisms in the samples. However, they want to make sure they are prepared in case anything in the samples might be harmful to people or the environment.

1 How might Mars samples help scientists?

2 What problems might Mars samples cause?

3 Write a sentence that is a generalization of the information in this article.

Internet Activity

To get help with vocabulary, people, and terms, select the dictionary or encyclopedia from *Social Studies Library* at **www.sfsocialstudies.com**.

End with a Song

The American flag has inspired artists and writers for more than two hundred years. In the early 1900s, American song-writer George M. Cohan wrote his own tribute to the flag. Read the words to "You're a Grand Old Flag." What was Cohan saying about the American flag and the nation it represents?

You're a Grand Old Flag

Words and Music by George M. Cohan

You're a grand old flag, you're a high - fly - ing flag;

And for - ev - er in peace may you wave;

You're the em - blem of the land I love,

The home of the free and the brave.

Ev - 'ry heart beats true un - der red, white, and blue,

Where there's nev - er a boast or brag;

But should auld ac - quaint - ance be for - got,

Keep your eye on the grand old flag.

Main Ideas and Vocabulary

TEST PREP

Read the passage below and use it to answer the questions that follow.

The nation's 50 states are grouped into five major regions based on geographical and cultural features. More than ever, Americans move from one region to another, often to find new jobs.

The United States is a <u>democracy</u>. Americans have both rights and responsibilities. Many of our basic rights are protected by the Constitution. They include the right to freedom of speech and freedom of religion. Participating in government is one of the responsibilities of American citizenship.

The Constitution set up the three branches of the federal government—the Legislative, Judicial, and Executive Branches. The United States Constitution has been called a "living document," because it is able to change over time.

On September 11, 2001, terrorists attacked the United States. Americans worked together to help the victims and their families. The United States attacked the countries of Afghanistan and Iraq as part of the war against terrorism.

The United States will face many other challenges in the future. One challenge will be conserving the environment. Some scientists are concerned that pollution of the atmosphere is causing <u>global warming</u>. New technology, such as hydrogen cars, may help.

1 In the passage, the word <u>democracy</u> means a
- **A** system in which few citizens have the right to vote
- **B** political party
- **C** system in which all people have a say in how the government works
- **D** region of the United States

2 The United States Constitution
- **A** cannot be changed.
- **B** set up the American government and can be changed over time.
- **C** set up the American government and does not guarantee rights to citizens.
- **D** set up four branches of government and guarantees rights to citizens.

3 According to the passage, how did the United States respond to the September 11 attacks?
- **A** The United States took military action against terrorists.
- **B** Americans did nothing to help citizens affected by the attacks.
- **C** A new amendment was added to the Constitution.
- **D** The United States surrendered to terrorists.

4 In the passage, the term <u>global warming</u> means—
- **A** the gases that surround a planet
- **B** a worldwide rise in temperature
- **C** the warming of climate caused by new hydrogen cars
- **D** a decrease in air pollution

Test Talk

Is your answer complete, correct, and focused?

People and Terms

Match each person and term to its definition.

1. **Esmeralda Santiago** (p. 477)

2. **popular sovereignty** (p. 481)

3. **interdependence** (p. 493)

4. **Saddam Hussein** (p. 507)

5. **Daniel Libeskind** (p. 508)

6. **artificial intelligence** (p. 516)

a. a system in which the people rule

b. an architect whose design will be used for the new buildings at the World Trade Center site

c. the former dictator of Iraq

d. what happens in one country can affect other countries

e. writer of *When I was Puerto Rican*

f. a machine's ability to learn and to imitate human thought

Apply Skills

Use Internet Skills for Research Choose one of the topics you have read about in Unit 6, such as international trade agreements or global warming. Use an Internet search engine to find out more information on the topic you have chosen. Remember to look for reliable sites such as those for encyclopedias or those that end in *.gov* or *.org*. Be sure to write down or print out the address of each Web site you use. Make a list of three new things you have learned about your topic using the Internet, and then share your list with the class.

Write and Share

Write a Speech The government of the United States depends on the participation of its citizens. Any American citizen born in the United States who is at least 35 years old and has lived in the country for at least fourteen years can run for President. But what if you could run for President right now? Write a campaign speech in which you try to convince others to elect you as President of the United States. Read your speech aloud to the class.

Read on Your Own

Look for these books in the library.

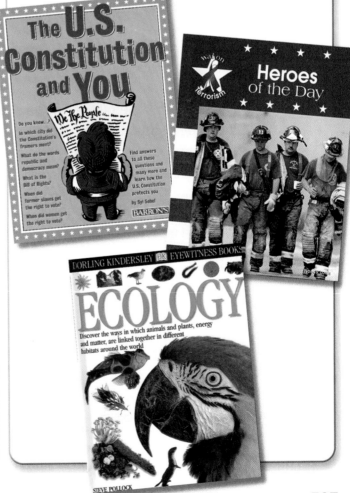

UNIT 6 Project

Explore a Business

Healthy businesses are good for the economy. Make your own presentation about a product or a business.

1 **Form** a group. Choose a product or a business.

2 **Research** the product or business and write a list of facts about it.

3 **Write** a script for a presentation about the product or business. Include the value and cost, as well as the history of the product or business. Give examples of its successes. Tell how it contributes to the economy.

4 **Make** an advertisement on a poster or banner to use in your presentation.

5 **Present** your business or product to the class.

Internet Activity

Explore events and issues in the United States. Go to **www.sfsocialstudies.com/activities** and select your grade and unit.

A Visual Introduction

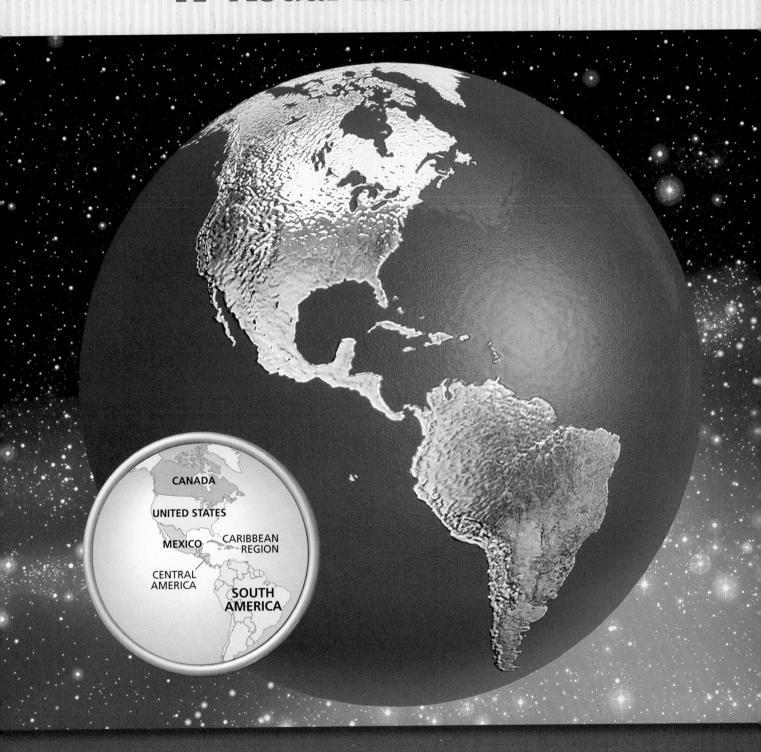

CANADA

UNITED STATES

MEXICO — CARIBBEAN REGION

CENTRAL AMERICA

SOUTH AMERICA

Who are our neighbors in the Western Hemisphere?

Canada

Capital
Ottawa

Population
31,278,097

Area
3,851,800
square miles

Official languages
English, French

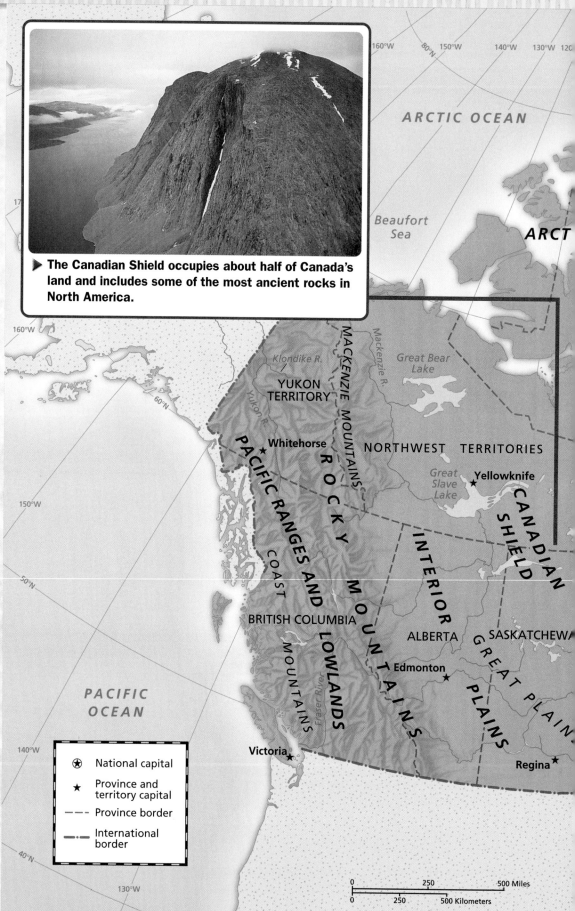

▶ The Canadian Shield occupies about half of Canada's land and includes some of the most ancient rocks in North America.

ARCTIC OCEAN

Beaufort Sea

ARCT

Great Bear Lake

Klondike R.

YUKON TERRITORY

MACKENZIE MOUNTAINS

Mackenzie R.

NORTHWEST TERRITORIES

Whitehorse ★

Yukon R.

Great Slave Lake

Yellowknife ★

CANADIAN SHIELD

ROCKY MOUNTAINS

PACIFIC RANGES AND LOWLANDS

COAST MOUNTAINS

INTERIOR

BRITISH COLUMBIA

MOUNTAINS

ALBERTA

SASKATCHEWA

Fraser River

Edmonton ★

GREAT PLAIN

PACIFIC OCEAN

Victoria ★

Regina ★

160°W
80°N
150°W
140°W
130°W
120

160°W
60°N
150°W
50°N
140°W
40°N
130°W

⊛	National capital
★	Province and territory capital
---	Province border
-·-	International border

0   250   500 Miles

0   250   500 Kilometers

90°W 80°W

ICELAND

20°W

20°W

Ellesmere
Island

Ellesmere Island is the northernmost area of
Canada and is close to the North Pole.

30°W

ISLANDS

Davis Strait

N

The Bay of Fundy has great
differences between high and
low tides. High tides have been
recorded more than 50 feet
above low tide.

40°W

50°N

NUNAVUT

Iqaluit

NEWFOUNDLAND AND LABRADOR

Hudson
Bay

Caniapiscau River

St. John's

HUDSON BAY
LOWLANDS

CANADIAN

SHIELD

QUEBEC

APPALACHIAN REGION

Gulf of
St. Lawrence

ST. PIERRE AND
MIQUELON (FR.)

MANITOBA

PRINCE EDWARD
ISLAND

50°W

Lake
Winnipeg

Albany River

LAURENTIAN MTS.

Charlottetown

ONTARIO

Quebec

NEW
BRUNSWICK
Fredericton

Halifax

Winnipeg

Ottawa R.

NOVA
SCOTIA

40°N

Lake Superior

Ottawa

St. Lawrence R.

Bay
of
Fundy

ATLANTIC
OCEAN

Lake
Huron

ST. LAWRENCE
LOWLANDS

Lake Michigan

Toronto

Lake Ontario

Lake Erie

531

UNITED STATES

70°W

60°W

Canada History

1896
Gold is discovered near Klondike River in present-day Yukon Territory.

1974
French is named Québec's official language.

1867
British North American Act establishes the Dominion of Canada.

40,000 to 10,000 years ago
People cross from Asia to North America.

1763
The Treaty of Paris gives Canada to Britain and expels France from much of North America.

| 1000 | 1200 | 1400 | 1600 | 1800 | 2000 |

1000
Viking explorers reach Newfoundland.

1608
Samuel de Champlain founds Québec City.

1885
Canada completes a transcontinental railroad.

1931
Canada is proclaimed a self-governing Dominion within the British Empire.

1999
Inuit land becomes new territory of Nunavut.

2003
Vancouver is selected to host the 2010 Olympic Winter Games.

Canada Today

▶ Iqaluit (ih cah LOO it) is the capital and largest community in the newly created territory of Nunavut (NOO nuh voot).

▶ Canada's natural beauty makes it a favorite place for vacations.

▶ Toronto is Canada's largest city.

Read on Your Own

Look for books like these in the library.

United States

Mexico

Capital
Mexico City

Population
100,349,766

Area
761,600
square miles

Official language
Spanish

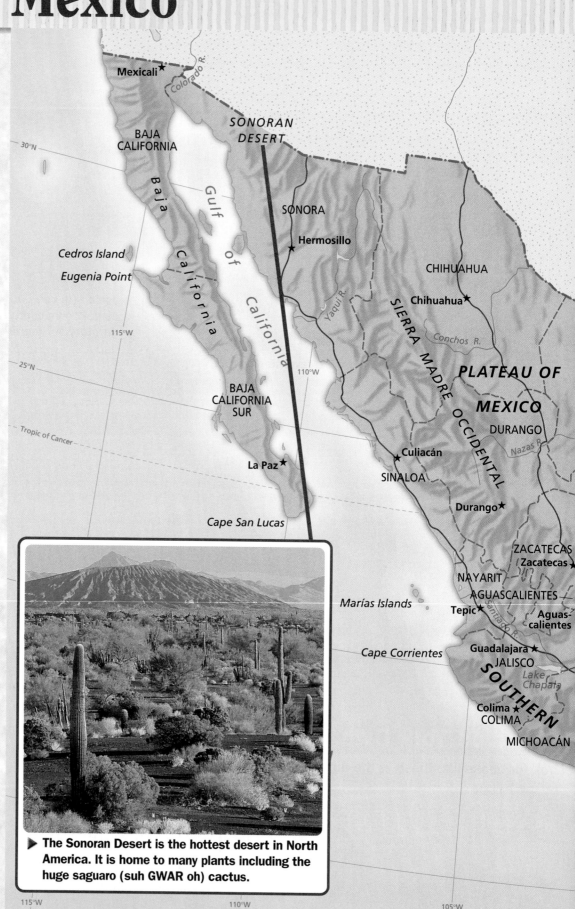

Mexicali

Colorado R.

BAJA
CALIFORNIA

SONORAN
DESERT

30°N

Baja
California

Gulf
of
California

SONORA

Hermosillo

Cedros Island

Eugenia Point

115°W

Yaqui R.

CHIHUAHUA

Chihuahua

SIERRA MADRE OCCIDENTAL

Conchos R.

25°N

110°W

PLATEAU OF
MEXICO

DURANGO

BAJA
CALIFORNIA
SUR

Nazas R.

Tropic of Cancer

Culiacán

SINALOA

La Paz

Durango

Cape San Lucas

ZACATECAS
Zacatecas

NAYARIT
AGUASCALIENTES

Marías Islands

Tepic

Aguas-
calientes

Cape Corrientes

Guadalajara
JALISCO

Lake
Chapala

SOUTHERN

Colima
COLIMA

MICHOACÁN

▶ **The Sonoran Desert is the hottest desert in North America. It is home to many plants including the huge saguaro (suh GWAR oh) cactus.**

115°W

110°W

105°W

▶ The volcano Orizaba (oh ree SAH bah) is the highest point in Mexico, at over 18,400 feet.

▶ The rain forests of the Yucatán (YOO cah tahn) Peninsula are home to many people and a variety of animals and plants.

30°N

CUBA

COAHUILA

SIERRA MADRE ORIENTAL

Río Grande
Río Bravo del Norte
Salado R.

NUEVO LEÓN
★ Monterrey

Saltillo ★

TAMAULIPAS

Ciudad Victoria ★

GULF COASTAL PLAIN

SAN LUIS POTOSÍ
★ San Luis Potosí

GUANAJUATO
★ Guanajuato
QUERÉTARO
★ Querétaro
HIDALGO
★ Pachuca
★ Morelia
México City
Toluca ★
MÉXICO D.F.
Cuernavaca ★
MORELOS
TLAXCALA
★ Tlaxcala
Puebla ★
PUEBLA
VERACRUZ
Pico de Orizaba
★ Jalapa Enríquez

Cuitzeo
Balsas River

UPLANDS
SIERRA MADRE DEL SUR
★ Chilpancingo
GUERRERO
Oaxaca ★
OAXACA Tuxtla Gutiérrez ★

Pan-American Highway

Gulf of Tehuantepec

Isthmus of Tehuantepec

CHIAPAS

CHIAPAS HIGHLANDS

GUATEMALA

Bay of Campeche

Campeche ★

TABASCO
Villahermosa ★

Grijalva R.

25°N

Tropic of Cancer

Yucatán Channel

★ Mérida
YUCATÁN

YUCATÁN PENINSULA

Cozumel Island

20°N

QUINTANA ROO
Chetumal ★

CAMPECHE

BELIZE

Gulf of Honduras

HONDURAS

85°W

95°W
90°W
100°W
95°W

N

535

Mexico History

1862
Mexicans defeat French in what is today celebrated as Cinco de Mayo.

2000
One-party rule ends with the election of President Vicente Fox Quesada.

1821
Mexico wins independence from Spain.

1300	1400	1500	1600	1700	1800	1900	2000

1325
Aztecs establish Tenochtitlan as the center of their empire.

1519–1521
Spanish conquistador Hernando Cortés conquers Aztecs and establishes Mexico City at site of Tenochtitlan.

1848
War between Mexico and United States results in Mexico's loss of land.

1910–1920
Mexican Revolution ends dictatorship and begins government reforms.

2003
About 21 million people live in or around Mexico City.

536

Mexico Today

▶ Densely populated Mexico City, the country's capital, is one of the largest cities in the world.

▶ Almost every city, town, and village in Mexico has a market, like this one in Chiapas, where farmers sell or trade their goods.

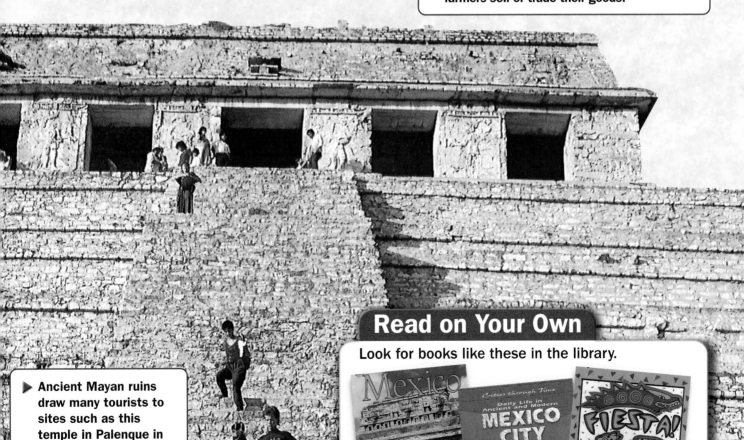

▶ Ancient Mayan ruins draw many tourists to sites such as this temple in Palenque in the state of Chiapas.

Read on Your Own

Look for books like these in the library.

Mexico

Cities through Time
Daily Life in Ancient and Modern
MEXICO CITY
by Steve Corey
illustrations by Kazu Webb

FIESTA!
Mexico's Great Celebrations
Elizabeth Silverthorne

537

The Countries of
Central America

Gulf of Mexico

92°W

MEXICO

BELIZE
⊛ Belmopan

Usumacinta River

SIERRA MADRE

GUATEMALA

Motagua River

Ulua

Guatemala City ⊛

San Salvador ⊛
EL SALVADOR

Belize	Capital	Belmopan
	Population	249,183
	Area	8,900 square miles
	Language	English

Costa Rica	Capital	San José
	Population	3,710,558
	Area	19,700 square miles
	Language	Spanish

El Salvador	Capital	San Salvador
	Population	6,122,515
	Area	8,100 square miles
	Language	Spanish

Guatemala	Capital	Guatemala City
	Population	12,639,939
	Area	42,000 square miles
	Language	Spanish

Honduras	Capital	Tegucigalpa
	Population	6,249,598
	Area	43,300 square miles
	Language	Spanish

Nicaragua	Capital	Managua
	Population	4,812,569
	Area	49,998 square miles
	Language	Spanish

Panama	Capital	Panama City
	Population	2,808,268
	Area	30,200 square miles
	Language	Spanish

▶ The Belize (buh LEEZ) Barrier Reef is the second-largest coral reef in the world, running for 180 miles across Belize's coast.

Read on Your Own

Look for books like these in the library.

Costa Rica
Enchantment of the

CULTURES OF THE WORLD
GUATEMALA

CULTURES OF THE WORLD
EL SALVADOR

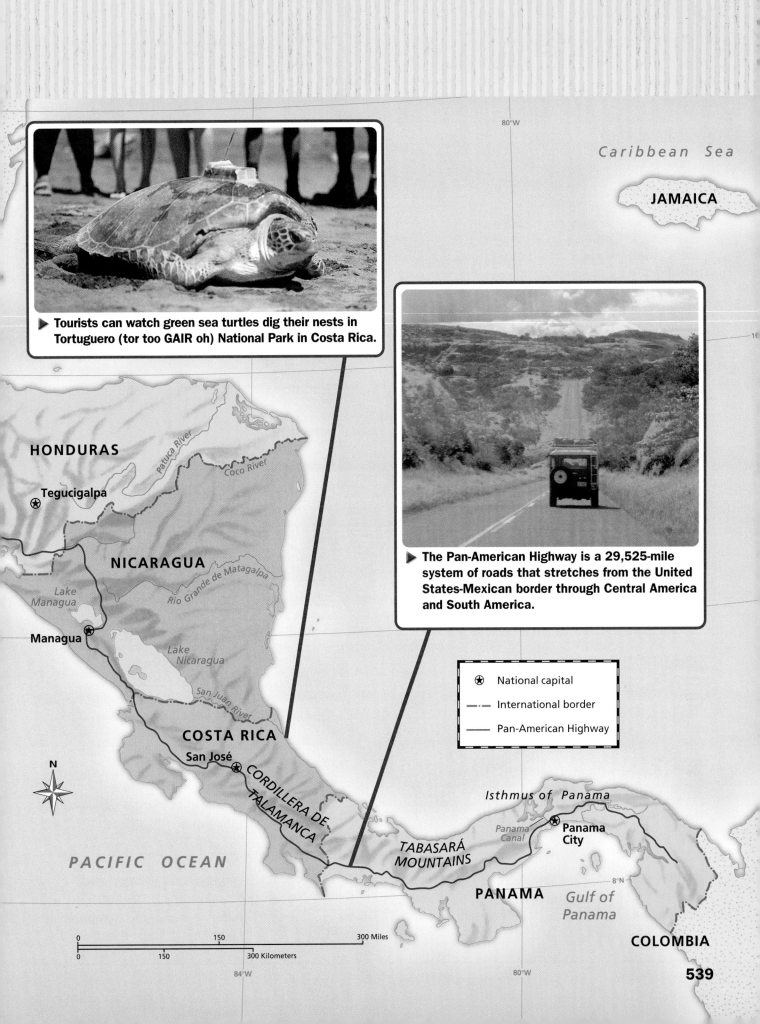

Tourists can watch green sea turtles dig their nests in Tortuguero (tor too GAIR oh) National Park in Costa Rica.

The Pan-American Highway is a 29,525-mile system of roads that stretches from the United States-Mexican border through Central America and South America.

Caribbean Sea

JAMAICA

HONDURAS

Tegucigalpa

Patuca River

Coco River

NICARAGUA

Lake Managua

Managua

Rio Grande de Matagalpa

Lake Nicaragua

San Juan River

COSTA RICA

San José

CORDILLERA DE TALAMANCA

PACIFIC OCEAN

N

Isthmus of Panama

Panama Canal

Panama City

TABASARÁ MOUNTAINS

PANAMA

Gulf of Panama

8°N

COLOMBIA

National capital
International border
Pan-American Highway

| 0 | | 150 | | 300 Miles |
| 0 | 150 | | 300 Kilometers | |

80°W

84°W

80°W

The Countries of the Caribbean Region

Antigua and Barbuda

Capital	Saint John's
Population	66,464
Area	170 square miles
Language	English

The Bahamas

Capital	Nassau
Population	294,982
Area	5,400 square miles
Language	English

Barbados

Capital	Bridgetown
Population	274,059
Area	170 square miles
Language	English

Cuba

Capital	Havana
Population	11,141,997
Area	42,800 square miles
Language	Spanish

Dominica

Capital	Roseau
Population	71,540
Area	300 square miles
Language	English

Dominican Republic

Capital	Santo Domingo
Population	8,442,533
Area	18,800 square miles
Language	Spanish

Grenada

Capital	Saint George's
Population	89,312
Area	130 square miles
Language	English

Haiti

Capital	Port-au-Prince
Population	6,867,995
Area	10,700 square miles
Languages	Haitian Creole, French

Jamaica

Capital	Kingston
Population	2,652,689
Area	4,200 square miles
Language	English

Puerto Rico (U.S.A.)

Capital	San Juan
Population	3,889,507
Area	3,508 square miles
Languages	Spanish, English

St. Kitts and Nevis

Capital	Basseterre
Population	38,819
Area	104 square miles
Language	English

St. Lucia

Capital	Castries
Population	156,260
Area	240 square miles
Language	English

St. Vincent and the Grenadines

Capital	Kingstown
Population	115,461
Area	130 square miles
Language	English

Trinidad and Tobago

Capital	Port-of-Spain
Population	1,175,523
Area	2,000 square miles
Language	English

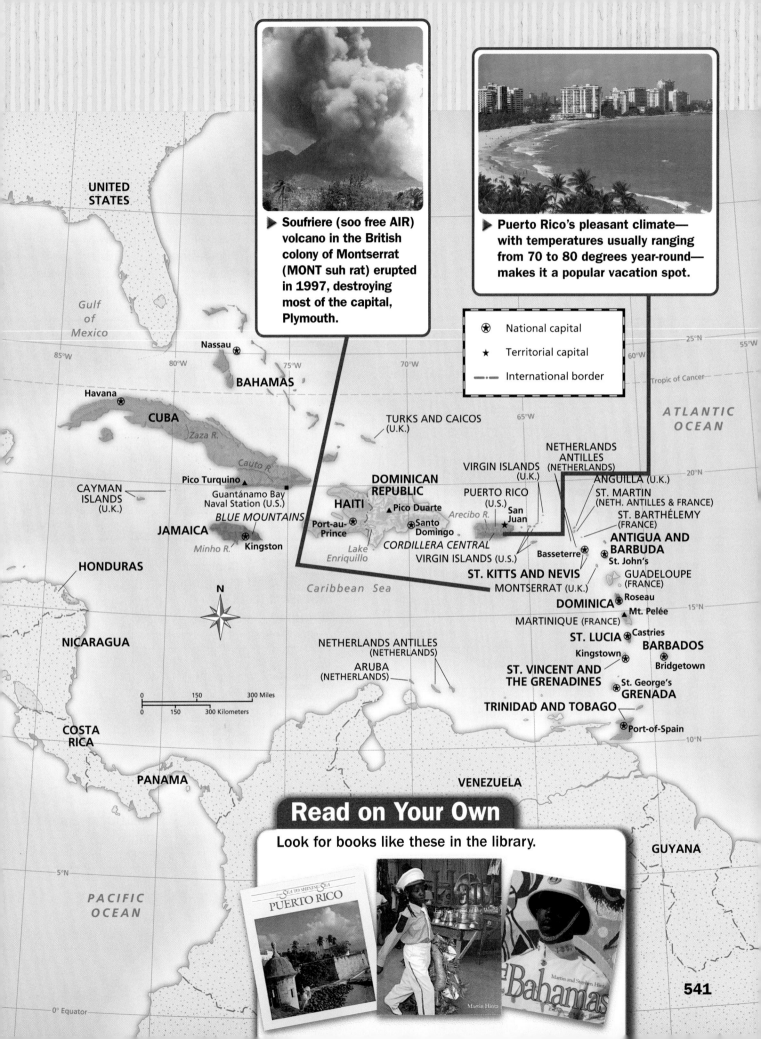

Soufriere (soo free AIR) volcano in the British colony of Montserrat (MONT suh rat) erupted in 1997, destroying most of the capital, Plymouth.

Puerto Rico's pleasant climate—with temperatures usually ranging from 70 to 80 degrees year-round—makes it a popular vacation spot.

National capital
Territorial capital
International border

UNITED STATES

Gulf of Mexico

Nassau

BAHAMAS

Havana

CUBA

Zaza R.

Cauto R.

CAYMAN ISLANDS (U.K.)

Pico Turquino

Guantánamo Bay Naval Station (U.S.)

BLUE MOUNTAINS

JAMAICA

Minho R.

Kingston

HONDURAS

N

Caribbean Sea

NICARAGUA

0   150   300 Miles
0   150   300 Kilometers

COSTA RICA

PANAMA

PACIFIC OCEAN

TURKS AND CAICOS (U.K.)

DOMINICAN REPUBLIC

HAITI

Pico Duarte

Port-au-Prince

Lake Enriquillo

Santo Domingo

CORDILLERA CENTRAL

VIRGIN ISLANDS (U.S.)

ST. KITTS AND NEVIS

MONTSERRAT (U.K.)

NETHERLANDS ANTILLES (NETHERLANDS)

ARUBA (NETHERLANDS)

VIRGIN ISLANDS (U.K.)

PUERTO RICO (U.S.)

Arecibo R.

San Juan

Basseterre

ATLANTIC OCEAN

NETHERLANDS ANTILLES (NETHERLANDS)

ANGUILLA (U.K.)

ST. MARTIN (NETH. ANTILLES & FRANCE)

ST. BARTHÉLEMY (FRANCE)

ANTIGUA AND BARBUDA

St. John's

GUADELOUPE (FRANCE)

DOMINICA

Roseau

Mt. Pelée

MARTINIQUE (FRANCE)

ST. LUCIA

Castries

BARBADOS

Kingstown

Bridgetown

ST. VINCENT AND THE GRENADINES

St. George's

GRENADA

TRINIDAD AND TOBAGO

Port-of-Spain

VENEZUELA

GUYANA

Tropic of Cancer

Equator

Read on Your Own

Look for books like these in the library.

PUERTO RICO

Bahamas

541

The Countries of
South America

Argentina

Capital	Buenos Aires
Population	36,955,182
Area	1,068,300 square miles
Language	Spanish

Guyana

Capital	Georgetown
Population	697,286
Area	83,000 square miles
Language	English

Bolivia

Capital	La Paz and Sucre
Population	8,152,620
Area	424,200 square miles
Languages	Spanish, Quechua, Aymara

Paraguay

Capital	Asunción
Population	5,585,828
Area	157,000 square miles
Language	Spanish

Brazil

Capital	Brasília
Population	172,860,370
Area	3,286,478 square miles
Language	Portuguese

Peru

Capital	Lima
Population	27,012,899
Area	496,200 square miles
Languages	Spanish, Quechua

Chile

Capital	Santiago
Population	15,153,797
Area	292,300 square miles
Language	Spanish

Suriname

Capital	Paramaribo
Population	431,303
Area	63,000 square miles
Language	Dutch

Colombia

Capital	Bogotá
Population	39,685,655
Area	439,700 square miles
Language	Spanish

Uruguay

Capital	Montevideo
Population	3,334,074
Area	68,000 square miles
Language	Spanish

Ecuador

Capital	Quito
Population	12,920,092
Area	109,500 square miles
Language	Spanish

Venezuela

Capital	Caracas
Population	23,542,649
Area	352,100 square miles
Language	Spanish

French Guiana (France)

Capital	Cayenne
Population	172,605
Area	33,399 square miles
Language	French

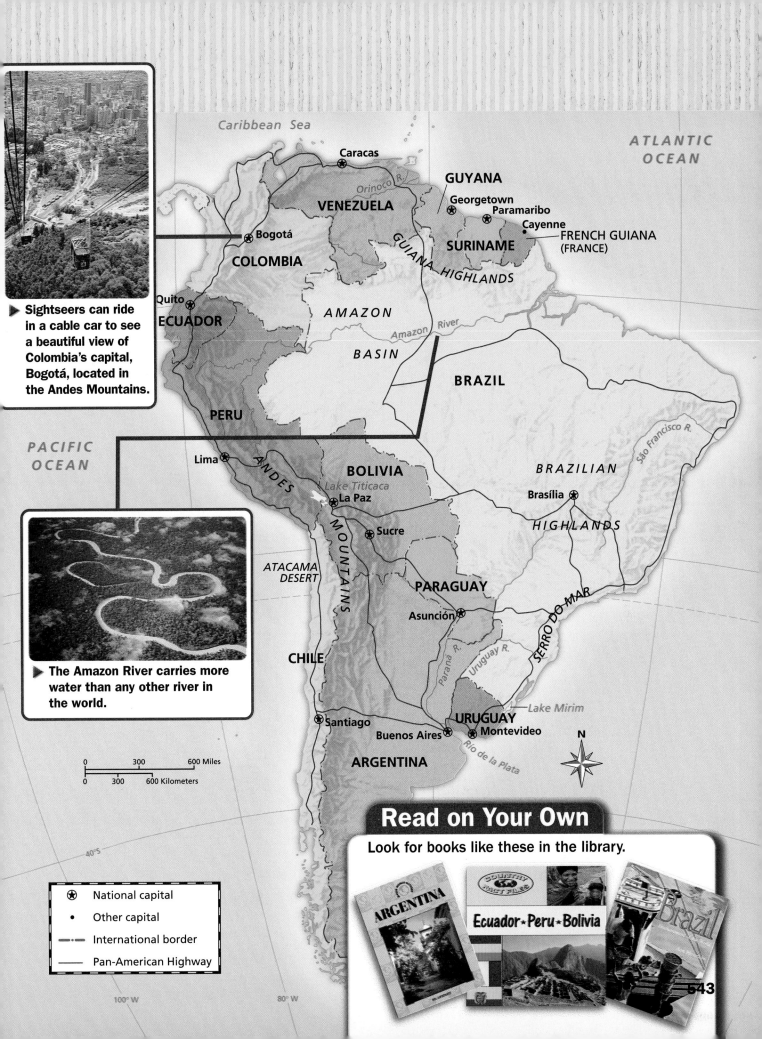

Caribbean Sea

ATLANTIC OCEAN

Caracas

GUYANA

Georgetown
Paramaribo
Cayenne
FRENCH GUIANA
(FRANCE)

Orinoco R.

VENEZUELA

GUIANA HIGHLANDS

SURINAME

Bogotá

COLOMBIA

Quito

ECUADOR

AMAZON

BASIN

Amazon River

BRAZIL

PERU

PACIFIC OCEAN

BRAZILIAN

São Francisco R.

Lima

Brasília

ANDES

BOLIVIA

Lake Titicaca
La Paz

HIGHLANDS

Sucre

ATACAMA DESERT

MOUNTAINS

PARAGUAY

SERRO DO MAR

Asunción

CHILE

Paraná R.

Uruguay R.

Lake Mirim

URUGUAY

Santiago

Montevideo

Buenos Aires

Río de la Plata

N

ARGENTINA

40°S

▶ Sightseers can ride in a cable car to see a beautiful view of Colombia's capital, Bogotá, located in the Andes Mountains.

▶ The Amazon River carries more water than any other river in the world.

0   300   600 Miles

0   300   600 Kilometers

National capital

Other capital

International border

Pan-American Highway

Read on Your Own

Look for books like these in the library.

ARGENTINA

COUNTRY FACT FILES

Ecuador★Peru★Bolivia

Brazil

100° W   80° W

543

Reference Guide

Table of Contents

Atlas

Photograph of the Continents   R2

Map of the World: Political   R4

Map of the Western Hemisphere: Political   R6

Map of the Western Hemisphere: Physical   R7

Map of North America: Political   R8

Map of North America: Physical   R9

Map of the United States of America   R10

Map of Our Fifty States: Political   R12

Map of Our Fifty States: Physical   R14

Geography Terms   **R16**

Facts About Our Fifty States   **R18**

Facts About Our Presidents   **R22**

United States Documents

The Declaration of Independence   R26

The Constitution of the United States of America   R30

Gazetteer   **R53**

Biographical Dictionary   **R59**

Glossary   **R68**

Index   **R80**

Credits   **R93**

Central America and the West Indies

ARCTIC OCEAN

SPITSBERGEN
(NORWAY)   SVALBARD
                  (NORWAY)

ICELAND

See inset below

RUSSIA

ASIA

EUROPE

KAZAKHSTAN

MONGOLIA

60°N

AZORES IS.
(PORTUGAL)

GEORGIA
ARMENIA
TURKEY

UZBEKISTAN
KYRGYZSTAN
TURKMENISTAN
TAJIKISTAN

NORTH
KOREA
SOUTH
KOREA

JAPAN

40°N

PACIFIC OCEAN

CANARY IS.
(SPAIN)

MOROCCO

TUNISIA

LEBANON SYRIA
ISRAEL   IRAQ
         JORDAN

AZERBAIJAN

IRAN

AFGHANISTAN

CHINA

WESTERN
SAHARA
(MOROCCO)

ALGERIA   LIBYA

EGYPT

KUWAIT
QATAR

BAHRAIN

PAKISTAN

NEPAL

BHUTAN

TAIWAN

Tropic of Cancer

20°N

MAURITANIA
CAPE VERDE
SENEGAL

MALI

NIGER   CHAD

SUDAN

SAUDI
ARABIA

UNITED
ARAB
EMIRATES

OMAN

INDIA

BANGLADESH

MYANMAR
(BURMA)

LAOS

WAKE ISLAND
(U.S.)

NORTHERN
MARIANA IS.
(U.S.)

MARSHALL ISLANDS

GUINEA
SIERRA
LEONE
LIBERIA

BURKINA
FASO
GHANA BENIN
       NIGERIA

AFRICA

CENTRAL
AFRICAN REP.

ERITREA
DJIBOUTI

YEMEN

THAILAND

VIETNAM

CAMBODIA

PHILIPPINES

PALAU

GUAM (U.S.)
FEDERATED STATES
OF MICRONESIA

KIRIBATI

CÔTE D'IVOIRE
SÃO TOMÉ AND PRÍNCIPE

TOGO
CAMEROON

ETHIOPIA

SOMALIA

SRI
LANKA

BRUNEI
MALAYSIA

SINGAPORE

Equator

NAURU

0°

GUINEA-
BISSAU
GAMBIA

EQUATORIAL
GUINEA

GABON
CONGO

DEM. REP.
CONGO

RWANDA
BURUNDI

UGANDA

KENYA

MALDIVES

INDONESIA

PAPUA
NEW
GUINEA

SOLOMON
ISLANDS

ATLANTIC
OCEAN

TANZANIA

SEYCHELLES

INDIAN
OCEAN

TUVALU

ANGOLA

ZAMBIA

MALAWI
MOZAMBIQUE

COMOROS

VANUATU

FIJI

20°S

NAMIBIA

ZIMBABWE

BOTSWANA

MADAGASCAR

MAURITIUS

RÉUNION (FR.)

AUSTRALIA

NEW
CALEDONIA
(FRANCE)

SOUTH
AFRICA

SWAZILAND
LESOTHO

NEW
ZEALAND

40°S

N

KERGUELEN
ISLANDS
(FRANCE)

0   1,000   2,000 Miles

0   1,000   2,000 Kilometers

Scale accurate at Equator

60°S

Antarctic Circle

80°S

ANTARCTICA

40°W   20°W   0°   20°E   40°E   60°E   80°E   100°E   120°E   140°E   160°E   180°

Europe

N

FINLAND

NORWAY

SWEDEN

ESTONIA

North
Sea

Baltic Sea

RUSSIA

IRELAND

UNITED
KINGDOM

DENMARK

LATVIA

LITHUANIA
RUSSIA

NETHERLANDS

BELGIUM   GERMANY

POLAND

BELARUS

LUXEMBOURG

CZECH
REPUBLIC

ATLANTIC
OCEAN

FRANCE LIECHTENSTEIN

SLOVAKIA

UKRAINE

SWITZERLAND

AUSTRIA

HUNGARY

MOLDOVA

SLOVENIA
CROATIA

ROMANIA

MONACO

SAN
MARINO

BOSNIA AND
HERZEGOVINA

SERBIA &
MONTENEGRO
(YUGOSLAVIA)

Black Sea

PORTUGAL

ANDORRA

SPAIN

CORSICA
(FR.)

ITALY

BULGARIA

MACEDONIA

BALEARIC IS.
(SP.)

SARDINIA
(IT.)

ALBANIA

GIBRALTAR (U.K.)

Mediterranean
Sea

SICILY
(IT.)

GREECE

40°N

CRETE
(GR.)

MALTA

0   250   500 Miles

0   250   500 Kilometers

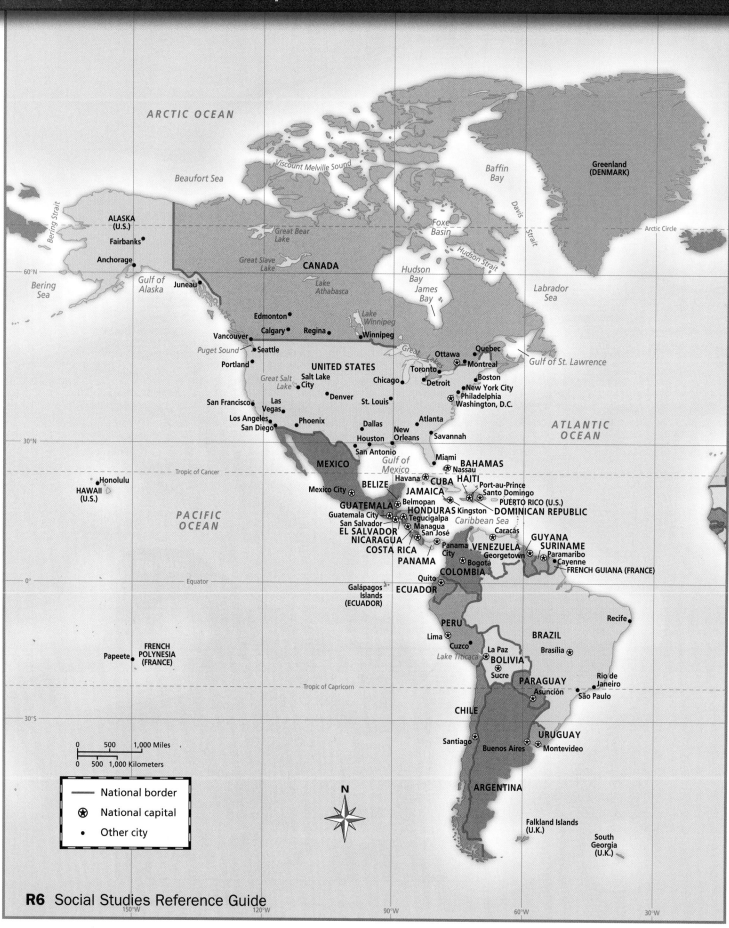

ARCTIC OCEAN

Beaufort Sea

Viscount Melville Sound

Baffin Bay

Greenland (DENMARK)

Davis Strait

Arctic Circle

Bering Strait

ALASKA (U.S.)

Fairbanks

Anchorage

Gulf of Alaska

Great Bear Lake

Great Slave Lake

CANADA

Foxe Basin

Hudson Strait

Bering Sea

60°N

Juneau

Lake Athabasca

Hudson Bay

James Bay

Labrador Sea

Edmonton

Calgary

Regina

Lake Winnipeg

Winnipeg

Vancouver

Puget Sound

Seattle

Portland

UNITED STATES

Great Salt Lake

Salt Lake City

Chicago

Ottawa

Toronto

Detroit

Quebec

Montreal

Gulf of St. Lawrence

Boston

New York City

Philadelphia

Washington, D.C.

San Francisco

Las Vegas

Los Angeles

San Diego

Denver

St. Louis

Phoenix

Dallas

Houston

Atlanta

New Orleans

Savannah

ATLANTIC OCEAN

30°N

San Antonio

Gulf of Mexico

Miami

BAHAMAS

Nassau

Tropic of Cancer

MEXICO

Havana

CUBA

HAITI

Honolulu

HAWAII (U.S.)

PACIFIC OCEAN

Mexico City

BELIZE

Belmopan

JAMAICA

GUATEMALA

Guatemala City

HONDURAS

Tegucigalpa

San Salvador

EL SALVADOR

NICARAGUA

Managua

COSTA RICA

PANAMA

Kingston

Port-au-Prince

Santo Domingo

PUERTO RICO (U.S.)

DOMINICAN REPUBLIC

Caribbean Sea

San José

Panama City

Caracás

VENEZUELA

GUYANA

SURINAME

Georgetown

Paramaribo

Cayenne

FRENCH GUIANA (FRANCE)

COLOMBIA

Bogotá

Quito

ECUADOR

0° Equator

Galápagos Islands (ECUADOR)

PERU

Recife

Lima

Cuzco

BRAZIL

FRENCH POLYNESIA (FRANCE)

La Paz

Brasília

Papeete

Lake Titicaca

BOLIVIA

Sucre

Rio de Janeiro

Tropic of Capricorn

PARAGUAY

Asunción

São Paulo

CHILE

30°S

Santiago

URUGUAY

Buenos Aires

Montevideo

N

500 1,000 Miles

500 1,000 Kilometers

National border

National capital

Other city

ARGENTINA

Falkland Islands (U.K.)

South Georgia (U.K.)

150°W   120°W   90°W   60°W   30°W

ARCTIC OCEAN

North Magnetic Pole+

Ellesmere Island

Queen Elizabeth Islands

Melville Island

Viscount Melville Sound

Devon Island

Baffin Bay

Greenland

Point Barrow

Beaufort Sea

Banks Island

Victoria Island

Baffin Island

Davis Strait

Arctic Circle

Brooks Range

Mt. McKinley 20,320 ft. (6,194 m)

Yukon River

Mackenzie Mts.

Mackenzie River

Great Bear Lake

CANADIAN

Foxe Basin

Hudson Strait

Cape Farewell

Bering Strait

Alaska Range

Yukon Plateau

Liard R.

Great Slave Lake

Peace River

Great Slave Lake

Hudson Bay

Labrador Sea

60°N

Bering Sea

Gulf of Alaska

Mt. Logan 19,524 ft. (5,951 m)

Coast Mountains

Athabasca R.

Lake Athabasca

Saskatchewan River

SHIELD

James Bay

Labrador

Alaska Peninsula

Kodiak Island

Queen Charlotte Islands

ROCKY

Lake Winnipeg

GREAT

Newfoundland

Gulf of St. Lawrence

Aleutian Islands

Vancouver Island

Coast Ranges

MOUNTAINS

PLAINS

NORTH AMERICA

Great Lakes

St. Lawrence R.

Nova Scotia

Puget Sound

Cascade Range

Black Hills

Missouri R.

Mississippi

Bay of Fundy

Cape Cod

Long Island

Snake R.

Sierra Nevada

Great Salt Lake

Platte R.

INTERIOR PLAINS

Ohio R.

APPALACHIAN MTS.

GREAT BASIN

Arkansas R.

Cape Hatteras

ATLANTIC OCEAN

Mt. Whitney 14,495 ft. (4,418 m)

Colorado R.

Ozark Plateau

Death Valley (lowest point in N.A.) -282 ft. (-86 m)

Sonoran Desert

Rio Grande

30°N

Baja California

Sierra Madre Occidental

Sierra Madre Oriental

COASTAL PLAIN

Gulf of Mexico

Bahamas

Hawaiian Islands

Tropic of Cancer

Citlaltépetl 18,701 ft. (5,700 m)

Yucatán Peninsula

Cuba

Greater Antilles

Hispaniola

Puerto Rico

Lesser Antilles

PACIFIC OCEAN

Lake Nicaragua

Caribbean Sea

Lake Maracaibo

Orinoco R.

Isthmus of Panama

Llanos

Guiana Highlands

Line Islands

Equator

Galápagos Islands

Chimborazo 20,561 ft. (6,267 m)

Rio Negro

Amazon R.

Cape São Roque

0°

AMAZON

Marquesas Islands

ANDES

BASIN

Tapajós R.

Xingu River

Tocantins R.

São Francisco R.

Huascarán 22,205 ft. (6,768 m)

Mato Grosso Plateau

Brazilian Highlands

Cook Islands

Tuamotu Archipelago

Society Islands

Lake Titicaca

MOUNTAINS

Altiplano

Paraguay R.

SOUTH AMERICA

Tropic of Capricorn

Gran Chaco

Iguazú Falls

30°S

Atacama Desert

Paraná R.

Uruguay R.

Mt. Aconcagua 22,831 ft. (6,959 m)

Pampa

0   500   1,000 Miles

0   500   1,000 Kilometers

Valdés Peninsula (lowest point in S.A.) -131 ft. (-40 m)

N

Patagonia

▲ Mountain peak

—— National border

Strait of Magellan

Tierra del Fuego

Falkland Islands

South Georgia

Cape Horn

150°W   120°W   90°W   60°W   30°W

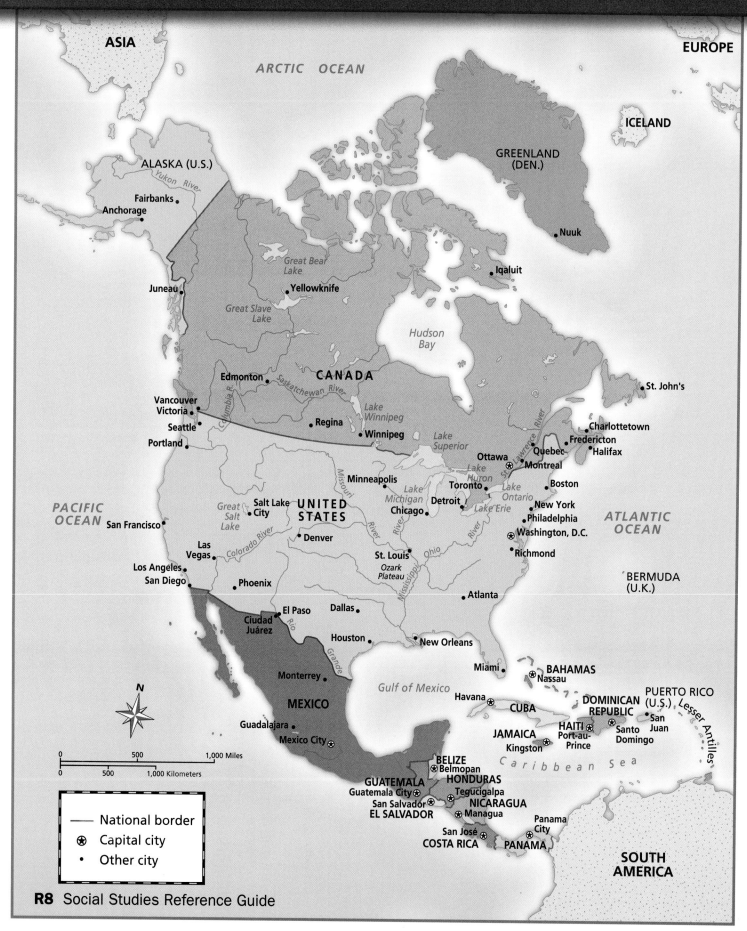

Atlas
Map of North America: Political

ASIA

EUROPE

ARCTIC OCEAN

ICELAND

ALASKA (U.S.)

GREENLAND (DEN.)

Fairbanks
Anchorage

Nuuk

Yukon River

Great Bear Lake

Juneau

Yellowknife

Iqaluit

Great Slave Lake

Hudson Bay

Edmonton

CANADA

St. John's

Saskatchewan River

Vancouver
Victoria

Lake Winnipeg

Charlottetown
Fredericton
Halifax

Seattle

Regina

Winnipeg

Lake Superior

St. Lawrence River

Quebec

Portland

Columbia R.

Lake Huron

Ottawa

Montreal

Boston

Minneapolis

Lake Michigan

Toronto

Detroit

Lake Ontario

New York

PACIFIC OCEAN

Missouri River

UNITED STATES

Chicago

Lake Erie

Philadelphia

ATLANTIC OCEAN

San Francisco

Great Salt Lake

Salt Lake City

Washington, D.C.

Denver

St. Louis

Richmond

Las Vegas

Colorado River

Ozark Plateau

Ohio River

Los Angeles
San Diego

Phoenix

Mississippi River

Atlanta

BERMUDA (U.K.)

El Paso

Dallas

Ciudad Juárez

Houston

New Orleans

Rio Grande

Miami

BAHAMAS

Monterrey

Gulf of Mexico

Nassau

PUERTO RICO (U.S.)

MEXICO

Havana

CUBA

DOMINICAN REPUBLIC

San Juan

Lesser Antilles

Guadalajara

JAMAICA

HAITI
Port-au-Prince

Santo Domingo

Mexico City

Kingston

Caribbean Sea

BELIZE
Belmopan

GUATEMALA

HONDURAS

Guatemala City

Tegucigalpa

San Salvador

NICARAGUA

EL SALVADOR

Managua

Panama City

San José

PANAMA

COSTA RICA

SOUTH AMERICA

N

0   500   1,000 Miles
0   500   1,000 Kilometers

— National border
⊛ Capital city
• Other city

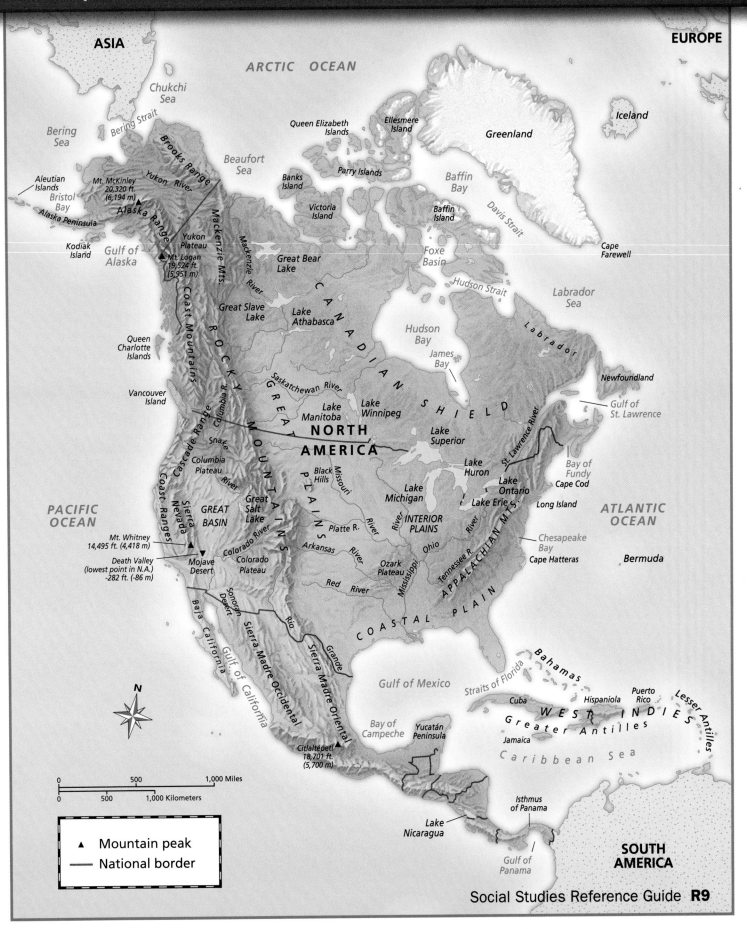

Map of North America: Physical

ASIA

EUROPE

ARCTIC OCEAN

Chukchi Sea

Bering Sea

Bering Strait

Queen Elizabeth Islands

Ellesmere Island

Iceland

Greenland

Beaufort Sea

Aleutian Islands

Bristol Bay

Alaska Peninsula

Brooks Range

Yukon River

Banks Island

Parry Islands

Baffin Bay

Davis Strait

Cape Farewell

Mt. McKinley 20,320 ft. (6,194 m)

Alaska Range

Kodiak Island

Gulf of Alaska

Yukon Plateau

Mt. Logan 19,524 ft. (5,951 m)

Mackenzie Mts.

Mackenzie River

Victoria Island

Baffin Island

Foxe Basin

Hudson Strait

Labrador Sea

Great Bear Lake

Great Slave Lake

Queen Charlotte Islands

Coast Mountains

Lake Athabasca

CANADIAN SHIELD

Hudson Bay

James Bay

Labrador

Newfoundland

Vancouver Island

ROCKY

Saskatchewan River

GREAT

Lake Manitoba

Lake Winnipeg

Gulf of St. Lawrence

Columbia R.

NORTH AMERICA

Lake Superior

St. Lawrence River

PACIFIC OCEAN

Cascade Range

Snake

Columbia Plateau

Columbia River

MOUNTAINS

PLAINS

Black Hills

Missouri

Lake Michigan

Lake Huron

Lake Ontario

Lake Erie

Long Island

Bay of Fundy

Cape Cod

ATLANTIC OCEAN

Coast Ranges

Sierra Nevada

GREAT BASIN

Great Salt Lake

River

INTERIOR PLAINS

River

APPALACHIAN MTS.

Chesapeake Bay

Cape Hatteras

Bermuda

Mt. Whitney 14,495 ft. (4,418 m)

Death Valley (lowest point in N.A.) -282 ft. (-86 m)

Mojave Desert

Colorado River

Colorado Plateau

Platte R.

Arkansas

River

Ozark Plateau

Ohio

Tennessee R.

Mississippi

Red

River

COASTAL

PLAIN

Baja California

Sonoran Desert

Sierra Madre Occidental

Gulf of California

Rio

Grande

Sierra Madre Oriental

Gulf of Mexico

Bay of Campeche

Yucatán Peninsula

Straits of Florida

Bahamas

Cuba

Jamaica

Greater Antilles

Hispaniola

WEST INDIES

Puerto Rico

Lesser Antilles

Caribbean Sea

Citlaltépetl 18,701 ft. (5,700 m)

Lake Nicaragua

Isthmus of Panama

Gulf of Panama

SOUTH AMERICA

N

| 0 | 500 | 1,000 Miles |
| 0 | 500 | 1,000 Kilometers |

▲ Mountain peak

— National border

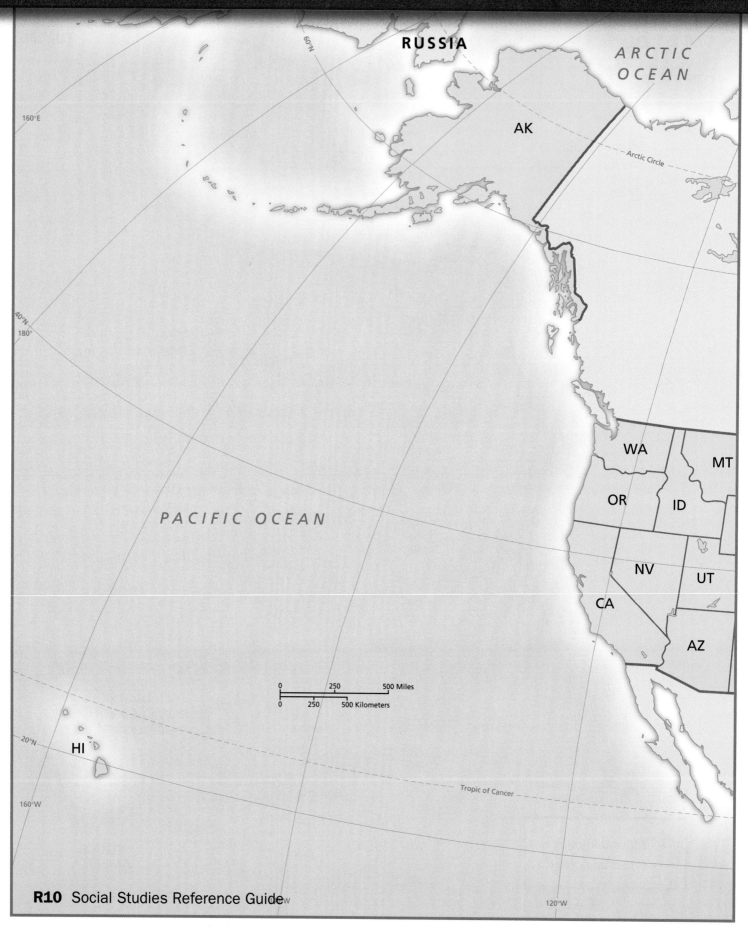

RUSSIA

ARCTIC OCEAN

AK

Arctic Circle

PACIFIC OCEAN

WA

MT

OR

ID

NV

UT

CA

AZ

0   250   500 Miles

0   250   500 Kilometers

Tropic of Cancer

HI

160°E

180°

40°N

60°N

20°N

160°W

120°W

State or area	Abbreviation
Alabama	AL
Alaska	AK
Arizona	AZ
Arkansas	AR
California	CA
Colorado	CO
Connecticut	CT
Delaware	DE
District of Columbia	DC
Florida	FL
Georgia	GA
Hawaii	HI
Idaho	ID
Illinois	IL
Indiana	IN
Iowa	IA
Kansas	KS
Kentucky	KY
Louisiana	LA
Maine	ME
Maryland	MD
Massachusetts	MA
Michigan	MI
Minnesota	MN
Mississippi	MS
Missouri	MO
Montana	MT
Nebraska	NE
Nevada	NV
New Hampshire	NH
New Jersey	NJ
New Mexico	NM
New York	NY
North Carolina	NC
North Dakota	ND
Ohio	OH
Oklahoma	OK
Oregon	OR
Pennsylvania	PA
Rhode Island	RI
South Carolina	SC
South Dakota	SD
Tennessee	TN
Texas	TX
Utah	UT
Vermont	VT
Virginia	VA
Washington	WA
West Virginia	WV
Wisconsin	WI
Wyoming	WY

Atlas
Map of Our Fifty States: Political

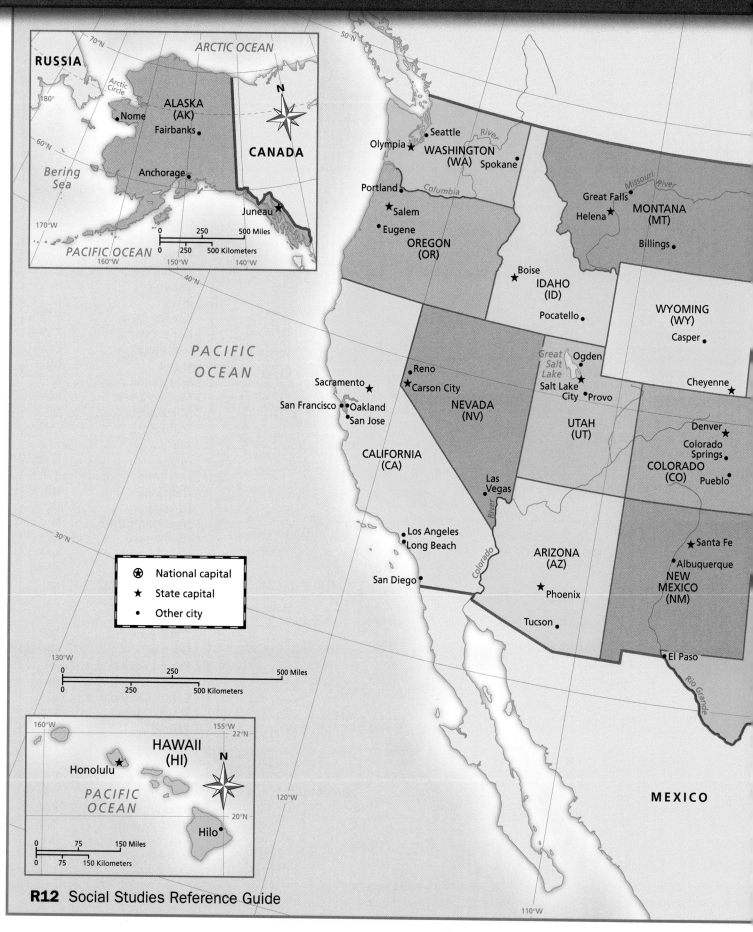

RUSSIA

ARCTIC OCEAN

ALASKA (AK)
Nome
Fairbanks

CANADA

Bering Sea

Anchorage

Juneau

PACIFIC OCEAN

National capital
State capital
Other city

HAWAII (HI)
Honolulu
PACIFIC OCEAN
Hilo

PACIFIC OCEAN

Seattle
Olympia ★ WASHINGTON (WA)
Spokane

Portland
Salem ★
Eugene
OREGON (OR)

Boise ★
IDAHO (ID)
Pocatello

Great Falls
Helena ★ MONTANA (MT)
Billings

WYOMING (WY)
Casper

Cheyenne ★

Sacramento ★
San Francisco
Oakland
San Jose

Reno
Carson City ★
NEVADA (NV)

Great Salt Lake
Ogden
Salt Lake City
Provo

UTAH (UT)

Denver ★
Colorado Springs
COLORADO (CO)
Pueblo

CALIFORNIA (CA)

Las Vegas

Los Angeles
Long Beach

San Diego

ARIZONA (AZ)

Phoenix ★

Tucson

Santa Fe ★
Albuquerque
NEW MEXICO (NM)

El Paso

MEXICO

Rio Grande

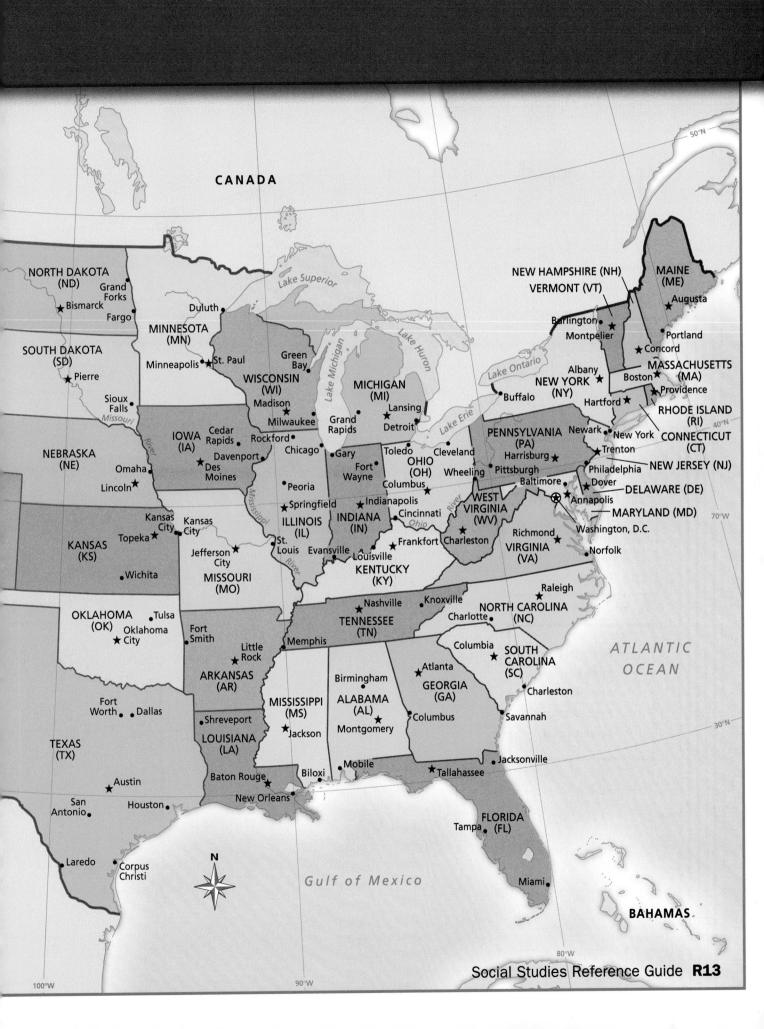

CANADA

NORTH DAKOTA (ND)
Grand Forks
Bismarck
Fargo

SOUTH DAKOTA (SD)
Pierre
Sioux Falls

NEBRASKA (NE)
Omaha
Lincoln

KANSAS (KS)
Topeka
Wichita

OKLAHOMA (OK)
Tulsa
Oklahoma City

TEXAS (TX)
Fort Worth
Dallas
Austin
San Antonio
Houston
Laredo
Corpus Christi

MINNESOTA (MN)
Duluth
Minneapolis
St. Paul

WISCONSIN (WI)
Green Bay
Madison
Milwaukee

IOWA (IA)
Cedar Rapids
Rockford
Davenport
Des Moines

MISSOURI (MO)
Kansas City
Kansas City
Jefferson City
St. Louis

ARKANSAS (AR)
Fort Smith
Little Rock

LOUISIANA (LA)
Shreveport
Jackson
Baton Rouge
New Orleans

Lake Superior

Lake Michigan

Lake Huron

MICHIGAN (MI)
Lansing
Grand Rapids
Detroit

ILLINOIS (IL)
Chicago
Gary
Peoria
Springfield

INDIANA (IN)
Fort Wayne
Indianapolis
Evansville

Lake Erie

Lake Ontario

OHIO (OH)
Toledo
Cleveland
Columbus
Cincinnati

KENTUCKY (KY)
Louisville
Frankfort

TENNESSEE (TN)
Memphis
Nashville
Knoxville

MISSISSIPPI (MS)
Biloxi
Mobile

ALABAMA (AL)
Birmingham
Montgomery
Columbus

GEORGIA (GA)
Atlanta
Columbus
Savannah

FLORIDA (FL)
Tallahassee
Jacksonville
Tampa
Miami

Gulf of Mexico

NEW HAMPSHIRE (NH)
VERMONT (VT)
Burlington
Montpelier
Concord

MAINE (ME)
Augusta
Portland

MASSACHUSETTS (MA)
Boston

NEW YORK (NY)
Buffalo
Albany
Hartford

RHODE ISLAND (RI)
Providence

CONNECTICUT (CT)

PENNSYLVANIA (PA)
Harrisburg
Pittsburgh
Wheeling
Newark
New York
Trenton

NEW JERSEY (NJ)
Philadelphia
Dover

DELAWARE (DE)

WEST VIRGINIA (WV)
Charleston

MARYLAND (MD)
Baltimore
Annapolis
Washington, D.C.

VIRGINIA (VA)
Richmond
Norfolk

NORTH CAROLINA (NC)
Raleigh
Charlotte

SOUTH CAROLINA (SC)
Columbia
Charleston

ATLANTIC OCEAN

BAHAMAS

Missouri River
Mississippi River
Ohio River

50°N
40°N
30°N
70°W
80°W
90°W
100°W

N

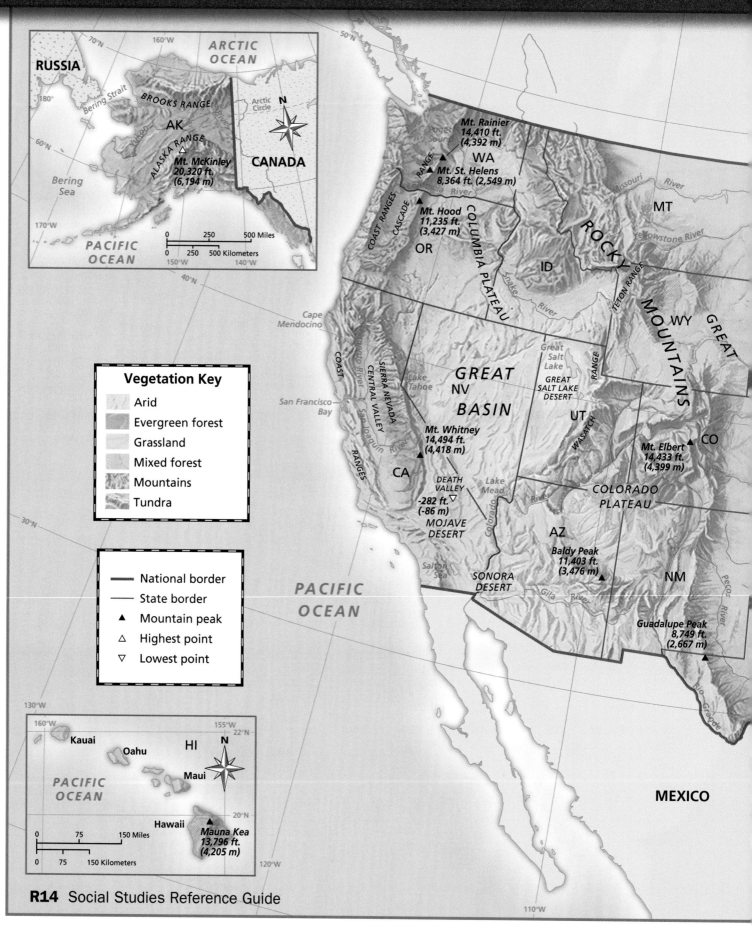

RUSSIA

ARCTIC
OCEAN

70°N   160°W

BROOKS RANGE

AK

ALASKA RANGE

Mt. McKinley
20,320 ft.
(6,194 m)

60°N

CANADA

N

Bering Strait

180°

Yukon

Arctic
Circle

Bering
Sea

170°W

PACIFIC
OCEAN

| 0 | 250 | 500 Miles |
| 0 | 250 | 500 Kilometers |

150°W   140°W

Vegetation Key

- Arid
- Evergreen forest
- Grassland
- Mixed forest
- Mountains
- Tundra

━━━ National border
──── State border
▲ Mountain peak
△ Highest point
▽ Lowest point

ARCTIC OCEAN

50°N

Mt. Rainier
14,410 ft.
(4,392 m)

Puget Sound

WA

RANGE

Mt. St. Helens
8,364 ft. (2,549 m)

Columbia River

Mt. Hood
11,235 ft.
(3,427 m)

COAST RANGES

CASCADE

COLUMBIA PLATEAU

OR

MT

ROCKY

Missouri   River

Yellowstone River

ID

Snake
River

40°N

Cape
Mendocino

COAST

SACRAMENTO River

SIERRA NEVADA
CENTRAL VALLEY

Lake
Tahoe

GREAT

NV

BASIN

Great
Salt
Lake

GREAT
SALT LAKE
DESERT

TETON RANGE

RANGE

WY

MOUNTAINS

GREAT

San Francisco
Bay

San Joaquin River

Mt. Whitney
14,494 ft.
(4,418 m)

UT

WASATCH

CA

RANGES

DEATH
VALLEY
-282 ft.
(-86 m)

MOJAVE
DESERT

Lake
Mead

Colorado River

COLORADO
PLATEAU

Mt. Elbert
14,433 ft.
(4,399 m)

CO

30°N

130°W

PACIFIC
OCEAN

AZ

Baldy Peak
11,403 ft.
(3,476 m)

NM

SONORA
DESERT

Salton
Sea

Gila   River

Pecos   River

Guadalupe Peak
8,749 ft.
(2,667 m)

Rio Grande

160°W   155°W   22°N

Kauai

Oahu   HI   N

Maui

PACIFIC
OCEAN

20°N

Hawaii

Mauna Kea
13,796 ft.
(4,205 m)

| 0 | 75 | 150 Miles |
| 0 | 75 | 150 Kilometers |

120°W

MEXICO

110°W

CANADA

Lake of
the Woods

ND

MN

Lake Superior

GREAT

MESABI RANGE

St. Lawrence River

Mt. Katahdin
5,267 ft.
(1,605 m)

ME

WHITE MTS.

Mt. Washington
6,288 ft.
(1,917 m)

VT

GREEN MTS.

NH

BLACK
HILLS

SD

WI

Lake Michigan

MI

Lake Huron

LAKES

ADIRONDACK
MTS.

Lake Ontario

NY

MA

Cape
Cod

CT

RI

Mississippi River

CENTRAL

PLAINS

Lake Erie

PA

MOUNTAINS

Long Island

40°N

NE

IA

Platte River

IL

IN

River

OH

WV

NJ

MD

DE

Delaware Bay

70°W

Missouri

ALLEGHENY MOUNTAINS

APPALACHIAN

VA

River

Chesapeake Bay

PLAINS

River

KS

MO

Ohio River

KY

PIEDMONT

COASTAL PLAIN

Cape
Hatteras

Arkansas

River

INTERIOR

PLAINS

OZARK
PLATEAU

Mt. Mitchell
6,684 ft.
(2,037 m)

NC

OK

TN

SC

Cape
Fear

OUACHITA
MOUNTAINS

AR

Stone
Mountain

Savannah River

Red

Tombigbee River

River

Mississippi River

MS

AL

GA

ATLANTIC
OCEAN

Alabama River

TX

LA

Chattahoochee River

30°N

Brazos

River

GULF COASTAL

PLAIN

Mobile Bay

Colorado River

Galveston
Bay

Mississippi
Delta

Cape
Canaveral

FL

Lake
Okeechobee

BAHAMAS

Tampa
Bay

N

Gulf of Mexico

Florida Keys

Straits of Florida

80°W

0   250   500 Miles

0   250   500 Kilometers

Social Studies Reference Guide **R15**

100°W

90°W

50°N

PLAINS

Geography Terms

basin bowl-shaped area of land surrounded by higher land

bay narrower part of an ocean or lake that cuts into land

canal narrow waterway dug across land mainly for ship travel

canyon steep, narrow valley with high sides

cliff steep wall of rock or earth, sometimes called a bluff

coast land at the edge of a large body of water such as an ocean

coastal plain area of flat land along an ocean or sea

delta triangle-shaped area of land at the mouth of a river

desert very dry land

fall line area along which rivers form waterfalls or rapids as the rivers drop to lower land

floodplain flat land, near a river, that is formed by dirt left by floods

foothills hilly land at the bottom of a mountain

glacier giant sheet of ice that moves very slowly across land

gulf body of water, larger than most bays, with land around part of it

harbor sheltered body of water where ships safely tie up to land

hill rounded land higher than the land around it

inlet narrow strip of water running from a large body of water either into land or between islands

island land with water all around it

lake large body of water with land all or nearly all around it

mesa flat-topped hill with steep sides

mountain a very tall hill; highest land on Earth

mountain pass narrow channel or path through a mountain range

mountain range long row of mountains

mouth place where a river empties into another body of water

ocean any of the four largest bodies of water on Earth

peak pointed top of a mountain

peninsula land with water on three sides

plain very large area of flat land

plateau high, wide area of flat land, with steep sides

prairie large area of flat land, with few or no trees, similar to a plain

river large stream of water leading to a lake, another river, or an ocean

riverbank land at a river's edge

sea large body of water somewhat smaller than an ocean

sea level an ocean's surface, compared to which land can be measured either above or below

source place where a river begins

swamp low, water-covered land filled with trees and other plants

tributary stream or river that runs into a larger river

valley low land between mountains or hills

volcano mountain with an opening at the top, formed by violent bursts of steam and hot rock

waterfall steep falling of water from a higher to a lower place

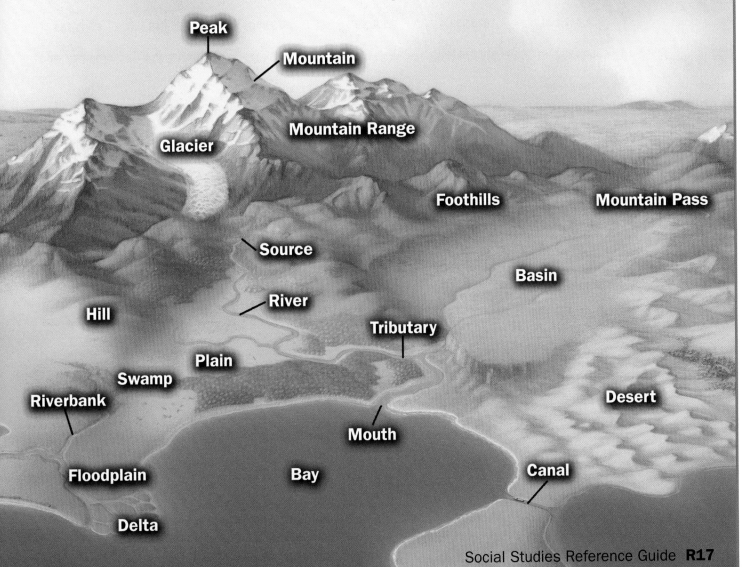

Facts About Our Fifty States

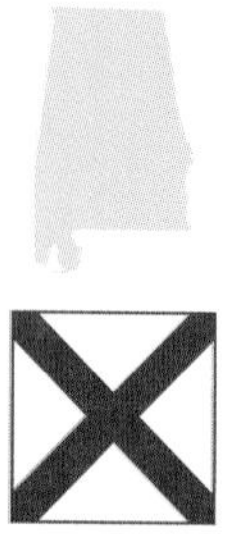

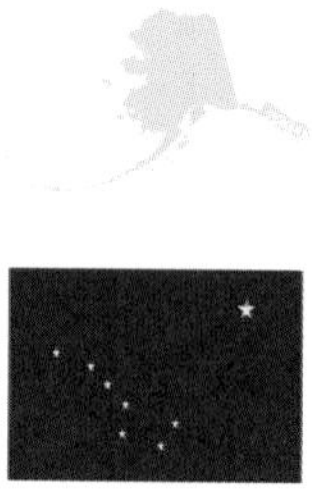

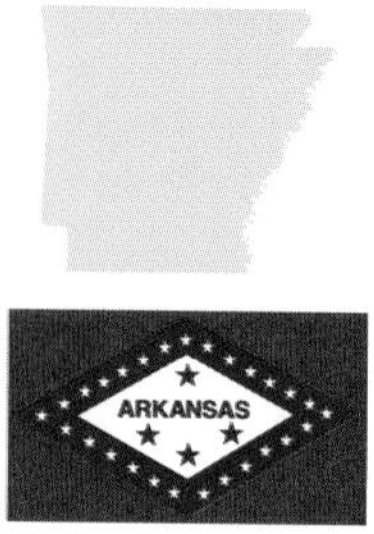

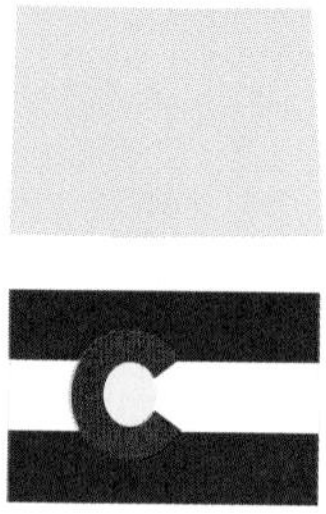

	AL Alabama	**AK** Alaska	**AZ** Arizona	**AR** Arkansas	**CA** California	**CO** Colorado
Capital	Montgomery	Juneau	Phoenix	Little Rock	Sacramento	Denver
Date and order of statehood	1819 (22)	1959 (49)	1912 (48)	1836 (25)	1850 (31)	1876 (38)
Nickname	Heart of Dixie	The Last Frontier	Grand Canyon State	Land of Opportunity	Golden State	Centennial State
Population	4,447,100	626,932	5,130,632	2,673,400	33,871,648	4,301,261
Square miles and rank in area	50,750 (28)	570,374 (1)	113,642 (6)	52,075 (27)	155,973 (3)	103,730 (8)
Region	Southeast	West	Southwest	Southeast	West	West

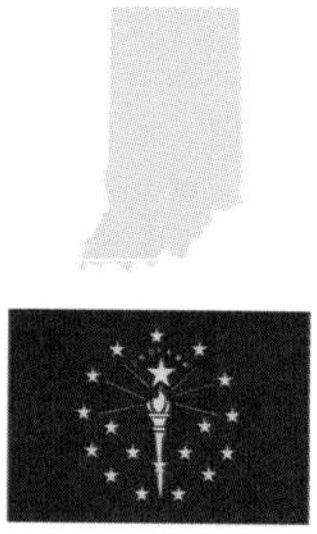

	IN Indiana	**IA** Iowa	**KS** Kansas	**KY** Kentucky	**LA** Louisiana	**ME** Maine
Capital	Indianapolis	Des Moines	Topeka	Frankfort	Baton Rouge	Augusta
Date and order of statehood	1816 (19)	1846 (29)	1861 (34)	1792 (15)	1812 (18)	1820 (23)
Nickname	Hoosier State	Hawkeye State	Sunflower State	Bluegrass State	Pelican State	Pine Tree State
Population	6,080,485	2,926,324	2,688,418	4,041,769	4,468,976	1,274,923
Square miles and rank in area	35,870 (38)	55,875 (23)	81,823 (13)	39,732 (36)	43,566 (33)	30,865 (39)
Region	Midwest	Midwest	Midwest	Southeast	Southeast	Northeast

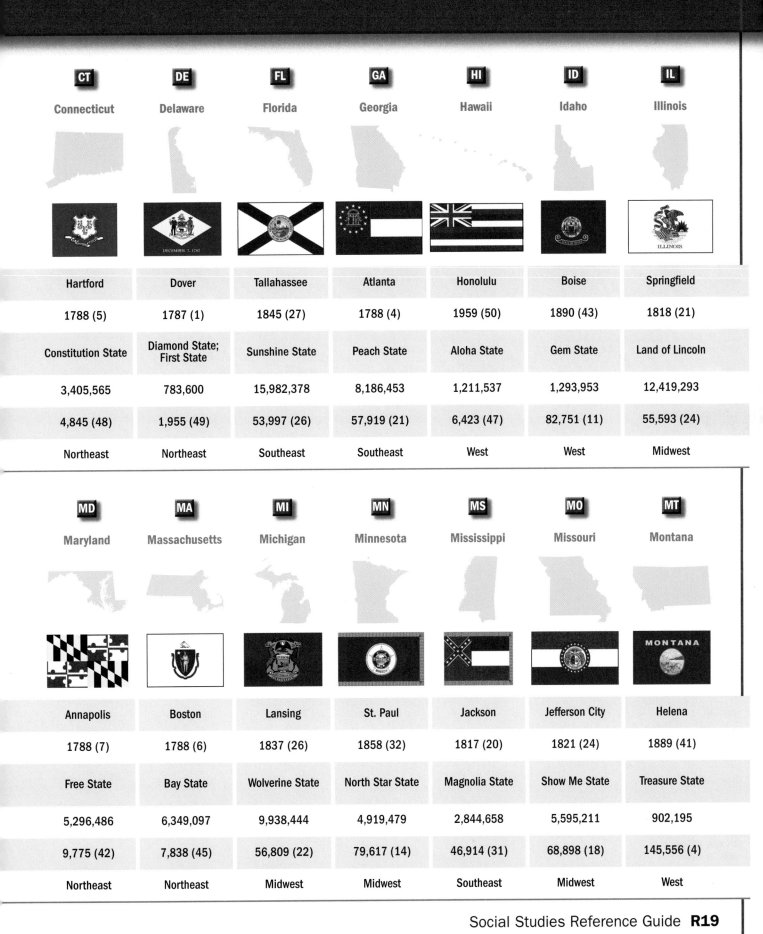

CT	**DE**	**FL**	**GA**	**HI**	**ID**	**IL**
Connecticut	Delaware	Florida	Georgia	Hawaii	Idaho	Illinois
Hartford	Dover	Tallahassee	Atlanta	Honolulu	Boise	Springfield
1788 (5)	1787 (1)	1845 (27)	1788 (4)	1959 (50)	1890 (43)	1818 (21)
Constitution State	Diamond State; First State	Sunshine State	Peach State	Aloha State	Gem State	Land of Lincoln
3,405,565	783,600	15,982,378	8,186,453	1,211,537	1,293,953	12,419,293
4,845 (48)	1,955 (49)	53,997 (26)	57,919 (21)	6,423 (47)	82,751 (11)	55,593 (24)
Northeast	Northeast	Southeast	Southeast	West	West	Midwest

MD	**MA**	**MI**	**MN**	**MS**	**MO**	**MT**
Maryland	Massachusetts	Michigan	Minnesota	Mississippi	Missouri	Montana
Annapolis	Boston	Lansing	St. Paul	Jackson	Jefferson City	Helena
1788 (7)	1788 (6)	1837 (26)	1858 (32)	1817 (20)	1821 (24)	1889 (41)
Free State	Bay State	Wolverine State	North Star State	Magnolia State	Show Me State	Treasure State
5,296,486	6,349,097	9,938,444	4,919,479	2,844,658	5,595,211	902,195
9,775 (42)	7,838 (45)	56,809 (22)	79,617 (14)	46,914 (31)	68,898 (18)	145,556 (4)
Northeast	Northeast	Midwest	Midwest	Southeast	Midwest	West

Facts About Our Fifty States

	NE Nebraska	NV Nevada	NH New Hampshire	NJ New Jersey	NM New Mexico	NY New York
Capital	Lincoln	Carson City	Concord	Trenton	Santa Fe	Albany
Date and order of statehood	1867 (37)	1864 (36)	1788 (9)	1787 (3)	1912 (47)	1788 (11)
Nickname	Cornhusker State	Silver State	Granite State	Garden State	Land of Enchantment	Empire State
Population	1,711,263	1,998,257	1,235,786	8,414,350	1,819,046	18,976,457
Square miles and rank in area	76,644 (15)	109,806 (7)	8,969 (44)	7,419 (46)	121,365 (5)	47,224 (30)
Region	Midwest	West	Northeast	Northeast	Southwest	Northeast

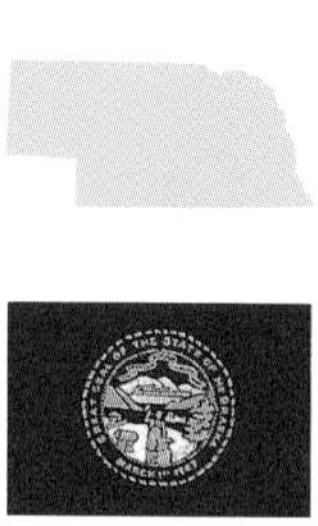

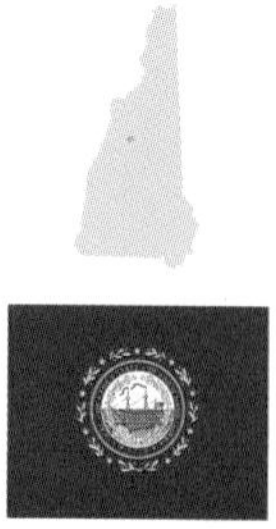

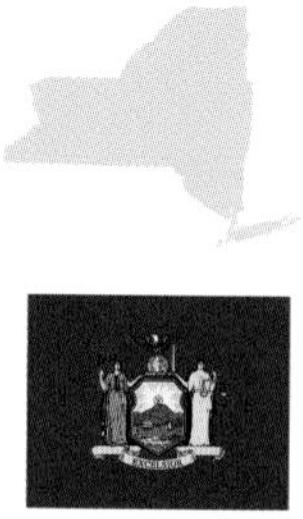

	SC South Carolina	SD South Dakota	TN Tennessee	TX Texas	UT Utah	VT Vermont
Capital	Columbia	Pierre	Nashville	Austin	Salt Lake City	Montpelier
Date and order of statehood	1788 (8)	1889 (40)	1796 (16)	1845 (28)	1896 (45)	1791 (14)
Nickname	Palmetto State	Mount Rushmore State	Volunteer State	Lone Star State	Beehive State	Green Mountain State
Population	4,012,012	754,844	5,689,283	20,851,820	2,233,169	608,827
Square miles and rank in area	30,111 (40)	75,898 (16)	41,220 (34)	261,914 (2)	82,168 (12)	9,249 (43)
Region	Southeast	Midwest	Southeast	Southwest	West	Northeast

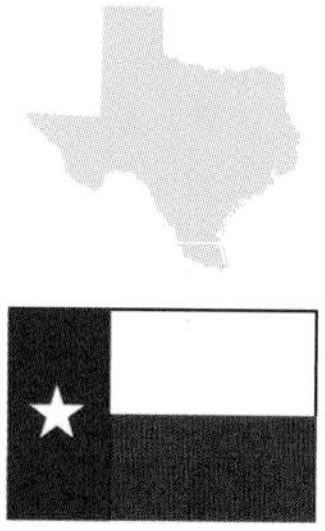

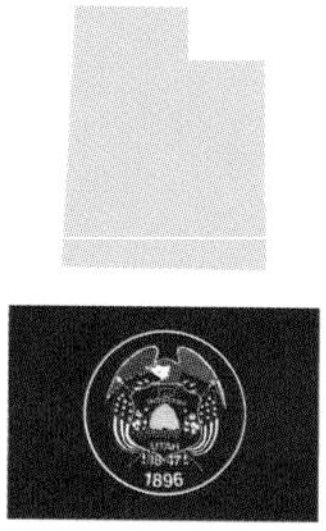

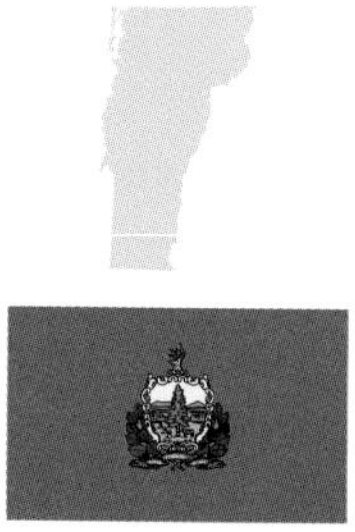

NC	ND	OH	OK	OR	PA	RI
North Carolina	North Dakota	Ohio	Oklahoma	Oregon	Pennsylvania	Rhode Island
Raleigh	Bismarck	Columbus	Oklahoma City	Salem	Harrisburg	Providence
1789 (12)	1889 (39)	1803 (17)	1907 (46)	1859 (33)	1787 (2)	1790 (13)
Tar Heel State	Sioux State	Buckeye State	Sooner State	Beaver State	Keystone State	Ocean State
8,049,313	642,200	11,353,140	3,450,654	3,421,399	12,281,054	1,048,319
48,718 (29)	68,994 (17)	40,953 (35)	68,679 (19)	96,003 (10)	44,820 (32)	1,045 (50)
Southeast	Midwest	Midwest	Southwest	West	Northeast	Northeast

VA	WA	WV	WI	WY
Virginia	Washington	West Virginia	Wisconsin	Wyoming
Richmond	Olympia	Charleston	Madison	Cheyenne
1788 (10)	1889 (42)	1863 (35)	1848 (30)	1890 (44)
Old Dominion	Evergreen State	Mountain State	Badger State	Equality State
7,078,515	5,894,121	1,808,344	5,363,675	493,782
39,598 (37)	66,582 (20)	24,087 (41)	54,314 (25)	97,105 (9)
Southeast	West	Southeast	Midwest	West

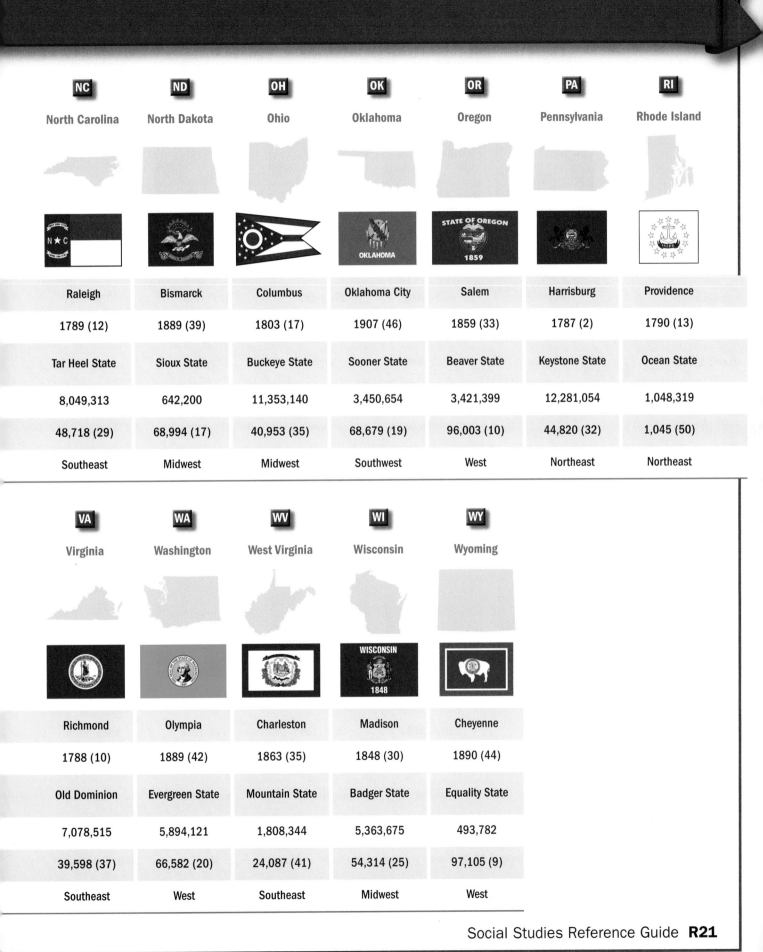

Facts About Our Presidents

	1 George Washington	**2** John Adams	**3** Thomas Jefferson	**4** James Madison	**5** James Monroe
Years in Office	1789–1797	1797–1801	1801–1809	1809–1817	1817–1825
Life Span	1732–1799	1735–1826	1743–1826	1751–1836	1758–1831
Birthplace	Westmoreland County, Virginia	Braintree County, Massachusetts	Albemarle County, Virginia	Port Conway, Virginia	Westmoreland County, Virginia
Home State	Virginia	Massachusetts	Virginia	Virginia	Virginia
Political Party	Federalist	Federalist	Democratic-Republican	Democratic-Republican	Democratic-Republican
First Lady	Martha Dandridge Washington	Abigail Smith Adams	None	Dolley Payne Madison	Elizabeth Kortright Monroe
Religion	Episcopalian	Unitarian	Deist	Episcopalian	Episcopalian

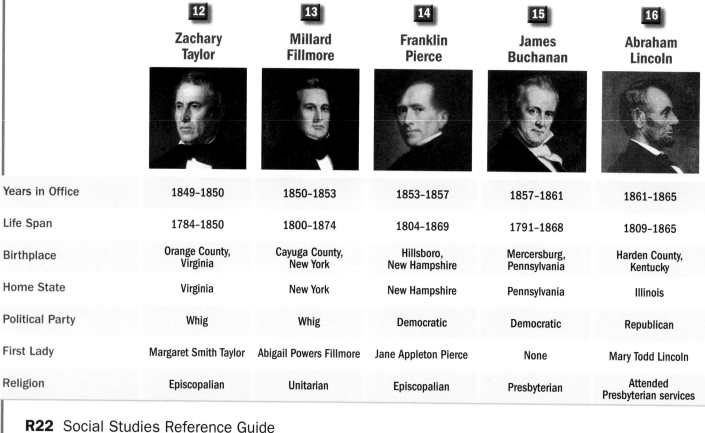

	12 Zachary Taylor	**13** Millard Fillmore	**14** Franklin Pierce	**15** James Buchanan	**16** Abraham Lincoln
Years in Office	1849–1850	1850–1853	1853–1857	1857–1861	1861–1865
Life Span	1784–1850	1800–1874	1804–1869	1791–1868	1809–1865
Birthplace	Orange County, Virginia	Cayuga County, New York	Hillsboro, New Hampshire	Mercersburg, Pennsylvania	Harden County, Kentucky
Home State	Virginia	New York	New Hampshire	Pennsylvania	Illinois
Political Party	Whig	Whig	Democratic	Democratic	Republican
First Lady	Margaret Smith Taylor	Abigail Powers Fillmore	Jane Appleton Pierce	None	Mary Todd Lincoln
Religion	Episcopalian	Unitarian	Episcopalian	Presbyterian	Attended Presbyterian services

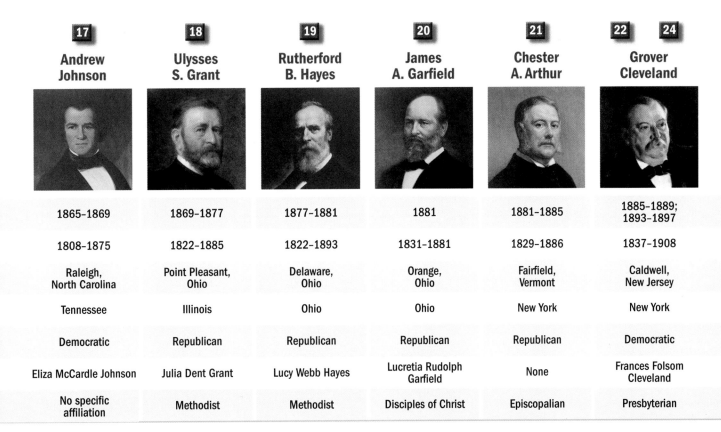

	6	7	8	9	10	11
	John Quincy Adams	**Andrew Jackson**	**Martin Van Buren**	**William H. Harrison**	**John Tyler**	**James K. Polk**
	1825–1829	1829–1837	1837–1841	1841	1841–1845	1845–1849
	1767–1848	1767–1845	1782–1862	1773–1841	1790–1862	1795–1849
	Braintree, Massachusetts	Waxhaw, South Carolina	Kinderhook, New York	Charles City County, Virginia	Charles City County, Virginia	Mecklenburg County, North Carolina
	Massachusetts	Tennessee	New York	Ohio	Virginia	Tennessee
	Democratic-Republican	Democratic	Democratic	Whig	Whig	Democratic
	Louisa Johnson Adams	None	None	Anna Symmes Harrison	Letitia Christian Tyler; Julia Gardiner Tyler	Sarah Childress Polk
	Unitarian	Presbyterian	Dutch Reformed	Episcopalian	Episcopalian	Presbyterian

	17	18	19	20	21	22 24
	Andrew Johnson	**Ulysses S. Grant**	**Rutherford B. Hayes**	**James A. Garfield**	**Chester A. Arthur**	**Grover Cleveland**
	1865–1869	1869–1877	1877–1881	1881	1881–1885	1885–1889; 1893–1897
	1808–1875	1822–1885	1822–1893	1831–1881	1829–1886	1837–1908
	Raleigh, North Carolina	Point Pleasant, Ohio	Delaware, Ohio	Orange, Ohio	Fairfield, Vermont	Caldwell, New Jersey
	Tennessee	Illinois	Ohio	Ohio	New York	New York
	Democratic	Republican	Republican	Republican	Republican	Democratic
	Eliza McCardle Johnson	Julia Dent Grant	Lucy Webb Hayes	Lucretia Rudolph Garfield	None	Frances Folsom Cleveland
	No specific affiliation	Methodist	Methodist	Disciples of Christ	Episcopalian	Presbyterian

Facts About Our Presidents

	23 Benjamin Harrison	**25** William McKinley	**26** Theodore Roosevelt	**27** William H. Taft	**28** Woodrow Wilson
Years in Office	1889–1893	1897–1901	1901–1909	1909–1913	1913–1921
Life Span	1833–1901	1843–1901	1858–1919	1857–1930	1856–1924
Birthplace	North Bend, Ohio	Niles, Ohio	New York, New York	Cincinnati, Ohio	Staunton, Virginia
Home State	Indiana	Ohio	New York	Ohio	New Jersey
Political Party	Republican	Republican	Republican	Republican	Democratic
First Lady	Caroline Scott Harrison	Ida Saxton McKinley	Edith Carow Roosevelt	Helen Herron Taft	Ellen Axson Wilson; Edith Galt Wilson
Religion	Presbyterian	Methodist	Dutch Reformed	Unitarian	Presbyterian

	35 John F. Kennedy	**36** Lyndon B. Johnson	**37** Richard M. Nixon	**38** Gerald R. Ford	**39** James E. Carter
Years in Office	1961–1963	1963–1969	1969–1974	1974–1977	1977–1981
Life Span	1917–1963	1908–1973	1913–1994	1913–2006	1924–
Birthplace	Brookline, Massachusetts	Stonewall, Texas	Yorba Linda, California	Omaha, Nebraska	Plains, Georgia
Home State	Massachusetts	Texas	California	Michigan	Georgia
Political Party	Democratic	Democratic	Republican	Republican	Democratic
First Lady	Jacqueline Bouvier Kennedy	Claudia "Lady Bird" Taylor Johnson	Thelma "Pat" Ryan Nixon	Elizabeth (Betty) Warren Ford	Rosalynn Smith Carter
Religion	Roman Catholic	Disciples of Christ	Quaker	Episcopalian	Southern Baptist

29	30	31	32	33	34
Warren G. Harding	**Calvin Coolidge**	**Herbert Hoover**	**Franklin D. Roosevelt**	**Harry S. Truman**	**Dwight D. Eisenhower**
1921–1923	1923–1929	1929–1933	1933–1945	1945–1953	1953–1961
1865–1923	1872–1933	1874–1964	1882–1945	1884–1972	1890–1969
Morrow County, Ohio	Plymouth, Vermont	West Branch, Iowa	Hyde Park, New York	Lamar, Missouri	Denison, Texas
Ohio	Massachusetts	California	New York	Missouri	Kansas
Republican	Republican	Republican	Democratic	Democratic	Republican
Florence DeWolfe Harding	Grace Goodhue Coolidge	Lou Henry Hoover	Anna Eleanor Roosevelt	Bess Wallace Truman	Marie "Mamie" Doud Eisenhower
Baptist	Congregational	Quaker	Episcopalian	Baptist	Presbyterian

40	41	42	43
Ronald Reagan	**George H. W. Bush**	**William J. Clinton**	**George W. Bush**
1981–1989	1989–1993	1993–2001	2001–
1911–2004	1924–	1946–	1946–
Tampico, Illinois	Milton, Massachusetts	Hope, Arkansas	New Haven, Connecticut
California	Texas	Arkansas	Texas
Republican	Republican	Democratic	Republican
Anne "Nancy" Davis Reagan	Barbara Pierce Bush	Hillary Rodham Clinton	Laura Welch Bush
Disciples of Christ	Episcopalian	Baptist	Methodist

Sometimes in history it becomes necessary for a group of people to break political ties with the country that rules it. When this happens, it is proper to explain the reasons for the need to separate.

We believe that all men are created equal and given by their Creator certain rights that cannot be taken away. People have the right to live, be free, and seek happiness.

Governments are established to protect these rights. The government gets its power from the support of the people it governs. If any form of government tries to take away the basic rights, it is the right of the people to change or end the government and to establish a new government that seems most likely to result in their safety and happiness.

Wise judgment will require that long-existing governments should not be changed for unimportant or temporary reasons. History has shown that people are more willing to suffer under a bad government than to get rid of the government they are used to. But when there are so many abuses and misuses of power by the government, it is the right and duty of the people to throw off such government and form a new government to protect their basic rights.

The colonies have suffered patiently, and now it is necessary for them to change the government. The king of Great Britain has repeatedly abused his power over these states. To prove this, the following facts are given.

In Congress, July 4, 1776
The unanimous Declaration of the thirteen United States of America

When, in the course of human events, it becomes necessary for one people to dissolve the political bands which have connected them with another, and to assume, among the powers of the earth, the separate and equal station to which the laws of nature and nature's God entitle them, a decent respect to the opinions of mankind requires that they should declare the causes which impel them to the separation.

We hold these truths to be self-evident, that all men are created equal, that they are endowed by their Creator with certain unalienable rights, that among these are life, liberty, and the pursuit of happiness.

That to secure these rights, governments are instituted among men, deriving their just powers from the consent of the governed; that whenever any form of government becomes destructive of these ends, it is the right of the people to alter or to abolish it, and to institute new government, laying its foundation on such principles, and organizing its powers in such form, as to them shall seem most likely to effect their safety and happiness.

Prudence, indeed, will dictate that governments long established should not be changed for light and transient causes; and accordingly all experience hath shown that mankind are more disposed to suffer, while evils are sufferable, than to right themselves by abolishing the forms to which they are accustomed. But when a long train of abuses and usurpations, pursuing invariably the same object, evinces a design to reduce them under absolute despotism, it is their right, it is their duty, to throw off such government, and to provide new guards for their future security.

Such has been the patient sufferance of these colonies; and such is now the necessity which constrains them to alter their former systems of government. The history of the present king of Great Britain is a history of repeated injuries and usurpations, all having in direct object the establishment of an absolute tyranny over these states. To prove this, let facts be submitted to a candid world.

He has refused his assent to laws the most wholesome and necessary for the public good. He has forbidden his governors to pass laws of immediate and pressing importance, unless suspended in their operation till his assent should be obtained; and when so suspended, he has utterly neglected to attend to them.

He has refused to pass other laws for the accommodation of large districts of people, unless those people would relinquish the right of representation in the legislature, a right inestimable to them, and formidable to tyrants only.

He has called together legislative bodies at places unusual, uncomfortable, and distant from the depository of their public records, for the sole purpose of fatiguing them into compliance with his measures.

He has dissolved representative houses repeatedly, for opposing, with manly firmness, his invasions on the rights of the people.

He has refused, for a long time after such dissolutions, to cause others to be elected; whereby the legislative powers, incapable of annihilation, have returned to the people at large for their exercise; the state remaining, in the meantime, exposed to all the dangers of invasion from without and convulsions within.

He has endeavored to prevent the population of these states; for that purpose obstructing the laws for the naturalization of foreigners, refusing to pass others to encourage their migrations hither, and raising the conditions of new appropriations of lands.

He has obstructed the administration of justice, by refusing his assent to laws for establishing judiciary powers.

He has made judges dependent on his will alone for the tenure of their offices, and the amount and payment of their salaries.

He has erected a multitude of new offices, and sent hither swarms of officers to harass our people and eat out their substance.

He has kept among us, in times of peace, standing armies, without the consent of our legislatures.

He has affected to render the military independent of, and superior to, the civil power.

He has combined with others to subject us to a jurisdiction foreign to our constitution and unacknowledged by our laws, giving his assent to their acts of pretended legislation:

The king has not given his approval to needed laws. He has not allowed his governors to pass laws needed immediately. The king has made the governors delay laws until they can get his permission, and then he has ignored the laws.

He has refused to pass other laws for the help of large districts of people, unless those people would give up the right of representation in the legislature, a right priceless to them, and threatening only to tyrants.

He has called together legislative bodies at unusual and uncomfortable places, far from where they store their public records, and only for the purpose of tiring them into obeying his measures.

He has repeatedly done away with legislative groups that firmly opposed him for taking away the rights of the people.

After he has dissolved these representative meetings, he has refused to allow new elections. Because of this lack of legislative power, the people are exposed to the dangers of invasion from outside the colonies and violence within the colonies.

He has tried to prevent people from immigrating to these states by blocking the process for foreigners to become citizens, refusing to pass laws to encourage people to travel to America, and making it harder to move to and own new lands.

He has interfered with the administration of justice, by refusing to approve laws for establishing courts.

He has made judges do what he wants by controlling how long they serve and how much they are paid.

He has created many new government offices, and sent many officials to torment our people and live off of our hard work.

In times of peace, he has kept soldiers among us, without the consent of our legislatures.

He has tried to make the military separate from, and superior to, the civil government.

He and others have made us live under laws that are different from our laws. He has given his approval to these unfair laws that Parliament has adopted:

For forcing us to feed and house many British soldiers;

For using pretend trials to protect British soldiers from punishment for murdering people in America;

For cutting off our trade with the world;

For taxing us without our consent;

For taking away, in many cases, the benefits of trial by jury;

For taking us to Great Britain to be tried for made-up offenses;

For doing away with the free system of English laws in a neighboring province, and establishing a harsh government there, and enlarging its boundaries, as a way to introduce the same absolute rule into these colonies;

For taking away our governing documents, doing away with our most valuable laws, and changing our governments completely;

For setting aside our own legislatures, and declaring that Great Britain has power to make laws for us in all cases whatsoever.

He has deserted government here, by not protecting us and waging war against us.

He has robbed our ships on the seas, destroyed our coasts, burned our towns, and destroyed the lives of our people.

He is at this time sending large armies of foreign hired soldiers to complete the works of death, destruction, and injustice he has already begun. These deeds are among the cruelest ever seen in history, and are totally unworthy of the head of a civilized nation.

He has forced our fellow citizens, who were captured on the high seas, to fight against America, to kill their friends and family, or to be killed themselves.

He has stirred up civil disorder among us, and has tried to cause the merciless killing of the people living on the frontiers by the Indians, whose rule of warfare includes the deliberate killing of people regardless of age, sex, or conditions.

In every stage of these mistreatments we have asked for a solution in the most humble terms; our repeated requests have been answered only by repeated injury. A leader who is so unfair and acts like a dictator is unfit to be the ruler of a free people.

For quartering large bodies of armed troops among us;

For protecting them, by a mock trial, from punishment for any murders which they should commit on the inhabitants of these states;

For cutting off our trade with all parts of the world;

For imposing taxes on us without our consent;

For depriving us, in many cases, of the benefits of trial by jury;

For transporting us beyond seas, to be tried for pretended offenses;

For abolishing the free system of English laws in a neighboring province, establishing therein an arbitrary government, and enlarging its boundaries, so as to render it at once an example and fit instrument for introducing the same absolute rule into these colonies;

For taking away our charters, abolishing our most valuable laws, and altering fundamentally the forms of our governments;

For suspending our own legislatures, and declaring themselves invested with power to legislate for us in all cases whatsoever.

He has abdicated government here, by declaring us out of his protection and waging war against us.

He has plundered our seas, ravaged our coasts, burned our towns, and destroyed the lives of our people.

He is at this time transporting large armies of foreign mercenaries to complete the works of death, desolation, and tyranny already begun with circumstances of cruelty and perfidy scarcely paralleled in the most barbarous ages, and totally unworthy the head of a civilized nation.

He has constrained our fellow citizens, taken captive on the high seas, to bear arms against their country, to become the executioners of their friends and brethren, or to fall themselves by their hands.

He has excited domestic insurrection among us, and has endeavored to bring on the inhabitants of our frontiers, the merciless Indian savages, whose known rule of warfare is an undistinguished destruction of all ages, sexes, and conditions.

In every stage of these oppressions we have petitioned for redress in the most humble terms; our repeated petitions have been answered only by repeated injury. A prince, whose character is thus marked by every act which may define a tyrant, is unfit to be the ruler of a free people.

Nor have we been wanting in attentions to our British brethren. We have warned them, from time to time, of attempts by their legislature to extend an unwarrantable jurisdiction over us. We have reminded them of the circumstances of our emigration and settlement here. We have appealed to their native justice and magnanimity; and we have conjured them, by the ties of our common kindred, to disavow these usurpations, which would inevitably interrupt our connections and correspondence. They, too, have been deaf to the voice of justice and consanguinity. We must, therefore, acquiesce in the necessity which denounces our separation, and hold them, as we hold the rest of mankind, enemies in war; in peace, friends.

We, therefore, the representatives of the United States of America, in General Congress assembled, appealing to the Supreme Judge of the world for the rectitude of our intentions, do, in the name and by the authority of the good people of these colonies, solemnly publish and declare that these United Colonies are, and of right ought to be, free and independent states; that they are absolved from all allegiance to the British crown, and that all political connection between them and the state of Great Britain is, and ought to be, totally dissolved; and that, as free and independent states, they have full power to levy war, conclude peace, contract alliances, establish commerce, and do all other acts and things which independent states may of right do. And, for the support of this declaration, with a firm reliance on the protection of Divine Providence, we mutually pledge to each other our lives, our fortunes, and our sacred honor.

We have also asked for help from the British people. We have warned them, from time to time, of attempts by their government to extend illegal power over us. We have reminded them of why we came to America. We have appealed to their sense of justice and generosity; and we have begged them, because of all we have in common, to give up these abuses of power. They, like the king, have not listened to the voice of justice and brotherhood. We must, therefore, declare our separation. In war the British are our enemies. In peace, they are our friends.

We, therefore, as the representatives of the people of the United States of America, in this General Congress assembled, appealing to God for the honesty of our purpose, do solemnly publish and declare that these United Colonies are, and rightly should be, free and independent states. The people of the United States are no longer subjects of the British crown. All political connections between the colonies and Great Britain are totally ended. These free and independent states have full power to declare war, make peace, make treaties with other countries, establish trade, and do all other acts and things that independent states have the right to do. To support this declaration, with a firm trust on the protection of Divine Providence, we pledge to each other our lives, our fortunes, and our sacred honor.

Button Gwinnett (GA)	Benjamin Harrison (VA)	Lewis Morris (NY)
Lyman Hall (GA)	Thomas Nelson, Jr. (VA)	Richard Stockton (NJ)
George Walton (GA)	Francis Lightfoot Lee (VA)	John Witherspoon (NJ)
William Hooper (NC)	Carter Braxton (VA)	Francis Hopkinson (NJ)
Joseph Hewes (NC)	Robert Morris (PA)	John Hart (NJ)
John Penn (NC)	Benjamin Rush (PA)	Abraham Clark (NJ)
Edward Rutledge (SC)	Benjamin Franklin (PA)	Josiah Bartlett (NH)
Thomas Heyward, Jr. (SC)	John Morton (PA)	William Whipple (NH)
Thomas Lynch, Jr. (SC)	George Clymer (PA)	Samuel Adams (MA)
Arthur Middleton (SC)	James Smith (PA)	John Adams (MA)
John Hancock (MA)	George Taylor (PA)	Robert Treat Paine (MA)
Samuel Chase (MD)	James Wilson (PA)	Elbridge Gerry (MA)
William Paca (MD)	George Ross (PA)	Stephen Hopkins (RI)
Thomas Stone (MD)	Caesar Rodney (DE)	William Ellery (RI)
Charles Carroll of Carrollton (MD)	George Read (DE)	Roger Sherman (CT)
George Wythe (VA)	Thomas McKean (DE)	Samuel Huntington (CT)
Richard Henry Lee (VA)	William Floyd (NY)	William Williams (CT)
Thomas Jefferson (VA)	Philip Livingston (NY)	Oliver Wolcott (CT)
	Francis Lewis (NY)	Matthew Thornton (NH)

"Among the natural rights of the Colonists are these: First, a right to life; Secondly, to liberty; Thirdly, to property; together with the right to support and defend them in the best manner they can."

Samuel Adams, The Report of the Committee of Correspondence to the Boston Town Meeting

"All, too, will bear in mind this sacred principle, that though the will of the majority is in all cases to prevail, that will to be rightful must be reasonable; that the minority possess their equal rights, which equal law must protect, and to violate would be oppression."

Thomas Jefferson, First Inaugural Address

We the people of the United States, in order to form a more perfect union, establish justice, insure peace in our nation, provide for our defense, promote the general welfare, and secure the blessings of liberty to ourselves and our descendants, do authorize and establish this Constitution for the United States of America.

ARTICLE 1
Legislative Branch

SECTION 1. Congress
Only the Congress of the United States has the power to make national laws. Congress is made up of a Senate and House of Representatives.

SECTION 2. House of Representatives
Members of the House of Representatives will be chosen every two years. People who are eligible to vote for state legislators are also eligible to vote for members of the House of Representatives.

To be a member of the House of Representatives, a person must be at least twenty-five years of age, must have been a citizen of the United States for at least seven years, and must live in the state the person is chosen to represent.

The number of representatives a state has is determined by the state's population. A census, or count, of the population must be taken every ten years. Each state shall have at least one representative.

W e the people of the United States, in order to form a more perfect union, establish justice, insure domestic tranquility, provide for the common defense, promote the general welfare, and secure the blessings of liberty to ourselves and our posterity, do ordain and establish this Constitution for the United States of America.

ARTICLE 1
Legislative Branch

SECTION 1. Congress
All legislative powers herein granted shall be vested in a Congress of the United States, which shall consist of a Senate and House of Representatives.

SECTION 2. House of Representatives
The House of Representatives shall be composed of members chosen every second year by the people of the several states, and the electors in each state shall have the qualifications requisite for electors of the most numerous branch of the State legislature.

No person shall be a representative who shall not have attained to the age of twenty-five years, and been seven years a citizen of the United States, and who shall not, when elected, be an inhabitant of that state in which he shall be chosen.

Representatives ~~and direct taxes~~ shall be apportioned among the several states which may be included within this Union, according to their respective numbers, ~~which shall be determined by adding to the whole numbers of free persons, including those bound to service for a term of years, and excluding Indians not taxed, three fifths of all other persons.~~* The actual enumeration shall be made within three years after the first meeting of the Congress of the United States, and within every subsequent term of ten years, in such manner as they shall by law direct. The number of representatives shall not exceed one for every thirty thousand, but each State shall have at least one representative; ~~and until such enumeration shall be made, the State of New Hampshire shall be entitled to choose three, Massachusetts eight, Rhode Island and Providence Plantations one, Connecticut five, New York six, New Jersey four, Pennsylvania eight, Delaware one, Maryland six, Virginia ten, North Carolina five, South Carolina five, and Georgia three.~~* (*Changed by the Fourteenth Amendment)

When vacancies happen in the representation from any state, the executive authority thereof shall issue writs of election to fill such vacancies.

The House of Representatives shall choose their speaker and other officers, and shall have the sole power of impeachment.

SECTION 3. Senate

The Senate of the United States shall be composed of two senators from each state, ~~chosen by the legislature thereof~~,* for six years; and each senator shall have one vote. *(*Changed by the Seventeenth Amendment)*

Immediately after they shall be assembled in consequence of the first election, they shall be divided as equally as may be into three classes. The seats of the senators of the first class shall be vacated at the expiration of the second year, of the second class at the expiration of the fourth year, and of the third class at the expiration of the sixth year, so that one third may be chosen every second year; ~~and if vacancies happen by resignation, or otherwise, during the recess of the legislature of any State, the executive thereof may make temporary appointments until the next meeting of the legislature, which shall then fill such vacancies.~~*

*(*Changed by the Seventeenth Amendment)*

No person shall be a senator who shall not have attained to the age of thirty years, and been nine years a citizen of the United States, and who shall not, when elected, be an inhabitant of that State for which he shall be chosen.

The Vice President of the United States shall be president of the Senate, but shall have no vote, unless they be equally divided.

The Senate shall choose their other officers, and also a president pro tempore, in the absence of the Vice President, or when he shall exercise the office of President of the United States.

The Senate shall have the sole power to try all impeachments. When sitting for that purpose, they shall be on oath or affirmation. When the President of the United States is tried, the Chief Justice shall preside: and no person shall be convicted without the concurrence of two thirds of the members present.

Judgment in cases of impeachment shall not extend further than to removal from office, and disqualification to hold any office of honor, trust or profit under the United States: but the party convicted shall nevertheless be liable and subject to indictment, trial, judgment and punishment, according to law.

When open positions occur happen in the representation from any state, the governor of the state will call a special election to fill the empty seat.

The House of Representatives shall choose their speaker and other officers, and only the House of Representatives may impeach, or accuse, government officials of crimes in office.

SECTION 3. Senate

The Senate of the United States shall be made up of two senators from each state. Each senator serves for six years; and each senator shall have one vote.

(Until the Seventeenth Amendment, the senators were chosen by the legislature of the state they represented).

Only one-third of the senators are up for election at one time.

(The remaining section was changed by the Seventeenth Amendment).

A senator must be at least thirty years old, a citizen of the United States for at least nine years, and live in the state the senator is chosen to represent.

The Vice-President of the United States is also the president of the Senate, but has no vote unless there is a tie.

The Senate chooses its own officers. The Senate also chooses a senator to be the president pro tempore who serves as the temporary president of the Senate in the absence of the Vice-President, or when the Vice-President acts as President of the United States.

Only the Senate has the power to bring all impeachments to trial. When meeting on an impeachment, the senators shall take an oath or affirmation. When the President of the United States is tried on impeachment charges, the Chief Justice shall be in charge, and no person shall be found guilty without the agreement of two-thirds of the members present.

Impeached officials who are convicted can be removed from office, and disqualified from holding any other government office. Other courts in the country may still try, judge, and punish the impeached official.

SECTION 4. Elections and Meetings of Congress

The state legislature determines the times, places, and method of holding elections for senators and representatives. Congress may make laws that change some of the regulations.

The Congress shall meet at least once in every year.

(Until the passing of the Twentieth Amendment, Congress met on the first Monday in December.)

SECTION 5. Rules for Congress

The Senate and House of Representatives judge the fairness of the elections and the qualifications of their own members. At least half of the members must be present to do business; but a smaller number may end the meeting from day to day, and may force absent members to attend and may penalize a member for not attending.

Each house may determine the rules of its proceedings and punish its members for disorderly behavior. Each house may, with the agreement of two-thirds of its members, force a member out of office.

Each house of Congress shall keep a record of its proceedings, and from time to time publish the record, except those parts that may need to be kept secret. If one-fifth of the members want it, the votes on any matter shall be published.

During the session of Congress, neither house shall adjourn for more than three days without the permission of the other, nor can either house decide to meet at any other place than where both houses agree.

SECTION 6. Rights and Restrictions of Members of Congress

The senators and representatives shall receive a payment for their services, to be decided by law, and paid out of the Treasury of the United States. Except for very serious crimes, senators and representatives are protected from arrest during their attendance at the session of Congress, and in going to and returning from Congress. Members of Congress shall not be arrested for anything they say in Congress.

No senator or representative shall be appointed to any government job while serving in Congress. No senator or representative is allowed to take a government job that is created or has its salary increased during the senator's or representative's term of office. While holding a government office, no person shall also be a member of Congress.

SECTION 4. Elections and Meetings of Congress

The times, places, and manner of holding elections for senators and representatives shall be prescribed in each State by the legislature thereof; but the Congress may at any time by law make or alter such regulations, except as to the places of choosing senators.

The Congress shall assemble at least once in every year, ~~and such meeting shall be on the first Monday in December,~~* unless they shall by law appoint a different day. (*Changed by the Twentieth Amendment)*

SECTION 5. Rules for Congress

Each house shall be the judge of the elections, returns and qualifications of its own members, and a majority of each shall constitute a quorum to do business; but a smaller number may adjourn from day to day, and may be authorized to compel the attendance of absent members, in such manner, and under such penalties as each house may provide.

Each house may determine the rules of its proceedings, punish its members for disorderly behavior, and, with the concurrence of two thirds, expel a member.

Each house shall keep a journal of its proceedings, and from time to time publish the same, excepting such parts as may in their judgment require secrecy; and the yeas and nays of the members of either house on any question shall, at the desire of one fifth of those present, be entered on the journal.

Neither house, during the session of Congress, shall, without the consent of the other, adjourn for more than three days, nor to any other place than that in which the two houses shall be sitting.

SECTION 6. Rights and Restrictions of Members of Congress

The senators and representatives shall receive a compensation for their services, to be ascertained by law, and paid out of the Treasury of the United States. They shall in all cases, except treason, felony and breach of the peace, be privileged from arrest during their attendance at the session of their respective houses, and in going to and returning from the same; and for any speech or debate in either house, they shall not be questioned in any other place.

No senator or representative shall, during the time for which he was elected, be appointed to any civil office under the authority of the United States, which shall have been created, or the emoluments whereof shall have been increased during such time; and no person holding any office under the United States shall be a member of either house during his continuance in office.

SECTION 7. How Laws Are Made

All bills for raising revenue shall originate in the House of Representatives; but the Senate may propose or concur with amendments as on other bills.

Every bill which shall have passed the House of Representatives and the Senate shall, before it become a law, be presented to the President of the United States; if he approve he shall sign it, but if not he shall return it, with his objections to that house in which it shall have originated, who shall enter the objections at large on their journal, and proceed to reconsider it. If after such reconsideration two thirds of that house shall agree to pass the bill, it shall be sent, together with the objections, to the other house, by which it shall likewise be reconsidered, and if approved by two thirds of that house, it shall become a law. But in all such cases the votes of both houses shall be determined by yeas and nays, and the names of persons voting for and against the bill shall be entered on the journal of each house respectively. If any bill shall not be returned by the President within ten days (Sundays excepted) after it shall have been presented to him, the same shall be a law, in like manner as if he had signed it, unless the Congress by their adjournment prevent its return, in which case it shall not be a law.

Every order, resolution, or vote to which the concurrence of the Senate and House of Representatives may be necessary (except on a question of adjournment) shall be presented to the President of the United States; and before the same shall take effect, shall be approved by him, or being disapproved by him, shall be repassed by two thirds of the Senate and House of Representatives, according to the rules and limitations prescribed in the case of a bill.

SECTION 8. Powers of Congress

The Congress shall have power:

To lay and collect taxes, duties, imposts and excises, to pay the debts and provide for the common defense and general welfare of the United States; but all duties, imposts and excises shall be uniform throughout the United States;

To borrow money on the credit of the United States;

To regulate commerce with foreign nations, and among the several States, and with the Indian tribes;

To establish a uniform rule of naturalization, and uniform laws on the subject of bankruptcies throughout the United States;

To coin money, regulate the value thereof, and of foreign coin, and fix the standard of weights and measures;

To provide for the punishment of counterfeiting the securities and current coin of the United States;

To establish post offices and post roads;

SECTION 7. How Laws Are Made

All bills for raising money shall begin in the House of Representatives. The Senate may suggest or agree with amendments to these tax bills, as with other bills.

Every bill that has passed the House of Representatives and the Senate must be presented to the President of the United States before it becomes a law. If the President approves of the bill, the President shall sign it. If the President does not approve, then the bill may be vetoed. The President then sends it back to the house in which it began, with an explanation of the objections. That house writes the objections on its record and begins to reconsider it. If two-thirds of each house agree to pass the bill, it shall become a law. But in all such cases the votes of both houses shall be determined by "yes" and "no" votes, and the names of persons voting for and against the bill shall be entered on the record of each house. If any bill is neither signed nor vetoed by the President within ten days (except for Sundays) after it has been sent to the President, the bill shall be a law. If Congress adjourns before ten days have passed, the bill does not become a law.

Every order, resolution, or vote that passes in the Senate and House of Representatives shall be presented to the President of the United States to be signed or vetoed. A bill that is vetoed by the President can become a law only if it is passed again by two-thirds of the Senate and House of Representatives.

SECTION 8. Powers of Congress

The Congress shall have power to:
- establish and collect taxes on imported and exported goods and on goods sold within the country. Congress also shall pay the debts and provide for the defense and general welfare of the United States. All federal taxes shall be the same throughout the United States;
- borrow money on the credit of the United States;
- make laws about trade with other countries, among the states, and with the American Indian tribes;
- establish one procedure by which a person from another country can become a legal citizen of the United States, and establish bankruptcy laws to deal with people and businesses who cannot pay what they owe;
- print or coin money and regulate its value. Congress has the power to determine how much foreign money is worth in American money. Congress sets the standard of weights and measures;

- establish punishments for counterfeiting, or making fake money, stocks, and bonds;
- establish post offices and roads for mail delivery;
- promote the progress of science and useful arts by protecting, for limited times, the writings and discoveries of authors and inventors by issuing copyrights and patents;
- create courts lower than the Supreme Court;
- define and punish crimes committed on the high seas, and crimes that break international laws;
- declare war and make rules about taking enemy property on land or sea;
- set up and supply armies. Congress cannot provide funding for the armies for more than two years at a time;
- set up and supply a navy;
- make rules for the armed forces;
- provide for calling the militia to action to carry out the laws of the country, put down revolts and riots and fight off invasions;
- provide for organizing, arming, and disciplining the militia, and for governing those employed in the armed service of the United States. The states have the right to appoint the officers, and the authority of training the militia according to the rules made by Congress;
- govern the nation's capital [Washington, D.C.] and military bases in the United States; and
- make all laws needed to carry out the powers mentioned earlier in the Constitution, and all other powers placed by this Constitution in the government of the United States, or in any department or officer of the government.

SECTION 9. Powers Denied to Congress

Congress does not have the power to prevent enslaved people from being brought into the country until 1808, but a tax may be placed on each imported person.

(Congress passed a law in 1808 forbidding the slave trade.)

Congress may not do away with laws that protect an individual from being jailed unless the person goes to trial or unless specific criminal charges are filed, unless the public safety requires it during a rebellion or invasion.

No law shall be passed that penalizes a person or group without the benefit of a trial or makes an action illegal after the action was taken.

To promote the progress of science and useful arts by securing for limited times to authors and inventors the exclusive right to their respective writings and discoveries;

To constitute tribunals inferior to the Supreme Court;

To define and punish piracies and felonies committed on the high seas, and offenses against the law of nations;

To declare war, grant letters of marque and reprisal, and make rules concerning captures on land and water;* *(*These powers are no longer exercised by Congress.)*

To raise and support armies, but no appropriation of money to that use shall be for a longer term than two years;

To provide and maintain a navy;

To make rules for the government and regulation of the land and naval forces;

To provide for calling forth the militia to execute the laws of the Union, suppress insurrections and repel invasions;

To provide for organizing, arming, and disciplining the militia, and for governing such part of them as may be employed in the service of the United States, reserving to the States respectively the appointment of the officers, and the authority of training the militia according to the discipline prescribed by Congress;

To exercise exclusive legislation in all cases whatsoever, over such district (not exceeding ten miles square) as may, by cession of particular States and the acceptance of Congress, become the seat of the government of the United States, and to exercise like authority over all places purchased by the consent of the legislature of the State in which the same shall be, for the erection of forts, magazines, arsenals, dockyards, and other needful buildings; and

To make all laws which shall be necessary and proper for carrying into execution the foregoing powers, and all other powers vested by this Constitution in the government of the United States, or in any department or officer thereof.

SECTION 9. Powers Denied to Congress

The migration or importation of such persons as any of the States now existing shall think proper to admit shall not be prohibited by the Congress prior to the year one thousand eight hundred and eight, but a tax or duty may be imposed on such importation, not exceeding ten dollars for each person.

The privilege of the writ of habeas corpus shall not be suspended, unless when in cases of rebellion or invasion the public safety may require it.

No bill of attainder or ex post facto law shall be passed.

No capitation, or other direct,* tax shall be laid, unless in proportion to the census or enumeration herein before directed to be taken.* (*Changed by the Sixteenth Amendment)

No tax or duty shall be laid on articles exported from any State.

No preference shall be given by any regulation of commerce or revenue to the ports of one State over those of another; nor shall vessels bound to, or from, one State be obliged to enter, clear, or pay duties in another.

No money shall be drawn from the Treasury, but in consequence of appropriations made by law; and a regular statement and account of the receipts and expenditures of all public money shall be published from time to time.

No title of nobility shall be granted by the United States; and no person holding any office of profit or trust under them, shall, without the consent of the Congress, accept of any present, emolument, office, or title of any kind whatever, from any king, prince, or foreign State.

SECTION 10. Powers Denied to the States

No State shall enter into any treaty, alliance, or confederation; grant letters of marque and reprisal; coin money; emit bills of credit; make anything but gold and silver coin a tender in payment of debts; pass any bill of attainder, ex post facto law, or law impairing the obligation of contracts, or grant any title of nobility.

No State shall, without the consent of the Congress, lay any imposts, or duties on imports or exports, except what may be absolutely necessary for executing its inspection laws; and the net produce of all duties and imposts, laid by any State on imports or exports, shall be for the use of the Treasury of the United States; and all such laws shall be subject to the revision and control of the Congress.

No State shall, without the consent of Congress, lay any duty of tonnage, keep troops, or ships of war in time of peace, enter into any agreement or compact with another State, or with a foreign power, or engage in war, unless actually invaded, or in such imminent danger as will not admit of delay.

ARTICLE 2

The Executive Branch

SECTION 1. The President and Vice President

The executive power shall be vested in a President of the United States of America. He shall hold his office during the term of four years, and, together with the Vice President, chosen for the same term, be elected as follows:

No person in the United States may be taxed unless everyone is taxed the same. *(The Sixteenth Amendment allowed an income tax.)*

No tax shall be put on articles exported from any state.

No laws shall be passed that give special treatment to one state over those of another in trade. Ships shall not be required to pay a tax to enter another state.

No money shall be taken from the Treasury, without a law passed by Congress. A public record must be kept of money raised and money spent.

The United States shall not give any titles of nobility, such as king or queen. No person holding any government office shall accept any present, payment, office, or title of any kind from another country, without the consent of the Congress.

SECTION 10. Powers Denied to the States

No state can make treaties or alliances with other nations or issue official documents permitting private citizens to capture merchant ships or engage warships of another nation. No state can issue its own money or make anything, other than gold or silver, legal as currency. No state can pass laws that apply to actions done before the law was passed. No state may allow a person to be punished without a fair trial. No state can pass laws that excuse anyone from a contract. No state can give anyone a title of nobility.

Without approval from Congress, no state can collect taxes on goods coming in or going out of the state, except those small fees needed for customs inspections. Any taxes from trade become the property of the United States government.

Without approval from Congress, states are forbidden to tax ships or keep troops or warships in peacetime, unless endangered by actual invasion. States may not enter into an agreement with another state or foreign nation.

ARTICLE 2
The Executive Branch

SECTION 1. The President and Vice-President

The President has the power to carry out the laws of Congress, and the President and Vice-President serve a four-year term.

The legislature of each state determines the process for electing its representatives in the Electoral College, which officially elects the President and the Vice-President. Each state's total number of electors is determined by the state's total number of members in Congress. No person holding any office in the federal government can become an elector.

(Until this was changed by the Twelfth Amendment, the person who received the most electoral votes became the President and the person with the next highest number became the Vice-President. The Twelfth Amendment overruled this clause and changed the way the election process worked.)

Congress determines the date and time when each state's electors are to cast their votes for President and Vice-President.

To become President a person must be born a citizen of the United States, be at least thirty-five years old, and have lived in the United States for at least fourteen years.

If a President dies, is disabled, or is removed from office, the Vice-President becomes President.

(The Twenty-Fifth Amendment changed the method for filling these offices if they become vacant.)

Each State shall appoint, in such manner as the legislature thereof may direct, a number of electors, equal to the whole number of senators and representatives to which the State may be entitled in the Congress, but no senator or representative, or person holding an office of trust or profit under the United States, shall be appointed an elector.

~~The electors shall meet in their respective States, and vote by ballot for two persons, of whom one at least shall not be an inhabitant of the same State with themselves. And they shall make a list of all the persons voted for, and of the number of votes for each; which list they shall sign and certify, and transmit sealed to the seat of the government of the United States, directed to the president of the Senate. The president of the Senate shall, in the presence of the Senate and House of Representatives, open all the certificates, and the votes shall then be counted. The person having the greatest number of votes shall be the President, if such number be a majority of the whole number of electors appointed; and if there be more than one who have such majority, and have an equal number of votes, then the House of Representatives shall immediately choose by ballot one of them for President; and if no person have a majority, then from the five highest on the list the said House shall in like manner choose the President. But in choosing the President, the votes shall be taken by States, the representation from each State having one vote; a quorum for this purpose shall consist of a member or members from two-thirds of the States, and a majority of all the States shall be necessary to a choice. In every case, after the choice of the President, the person having the greatest number of votes of the electors shall be the Vice President. But if there should remain two or more who have equal votes, the Senate shall choose from them by ballot the Vice President.~~* (*Changed by the Twelfth Amendment*)

The Congress may determine the time of choosing the electors, and the day on which they shall give their votes; which day shall be the same throughout the United States.

No person except a natural-born citizen, or a citizen of the United States, at the time of the adoption of this Constitution, shall be eligible to the office of President; neither shall any person be eligible to that office who shall not have attained to the age of thirty-five years, and been fourteen years a resident within the United States.

In case of the removal of the President from office, or of his death, resignation, or inability to discharge the powers and duties of the said office, the same shall devolve on the Vice President~~, and the Congress may by law provide for the case of removal, death, resignation, or inability, both of the President and Vice President, declaring what officer shall then act as President, and such officer shall act accordingly, until the disability be removed, or a President shall be elected.~~* (*Changed by the Twenty-Fifth Amendment*)

The President shall, at stated times, receive for his services a compensation, which shall neither be increased nor diminished during the period for which he shall have been elected, and he shall not receive within that period any other emolument from the United States, or any of them.

Before he enter on the execution of his office, he shall take the following oath or affirmation: — "I do solemnly swear (or affirm) that I will faithfully execute the office of President of the United States, and will to the best of my ability, preserve, protect and defend the Constitution of the United States."

SECTION 2. Powers of the President

The President shall be Commander in Chief of the Army and Navy of the United States, and of the militia of the several States, when called into the actual service of the United States; he may require the opinion, in writing, of the principal officer in each of the executive departments, upon any subject relating to the duties of their respective offices, and he shall have power to grant reprieves and pardons for offenses against the United States, except in cases of impeachment.

He shall have power, by and with the advice and consent of the Senate, to make treaties, provided two-thirds of the senators present concur; and he shall nominate, and by and with the advice and consent of the Senate, shall appoint ambassadors, other public ministers and consuls, judges of the Supreme Court, and all other officers of the United States, whose appointments are not herein otherwise provided for, and which shall be established by law; but the Congress may by law vest the appointment of such inferior officers, as they think proper, in the President alone, in the courts of law, or in the heads of departments.

The President shall have power to fill up all vacancies that may happen during the recess of the Senate, by granting commissions which shall expire at the end of their next session.

SECTION 3. Duties of the President

He shall from time to time give to the Congress information of the state of the Union, and recommend to their consideration such measures as he shall judge necessary and expedient; he may, on extraordinary occasions, convene both houses, or either of them, and in case of disagreement between them, with respect to the time of adjournment, he may adjourn them to such time as he shall think proper; he shall receive ambassadors and other public ministers; he shall take care that the laws be faithfully executed, and shall commission all the officers of the United States.

The President will receive a salary, but it cannot be increased or decreased during the term(s) of office. The President cannot have another occupation or receive outside compensation while in office.

Before assuming the duties of the office, the President must take the following oath or affirmation: "I do solemnly swear (or affirm) that I will faithfully execute the office of President of the United States, and will to the best of my ability, preserve, protect and defend the Constitution of the United States."

SECTION 2. Powers of the President

The President is the leader of the armed forces of the United States and of the state militias during times of war. The President may require the principal officer in each of the executive departments to write a report about any subject relating to their duties, and can grant delays of punishment or pardons for criminals, except in cases of impeachment.

With the advice and consent of two-thirds of the members of the Senate, the President can make treaties with foreign nations and can appoint ambassadors and other officials as necessary to handle the countries diplomatic affairs with other countries. The President can appoint federal judges and other key officers in the executive branch of government, with the consent of two-thirds of the Senate. Congress may give power to the President to appoint minor government officials and heads of departments.

When the Senate is not in session, the President can make temporary appointments to offices that require Senate approval. These appointments expire when the next session ends.

SECTION 3. Duties of the President

The President must make a report to Congress on a regular basis, providing information concerning important national developments and goals. Lawmaking requests for Congress should be given as well. The President can call for special sessions of one or both houses of Congress for special reasons. If the houses of Congress cannot agree on a common date for adjournment, the President has the power to make that decision. The President is to officially receive foreign ambassadors and other public ministers. The President is to fully and faithfully carry out the laws of Congress and sign the documents required to give officers the rights to perform their duties.

SECTION 4. Removal from Office

The President, Vice-President, and all civil officers can be removed from office if convicted on impeachment charges for treason, bribery, or other high crimes and misdemeanors.

ARTICLE 3
The Judicial Branch

SECTION 1. Federal Courts

The Supreme Court is the highest court in the land. Congress has the power to create all other federal courts. Federal judges may hold office for life as long as they act properly, and they shall receive a salary that cannot be lowered during the judge's time of service.

SECTION 2. Powers of Federal Courts

The power of the federal courts covers two types of cases: (1) those involving the interpretation of the Constitution, federal laws, treaties, and laws relating to ships on the high seas; and (2) those involving the United States government itself, foreign diplomats, two or more state governments, citizens of different states, and a state or its citizens versus foreign countries or their citizens.

Cases involving foreign diplomats and any state in the United States will be tried by the Supreme Court. Other cases tried by the Supreme Court are those appealed or brought forward from lower federal courts or from state courts. Congress can decide to make exceptions to these regulations.

Except for those trials involving impeachment, all persons accused of crimes are guaranteed a jury trial in the same state where the crime was committed. When a crime is committed outside of any state, such as on a ship at sea, Congress will decide where the trial will take place.

SECTION 3. Treason

Anyone who makes war against the United States or gives help to the nation's enemies, can be charged with treason. No one can be convicted of treason unless two witnesses support the charge or unless the person confesses to the charge in open court.

SECTION 4. Removal from Office

The President, Vice President, and all civil officers of the United States, shall be removed from office on impeachment for, and conviction of, treason, bribery, or other high crimes and misdemeanors.

ARTICLE 3
The Judicial Branch

SECTION 1. Federal Courts

The judicial power of the United States shall be vested in one Supreme Court, and in such inferior courts as the Congress may from time to time ordain and establish. The judges, both of the Supreme and inferior courts, shall hold their offices during good behavior, and shall, at stated times, receive for their services a compensation, which shall not be diminished during their continuance in office.

SECTION 2. Powers of Federal Courts

The judicial power shall extend to all cases, in law and equity, arising under this Constitution, the laws of the United States, and treaties made, or which shall be made, under their authority; — to all cases affecting ambassadors, other public ministers and consuls; — to all cases of admiralty and maritime jurisdiction; — to controversies to which the United States shall be a party; — to controversies between two or more States; — between a State and citizens of another State; —between citizens of different states — between citizens of the same State claiming lands under grants of different States, and between a State, or the citizens thereof, and foreign States, citizens or subjects.

In all cases affecting ambassadors, other public ministers and consuls, and those in which a State shall be party, the Supreme Court shall have original jurisdiction. In all the other cases before mentioned, the Supreme Court shall have appellate jurisdiction, both as to law and fact, with such exceptions, and under such regulations as the Congress shall make.

The trial of all crimes, except in cases of impeachment, shall be by jury; and such trial shall be held in the State where the said crimes shall have been committed; but when not committed within any State, the trial shall be at such place or places as the Congress may by law have directed.

SECTION 3. Treason

Treason against the United States shall consist only in levying war against them, or in adhering to their enemies, giving them aid and comfort. No person shall be convicted of treason unless on the testimony of two witnesses to the same overt act, or on confession in open court.

The Congress shall have power to declare the punishment of treason, but no attainder of treason shall work corruption of blood, or forfeiture except during the life of the person attainted.

Congress has the power to decide punishments for acts of treason. The family of the traitor does not share in the guilt.

ARTICLE 4
Relations Among the States

SECTION 1. Recognition by Each State
Full faith and credit shall be given in each State to the public acts, records, and judicial proceedings of every other State. And the Congress may by general laws prescribe the manner in which such acts, records, and proceedings shall be proved, and the effect thereof.

SECTION 2. Rights of Citizens in States
The citizens of each State shall be entitled to all privileges and immunities of citizens in the several States.

A person charged in any State with treason, felony, or other crime, who shall flee from justice, and be found in another State, shall on demand of the executive authority of the State from which he fled, be delivered up to be removed to the State having jurisdiction of the crime.

No person held to service or labor in one State, under the laws thereof, escaping into another, shall, in consequence of any law or regulation therein, be discharged from such service or labor, but shall be delivered up on claim of the party to whom such service or labor may be due. *
(*Changed by the Thirteenth Amendment)

SECTION 3. New States
New States may be admitted by the Congress into this Union; but no new State shall be formed or erected within the jurisdiction of any other State; nor any State be formed by the junction of two or more States, or parts of States, without the consent of the legislatures of the States concerned as well as of the Congress.

The Congress shall have power to dispose of and make all needful rules and regulations respecting the territory or other property belonging to the United States; and nothing in this Constitution shall be so construed as to prejudice any claims of the United States, or of any particular State.

SECTION 4. Guarantees to the States
The United States shall guarantee to every State in this Union a republican form of government, and shall protect each of them against invasion; and on application of the legislature, or of the executive (when the legislature cannot be convened), against domestic violence.

ARTICLE 4
Relations Among the States

SECTION 1. Recognition by Each State
Each state must recognize the laws, records, and legal decisions made by all the other states. Congress has the power to make laws to determine how these laws, records, and legal decisions can be proved.

SECTION 2. Rights of Citizens in States
States must give the same rights to citizens from other states that they give their own citizens.

If a person charged with a crime runs away to another state, the person must be returned to the original state for a trial.

No person who was a slave in one state may become free by escaping to a different state.
(This was changed by the Thirteenth Amendment, which made slavery illegal in all states.)

SECTION 3. New States
New states may become part of the United States with the permission of Congress. New states cannot be formed from land in an existing state, nor can two or more states or their parts join to create a new state without the consent of the states involved and of Congress.

Congress may sell or give away land or property belonging to the United States. Congress has the power to make all laws related to territories or other property owned by the United States and to make laws to govern federal territories and possessions.

SECTION 4. Guarantees to the States
The United States government is required to guarantee that each state has a republican form of government, a government that is responsible to the will of its people through their elected representatives. The federal government also must protect the states if they are invaded by foreign nations, and to do the same in case of riots, if requested by the governor or legislature of the state.

ARTICLE 5
Amending the Constitution

Amendments may be proposed by a two-thirds vote of each house of Congress or by a national convention called by Congress at the request of two-thirds of the states. To add an amendment to the Constitution, the legislatures or special conventions of three-fourths of the states must give approval or ratify it. However, no amendment can be added that keeps a state from having an equal vote in the United States Senate. No amendment may be added before 1808 that affects the slave trade or certain taxes. *(Congress passed a law in 1808 forbidding the slave trade protected under Article 1.)*

ARTICLE 6
Debts, Federal Supremacy, Oaths of Office

The federal government must pay all debts owed by the United States, including those debts which were taken on under the Articles of Confederation.

The Constitution and the laws of the United States are the supreme, or highest, laws of the land. All public officials in the federal government or within the states, regardless of other laws to the contrary, are bound by the Constitution and the national laws.

All officials in both federal and state governments must promise to obey and support the Constitution. No religious qualifications can be required as a condition for holding public office.

ARTICLE 7
Ratifying the Constitution

The Constitution will take effect when it is approved by at least nine of the thirteen states.

On September 17, 1787, all twelve state delegations present have given approval for adopting the Constitution. As proof, the delegates have each placed their signatures on the document.

ARTICLE 5
Amending the Constitution

The Congress, whenever two thirds of both houses shall deem it necessary, shall propose amendments to this Constitution, or, on the application of the legislatures of two thirds of the several States, shall call a convention for proposing amendments, which, in either case, shall be valid to all intents and purposes, as part of this Constitution, when ratified by the legislatures of three fourths of the several States, or by conventions in three fourths thereof, as the one or the other mode of ratification may be proposed by the Congress; provided ~~that no amendment which may be made prior to the year one thousand eight hundred and eight shall in any manner affect the first and fourth clauses in the ninth section of the first article and~~ that no State, without its consent, shall be deprived of its equal suffrage in the Senate.

ARTICLE 6
Debts, Federal Supremacy, Oaths of Office

All debts contracted and engagements entered into, before the adoption of this Constitution, shall be as valid against the United States under this Constitution, as under the Confederation.

This Constitution, and the laws of the United States which shall be made in pursuance thereof, and all treaties made, or which shall be made, under the authority of the United States, shall be the supreme law of the land; and the judges in every State shall be bound thereby, anything in the Constitution or laws of any State to the contrary notwithstanding.

The senators and representatives before mentioned, and the members of the several State legislatures, and all executive and judicial officers, both of the United States, and of the several States, shall be bound by oath or affirmation to support this Constitution; but no religious test shall ever be required as a qualification to any office or public trust under the United States.

ARTICLE 7
Ratifying the Constitution

The ratification of the conventions of nine States shall be sufficient for the establishment of this Constitution between the States so ratifying the same.

Done in Convention by the unanimous consent of the States present the seventeenth day of September in the year of our Lord one thousand seven hundred and eighty-seven and of the independence of the United States of America the twelfth. In witness whereof we have hereunto subscribed our names.

George Washington, *President* (Virginia)

Massachusetts
Nathaniel Gorham
Rufus King

New York
Alexander Hamilton

Georgia
William Few
Abraham Baldwin

Delaware
George Read
Gunning Bedford, Jr.
John Dickinson
Richard Bassett
Jacob Broom

Virginia
John Blair
James Madison, Jr.

Pennsylvania
Benjamin Franklin
Thomas Mifflin
Robert Morris
George Clymer
Thomas FitzSimons
Jared Ingersoll
James Wilson
Gouverneur Morris

New Hampshire
John Langdon
Nicholas Gilman

New Jersey
William Livingston
David Brearley
William Paterson
Jonathan Dayton

Connecticut
William Samuel Johnson
Roger Sherman

North Carolina
William Blount
Richard Dobbs Spaight
Hugh Williamson

South Carolina
John Rutledge
Charles Cotesworth Pinckney
Charles Pinckney
Pierce Butler

Maryland
James McHenry
Daniel of St. Thomas Jenifer
Daniel Carroll

"Let virtue, honor, and love of liberty and of science be and remain the soul of this constitution, and it will become the source of great and extensive happiness to this and future generations."

From Jay's charge to the Grand Jury of Ulster County. The Correspondence and Public Papers of John Jay, *Henry P. Johnston, editor (New York: Burt Franklin, 1970), Vol. I, pp. 158–165, September 9, 1777.*

"The power under the Constitution will always be in the people."

George Washington, The Writings of George Washington, *Jared Sparks, editor (Boston: Russell, Odiorne and Metcalf, 1835), Vol. IX, p. 279, to Bushrod Washington on November 10, 1787.*

FIRST AMENDMENT—1791
Freedom of Religion, Speech, Press, Assembly, and Petition

Congress shall not make any laws that set up an official national religion or that keeps people from worshiping according to their conscience. Congress may not limit the freedom of speech or the press, or the freedom to meet peaceably. People must have the right to ask the government to correct a problem.

SECOND AMENDMENT—1791
Right to Have Firearms

Because an organized militia is needed to protect the states, the right of people to keep and bear firearms shall not be violated.

THIRD AMENDMENT—1791
Right Not to House Soldiers

Soldiers may not be housed in private homes, without the consent of the owner, unless a law for that purpose is passed during a time of war.

FOURTH AMENDMENT—1791
Freedom from Unreasonable Search and Seizure

People and their property are to be protected from unreasonable search and seizure. Government authorities must have good cause and have a written order from a judge describing the place to be searched and the person or things to be seized.

FIFTH AMENDMENT—1791
Rights of People Accused of Crimes

A person may not be put on trial for a crime that is punishable by death or imprisonment without first being accused by a grand jury. [A grand jury is a group of citizens selected to decide whether there is enough evidence against a person to hold a trial.] However, during wartime or a time of public danger, people in military service may not have that right.

A person may not be put on trial twice for the same crime.

FIRST AMENDMENT—1791
Freedom of Religion, Speech, Press, Assembly, and Petition

Congress shall make no law respecting an establishment of religion, or prohibiting the free exercise thereof; or abridging the freedom of speech, or of the press; or the right of the people peaceably to assemble, and to petition the government for a redress of grievances.

SECOND AMENDMENT—1791
Right to Have Firearms

A well-regulated militia, being necessary to the security of a free state, the right of the people to keep and bear arms shall not be infringed.

THIRD AMENDMENT—1791
Right Not to House Soldiers

No soldier shall, in time of peace, be quartered in any house, without the consent of the owner, nor in time of war, but in a manner to be prescribed by law.

FOURTH AMENDMENT—1791
Freedom from Unreasonable Search and Seizure

The right of the people to be secure in their persons, houses, papers, and effects, against unreasonable searches and seizures, shall not be violated, and no warrants shall issue, but upon probable cause, supported by oath or affirmation, and particularly describing the place to be searched, and the persons or things to be seized.

FIFTH AMENDMENT—1791
Rights of People Accused of Crimes

No person shall be held to answer for a capital or otherwise infamous crime, unless on a presentment or indictment of a grand jury, except in cases arising in the land or naval forces, or in the militia, when in actual service in time of war or public danger; nor shall any person be subject for the same offense to be twice put in jeopardy of life or limb; nor shall be compelled in any criminal case to be a witness against himself, nor be deprived of life, liberty, or property, without due process of law; nor shall private property be taken for public use without just compensation.

SIXTH AMENDMENT—1791
Right to a Jury Trial in a Criminal Case

In all criminal prosecutions, the accused shall enjoy the right to a speedy and public trial, by an impartial jury of the state and district wherein the crime shall have been committed, which district shall have been previously ascertained by law, and to be informed of the nature and cause of the accusation; to be confronted with the witnesses against him; to have compulsory process for obtaining witnesses in his favor, and to have the assistance of counsel for his defense.

SEVENTH AMENDMENT—1791
Right to a Jury Trial in a Civil Case

In suits at common law, where the value in controversy shall exceed twenty dollars, the right of trial by jury shall be preserved, and no fact tried by a jury shall be otherwise reexamined in any court of the United States, than according to the rules of the common law.

EIGHTH AMENDMENT—1791
Protection from Unfair Bail and Punishment

Excessive bail shall not be required, nor excessive fines imposed, nor cruel and unusual punishments inflicted.

NINTH AMENDMENT—1791
Other Rights

The enumeration in the Constitution of certain rights shall not be construed to deny or disparage others retained by the people.

TENTH AMENDMENT—1791
Powers of the States and People

The powers not delegated to the United States by the Constitution, nor prohibited by it to the States, are reserved to the states respectively, or to the people.

People cannot be required to give evidence against themselves.

People may not have their lives, liberty, or property taken away without fair and equal treatment under the laws of the land.

People may not have their property taken for public use without receiving reasonable payment.

SIXTH AMENDMENT—1791
Right to a Jury Trial in a Criminal Case

A person accused of a crime must have a speedy, public trial held before an open-minded jury made up of citizens living in the community where the crime occurred. The accused person must also be told about the nature of the charge of wrongdoing. Accused people are allowed to meet and question witnesses against them, to have witnesses testify in their favor, and to have the services of a lawyer.

SEVENTH AMENDMENT—1791
Right to a Jury Trial in a Civil Case

In civil cases, where the value of the property in question is over $20, the right to a jury trial is guaranteed. The decision of the jury is final and cannot be changed by a judge but only by a new trial.

EIGHTH AMENDMENT—1791
Protection from Unfair Bail and Punishment

Bails and fines must not be too large, and punishments may not be cruel and unusual.

NINTH AMENDMENT—1791
Other Rights

Fundamental rights not listed in the Constitution remain guaranteed to all citizens.

TENTH AMENDMENT—1791
Powers of the States and People

The states or the people keep all powers not granted to the federal government and not denied to the states by the Constitution.

ELEVENTH AMENDMENT—1795
Limits on Right to Sue States

A state government cannot be sued in a federal court by people from a different state or from a foreign country.

TWELFTH AMENDMENT—1804
Election of President and Vice-President

In each state, members of the Electoral College vote on separate ballots for one person as President and another person as Vice-President. At least one of these choices may not live in the same state as the electors. Each person on the ballot receiving votes in a given state must be listed by the total numbers of votes. Final counts of votes from each state must be signed and officially recognized as accurate and complete. These results must be delivered to the national capital to be opened and read aloud by the president of the Senate at a joint session of Congress.

If a person receives a majority of votes for President, that person shall be the President. If no person has a majority, then from the three who received the most votes, the House of Representatives will immediately choose the President by ballot. But in choosing the President, the votes shall be taken by states, with each state having one vote. Two-thirds of the states must participate in this choice. *(Until changed by the Twentieth Amendment, if the House of Representatives failed to elect a President by March 4, the Vice-President served as President.)*

If a person receives a majority of votes as Vice-President, that person shall be the Vice-President. If no person has a majority, then from the two highest numbers on the list, the Senate will choose the Vice-President, provided that two-thirds of the senators are present to vote. A simple majority, with each senator voting individually, is necessary to make a final choice. A person who is not eligible to be President cannot be eligible for the office of Vice-President.

ELEVENTH AMENDMENT—1795
Limits on Right to Sue States

The judicial power of the United States shall not be construed to extend to any suit in law or equity, commenced or prosecuted against one of the United States by citizens of another State, or by citizens or subjects of any foreign State.

TWELFTH AMENDMENT—1804
Election of President and Vice President

The electors shall meet in their respective States, and vote by ballot for President and Vice President, one of whom, at least, shall not be an inhabitant of the same State with themselves; they shall name in their ballots the person voted for as President, and in distinct ballots the person voted for as Vice President, and they shall make distinct lists of all persons voted for as President, and of all persons voted for as Vice President, and of the number of votes for each, which lists they shall sign and certify, and transmit sealed to the seat of the government of the United States, directed to the president of the Senate;—The president of the Senate shall, in the presence of the Senate and House of Representatives, open all the certificates and the votes shall then be counted;—The person having the greatest number of votes for President shall be the President, if such number be a majority of the whole number of electors appointed; and if no person have such majority, then from the persons having the highest numbers not exceeding three on the list of those voted for as President, the House of Representatives shall choose immediately, by ballot, the President. But in choosing the President, the votes shall be taken by States, the representation from each State having one vote; a quorum for this purpose shall consist of a member or members from two thirds of the States, and a majority of all the States shall be necessary to a choice. ~~And if the House of Representatives shall not choose a President whenever the right of choice shall devolve upon them, before the fourth day of March next following,~~* then the Vice President shall act as President, as in the case of the death or other constitutional disability of the President. The person having the greatest number of votes as Vice President shall be the Vice President, if such number be a majority of the whole number of electors appointed, and if no person have a majority, then from the two highest numbers on the list, the Senate shall choose the Vice President; a quorum for the purpose shall consist of two thirds of the whole number of senators, and a majority of the whole number shall be necessary to a choice. But no person constitutionally ineligible to the office of President shall be eligible to that of Vice President of the United States. *(*Changed by the Twentieth Amendment)*

THIRTEENTH AMENDMENT—1865
Abolition of Slavery

SECTION 1. Slavery Outlawed
Neither slavery nor involuntary servitude, except as a punishment for crime whereof the party shall have been duly convicted, shall exist within the United States, or any place subject to their jurisdiction.

SECTION 2. Enforcement
Congress shall have power to enforce this article by appropriate legislation.

FOURTEENTH AMENDMENT—1868
Rights of Citizens

SECTION 1. Citizenship
All persons born or naturalized in the United States, and subject to the jurisdiction thereof, are citizens of the United States and of the State wherein they reside. No State shall make or enforce any law which shall abridge the privileges or immunities of citizens of the United States; nor shall any State deprive any person of life, liberty, or property, without due process of law; nor deny to any person within its jurisdiction the equal protection of the laws.

SECTION 2. Representation in Congress
Representatives shall be apportioned among the several States according to their respective numbers, counting the whole number of persons in each State, excluding Indians not taxed. But when the right to vote at any election for the choice of electors for President and Vice President of the United States, representatives in Congress, the executive and judicial officers of a State, or the members of the legislature thereof is denied to any of the male inhabitants of such State, being twenty-one years of age, and citizens of the United States, or in any way abridged, except for participation in rebellion, or other crime, the basis of representation therein shall be reduced in the proportion which the number of such male citizens shall bear to the whole number of male citizens twenty-one years of age in such State.* (*Restriction on race and ethnicity changed by the Fifteenth Amendment; restriction on gender changed by the Nineteenth Amendment; restriction regarding taxation changed by the Twenty-Fourth Amendment; restriction on age changed by the Twenty-Sixth Amendment)

THIRTEENTH AMENDMENT—1865
Abolition of Slavery

Slavery shall not exist anywhere in the United States or anyplace governed by the United States. Forced labor may only be required after a person has been fairly convicted of a crime.

Congress may make laws to enforce this article.

FOURTEENTH AMENDMENT—1868
Rights of Citizens

All persons born in the United States or granted citizenship are citizens of both the United States and of the states in which they live.
No state may pass laws that take away or limit the freedoms or privileges of any of its citizens. Citizens may not have their lives, liberties, or property taken away without access to a regular judicial process conducted according to the laws. All people must be protected equally by the laws.

A state's representation in Congress is determined by the state's population. A state which does not allow qualified voters to vote may have its representation in Congress reduced. (Other provisions of this section were changed by the Fifteenth, Nineteenth, Twenty-Fourth, and Twenty-Sixth Amendments.)

No person may hold a civil or military office in the federal or a state government who had previously taken an oath to uphold the Constitution and then aided or helped the Confederacy during the Civil War or other rebellions against the United States.

Congress may remove this provision by a two-thirds vote of both houses.

Any federal debts resulting from fighting to end a civil war or put down a rebellion must be paid in full. However, the federal or state government shall not pay debts made by those who participate in a rebellion against the United States.

Former owners of slaves shall not be paid for the financial losses caused by the freeing of slaves.

Congress has the power to pass laws to enforce the provisions of this article.

SECTION 3. Penalties for Leaders of the Confederacy

No person shall be a senator or representative in Congress, or elector of President and Vice President, or hold any office, civil or military, under the United States, or under any State, who, having previously taken an oath, as a member of Congress, or as an officer of the United States, or as a member of any State legislature, or as an executive or judicial officer of any State, to support the Constitution of the United States, shall have engaged in insurrection or rebellion against the same, or given aid or comfort to the enemies thereof. But Congress may by a vote of two thirds of each house, remove such disability.

SECTION 4. Responsibility for the Public Debt

The validity of the public debt of the United States, authorized by law, including debts incurred for payment of pensions and bounties for services in suppressing insurrection or rebellion, shall not be questioned. But neither the United States nor any State shall assume or pay any debt or obligation incurred in aid of insurrection or rebellion against the United States, or any claim for the loss or emancipation of any slave; but all such debts, obligations and claims shall be held illegal and void.

SECTION 5. Enforcement

The Congress shall have power to enforce, by appropriate legislation, the provisions of this article.

FIFTEENTH AMENDMENT—1870
Voting Rights

A citizen's right to vote in any election cannot be denied based on the person's race or color, or because they were once enslaved.

Congress has the power to pass laws to enforce the provisions of this article.

FIFTEENTH AMENDMENT—1870
Voting Rights

SECTION 1. Suffrage for African Americans

The right of citizens of the United States to vote shall not be denied or abridged by the United States or by any State on account of race, color, or previous condition of servitude.

SECTION 2. Enforcement

The Congress shall have power to enforce this article by appropriate legislation.

SIXTEENTH AMENDMENT—1913
Income Tax

Congress has the power to tax all individuals directly based on their personal incomes, without collecting taxes based on a division among the states or in consideration of a state's population.

SIXTEENTH AMENDMENT—1913
Income Tax

The Congress shall have power to lay and collect taxes on incomes, from whatever source derived, without apportionment among the several States, and without regard to any census or enumeration.

SEVENTEENTH AMENDMENT—1913
Direct Election of Senators

The Senate of the United States shall be composed of two senators from each State, elected by the people thereof, for six years; and each senator shall have one vote. The electors in each State shall have the qualifications requisite for electors of the most numerous branch of the State legislatures.

When vacancies happen in the representation of any State in the Senate, the executive authority of such State shall issue writs of election to fill such vacancies: Provided, that the legislature of any State may empower the executive thereof to make temporary appointments until the people fill the vacancies by election as the legislature may direct.

This amendment shall not be so construed as to affect the election or term of any Senator chosen before it becomes valid as part of the Constitution.

EIGHTEENTH AMENDMENT*—1919
Prohibition

SECTION 1. Liquor Banned
After one year from the ratification of this article, the manufacture, sale, or transportation of intoxicating liquors within, the importation thereof into, or the exportation thereof from the United States and all territory subject to the jurisdiction thereof for beverage purposes is hereby prohibited.*

SECTION 2. Enforcement
The Congress and the several States shall have concurrent power to enforce this article by appropriate legislation.*

SECTION 3. Time Limit for Ratification
This article shall be inoperative unless it shall have been ratified as an amendment to the Constitution by the legislatures of the several States, as provided in the Constitution, within seven years from the date of the submission hereof to the States by the Congress.* (*Repealed by the Twenty-First Amendment)

SEVENTEENTH AMENDMENT—1913
Direct Election of Senators

Two senators will represent each state in Congress, each elected for six-year terms and having one vote in the Senate. They will be elected directly by the qualified voters in the states (not by state legislatures, which was originally provided for in Article I, Section 3, Clause 1).

When vacancies occur in the Senate, the governor of the state will call for an election to fill the vacancy. In the meantime the state legislature will permit the governor to make a temporary appointment until the election occurs. The legislature organizes the election.

This amendment shall not affect the election or term of any Senator chosen before it becomes part of the Constitution.

EIGHTEENTH AMENDMENT*—1919
Prohibition

The making, selling, and transporting of alcoholic beverages anywhere in the United States and its territories is outlawed. This amendment takes effect one year after the amendment is passed.

Congress and the states will share lawmaking powers to enforce this article.

This amendment will become part of the Constitution only if it is ratified within seven years after Congress has sent it to the States.
(This amendment was repealed by the Twenty-First Amendment.)

NINETEENTH AMENDMENT—1920
Women's Right to Vote

A citizen's right to vote in any election cannot be denied based on the person's sex.

Congress shall have power to pass laws to enforce the provisions of this article.

TWENTIETH AMENDMENT—1933
Terms of Office

The terms of the President and Vice-President end at noon on January 20th, and the terms of senators and representatives end at noon on January 3rd, following the federal elections held the previous November. The terms of their successors begin at that time.

Congress must meet at least once a year, and the session will begin at noon on January 3rd unless a law is passed to change the day.

If the President-elect dies before taking office, the Vice-President-elect becomes President. If a President has not been chosen before January 20, or if the President-elect has not qualified, then the Vice-President-elect acts as President until a President becomes qualified. If neither the President-elect or Vice-President-elect is able to take office on the designated date, then Congress will decide who will act as President until a President or Vice-President has been qualified.

If a candidate fails to win a majority in the Electoral College, and then dies while the election is being decided in the House of Representatives, Congress will have the power to pass laws to resolve the problem. Congress has similar power in the event that a candidate for Vice-President dies while the election is in the Senate.

NINETEENTH AMENDMENT—1920
Women's Right to Vote

SECTION 1. Suffrage for Women

The right of citizens of the United States to vote shall not be denied or abridged by the United States or by any State on account of sex.

SECTION 2. Enforcement

Congress shall have power to enforce this article by appropriate legislation.

TWENTIETH AMENDMENT—1933
Terms of Office

SECTION 1. Start and End of Terms

The terms of the President and Vice President shall end at noon on the 20th day of January, and the terms of senators and representatives at noon on the third day of January, of the year in which such terms would have ended if this article had not been ratified; and the terms of their successors shall then begin.

SECTION 2. Congressional Meeting

The Congress shall assemble at least once in every year, and such meeting shall begin at noon on the third day of January, unless they shall by law appoint a different day.

SECTION 3. Successor for the President-Elect

If, at the time fixed for the beginning of the term of the President, the President-elect shall have died, the Vice President-elect shall become President. If a President shall not have been chosen before the time fixed for the beginning of his term, or if the President-elect shall have failed to qualify, then the Vice President-elect shall act as President until a President shall have qualified; and the Congress may by law provide for the case wherein neither a President-elect nor a Vice President-elect shall have qualified, declaring who shall then act as President, or the manner in which one who is to act shall be selected, and such persons shall act accordingly until a President or Vice President shall have qualified.

SECTION 4. Elections Decided by Congress

The Congress may by law provide for the case of the death of any of the persons from whom the House of Representatives may choose a President whenever the right of choice shall have devolved upon them, and for the case of the death of any of the persons from whom the Senate may choose a Vice President whenever the right of choice shall have devolved upon them.

SECTION 5. Effective Date
Sections 1 and 2 shall take effect on the 15th day of October following the ratification of this article.

Sections 1 and 2 of this amendment shall take effect on October 15, after this amendment is ratified.

SECTION 6. Time Limit for Ratification
This article shall be inoperative unless it shall have been ratified as an amendment to the Constitution by the legislatures of three fourths of the several States within seven years from the date of its submission.

This amendment will become part of the Constitution only if it is ratified by three-fourths of the states within seven years after Congress has sent it to the States.

TWENTY-FIRST AMENDMENT—1933
Repeal of Prohibition Amendment

TWENTY-FIRST AMENDMENT—1933
Repeal of Prohibition Amendment

SECTION 1. End of Prohibition
The eighteenth article of amendment to the Constitution of the United States is hereby repealed.

The Eighteenth Amendment, prohibiting the making, sale, and transportation of alcoholic beverages in the United States and its possessions, is repealed.

SECTION 2. Protection of State Prohibition Laws
The transportation or importation into any State, territory, or possession of the United States for delivery or use therein of intoxicating liquors, in violation of the laws thereof, is hereby prohibited.

Individual states may prohibit the transporting or importing of alcoholic beverages.

SECTION 3. Time Limit for Ratification
This article shall be inoperative unless it shall have been ratified as an amendment to the Constitution by conventions in the several States, as provided in the Constitution, within seven years from the date of submission hereof to the States by the Congress.

This amendment will become part of the Constitution only if it is ratified in seven years.

TWENTY-SECOND AMENDMENT—1951
Limit on Terms of the President

TWENTY-SECOND AMENDMENT—1951
Limit on Terms of the President

SECTION 1. Two-Term Limit
No person shall be elected to the office of the President more than twice, and no person who has held the office of President, or acted as President, for more than two years of a term to which some other person was elected President shall be elected to the office of the President more than once.

No person can be elected to the office of the President more than twice. If a President has served two or more years of a previous President's term, then the President may be reelected for one additional term.

The current President in office at the time of this amendment's ratification process is not limited to term restrictions.

But this Article shall not apply to any person holding the office of President when this Article was proposed by the Congress, and shall not prevent any person who may be holding the office of President, or acting as President, during the term within which this Article becomes operative from holding the office of President or acting as President during the remainder of such term.

SECTION 2. Time Limit on Ratification

This article shall be inoperative unless it shall have been ratified as an amendment to the Constitution by the legislatures of three-fourths of the several States within seven years from the date of its submission to the States by the Congress.

This amendment will become part of the Constitution only if it is ratified by three-fourths of the States within seven years after Congress has sent it to the States.

TWENTY-THIRD AMENDMENT—1961
Presidential Elections for District of Columbia

TWENTY-THIRD AMENDMENT—1961

Presidential Elections for District of Columbia

Citizens living in the District of Columbia may elect members to the Electoral College to vote in federal elections for President and Vice-President. The number of electors is limited to the number of votes of the least populated state. The voters must live in the district and follow all duties and procedures outlined in the Twelfth Amendment.

SECTION 1. Presidential Electors

The District constituting the seat of government of the United States shall appoint in such manner as the Congress may direct:

A number of electors of President and Vice President equal to the whole number of senators and representatives in Congress to which the District would be entitled if it were a State, but in no event more than the least populous state; they shall be in addition to those appointed by the States, but they shall be considered, for the purposes of the election of President and Vice President, to be electors appointed by a State; and they shall meet in the District and perform such duties as provided by the twelfth article of amendment.

SECTION 2. Enforcement

The Congress shall have power to enforce this article by appropriate legislation.

Congress has the power to make laws necessary to enforce this amendment.

TWENTY-FOURTH AMENDMENT—1964
Outlawing of Poll Tax

TWENTY-FOURTH AMENDMENT—1964

Outlawing of Poll Tax

United States citizens may not have their voting rights restricted in federal elections by the establishment of a poll tax or other tax.

SECTION 1. Ban on Poll Tax in Federal Elections

The right of citizens of the United States to vote in any primary or other election for President or Vice President, for electors for President or Vice President, or for senator or representative in Congress, shall not be denied or abridged by the United States or any State by reason of failure to pay any poll tax or other tax.

SECTION 2. Enforcement

The Congress shall have power to enforce this article by appropriate legislation.

TWENTY-FIFTH AMENDMENT—1967

Presidential Succession

SECTION 1. Filling Vacant Office of President

In case of the removal of the President from office or his death or resignation, the Vice President shall become President.

SECTION 2. Filling Vacant Office of Vice President

Whenever there is a vacancy in the office of the Vice President, the President shall nominate a Vice President who shall take the office upon confirmation by a majority vote of both houses of Congress.

SECTION 3. Disability of the President

Whenever the President transmits to the president pro tempore of the Senate and the Speaker of the House of Representatives his written declaration that he is unable to discharge the powers and duties of his office, and until he transmits to them a written declaration to the contrary, such powers and duties shall be discharged by the Vice President as Acting President.

SECTION 4. When Congress Names an Acting President

Whenever the Vice President and a majority of either the principal officers of the executive departments or of such other body as Congress may by law provide, transmit to the president pro tempore of the Senate and the Speaker of the House of Representatives their written declaration that the President is unable to discharge the powers and duties of his office, the Vice President shall immediately assume the powers and duties of the office as Acting President.

Thereafter, when the President transmits to the president pro tempore of the Senate and the Speaker of the House of Representatives his written declaration that no inability exists, he shall resume the powers and duties of his office unless the Vice President and a majority of either the principal officers of the executive department or of such other body as Congress may by law provide, transmit within four days to the president pro tempore of the Senate and the Speaker of the House of Representatives their written declaration that the President is unable to discharge the powers and duties of his office. Thereupon Congress shall decide the issue, assembling within forty-eight hours for that purpose if not in session. If

---

Congress has the power to make laws necessary to enforce this amendment.

TWENTY-FIFTH AMENDMENT—1967
Presidential Succession

If a President dies or is removed from office, then the Vice-President will become President.

If the office of Vice-President becomes vacant, the President may nominate a new Vice-President. The person nominated must be approved by a majority vote in both houses of Congress.

If the President sends a written notice to officers of both houses of Congress that the President is unable to perform the duties of the office, then the Vice-President will become Acting President. The Vice-President will act as the President until the President informs Congress that the President is again ready to take over the presidential responsibilities.

If the President is unconscious or has a disabling illness, the Vice-President and a majority of the Cabinet have the right to inform Congress in writing that the President is unable to carry out the duties of being President. The Vice-President then becomes Acting President until the President can return to work.

When the President informs the leaders of Congress in writing that the disability no longer exists, the President shall resume the office. But if there is a disagreement between the President and the Vice-President and a majority of the Cabinet about the President's ability to carry out the duties of being President, the Vice-President, or other appropriate authority, has four days to notify Congress, and Congress has the power to decide the issue. If not in session, both houses of Congress must meet within 48 hours for that purpose and will have 21 days to make a decision. A two-thirds vote in both houses of Congress is required to find the President unfit to perform the duties of the office.

the Congress, within twenty-one days after receipt of the latter written declaration, or, if Congress is not in session, within twenty-one days after Congress is required to assemble, determines by two-thirds vote of both houses that the President is unable to discharge the powers and duties of his office, the Vice President shall continue to discharge the same as Acting President; otherwise, the President shall resume the powers and duties of his office.

TWENTY-SIXTH AMENDMENT—1971
Voting Rights for Eighteen-Year-Olds

SECTION 1. New Voting Age
The right of citizens in the United States, who are eighteen years of age or older, to vote shall not be denied or abridged by the United States or by any State on account of age.

SECTION 2. Enforcement
The Congress shall have power to enforce this article by appropriate legislation.

TWENTY-SEVENTH AMENDMENT—1992
Limits on Congressional Salary Changes

No law varying the compensation for the services of the Senators and Representatives shall take effect, until an election of Representatives shall have intervened.

TWENTY-SIXTH AMENDMENT—1971
Voting Rights for Eighteen-Year-Olds

Citizens who are eighteen years of age or older have the right to vote in all elections.

Congress has the power to make laws necessary to enforce this amendment.

TWENTY-SEVENTH AMENDMENT—1992
Limits on Congressional Salary Changes

Salary changes for Congress cannot take effect until after the next federal election.

Gazetteer

This Gazetteer is a geographic dictionary that will help you locate and pronounce the names of places in this book. Latitude and longitude are given for cities. The page numbers tell you where each place appears on a map (m.) or in the text (t.).

 **A**

Afghanistan (af gan′ ə stan) Country in Southwest Asia where United States soldiers defeated Taliban troops in 2001. (m. 449, 506; t. 448, 506)

Africa (af′ rə kə) Second largest of Earth's seven continents. (m. 9, t. 9)

Ahwahnee Valley (ä wä′ nē) Valley in California that was one of the first rural places with phone access; part of Yosemite National Park. (m. 216, t. 219)

Anaheim (an′ ə hīm) City in southwestern California where the first theme park in the world, Disneyland, opened in 1955; 34°N, 118°W. (m. 394, t. 401)

Angel Island (ān′ jəl ī′ lənd) Island in San Francisco Bay, California, that was the entry point for immigrants from Asia from 1910 to 1940. (m. 184, t. 187)

Antarctica (ant′ ärk′ tə kə) One of Earth's seven continents, around the South Pole. (m. R4–5)

Appleton (ap′ əl tən) Town in eastern Wisconsin where the first hydroelectric power plant in the United States was built in 1882; 44°N, 88°W. (m. 216, t. 220)

Appomattox Court House (ap′ ə mat′ əks kôrt′ hous) Town in central Virginia, site of Confederate General Lee's surrender to Union General Grant on April 9, 1865, ending the Civil War; 37°N, 79°W. (m. 99, t. 101)

Arctic Ocean (ärk′ tic ō′ shən) Smallest of Earth's four oceans. (m. R4–5)

Argonia (är gō′ nē ə) Town in southern Kansas where the first woman mayor in the United States was elected in 1887; 37°N, 98°W. (m. 240, t. 242)

Asia (ā′ zhə) Largest of Earth's seven continents. (m. 6, t. 7)

Atlanta (at lan′ tə) Capital and largest city in Georgia; 33°N, 84°W. (m. 99, 113; t.100)

Atlantic Ocean (at lan′ tik ō′ shən) One of Earth's four oceans. (m. R4–5)

Australia (ȯ strā′ lyə) Smallest of Earth's seven continents. (m. R5)

Austria-Hungary (ȯ′ strē ə hung′ gar ē) Country in south central Europe that declared war on Serbia, starting World War I. (m. 273, t. 273)

 **B**

Bering Strait (bir′ ing strāt′) Narrow body of water that separates Asia from North America. During the Ice Age, it was a land bridge connecting the two continents. (m. 7, t. 7)

Black Hills (blak hilz) Mountain range in South Dakota and Wyoming, where gold was discovered in 1874. (m. 154, t. 155)

Boston (bȯ′ stən) Capital and largest city of Massachusetts; 42°N, 71°W. (m. 16; t. 23, 229, 494)

 **C**

Chicago (shə kä′ gō) Largest city in Illinois, located on Lake Michigan; 41°N, 87°W. (m. 134, t. 150, 223, 235)

Cleveland (klēv′ lənd) Port city in Ohio, on Lake Erie; 41°N, 81°W. (m. 176, t. 179)

Coast Ranges (kōst rān′ jəz) Mountains extending along the Pacific coast of North America. (m. R14)

Cuba (kyü′ bə) Largest country in the West Indies. (m. 255, t. 253)

Pronunciation Key

a in hat	ō in open	sh in she
ā in age	ȯ in all	th in thin
â in care	ô in order	ᵀʜ in then
ä in far	oi in oil	zh in measure
e in let	ou in out	ə = a in about
ē in equal	u in cup	ə = e in taken
ėr in term	u̇ in put	ə = i in pencil
i in it	ü in rule	ə = o in lemon
ī in ice	ch in child	ə = u in circus
o in hot	ng in long	

Gazetteer

Dallas (dal′ əs) City in northeastern Texas; 33°N, 97°W. (m. R13)

Death Valley (deth val′ ē) Lowest point in North America, located in the Mojave Desert in California. (m. R14)

Denver (den′ vər) Capital and largest city in Colorado; 40°N, 105°W. (m. 134, t. 151)

Detroit (di troit′) Largest city in Michigan, site of Henry Ford's automobile factory; 42°N, 83°W. (m. 298, t. 299, 402)

Dodge City (doj sit′ ē) City in southern Kansas, located on the Arkansas River; formerly a stop along a cattle trail in the late 1800s; 38°N, 100°W (m. 148, 328; t. 149, 332)

East Berlin (ēst bər lin′) Eastern section of the city of Berlin, Germany, divided from the western section by the Berlin Wall from 1961 to 1989. (m. 384, t. 389)

Eastern Hemisphere (ē′ stərn hem′ ə sfir) Half of Earth east of the prime meridian, including the continents of Africa, Asia, Europe, and Australia. (m. H10, t. H10)

Ellis Island (el′is ī′lənd) Island in New York Harbor, which was the entry point for immigrants from Europe from 1892 to 1954. (m. 184, t.186)

Europe (yùr′ əp) One of Earth's seven continents. (m. 17, t. 10)

Fort Sumter (fôrt sum′ tər) Fort in Charleston Harbor, South Carolina, site of the first battle of the Civil War in 1861. (m. 99, t. 75)

Fort Wagner (fôrt wag′ nər) Fort that protected the harbor of Charleston, South Carolina, attacked by the African American 54th Regiment in the Civil War in July 1863. (m. 88, t. 91)

France (frans) Country in Western Europe. (m. 273, t. 32)

Gettysburg (get′ ēz bėrg′) Town in southern Pennsylvania, site of a major Union victory during the Civil War in 1863; 40°N, 77°W. (m. 99, t. 97)

Grand Canyon National Monument (grand kan′ yən nash′ ə nəl mon′ yə mənt) Large wildlife area in Arizona set aside by President Theodore Roosevelt in 1908; the area later become a national park. (m. 262, t. 267)

Great Plains (grāt plānz) Region in central North America, east of the Rocky Mountains and extending from Canada to Texas. (m. 138, t. 139)

Great Salt Lake (grāt sȯlt lāk) Lake in northwestern Utah, largest salt lake in North America. (m. R14)

Greensboro (grēnz′ bėr ō) City in north central North Carolina where four African American students staged a sit-in for equal rights in 1960; 36°N, 80°W. (m. 418, t. 423)

Harlem (här′ ləm) Neighborhood in New York City where many African American artists lived and worked in the 1920s. (m. 310, t. 314)

Harpers Ferry (här′ pərz fer′ ē) Town in northeastern West Virginia, site of federal arsenal raided by abolitionist John Brown in 1859; 39°N, 78°W. (m. 66, t. 70)

Hawaii (hə wī′ ē) Group of volcanic islands in the central Pacific Ocean that became a state in 1959. (m. 255, t. 252)

Hiroshima (hir′ ō shē′ mə) City in southwestern Japan; the first city where an atomic bomb was dropped, on August 6, 1945; 35°N, 132°E. (m. 367, t. 361)

Homestead (hōm′ sted) Town in southwest Pennsylvania; site of a major labor strike at Andrew Carnegie's Homestead Steel Works in 1892; 40°N, 80°W. (m. 192, t. 193)

I

Iraq (i rak′) Country in Asia, site of the 1991 Persian Gulf War; invaded by the United States and other nations as part of the war on terrorism in 2003. (m. 506, t. 507)

Iwo Jima (ē′ wō jē′ mə) Small Pacific island off of Japan, site of major battle during World War II; 25°N, 141°E. (m. 359, t. 361)

J

Jamestown (jāmz′ toun) First permanent English colony in North America, founded in 1607 in eastern Virginia; 37°N, 77°W. (m. 13, t. 14)

K

Kansas Territory (kan′ zəs ter′ ə tôr′ ē) Territory created in 1854 by the Kansas-Nebraska Act; part of it became the state of Kansas. (m. 69, t. 69)

Kitty Hawk (kit′ ē hȯk) Town in North Carolina where the Wright Brothers flew the first powered airplane in 1903; 36°N, 76°W. (m. 166, t. 172)

Kuwait (kü wāt′) Country in Asia that was invaded by Iraq in 1990, leading to the Persian Gulf War. (m. 446, t. 450)

L

Los Alamos (lōs al′ ə mōs) City in northern New Mexico that was the site of a major atomic bomb research laboratory; 36°N, 106°W. (m. 348, t. 354)

Los Angeles (los an′ jə ləs) Largest city in California, located in southern part of the state; 34°N, 118°W. (m. 130, t. 304)

M

Manassas Junction (mə nas′ əs jungk′ shən) Town in Virginia near the site of the First Battle of Bull Run in 1861; 39°N, 78°W. (m. 82, t. 85)

Menlo Park (men′ lō pärk) Community in central New Jersey, site of inventor Thomas Edison's laboratory. (m. 166, t. 168)

Middle East (mid′ l ēst) A group of countries in Southwest Asia, including Iraq, Afghanistan, Egypt, and Israel. (m. 446, t. 448)

Midwest (mid′ west′) Region of the north central United States. (m. 473, t. 473)

Montgomery (mont gum′ ər ē) Capital of Alabama, site of African American bus boycott for equal rights from 1955 to 1956; 32°N, 86°W. (m. 418, t. 422)

Moscow (mos′ cō) Capital of Russia, located in the western part of the country; 56°N, 37°E. (m. 389, t. 388)

Mount Whitney (mount wit′ nē) Highest mountain in the contiguous states, located in southeastern California. (m. R14)

Pronunciation Key		
a in hat	ō in open	sh in she
ā in age	ȯ in all	th in thin
â in care	ô in order	ŦH in then
ä in far	oi in oil	zh in measure
e in let	ou in out	ə = a in about
ē in equal	u in cup	ə = e in taken
ėr in term	u̇ in put	ə = i in pencil
i in it	ü in rule	ə = o in lemon
ī in ice	ch in child	ə = u in circus
o in hot	ng in long	

Gazetteer

Nebraska Territory (nə bras′ kə ter′ ə tôr′ ē) Territory created in 1854 as a result of the Kansas-Nebraska Act; part of it became the state of Nebraska. (m. 69, t. 69)

New Amsterdam (nü am′ stər dam) Settlement founded by the Dutch on Manhattan Island; became present-day New York City. (m. 13, t. 13)

New Haven (nü hā′ vən) City in southern Connecticut, site of the trial of Africans who in 1839 took control of the Spanish slave ship *Amistad;* 41ºN, 72ºW. (m. 60, t. 62)

New Orleans (nü ôr′ lē ənz) Port city in Louisiana, largest city in the state; 30ºN, 90ºW. (m. 310, t. 312)

New York City (nü yôrk sit′ ē) Largest city in the United States, located in southeastern New York; 40ºN, 73ºW. (m. 223, t. 193, 223, 322, 443)

Nicodemus (nik ə dē′ məs) Town in Kansas that was founded by African American pioneers; 39ºN, 100ºW. (m. 138, t. 141)

Normandy (nôr′ mən dē) Region in northern France along the English Channel, where the Allies invaded Axis-occupied France in World War II; 49ºN, 2ºE. (m. 360, t. 360)

North America (nôrth ə mer′ ə kə) One of Earth's seven continents. (m. 7, t. 7)

Northeast (nôrth′ ēst′) Region in the northeastern United States. (m. 473, t. 473)

Northern Hemisphere (nôr′ ŦHərn hem′ ə sfir) Half of Earth north of the equator. (m. H13, t. H13)

North Korea (nôrth kô rē′ ə) Country occupying the northern part of the Korean peninsula. (m. 407, t. 407)

North Pole (nôrth pōl) Northernmost point on Earth; 90ºN. (m. H13–15, t. H13–14)

North Vietnam (nôrth vē et′ näm′) Northern part of Vietnam that was a separate nation from 1954 to 1975. (m. 431, t. 431)

Omaha (ō′ mə hä) Largest city in Nebraska, located in the eastern part of the state; 41ºN, 96ºW. (m. 130, t. 130)

Pacific Ocean (pə sif′ ik ō′ shən) Largest of Earth's four oceans. (m. R4–5)

Panama Canal (pan′ ə mä kə nal′) Canal through the Isthmus of Panama, connecting the Atlantic and Pacific Oceans. (m. 250, t. 257)

Pearl Harbor (pėrl här′ bər) Harbor in Hawaii, where Japanese planes bombed the United States naval base in a surprise attack on December 7, 1941. (m. 344, 346; t. 344)

Philadelphia (fil′ ə del′ fē ə) City in southeastern Pennsylvania, which was the capital of the United States from 1790 to 1800; 40ºN, 75ºW. (m. 16, t. 23, 223)

Pittsburgh (pits′ bėrg) City in southwestern Pennsylvania, site of Andrew Carnegie's steel mill; 40ºN, 79ºW. (m. 176, t. 177)

Plymouth (plim′ əth) Town in southeastern Massachusetts, founded by the Pilgrims in 1620; 42ºN, 71ºW. (m. 13, t. 15)

Promontory Point (prom′ ən tôr′ ē point) Place in northwestern Utah where tracks of the Union Pacific and Central Pacific railroads met in 1869 to complete the transcontinental railroad; 41ºN, 112ºW. (m. 128, t. 133)

Puerto Rico (pwär′ tō rē′ kō) Island in the West Indies, a commonwealth of the United States. (m. 255, t. 253)

Quebec (kwi bek′) Capital of the Canadian province of Quebec, the first French colony in the Americas; 46°N, 71°W. (m. 13, t. 13)

Queens (kwēnz) Borough of New York City, site of the 1939 World's Fair. (m. 328, t. 334)

Richmond (rich′ mənd) Capital of Virginia, was capital of the Confederacy during the Civil War; 37°N, 77°W. (m. 99, t. 85, 170)

Sacramento (sak′ rə men′ tō) Capital of California; 38°N, 121°W. (m. 128, t. 130)

San Diego (san dē ā′ gō) Port city in southern California; 32°N, 117°W. (m. R12)

Savannah (sə van′ ə) Port city on the coast of Georgia; 32°N, 81°W. (m. 99, t. 100)

Seneca Falls (sen′ ə kə fȯlz) Town in west central New York, site of the first women's rights convention in the United States, in 1848; 43°N, 77°W. (m. 240, t. 242)

Serbia (sėr′ bē ə) Country in southern Europe where Archduke Franz Ferdinand of Austria-Hungary was assassinated, leading to World War I. (m. 273, t. 273)

Southampton County (south amp′ tən koun′ tē) County in southeastern Virginia, location of Nat Turner's slave rebellion in 1831. (m. 60, t. 62)

Southeast (south′ ēst′) Region in the southeastern United States. (m. 473, t. 473)

Southern Hemisphere (suᴛʜ′ ərn hem′ ə sfir) Half of Earth south of the equator. (m. H13, t. H13)

South Korea (south kô rē′ ə) Country occupying the southern part of the Korean peninsula. (m. 407, t. 407)

South Pole (south pōl) Southernmost point on Earth; 90°S. (m. H13–15, t. H13–14)

South Vietnam (south vē et′ näm′) Southern part of Vietnam that was a separate nation from 1954 to 1975. (m. 431, t. 431)

Southwest (south′ west′) Region in the southwestern United States. (m. 473, t. 473)

St. Louis (sānt lü′ is) City in eastern Missouri; 39°N, 90°W. (m. 222, t. 228)

Tuskegee (təs kē′ gē) City in central Alabama, site of Booker T. Washington's college for African Americans, Tuskegee Institute; 32°N, 86°W. (m. 232, t. 237, 239, 352)

Versailles (ver sī′) City in north central France, where treaty was signed ending World War I; 49°N, 2°E. (m. 272, t. 280)

Vicksburg (viks′ bərg) City in western Mississippi on the Mississippi River, site of major Union victory during the Civil War in 1863; 32°N, 91°W. (m. 99, t. 99)

Virginia City (vər jin′ yə sit′ ē) Town in western Nevada on the eastern slope of the Sierra Nevada mountain range; 39°N, 120°W. (m. 148, t. 152)

Pronunciation Key

a in hat	ō in open	sh in she
ā in age	ȯ in all	th in thin
â in care	ô in order	ᴛʜ in then
ä in far	oi in oil	zh in measure
e in let	ou in out	ə = a in about
ē in equal	u in cup	ə = e in taken
ėr in term	u̇ in put	ə = i in pencil
i in it	ü in rule	ə = o in lemon
ī in ice	ch in child	ə = u in circus
o in hot	ng in long	

Gazetteer

Walnut Grove (wäl′ nət grōv) Estate in southwestern Virginia, where the mechanical reaper was perfected. (m. 216, t. 217)

Washington, D.C. (wäsh′ ing tən dē cē) Capital of the United States of America; 38°N, 77°W. (m. 30, 99; t. 31, 107, 484)

West (west) Region in the western United States. (m. 473, t. 473)

West Berlin (west bėr lin′) Western section of the city of Berlin, Germany, divided from the eastern section by the Berlin Wall from 1961 to 1989. (m. 384, t. 389)

Western Hemisphere (west′ ərn hem′ ə sfir) Half of Earth west of the prime meridian; includes South America and North America. (m. H14, t. H14)

Yorktown (yôrk′ toun) Town in southeastern Virginia near Chesapeake Bay, which was the site of the last major battle of the American Revolution; 37°N, 76°W. (m. 22, t. 25)

Yosemite National Park (yō sem′ i tē nash′ ə nəl pärk) National Park in California, established in 1890. (m. 262, t. 266)

Biographical Dictionary

This Biographical Dictionary tells you about the people in this book and how to pronounce their names. The page numbers tell you where the person first appears in the text.

 **A**

Adams, Abigail (ad′ əmz) 1744–1818 Wife of second President John Adams, she was the first First Lady to live in what later became known as the White House. (p. 25)

Adams, John (ad′ əmz) 1735–1826 Second President of the United States, from 1797 to 1801. Member of committee that drafted the Declaration of Independence and Patriot leader during the American Revolution. (p. 24)

Adams, Samuel (ad′ əmz) 1722–1803 Political leader in the American Revolution who organized the Sons of Liberty in Boston; helped plan the Boston Tea Party. (p. 23)

Addams, Jane (ad′ əmz) 1860–1935 Social worker and reformer who founded Hull House in Chicago in 1889. (p. 226)

Albright, Madeleine (äl′ brīt) 1937– Former United States ambassador to the United Nations and the first woman to serve as secretary of state, appointed 1997. (p. 451)

Aldrin, Edwin "Buzz" (äl′ drin) 1930– Astronaut on the *Apollo 11* who was the second person to walk on the moon, in 1969. (p. 430)

Anthony, Susan B. (an′ thə nē) 1820–1906 Women's suffrage leader who fought for voting rights for women and the abolition of slavery. (p. 242)

Antin, Mary (an′ tin) 1881–1949 Russian-born writer who published *The Promised Land,* an autobiography about her experiences as an immigrant in the United States. (pp. 185, 191)

Armstrong, Louis (ärm′ strȯng) 1901–1971 Trumpeter and singer who was the first major jazz soloist. (p. 312)

Armstrong, Neil (ärm′ strȯng) 1930– Astronaut who was the first person to walk on the moon, in 1969. (p. 430)

 **B**

Barton, Clara (bärt′ n) 1821–1912 Nurse during the Civil War who founded the American Red Cross. (p. 92)

Bell, Alexander Graham (bel) 1847–1922 Inventor and educator of the deaf who built the first telephone in 1876. (p. 167)

bin Laden, Osama (bin lä′ dən) 1957– Leader of the terrorist organization al Qaeda, which planned and carried out the September 11, 2001, attacks on New York City and the Pentagon. (p. 506)

Boyd, Belle (boid) 1844–1900 Confederate spy during the Civil War. (p. 92)

Brady, Mathew (brā′ dē) 1823–1896 Civil War photographer. (p. 89)

Brown, John (broun) 1800–1859 Abolitionist who led attacks on supporters of slavery in Kansas and led a raid on Harpers Ferry, Virginia, in 1859. (p. 70)

Bruce, Blanche K. (brüs) 1841–1898 Former slave who was elected to the United States Senate in 1874. (p. 108)

Bush, George H. W. (bu̇sh) 1924– 41st President of the United States, from 1989 to 1993. (p. 449)

Bush, George W. (bu̇sh) 1946– Became 43rd President of the United States in 2001, governor of Texas from 1995 to 2000 and son of 41st President George H. W. Bush. (pp. 452, 505)

Pronunciation Key

a in hat	ō in open	sh in she
ā in age	ȯ in all	th in thin
â in care	ô in order	ŦH in then
ä in far	oi in oil	zh in measure
e in let	ou in out	ə = a in about
ē in equal	u in cup	ə = e in taken
ėr in term	u̇ in put	ə = i in pencil
i in it	ü in rule	ə = o in lemon
ī in ice	ch in child	ə = u in circus
o in hot	ng in long	

Biographical Dictionary

★ C ★

Calhoun, John C. (kal hün′) 1782–1850 United States senator from South Carolina who believed in states' rights. (p. 67)

Carnegie, Andrew (kär′ nə gē) 1835–1919 Industrialist who made steel a major industry in the United States. (p. 177)

Carney, William (kär′ nē) 1840–1908 Civil War hero who was one of 16 African Americans to win the Congressional Medal of Honor for heroism in the Civil War. (p. 91)

Carson, Rachel (kär′ sən) 1907–1964 Biologist who wrote *The Silent Spring* in 1962, a book that helped make more people aware of growing environmental problems. (p. 443)

Carter, Jimmy (kär′ tər) 1924– 39th President of the United States, from 1977 to 1981. Awarded the Nobel Peace Prize in 2002 for his work promoting peace around the world. (pp. 448, 514)

Carver, George Washington (kär′ vər) 1861?–1943 Agricultural scientist and educator who taught at Tuskegee Institute, an African American college. He discovered hundreds of new uses for peanuts, sweet potatoes, and other crops. (p. 237)

Cather, Willa (kath′ ər) 1873–1947 Novelist who moved to the Great Plains as a child in the 1800s. Her writing was strongly influenced by Nebraska's immigrant settlers. (p. 140)

Catt, Carrie Chapman (kat) 1859–1947 Women's rights leader who helped win the passage of the Nineteenth Amendment. (p. 243)

Chávez, César (shä′ vez) 1927–1993 Mexican American leader who formed the National Farm Workers Association to gain rights for migrant workers. (p. 441)

Churchill, Winston (chėr′ chil) 1874–1965 British leader during World War II. (p. 343)

Cinque, Joseph (sin′ kā) 1813(?)–1879(?) West African captive who led the 1839 slave revolt on the Spanish slave ship *Amistad* and was allowed by the Supreme Court to return home to Africa. (p. 62)

Clark, William (klärk) 1770–1838 Shared command of the expedition to explore the Louisiana Territory with Meriwether Lewis. (p. 32)

Clay, Henry (klā) 1777–1852 United States senator who was nicknamed "The Great Compromiser" for organizing important agreements such as the Missouri Compromise in 1820 and the Compromise of 1850. (p. 67)

Clinton, Bill (klin′ tən) 1946– 42nd President of the United States, from 1993 to 2001. (p. 450)

Coffin, Catherine (ko′ fin) 1803–1881 Conductor on the Underground Railroad who, with her husband, Levi Coffin, helped more than 2,000 people escape from slavery to freedom. (p. 63)

Coffin, Levi (ko′ fin) 1798–1877 White teacher who became conductor on the Underground Railroad; married to Catherine Coffin. (p. 63)

Collins, Michael (ko′ lənz) 1930– One of the first astronauts to travel to the moon, with Neil Armstrong and Buzz Aldrin, in 1969. (p. 430)

Columbus, Christopher (kə lum′ bəs) 1451(?)–1506 Italian-born explorer who sailed across the Atlantic Ocean to the Americas in 1492. He was the first European to establish lasting contact between Europe and the Americas. (p. 10)

Colvin, L. O. (kōl′ vən) 1800s Farmer who developed the first cow-milking machine in 1862. (p. 217)

Conrad, Frank (kon′ rad) 1874–1941 Engineer for Westinghouse Electric whose work with radios led to the development of the first commercial radio station, KDKA in Pittsburgh, Pennsylvania, in 1920. (p. 302)

Cooper, Jack L. (kü′ pər) 1900s First African American radio disc jockey. (p. 236)

Crazy Horse (krā′ zē hôrs) 1842(?)–1877 Lakota leader who helped defeat Colonel George Custer at the Battle of Little Bighorn. (p. 156)

Cronkite, Walter (kron′ kīt) 1916– Journalist and television newscaster who was a war correspondent during World War II. (p. 402)

Custer, George (kus′ tər) 1839–1876 United States military leader who was defeated by the Lakota at the Battle of Little Bighorn in 1876. (p. 156)

D

Davis, Benjamin O., Jr., (dā′ vis) 1912–2002 Pilot who was the first African American general in the United States Air Force. He organized and commanded the Tuskegee Airmen in 1943. (p. 352)

Davis, Jefferson (dā′ vis) 1808–1889 President of the Confederacy during the Civil War and former United States senator from Mississippi. (p. 75)

Douglas, Stephen (dug′ ləs) 1813–1861 United States senator from Illinois who helped create the Kansas-Nebraska Act. (p. 69)

Douglass, Frederick (dug′ ləs) 1817–1895 Leading abolitionist who spoke and wrote about his life as a former slave. (p. 36)

Du Bois, W. E. B. (dü boiz′) 1868–1963 African American writer who helped start the National Association for the Advancement of Colored People (NAACP) in 1909. (p. 237)

Duryea, Charles (dər′ yā) 1861–1938 Inventor who, with his brother Frank, built the first working car in the United States in 1893. (p. 170)

Duryea, Frank (dər′ yā) 1869–1967 Inventor who, with his brother Charles, built the first working car in the United States in 1893. He produced an improved version in 1895 and won several races. (p. 170)

E

Eads, James Buchanan (ēdz) 1820–1887 Engineer who built the first bridge made entirely of steel, over the Mississippi River, in 1874. (p. 228)

Earhart, Amelia (âr′ härt) 1897–1937(?) Pilot who was the first woman to fly alone over the Atlantic Ocean in 1932. In 1937 she attempted to fly around the world and her plane mysteriously disappeared. (p. 315)

Edison, Thomas (ed′ ə sən) 1847–1931 Inventor whose many creations included the light bulb, the phonograph, and the microphone. (p. 168)

Eglui, Ellen (eg′ lü ē) 1800s Inventor who created a clothes wringer for washing machines in the late 1800s. (p. 218)

Einstein, Albert (īn′ stīn) 1879–1955 German-born physicist who told President Franklin D. Roosevelt about the possibility of atomic bombs. He made some of the most important contributions to science in the twentieth century. (p. 354)

Eisenhower, Dwight D. (ī′ zn hou′ ər) 1890–1969 34th President of the United States, from 1953 to 1961. Commander of Allied forces in western Europe during World War II. In 1957 he sent troops to a high school in Little Rock, Arkansas, to enforce desegregation. (p. 360)

Ellington, Duke (el′ ing tən) 1899–1974 Jazz composer, bandleader, and pianist who wrote over 2,000 pieces of music. (p. 312)

F

Fitzgerald, F. Scott (fits jer′ əld) 1896–1940 Writer famous for his novels and short stories about the 1920s. (p. 313)

Ford, Gerald (fôrd) 1913–2006 38th President of the United States, from 1974 to 1977. Took office when Richard Nixon resigned, becoming the nation's only President not elected. (p. 447)

Ford, Henry (fôrd) 1863–1947 Entrepreneur and inventor who built the Model T, the first car to become widely available in the United States. His method of assembly-line production was faster and cheaper than previous methods, forever changing factories in the United States. (p. 299)

Pronunciation Key

a in hat	ō in open	sh in she
ā in age	ȯ in all	th in thin
â in care	ô in order	ᴛʜ in then
ä in far	oi in oil	zh in measure
e in let	ou in out	ə = a in about
ē in equal	u in cup	ə = e in taken
ėr in term	ù in put	ə = i in pencil
i in it	ü in rule	ə = o in lemon
ī in ice	ch in child	ə = u in circus
o in hot	ng in long	

Biographical Dictionary

Frank, Anne (frangk) 1929–1945 Jewish girl whose diary was published in 1947 and became a literary classic of the Holocaust. She hid with her family from the Nazis in Amsterdam during World War II before being captured. She died in a Nazi concentration camp. (p. 362)

Franklin, Benjamin (frang′ klən) 1706–1790 Writer, printer, scientist, and inventor in Pennsylvania, and member of the committee that drafted the Declaration of Independence; a leading Patriot during the American Revolution. (p. 24)

Geronimo (jə ron′ ə mō) 1829–1909 Apache leader who fought United States soldiers to keep his land. He led a revolt of 4,000 of his people after they were forced to move to a reservation in Arizona. (p. 158)

Giuliani, Rudolph (jü lē ä′ nē) 1944– Mayor of New York City, from 1993 to 2002. He was praised for his handling of the city after the September 11, 2001; terrorist attacks. (p. 504)

Glenn, John (glen) 1921– First American astronaut to orbit Earth, in 1962. (p. 429)

Gompers, Samuel (gom′ pərz) 1850–1924 Labor leader who, in 1886, founded the American Federation of Labor, which fought for better working conditions. (p. 195)

Goodnight, Charles (gu̇d′ nīt) 1836–1929 Rancher who established the Goodnight-Loving Trail, a cattle trail from Texas to Colorado, in 1866. (p. 149)

Gorbachev, Mikhail (gôr′ bə chȯf) 1931– Last leader of the Soviet Union, from 1985 to 1991. (p. 448)

Grant, Ulysses S. Grant (grant) 1822–1885 18th President of the United States, from 1869 to 1877. Commander of Union forces during the Civil War. (p. 99)

Hamilton, Alexander (ham′ əl tən) 1755(?)–1804 Delegate to the Constitutional Convention and leader of the Federalists; first secretary of the treasury. (p. 31)

Hearst, William Randolph (hėrst) 1863–1951 Newspaper publisher who built the leading newspaper chain in the United States in the early 1900s. (p. 180)

Hine, Lewis (hīn) 1874–1940 Photographer who used his pictures to draw attention to social problems such as child labor and the poor living conditions of immigrants in New York City. (p. 194)

Hitler, Adolf (hit′ lər) 1889–1945 Nazi dictator of Germany during World War II. (p. 341)

Hoover, Herbert (hü′ vər) 1874–1964 31st President of the United States, from 1929 to 1933. (p. 321)

Huerta, Dolores (wer′ tä) 1930– Mexican American leader who helped establish the United Farm Workers of America, a group that fought for rights for migrant farm workers. (p. 441)

Hughes, Langston (hyüz) 1902–1967 Writer who was an important figure in the Harlem Renaissance. His poems often addressed race and discrimination. (p. 314)

Hurston, Zora Neale (hėr′ stən) 1891–1960 Writer who was an important figure in the Harlem Renaissance. (p. 314)

Hussein, Saddam (hu̇ sān′) 1937– Dictator of Iraq who was removed from power by the United States in 2003. (pp. 450, 507)

Jackson, Andrew (jak′ sən) 1767–1845 seventh President of the United States, from 1829 to 1837, and war hero from the War of 1812. (p. 33)

Jackson, Thomas "Stonewall" (jak′ sən) 1824–1863 Confederate general who led the Confederate army to victory in several battles early in the Civil War. (p. 85)

Jefferson, Thomas (jef′ ər sən) 1743–1826 third President of the United States, from 1801 to 1809. He wrote the first draft of the Declaration of Independence. (p. 24)

Johnson, Andrew (jon′ sən) 1808–1875 17th President of the United States, from 1865 to 1869; became President after Abraham Lincoln's assassination. (p. 107)

Jones, Mary Harris (jōnz) 1830–1930 Labor organizer, known as "Mother Jones." She fought for coal workers' rights by speaking in Appalachian mining towns, encouraging them to join unions. (p. 195)

Joseph, Chief (jō′ zəf) 1840–1904 Nez Percé leader who led his people in their unsuccessful effort to escape to Canada to avoid being forced onto a reservation. (p. 157)

Kennedy, John F. (ken′ ə dē) 1917–1963 35th President of the United States, from 1961 to 1963. He was the youngest person ever to be elected President, and was assassinated in 1963. (p. 410)

King, Martin Luther, Jr., (king) 1929–1968 Minister who led the Civil Rights movement during the 1950s and 1960s and believed in peaceful protests. He was assassinated in 1968. (p. 422)

Lange, Dorothea (lang) 1895–1965 Photographer whose pictures helped draw attention to the living conditions of the poor during the Great Depression. (p. 333)

Latimer, Lewis (lat′ ə mėr) 1848–1928 Inventor who improved Thomas Edison's light bulb, making electric lighting more practical. (p. 168)

Laval, Gustav de (di läv äl′) 1845–1913 Farmer who invented the cream separator in 1879. (p. 217)

Lawrence, Jacob (lôr′ əns) 1917–2000 Painter whose work shows African American life and history. His best known works are *Life in Harlem* and his *Great Migration* series. (p. 314)

Lee, Robert E. (lē) 1807–1870 Commander of the Confederate forces in the Civil War. (p. 85)

Lewis, Meriwether (lü′ is) 1774–1809 Army captain appointed by Thomas Jefferson to lead the Lewis and Clark expedition to explore the lands gained in the Louisiana Purchase. (p. 32)

Libeskind, Daniel (lēbz′ kind) 1946– Architect whose plan was chosen as part of the design for the rebuilding of the World Trade Center site in New York City. (p. 508–509)

Liliuokalani (lē lē ü ō kä lä′ nē) 1838–1917 Last queen of the Hawaiian Islands, she protested the American takeover of Hawaii in the 1890s. (p. 252)

Lin, Maya Ying (lin) 1959– Architect and sculptor who designed the Vietnam Veterans Memorial in Washington, D.C. (p. 434)

Lincoln, Abraham (ling′ kən) 1809–1865 16th President of the United States, from 1861 to 1865, who led the United States during the Civil War and was assassinated in 1865. (p. 71)

Lindbergh, Charles (lind′ bėrg) 1902–1974 Pilot who was the first to fly solo across the Atlantic Ocean in 1927. (p. 315)

Love, Nat (luv) 1854–1921 Former slave who became a cowboy at fifteen and wrote a popular autobiography. (p. 149)

MacArthur, Douglas (mək är′ thər) 1880–1964 General who commanded American forces in the southwest Pacific during World War II. (p. 361)

Malcom X (mal′ kəm eks) 1925–1965 Civil rights activist in the 1960s who urged African Americans to rely on themselves. (p. 425)

Marconi, Guglielmo (mär kō′ nē) 1874–1937 Italian physicist and inventor who sent the first radio message across the Atlantic Ocean. (p. 302)

Marshall, George C. (mär′ shəl) 1880–1959 World War II general and United States secretary of state from 1947 to 1949 who created the Marshall Plan, which aided Europe after World War II. (p. 386)

Marshall, Thurgood (mär′ shəl) 1908–1993 Lawyer and civil rights activist who was the first African American justice appointed to the Supreme Court, serving from 1967 to 1991. (p. 421)

Pronunciation Key

a in hat	ō in open	sh in she
ā in age	ȯ in all	th in thin
â in care	ô in order	ᴛʜ in then
ä in far	oi in oil	zh in measure
e in let	ou in out	ə = a in about
ē in equal	u in cup	ə = e in taken
ėr in term	u̇ in put	ə = i in pencil
i in it	ü in rule	ə = o in lemon
ī in ice	ch in child	ə = u in circus
o in hot	ng in long	

Biographical Dictionary

McCarthy, Joseph (mə kär′ thē) 1908–1957 United States senator who, in the 1950s, claimed that communists were working inside the United States government. (p. 409)

McCormick, Cyrus (mə kôr′ mik) 1809–1884 Farmer and inventor who perfected the mechanical reaper, a machine that cuts wheat. (p. 217)

Monroe, James (mən rō′) 1758–1831 fifth president of the United States, from 1817 to 1825. Issued the Monroe Doctrine in 1823, warning European nations against interfering in the Western Hemisphere. (p. 33)

Morgan, J. P. (môr′ gən) 1837–1913 Banker who invested millions in railroads, steel mills, and other companies, helping American industries to grow. (p. 181)

Morse, Samuel (môrs) 1791–1872 Inventor who helped develop the Morse code, which was used to send messages by telegraph. (p. 129)

Mott, Lucretia (mot) 1793–1880 Social reformer who fought to abolish slavery and to give women the right to vote. (p. 242)

Muir, John (myür) 1838–1914 Naturalist and conservationist who helped establish Sequoia and Yosemite national parks. (p. 266)

Murrow, Edward R. (mėr′ ō) 1908–1965 Radio and television broadcaster who became famous for his World War II coverage. (p. 402)

Mussolini, Benito (mü sə lē′ nē) 1883–1945 Italian dictator who led his country during World War II. (p. 341)

Nimitz, Chester (nim′ its) 1885–1966 Military commander of the United States Pacific Fleet during World War II; helped the United States win the Battle of Midway. (p. 358)

Nixon, Richard (nik′ sən) 1913–1994 37th President of the United States, from 1969 to 1974; first President to resign from office. (p. 430)

O'Connor, Sandra Day (ō kon′ ər) 1930– Judge who was the first woman appointed to the United States Supreme Court. (pp. 439, 484)

O'Keeffe, Georgia (ō kēf′) 1887–1986 Painter famous for her colorful flowers and natural scenes. (p. 316)

Otis, Elisha Graves (ō′ tis) 1811–1861 Inventor who developed the first safety elevator in 1852. (p. 228)

Parks, Rosa (pärks) 1913–2005 Civil rights leader arrested for protesting bus segregation in Montgomery, Alabama, in 1955. Her actions helped end the segregation of public buses. (p. 422)

Patton, George S. (pat′ n) 1885–1945 General in the United States Army who helped lead the Allies to victory in the Battle of the Bulge. (p. 360)

Pershing, John J. (pėr′ shing) 1860–1948 Army general who led American forces in Europe during World War I. (p. 276)

Pocahontas (pō′ kə hon′ təs) 1595(?)–1616 Native American woman who married John Rolfe and helped create peace between the Powhatan and the English. (p. 14)

Powell, Colin (pou′ əl) 1937– Highest-ranking American military leader during the Persian Gulf War; became the first African American secretary of state in 2001. (p. 450)

Reagan, Ronald (rā′ gən) 1911–2004 40th President of the United States, from 1981 to 1989. (p. 448)

Red Cloud (red kloud) 1822–1909 Lakota chief who objected to the United States forts and railroads being built on Lakota lands. (p. 131)

Reed, Walter (rēd) 1851–1902 United States Army doctor and medical researcher who proved diseases such as yellow fever and malaria are spread by mosquitoes. (p. 256)

Revels, Hiram R. (rev′ əlz) 1822–1901 First African American elected to the United States Senate in 1870. (p. 108)

Rice, Condoleezza (rīs) 1954– First woman appointed as national security advisor, by President George W. Bush, in 2001. (pp. 449, 507)

Rickenbacker, Eddie (rik′ ən bä kər) 1890–1973 Pilot for the United States Army who shot down several German planes during World War I. (p. 276)

Riis, Jacob (rēs) 1849–1914 Newspaper reporter who wrote *How the Other Half Lives,* a book that revealed the living conditions of the poor in New York City. (p. 226)

Robinson, Jackie (rob′ ən sən) 1919–1972 Baseball player who became the first African American player in the United States Major Leagues in 1947, playing for the Brooklyn Dodgers; elected to the Baseball Hall of Fame in 1962. (p. 420)

Rockefeller, John D. (rok′ ə fel ər) 1839–1937 Industrialist who founded the Standard Oil Company, which had a near monopoly on the petroleum industry in the United States by 1881. (p. 179)

Roebling, John (rō′ bling) 1806–1869 German-born engineer who designed the world's first suspension bridge in Cincinnati and went on to design the Brooklyn Bridge in New York City. (p. 228)

Roebuck, Alvah C. (rō′ buk) 1864–1948 Businessman who, along with Richard Sears, founded the national mail-order company Sears, Roebuck, and Company. (p. 218)

Rolfe, John (rälf) 1585–1622 Colonist in Jamestown, Virginia, who grew tobacco, which became a valuable cash crop for Jamestown. In 1614 he married Pocahontas, a Native American woman, and their union led to a period of peace between the settlers and Native Americans. (p. 14)

Roosevelt, Eleanor (rō′ zə velt) 1884–1962 First Lady who traveled around the country during the Great Depression to report Americans' living conditions to her husband, President Franklin D. Roosevelt. In 1948 she helped draft the Universal Declaration of Human Rights. (p. 333)

Roosevelt, Franklin D. (rō′ zə velt) 1882–1945 32nd President of the United States, from 1933 to 1945. Created a group of programs called the New Deal to try to help the United States recover from the Great Depression; led the United States during World War II. (pp. 329, 341)

Roosevelt, Theodore (rō′ zə velt) 1858–1919 26th President of the United States, from 1901 to 1909. Led a group of soldiers called the Rough Riders during the Spanish-American War. As President, he established national forest reserves and parks. (p. 254)

Sacagawea (sa kä′ gä wä ə) 1786(?) –1812 Shoshone woman who was an interpreter and guide on the Lewis and Clark expedition. (p. 32)

Salem, Peter (sā′ ləm) 1750(?)–1816 Soldier in the Continental Army. One of about 5,000 African Americans to serve in the American Revolution, he gained recognition for his heroism in battle. (p. 25)

Salter, Susannah Medora (sȯlt′ ər) 1800s Politician who was elected mayor of Argonia, Kansas, in 1887, becoming the first female mayor in the United States. (p. 242)

Santiago, Esmeralda (sän tē ä′ gō) 1948– Writer who published books about her experience moving from Puerto Rico to New York City. (p. 477)

Sarnoff, David (sär′ nôf) 1891–1971 Russian-born radio pioneer who proposed selling radios for entertainment in 1916. By 1924 millions of radios had been sold. (p. 302)

Schlafly, Phyllis (shla′ flē) 1924– Lawyer, political leader, and author who wrote books and articles supporting women who focused on traditional roles and values. (p. 440)

Scott, Blanche Stuart (skot) 1889–1970 Pilot who was the first American woman to fly an airplane. She was the first woman to drive across the United States. (p. 173)

Scott, Dred (skot) 1795(?)–1858 Enslaved African American who claimed he was free because he had lived in a free state. His case reached the Supreme Court, which decided against him. (p. 70)

Pronunciation Key

a in hat	ō in open	sh in she
ā in age	ȯ in all	th in thin
â in care	ô in order	ᴛʜ in then
ä in far	oi in oil	zh in measure
e in let	ou in out	ə = a in about
ē in equal	u in cup	ə = e in taken
ėr in term	u̇ in put	ə = i in pencil
i in it	ü in rule	ə = o in lemon
ī in ice	ch in child	ə = u in circus
o in hot	ng in long	

Biographical Dictionary

Scott, Winfield (skot) 1786–1866 General who fought in the Mexican War, and Union general in the Civil War; creator of the Anaconda Plan. (p. 84)

Sears, Richard (sērz) 1863–1914 Merchant who turned his small jewelry business into the national mail-order company Sears, Roebuck and Company. (p. 218)

Sequoyah (si kwoiʹ ə) 1770(?)–1843 Cherokee chief and scholar who developed a written alphabet for the Cherokee language. (p. 33)

Seward, William (süʹ wərd) 1801–1872 Secretary of state from 1861 to 1869. He negotiated the United States' purchase of Alaska from Russia in 1867. (p. 251)

Sherman, William Tecumseh (sherʹ mən) 1820–1891 Union general in the Civil War who helped defeat the Confederacy. (p. 100)

Shima, George (shēʹ mä) 1863(?)–1926 Immigrant farmer from Japan who produced 80 percent of California's potato crop, becoming known as the "Potato King." (p. 144)

Sinclair, Upton (sin klärʹ) 1878–1968 Writer of *The Jungle*, a book about poor conditions in the meat-packing plants in Chicago. (p. 264)

Singleton, Benjamin (singʹ gəl tən) 1809–1892 Leader of African American pioneers known as exodusters, who moved to the Great Plains after the Civil War. (p. 141)

Sitting Bull (sitʹ ing bùl) 1831?–1890 Lakota leader who defeated American soldiers at the Battle of Little Bighorn in 1876. (p. 155)

Slater, Samuel (slāʹ tər) 1768–1835 British mechanic who built the country's first cotton-spinning factory in Rhode Island in 1790, bringing the Industrial Revolution to the United States. (p. 34)

Smith, Bessie (smith) 1894(?)–1937 Blues singer who often recorded with jazz legend Louis Armstrong. (p. 312)

Smith, John (smith) 1580–1631 Leader of the Jamestown colony. (p. 14)

Sprague, Frank (sprāg) 1857–1934 Inventor who designed the world's first system of electric streetcars in Richmond, Virginia, in 1888. (p. 170)

Squanto (skwonʹ tō) 1590(?)–1622 Native American who helped the Pilgrims by teaching them key survival skills, such as how to grow corn. (p. 15)

Stalin, Joseph (stäʹ lin) 1879–1953 Communist dictator of the Soviet Union, from 1923 to 1953. (p. 346)

Stanton, Elizabeth Cady (stanʹ tən) 1815–1902 Women's suffrage leader and abolitionist who helped begin the women's rights movement in the United States. (p. 242)

Steinbeck, John (stīnʹ bek) 1902–1968 Writer who described the hardships faced by migrant workers during the Great Depression in his novel, *The Grapes of Wrath.* (p. 333)

Stevens, John (stēʹ vənz) 1853–1943 Chief engineer of the Panama Canal, from 1905 to 1907. His improvements of the working conditions there helped the project to be completed successfully. (p. 257)

Stone, Lucy (stōn) 1818–1893 American suffragist who founded the American Woman Suffrage Association. (p. 242)

Stowe, Harriet Beecher (stō) 1811–1896 Author of *Uncle Tom's Cabin,* a novel that described the cruelties of slavery and which sold over 300,000 copies. (p. 70)

Strauss, Levi (strous) 1829–1902 Immigrant from Germany who produced the first denim pants in San Francisco during the California gold rush. (p. 152)

T

Tarbell, Ida (tärʹ bəl) 1857–1944 Writer and journalist who exposed the unfair practices of large companies. (p. 264)

Tojo, Hideki (tōʹ jō) 1884–1948 Military leader of Japan during World War II. (p. 344)

Truman, Harry S. (trüʹ mən) 1884–1972 33rd President of the United States, from 1945 to 1953. In 1945 he decided to use atomic bombs against Japan, leading to the end of World War II. (pp. 361)

Tubman, Harriet (tubʹ mən) 1820(?)–1913 Abolitionist who escaped from slavery in about 1849 and became a conductor on the Underground Railroad; she led more than 300 people to freedom. (p. 63)

Turner, Nat (terʹ nər) 1800–1831 Leader of an 1831 slave rebellion in Southampton County, Virginia. (p. 62)

Twain, Mark (twān) 1835–1910 Pen name of American writer Samuel L. Clemens, who wrote *The Adventures of Huckleberry Finn* and *The Adventures of Tom Sawyer*. (p. 152)

Tweed, "Boss" William M. (twēd) 1823–1878 One of the leaders of the New York political group called Tammany Hall. He stole million of dollars from the city of New York and was eventually sent to prison. (p. 227)

Walker, David (wȯ′ kər) 1785–1830 Abolitionist who wrote a pamphlet in 1829 urging slaves to rebel. (p. 57)

Walker, Madame C. J. (wȯ′ kər) 1867–1919 Entrepreneur who was the first African American woman to become a millionaire. (p. 180)

Wang, An (wang) 1920–1990 Engineer and inventor who invented technology that improved computer memory. (p. 494)

Ward, Aaron Montgomery (wôrd) 1843–1913 Merchant who developed the first mail-order business in 1872. (p. 218)

Washington, Booker T. (wäsh′ ing tən) 1856–1915 Educator who founded the Tuskegee Institute, a college for African Americans, in Tuskegee, Alabama. (p. 237)

Washington, George (wäsh′ ing tən) 1732–1799 First President of the United States, from 1789 to 1797. Commander-in-chief of the Continental Army during the American Revolution. (p. 24)

Webster, Daniel (web′ stər) 1782–1852 Senator from Massachusetts and opponent of slavery who supported the Compromise of 1850. (p. 68)

Wells-Barnett, Ida (welz bär net′) 1862–1931 Journalist who helped to start an African American newspaper and fought against discrimination. (p. 238)

Westinghouse, George (wes′ ting hous) 1846–1914 Inventor and entrepreneur who developed a new technology called alternating current to deliver electricity to customers. (p. 180)

Westmoreland, William (west môr′ lənd) 1914– United States Army general who led American troops in Vietnam from 1964 to 1968. (p. 432)

Wilson, Luzena Stanley (wil′ sən) 1800s Settler whose family went to California during the 1849 gold rush. (p. 151)

Wilson, Woodrow (wil′ sən) 1856–1924 28th President of the United States, from 1913 to 1921; led the United States during World War I. (p. 275)

Wright, Orville (rīt) 1871–1948 Inventor who, with his brother Wilbur, built the first successful airplane in 1903. (p. 172)

Wright, Wilbur (rīt) 1867–1912 Inventor who, with his brother Orville, built the first successful airplane in 1903. (p. 172)

York, Alvin C. (yôrk) 1887–1964 War hero from World War I, known for his bravery and expert shooting. (p. 276)

Pronunciation Key

a in hat	ō in open	sh in she
ā in age	ȯ in all	th in thin
â in care	ô in order	ᴛʜ in then
ä in far	oi in oil	zh in measure
e in let	ou in out	ə = a in about
ē in equal	u in cup	ə = e in taken
ėr in term	ù in put	ə = i in pencil
i in it	ü in rule	ə = o in lemon
ī in ice	ch in child	ə = u in circus
o in hot	ng in long	

Glossary

This Glossary will help you understand the meanings and pronounce the vocabulary words in this book. The page number tells you where the word first appears.

A

abolitionist (ab′ ə lish′ ə nist) Person who wants to abolish, or end, slavery. (p. 36)

AFL-CIO Largest labor organization in the nation, formed in 1955 by the merging of the American Federation of Labor and the Congress of Industrial Organizations. (p. 396)

aggressor (ə gres′ ər) Nation that starts war. (p. 385)

agriculture (ag′ rə kul′ chər) Science of farming, including growing crops and raising animals. (p. 7)

alliance (ə li ′ əns) Agreement among nations to defend one another. (p. 273)

Allies (al′ īz) Alliance among Great Britain, France, the United States, Canada, the Soviet Union, and other nations during World War II. (p. 342)

almanac (ȯl′ mə nak) Reference book with helpful facts and figures. (p. H6)

Americans with Disabilities Act (ə mer′ ə kəns with dis′ ə bil′ i tēz akt) Law passed in 1990 that protects people with disabilities from discrimination in employment and requires public services to be accessible. (p. 441)

Anaconda Plan (an′ ə kon′ də plan) Union strategy for defeating the Confederacy during the Civil War. (p. 84)

arms control (ärmz kən trōl′) Agreement to limit the production of weapons. (p. 447)

arms race (ärmz rās) Race to build more and better weapons than the enemy has. (p. 410)

artificial intelligence (är′ tə fish′ əl in tel′ ə jəns) The ability of a machine to learn and imitate human thought. (p. 516)

assassination (ə sas ə nā′ shən) Killing of a government or political leader. (p. 107)

assembly line (ə sem′ blē lin) Method of mass production in which a product is put together as it moves past a line of workers. (p. 299)

atlas (at′ ləs) Book of maps. (p. H6)

atmosphere (at′mə sfir) Gasses that surround a planet. (p. 513)

atomic bomb (ə tom′ ik bom) Type of bomb built during World War II that was more powerful than any built before it. (p. 354)

Axis (ak′ sis) Alliance of Germany, Italy, and Japan during World War II. (p. 342)

B

Battle of Antietam (bat′ l uv an tē′ təm) Civil War battle fought in 1862 near Sharpsburg, Maryland, that was an important victory for the Union. (p. 85)

Battle of Bull Run, First (fėrst bat′ l uv bùl run) First major battle of the Civil War, fought near Manassas Junction, Virginia, on July 21, 1861. (p. 85)

Battle of Gettysburg (bat′ l uv get′ ēz bėrg′) Union victory over Confederate forces in 1863 in Gettysburg, Pennsylvania, that was a turning point in the Civil War. (p. 97)

Battle of Little Big Horn (bat′ l uv lit′ l big′ hôrn′) Lakota victory over United States soldiers on June 25, 1876. (p. 156)

Battle of Midway (bat′ l uv mid′ wā′) World War II naval battle between the United States and Japan in 1942, which weakened the Japanese threat in the Pacific. (p. 358)

Battle of Stalingrad (bat′ l uv stä′ lin grad) Unsuccessful German attack on the city of Stalingrad during World War II, from 1942 to 1943, that was the furthest extent of German advance into the Soviet Union. (p. 359)

Battle of the Bulge (bat′ l uv ᴛʜə bulj) World War II battle in December 1944 between Germany and Allied troops that was the last German offensive in the West. General George S. Patton led the Allies to victory. (p. 360)

Battle of Vicksburg (bat′ l uv viks′ bərg) Union victory over Confederate forces in 1863 at Vicksburg, Mississippi, that gave the Union control of the Mississippi River. (p. 99)

Berlin Airlift (bər lin′ âr′ lift′) Program under which the United States aided West Berlin by flying in food and fuel when Soviet troops cut off the city from Western trade. (p. 389)

Berlin Wall (bər lin′ wȯl) Barrier that divided communist East Berlin from non-communist West Berlin from 1961 to 1989. (p. 412)

Bill of Rights (bil uv rīts) First ten amendments to the Constitution, ratified in 1790. (p. 28)

black codes (blak kōdz) Laws that denied African Americans many civil rights. (p. 107)

blockade (blo kād′) Shutting off of an area by troops or ships to keep people and supplies from moving in or out. (p. 84)

Blue Laws (blü lȯs) Laws introduced by Progressives in the early 1900s designed to solve social problems, such as alcohol abuse. (p. 265)

border state (bôr′ dər stāt) During the Civil War, a state located between the Union and the Confederacy that allowed slavery but remained in the Union. (p. 76)

Buffalo Soldiers (buf′ ə lō sōl′ jərz) Nickname for African American soldiers who fought in the wars against Native Americans living on the Great Plains during the 1870s. (p. 254)

★ C ★

Cabinet (kab′ ə nit) Officials appointed by the President as advisors and to head the departments in the Executive Branch. (p. 31)

capital resource (kap′ ə təl ri′ sôrs) Money, tools, and machines a company uses to produce goods and services. (p. 181)

cardinal direction (kärd′ n əl də rek′ shən) One of the four main directions on Earth: north, south, east, and west. (p. H17)

caring (kâr′ ing) Being interested in the needs of others. (p. H2)

cash crop (kash krop) Crop grown to be sold for a profit. (p. 14)

cattle drive (kat′ l drīv) Method cowboys used to move large herds of cattle north from ranches in Texas to towns along the railroads in the late 1800s. (p. 149)

century (sen′ chər ē) Period of 100 years. (p. 38)

checks and balances (cheks and bal′ ən səz) System set up by the writers of the Constitution that gives each of the three branches of government the power to check, or limit, the power of the other two. (p. 26)

circle graph (sėr′ kəl graf) Graph that shows how a whole is divided into parts. (p. 230)

citizen (sit′ ə zən) Member of a country. (p. 482)

Pronunciation Key

a	in hat	ō	in open	sh	in she
ā	in age	ȯ	in all	th	in thin
â	in care	ô	in order	ᴛʜ	in then
ä	in far	oi	in oil	zh	in measure
e	in let	ou	in out	ə	= a in about
ē	in equal	u	in cup	ə	= e in taken
ėr	in term	ů	in put	ə	= i in pencil
i	in it	ü	in rule	ə	= o in lemon
ī	in ice	ch	in child	ə	= u in circus
o	in hot	ng	in long		

Glossary

civil rights (siv′ əl rīts) Rights guaranteed to all United States citizens by the Constitution. (p. 420)

civil war (siv′ əl wôr) War between people of the same country. (p. 77)

climograph (klī′ mə graph) Graph that shows the average temperature and average precipitation for a place over time. (p. 146)

Cold War (kōld wôr) Struggle between the United States and the Soviet Union from the late 1940s to the early 1990s that was fought with ideas, words, and money, with no direct conflict between the two countries. (p. 390)

colony (kol′ ə nē) Settlement far from the country that rules it. (p. 10)

Columbian Exchange (kə lum′ bē ən eks chānj′) Movement of people, animals, plants, diseases, and ways of life between the Eastern and Western Hemispheres following the voyages of Christopher Columbus. (p. 10)

communism (kom′ yə niz′ əm) Political and economic system in which the government owns all businesses and land. (p. 388)

commute (kə myüt′) Trip to work, such as from the suburbs to a nearby city. (p. 401)

compass rose (kum′ pəs rōz) Pointer that shows directions on a map. (p. H17)

Compromise of 1850 (kom′ prə mīz uv) Law under which California was admitted to the Union as a free state and the Fugitive Slave Law was passed. (p. 68)

concentration camp (kon′ sən trā′ shən kamp) Prison in which the Nazis enslaved and murdered millions of Jews and other groups during World War II. (p. 362)

Confederacy (kən fed′ ər ə sē) Confederate States of America formed by the 11 Southern states that seceded from the Union after Abraham Lincoln was elected President. (p. 75)

conservation (kon′ sər vā′ shən) Protection and careful use of natural resources. (p. 266)

constitution (kon′ stə tü′ shən) Written plan of government. The United States Constitution, adopted in 1789, is the foundation of the national government. (p. 26)

consumer (kən sü′ mər) Person who buys or uses goods and services. (p. 180)

consumer credit (kən sü′ mər kre′d it) Credit used to buy goods that are consumed, such as clothing, rather than for investments, such as business equipment. (p. 398)

corporation (kôr′ pə rā′ shən) Business owned by investors. (p. 178)

courage (kėr′ ij) Doing what is right even when it is frightening or dangerous. (p. H2)

credible (kred′ ə bəl) Reliable. (p. 260)

credit (kred′ it) Borrowed money. (p. 323)

credit card (kred′ it kärd) Card that allows the cardholder to charge goods and services and then pay off the charge, along with an extra fee, over a period of time. (p. 398)

Cuban Missile Crisis (kyü′ bən mis′ əl krī′ sis) Tension between the United States and the Soviet Union in 1962 over nuclear missiles in Cuba. (p. 411)

culture (kul′ chər) Way of life of a group of people, including their religion, customs, and language. (p. 8)

decade (dek′ ād) Period of ten years. (p. 38)

Declaration of Independence (dek′ lə rā′ shən uv in′ di pen′ dəns) Document that declared the 13 Colonies independent from Great Britain, written mainly by Thomas Jefferson and approved on July 4, 1776. (p. 24)

degree (di grē′) Unit of measuring, used in latitude and longitude. (p. H15)

demand (di mand′) Amount of a product that people are willing to buy. (p. 489)

democracy (di mok′ rə sē) Government run by the people. (p. 481)

dictator (dik′ tā tər) Leader with complete control of a country's government. (p. 341)

dictionary (dik′ shə ner′ ē) Alphabetical collection of words that includes the meaning and pronunciation of each word. (p. H6)

discrimination (dis krim′ ə nā′ shən) Unfair treatment of a group or individual. (p. 108)

distribution map (dis′ trə byü′ shən map) Map that shows patterns of how things such as population or natural resources are spread out over an area. (p. 478)

diversity (də vėr′ sə tē) Variety. (p. 190)

draft (draft) Law that requires men of a certain age to serve in the military, if called. (p. 89)

drought (drout) Long period without rain. (p. 332)

Dust Bowl (dust bōl) Name given to much of the Great Plains during the long drought of the 1930s. (p. 332)

Earth Day (ėrth dā) Annual day of awareness to encourage respect for the environment. The first Earth Day celebration was held on April 22, 1970. (p. 443)

economist (i kon′ ə mist) Person who studies the economy. (p. 181)

economy (i kon′ ə mē) System for producing and distributing goods and services. (p. 16)

Eighteenth Amendment (ā′ tēnth ə mend′ mənt) Amendment to the Constitution, also called the Prohibition Amendment, passed in 1919, that outlawed the making, sale, and transporting of alcoholic beverages. (p. 311)

electoral college (i lek′ tər əl kol′ ij) Group of people chosen by the voters of each state who elect the President and Vice-President of the United States. (p. 483)

elevation (el′ ə vā′ shən) Height of the land above sea level. (p. H22)

elevation map (el′ ə vā′ shən map) Physical map that uses color to show elevation. (p. H22)

Emancipation Proclamation (i man′ sə pā′ shən prok′ lə mā′ shən) Statement issued by President Abraham Lincoln on January 1, 1863, freeing all slaves in Confederate states still at war with the Union. (p. 90)

encyclopedia (en sī′ klə pē′ dē ə) Book or set of books with articles, alphabetically listed, on various topics. (p. H6)

enfranchise (ən fran′ chīz) To give the right to vote. (p. 233)

entrepreneur (än′ trə prə nėr′) Person who starts a new business, hoping to make a profit. (p. 152)

Environmental Protection Agency (EPA) (en vī′ rən men′ təl prə tek′ shən ā′ jen sē) Federal agency formed in 1970 to enforce environmental laws. (p. 443)

Equal Employment Opportunity Commission (ē′ kwəl em ploi′ mənt op′ ər tü′ ni tē kə mish′ ən) Federal agency formed in 1965 that enforces civil rights laws that have to do with the workplace. (p. 442)

Pronunciation Key

a in hat	ō in open	sh in she
ā in age	ȯ in all	th in thin
â in care	ô in order	ŦH in then
ä in far	oi in oil	zh in measure
e in let	ou in out	ə = a in about
ē in equal	u in cup	ə = e in taken
ėr in term	u̇ in put	ə = i in pencil
i in it	ü in rule	ə = o in lemon
ī in ice	ch in child	ə = u in circus
o in hot	ng in long	

Glossary

equator (i kwā′ tər) Imaginary line around the middle of Earth, halfway between the North Pole and the South Pole; 0° latitude. (p. H12)

ethnic group (eth′ nik grüp) Group of people who share the same customs and language. (p. 476)

Executive Branch (eg zek′ yə tiv branch) Part of the federal government, led by the President, that makes sure the laws are carried out. (p. 484)

exoduster (ek′ sə dus tər) Name for African American pioneers who moved to the Great Plains after the Civil War. (p. 141)

export (ek′ spôrt) Good that one country sells to another country. (p. 492)

fact (fakt) Statement that can be proved to be true. (p. 306)

fairness (fâr′ nes) Not favoring one more than others. (p. H2)

fascism (fash′ iz′ əm) Form of government in which individual freedoms are denied and the government has complete power. (p. 341)

Fifteenth Amendment (fif′ tēnth ə mend′ mənt) Amendment to the United States Constitution, ratified in 1870, that gave male citizens of all races the right to vote. (p. 109)

Fourteenth Amendment (fôr′ tēnth ə mend′ mənt) Amendment to the United States Constitution, ratified in 1868, that gave African Americans citizenship and equal protection under the law. (p. 109)

Freedmen's Bureau (frēd′ mənz byür′ ō) Federal agency set up in 1865 to provide food, schools, and medical care to freed slaves in the South. (p. 108)

free enterprise (frē en′ tər prīz) Economic system in which people are free to start their own businesses and own their own property. (p. 180)

free state (frē stāt) State in which slavery was not allowed. (p. 67)

French and Indian War (french and in′ dē ən wôr) War fought by the British against the French and their Native American allies in North America, from 1754 to 1763. (p. 18)

Fugitive Slave Law (fyü′ jə tiv slāv lò) Law passed in 1850 that said escaped slaves had to be returned to their owners even if they reached free states. (p. 68)

generalization (jen′ ər ə lə zā′ shən) Broad statement or idea about a subject. (p. 518)

Gettysburg Address (get′ ēz bérg ə dres′) Civil War speech given by President Abraham Lincoln in 1863 at the site of the Battle of Gettysburg. (p. 98)

G.I. Bill of Rights (jē ī bil uv rīts) Law passed during World War II that provided benefits to help veterans return to civilian life. (p. 397)

glacier (glā′ shər) Thick sheet of ice. (p. 7)

globalization (glō′ bə li zā′ shən) Development of a world economic system in which people and goods move freely from one country to another. (p. 493)

global warming (glō′ bəl wôr′ ming) Idea that the increase in carbon dioxide in the atmosphere is leading to a slow warming of the global climate, which would cause environmental problems around the world. (p. 513)

globe (glōb) Round model of Earth. (p. H12)

gold rush (gōld rush) Sudden movement of many people to an area where gold has been found. (p. 151)

Great Depression (grāt di presh′ ən) Period of severe economic hardship that began in the United States in 1929. (p. 323)

Great Migration (grāt mī grā′ shən) Movement of millions of African Americans to the northern United States between 1915 and the 1940s in search of work and fair treatment. (p. 235)

grid (grid) Pattern of criss-crossing lines that can help find locations on a map. (p. 366)

guerrilla warfare (gə ril′ ə wôr′ fâr) Form of warfare that includes surprise, random attacks, often by fighters not in uniform. (p. 432)

Harlem Renaissance (här′ ləm ren′ ə säns) Artistic movement centered in Harlem, an African American neighborhood in New York City. (p. 314)

hemisphere (hem′ ə sfir) Half of a sphere or globe. Earth can be divided into hemispheres. (p. H13)

Holocaust (hol′ ə kȯst) Murder of about 12 million people, including 6 million Jews, by the Nazis during World War II. (p. 362)

Homestead Act (hōm′ sted′ akt) Law signed in 1862 offering free land to people willing to start new farms on the Great Plains. (p. 139)

homesteaders (hōm′ sted ərz) Settlers who claimed land on the Great Plains under the Homestead Act. (p. 139)

honesty (on′ ə stē) Truthfulness. (p. H2)

House of Burgesses (hous uv bėr′ jis ez) Law-making assembly in colonial Virginia, the first in an English colony. (p. 14)

human resource (hyü′ mən ri sôrs′) People. (p. 181)

Ice Age (īs āj) Long period of time when Earth's climate was much colder than it is today. (p. 7)

ideals (ī dē′ əlz) Important beliefs. (p. 475)

ideology (ī′ dē ol′ ə jē) Set of beliefs. (p. 388)

impeachment (im pēch′ mənt) Bringing of charges of wrongdoing against an elected official by the House of Representatives. (p. 109)

import (im′ pôrt) Good that one country buys from another country. (p. 492)

Industrial Revolution (in dus′ trē əl rev′ ə lü′ shən) Period of change from making goods by hand to producing them with machines. (p. 34)

inflation (in flā′ shən) Rapid rise in prices. (p. 335)

inset map (in′ set′ map) Small map within a larger map. Shows areas outside of or in greater detail than the larger map. (p. H19)

interdependence (in′ tər di pen′ dəns) Result of globalization in which changes to the economy of one country can affect the economies of other countries. (p. 493)

intermediate direction (in′ tər mē′ dē it də rek′ shən) Pointer halfway between the main directions: northeast, northwest, southeast, southwest. (p. H17)

International Date Line (in′ tər nash′ ə nəl dāt līn) An imaginary line running along latitude 180°, in the middle of the Pacific Ocean, marking the time boundary between one day and the next. (p. 367)

Internet (in′ tər net′) Worldwide network of computers. (p. H7)

Pronunciation Key

a in hat	ō in open	sh in she
ā in age	ȯ in all	th in thin
â in care	ô in order	ŦH in then
ä in far	oi in oil	zh in measure
e in let	ou in out	ə = a in about
ē in equal	u in cup	ə = e in taken
ėr in term	u̇ in put	ə = i in pencil
i in it	ü in rule	ə = o in lemon
ī in ice	ch in child	ə = u in circus
o in hot	ng in long	

Glossary

interstate highway (in′ tər stāt hī′ wā′) Road that connects cities in different states. (p. 102)

investor (in vest′ ər) Person who gives money to a business or project, hoping to make a profit. (p. 168)

isolationism (ī′ sə lā′ shə niz′ əm) Policy in which a nation prefers to remain neutral and let other countries handle their own affairs. (p. 275)

isthmus (is′ məs) A narrow strip of land that connects two larger areas. (p. 256)

jazz (jaz) Musical form that began in New Orleans, Louisiana, and was influenced by African American musical traditions. (p. 312)

Jim Crow laws (jim krō lōz) Laws passed in the South after Reconstruction enforcing the segregation of blacks and whites. (p. 110)

Judicial Branch (jü dish′ əl branch) Part of the federal government, made up of the court system, that decides the meaning of the laws. (p. 484)

Kansas-Nebraska Act (kan′ zəs nə bras′ kə akt) Law passed in 1854 allowing the people of these two territories to decide for themselves whether to allow slavery. (p. 69)

key (kē) Box explaining the symbols on a map. It is also known as a legend. (p. H16)

Korean War (kô rē′ ən wôr) War between South Korea, supported by the United States and the United Nations, and North Korea, supported by China, from 1950 to 1953. (p. 407)

labor union (lā′ bər yü′ nyən) Group of workers joined together to fight for improved working conditions and better wages. (p. 195)

large-scale map (lärj skāl map) Map showing a small area in detail. (p. 20)

latitude (lat′ ə tüd) Distance north or south of the equator, measured in degrees. (p. H15)

League of Nations (lēg uv nā′ shənz) International organization formed after World War I to prevent wars. (p. 280)

Legislative Branch (lej′ ə slā′ tiv branch) Part of the federal government, led by Congress, that makes the laws. (p. 484)

Lend-Lease (lend′ lēs) Policy that allowed Great Britain to borrow military supplies from the United States during World War II. (p. 343)

line graph (līn graf) Graph that shows change over time. (p. 230)

locator map (lō′ kā tər map) Small map that appears with a larger map; shows where the subject area of the larger map is located on Earth. (p. H16)

longitude (lon′ jə tüd) Distance east or west of the prime meridian, measured in degrees. (p. H15)

Manhattan Project (man hat′ n proj′ ekt) Code name given to the effort to build an atomic bomb in the United States. (p. 354)

manifest destiny (man′ ə fest des′ tə nē) Belief that the United States should expand west to the Pacific Ocean. (p. 35)

manual labor (man′ yü əl lā′ bər) Work done by hand without machines. (p. 217)

map projection (map prə jek′ shen) Way of showing Earth as a flat surface. (p. 454)

Marshall Plan (mär′ shəl plan) Program under which the United States provided funds to help European countries rebuild after World War II. (p. 386)

mass media (mas mē′ dē ə) Public forms of communication that reach large audiences. (p. 303)

mass production (mas prə duk′ shən) Making of a large number of goods that are exactly alike. (p. 302)

mechanization (mek′ ə ni zā′ shən) Using machines to do work. (p. 217)

meridian (mə rid′ ē ən) Imaginary line extending from the North Pole to the South Pole, also called longitude line. (p. H15)

migrant worker (mī′ grənt wėr′ kər) Person who moves from place to place harvesting crops. (p. 332)

migrate (mī′ grāt) To move from one area to another. (p. 7)

Missouri Compromise (mə zùr′ ē kom′ prə mīz) Law passed in 1820 that divided the Louisiana Territory into a southern area that allowed slavery and a northern area that did not. (p. 67)

monopoly (mə nop′ ə lē) A company that has control of an entire industry. (p. 179)

muckraker (muk′ rā′ kər) Writer or journalist of the early 1900s who uncovered shameful conditions in business and other areas of American life. (p. 264)

nationalism (nash′ ə nə liz′ əm) Love of country and the desire to have one's country free from the control of another. (p. 273)

National Organization for Women (nash′ ə nəl ôr′ gə nə zā′ shən fôr wim′ ən) Group founded in 1966 to work for equal rights and opportunities for women. (p. 440)

NATO (nā′ tō) North Atlantic Treaty Organization, a military alliance among the nations of Western Europe, United States, and Canada in which they agreed to help each other if attacked by the Soviet Union. (p. 389)

natural resource (nach′ ər əl ri sôrs′) Materials found in nature that people can use such as trees and water. (p. 16)

New Deal (nü dēl) Series of programs started by President Franklin D. Roosevelt in 1933 to try to help the nation recover from the Great Depression. (p. 329)

Nineteenth Amendment (nīn′ tēnth ə mend′ mənt) Amendment to the Constitution, ratified in 1920, that gave women the right to vote. (p. 243)

nonfiction book (non fik′ shən bùk) Book that is based on fact. (p. H6)

North American Free Trade Agreement (NAFTA) (nôrth ə mer′ ə kən frē trād ə grē′ mənt) Agreement among the United States, Canada, and Mexico that allows them to import and export goods with each other without having to pay taxes or fees. (p. 492)

Pronunciation Key		
a in hat	ō in open	sh in she
ā in age	ȯ in all	th in thin
â in care	ô in order	ᴛʜ in then
ä in far	oi in oil	zh in measure
e in let	ou in out	ə = a in about
ē in equal	u in cup	ə = e in taken
ėr in term	ù in put	ə = i in pencil
i in it	ü in rule	ə = o in lemon
ī in ice	ch in child	ə = u in circus
o in hot	ng in long	

Glossary

opinion (ə pin′ yən) Personal view about an issue. (p. 306)

opportunity cost (op′ ər tü′ nə tē kȯst) Value of what must be given up in order to produce a certain good. (p. 489)

outline (out′ līn′) Written plan for organizing information about a subject. (p. 174)

parallel (pȧr′ ə lel) Imaginary circle around the Earth, also called latitude lines. (p. H15)

parallel time lines (pȧr′ ə lel tīm līnz) Two or more time lines grouped together. (p. 38)

passive resistance (pas′ iv ri zis′ təns) Form of protest that does not use violence. (p. 423)

periodical (pir′ ē od′ ə kəl) Newspaper or magazine that is published on a regular basis. (p. H6)

Persian Gulf War (pėr′ zhən gulf wȯr) War involving the United States and its allies against Iraq, triggered by Iraq's invasion of Kuwait in 1990. (p. 450)

physical map (fiz′ ə kəl map) Map showing geographic features, such as mountains and rivers. (p. H17)

pioneer (pī ′ ə nir′) Early settler of a region. (p. 139)

plantation (plan tā′ shən) Large farm with many workers who live on the land they work. (p. 16)

point of view (point uv vyü) A person's own opinion on an issue or event. (p. 58)

political cartoon (pə lit′ ə kəl kär tün′) Drawing that shows people or events in the news in a funny way. (p. 268)

political machine (pə lit′ ə kəl mə shēn′) Organization of people that controls votes to gain political power. (p. 227)

political map (pə lit′ ə kəl map) Map that shows borders between states or countries. (p. H16)

political party (pə lit′ ə kəl pär′ tē) Organized group of people who share a similar view of what government should do. (p. 31)

Pony Express (pō′ nē ek spres′) Service begun in 1860 that used a relay of riders on horses to deliver mail from Missouri to California in ten days. (p. 129)

popular sovereignty (pop′ yə lər sov′ rən tē) Idea that all people have a say in how the government is run. (p. 481)

population density map (pop′ yə lā′ shən den′ sə tē map) Map that shows the distribution of population over an area. (p. 478)

prejudice (prej′ ə dis) Unfair negative opinion about a group of people. (p. 189)

primary source (prī′ mer ē sôrs) Eyewitness account of a historical event. (p. H6)

prime meridian (prīm mə rid′ ē ən) Line of longitude marked 0 degrees. Other lines of longitude are measured in degrees east or west of the prime meridian. (p. H12)

producer (prə dü′ sər) Person who makes goods. (p. 489)

Progressives (prə gres′ ivz) Reformers who worked to stop unfair practices by businesses and improve the way government works. (p. 264)

Prohibition (prō′ ə bish′ ən) Complete ban on the making, transporting, and sale of alcoholic beverages in the United States from 1920 to 1933. (p. 311)

propaganda (prop′ ə gan′ də) Systematic effort to spread opinions or beliefs. (p. 390)

rationing (rash′ ən ing) Government limiting of the amount of food each person in the United States could buy during World War II. (p. 351)

reaper (rē′ pər) Machine that cuts wheat. (p. 217)

Reconstruction (rē′ kən struk′ shən) Period of rebuilding after the Civil War, during which the Southern states rejoined the Union. (p. 107)

Red Scare (red skâr) Period of panic and fear that communism was spreading in the United States in the early twentieth century. (p. 409)

region (rē′ jən) Large area that has common features that set it apart from other areas. (p. 473)

republic (ri pub′ lik) Form of government in which people elect representatives to make laws and run the government. (p. 26)

research (rē′ sėrch′) Way of gathering information to learn more about a subject. (p. 496)

reservation (rez′ ər vā′ shən) Land set aside by the government for Native Americans. (p. 155)

respect (ri spekt′) Consideration for others. (p. H2)

responsibility (ri spon′ sə bil′ ə tē) Doing what you are supposed to do. (p. H2)

road map (rōd map) Map showing roads, cities, and places of interest. (p. H24)

Rough Riders (ruf rī′ dərz) Volunteer soldiers led by Theodore Roosevelt during the Spanish-American War. (p. 254)

scale (skāl) Tool that helps you measure distances on a map. (p. H18)

search engine (sėrch en′ jən) Computer site that searches for information from numerous Internet Web sites. (p. H7)

secede (si sēd′) To break away from a group, as the Southern states broke away from the United States in 1861. (p. 75)

secondary source (sek′ ən der′ ē sôrs) Description of events written by a person who did not witness the events. (p. H6)

sectionalism (sek′ shə nə liz′ əm) Loyalty to a part of a country rather than to the country itself. (p. 55)

segregation (seg′ rə gā′ shən) Separation of people of different races. (p. 110)

settlement house (set′ l mənt hous) Center that provides help for immigrants and the poor. (p. 226)

sharecropping (shâr′ krop′ ing) System of farming in which farmers rent land and pay the landowner with a share of the crops they raise. (p. 110)

slave codes (slāv kōdz) Laws designed to control the behavior of enslaved people. (p. 61)

slave state (slāv stāt) State in which slavery was allowed before the Civil War. (p. 67)

small-scale map (smôl′ skāl map) Map showing a large area of land but not much detail. (p. 20)

Social Security (sō′ shəl si kyùr′ ə tē) New Deal program that provides monthly payments to people who are elderly, disabled, or unemployed. (p. 329)

sodbuster (sod′ bus tər) Great Plains farmer of the late 1800s who had to cut through sod, or thick grass, before planting crops. (p. 140)

source (sôrs) Written or oral account that may provide information. (p. 260)

Pronunciation Key

a in hat	ō in open	sh in she
ā in age	ȯ in all	th in thin
â in care	ô in order	ᴛʜ in then
ä in far	oi in oil	zh in measure
e in let	ou in out	ə = a in about
ē in equal	u in cup	ə = e in taken
ėr in term	ù in put	ə = i in pencil
i in it	ü in rule	ə = o in lemon
ī in ice	ch in child	ə = u in circus
o in hot	ng in long	

Glossary

space race (spās rās) Race between the United States and the Soviet Union to explore outer space during the Cold War. (p. 429)

Spanish-American War (span′ ish ə mer′ ə kən wôr) War between the United States and Spain in 1898 in which the United States gained Spanish territory. (p. 253)

Stamp Act (stamp akt) British law approved in 1765 that taxed printed materials in the 13 Colonies. (p. 23)

standard time (stan′ dərd tīm) Time set by law for all places in a time zone. (p. 134)

states' rights (stāts rīts) Idea that states have the right to make decisions about issues that concern them. (p. 67)

stock (stok) A share of a company that is sold to an investor. (p. 178)

stock market (stok mär′ kit) Place where stocks are bought and sold. (p. 322)

strike (strīk) Refusal of workers to work until business owners meet their demands. (p. 195)

suburb (sub′ ėrb′) Community just outside or near a city. (p. 395)

suffrage (suf′ rij) Right to vote. (p. 242)

suffragist (suf′ rə jist) Person working for women's voting rights. (p. 242)

Sunbelt (sun′ belt′) An area of the United States made up of the Southeast and Southwest regions. (p. 474)

supply (sə plī′) Amount of a product that is available. (p. 489)

suspension bridge (sə spen′ shən brij) Bridge that hangs from steel cables. (p. 228)

sweatshop (swet′ shop′) Factory or workshop where people work under poor conditions. (p. 193)

symbol (sim′ bəl) Something that stands for something else. (p. H16)

technology (tek nol′ ə jē) Use of new ideas to make tools that improve people's lives. (p. 142)

telegraph (tel′ ə graf) Device that sends messages through wires using electricity. (p. 129)

tenant (ten′ ənt) Person who pays rent to use land or buildings that belong to someone else. (p. 233)

tenement (ten′ ə mənt) Building, especially in a poor section of a city, divided into small apartments. (p. 224)

terrorist (ter′ ər ist) Person who uses violence and fear to try to achieve goals. (p. 503)

Thirteenth Amendment (thėr′ tēnth ə mend′ mənt) Amendment to the United States Constitution that abolished slavery in 1865. (p. 107)

threshing machine (thresh′ ing mə shēn′) Machine that separates the grain from plant stalks. (p. 217)

time zone (tīm zōn) Region in which one standard of time is used. There are 24 time zones around the world. (p. 134)

time zone map (tīm zōn map) Map showing the world's or any country's time zones. (p. H21)

title (tī′ tl) Name of something, such as a book or map. (p. H16)

total war (tō′ təl wôr) Method of warfare that involves civilians as targets and is designed to destroy the opposing army and the people's will to fight. (p. 100)

transcontinental railroad (tran′ skon tə nen′ tl rāl′ rōd′) Railroad that crosses a continent. The first transcontinental railroad in the United States was completed in 1869. (p. 130)

Treaty of Versailles (trē′ tē uv ver sī′) Treaty signed in 1919 that officially ended World War I. (p. 280)

triangular trade route (trī ang′ gyə lər trād rout) Three-sided trade route among England, Africa, and the North American colonies; included the slave trade. (p. 17)

trust (trust) Large companies with the power to drive out competition in an industry. (p. 263)

Tuskegee Airmen (təs kē′ gē âr′ men) First African American fighter pilots. (p. 352)

Twenty-first Amendment (twen′ tē fėrst ə mend′ mənt) Amendment to the United States Constitution, adopted in 1933, that ended Prohibition. (p. 311)

Underground Railroad (un′ dər ground′ rāl′ rōd′) Organized system of secret routes used by people escaping slavery that led from the South to the North or Canada. (p. 63)

unemployment (un′ em ploi′ mənt) Number or percentage of workers without jobs. (p. 321)

Union (yü′ nyən) States that remained loyal to the United States government during the Civil War. (p. 75)

United Farm Workers of America (yü nī′ tid färm wėr′ kərs uv ə mer′ ə kə) Labor union founded by César Chávez and Dolores Huerta that works for the rights of migrant farm workers. (p. 441)

United Nations (yü nī′ tid nā′ shəns) International organization formed in 1945 to promote peace and end conflicts between countries. (p. 387)

urbanization (ėr bə niz ā′ shən) Movement of people from rural areas to cities. (p. 224)

Vietnam Conflict (vē et′ näm′ kon′ flikt) Conflict in the 1960s and 1970s during which the United States sent soldiers to South Vietnam to try to prevent communists from taking over the nation. (p. 432)

weapons of mass destruction (wep′ ənz uv mas di struk′ shən) Nuclear weapons and weapons that spread poison chemicals or deadly diseases. (p. 507)

World War I (wėrld wôr wun) War fought from 1914 to 1918 between the Central and Allied Powers. The United States joined the Allied Powers in 1917, helping them to victory. (p. 273)

World War II (wėrld wôr tü) War fought from 1939 to 1945 between the Allies and the Axis, involving most of the countries in the world. The United States joined the Allies in 1941, helping them to victory. (p. 342)

yellow journalism (yel′ ō jėr′ nl iz′ əm) False or exaggerated reporting. (p. 253)

Pronunciation Key

a in hat	ō in open	sh in she
ā in age	ȯ in all	th in thin
â in care	ô in order	ŦH in then
ä in far	oi in oil	zh in measure
e in let	ou in out	ə = a in about
ē in equal	u in cup	ə = e in taken
ėr in term	ů in put	ə = i in pencil
i in it	ü in rule	ə = o in lemon
ī in ice	ch in child	ə = u in circus
o in hot	ng in long	

Index

This Index lists the pages on which topics appear in this book. Page numbers after an *m* refer to a map. Page numbers after a *p* refer to a photograph. Page numbers after a *c* refer to a chart or graph.

abolitionist, 36, 57, 62, 245

Adams, Abigail, 25, 29, *p29*

Adams, John, 24, 29, R22, *pR22*

Adams, John Quincy, 62, R23, *pR23*

Adams, Samuel, 23

Addams, Jane, 226, *p226*

Afghanistan, 448, 506–507, *m506*

AFL-CIO, 396

Africa, 9–10, 17, 514, *m9, m17, R5*

African Americans
in American Revolution, 25

artists, 293, 295, 314, 318–319

Buffalo Soldiers, 254, *p254*

civil rights of, 413, 418–426

in Civil War, 90–91, *p91*

discrimination against, 108, 233–234, 236–237, 352, 418–424

education and, 51, 237, 239, 418–419, 421, *p237, 421*

entertainers, 312, 419, *p312*

entrepreneur, 180

exodusters, 141

in government, 108, 449, 453, 467, 507

migration of, 235, 314, 318, 474, *m235*

Reconstruction and, 107–111

resistance to slavery by, 60–63

slavery and, 56–57, 61

voting rights of, 56, 107–110, 215, 242, 424–425, *p109, 425, c245*

World War I and, 235, 278

World War II and, 352

Africans, 16–17

aggressor, 385

agriculture, 7. *See also* farming

Agriculture Adjustment Administration (AAA), 330, *p330*

Ahwahnee Valley, California, 219, *m216*

AIDS, 514

airplane, 171–172, 277, 309, 349, 402, 516, *p172, 309, 402*

Alabama, R18, *m473*

Alaska, 250–251, R18, *p250–251, m473*

Albright, Madeleine, 451, 486–487, *p487*

Aldrin, Edwin, 428, 430, 458–459

alliance, 273

Allied Powers, 273, 275–277, 279, 321, *m273*

Allies, 342, 345–346, 349, 354–355, 358, 360, 365, 385, 395, *m346, c345*

almanac, H6

al Qaeda, 506–507

amendment, 484. *See also* specific amendments

American Association of the Red Cross, 92, 278

American Federation of Labor (AFL), 195, 396

American Indians, *See* Native Americans, *as well as specific groups*

American Revolution, 24–25

Americans with Disabilities Act, 441

Amistad, 62, *p62*

Anaconda Plan, 84, 99, *m84*

Anaheim, California, 401, *m394*

Anderson, Mary, 174–175

Angel Island, 187, *p187, m184*

Antarctica, *mR4–5*

Anthony, Susan B., 210, 242, 245, *p210, 245*

Antietam, Battle of, 85, *p85, m99*

Antin, Mary, 123, 185, 191, *p123, 191*

ANZACs, 277, *p277*

Apache, 158, *m8*

apartheid, 451

Apollo 11, 428, 430, 458–459

Appleton, Wisconsin, 220, *m216*

appliances, electric, 220–221, 399–400, *p220, 399*

Appomattox Court House, Virginia, 101, *m99*

Appleton, Wisconsin, 220, *m216*

Arctic Ocean, *mR4–5*

Argonia, Kansas, 242, *m240, p214*

Arizona, R18, *m473*

Arkansas, R18, *m473*

arms control, 447, 449

arms race, 410–412

Armstrong, Louis, 312, *p312*

Armstrong, Neil, 379, 428, 430, 458–459, *p379*

Arthur, Chester A., R23, *pR23*

Articles of Confederation, 26

artificial intelligence, 516

Ashe, Arthur, 426

Asia, 7, 10, *m6, R5, R6*

assassination, 107

assembly line, 299, *p299*

Atlanta, Georgia, 100, 223, 427, 474, *m99, 113*

Atlantic Ocean, *mR4–5*

atlas, H17, *mR2–R15*

atmosphere, 513

atomic bomb, 354, 361, 364

Australia, *mR5*

Austria-Hungary, 273–274, *m273*

automobile, 125, 170–171, 298–301, 402, 489, *p170, 171, 298, 299, 300*

Axis, 342–343, 346, 349, 354, 358, 360, *m346, c345*

Baby Boomers, 400, 452, *p400, c400*

barbed wire, 143, 150, *p143*

Barton, Clara, 49, 92, *p49*

baseball, 315, 350, 420, 426

Battle of Bull, First1 Run, 85, 92, *m99*

battles. *See* specific battles

Belgium, 273–274, *m273*

Bell, Alexander Graham, 123, 125, 166–167, 219, *p123, 167*

Bering Strait, 7, *m7*

Berlin, Germany, 389, *m389*

Berlin Airlift, 389

Berlin Wall, 412, 446, 449, *p448*

Bessemer, Henry, 177

Bessemer process, 177

Bill of Rights, 28, R42–R43

bin Laden, Osama, 506

black codes, 107

Black Hills, 155, *m154, p156*

Black Tuesday, 322

blockade, 84, 86, 89, 99

Blue Laws, 265, 311

Booth, John Wilkes, 107

border states, 76, *m76*

Bosnia-Herzegovina, 451, *m449, R5*

Boston, Massachusetts, 17, 22–24, 54, 229, 494, *m16*

Boston Massacre, *c23*

Boston Tea Party, *c23*

boycott, 422, *p422*

Boyd, Belle, 92, *p92*

Brady, Mathew, 89

Brazil, 475, *m475, p475*

Britain. *See* England, Great Britain

Brooklyn Bridge, 228–229

Brown, John, 70

Brown, Linda, 421, *p421*

Bruce, Blanche K., 108

Buchanan, James, R22, *pR22*

buffalo, 154, *p155*

Buffalo Soldiers, 254, *p254*

Bulgaria, 273, *m273, p388,*

Bulge, Battle of the, 360, *m358*

Bull Run First Battle of, 85, 92, *m99*

Bunche, Ralph, 426

Bush, George H. W., 449–450, R25, *pR25*

Bush, George W., 442, 452–453, 467, 483, 505–507, 513, R25, *p453, 467, 504, R25*

Cabinet, 31, *p31*

Calhoun, John C., 67–68

California, 68, 144–145, 151, 179, 332–333, R18, *m473*

Canada, 63, *m63, mR6, c345*

capital resource, 181

cardinal directions, H12

Carnegie, Andrew, 122, 177, 181, 183, 193, 196, *p122, 183*

Carney, William, 91

Carson, Rachel, 443

Carter, James E. (Jimmy), 448, 451, 466, 514, R24, *p466, R24*

Carver, George Washington, 237

cash crop, 14

Cather, Willa, 140

Catt, Carrie Chapman, 243

cattle drive, 149–150, 202, *m150*

cause and effect, 229, 258, 326, 380–381, 391, 403, 426, 444, 453, 494

Central Pacific, 130–133, *m130*

Central Powers, 273, 275, 279–280, *m273*

century, 38

character traits

caring, H2, 94–95

courage, H2, 510–511

fairness, H2, 160–161

honesty, H2, 318–319

respect, H2, 436–437

responsibility, H2, 270–271

Charleston, South Carolina, 17, 54, 74–75, *m16*

Chávez, César, 441, 445, *p441*

checks and balances, 26–27, *c27*

Cherokee, 33, 37, *m8*

Chestnut, Mary Boykin, 74

Cheyenne, 131, 155–156, *m8*

Chicago, Illinois, 150, 178, 198, 223, 226, 228, 235, *m134, 223*

child labor, 194–199, 259, 263, 265, *p194, 199, 263*

China, 9–10, 187, 342, 344, 390, 409, 447, 493, 495, *m9, R5*

Chinese Americans, 185, 187, *p130*

Churchill, Winston, 343, 345, 385, 388, *p343*

Cinque, Joseph, 49, 62, *p49, 62*

circle graphs, reading, 230–231, *c231*

cities, growth of, 213, 215, 222–229, 474, *m223, p224, c474*

citizen

definition of, 482

naturalized, 486–487, *p486, 487*

Index

citizenship

caring, H2, 94–95

courage, H2, 510–511

decision making, H5

fairness, H2, 160–161

honesty, H2, 318–319

problem solving, H5

respect, H2, 40–41, 436–437

responsibility, H2, 270–271

civil rights

of African Americans, 413, 418–426

definition of, 420

Civil Rights Act of 1964, 424

civil war, 77

Civil War, American

African Americans in, 90–91, *p91*

attack on Fort Sumter, 74–77, 84, *p75*

battles of, 85–86, 97, 99, *m97, m99*

communications during, 104–105, *p104–105*

life during, 88–93

secession of Southern states, 75

strategies of, 84, *p84*

summary, 51

technology, 86, 89

women and, 92

Civilian Conservation Corps (CCC), 330, *p330*

Clark, William, 32, 160

Clay, Henry, 48, 67–68, *p48*

Cleveland, Grover, R23, *pR23*

Cleveland, Ohio, 179, *p443, m176*

climograph, 146–147, *c146, 147*

Clinton, William J. (Bill), 450–451, R25, *pR25*

Coast Ranges, *R14*

Code Talkers, 357, 442, *p357*

Coffin, Catherine, 63

Coffin, Levi, 63

Cohan, George M., 284–285, 524–525

Cold War, 390–391, 395, 406–413, 417, 428–434, 446, 448–449, 452, 493

Cole, Nat King, 419

Coleman, Bessie, 420

Collins, Michael, 430, 458–459

colony

definition of, 10

English, 14–16, *m16*

European, 13, *m13*

life in, 12–18

Colorado, R18, *m473*

Columbian Exchange, 10–11, *c10*

Columbus, Christopher, 10, *p11*

Colvin, L. O., 217

commercials, 303

communication. *See* Internet, Pony Express, radio, satellite, telegraph, telephone, television

communism, 381, 385, 388, 390, 408–409, 412, 431, 433, 448

commute, 401

compare and contrast, 212–213, 221, 267, 280

compass, magnetic, 10, *p10*

compass rose, H17

Compromise of 1850, 68

computer, 490–491, 494–495, 515–516, *p490, 515*

concentration camp, 362–363

conclusions, draw, 197, 294–295, 305, 316, 347

Confederacy, 75–77, 83–90, 92–93, 99–101, 107, *m76, c83*

Congress, United States, 107–109, 251, 257, 275, 324, 329, 343, 345, 386, 424, 440, 443, 506, *p275*

Congress of Industrial Organizations (CIO), 396

Connecticut, R19, *m473*

Conrad, Frank, 302

conservation, 266–267, 443

constitution, 26

Constitution, United States, 26–28, 109–111, 311, 420–421, 481–482, 484, R30–R52

Constitutional Convention, 26, 28, *p26*

consumer, 180, 395, 489

consumer credit, 398

Continental Army, 24–25

Continental Congress, 23–24, 26

Coolidge, Calvin, R25, *pR25*

Cooper, Jack L., 236

Cooper, Peter, 34

Cornwallis, Charles, 5

corporation, 178

cotton gin, 34, *p34*

cotton production, 34, 56, *c34, p56*

cowboy, 148–150, *p149*

Crazy Horse, 156

credit, 323

credible, 260

credit card, 398, 400, *p398*

Croatia, 450, *mR5*

Cronkite, Walter, 402

Crow, 155, *m8*

Cuba, 253–255, *m255*

Cuban Missile Crisis, 410–411, 413, *m411*

culture

American, 303–304, 491

definition of, 8

global, 493

Native American, 8–9, *m8*

Custer, George, 156, *p156*

Dallas, Texas, *mR13*

Davis, Benjamin O., Sr., 420

Davis, Benjamin O., Jr., 293, 352, *p293, 352*

Davis, Jefferson, 48, 75–76, *p48, 75*

D-Day, 360, 365, *m360*

decade, 38

decision making, H5

Declaration of Independence, 3, 24, 29, 503, R26–R29, *p1–3, 24*

Deere, John, *c143*

degrees, H15

Delaware, 76, R19, *m473*

delegate. *See* representative

demand, 489

democracy, 388, 390, 417, 469, 481–482

Democratic Party, 71–72

Denver, Colorado, 151, 153, *m134*

Department of Homeland Security, 508

details. *See* main idea and details

Detroit, Michigan, 299, 301, 402, 474, *m298, 301*

Dewey, George, 254

dictator, 341

dictionary, H6

discrimination, 56, 108, 145, 213, 233–234, 236–237, 352–353, 418–423, 477

distribution map, 478, *m478, 479*

diversity, 190, 475–476

Dodge City, Kansas, 149, 332, *m148, 328*

Douglas, Stephen, 69, 71–72, *p71*

Douglass, Frederick, 36, 70, 90, 242, *p36*

draft, 89, 347

drought, 332, *m332*

Du Bois, W. E. B., 237, *p237*

Duncan, Isadora, 313, *p313*

Duryea, Charles, 170

Duryea, Frank, 170

Dust Bowl, 332–333, *m332–333, p333*

Eads, James Buchanan, 228

Earhart, Amelia, 310, 315

Earth Day, 443

East Berlin, Germany, 389

Eastern Hemisphere, H14

economist, 181

economy

 1900s, 182

 colonial, 16–17

 definition of, 16

 post-World War II, 395

 United States, 488–494

Edison, Thomas, 168, 304, 494, *p168*

education

 African Americans and, 51, 237, 239, 418–419, 421, *p237*

 Carnegie, Andrew, and, 183

 public, 110, 399–400, 441

 Reconstruction and, 108, *p108*

 segregation and, 421, *p421*

 veterans and, 397

 women and, 244, 270–271, *p244*

Eglui, Ellen, 218

Eighteenth Amendment, 311

Einstein, Albert, 354, *p354*

Eisenhower, Dwight D., 292, 360, 365, 407, 410, 431, R25, *p292, 365, 407, R25*

election of 2000, 452–453, 483, *m483*

electoral college, 452–453, 483

electricity, 169–170, 179, 213, 220–221, 490, *c169*

elevation, H22

elevation map, H22

elevator, 228, *p228*

Ellington, Duke, 312, *p312*

Ellis Island, 186, *p186, m184*

Emancipation Proclamation, 90

encyclopedia, H6

energy, sources of, 513, 518–519, *c513*

enfranchised, 233

England, 13, *m17. See also* Great Britain

entrepreneur, 152, 169, 177, 180–181, 299

environment, 417, 443–444, 452, 513, 518–519

Environmental Protection Agency (EPA), 443

E Pluribus Unum, 475

Equal Employment Opportunity Commission, 442

Equal Rights Amendment (ERA), 440, *m440*

equator, H12–H13, H15

ethnic group, 476

Executive Branch, 26–27, 484, *c27*

exoduster, 141

expansion, of United States, 35, *m35*

export, 492–493, *p492–493, c493*

fact, 306–307

fact and opinion, 306–307

farming, 7, 16, 55, 139–143, 217, 321, 332, 441, *p142, 217. See also* agriculture

fascism, 341

Federal Aid Highway Act, 402

Fifteenth Amendment, 109–111, 242, *c109*

Fillmore, Millard, R22, *pR22*

firefighter, 504, 510–511

First Amendment, 28

Fitzgerald, F. Scott, 295, 313

Fitzhugh, George, 58–59

flag, United States, 40–41, *p41*

Florida, R19, *m473*

Ford, Gerald, 447, *pR24*

Ford, Henry, 292, 299, *p292*

Index

Fort Sumter, 74–77, 84, *m99, p75*

Fort Wagner, 91, *m88, p91*

Fourteenth Amendment, 109–111, *c109*

France, 13, 18, 25, 32, 40, 273–274, 276, 279, 342, 350, 360, 408, 431, *mR5*

Frank, Anne, 362–363, *p363*

Franklin, Benjamin, 24, *p26–27*

Freedmen's Bureau, 51, 108

freedom, political, 341, 391, 469, 482. *See also* specific freedoms

freedom rides, 423, *p423*

free enterprise, 180, 388, 390, 449, 471, 489–490, 493

free states, 67, *m67, 69*

French and Indian War, 18, 22

Fugitive Slave Law, 68, *p68*

Fulton, Robert, 34

Gallipoli, Turkey, 277, *p277, m277*

Garfield, James A., R23, *pR23*

generalizations, making, 518–519

geography, H10–H11, H15–H24. *See also* specific themes

Georgia, R19, *m473*

Germany, 273–275, 280, 335, 341–342, 345–346, 349, 354, 359–360, 365, 385, *mR5*

Geronimo, 158, *p159*

Gershwin, George, 313, *p313*

Gershwin, Ira, 313, *p313*

Gettysburg, Battle of, 97, 99, *m97, 99*

Gettysburg, Pennsylvania, 81, 96–97, *m96, 99, p102*

Gettysburg Address, 47, 81, 98

G.I. Bill of Rights, 397

Giuliani, Rudolph, 466, 504, 511, *p466, 504*

glacier, 7

Glenn, John, 429, *p429*

Glidden, Joseph, *c143*

globalization, 493

Global Positioning System (GPS), 491, *p491*

global warming, 513

globe, H8

gold rush, 151–153

Gompers, Samuel, 195, *p195*

Goodnight, Charles, 149

Goodnight-Loving Trail, 149, *m150*

Gorbachev, Mikhail, 448–449

Gorgas, W. C., 257

Gore, Al, 452–453, 483

government, United States, 480–484

Grand Canyon National Monument, 267, *m262, p266*

Grant, Ulysses S., 49, 99–101, R23, *p49, 100, R23*

Grapes of Wrath, The, 333, 370–371

graphs, reading

　circle, 230–231, *c231*

　line, 230–231, *c230*

Graveley, Samuel Lee, Jr., 426

Great Britain, 18, 34–35, 40, 55, 84–85, 273–274, 342–345, 351, 388, 408, 505, 507, *m351. See also* England

Great Depression, 323–329, 333–335, 343, 349, 395, 400, *p323, 324, 325*

Great Migration, 235, 314, 318, *m235*

Great Plains, 138–144, 150–151, 155–156, 178, *m138, p139, 140, 142,*

Great Salt Lake, *mR14*

Great Seal of the United States, 475

Greensboro, North Carolina, 423, *m418*

grid, 366

Guam, 254–255, *m367*

guerrilla warfare, 432

Hamilton, Alexander, 31, *p31*

Harding, Warren G., R25, *pR25*

Harlem, 295, 314, 318, *p314, m310*

Harlem Renaissance, 295, 314

Harper's Ferry, Virginia, 70, *m66*

Harrison, Benjamin, R24, *pR24*

Harrison, William Henry, R23, *pR23*

Hawaii, 252, R19, *p252, m473*

Hayes, Rutherford B., R23, *pR23*

Hearst, William Randolph, 180

hemisphere, H9

hijack, 503

Hine, Lewis, 194

Hiroshima, Japan, 361, *m367*

Hispanics. *See* Latinos

Hitler, Adolf, 341–342, 346, 354, 359–360, 391, *p341*

Ho Chi Minh, 431–432, *p431*

Holocaust, 362–363

Homestead, Pennsylvania, 193, *m192*

Homestead Act, 139, 141

homesteader, 139–142, 150

Homestead Strike, 196

Hoover, Herbert, 321, 324–326, R25, *p321, R25*

House of Burgesses, 14

Huerta, Dolores, 379, 441, 445, *p379, 445*

Hughes, Langston, 295, 314, 325, *p314*

Hull House, 226, *p226*

human-environment interaction (as geographical theme), H10

human resource, 181

human rights, 387

Hurston, Zora Neale, 293, 314, *p293*

Hussein, Saddam, 450, 507

Ice Age, 7

Idaho, 160, R19, *m473*

ideals, 475, 505

ideology, 388, 390–391

Illinois, R19, *m473*

immigrants

    Africans, 16–17, 476

    Asian, 7, 185, 187, 476

    becoming a citizen, 486–487

    Chinese, 132, 187, 234, *p187*

    European, 184–186, 188–190

    Irish, 131, 185, 190, *p185*

    Japanese, 144, 145, *p187*

    Jewish, 184–185, 191

    life of, 184–190, 215, 476

    Mexican, 185, 190

    Russian, 141, 185, 191

    twentieth century, *c188*

    urbanization and, 224–227

impeachment, 109, 451

import, 492–493, *p492–493, c492*

inauguration, 328

income tax, 265

Indiana, R18, *m473*

Indians. *See* Native Americans

Indian Territory, *m8, c33*

Industrial Revolution, 34, 55

"In Flanders Fields," 279, *p279*

inflation, 335

inset map, H19

interdependence, 493

intermediate directions, H17

International Date Line, 367, *m367*

International Space Station, 430, 521, *p521*

Internet, H17, 452, 491, 496–497, 516

internment, 353, *p353*

interstate highway, 102

interview, H8

Intolerable Acts, *c23*

inventions, 10, 34, 166–173, 181, 213, 241, 297, 299, 302, 304, 308–309, 490, 495, *p308–309, c171.* *See also* technology

investor, 168, 322

Iowa, R18, *m473*

Iraq, 450, 507, *m506*

Ireland, 185, *m185*

Irish potato famine, 185

Iron Curtain, 388, 390, *m389*

Iroquois, 8–9, *m8, p9*

isolationism, 275, 280, 343–344, *p343*

isthmus, 256, *m256*

Italy, 341–342, 345, 356, 360, *mR5*

"I, too," 295, 314

Iwo Jima, 361, *p361, m359*

Jackson, Andrew, 33, R23, *p33, R23*

Jackson, Mahalia, 419

Jackson, Thomas "Stonewall," 85

Jamestown, Virginia, 14, 19, *m13, p14*

Japan, 341–342, 344–345, 349, 358–359, 361, 385–386, *mR5*

Japanese Americans, 353, *p353*

jazz, 310, 312

Jazz Age, 312–313

Jefferson, Thomas, 24, 29, 31–32, R22, *p31, R22*

Jews, 184–185, 191, 341, 362–363

Jim Crow laws, 51, 110, 234, 236

jobs, 490, *c490*

Johnson, Andrew, 107, 109, 251, R23, *pR23*

Johnson, Lyndon B., 413, 424, 431–432, 434, R24, *pR24*

Jones, Mary Harris, 195, *p195*

Joseph, Chief, 122, 157, 160–161, *p122, 157, 160*

Judicial Branch, 26–27, 484, *c27*

Jungle, The, 264, *p264*

jury, trial by, 469, 482

Kansas, 66, 69, 141, R18, *m473*

Kansas-Nebraska Act, 69, *m69*

Kansas Territory, 69, *m69*

Kelley, Florence, 198, *p198*

Kemble, Fanny, 58–59, *p58*

Kennedy, John F., 378, 410–413, 424, 431, R24, *p378, 413, R24*

Kentucky, 76, R18, *m473*

Key, Francis Scott, 40–41, *p40*

key, map, H16

Kielburger, Craig, 199, *p199*

King, Martin Luther, Jr., 379, 422–425, 427, 441, *p379, 424, 427*

Kitty Hawk, North Carolina, 172, *m166*

Korea, 381, 385, 407, *m407*

Korean War, 407–409

Ku Klux Klan, 108

Kuwait, 450, *m446*

Index

Labor Day, 197, *p197*

labor union, 195–197, 396, *p396*

Lakota, 9, 131, 154–156, *m8*

landmine, 94–95

Lange, Dorothea, 293, 333, *p293, 333*

Lantos, Tom, 487, *p487*

large-scale map, 20–21, *m21*

Latimer, Lewis, 123, 168, *p123, 168*

Latinos, 185, 190, 441, 445, 476–477, *p441, 445, 467, c188*

latitude, H15, 366–367, *m366, 367*

Laval, Gustav de, 217

Lawrence, Jacob, 293, 314, 318–319, *p293, 318*

Lazarus, Emma, 165

League of Nations, 280

Lee, Robert E., 48, 85, 87, 97, 99–101, *p48, 87, 100*

Legislative Branch, 26–27, 484, *c27. See also* Congress, United States

Lend-Lease, 343, 346

Lewis, Meriwether, 32, 160

Libeskind, Daniel, 467, 508–509, *p467, 509*

light bulb, electric, 168, 171, *p168, 171*

Liliuokalani, 210, 252, *p210, 252*

Lin, Maya Ying, 379, 434, 437, *p379*

Lincoln, Abraham, 47–48, 51, 71–73, 75–76, 83–85, 96, 98, 100–101, 106–107, 130, 251, 481, R22, *p48, 71, 73, R22*

Lindbergh, Charles, 315, *p315*

line graphs, reading, 230–231, *c230*

literature

Declaration of Independence, 24, R26–R29

Grapes of Wrath, The, 333, 370–371

"I, too," 295, 314

"In Flanders Fields," 279, *p279*

Roughing It, 152

Silent Spring, 443

To Build a Fire, 251

Uncle Tom's Cabin, 70, *p70*

When I Was Puerto Rican, 476

Little Big Horn, Battle of, 156

location (as geographical theme), H10

locator map, H16

locks, 257

London, Jack, 251

longhouse, 9, *p9*

longitude, H15, 366–367, *m366–367*

Los Alamos, New Mexico, 354, *m348*

Los Angeles, California, 144, 190, 304, *m130*

Louisiana, R18, *m473*

Louisiana Purchase, 32, 67, *m32*

Love, Nat, 148–149, *p149*

MacArthur, Douglas, 361

Macedonia, 451, *mR5*

Madison, James, R22, *pR22*

mail-order catalog, 218, 241

main idea and details, 50–51, 57, 64, 72, 86, 93, 101, 111, 182, 238, 335, 355, 517

Maine, 67, R18, *m473*

Maine, 253, 260–261, *p253, 260*

malaria, 256–257

Malcolm X, 425, *p425*

Manassas Junction, Virginia, 85, *m82*

Mandela, Nelson, 451, *p451*

Manhattan Island, 13, *m227*

Manhattan Project, 354

manifest destiny, 35

manual labor, 217

map projection, 454–455, *m454, 455*

maps

elevation, H22

latitude on, H15, 366–367, *m366, 367*

longitude on, H15, 366–367, *m366, 367*

physical, H17

political, H16

population density, H23, 478–479, *m478, 479*

projections of, 454–455, *m454, 455*

road, H24, 102–103, *m103*

scales of, comparing, H18, 20–21, *m20, 21*

time zone, H21, 134–135, *m134*

Marconi, Guglielmo, 302, *p302*

Marshall, Eliza, 199, *p199*

Marshall, George C., 386

Marshall Plan, 386, 389, *p386*

Marshall, Thurgood, 378, 418, 421, 426, *p378, 418*

Maryland, 76, R19, *m473*

Masih, Iqbal, 199, *p199*

mass media, 303, 315

mass production, 302

Massachusetts, 15, 24, R19, *m473*

Mayflower, 15, *p15*

McCarthy, Joseph, 409, *p409*

McCormick, Cyrus, 217

McKinley, William, R24, *p180, R24*

mechanization, 217

Menlo Park, New Jersey, 168, *m166*

meridian, H12, H14–H15, 366–367, *m366*

Merrimack, 86

Mexican War, 35, 68, 84, 99

Mexico, 7, 35, 68, 275, *mR4*

Michigan, R19, *m473*

Middle Colonies, 16, 38, *m16, c38–39*

Middle East, 448, 450, *m446*

Midway, Battle of, 358–359, *m359*, 367

Midwest, 473, *m473*

migrant worker, 332–333, 441, 445

migrate, 7, *m7*

migration, 7, 235, 314, 318, 474, *m7, 235*

Miles, Nelson, 157

Minnesota, R19, *m473*

Mississippi, R19, *m473*

Mississippi River, 84, 99, 129, 228, *m32*

Missouri, 67, 76, R19, *m473*

Missouri Compromise, 67–68, *m67*

Model T, 298–299, *p298*

Monitor, 86

monopoly, 179

Monroe, James, 33, R22, *pR22*

Monroe Doctrine, 33

Montana, R19, *m473*

Montgomery, Alabama, 422, *m418*

Moody, Dwight L., 226

Morgan, J. P., 181, *p181*

Morse, Samuel, 122, 129, *p122*

Moscow, Soviet Union (now Russia), 388, *m389*

Mott, Lucretia, 242, *p242*

Mount Whitney *mR14*

Movement (as a geographical theme), H11

movies, 304–305, 307, 334, *p304, 334, c305*

muckraker, 264

Muir, John, 210, 266, *p210, 267*

Murrow, Edward R., 402

Mussolini, Benito, 341–342

Naismith, James, 226

National Aeronautics and Space Administration (NASA), 429, 439, 452, 516

National Association for the Advancement of Colored People (NAACP), 237, 423

nationalism, 273

National Organization for Women (NOW), 440

national park, 266

National Road, 125

Native Americans. *See also* specific groups

colonists and, 14–15, 18–19

conflicts and, 131, 154–158

cultures of, 8–9, *m8*

enslavement of, 11

opportunities for, 441

population, 158–159

removal of, 33, *p33*

reservation, 155–161, *m158*

transcontinental railroad and, 131

in World War II, 357, 442, *p357*

NATO, 389, 408

natural resource, 16, 181, 251, 259, 301, 513, *c513*

Navajo, 357, 442, *m8, p357*

Nazis, 341, 362–363

Nebraska, R20, *m473*

Nebraska Territory, 69, *m69*

Netherlands, The, 13, *mR5*

Nevada, R20, *m473*

New Amsterdam, 12–13, *m13*

New Deal, 329–333

New England Colonies, 16, 38, *m16, c38–39*

New Hampshire, R20, *m473*

New Haven, Connecticut, 62, *m60*

New Jersey, R20, *m473*

New Mexico, R20, *m473*

New Orleans, Louisiana, 64, 312, *m310*

New York, 25, R20, *m473*

New York, New York, 17, 31, 169, 186, 193, 223, 226, 227, 322, 387, 443, 503–504, 509, 510–511, *m192, 227, p169, 224, 503*

newsies, 196

Nez Percé, 157–158, 160–161, *p161*

Nicodemus, Kansas, 141, *m138, p141*

Nimitz, Chester, 358

Nineteenth Amendment, 243, 245

Nixon, Richard, 430, 433–434, 447, R24, *p447, R24*

Nobel Peace Prize, 426, 514

nonfiction book, H6

Normandy, France, 360, *m360*

North America, 7, *m7*

North American Free Trade Agreement (NAFTA), 492

North Atlantic Treaty Organization (NATO), 389, 408

North Carolina, R21, *m473*

North Dakota, R21, *m473*

Northeast, 473, *m473*

Northern Hemisphere, H9

North Korea, 390, 407–408, *m407*

North Pole, H13–H14, *mH13–H15*

North Vietnam, 431–434, *m431*

nuclear power, 513, *c513*

O'Connor, Sandra Day, 439–440, 466, 484, 485, *p442, 466, 485*

Ohio, R21, *m473*

Index

oil industry, 179, 321, 489

O'Keeffe, Georgia, 292, 316, 317, *p292, 317*

Oklahoma, 157, 179, R21, *m473*

Omaha, Nebraska, 130, *m130*

opinion, 306–307

opportunity cost, 489

Oregon, 144, R21, *m473*

Oregon Territory, 35, *m35*

Otis, Elisha Graves, 228, *p228*

outline, writing, 174–175

"Over There," 278, 284–285

Pacific Ocean, *mR4–5*

Panama, 256–258, *mR4*

Panama Canal, 256–258, *m250, 256, p257, 258*

parallel, H15, 366

parallel time lines, 38

Parks, Rosa, 378, 422, *p378, 422*

passive resistance, 423, 427, 441

Patton, George S., 360

Pearl Harbor, 344, 353, 358, 503, *m339, 344, 364, p344*

Pennsylvania, 23–24, R21, *m473*

Pentagon, 503, 508

periodical, H6

Pershing, John J., 276

Persian Gulf War, 450, 507

Philadelphia, Pennsylvania, 17, 23, 26, 63, 222–223, *m16, 63, 223*

Philippines, 254–255, 358, 408, *mR5*

photography, 89

physical map, H17

Pickett, George, 97

Pickett's Charge, 97, *m97*

Pierce, Franklin, R22, *pR22*

Pilgrim, 15

pioneer, 139, 241, *p140*

Pittsburgh, Pennsylvania, 177, 183, *m176*

place (as geographical theme), H10

plantation, 16–17, 56

Pledge of Allegiance, 53

Plessy, Homer, 234

plow, steel, 143, *p143*

Plymouth, Massachusetts, 15, *m13*

Pocahontas, 14, 19

point of view, recognizing, 58–59

Poland, 342, 346, *mR5*

political cartoons, interpreting, 268–269

political machine, 227

political map, H16

political party, 31, 71–72

Polk, James K., R23, *pR23*

pollution, 443, 452, 513, *p443*

Pony Express, 125, 129, *p129*

popular sovereignty, 481

population

free and enslaved African Americans, 56, *c56*

Native American, 158–159, *m158*

United States, 1850, 55, *c55*

United States, 1861, *c83*

United States cities, 474, *c474*

population density map, H23, 478–479, *m478, 479*

potatoes, 145, 185

potato famine, Irish, 185

Powell, Colin, 450, 453, *p450*

Powhatan, 14, 19, *m8*

prejudice, 189, 225, 234, 477

President, *c27.* See also specific names of

press, freedom of, 28

primary source, H6, 392–393

prime meridian, H12, H14–H15, 366–367, *m366*

problem solving, H3

producer, 489

profit, 13, 19

Progressives, 264–265, 311, 443

Prohibition, 311

Promontory Point, Utah Territory, 133, *m128*

propaganda, 390

public health, 225

Puerto Rico, 253–255, 476–477, *m255*

Puritan, 15

Quebec, Canada, 13, *m13*

Queens, New York City, 334, *m328*

radar, 355, *p355*

radio, 125, 171, 302–303, 315, 491, *p171, 303*

Radio Corporation of America (RCA), 302

railroad, 34, 125, 127, 129–133, 136–137, 144, 150, 154, 178, 181, *m130, 178*

rationing, 351, 395

Reagan, Ronald, 378, 448, 484–485, R25, *p378, 448, R25*

reaper, 217, 221, *p217*

Reconstruction, 51, 107–111, 233

Red Cloud, 131, *p131*

Red Cross. *See* American Association of the Red Cross

"Red River Valley," 202–203

Red Scare, 409

Reed, Walter, 256

region (as geographical theme), H11, 473, *m473*

religion, freedom of, 13, 15, 28, 475, 482

representative, 26, 481, 483

republic, 26, 481

Republican Party, 71, 107, 268

research, Internet, 496–497, *p496, 497*

research report, writing, H9

research skills, H4–H9

reservation, 155–161, *m158*

resource

   capital, 181

   definition of, 16

   human, 181

   natural, 16, 181, 251, 259, 301, 513, *c513*

resource, research,

   community, H8

   print, H6

   technology, H7

responsibilities, of citizens, 469, 482

Revels, Hiram R., 108, *p108*

Rhode Island, 34, R21, *m473*

Rice, Condoleezza, 449, 453, 467, 507, *p467*

Richmond, Virginia, 85, 170, *m99*

Rickenbacker, Eddie, 276

Ride, Sally, 440

rights, of citizens, 391, 469, 482

Riis, Jacob, 226

road map, H24, 102–103, *m103*

Roaring Twenties, 295, 310–316

Robinson, Jackie, 420, 426, *p420*

Rockefeller, John D., 179–181, 264, 270, *p179*

Roebling, John, 228–229

Roebuck, Alvah C., 218

Rolfe, John, 14, 19, *p19*

Roosevelt, Eleanor, 333, 387, 399, *p329, 399*

Roosevelt, Franklin D., 292, 326–329, 333–334, 339, 340–341, 343, 345, 349, 353–354, 361, 385, 387, 397, 420, R25, *p292, 327, 328, 329, R25*

Roosevelt, Theodore, 211, 226, 254–256, 259, 264–267, 269, 271, 469, R24, *p211, 254, 257, 259, 267, R24*

Roughing It, 152

Rough Riders, 254, *p254*

Route 66, 401, *m401*

Rural Electrification Act, 220

Russia, 90, 141, 251, 273–274, 409, *mR5. See also* Soviet Union

Ruth, Babe, 310, 315, *p315*

Sacagawea, 32

Sacramento, California, 130, *m128*

safety, worker, 265, *p265*

Salem, Peter, 25

Salter, Susannah Medora, 242

San Diego, California, *mR12*

San Francisco, California, 153, 187, 220, 223, 234, *m130*

Santiago, Esmeraldo, 467, 476–477, *p467*

Saratoga, Battle of, 25

Sarnoff, David, 302, *p302*

satellite, 429–430, 491, *p429, 491*

Savannah, Georgia, 100, *m99*

scale, map, H18

Schlafly, Phyllis, 440

Scott, Blanche Stuart, 173

Scott, Dred, 70

Scott, Winfield, 84

Scruggs, Jan, 434, 436–437, *p436*

search engine, H17

Sears, Richard, 218

SEATO, 408

Seattle, Washington, 144, *m471*

secede, 75

secondary source, H6, 392–393

sectionalism, 55

segregation, 110, 233–234, 236, 352, 418–424, *m419, p234*

Seneca Falls, New York, 242, *m240*

September 11, 2001, 502–505, 509–511, *p503, 504, 505*

sequence, 77, 124–125, 133, 144, 153, 159, 173, 244, 364

Sequoyah, 33, 37, *p37*

Serbia, 273, 451, *m273, R5*

serfs, 90, *p90*

settlement house, 226, *p226*

Seward, William, 251, *p251*

sharecropping, 110–111, 232–233

Sherman, William Tecumseh, 100, 131

Sherman Antitrust Act, 264

Shima, George, 123, 144, 145, *p123, 145*

Sierra Club, 266

Sierra Nevada, 131–132

Silent Spring, 443

Silk Road, 9, *m9*

Sinclair, Upton, 264

Singleton, Benjamin, 141

Sitting Bull, 154–157, *p154*

Sixteenth Amendment, 265

Sixth Amendment, 469

skyscraper, 228, *p176*

Slater, Samuel, 34

slave codes, 61

slave states, 67, *m67, 69*

slavery

   abolitionists and, 36

   Civil War and, 75–77

   colonial, 13, 16

Compromise of 1850 and, 68

Emancipation Proclamation and, 90

end of, 106–111

Missouri Compromise and, 67

Native American, 11

resisting, 60–65

Southern states and, 53, 56–57

trade and, 17, *m17*

Slovenia, 450, *mR5*

small-scale map, 20–21, *m20*

Smith, Bessie, 312, *p312*

Smith, John, 14

Social Security, 329, 331

sodbuster, 140

songs

"Over There," 278, 284–285

"Red River Valley," 202–203

"Star-Spangled Banner, The," 40–41

"When Johnny Comes Marching Home," 114–115

"You're a Grand Old Flag," 524–525

Sons of Liberty, 23

source, credibility of, 260–261

sources, comparing primary and secondary, 392–393

South Africa, 451, *m451*

Southampton County, Virginia, 62

South Carolina, 75, 100, R20, *m473*

South Dakota, R20, *m473*

Southeast, 473, *m473*

South East Asia Treaty Organization (SEATO), 408

Southern Colonies, 16, 38, *m16, c38–39*

Southern Hemisphere, H13, *mH13*

South Korea, 407–408, *m407, p408*

South Vietnam, 431–434, 436, *m431*

Southwest, 473, *m473*

Soviet Union, 346, 358–360, 381, 385–386, 388–391, 417, 429–431, 447–449, *m389. See also* Russia

space race, 429–430

space shuttle, 430

Spain, 10, 13, 62, 253–255, *mR5*

Spanish-American War, 253–256, 264, *p254*

speech, freedom of, 28, 475, 482

Sprague, Frank, 170

Sputnik, 429, *p429*

Squanto, 15

stagecoach, 128–129, *p128*

Stalin, Joseph, 346, 385, 388–389, 391

Stalingrad, Battle of, 359, *m358*

Stamp Act, 22–23, *c23*

Standard Oil Company, 179, 264, 270–271

standard time, 134–135

Stanton, Elizabeth Cady, 210, 242, 245, *p210, 242*

"Star-Spangled Banner, The," 40–41

states' rights, 67, 75, 77

Statue of Liberty, 165, 186

steel, 143, 177, 228, *p177, 228*

Steinbeck, John, 333, 370

Stevens, John, 257

St. Louis, Missouri, 228, *m222*

stock market, 322, *c322*

stocks, 178, 322, *c322*

Stone, Lucy, 242

Stowe, Harriet Beecher, 70

Strauss, Levi, 122, 152, *p122, 152*

streetcar, 170, *p170*

strike, 195–196, 396, *p196, 396*

Suarez, Benjamin, 510–511

submarine, 86, 275

suburb, 395, 400, *p395*

suffrage, 242

suffragists, 242

summarize, 4–5, 11, 18, 28, 36, 190, 412, 435, 468–469, 477, 484, 508

Sunbelt, 474

supply, 489

Supreme Court, 421

surplus, 321

survey, H19

suspension bridge, 228

sweatshop, 193, *p193*

Sweden, 13, *mR5*

symbol, map, H16

Taft, William H., R24, *pR24*

Taliban, 506

Taney, Roger, 70

tank, 277, *p277*

Tarbell, Ida, 264, 270–271, *p270*

tariff, 55, 323–324, 492

taxes, 265, 324, 400, 482

Taylor, Zachary, R22, *pR22*

technology. *See also* inventions

1950s, 402–403, *p402–403*

Civil War, 86, 89

current, 491–492, 494, 495, 501

definition of, 142

farming, 142–143, 213, 217, *p143*

future and, 516–517, 520–521, *p520–521*

Internet, 452, 491, 496–497, 516

World War I, 277, *p276, 277*

World War II, 354–355, *p354, 355*

telegraph, 104–105, 125, 127, 129, 154, *p104, 105*

telephone, 125, 167, 171, 219, 403, 491, 521, *p166, 167, 171, 219, 521*

television, 402, 428, 433, 491, 521, *p402, 491, 521*

temperance movement, 242

tenant, 233

tenement, 224–225, *p225*

Tennessee, R20, *m473*

Tennessee Valley Authority (TVA), 331

territories, United States, 255, *m255*

terrorism, 451, 503, 506

terrorist, 503, 506

Texas, 35, 149–150, 179, R20, *m473*

Third World countries, 391

Thirteenth Amendment, 107, 110, *c109*

threshing machine, 217, 221

time lines, parallel, 38–39, *c38–39*

time zone, 134–135, *m134*

time zone map, H21, 134–135, *m134*

time zone map, reading, 135

title, map, H16

Title 9, 440

To Build a Fire, 251

Tojo, Hideki, 344

total war, 100

Toussaint, Lorraine, 487, *p487*

Townshend Act, *c23*

trade

    Asian, 9–10

    colonial, 13

    European, 9–10

    international, 492–493, *c492, 493*

    NAFTA, 492

    slave, 17, *m17*

transcontinental railroad, 125, 130–133, 178, *m130*

transportation. *See* automobile, railroad, stagecoach, streetcar, railroad

Treaty of Versailles, 280

Triangle Shirtwaist Company, 193, 195

triangular trade route, 17, *m17*

Truman, Harry S., 361, 386–387, 389, 407, 420, R25, *p386, R25*

trust, 263–265, 270–271

Truth, Sojourner, 109

Tubman, Harriet, 49, 63, 65, *p49, 65*

Turkey, 273, 277, *mR5*

Turner, Nat, 62

Tuskegee, Alabama, 237, 239, *m232*

Tuskegee Airmen, 352, *p352*

Tuskegee Institute, 237, 239, *p237*

Twain, Mark, 152–153

Tweed, William M., 227, *p227*

Twenty-first Amendment, 311

Twenty-sixth Amendment, 484

Tyler, John, R23, *pR23*

Uncle Tom's Cabin, 70, *p70*

Underground Railroad, 63, 65, *m63*

unemployment, 321, 324, 329, 335, 349, *c349*

Union, 75–77, 83, 88–93, 98–100, *m76, c83*

union labor, 195–197, 396, *p396*

Union Pacific, 130–133, *m130*

Union of Soviet Socialist Republics (USSR). *See* Soviet Union

United Farm Workers of America (UFW), 441

United Nations, 387, 399, 407, 450–451, 506–507, *p387*

urbanization, 224. *See also* cities, growth of

Utah, R20, *m473*

Values. *See* ideals

Van Buren, Martin, R23, *pR23*

Vermont, 33, R20, *m473*

Versailles, France, 280, *m272*

veteran, 279, 397–398

Veterans Day, 279

veto, *c27*

Vicksburg, Battle of, 99, *m99*

Vicksburg, Mississippi, 99, *m99*

Vietnam, 381, 431, 435, *m431*

Vietnam Conflict, 432–434, *p432*

Vietnam Veterans Memorial, 434, 436–437, *p434, 437*

Virginia, 24, 85, 97, 100, 472, 503, R21, *m20, 473*

Virginia, 86

Virginia City, Nevada, 152–153, *m148*

vote

    African Americans and, 56, 107–110, 215, 242, 424–425, *p109, c425*

    18 year olds and, 471, 482, 484

    right to, 469, 482, *p482*

    women and, 109, 215, 240–243, 245, *p243*

Voting Rights Act of 1965, 424–425, *c425*

Walker, David, 57

Walker, Madame C. J., 180

Walnut Grove, Virginia, 217, *m216*

Wang, An, 466, 494–495 *p466, 495*

War of 1812, 33, 40

War Between the States. *See* Civil War, American

Ward, Aaron Montgomery, 218

Washington, Booker T., 211, 237, 239, *p211, 239*

Washington, D.C., 31, 107, 424, 434, 437, 484, *m30, 99, p424*

Index

Washington, Dinah, 419

Washington, George, 5, 24–25, 30–31, R22, *p26, 27, 31, R22*

Washington State, 144, R21, *m473*

Watergate scandal, 447

Waters, Ethel, 419

weapons of mass destruction, 507

Web site, 497

Webster, Daniel, 68

Wells-Barnett, Ida, 211, 238, *p211, 238*

West, 473, *m473*

West Berlin, Germany, 389

Western Hemisphere, H14, *mH14, R6–R7*

Westinghouse, George, 180

Westmoreland, William, 432

West Virginia, R21, *m473*

Wharton, Clifton R., Sr., 426

wheat, 141, *p330*

When I Was Puerto Rican, 476

"When Johnny Comes Marching Home," 114–115

White House, *p29*

Whitney, Eli, 34

Wilder, L. Douglas, 426

Williams, Jody, 94–95, *p94*

Wilson, Luzena Stanley, 151–152

Wilson, Woodrow, 211, 275, 280, R24, *p211, 275, R24*

windmill, 143, *p143*

Wisconsin, 220, R21, *m216, 473*

women

in American Revolution, 25, 29

artists, 316–317

in Civil War, 92

education and, 244, 270–271, *p244*

rights of, 109, 215, 240–245, *p243*

workers, 241, 243–244, 278, 316, 325, 339, 348, 350, 396, 399, 439–440, *p349, 350, 439, c439*

World War I and, 243, 278

World War II and, 339, 348, 350, *p349, 350*

Word Exercise, 4, 50, 124, 212, 294, 380, 468

Works Progress Administration (WPA), 330, *p289–291, 330–331*

World's Fair, 334, *p334*

World Trade Center, 451, 503–504, 508, 509, 510–511, *p503*

World War I, 235, 243, 272–273, 281, 321, *p274, 275, 276, 277, 281*

World War II, 339, 340, 342–365, 381, 383, 384–388, 395, 407, 409, 420, 431, 442, 495, *m334, 346, 351, 358–359, 360, 367, p342, 343, 344, 347, 348, 349, 350, 351, 352, 353, 354, 355, 356, 357, 361, 362, 363, c345*

Wounded Knee, South Dakota, 158, *m127*

WPA, 330, *p289–291, 330*

Wright, Orville, 171, 172, 309

Wright, Wilbur, 171, 172, 309

Wyoming, 242, R21, *m473*

yellow fever, 256–257

yellow journalism, 253

Yellowstone National Park, 266

York, Alvin C., 276

Yorktown, Battle of, 5, 25

Yorktown, Virginia, 25, *m22, p25*

Yosemite National Park, 266, *m262*

"You're a Grand Old Flag," 524–525

Yugoslavia, 450

Credits

TEXT:

Dorling Kindersley (DK) is an international publishing company specializing in the creation of high quality reference content for books, CD-ROMs, online materials, and video. The hallmark of DK content is its unique combination of educational value and strong visual style. This combination allows DK to deliver appealing, accessible, and engaging educational content that delights children, parents, and teachers around the world. Scott Foresman is delighted to have been able to use selected extracts of DK content within this Scott Foresman Social Studies program.

104–105 from *The Visual Dictionary of the Civil War* by John Stanchak. Copyright 2000 Dorling Kindersley Limited.

281 from *World War I* by Simon Adams. Copyright 2001 Dorling Kindersley Limited.

308–309 from *Invention* by Lionel Bender. Copyright 2000 Dorling Kindersley Limited.

404–405 from *Music* by Neil Ardley. Copyright 2000 Dorling Kindersley Limited.

520–521 from *Future* by Michael Tambini. Copyright 1998 Dorling Kindersley Limited.

Excerpts from a letter by Hiram Dwight Pierce to his wife Sara Jane Pierce, dated October 18, 1849. Courtesy of California State Library.

From *Island, Poetry and History of Chinese Immigrants on Angel Island* by Him M. Lai, Genny Lim and Judy Yung. Reprinted by permission of The University of Washington Press.

From *Great Migration: An American Story,* paintings by Jacob Lawrence, poem by Walter Dean Myers. Copyright © 1993 by The Museum of Modern Art, New York, and The Phillips Collection. "Migration" copyright © 1993 by Walter Dean Myers.

"I, Too" from *The Collected Poems of Langston Hughes* by Langston Hughes. Copyright © 1994 by The Estate of Langston Hughes. Used by permission of Alfred A. Knopf, a division of Random House, Inc.

"Chapter 1," from *The Grapes of Wrath* by John Steinbeck, copyright 1939, renewed © 1967 by John Steinbeck. Used by permission of Viking Penguin, a division of Penguin Group (USA) Inc.

From *Anne Frank: The Diary of a Young Girl,* translated from the Dutch by B.M. Mooyaart-Doubleday. Copyright 1952 by Otto H. Frank.

From a CNN interview with Col. Gail Halvorsen, U.S. Air Force Pilot, found at Web site www.cnn.com.

From "Coffee, Doughnuts, and a Witty Line of Chatter: The Photos and Letters of Helen Stevenson Meyner in Japan and Korea, 1950–1952." Reprinted by permission of the Lafayette College Special Collections & Archives.

From "Secretary of State Speaks at Naturalization Ceremony" from the *Monticello Newsletter*. Reprinted by permission of The Thomas Jefferson Foundation.

From "Pastures of Plenty" by Woody Guthrie. © TRO/Ludlow Music.

From "In Defense of the Electoral College" by John Samples, November 10, 2000, as appears on Web site www.cato.org/dailys/11-10-00.html. Reprinted by permission of The Cato Institute.

FAIR USE:

Excerpts from "Theater, TV Veteran Toussaint Is Proud to Be an American"

Excerpt from *Silent Spring* by Rachel Carson, p. 6

Excerpt from *Factsheet: The American Red Cross During the Korean War,* found on Web site http://korea50.army.mil/history/factsheets/amer-red-cross.shtml

Excerpt from "The Wall That Heals" by Beth Bruno

Excerpts from *Charter of the United Nations: Preamble*

Excerpts from "Airlift to Berlin" from *National Geographic*

"Rep. Tom Lantos' Rock-Solid Views Grounded in History," found at Web site http://www.sfgate.com/cgi-bin/article

Excerpt from *Visions: How Science Will Revolutionize the 21st Century* by Michio Kaku, p. 10

Excerpt from "Introduction" by Rudolph W. Giuliani, from *One Nation: America Remembers September 11, 2001*

Excerpt from "Libeskind's WTC Vision Was Born of Socialist Bronx" by Lisa Keys, found at www.forward.com/issues/2003/0303.07/faces.html

Quotation by An Wang, as found on Web site www.creativequotations.com

Excerpts from "My First Job" by Rosa Cohen

Excerpt from *You Must Remember This* by Jeff Kisseloff

Excerpt from *Making America: A History of the United States,* second edition, by Carol Berkin, et al.

Excerpt from *Kids on Strike!* by Susan Campbell Bartoletti

Excerpt from *Immigrant Kids* by Russell Freedman

Excerpt from *The Picture History of Photography* by Peter Pollack

Excerpt from "The Exodus to Freedom" from Web site http://www.nps.gov/untold/banners-_and_backgrounds/expansionbanner/exoduster.htm

Excerpts from "How to Succeed in Life" by Andrew Carnegie

Quote from *Madam C.J. Walker, Entrepreneur,* "I got my start by giving myself a start."

Excerpt from *Carriages Without Horses,* by Richard Scharchburg

Excerpt from *The Wright Brothers: How They Invented the Airplane* by Russell Freedman

Excerpt from *Tomboy of the Air: Daredevil Pilot Blanche Stuart Scott* by Julie Cummins

Excerpts from *To Speak for My People* from Web site http://www.pbs.org/weta/thewest/program/episodes/eight/tospeak.htm

Excerpts from *Luzena Stanley Wilson 49er, Her Memoirs as Taken Down by Her Daughter in 1881*

Excerpt from *Gold and Silver in the West: The Illustrated History of an American Dream* by T.H. Watkins

Excerpt from "A Practical Plan for Building a Pacific Railroad, Part II" by Theodore Judah

Excerpt from *Nothing Like It in the World* by Stephen E. Ambrose

Excerpt from text found at Web site http://history.acusd.edu/gen/text/ww1/sgtyork.html

Excerpt from subject heading "World War I" from the *World Book Encyclopedia*

"The College Graduate in Her Community" by Ida Tarbell

Excerpt from *Afterthoughts. Rochefort on: The Battle of Midway—June 1942* by Pete Azzole, found on Web site www.usncva.org/clog/midway.html

Except from *From Slavery to Freedom: A History of Negro Americans,* sixth edition, by John Hope Franklin and Alfred A. Moss, Jr.

Excerpt from *Anxious Decades: America in Prosperity and Depression 1920–1941* by Michael E. Parrish

Excerpt from *Great Issues in American History: From Reconstruction to the Present Day, 1864–1981,* edited Richard Hofstadter and Beatrice K. Hofstadter

Excerpt from *Freedom from Fear: The American People in Depression and War, 1929–1945,* by David M. Kennedy

Excerpts from *We Were There, Too! Young People in U.S. History* by Phillip Hoose

Excerpt from *They Also Served: American Women in World War II* by Olga Gruhzit-Hoyt

Excerpt from *The Good War: An Oral History of World War Two* by Studs Terkel

Excerpt from *O Pioneers!* by Willa Cather

Excerpts from *The West: An Illustrated History,* by Geoffrey C. Ward

Excerpts from *Bury My Heart at Wounded Knee,* by Dee Brown

Excerpts from *Up from Slavery* by Booker T. Washington

Excerpt from preface to the *1897 Sears Roebuck Catalog*

Excerpt from *When I Was Puerto Rican* by Esmeralda Santiago

Excerpts from *World Almanac and Book of Facts 2003*

Excerpt from *Jacob Riis: Reformer and Photographer*

Excerpts from *This Fabulous Century: 1870–1900,* by the editors of Time-Life Books

Excerpt from *California As I Saw It, 1849–1900,* reprinted from *California and the West (1881),* by L. Vernon Briggs, as found on Web site http://memory.loc.gov/ammem/ndlpedu/features/timeline/risInd/chinimms/briggs.html

Excerpt from *Talking It Over* by Hillary Rodham Clinton

Excerpt from *Georgia O'Keeffe: The "Wilderness and Wonder" of Her World* by Beverly Gherman

"I Shall Run in 1948" speech given by Henry A. Wallace, delivered over the Mutual Broadcasting System, Chicago, IL, December 29, 1947. From *Vital Speeches of the Day* (January 1, 1948), v. 14, n. 6, p. 172

Excerpt from *The Road Ahead* by Bill Gates

MAPS:

Mapquest.com, Inc. See pages 3–10

ILLUSTRATIONS:

10 Albert Lorenz
19, 492–4493 Darch Clampitt
32 Guy Porfirio
97 Barbara Emmons
114 John Berkey
123 Kent Barton
145 Robert Gunn
150 Troy Howell
199 David Cunningham
202 Wayne Parmenter
268 Tom Herzberg
301, 401, 483 John Sandford
525–6 Russell Charpentier
R16 Leland Klanderman

PHOTOGRAPHS:

Every effort has been made to secure permission and provide appropriate credit for photographic material. The publisher deeply regrets any omission and pledges to correct errors called to its attention in subsequent editions.

Unless otherwise acknowledged, all photographs are the property of Scott Foresman, a division of Pearson Education.

Photo locators denoted as follows: Top (T), Center (C), Bottom (B), Left (L), Right (R), Background (Bkgd).

Cover and End Sheets:
©Craig Aurness/Corbis, Getty Images

Front Matter:
E1 (T) ©Nik Wheeler/Corbis, (TC) ©Frank Chmura/ImageState/Alamy.com, (CL) Getty Images, (CR) ©Chad Ehlers/Alamy.com, (BC) ©Thomas E. Arthur/Kunta Kinte Celebrations, Inc., (B) ©Flip Schulke/Corbis, (BR) Craig Aurness/Corbis; E2 (Border) Getty Images, (L) ©David Falconer/Folio, Inc., (C) AP/Wide World Photos, (BL, BC, BR, R) Courtesy of Crazy Horse Memorial; E3 (TL ©Nik Wheeler/Corbis, (C, BL, BC, BR) Courtesy of Crazy Horse Memorial, (R) Getty Images; E4 ©Shaul Schwarz/Corbis, (B) ©James Leynse/Corbis, (Bkgd) Folio, Inc., (T) ©Neil Selkirk/Getty Images; E5 (CL) ©Jean Miele/Corbis, (BC) ©Frank Chmura/Imagestate/Alamy.com, (CC) ©Mark Lewis/Getty Images, (BR) ©Bettmann/Corbis; E6 (BL) Getty Images, (BR) ©Roger Ressmeyer/Corbis; E7 (Bkgd) ©Tony Freeman/PhotoEdit, (BR) Brand X Pictures; E8 (BL) ©Danny Lehman/Corbis, (BR) ©William A. Bake/Corbis, (C) ©Mark Goebel/Painet Stock Photos, (T) ©Virginia P. Weinland/Photo Researchers, Inc.; E9 (TC) ©Merlin D. Tuttle/Bat Conservation International, (C) ©Chad Ehlers/Alamy.com, (BC) ©Gail Shumway/Getty Images, (BR) ©David Muench/Corbis; E10 (BL) AP/Wide World Photos, (TC) ©Bettmann/Corbis, (B) ©Thomas E. Arthur/Kunta Kinte Celebrations, Inc., (Bkgd) ©Lawrence Migdale/Getty Images; E11 Getty Images; E12 (BL) ©Flip Schulke/Corbis; E13 (BC) ©Bettmann/Corbis, (BL) Corbis, (BC) ©David J. Janice L. Frent Collection/Corbis, (C) AP/Wide World Photos, (TC) ©David J. & Janice L. Frent Collection/Corbis, (TR) Photri, Inc.; E14 (BL) ©Don Mason/Corbis, (T) ©Joseph Sohm/The Image Works, Inc., (B) AP/Wide World Photos; E15 (BL) ©Craig Aurness/Corbis, (C) Corbis, (BR) ©Joseph Sohm; Visions of America/Corbis; E16 (TL) ©Wendell Metzen/Bruce Coleman, Inc., (BL) ©Rudi Von Briel/Index Stock Imagery, (CR) ©U.S. Department of State, Office of Multi-Media Services H2 (TL) ©Michael Newman/PhotoEdit, (TC) ©Bill Aron/PhotoEdit, (TR) ©Myrleen Cate/Index Stock Imagery, (BL) ©Larry Dale Gordon/Getty Images, (BC) ©Spencer Grant/PhotoEdit, (BR) ©Richard Hutchings/PhotoEdit; H3 (R) Mug Shots/Corbis Stock Market, (L) ©Bob Daemmrich/Stock Boston; H4–5 Colonial Williamsburg Foundation; H10 (Bkgd) ©Toyohiro Yamada/Getty Images, (BR) Corbis; H11 (BL) ©Andrea Wells Photography, (BR) ©Steven Simpson/Getty Images; H12 (TL) Earth Imaging/Stone

Overview:
1–3 ©Bettmann/Corbis, 5 The Granger Collection, New York; 6 (BR) Culver Pictures Inc, (BL) American Museum of Natural History/©Dorling Kindersley; 8 ©Richard T. Nowitz/Corbis; 9 (R) ©Werner Forman/Art Resource, NY, (C) American Museum of Natural History/©Dorling Kindersley; 10 (T) Pitt Rivers Museum/©Dorling Kindersley; 11 (T) Architect of the Capitol; 12 Alamy.com; 14 (C) SuperStock, (BR, CR) APVA Preservation Virginia, (BL) Nativestock; 15 (TR, BR) Getty Images, (TL) ©James Griffiths; 19 (Bkgd) ©N. Carter/North Wind Picture Archives, (C) ©David Muench/Corbis; 22 (B) ©Thomas Addis Emmet Collection, Manuscripts & Archives Division/New York Public Library Picture Collection; 23 Colonial Williamsburg Foundation; 24 ©Jean Leone Gerome Ferris/SuperStock; 25 The Granger Collection, New York; 26 (T) The Granger Collection, New York, (BR) North Wind Picture Archives; 27 SuperStock; 29 (R, CL) The Granger Collection, NY, (Bkgd) ©Kindra Clineff/Index Stock Imagery; (R) Hemera Technologies; 30 National Museum of American History/Smithsonian Institution/Behring Center; 31© Bettmann/Corbis; 33 (TL) United States Mint, (CR) Corbis, (L) Peter Newark's American Pictures, (R) Getty Images; 34 (TR) Corbis, (B) ©Bettmann/Corbis; 36 The Granger Collection, New York; 37 (BR) North Wind Picture Archives, (Bkgd) Getty Images, (CL) The Granger Collection, NY; 38 (TL) ©James Griffiths, (C) ©David Muench/Corbis; 39 The Granger Collection, New York; 40 The Granger Collection, New York; 41 Smithsonian National Museum of American History

Unit 1:
45–47 The Granger Collection, New York; 48 (L) The Granger Collection, New York, (CL) The Corcoran Gallery of Art/Corbis, (CR) ©Bettmann/Corbis, (R) Stock Montage Inc; 49 (L) The Granger Collection, New York, (R) Stock Montage Inc; 51 The Granger Collection, New York; 52 (T, B) The Granger Collection, New York, (TC) Sophia Smith Collection, Smith College, (BC) SuperStock; 54 (BL) ©Richard Hamilton Smith/Corbis; 55 (BL) North Wind Picture Archives; 56 (B) The Granger Collection, New York; 58 (CL, CR) The Granger Collection, New York, (L) Getty Images; 59 The Granger Collection, New York; 60 ©Adam Woolfitt/Corbis; 61 The Granger Collection, New York; 62 (BR) The Granger Collection, New York, (B) ©Bill Grant/©AFP; 65 (R) North Wind Picture Archives, (CL) ©Tria Giovan/Corbis, (Bkgd) SuperStock; 68 Corbis; 70 Private Collection/Bridgeman Art Library International Ltd; 71 The Granger Collection, New York; 73 ©Bettmann/Corbis, (L) Stock Montage Inc, (R) Library of Congress; 75 The Granger Collection, New York, (BR) ©Bettmann/Corbis; 78 (CL) North Wind Picture Archives; 80 (T, B) ©Bettmann/Corbis, (TC, BC) The Granger Collection, New York; 82 North Carolina Museum of History; 84 The Granger Collection, New York; 85 The Granger Collection, New York; 87 ©Joseph Sohm/ChromoSohm Inc/Corbis; (CL) Corbis, (R) U.S. Signal Corps/Brady Collection/National Archives; 89 The Granger Collection, New York; 90 North Wind Picture Archives; 91(T) Library of Congress, (TR) The Granger Collection, New York; 92 (TR) Corbis, (TL) Bettmann/Corbis; 93 North Wind Picture Archives; 94 AP/WideWorld; 95 (TR) ©Jim Lukoski/Black Star Publishing/PictureQuest, (B) AP/Wide World; 98 SuperStock; 100 North Wind Picture Archives; 102 North Wind Picture Archives; 104 (TR) The State Museum of Pennsylvania, Pennsylvania Historical and Museum Commission, (CL) National Maritime Museum/©Dorling Kindersley, (BR) Library of Congress; 105 (TR) Library of Congress, (C, BL, BR) U.S. Army Signal Corps Museum; 106 (BR) ©Bettmann/Corbis; 107 negative no. 21184/Collection of The New-York Historical Society; 108 (BL) Corbis, (TR) The Granger Collection, New York; 109 Harper's Weekly, November 16, 1867; 110 Library of Congress; 112 The Granger Collection, New York

Unit 2:
119–121 Hulton Archive/Getty Images; 122 (L) Hulton-Deutsch Collection/Corbis, (CL, CR) The Granger Collection, New York, (R) SuperStock; 123 Brown Brothers, (CL) Latimer Family Papers/Long Island Division/Queens Borough Public Library, (L) The Granger Collection, New York; 126 (B) ©D. Furlong/Robert Harding Picture Library Ltd, (TC) Kansas Historical Society, (BC) Max Alexander/©Dorling Kindersley; 128 The Granger Collection, New York; 129 (BR) The Granger Collection, New York, (B) North Wind Picture Archives; 130 Union Pacific Historical Collection; 131(T) Union Pacific Historical Collection, (BR) Corbis; 132 (B) Hulton Archive/Getty Images, (TR) ©Joseph Barnell/SuperStock; 133 The Granger Collection, New York; 136 Colonial Williamsburg Foundation; 138 The Granger Collection, New York; 139 ©Daniel J. Cox/Natural Exposures; 140 The Granger Collection, New York; 141(BR) Kansas State Historical Society, (B) ©Barbara Laing/Getty Images; 142 (CR) ©Darlyne A/Dr. Murawski/NGS Image Collection, (BL) Francis G. Mayer/Corbis, (TR) The Granger Collection, New York; 143 (TR) Courtesy of Deere & Company, (L) Corbis, (BR) North Wind Picture Archives; 145 (Bkgd) ©Craig Aurness/Corbis; (TL) SuperStock; 146 Corbis; 147 ©Richard T. Nowitz/Corbis; 148 Brand X Pictures; 149

Credits

The Granger Collection, New York, (T) SuperStock; 151 (T) Hulton Archive/Getty Images, (TR) Max Alexander/©Dorling Kindersley; 152 The Granger Collection, New York; 154 Getty Images; 155 North Wind Picture Archives; 156 (TR) AP/Wide World Photos, (B) ©Phil Schermeister/Corbis; 157 (BR) Brown Brothers, (BL) The Granger Collection, NY; 159 Corbis; 160 (R) Corbis, (CL) ©Jeffrey Torretta Photography; 161 Smithsonian Institution, Washington DC, USA/Bridgeman Art Library; 162 North Wind Picture Archives; 164 (TC) Corbis, (BC, B) Brown Brothers; 166 Smithsonian Institution; 167 (BR) ©Bettmann/Corbis, (BL) The Granger Collection, New York; 168 (TR) Brown Brothers, (BL) Latimer Family Papers/Long Island Division/Queens Borough Public Library; 169 Bettmann/Corbis; 170 (T) Hulton Archive/Getty Images, (BR) Brown Brothers; 171 (TL) Hulton Archive/Getty Images, (BCL) Beaulieu Motor Museum/©Dorling Kindersley, (B) The Granger Collection, New York, (TR) ©Frank J. Forte/Herkimer County Historical Society, NY, (BL) ©E.O. Hoppé/Corbis, (CR) Brown Brothers, (TCL) Smithsonian Institution; 172 (TR) Photri–Microstock, (B) The Granger Collection, New York; 176 ©Bettmann/Corbis; 177 (L) Mary Evans Picture Library, (B) Corbis; 179 (BR) ©Bettmann/Corbis, (L) Getty Images; 180 (BR) Harry Ransom Humanities Research Center; 181(C) ©Joseph Barnell/SuperStock, (B) ©Rensselaer County Historical Society; 183 (Bkgd) PictureHistory, (TL) ©Lynne S. Comunale/Glenn A. Walsh, (BR) Museum of the City of New York/Archive Photos/ Getty Images; 184 (BL) Bud Freund/Index Stock Imagery; 185 Corbis; 186 (BR) Corbis, (B) ©Tony Perrottet/Ambient Images, Inc; 187(TR) Brown Brothers, (BL) ©Lee Foster/Lonely Planet Images; 188 Corbis; 189 (T) Huntington Library/SuperStock, (BR) Photo Collection Alexander Alland, Sr./Corbis; 191 (Bkgd) ©Bettmann/ Corbis, (BR) Brown Brothers; 193 (T) Brown Brothers, (R) The Granger Collection, NY; 194 (BL) Brown Brothers, (TR) Corbis; 195 (BL) ©Bettmann/Corbis, (TR) The Granger Collection, New York; 196 Brown Brothers; 197 (TR) The Granger Collection, New York; 198 (BL) Brown Brothers; 199 (C) Broad Meadows Middle School/ Ron Adams, (BC) AP/Wide World, (Bkgd) The Granger Collection, New York; 200 ©E.O. Hoppé/Corbis; 207 The Granger Collection

Unit 3:
207–209 The Granger Collection; 210 (R, CL) The Granger Collection, New York, (CR) Corbis; 211 (CL) Stock Montage Inc., (CR, R, L) The Granger Collection, New York; 213 (T) The Granger Collection, New York; 214 (B) Russell Crump's Santa Fe Archive, www.atsfry.com, (T) Hulton-Deutsch Collection/Corbis, (BC) Corbis; 216 Bohemian Nomad Picturemakers/Corbis; 217 Hulton-Deutsch Collection/Corbis; 218 (BR) The Granger Collection, (B) Brown Brothers; 219 (TR) ©Vintage Image/Retrofile.com, (B) Getty Images; 220 (L) ©Schenectady Museum/Hall of Electrical History Foundation/Corbis, (C)Brown Brothers, (TR) Mary Evans Picture Library; 221 Stock Montage Inc; 222 © Railroad Museum of Pennsylvania; 224 (TR) Brown Brothers, (B) The Granger Collection; 225 The Granger Collection, New York; 226 (TR) Wallace Kirkland/ Getty Images, (BL) ©Bettmann/Corbis; 227 ©Bettmann/Corbis; 228 (CL) ©Bettmann/Corbis, (BR) Getty Images; 232 (BL) ©Gifts of Alexander Hay and Mark E. Charbonnet/Louisiana State Museum; 233 (B) Library of Congress; 234 (CL) AP/Wide World Photos, (TR) ©Bettmann/Corbis, (BL) Mary Evans Picture Library; 236 (T) Lawrence, Jacob. "The Migrants Arrived in Great Numbers" Panel 40 from "The Migration Series". (1940–41; text and title revised by the artist, 1993). Tempera on gesso on composition board 12 x 18" (20.5 x 45.7cm). The Museum of Modern Art, New York Gift of Mrs. David M. Levy, Photograph ©2001, The Museum of Modern Art, New York; 237 (T) Hulton Archive/Getty Images, (B) Corbis; 238 (CL) The Granger Collection, New York; 239 (C) Tuskegee Institute National Historic Site (TUIN888)/The National Park Service, Museum Management Program, (Bkgd) ©Bettmann/Corbis, BR Corbis; 240 Retrofile.com; 241 (B) Brown Brothers, (TR) Hulton Archive/Getty Images; 242 (BL) ©Bettmann Archive/Corbis, (BC) ©Bettmann/Corbis; 243 SuperStock; 244 (CL) ©Bettmann/Corbis; 245 (BR) Corbis, (CL) ©Bettman/Corbis, (Bkgd) The Granger Collection; 247 ©Schenectady Museum/Hall of Electrical History Foundation/Corbis; 248 ©Bettmann/Corbis; 250 SuperStock; 251 Corbis; 252 (B) Robertstock.com, (BR) The Granger Collection, New York; 253 (T, TR) The Granger Collection, New York; 254 (BL) OnRequest Images, (BR) Corbis; 257 (BL) ©Will & Deni McIntyre/ Stone/Getty Images, (TR) The Granger Collection, New York; 258 (TL) ©John Davenport/Getty Images; 259 (Bkgd) ©Charles O'Rear/Corbis, The Granger Collection, New York; 260 The Granger Collection, New York; 261(TR) The Granger Collection, New York; 263 (B) ©E.O. Hoppé/Corbis, (TR) Prints & Photographs Division, National Child Labor Committee Collection, [LC-USZ62-105651]/ Library of Congress; 264 ©Bettmann/Corbis; 265 (TR) Brown Brothers, (CR) Corbis; 266 (B) Lake County Museum/Corbis; 267 Corbis; 269 (T) ©Bettmann/Corbis; 270 (L) Corbis; 271 ©Michael Newman/PhotoEdit; 272 ©Bettmann/Corbis; 274 Corbis; 275 (B) Courtesy of The First Division Museum at Cantigny/The First Division Museum at Cantigny; (TR) Stock Montage Inc; 276 Getty Images; 277 (CL) Brown Brothers, (CR) ©Bettmann/Corbis, (BR) Getty Images; 278 (TR) Corbis, (CL) The Granger Collection, New York, (BL) Brown Brothers; 279 (CL) Getty Images, (B) American Battle Monuments Commission, Arlington, VA; 281 (BR) Imperial War Museum, (CR) ©Hulton Archive/Getty Images, (C, TL, TCL, L, CL) RAF Museum, Hendon/©Dorling Kindersley; 284 (Bkgd) PictureHistory

Unit 4:
292 (L) Corbis, (CL) Stock Montage Inc, (R) The Granger Collection, New York, (CR) © Joe Munroe/Getty Images; 293 (L) The Granger Collection, NY, (CL) Corbis, (CR) ©Gabriel Benzur/Getty Images, (R) ©Martha Holmes/Getty Images; 295 Getty Images; 296 ©Bettmann/Corbis; 298 ©Bettmann/Corbis; 299 (BL) Mary Evans Picture Library, (BR) Bettmann/Corbis; 300 (CR) Lake County Museum/Corbis, (B) Corbis; 302 (BR) ©Hulton Archive/Getty Images, (L) Everett Collection, Inc; 303(T) Hulton-Deutsch Collection/Corbis, (CR) Advertising Archive; 304 Bettmann/Corbis; 305 ©First National/Charles Chaplin/Kobal Collection; 306 AKG London Ltd; 308 (CR) Science Museum/©Dorling Kindersley, (B)Wright State University Library; 309 (TL) Science Museum, London/©Dorling Kindersley, (TR) Gaslight Ad Archives, Commack NY, (CL) Science Museum/©Dorling Kindersley; 311 (BL) ©Bettmann/Corbis; 312 (CR) ©Bettmann/Corbis, (TR) Lebrecht Collection, (BL) Photofest, (BR) ©Bettmann/Corbis; 313 Lebrecht Collection; 314 (BL) ©Bettmann/Corbis, (BR) Corbis; 315 ©Bettmann/Corbis, 316 (CL) ©Dorling Kindersley; 317 (BR) ©Joe Munroe/Getty Images, (Bkgd) ©James Randklev/Corbis, (CL) Getty Images; 318 (BR) ©Robert W. Kelley/Getty Images; 319 (B) ©Library class/Corbis, (T) ©Jacob Lawrence, courtesy of the Jacob and Gwendolyn Lawrence Foundation/Digital Image (c) The Museum of Modern Art/Licensed by SCALA/Art Resource, NY; 320 (BL) SuperStock; 321 (TR) Hulton-Deutsch Collection/Corbis, (BL) ©Michael A. Murphy/Texas Department of Transportation, (BC) ©Breck P. Kent/Animals Animals/Earth Scenes; 322 (T) The Granger Collection, New York; 323 (T) ©Bettmann/Corbis; 324 (B) ©Bettmann/Corbis; 325 (TR) Underwood & Underwood/Corbis, (B) Minnesota Historical Society/Corbis; 326 Getty Images; 327 (Bkgd) ©Bettmann/Corbis, (CL) ©Alex Wong/Getty Images, (R)Underwood & Underwood/Corbis; 328 ©Bettmann/Corbis; 329 ©Bettmann/ Corbis; 330 (BR) Corbis, (TR) The Granger Collection, NY, (TCL) ©Larry Lefever/Grant Heilman Photography, (BCL) Getty Images; 331 (TL) ©Charles E. Rotkin/Corbis, (BR) The Granger Collection, NY; 332 (BR) ©Dorothea Lange/Corbis; 333 (T) Getty Images, (B) The Granger Collection, NY; 334 (TR) Corbis, (BL) Everett Collection, Inc, (B) ©Bettmann/Corbis; 336 ©Bettmann/Corbis; 338 (C) ©Gabriel Benzur/Getty Images; 338 (T) Superstock; 340 Getty Images; 341 (B) Corbis; 342 (TR) ©Bettmann/Corbis, (BL) ©Eileen Tweedy/The Art Archive, (BR) The Granger Collection, NY; 343 (TR) Culver Pictures Inc, (BL) The Granger Collection, NY; 344 (TR) Superstock, (B) Michael T. Sedam/Corbis; 345 (CR) Mary Evans Picture Library, (TR, BR, CL, BC, CC) ©Dorling Kindersley, (BL) The Granger Collection, NY; 347 (TL) Corbis, 348 (BL) ©Richard Cummins/Corbis; 349 (BR) The Granger Collection, NY; 350 (TR) The Granger Collection, New York, (TL) Getty Images, 351(BR) Hulton-Deutsch Collection/Corbis, 352 ©Gabriel Benzur/Getty Images; 353 (BL) Seattle Post-Intelligencer Collection; Museum of History & Industry/Corbis, (TR) The Mariners' Museum/Corbis; 354 (BL) ©Bettmann/Corbis, (TR) Jerry Proc; 355 (TL) Underwood Photo Archives/SuperStock; 356 (BL) ©2002 Black Box/Retrofile.com; 357 (BR) Marine Corps/Department of Defense; 361 (TR) Everett Collection, Inc, (BL) The Granger Collection, New York; 362 (T) ©Hulton-Deutsch Collection/Corbis, (CL) Bettmann/Corbis; 363 (TR) AP/Wide World, (BC) ©Bettmann/Corbis; 365 (Bkgd) ©Lee Snider/Corbis, (BR) The Granger Collection, New York, (CL) Corbis; 369 Jerry Proc; 371 (BR) The Granger Collection, NY, (Bkgd) ©FSA photo/Arthur Rothstein/Stock Montage Inc

Unit 5:
375–377 ©Frank Whitney/Brand X Pictures; 378 (R) Corbis, (L, CL) ©Bettmann/Corbis, (CR) ©Reuters NewMedia Inc./Corbis, 379 (CL, C) 1999 NASA/Black Star, (L) Topham/Image Works, (CR) AP/Wide World, (R) ©Richard Howard/Black Star; 382 (C) H. Armstrong Roberts/Robertstock.com, (B) ©Bettmann/Corbis; 384 Corbis; 385 (B) Hulton-Deutsch Collection/Corbis; 386 (BR) Corbis, (TR) AP/Wide World Photos, (CL) ©Bettmann/Corbis, (BL) Corbis; 387 (BC) The Military Picture Library/Corbis, (BR) Chris Ballentine/ Alamy.com; 388 (B) David King Collection; 390 (B) ©Bettmann/ Corbis, (CR) Hulton Archive/Getty Images; 394 (BL) SuperStock; 395 (TL) R. Krubner/Retrofile.com, (TR) H. Armstrong Roberts/ Retrofile.com, 396 Brown Brothers, 397 (T) ©Bettmann/Corbis; 398 (TR) AP/Wide World Photos, (TC) Courtesy Citicorp Diners Club Inc; 399 (TR) AP/Wide World Photos, (BL) Hulton Archive/Getty Images; 400 (CR) ©Bettmann/Corbis, 400 (TR, BR, BL,) ©H. Armstrong Roberts/Retrofile.com; 402 (B) Boeing Commercial Airplane Group, (TR) ©Bettmann/Corbis; 403 (TL) Corbis; 404 (L, C) ©Dorling Kindersley; 405 (TL, R, TR, C) ©Dorling Kindersley; 406 Bill Pierce/Rainbow/PictureQuest, (TR) SuperStock; 407 (BR) ©Bettmann/Corbis; 408 (BR) ©Michel Setboun/Getty Images, (CR) ©Michael Rougier/Getty Images; 409 (TR) ©Bettmann/Corbis, (TC) Chicago Tribune; 410 (BL) ©Bettmann/Corbis, (BR) Getty Images; 412 (T) Brown Brothers; 413 (BR) Underwood & Underwood/Corbis, (Bkgd) Brand X Pictures, (C) Brand X Pictures; 416 (BC) AP/Wide World Photos, (B) ©Tannen H. Maury/The Image Works, Inc, (TC) ©Ivan Massar/Black Star; 418 ©Bettmann/Corbis; 419 (TR) Hulton Archive/Getty Images, (BR) Hulton-Deutsch Collection/Corbis; 420 (TR) Brown Brothers, (BR) Corbis; 421 (BR) ©Bettmann/Corbis, (C) ©Carl Iwasaki/Getty Images; 422 (TR) ©Don Cravins/Getty Images, (BR) AP/Wide World Photos, (BL) Bettmann/Corbis; 423 (TR) ©Jack Moebes/Corbis, (BL) ©Bettmann/Corbis; 424 (B) Getty Images, (TR) ©Flip Schulke/Corbis; 425 (TR) Bettmann/Corbis; 427 (BR) Topham/Image Works, (Bkgd) Underwood & Underwood/Corbis, (CL) AP/Wide World; 428 Getty Images; 429 (TR) AP/Wide World Photos; 429 (BC) Photri–Microstock, (TL) Getty Images; 430 (B) Getty Images; 431 (BCL) Hulton Archive/Getty Images; 432 (BL) ©Ivan Massar/Black Star; 433 (BL) ©Arthur Henrikson/AAEC Editorial Cartoon Collection, McCain Library & Archives, The University of Southern Mississippi, (TR) ©Eddie Germano/AAEC Editorial Cartoon Collection, McCain Library & Archives, The University of Southern Mississippi; 434 (B) ©James P. Blair/Corbis, (CL) Photri-Microstock; 435 (TR) AP/Wide World Photos; 436 (BL) ©Bettmann/Corbis; 437 ©James P. Blair/Corbis; 438 (BR) ©Francis Miller/Getty Images; 439 (TR) ©William Gottlieb/Corbis, (BR) Brown Brothers; 440 Icon Sports Media; 441 (TR) The Image Works, Inc, (CL) ©Hulton-Deutsch Collection/Corbis; 442 (BR) ©Chuck Savage/ Corbis, (BL) ©Catherine Ursillo/Photo Researchers, Inc, (T) ©Mark Wilson/Getty Images; 443 (TR) James Thomas/Special Collections/ Cleveland State University Library, (TCR) ©Andre Jenny/Alamy.com; 444 (TR) ©John Henley/Corbis, 445 (R) ©Michael Smith/Getty Images, (Bkgd) Joseph Rodriguez/Black Star, (CL) Japack Company/Corbis; 447 ©Bettmann/Corbis; 448 (BR) Getty Images, (BL) ©Chris Niedenthal/Black Star; 450 (T) ©Jonathon Bainbridge/Reuters/ Getty Images; 451(BR) Gallo Images/Corbis; 452 (BR) The New Yorker Collection 2000 Danny Shanahan from cartoonbank.com. All Rights Reserved/Cartoon Bank (Div of New Yorker Magazine); 453 ©Alex Wong/Getty Images; 459 (T) ©Bettmann/Corbis, (Bkgd, TR) NASA

Unit 6:
463–465 ©Diaphor Agency/Index Stock Imagery; 466 (CL) ©Bettmann/Corbis, (R) ©Andrea Renault/Globe Photos, Inc, (CR) Reuters/Corbis; 467 (L, CL) AP/Wide World Photos, (R) Corbis, (CR) Frank Cantor, 469 (T) ©Bob Daemmrich/The Image Works, Inc; 470 (B) Corbis, (T) ©Ron Sherman; 475 Corbis; 476 ©Rudi Von Briel/ PhotoEdit; 481(B) SuperStock; 482 (BR) ©Journal-Courier/Steve Warmowski/The Image Works, Inc, (T) ©Andy Sacks/Stone; 485 (BR) ©Fred Ward/Black Star, (Bkgd) ©Wendell Metzen/Bruce Coleman Inc; 486 (TCR) Corbis, (Bkgd) Getty Images; 487 (TL) ©Wally McNamee/Corbis, (CR) ©William Morris Agency, Inc, (BL) ©Congressman Tom Lantos; 489 (B) Jeff Greenberg/Visuals Unlimited; 490 (BL) Corbis; (BC) Getty Images; 491(BL) Getty Images, (TR) Corbis, (CR) ©Bill Aron/PhotoEdit, (B) ©Corbis; 495 (BR) Corbis, (Bkgd) ©Court Mast/Getty Images, (CL) Getty Images; 497 (BL) ©Ed Lallo/Index Stock Imagery; 500 (B) ©Chris Lundy/ Index Stock Imagery, (T) Thomas E. Franklin/The Record (Bergen County, NJ)/Corbis; 503 (BL) ©Enrique Shore/Reuters/ Getty Images, (BR) ©Mike Segar/Reuters/Getty Images; 504 (B) AP/Wide World Photos; 505 (CR) AP/Wide World, (CL) Gerardo Mora/epa/Corbis (B) ©Gene Blevins/Getty Images; 507 (B) ©Wesley Bocxe/The Image Works, Inc, (TR) The Image Works, Inc; 509 (BR) AP/Wide World Photos, (Bkgd) ©Archimation/Studio Daniel Libeskind, (CL) Getty Images; 512 (BL) NASA Image Exchange; 513 (B) Getty Images; 514 (BL) Corbis, (BR) ©Paul Conklin/PhotoEdit; 515 (B) © Mike Johnson Marine Natural History Photography, (TL) Getty Images, (TR) ©Alex Wong/Getty Images, (CR) ©Richard T. Nowitz/Corbis, (CL) Corbis, (B) ©Chris Lundy/Index Stock Imagery; 517 NASA Image Exchange; 518 (B) Corbis; 520 (CL) ©Michael S. Yamashita/Corbis, (TR) Courtesy of Panasonic (UK), (BR) ©James King-Holmes/Photo Researchers, Inc; 521 (TL) ©Dorling Kindersley, (TR) NASA Image Exchange, (CR) Science & Society Picture Library, (CL) Department of Cybernetics, University of Reading/©Dorling Kindersley, (B) Courtesy of Honda (UK); 524–525 Ron Sherman/Stone; 529 John Harwood/Science Photo Library/Photo Researchers, Inc; 530 (T) ©Jerry Kobalenko/ First Light; 531 (T) ©Dan Guravich/Corbis, (CR) ©Paul A. Souders/ Corbis; 532 (TL) The Granger Collection, New York, (TR) ©Robert Estall/Corbis, (B) The Granger Collection, New York; 533 (TR) ©Alison Wright/Corbis, (TL) ©Don McPhee/Valan Photos, (B) ©Layne Kennedy/Corbis; 534 (BL) ©Robert Frerck/Odyssey Productions; 535 (T) ©Robert Frerck/Odyssey Productions, (C) ©John Cancalosi/Valan Photos; 536 (TL, B) The Granger Collection, New York, (TR) AP/Wide World; 537 (TR, B) Daemmrich Photography, (TL) Chip and Rosa Maria de la Cueva Peterson; 538 (CR) ©Kevin Schafer/Corbis; 539 (TL) Teresita Chavarria/© AFP, (CR) ©Tim Page/Corbis; 541 (TC) AP/Wide World, (TR) ©Bob Krist/Corbis; 543 (CL) Frans Lanting, (TL) Chip and Rosa Maria de la Cueva Peterson

End Matter:
R1 Earth Imaging/Stone; R2 Earth Imaging/Stone; R18–R21 One Mile Up, Inc; R19 Georgia Secretary of State Cathy Cox